Logotherapy and Existential Analysis: Proceedings of the Viktor Frankl Institute Vienna

Series Editor
Alexander Batthyány

More information about this series at http://www.springer.com/series/13368

Alexander Batthyány
Editor

Logotherapy and Existential Analysis

Proceedings of the Viktor Frankl Institute Vienna, Volume 1

Springer

Editor
Alexander Batthyány
Viktor Frankl Chair of Philosophy and Psychology
International Academy of Philosophy
Bendern, Principality of Liechtenstein

Viktor Frankl Institute Vienna
Vienna, Austria

Logotherapy and Existential Analysis: Proceedings of the Viktor Frankl Institute Vienna
ISSN 2366-7559 ISSN 2366-7567 (electronic)
ISBN 978-3-319-29423-0 ISBN 978-3-319-29424-7 (eBook)
DOI 10.1007/978-3-319-29424-7

Library of Congress Control Number: 2016934054

Printed on acid-free paper

This Springer imprint is published by Springer Nature
The registered company is Springer International Publishing AG Switzerland

Preface

After several years of preparatory work, we are proud to present the first edition of the Proceedings of the Viktor Frankl Institute. They are the natural outgrowth of three parallel movements in logotherapy. The first reflects a rediscovery of Frankl's work in the behavioral and clinical sciences, especially in positive and existential psychology (Bretherton and Ørner 2004; Wong 1998; 2009; for a comprehensive overview on the current reception of Frankl's work in positive and existential psychology, see Batthyány and Russo-Netzer 2014). The second movement reflects the growing dialogue between logotherapists and representatives of neighboring schools of psychotherapy and counseling (e.g., Corrie and Milton 2000; Ameli and Dattilio 2013) and psychology in general (Baumeister 1991; Baumeister and Vohs 2002), and the third movement refers to a growing trend towards collaboration and networking *within* the logotherapy community itself.

Arguably, neither the first nor the second movements were foreseeable when Frankl developed logotherapy and existential analysis in the first half of the past century, nor was it foreseeable that logotherapeutic concepts should one day become as prominent in academic and empirical psychology as they are today. Indeed, it appears as if Frankl's logotherapy, once only one single psychiatrist's "courageous rebellion against the […] paradigms that dominated psychological theorizing" (Baumeister and Vohs 2002), has now, albeit belatedly, arrived at the research front of experimental, empirical, and clinical psychology.

The discovery, or rediscovery, of Frankl's work within academic psychology, however, comes with a number of scientific challenges and intellectual obligations. For once logotherapy's main tenets are scrutinized by colleagues whose approach is evidence- rather than theory-based, logotherapists will need to be able to assign a place to logotherapy and existential analysis within the larger canon of psychological theory and empirical data; and they will need to relate logotherapy to other psychological and clinical theories which have broad overlaps with Franklian psychology (such as self-determination theory [e.g., Deci and Ryan 2000; Ryan and Deci 2000], resilience and hardiness research [e.g., Maddi 2004], Self-Efficacy Theory [e.g., Bandura 1997], and Moral Reconation Therapy [e.g., Little and Robinson 1988]). Since these models also come with a large stock of experimental designs and empirical data directly relevant for logotherapy, logotherapists will, in all likelihood, profit considerably from a dialogue with these neighboring schools. Indeed, a significant number of the research findings of most of the above-mentioned schools support some of the core ideas of logotherapy, but surprisingly, until now, it seems as if their work has rarely been fully acknowledged, let alone adopted, by logotherapists for their own research or clinical practice—at least not on a large scale.

There might be several reasons for the relative nonchalance with which significant research from other psychological research traditions has been greeted in our field. One is tempted to speculate that perhaps to some degree, logotherapists have become so accustomed to be, as Baumeister puts it, in constant "courageous rebellion against the […] paradigms that dominate psychological theorizing" (Baumeister and Vohs 2002) that they also have become used to just don't expect relevant or supporting input from current research in the behavioral and clinical sciences. Or perhaps some are simply not overly impressed when researchers and clinicians from very different backgrounds "discover" that meaning awareness and purpose do play important roles both in human coping and striving after all—and that they do so throughout the entire lifespan. Given the fact that during the past four decades, several hundreds of studies on the psychological relevance of meaning motivation and awareness have been conducted mostly by logotherapists or others influenced by Frankl's work, which consistently support the basic tenets of Franklian psychology (for research overviews spanning the years 1975–2014, see Schulenberg 2003; Batthyány and Guttmann 2005; Batthyány 2009; Thir 2012; Thir and Batthyány 2014), the logotherapists' reluctant reaction to non-logotherapeutic meaning research is perhaps comprehensible. And yet: comprehensible it perhaps may be—but it is not necessary, and neither is it too healthy for the intellectual and scientific development of a discipline to remove itself from current scientific debate and development. Perhaps nobody saw this clearer than Frankl himself, who hinted at the inherent dangers of scientific and philosophical isolationism within the field, when he told the editor of the then newly established *International Forum*:

> Why should we lose, unnecessarily and undeservedly, whole segments of the academic community, precluding them a priori from understanding how much logotherapy "speaks to the needs of the hour"? Why should we give up, right from the beginning, getting a hearing from modern researchers by considering ourselves above tests and statistics? We have no reason not to admit our need to find our discoveries supported by strictly empirical research. […]
>
> You cannot turn the wheel back and you won't get a hearing unless you try to satisfy the preferences of present-time Western thinking, which means the scientific orientation or, to put it in more concrete terms, our test and statistics mindedness […]. That's why I welcome all sober and solid empirical research in logotherapy, however dry its outcome may sound. (Frankl in Fabry 1978/79, 5–6)

Clearly, when Frankl deposited this in the *Forum*, he not only referred to *conducting* research but also encouraged both researchers and clinicians to also make available (i.e., *publish*) their findings and thus make them accessible to logotherapists and proponents of neighboring schools of thought.

Given the noticeable tendency towards a renewed interest in existential issues in psychology and psychiatry, the idea to launch an interdisciplinary sister periodical to logotherapy's long-standing excellent *Forum of Logotherapy* (published under the auspices of the Viktor Frankl Institute of Logotherapy in Abilene, Texas) was born. We hope that these Proceedings will supplement its esteemed older sister as a new international peer-reviewed periodical—one which is forthright about being dedicated to the advancement of logotherapeutic theory and practice and to the same measure open to dialogue and new developments within the larger context of the behavioral and clinical sciences and the humanities in general.

Once the idea was born, the concept of the Proceedings matured during discussions at the two past biannual International Congresses on *The Future of Logotherapy* in Vienna (2012 and 2014). Here, as well as at the 2013 *World Congress of Logotherapy* in Dallas, we were pleased to witness an unprecedented growth and development of the scientific and clinical work within our field, and hence all the more felt that a dedicated international periodical would be the ideal vehicle to capture and make accessible the diverse scholarly interests of an ever more vibrant logotherapy and logotherapy-inspired research and clinical community. A further impulse to launch the Proceedings was the founding of the *International Association of Logotherapy and Existential Analysis* at the Viktor Frankl Institute Vienna last year. This initiative—arguably yet another sign of the maturation and professionalization of our field—was extremely well received, with almost all of the 120 worldwide institutes and societies (and several hundreds of individual members) applying for accreditation and membership in the *International Association*.

In brief, during the past few years since the conception of the idea of the Proceedings, we were increasingly confronted with signals that we should indeed offer a new international and interdisciplinary forum to our worldwide community, which, at the same time, is set out to be a forum of, but not only for, logotherapists. Rather, in order to take account of the developments within the behavioral sciences and the humanities mentioned above, we felt that the field needs a periodical directed towards a broad interdisciplinary readership with a wide range of intellectual and academic backgrounds and interests. In other words, the Proceedings are not an in-house publication of and for logotherapists. Rather they are equally directed towards the growing number of our colleagues who are not logotherapists themselves, but are interested in, or perhaps even intrigued by, what logotherapists have to offer to current debates within the behavioral sciences, the humanities, and the helping professions.

Next to offering a forum for presenting and discussing new empirical and theoretical research, the Proceeding's second intention is to facilitate dialogue across disciplines and research traditions. Now, it seems obvious that dialogue between and across disciplines and schools of thought has to, should, and does cut both ways, and only then deserves the term "dialogue." It is not only that "they" learn from "us," but that "we" learn from "them," too—and indeed the whole concept of "us" and "them" looses much of its former force once one enters into a sincere dialogue. For sincere dialogue means that one inevitably encounters and learns about new concepts, challenges, and ideas (or rediscovers some old concepts, challenges, and ideas), which may well broaden or change one's own perspective on long-held and rarely questioned propositions.

This principle applies to all scientific dialogue, and, again, logotherapy is no exception. Indeed, analysis of the history of ideas in logotherapy clearly shows that especially since around the late 1960s, logotherapy steadily moved along the trajectory of many a psychotherapy tradition, i.e., from a school of thought into a research discipline. Thus we can observe a keen interest in the intellectual encounter of logotherapy with other ideas and trends within the behavioral sciences in Frankl's own work. Furthermore, once the core concepts of logotherapy were developed (around the mid-1950s), invariably each new development *within* logotherapy was triggered by developments from *without* logotherapy (Batthyány 2007). Frankl's critique of the affect-over-cognition approach of the 1960s human potential movement, for example, was instrumental for the development of logotherapy's model of meaning discovery and perception as being neither purely affect- nor cognition-based, but rather being akin to the gestalt perception process (Frankl 1966). In a similar vein, Frankl's skepticism towards the inherent epistemological constructionism of the humanistic and transpersonal psychology movements was instrumental for his coining of some of his finest and most elaborate arguments for epistemological and ontological value realism in therapeutic dialogue, which are now core elements of contemporary logotherapy and existential analysis (Frankl 1973, 1979; for more examples, see Batthyány 2013).

In brief, logotherapy owes much of its depth, growth, and maturation to the fact that Frankl and other early pioneers and proponents of logotherapy (such as J.C. Crumbaugh, L.T. Maholick, E. Weiskopf-Joelsson, E. Lukas) never shied away from entering into a constructive dialogue with, and studying and learning from, models and schools of thought which were often totally foreign, and sometimes even outright hostile to the larger non-reductionist existential tradition of which logotherapy is a part.

As I already pointed out, there is no reason to believe that the principle of growth by dialogue should have changed or that it should not also apply to contemporary logotherapy and existential analysis. Hence one hope we connect with the launching of these Proceedings is that it may help strengthen the academic exchange and debate with other schools of thought, both with those with whom we share much common ground, but also, and perhaps especially with those which may seem particularly different from logotherapy. To this end, the Proceedings not only carry articles, which engage in cross-disciplinary debate and dialogue, but also have a book review section, which covers primarily non-logotherapeutic publications.

At the same time, we also felt the necessity to collect essays on current trends and topics in applied logotherapy and existential analysis in order to provide our readers with relevant up-to-date, well-integrated, and technically sound papers that will enhance the knowledge and skills of anyone, who in one way or another applies logotherapy and existential analysis in his or her professional work and/or personal life. Thus, a further objective of the Proceedings is to bring together a wide range of views and approaches, new ideas and methods, and new applications for logotherapy and existential analysis.

The decision to regularly publish articles on research and developments in logotherapy, however, depends on whether sufficient new substantive knowledge and insight have accumulated to warrant it.

It is reassuring to see that indeed much substantive knowledge has been and continues to be accumulated—in fact, much more than we expected and much more than we were able to include in this first volume of the Proceedings. So, our task was to find a compromise between two objectives: on the one hand, we wanted to present a considerable amount of new ideas and research; on the other hand, we had to keep the size of this first volume manageable. Since the majority of the submissions were consistently and uniformly high in quality, our peer reviewers and we were forced to make some very difficult editorial decisions. Thus many papers had to be rejected which, had we had more space available, certainly would have made it into this first volume of the Proceedings. The decision on which papers to include was made between peer reviewers and the editors after careful consideration and discussion. In general, we tended to favor papers that proposed new ideas, applications, methods, or research strategies.

At the same time, we also included some core texts of logotherapy in this volume which haven't yet been available to a larger English-speaking readership—among them hitherto untranslated or privately published articles by Viktor E. Frankl and a brief but important article by Elisabeth Lukas on how to update logotherapy's model of the pathogenesis of neuroses against the background of recent findings on the neuropsychological underpinnings of a number of neuroses and personality disorders.

In brief, this first volume of the Proceedings—and many more to come—presents a wide variety of interesting and intellectually stimulating reading material for both logotherapists and non-logotherapists alike. We hope that you will be pleased with and inspired by this historical first volume. As editor-in-chief, I am happy to receive all your comments and suggestions on how to improve what is intended to be a new prime resource on anything related to logotherapy and beyond.

Vienna, Austria Alexander Batthyány

References

Ameli, M., & Dattilio, F. M. (2013). Enhancing cognitive behavior therapy with logotherapy: Techniques for clinical practice. *Psychotherapy*, *50* (3), 387–391.

Bandura, A. (1997). *Self-Efficacy: The exercise of control*. New York: Freeman.

Batthyány, A. (2007)."... immer schon ist die Person am Werk". Zur Ideengeschichte der Logotherapie und Existenzanalyse. In O. Wiesmeyer, A. Batthyány (Eds.) (2007). *Sinn und Person. Beiträge zur Logotherapie und Existenzanalyse*. Weinheim: Beltz.

Batthyány, A. (2011). Over thirty-five years later: Research in logotherapy since 1975. New afterword to: Frankl, V. E. (2011). *Man's search for ultimate meaning*. London: Rider.

Batthyány, A. (2013). Logotherapy and the cognitive neurosciences. *The 2013 World Congress of Logotherapy*. Viktor Frankl Institute of Logotherapy, Dallas, Texas.

Batthyány, A., & Guttmann, D. (2005). *Empirical research in logotherapy and meaning-oriented psychotherapy*. Phoenix: Zeig, Tucker & Theisen.

Batthyány, A., & Russo-Netzer, P. (2014). Psychologies of meaning. In A. Batthyány, P. Russo-Netzer, (Eds.), *Meaning in existential and positive psychology.* New York: Springer.

Batthyány, A., & Russo-Netzer, P. (2014). *Meaning in existential and positive psychology.* New York: Springer.

Baumeister, R. F. (1991). *Meanings of life.* New York: Guilford.

Baumeister, R. F., & Vohs, K. D. (2002). The pursuit of meaningfulness in life. In C. R. Snyder & S. J. Lopez (Eds.), *Handbook of positive psychology* (pp. 608–628). New York: Oxford University Press.

Bretherton, R. & Ørner, R. J. (2004). Positive psychology and psychotherapy: An existential approach. In P.A. Linley & S. Joseph (Eds.), *Positive psychology in practice* (pp. 420–430). Hoboken: Wiley.

Corrie, S., & Milton, M. (2000). The relationship between existential-phenomenological and cognitive-behavior therapies. *The European Journal of Psychotherapy, Counseling & Health,* 3, 7–24.

Crumbaugh, J. C., & Maholick, L. T. (1964). An experimental study in existentialism: The psychometric approach to Frankl's concept of noogenic neurosis. *Journal of Clinical Psychology, 20,* 200–207.

Damon, W., Menon, J., & Bronk, K. C. (2003). The development of purpose during adolescence. *Applied Developmental Science, 7* (3).

Deci, E. L., & Ryan, R. M. (2000). The "What" and "Why" of goal pursuits: Human needs and the self-determination of behavior. *Psychological Inquiry, 11*, 227–268.

Fabry, J. B. (1978-1979). Aspects and prospects of logotherapy: A dialogue with Viktor Frankl. *The International Forum for Logotherapy Journal of Search for Meaning*, 2, 8–11.

Frankl, V. E. (1966). What is meant by meaning? *Journal of Existentialism* 7, 21–28.

Frankl, V. E. (1973). Encounter: The concept and its vulgarization. *The Journal of The American Academy of Psychoanalysis, 1*(1), 73–83.

Frankl, V. E. (1979). Reply to Rollo May. *Humanistic Psychology*, *19*, 4, pp. 85–86.

Koole, S. L., Greenberg, J., & Pyszczynski, T. (2006). Introducing science to the psychology of the soul: Experimental existential psychology. *Current Directions in Psychological Science*, *15*, 212–216.

Little, G. L., & Robinson, K. D. (1988). Moral Reconation Therapy: A systematic step-by-step treatment system for treatment-resistant clients. *Psychological Reports*, *62*, 135–151.

Lopez, S. J., & Snyder, C. R. (2006). *Oxford handbook of positive psychology*. New York: Oxford University Press.

Maddi, S. R. (2004). Hardiness: An operationalization of existential courage. *Journal of Humanistic Psychology, 44*(3): 279–298.

Ryan, R. M., & Deci, E. L. (2000). Self-determination theory and the facilitation of intrinsic motivation, social development, and well-being. *American Psychologist, 55*, 68–78.

Schulenberg, S. E. (2003). Empirical research and logotherapy. *Psychological Reports, 93,* 307–319.

Thir, M. (2012). *Überblick zum gegenwärtigen Stand der empirischen Evaluierung der psychotherapeutischen Fachrichtung "Logotherapie und Existenzanalyse"*. Wels: Ausbildungsinstitut für Logotherapie und Existenzanalyse, Abile.

Thir, M., & Batthyány, A. (2014). *Clinical efficacy of logotherapy and existential analysis: An updated research overview*. Vienna: The 2nd Future of Logotherapy Congress.

Wong, P. T. P. (1998). Implicit theories of meaningful life and the development of the personal meaning profile. In P. T. P. Wong & P.S. Fry (Eds.), *The human quest for meaning* (pp. 111–140). Mahwah: Erlbaum.

Wong, P. T. P. (2009). Existential positive psychology. In S. Lopez (Ed.), *Encyclopedia of positive psychology* (vol. 1, pp. 361–368). Oxford: Wiley Blackwell.

Acknowledgements

The planning and editing of this first volume during the past 2 years required an immense amount of time and work on the part of many people. I am especially indebted to all the contributors for their splendid cooperation and to the peer reviewers for their diligent and careful work and for dedicating many reading hours to this project.

I would also like to thank my assistant editors, Jutta Jank Clarke, Michael Thir, and Sabina Menotti, without whose help the editing of this volume simply wouldn't have been possible. Thank you not only for the wonderful cooperation, but also for the many inspiring off-topic conversations without which the editing of this volume would have probably taken half of the time, but would also have been half as fun and interesting. I would also like to thank Marshall H. Lewis, co-editor of the esteemed partner periodical of the Proceedings, *The International Forum for Logotherapy*, for his never-ending support, valuable advice, the proofreading work, friendship, and help.

Many thanks go to Stefan Schulenberg for his valuable and wise advice and for the copy-editing and proofreading, and to L. T. Stephens, Mathew A. Tkachuck, Marcela C. Weber, and Heather N. Bliss for the copy-editing of many of the papers collected in this volume. I should also like to thank Christian Perring, Ph.D., editor-in-chief of the online Journal *Metapsychology*, for granting us reprint permissions for a number of the book reviews included in this volume. Thanks also go to Beacon Press for granting us permission to reprint the English translations of Frankl's *Türkheim* and the *Rathausplatz Vienna speeches* and the two letters written in 1945 after his return to Vienna.

Warm thanks go to Zoe Beloff for allowing including her late father's unpublished paper *What are minds for?* in this volume. I would also express my gratitude to Franz J. Vesely for the excellent translation of *Economic Crisis and Mental Health*, and to Stephen Reysen, editor-in-chief of the *Journal of Articles in Support of the Null Hypothesis*, for granting us permission to reprint Brouwers' and Tomic's study on the *Factorial Structure of Längle's Existence Scale*, as well as to Springer NY for allowing us to include Brock's chapter on measuring meaning in this volume.

A very special thanks goes out to Sylvana Ruggirello, Editorial Assistant Psychology at Springer, for her unending support and enthusiasm for this and several other books on logotherapy which we have brought, or are about to bring to fruition together: Thank you!

Finally, I wish to thank Juliane for her patience, support, and, in fact, for everything she is and does. And my daughters Leonie and Larissa I thank both for distracting me from the editing work and for your forbearance on the rare occasions when I proved resistant to your ever more refined distraction attempts.

Contents

Contributors

Leo Michel Abrami Arizona Institute of Logotherapy, Sun City West, AZ, USA

Matti Ameli Calle de Ribera, Valencia, Spain

Alexander Batthyány Viktor Frankl Institute Vienna, Vienna, Austria and Viktor Frankl Chair of Philosophy and Psychology, International Academy of Philosophy, Bendern, Principality of Liechtenstein

Willliam S. Breitbart Department of Psychiatry and Behavioral Sciences, Memorial Sloan-Kettering Cancer Center, New York, NY, USA

Kendall Cotton Bronk Claremont Graduate University School of Social Science, Policy, and Evaluation Division of Behavioral and Social Sciences Department of Psychology, Claremont, CA

André Brouwers Department of Psychology, The Open University, Heerlen, The Netherlands

Marianna D. Falcón Cooper Centro Nous, Mexico City, Mexico

Stephen J. Costello Viktor Frankl Institute of Ireland, Dublin 6, Ireland

Beate von Devivere Hansaallee 22, Frankfurt am Main, Germany

William F. Evans Department of Psychology, James Madison University, Harrisonburg, VA, USA

Ivonne A. Florez Department of Psychology, The University of Mississippi, University, MS, USA

Joaquín García-Alandete Dpto. de Neuropsicobiología, Metodología y Psicología Social, Universidad Católica de Valencia “San Vicente Mártir”, Valencia, Spain

S. Nassir Ghaemi Sackler School of Biomedical Sciences, Tufts University, Boston, MA, USA

Ann V. Graber Graduate Center for Pastoral Logotherapy, Graduate Theological Foundation, Mishawaka, IN, USA

Marnin J. Heisel Department of Psychiatry, London Health Sciences Centre-Victoria Hospital, The University of Western Ontario, London, ON, Canada

Shulamith Kreitler The School of Psychological Sciences, Tel Aviv University, Tel Aviv, Israel

Dmitry Leontiev Department of Psychology, Moscow State University, Moscow, Russia

Marshall H. Lewis LogoTalk, Ulysses, KS, USA

Bernadette T. Lowthert New York, NY, USA

Beatriz Soucase Lozano Dpto. de Neuropsicobiología, Metodología y Psicología Social, Universidad Católica de Valencia "San Vicente Mártir", Valencia, Spain

Elisabeth Lukas Perchtoldsdorf, Austria

Eva Rosa Martínez Dpto. de Neuropsicobiología, Metodología y Psicología Social, Universidad Católica de Valencia "San Vicente Mártir", Valencia, Spain

Pilar Maseda C.E.S. Don Bosco, Universidad Complutense de Madrid, Madrid, Spain

Charles McLafferty Jr. Purpose Research, LLC, Birmingham, AL, USA

Lucrecia Mollinedo de Moklebust Instituto de Ciencias de la Familia (ICF), Guatemala/Asociación Guatemalteca de Logoterapia, Guatemala C.A., Guatemala

Maria Ángeles Noblejas Equipo Específico de Alteraciones Graves de Desarrollo, Comunidad de Madrid. Asociación Española de Logoterapia, Madrid, Spain

Pilar Sellés Nohales Dpto. de Neuropsicobiología, Metodología y Psicología Social, Universidad Católica de Valencia "San Vicente Mártir", Valencia, Spain

Sharon Packer Private Practice, New York, NY, USA

Isabel Pérez CEPRI (Asociación para la investigación y el estudio de la deficiencia mental), Colegio Concertado de Educación Especial CEPRI, Madrid, Spain

Christian Perring Department of Philosophy, Dowling College, Oakdale, NY, USA

Pilar Pozo Facultad de Psicología, Universidad Nacional de Educación a Distancia, Ciudad Universitaria, Madrid, Spain

Georges-Elia Sarfati French School for Existential Analysis and Therapy (Logotherapy) V. Frankl—EFRATE (EFRATE), Charenton-le-Pont, France

Stefan E. Schulenberg Department of Psychology, The University of Mississippi, University, MS, USA

Steven M. Southwick VA Connecticut Healthcare System, Yale University School of Medicine, West Haven, CT, USA

Jacob Stegenga Department of Philosophy, University of Utah, Salt Lake City, UT, USA

Tracie L. Stewart Social Sciences (SO 402), Department of Psychology, Kennesaw State University, Kennesaw, GA, USA

Michael Thir Viktor Frankl Institute Vienna, Vienna, Austria

Marinka Tomic Van Hövell tot Westerflierhof 31a, Hoensbroek, Netherlands

Welko Tomic Department of Psychology, The Open University, Heerlen, The Netherlands

Gloria Bernabé Valero Dpto. de Neuropsicobiología, Metodología y Psicología Social, Universidad Católica de Valencia "San Vicente Mártir", Valencia, Spain

Paul T.P. Wong International Network on Personal Meaning (INPM), Toronto, ON, Canada

Robert Zaborowski Department of Philosophy, University of Warmia and Mazury, Olsztyn, Poland

Part I
From the Archives

Economic Crisis and Mental Health from the Viewpoint of the Youth Counselor, 1933

Viktor E. Frankl

Of the approximately 3700 young people who called on the Vienna Youth Counseling Service in the course of the five years of its existence, probably relatively few came due to the immediate issue of their economic plight. In order to prevent unjustified hopes and unnecessary effort, the management of the counseling center stresses in its announcements the words "*mental* distress" as the subject of its aid efforts. Still, it is just the youth consultant who can appreciate to what extent and in what way the economic crisis profoundly affects the life of the young people.

Even in the group of cases, which call on us in consequence of a conflict with the parents, the impact of unemployment on the psyche shows clearly. The generations of parents and children had already been moved apart ideologically and psychologically by the breach caused by the World War, and they would face each other with little understanding and trust; but it was the economic crisis that somehow pitted the two generations against each other and exacerbated the age-old conflict of generations. The psychological basis is probably to be found in the feeling of powerlessness with which unemployed fathers are facing their situation. As an additional grievance, one or the other child is also unemployed and can contribute nothing to the cost of the familial economy. These bitter and angry fathers are usually at home during the day, and having reason enough internally to be disgruntled, they also have, externally, more than enough time at their hands to make their bad mood felt to their loved ones. In the concerned families there is a constant nervous tension and unrest, which represents a risk in terms of mental hygiene for young people.

From: *Sozialärztliche Rundschau,* 4 [1933] no. 3, pp. 43-46. Translated by Franz J. Vesely

V.E. Frankl

A. Batthyány (ed.), *Logotherapy and Existential Analysis*, Logotherapy and Existential Analysis: Proceedings of the Viktor Frankl Institute Vienna 1,
DOI 10.1007/978-3-319-29424-7_1

In a further category of our consultees, where sexual problems are involved, the economic crisis sometimes confronts us in tragic ways. For instance, when young fellows report that they have voluntarily renounced on the beloved girl, in order to spare her the misfortune of living at the side of the unemployed! Or the girl, whose parents have placed a ban on her dealing with an unemployed young man "because he has no future". On this occasion, I wish to remark that we can hardly imagine the heroism with which young people bear their tragic fate, but also the great sense of responsibility and maturity displayed by many of these - mostly proletarian - young people.

Finally, with respect to the cases of neurosis, the following principal remarks are to be noted. The economic situation is in interplay with the human psyche. It is partly cause, partly consequence of mental disorders. In cases where economic need is based on mental disorders, we have to discriminate between direct and indirect causation. Insofar as we deal with neuroses, i.e. the latter, only indirect causation will represent the more common type. It seems that the individual has some leeway, within which he is conditionally free to move. In other words: the impact of the economic crisis on the neurotic person is not direct, but first passes through a kind of intermediary zone, in which it interacts with preformed psychopathological mechanisms, with a neurotic *disposition*, so to speak. In this context we have the opportunity to observe certain attitudes, which have been described in recent psychotherapeutic research, for example the "arrangements" in the sense of Individual Psychology, which are so familiar to every psychotherapist. The respective type of client will find in his economic plight a pretext towards his peers and an excuse towards himself, for his complete failure. I would say that it apparently is a demand of spiritual economy to ensure that the shoe will pinch on one place only; with the help of the thought: "yes, if I were not unemployed, then everything would be quite different" - the type in question can concentrate his whole suffering on one single point, and one of which he can safely assume that it cannot serve as the starting point of cure. In other words, the economic emergency gains the character of a scapegoat on which to push the blame for the botched existence.

But the economic crisis not only enables typical forms of neuroses, by providing them with fuel, it also makes them – necessary. In this regard we may rightly speak of a provocation of neurotic reactions: the difficult human situation will actually *suggest* an escape into neurosis. All the more it is a very *specific psychotherapeutic task of our time* to attempt to eliminate the psychological overlay of economic distress, to delete its psychological aspect, so to speak. We have to keep in mind that a neurosis will retroactively increase the economic hardship, that for example a discouraged, depressed unemployed will have, *ceteris paribus,* lower chances to find a job than another, who has been relieved from the unnecessary "ballast" of a neurosis. In this respect, economic distress is at least in part the consequence of a neurosis.

A further, non-specific form of the neurosis of the unemployed should finally be mentioned, and one which may duly be called the unemployment neurosis proper. It is usually characterized by a general apathy of alarming level. An everyday figure in our offices is the youth who – often since leaving school – is unemployed and remains in bed until noon, firstly because he has nothing really to do, secondly because he gets less hungry or at least can overcome his hunger more easily. Afternoons and evenings he will sit around in a small coffee house and spend his last dime for a black coffee, which buys him the stay in the warm room, the distraction by a newspaper and society and maybe a card game. There he meets a circle of dubious characters whose demoralizing influence he cannot resist, just because of his apathy. I remember the case of a boy who in this manner was drawn into a real criminal gang whose members were recruited from unemployed young people, some of them high school graduates. The tragic aspect of such apathy is that it prevents these young people from even *letting* themselves be helped, from taking and holding the hand you extend to them. In the cited case the youth counseling service had already helped the teenager also in the way of economic support when he undertook a suicide attempt; when he subsequently once again visited the youth consultant, he reported that at the time he had been simply too apathetic to get to him in time, although he knew that he would maybe obtain help again.

In stark contrast, we also get to know boys and girls who can only be described as true heroes. With rumbling stomach they work in some organization, are active as volunteers in libraries or do assistant service in adult education centers. They are replete with devotion to a cause, an idea, maybe even to a struggle for better times, to build a new world, which would also solve the problem of unemployment. Their leisure time, of which they have an unfortunate abundance, is filled by useful employment: they read and learn, listen to lectures and courses, play and take part in sports. (In this context I wish to recall the exemplary effectiveness of the initiative "Youth in Need" [Jugend in Not] and its day centers.)

Evidently, the opposite type of youth, who may be described as apathetic, depressed, neurotic, is lacking – and this cannot be stressed enough – not so much the work itself, the professional activity as such, as the feeling to achieve anything at all, but the awareness that their life is not without meaning or purpose. The young are *crying out, at least as much as for work and bread, for a goal and purpose of life, for a meaning of existence*. Young people who approached me in the youth counseling center, desperately asked me to employ them with some errand, or made quite grotesque offers to me. (One wanted to clean the hall always after the office hours, that is to say, after many people had been through my apartment). I have the feeling that the young generation is underestimated: with regard to their endurance (just look at so many cheerful faces, despite everything) and with regard to their efficiency (consider with what zeal some are pursuing their studies). The new generation is setting forth from a new objectivity and yearns for a new – morality; for ways to realize values. This should be taken into account; for I cannot imagine that anything would be more suited to enable people to endure and to overcome subjective complaints and objective difficulties than *the feeling to have a task* – a mission!

With this in mind, I usually ask the discouraged young unemployed whether they really believe that life becomes worth living by the bare fact that you work eight hours a day in a grocery, or toil for some employer or the like. The answer is "no", and I clarify to them what this "no" means, in a positive way: professional work does not represent the only chance to make life meaningful! Indeed, the spiritual cause for the described apathetic state is the erroneous identification of profession and vocation. From the foregoing it is imperative for every young unemployed to find a suitable *life purpose*; to *search* for it – this is the immediate specific task! He is called to organize and rationalize his private life, and to make the best use of his time, even if it means just beginning to study English, for example. (A week later he may already have knowledge of 100 words; he will be no less hungry, but he will have gained a sense of having achieved something.)

The consultant is regrettably hardly able to change the economic *position* of the young; however, in most instances he will be able to influence the *attitude* towards it. The consultant should bring about such a change in the person concerned that he or she gains the ability to endure the economic plight if it is necessary, and to resolve it if that is possible.

Questions and Answers, June, 30, 1966

Viktor E. Frankl

Question: *How does man work for self-transcendence as contrasted with self-actualization?*
VF: I do not wish to debase the concept of self-actualization. I am in touch with Abraham Maslow and admire him very much. We both agree that self-actualization is an excellent thing. However, self-actualization is only obtainable to the extent to which a man fulfills the meaning of his life or for that matter, the unique meaning of each unique life situation. Then self-actualization occurs automatically and spontaneously, as it were, while it would be spoiled and destroyed and would be self-defeating if I tried to attempt to obtain it in a direct way, by way of direct intention. Only to the extent to which I fulfill a meaning do I also actualize myself. *Per effectum* rather than *per intentionem.*

Question: *You say meaning is inherent in a situation and therefore distinct from values?*
VF: I would say that values are general universal meanings and by being universal meanings, they alleviate the human situation. Being guided by universal values, we are not compelled incessantly to make existential decisions. In the final analysis, man is finding and fulfilling meanings, guided and sometimes also misled by his finite conscience. Conscience is creative in that a man might find that the meaning of which he becomes aware through conscience contradicts any general or universal values. Then he is creating a new value because the meaning discovered through creative conscience today becomes the universal values of tomorrow.

June 30, 1966 at Horace Mann Auditorium, Teachers College, Columbia University, sponsored by the International Center for Integrative Studies

V.E. Frankl

A. Batthyány (ed.), *Logotherapy and Existential Analysis*, Logotherapy and Existential Analysis: Proceedings of the Viktor Frankl Institute Vienna 1,
DOI 10.1007/978-3-319-29424-7_2

Question: *Does your concept of meaning through suffering not give rise to the danger of masochism?*

VF: There is no danger of masochism because meaning, potential meaning, is only available in indispensable, inescapable, unavoidable suffering. To needlessly shoulder the cross of suffering in the case of an operable cancer when pain relief is available doesn't constitute any meaning. This would be sheer masochism rather than heroism. Nowhere have I found a clearer differentiation between unavoidable, necessary suffering (which gives an opportunity to transmutation into a meaningful achievement) on the one hand, and on the other hand, unnecessary, avoidable suffering (which does not yield any meaning) than in an advertisement which I read in a New York newspaper. It was written in German but an American friend translated it into English. It was couched in the form of a poem and this poem read as follows:

> *"Calmly bear without ado*
> *That which fate imposed on you"*

That is to say, unavoidable suffering should be borne courageously and thereby made into a human heroic achievement:

> *"Calmly bear without ado*
> *That which fate imposed on you,*
> *But to bedbugs don't resign*
> *Turn for help to Rosenstein."*

Question: *Doesn't your view of the noological dimension imply that the psychiatrist is not competent to administer existential therapy in the noological dimension?*

VF: This is not true. The job assigned to psychiatrists is to make a clinical symptom transparent against the higher dimension, the intrinsically human dimension and thus it *is* the job of the psychiatrist to treat noogenic neurosis. Particularly, this is his assignment in an age like ours in which, as the famous German Catholic psychiatrist, Viktor von Gebsattel, says men are migrating from the priest, pastor or rabbi toward the psychiatrist. A psychiatrist today has to play the role of a substitute for ministry or as I have called it, the role of the medical ministry. No one is justified in saying: "Oh, these people are confronted with existential or philosophical or spiritual problems; we don't wish to embark on dealing with such problems. They should go to a priest, or if they are non-believers then I don't care." These people confront us and we have to do our best. This is not just my personal conviction. There is even a paragraph in the constitution of the world's largest medical association, the American Medical Association, which states that a doctor, when he is not able to cure a patient or even to bring relief from pain, is entitled and even obliged to try to offer some consolation. So this area still pertains to the realm of the medical profession.

Question: *Two people have asked whether you have been in touch with Rabbi Leo Baeck.*

VF: I met Rabbi Leo Baeck in a concentration camp. It was more than just a meeting, it was a true encounter. From then on, I kept in touch with him. Rabbi Leo Baeck was assigned to write a chapter on the borderlines between Judaism and psychotherapy in a five-volume encyclopedia of neurosis theory and psychotherapy, which I edited with V.E. von Gebsattel and J. H. Schultz from Berlin. While working on that manuscript, Rabbi Baeck died in London and thus he could not complete his assignment.

Question: *Is there a place for religion in your theory?*
VF: There cannot be a place for religion in a psychiatric school or theory, precisely because of the difference of dimension. The only thing that can be demanded of a psychiatric approach is that it be left open toward a higher dimension. Psychiatry is no closed system. Psychiatry must remain open so that the religious patient is not done an injustice, but is understood in intrinsically human terms rather than becoming a victim of a reductionist approach to neurosis and psychotherapy. If for no other reason, I am compelled by the Hippocratic Oath on which I had to swear when I took the medical degree, to guarantee that Logotherapy be available for each and every patient, including the agnostic patient and usable by each and every doctor, including the atheistically oriented doctor. Psychotherapy belongs to medicine, at least according to the legislation of Austria, and so the Hippocratic Oath is applicable to psychotherapy, including Logotherapy. Thus I have to be available for each and every suffering human being.

Question: *Do you believe man can overcome despair without a personal God or religious orientation?*
VF: It does not matter what I personally believe. I speak and stand for a school called Logotherapy. Logotherapy seeks to know, not to believe. The ultimate decision, the most personal decision for or against a religious *Weltanschauung* or philosophy of life is up to the patient rather than to the doctor. Logotherapy doesn't have the answers, but Logotherapyis education toward responsibility and thus the Logotherapist is least in danger, of all psychiatric schools, of taking responsibility for such a decision from the shoulders of the patient. He will try to enable the patient to make a decision of his own.

Question*: How can you explain the concept of God?*
VF: Of course, as a Logotherapist, as a psychiatrist for that matter, I cannot explain it. And it would be a very dangerous venture to try to explain it. An apropos example was given by Sigmund Freud in a letter addressed to the great, late famous Swiss psychiatrist, the creator of *Daseinsanalyse* Ludwig Binswanger. Freud said that all his life he had restricted his view to the basement and ground floor of the edifice - that is to say, to a lower dimension. This is not a debasing expression; it doesn't imply any value judgment. It is just that the less inclusive dimension is overarched and humanized by adding the intrinsically human dimension. So Freud was aware of the limitation of his view and was no reductionist when saying so. He only became the victim of the reductionism of his era when he continued his first sentence by saying: "I also believe that I have found a place for religion in that edifice, in that basement, by disposing of it in terms of the collective neurosis of mankind." Only in that moment, even a genius such as Freud could not fully resist the temptation of reductionism.

Question: *Did you intend your last symbol to be a cross?*[1]
VF: I wonder if you know that I am not a Christian. It just happens that this diagram is a cross; but I don't mind that it is a cross. And further, viewed in terms of dimensional ontological teachings, I would have to say it may well be that in a higher dimension, this "happening" that the figure is a cross has a deeper or a higher meaning.

Question: *How do you counteract existential vacuum? How do you give meaning to a patient?*
VF: Despite my insistence that we do not *give* meaning, *we do* have to promote the patient to that point where he spontaneously *finds* meaning, because meaning is something to be found rather than to be given. You do not give meanings, attribute meanings, ascribe meanings, attach meanings to things or happenings as if reality were just a projective test. Reality is no neutral screen upon which you project your wishful thinking or upon which you express your inner makeup by attaching meanings. We cannot give meanings in an arbitrary way but if at all, in the way in which we give answers. In the final analysis there is one answer only to each question. There is one solution only to each problem and likewise in the final analysis there is one meaning only to each situation - the right meaning, the true meaning. Reality, rather than being a Rorschach blot into which we project our wishful thinking, expressing ourselves, is rather a hidden figure and we have to find out the meaning. I made the statement that giving meanings is something like giving answers. Let me explain this by evoking something, which happened a few years ago on a theological campus. People in the audience were given cards and invited to write their questions in block letters - printed. Then a theologian gathered the questions and in passing them to me, singled out one and wanted to skip it. I asked why. He said, "It's sheer nonsense. 'Dr. Frankl, how do you interpret 600 in your theory of existence?" I looked at it and said, "Excuse me, I read it in a different way: 'Dr. Frankl, how do you interpret GOD in your theory of existence?'"

It is a projective test, isn't it? The theologian read "600" and the neurologist read "GOD', an unintentional projective test. I made a slide of it and used it as a projective test in classes of American students studying at the Vienna University. I showed them the slide and then invited them to vote on what it meant. Believe it or not, nine students said "GOD", nine others said "600" and four students oscillated between the two interpretations. What do I wish to convey to you? Only one mode of interpretation of the question was the right one. The way in which I understood the question was the right one. What do I mean by that? That each situation in life implies a question, a call. And we have to try to find out the meaning. You may now understand how I arrive at the definition of meaning. Meaning is that which is meant either by the man who asks a question or by life, which incessantly raises questions, existential questions, to be answered in an existential way by making decisions. But these decisions cannot be made arbitrarily, they must be made responsibly. That is to say, our answer is a call from life or from that super-personal entity called God,

[1] This refers to a diagram Frankl showed during his lecture.

which stands behind life asking questions. Our answer has to be an existential, responsible action; our answer is action rather than just an intellectual or rational answer.

Question: *What is your solution for ending the existential vacuum and how does it tie in with the religious feeling?*
VF: I have spoken of meanings to be found and have made the clear-cut statement that meaning cannot be given, least of all by a doctor, to the life of a patient. A book has recently been published by Redlich and Friedman and unfortunately both authors dismiss Logotherapy as an attempt to give meanings to patients. Thus you see, one cannot but be misunderstood again and again, even by people who receive reprints of your writings for years in which they may read: "Meaning cannot be given; meaning must not be given by a doctor; meaning must be found by the patient himself." If you think it was a Logotherapist who contended that he had the answers, you are mistaken. It was not a Logotherapist, but a serpent in Paradise who said: "I tell people what is wrong and what is right and what is meaningful and what is meaningless."

Let me conclude. What is to be done for a young man, for instance, who cannot see any meaning in life, at least not immediately? He should be made aware that this condition, which is called existential vacuum, is no neurotic symptom. Rather than being something to be ashamed of, it is something to be proud of. It is a human achievement. It is above all, particularly a prerogative of young people; not to take for granted that there is meaning inherent in human existence, but rather to try, to venture, to question and to challenge the problem of meaning of existence. This is an achievement to be proud of rather than a neurosis to be ashamed of. If a neurosis at all, it is a collective neurosis. It is a neurosis of mankind. But if such a young man has the courage to pose such questions, he should also have the patience to wait until meaning will dawn upon him. And until that time - if he is caught in the existential vacuum, in this abysmal feeling (this abyss experience, to put it alongside the peak experience so beautifully elaborated on by Abraham Maslow) - if need be, he should tell himself: This dreadful experience is exactly what Jean Paul Sartre describes so beautifully in his work on *Being and Nothingness*. In this way, he is enabled to put distance between this dreadful experience and himself. There are two main features and traits, which characterize and constitute human existence. The first is self-transcendence - the fact that man is always reaching beyond himself, reaching out for meaning to fulfill, for other beings to encounter. The second is self-detachment, the intrinsically human capacity to rise above the level of somatic and psychic data, above the plane within which an animal being moves and to which an animal being is bound. Man is by no means fully free. Man is not free from determinants. Man's freedom is a finite freedom, not freedom from conditions; his freedom lies in the potentiality for taking a stand toward whatever conditions might confront him.

When Professor Huston C. Smith interviewed me on this matter of human freedom I said, "Man is determined but he is not pan-determined." Then Professor Smith said, "You, Dr. Frankl, as a professor of neurology and psychiatry are certainly aware that there are conditions and determinants to which man is bound." I replied: "Well, Dr. Smith, you are right. I am a neurologist and a psychiatrist and as such I know very well the huge extent to which man is conditioned - is subject to biological, psychological and sociological conditions. But apart from being a professor in two fields, I am also a survivor of four concentration camps, and as such, I bear witness to the incredible and unexpected extent to which man is also capable of braving conditions, be they the worst conditions, including those of a camp such as Auschwitz."

Memorial Speech on the 40th Anniversary of the Liberation of the Türkheim Concentration Camp (Dachau Complex), April 27, 1985

Viktor E. Frankl

Honored guests,

First, I thank you for the honor you have shown me by inviting me. You have given me the power to speak, and so I may also speak on behalf of the dead. The city of my birth is Vienna, but Türkheim is the place of my rebirth. Rebirth after the fist half of my life. A short while ago I turned eighty, and my fortieth birthday was spent in the concentration camp at Türkheim. My birthday gift then was, that after weeks of typhus fever, I became free of the fever for the first time.

So my first greeting is to my dead companions. My fist thanks, however, go to the high school students, who had the memorial stone made. And I also thank them in the name of the dead, to whom it is dedicated. But I must also say thank you, to those who liberated us, who saved the lives of us, survivors, and I want to tell you a little story. When a couple of years ago I was in the capital of Texas, giving a lecture at its university on the psychotherapy I founded, Logotherapy as it is called, the mayor made me an honorary citizen. I replied that rather than make me an honorary citizen of his town, I should really name him an Honorary Logotherapist. For if young men from Texas had not risked their lives and some of them also sacrificed their life to liberate us, then as of 27 April 1945 there would have been no Viktor Frankl, to say nothing of any Logotherapy. Tears came to the mayor's eyes.

Now I also have to thank the people of Türkheim. Whenever I gave the last lecture of the semester at the United States International University in California, I would show, at the request of the students, a series of slides: photos [of the camps] I had taken – after the war. And at the end I always showed them a slide that I had taken on the other side of the railway embankment, showing the front of a large farmhouse, in front of which I had gathered the large extended family that lived there. These were the people who, during the last days of the war, risked their lives by hiding Hungarian Jewish girls who had escaped from the camp! With this slide

V.E. Frankl

A. Batthyány (ed.), *Logotherapy and Existential Analysis*, Logotherapy and Existential Analysis: Proceedings of the Viktor Frankl Institute Vienna 1,
DOI 10.1007/978-3-319-29424-7_3

I wanted to show what my deepest conviction is – and has been from the very first day after the war: namely that there is no collective guilt! Let alone – if I may so call it – retroactive collective guilt, in which someone is held responsible for what their parents' or even grandparents' generation may once have done.

Guilt can only be personal guilt - guilt for what one has done oneself or even not done, neglected to do. But even then we must have some understanding of the fears of those concerned – fear for their freedom, even their lives, and not least fear for the fate of their families. Certainly, there have been those that have nonetheless preferred to let themselves be put in a concentration camp, rather than be unfaithful to their convictions. But actually, one may only demand heroism of one person - and that person is oneself. At the very least, a person is only really justified in asking heroism of others if that person has proved that they preferred to go into a concentration camp rather then conform or make compromises. But those who sat safely abroad, they cannot ask of others that they should prefer to go to their deaths rather then pursue opportunism. And consider this: those who were in the camps judge in general much more mildly than say, the émigrés who were able to secure their freedom, or those who were not even born until decades later.

Finally I cannot help but also thank a man who unfortunately could not attend this thanksgiving. I mean the commandant of the Türkheim camp, Herr Hofmann. I can still see him standing in front of me, as we arrived from the camp of Kaufering III, in ragged clothes, freezing, without blankets; and hear as he began to curse most heartily because he was so appalled that we had been sent there in this state. It was also he who secretly, as we later found out, bought medicines from his own pocket for his Jewish prisoners.

A few years ago I invited some Türkheim citizens who had helped camp inmates to a get-together at a local inn; I wanted Herr Hofmann to come too, but, as it turned out, he had died shortly before. From a certain spiritual advisor whom you all surely know (he, too, has died in the meantime) I now know that Herr Hofmann himself, he who should have had the very least need, was until the end of his life plagued by self-reproach. How willingly, and with what conviction, would I have eased his mind.

Now you will surely object: that's all well and good, but people like Herr Hofmann are exceptions. Maybe. But *they* are what counts. At least when it comes to understanding, forgiveness, reconciliation! And I feel it legitimate to say this, for it was no lesser person than the famous, late Rabbi Leo Baeck, who back in 1945 – just imagine, 1945! – wrote a "Prayer for Reconciliation", in which he explicitly says: 'Only goodness shall count.'

And if you point out to me that there was in fact so little goodness, then I can only answer with the words of another great Jewish thinker, namely the philosopher Benedictus de Spinoza, whose main work, *Ethics*, concludes with the words: *ed omnia praeclara tam difficilia, quam rara sunt.* "Everything that is great is as rare to find, as it is difficult to do." In fact, I myself believe that decent people are in the minority, have always been and will always be. But that's nothing new. There is an ancient Jewish legend, according to which the existence of the world depends on there always being thirty-six – no more than thirty-six! - righteous people in the world. Well, I cannot tell you exactly how many there are, but I am convinced that in Türkheim there were, and there certainly still are, a couple of righteous people. And when we now remember the dead of the Türkheim camp, I would like also to thank in the name of these dead the righteous people of the town of Türkheim.

Memorial Speech on the 50th Anniversary of Austria's Incorporation into Germany: Rathausplatz, Vienna, March 10, 1988

Viktor E. Frankl

Ladies and Gentleman,

I hope for your understanding when I ask you in this hour of remembrance to join me in thinking of: my father – he perished in the Theresienstadt camp; my brother – he died in Auschwitz; my mother - she was killed in the gas chamber in Auschwitz; and my first wife – she lost her life in Bergen-Belsen. And yet, I must ask you to expect no words of hatred from me. Whom should I hate? I know only the victims, not the perpetrators, at least I do not know them personally – and I refuse to call people collectively guilty. There is no collective guilt, it does not exist, and I say this not only today, but I've said so from day one when I was liberated from my last concentration camp – and at that time it was definitely not a way to make oneself popular - to dare publicly to oppose the idea of collective guilt.

Guilt can in any case only be personal guilt – the guilt for something I myself have done – or may have failed to do! But I cannot be guilty of something that other people have done, even if it is my parents or grandparents. And to try to persuade today's Austrians between the ages of naught and fifty of a sort of "retroactive collective guilt", I consider to be a crime and an insanity – or, to put it in a psychiatrist's terms, it would be a crime, were it not a case of insanity. And a return to the so-called "kin liability" of the Nazis. And I think that the victims of former collective persecution should be the first to agree with me. Otherwise it would be as if they set great store by driving young people into the arms of the old Nazis or the neo-Nazis!

I shall now come back to my liberation from the concentration camp: I then took the first possible lift I could get (even if only illegally possible) on a truck back to Vienna. In the intervening years I have been to America sixty-three times; but every time I returned to Austria. Not because the Austrians loved me especially, but rather, the other way round, because I love Austria so much, and we know that love

V.E. Frankl

A. Batthyány (ed.), *Logotherapy and Existential Analysis*, Logotherapy and Existential Analysis: Proceedings of the Viktor Frankl Institute Vienna 1,
DOI 10.1007/978-3-319-29424-7_4

is not always based on reciprocity. Well, whenever I am in America, the Americans ask me: "Mr. Frankl, why didn't you come to us *before* the war – you could have spared yourself a great deal." And I then have to explain to them, that I had to wait for years to get a visa, and how when it finally arrived, it was already too late, because I simply could not bring myself, in the middle of the war, to leave my elderly parents to their fate. And then the Americans ask me: "Well, why didn't you at least come to us *after* the war - hadn't the Viennese done enough to you - you and yours?"

"Well," I then say to these people, "in Vienna there was, for example, a Catholic baroness, who at the risk of her own life hid a cousin of mine as a 'U-boat' (an illegal) and thus saved my cousin's life. And then in Vienna there was a certain socialist lawyer who at great personal risk gave me food whenever he could." Do you know who that was? Bruno Bittermann, subsequently Vice-Chancellor of Austria. Now I go on to ask the Americans why should I *not* return to such a city, where there are such people?

Ladies and Gentlemen, I hear you say: that's all well and good, but those were only exceptions – exceptions to the rule, and as a rule people were just opportunists – they should have shown resistance. Ladies and gentlemen, you are right, but consider: resistance presupposes heroism, and in my opinion one may demand heroism only of a single person, and that is – oneself! And whoever then says that someone should have preferred to be locked up rather than get on with the Nazis, then that person can only actually say this if they themselves have proved that they preferred to let themselves be put in a concentration camp, and consider this: those who were in concentration camps do in general judge the opportunists far more lightly – more lightly than those who stayed abroad for the duration. Not to mention the younger generation – how can they imagine how afraid people were and how they trembled for their freedom, for their very lives and for the fate of their families, for whom they were always responsible. We can only admire all those who dared to join the resistance movement. I am thinking here of my friend Hubert Gsur, who was sentenced to death for undermining the military and executed by the guillotine.

National Socialism nurtured racism. In reality there are only two races, namely the "race" of decent people and the "race" of people who are not decent. And "segregation" runs through all nations and within every single nation straight through all parties. Even in the concentration camps one came across halfway decent fellows here and there among the SS men – just as one came across the odd scoundrel or two among the prisoners. Not to mention the Capos. That decent people are in the minority that they have always been a minority and are likely to remain so – is something we must come to terms with. Danger only threatens, when a political system sends those non–decent people, i.e. the negative elements of a nation, to the top. And no nation is immune from doing this, and in this respect every nation is in principle capable of a Holocaust. In support of this we have the sensational results of scientific experiments in the field of social psychology, for which we owe thanks to an American (they are known as the Milgram Experiment).

If we want to extract the political consequences from all this, we should assume that there are basically only two styles of politics, or perhaps better said, only two types of politicians: the first are those who believe that the end justifies the means, and that could be *any* means.. While the other type of politician knows very well that there are means that could desecrate the holiest end. And it this type of politician whom I trust, despite the clamor around the year 1988, and the demands of the day, not to mention of the anniversary, trust to hear the voice of reason and to ensure that all who are of good will, stretch out their hands to each other, across all the graves and across all divisions.

Thank you for your attention.

Two Letters after the Liberation from the last Concentration Camp, Türkheim (Dachau Complex), 1945

Viktor E. Frankl

Dear Stepha and dear Wilhelm,

I am writing this letter to you today with every haste. I am currently in Bad Wörishofen, the famous Kneipp spa resort in Bavaria, in a large, elegant hotel which until recently was being used as a German hospital and is now a hospital and accommodation for Jewish prisoners brought here from the many surrounding concentration camps. I'm now working here as the supervising doctor on the medical side of things for the Jewish patients as well as for the American authorities, after having myself been in a nearby concentration camp (Türkheim). This is what happened: in September 1942 my parents, my young wife and I went to the Theresienstadt ghetto, unlike the majority of Viennese Jews who were sent to Poland (my position at the hospital meant that we were to that extent "privileged"). In February 1943 my poor father died, from starvation. I could at least spare him the final agony with an injection of morphine in his last hour. Later, in particular when packages from Vienna and parcels of sardines via Portugal got through, things were much better. Until suddenly the mass deportations began. In October 1944 I had to go, leaving my poor mother alone, while my wife voluntarily gave her name to come with me. After days of travelling in unimaginable circumstances, we arrived at the infamous concentration camp of Auschwitz. Apart from about 100 of us, every one of the 1,500 people on my transport were gassed and burned on the same day. My wife and I appeared fit enough for work to the SS doctor sorting people on the platform and so we were sent to the side of the station for those who – as we later learned – were destined to remain alive. In the disinfection process, we all lost everything that we had, we kept only our spectacles and our belts – and everything else, all documents, photos, clothes, belongings, my academic life's work (a print-ready manuscript) – they were all lost in a minute, along with the hair on our heads, which was sheared off us. We were given impossibly old shoes and worn trousers and jackets – which

V.E. Frankl

A. Batthyány (ed.), *Logotherapy and Existential Analysis*, Logotherapy and Existential Analysis: Proceedings of the Viktor Frankl Institute Vienna 1,
DOI 10.1007/978-3-319-29424-7_5

had to last for half a year! Once in four days, a small piece of bread. What else can I tell you – there would be no end to it. After four days we were lucky enough to be transferred to a different camp, one where there is *no* crematorium – after a terrible journey of three days and nights to Kaufering in Bavaria – like the Türkheim concentration camp a sub-camp of Dachau, where I now had the honor of receiving prisoner number 119104. Now I had become a laborer. In minus 20 degrees of frost, in open shoes (they did not fasten and I could not wear foot rags, because like almost all of us I had serious oedema caused by hunger), with no underwear, on a daily ration of 20g of bread and some watery soup. I had to hack at the frozen ground with picks and pickaxes to dig water pipes etc. for mysterious underground factories that were being planned. In the earthen huts in the camp, where the icicles hung down from the roof (on the inside!), my companions simply dies right and left alongside me, many stronger than I, many Viennese physicians among them. That I am alive can only be described as a series of 1001 of God's miracles. We were of course also beaten hard. In March I was finally transferred to a "better" camp, in Türkheim. There I worked as a doctor. I caught typhus (epidemic typhus). Sixteen days of fever up to 40 degrees in my then physical condition! On my fortieth birthday I was free from fever for the first time and out of life-threatening danger. I then continued to work as a doctor with my remaining strength, often still with a fever and with the most severe neuralgia. Even today, my heart muscle is somewhat damaged. You can imagine how happy one is (in my situation), simply to still be alive. On 27 April the Americans liberated us. (Immediately before that I had already made an attempt to escape, when I had to bury one of the many dead bodies outside the barbed wire.) In a very short time I had regained kilo after kilo, everything was like a dream in the first days, one could not actually be happy about anything – believe me, one had literally forgotten how! Unfortunately, to this day I am still unclear about the fate of my people, whether my mother remained in Theresienstadt, whether my wife has come from a concentration camp back to Vienna. I cannot go there for the present, not even write. Also, I know nothing about Walter! My mother-in-law, who was deported from Theresienstadt in June 1944 (she had come there with us, along with my wife's grandmother), has not been heard from, except once. Hopefully everyone is alive. I fear the moment of certainty … when one comes home.

Since the day before yesterday, I have been re-dictating my manuscript in shorthand and so my mind has been on other thoughts. Maybe I'll be able to continue my scientific work in Vienna again, for as long as I can or must stay there. It all depends on how things are looking for my mother and my wife: the former will surely want to go to Australia, and Tilly to her people in Brazil.

I would ask you to inform Stella if possible, sparing some of the details; also my father-in-law, Professor Ferdinand Grosser, Porto Allegre, Brazil, my brother-in-law Gustav Grosser in Zurich, who is employed by a Jewish Relief Committee there, perhaps still living in Manessestrasse (?).

God knows what other urgent and important matters I have forgotten to tell you in my haste! I am still tired from today's dictation – for my book "The Doctor and the Soul", which hopefully may soon be published somewhere, so I can finally have this mental confinement behind me. So keep your fingers crossed for me that all things concerning my relatives turn out well, and hopefully you have not already forgotten...

Your Viktor

My dears!

I've been in Vienna for four weeks now. Finally there is an opportunity to write to you. But I have only sad news to communicate: shortly before my departure from Munich, I learned that my mother was sent to Auschwitz a week after me. What that means, you know all too well. And I had scarcely arrived in Vienna when I was told that my wife is also dead. She was sent from Auschwitz to work in the trenches at Trachtenberg in Breslau, and then on to the infamous concentration camp of Bergen-Belsen. There, the women endured 'terrible, indescribable suffering', as it was put in a letter from a former colleague of Tilly's, in which Tilly's name is listed as one of those who died of typhus (the letter comes from the only survivor of the former hospital nurses, such as there were in Bergen-Belsen). I have had the 'indescribable' depicted to me by a survivor of Bergen-Belsen. I cannot repeat it.

So now I'm all alone. Whoever has not shared a similar fate cannot understand me. I am terribly tired, terribly sad, terribly lonely. I have nothing more to hope for and nothing more to fear. I have no pleasure in life, only duties, and I live out of conscience.. And so I have re-established myself, and now I am re-dictating my manuscript, both for publication and for my own rehabilitation. A couple of well-placed old friends have taken on my cause in the most touching way. But no success can make me happy, everything is weightless, void, vain in my eyes, I feel distant from everything. It all says nothing to me, means nothing. The best have not returned (also, my best friend [Hubert Gsur] was beheaded) and they have left me alone. In the camp, we believed that we had reached the lowest point – and then, when we returned, we saw that nothing has survived, that that which had kept us standing has been destroyed, that at the same time as we were becoming human again it was possible to fall deeper, into an even more boundless suffering. There remains perhaps nothing more to do than cry a little and browse a little through the Psalms.

Perhaps you will smile at me, maybe you will be angry with me, but I do not contradict myself in the slightest, I take nothing away from my former affirmation of life, when I experience the things I have described. On the contrary, if I had not had this rock-solid, positive view of life – what would have become of me in these last weeks, in those months in the camp? But I now see things in a larger dimension. I see increasingly that life is so very meaningful, that in suffering and even in failure there must still be meaning. And my only consolation lies in the fact that I can say in all good conscience, that I realized the opportunities that presented themselves to me, I mean to say, that I turned them into reality. This is the case with respect to my short marriage to Tilly. What we have experienced cannot be undone, it has been, but this Having-been is perhaps the most certain form of being.

To finish, some happy news: Vally Laufer is alive and well in Vienna, stayed here in hiding as a "U-Boot" [an illegal)! I leave it to you to let Stella and my father-in-law, as well as my brother-in-law Gustav D. Grosser, gradually know the truth. Sadly Walter also probably died at Auschwitz. And Tilly's aunt, Hertha Weiser, lost her husband in a shootout in the final days of fighting in Vienna. Are you in contact with EH, EK, TK? – Have you received my second letter via Berman? Forgive these disjointed scribblings but I have to write bit by bit during my surgery hours.

With warmest greetings!

Your Viktor

Part II
Research

Measuring Purpose

Kendall Cotton Bronk

Given the multiple dimensions and subjective nature of the purpose in life construct, measuring it presents a challenge (Melton and Schulenberg 2008). Perhaps because of that, a range of methodological approaches has been used to study purpose. Surveys, interviews, rankings, diary studies, and historical document reviews have been utilized to assess purpose and related constructs. Additionally, measures have been created for use with adolescent, emerging adult, and adult samples.

In line with the history of psychological research, early measures of purpose focused on assessing areas of deficit (Melton and Schulenberg 2008). Tools were developed to study purposelessness among individuals who were depressed, addicted to drugs or alcohol, or otherwise psychologically unfit (e.g., Crumbaugh 1968; Crumbaugh and Maholick 1964; Reker 1977). However, in conjunction with the growth of positive psychological research, more recent assessments of purpose tend to be growth-oriented (e.g., Bronk 2008, 2011, 2012; Bronk et al. 2009, 2010; Damon 2008). Rather than emphasizing the lack of purpose, these studies focus on the positive correlates of leading a life of purpose.

Following is an overview of the tools most commonly used to measure purpose from both deficit and growth-oriented perspectives. The following discussion features measurement tools that have been used with some regularity in empirical studies and that were designed to assess a conception of purpose similar to one put forth in this book.

Reprint of Chapter 2, Bronk, K. C. (2013). Purpose in life: A component of optimal youth development. New York: Springer. With kind permission from Springer, New York.

K.C. Bronk (✉)
Division of Behavioral and Social Sciences Department of Psychology,
Claremont Graduate University School of Social Science, Policy, and Evaluation,
150 E. 10th Street, CA 91711, Claremont
e-mail: kcbronk@cgu.edu

A. Batthyány (ed.), *Logotherapy and Existential Analysis*, Logotherapy and Existential Analysis: Proceedings of the Viktor Frankl Institute Vienna 1,
DOI 10.1007/978-3-319-29424-7_6

Surveys Aligned with Frankl's Conception of Purpose

Surveys are the most common assessment tool for the study of purpose, and Viktor Frankl (1959) developed the first psychological survey of purpose in life. Called the Frankl Questionnaire, this self-report measure consists of a relatively informal set of 13 questions. It was created to both assess Frankl's Will to Meaning assumption and to evaluate the degree of purpose present among his patients. He believed that when individuals were unable to find a purpose for their lives they suffered varying degrees of existential frustration, typically manifest as boredom, apathy, or depression. According to Frankl approximately 20 % of patients seeking psychological counseling suffer from a severe lack of purpose in life (noogenic neurosis) and 55 % of the general public suffers from at least some degree of purposelessness (existential vacuum) (Crumbaugh and Maholick 1964; Crumbaugh 1968). Frankl's evaluation of the presence of purpose depended largely on an individual's response to one questionnaire item, "Do you feel your life is without purpose?" (Crumbaugh and Maholick 1964). Participant responses are coded from "1: no or very low level of purpose or meaning" to "3: high purpose in life present" and are added to scores on the other 12 questions to determine the individual's purpose level.

Frankl used his measure for clinical rather than research purposes. However, two individuals used the measure to conduct empirical studies. Crumbaugh and Maholick (1964) administered the Frankl Questionnaire to a population of psychiatric and more typical adults and found more typical individuals consistently scored higher on purpose than psychiatric patients did, supporting Frankl's theory about the relationship between purpose and mental health. However, given that the measure's reliability and validity have not been assessed, researchers (Reker 1977) have called into question the adequacy of the Frankl Questionnaire as an independent measure of purpose.

Crumbaugh and Maholick agreed that the Frankl Questionnaire was limited as a research tool, so they created a new survey of purpose designed to apply "the principles of existential philosophy to clinical practice" (1964, p. 200). The idea that mental illness could result from existential factors, such as a lack of purpose, went against conventional wisdom at the time (Damon et al. 2003; Kotchen 1960). Behaviorism and psychoanalytical theories prevailed, but Crumbaugh and Maholick, were eager to further test Frankl's controversial thesis.

In consultation with Frankl, Crumbaugh and Maholick (1964) developed the most widely used measure of purpose to date (Pinquart 2002). Their Purpose in Life Test (PIL) improves upon the Frankl Questionnaire, and as such it relies on Frankl's conception of purpose, or "the ontological significance of life from the point of view of the experiencing individual" (Crumbaugh and Maholick 1964, p. 201), and tests Frankl's Will to Meaning assumption (Crumbaugh and Maholick 1964, 1981). In particular, the survey assesses the degree to which individuals strive to make meaning of their conscious experiences and the degree to which that meaning leaves individuals feeling as though their lives are worthwhile and significant (Crumbaugh and Henrion 2001). However, it does not assess an individual's commitment to issues beyond-the-self (Damon et al. 2003).

The PIL consists of three parts: parts A, B, and C. Since only part A is objectively scored, it is the only part that is regularly used in empirical studies of purpose. Part B asks participants to complete 13 sentences about purpose and Part C asks them to compose a paragraph about their personal aspirations. Part A originally consisted of 25 items, but following pilot tests about half of the items were discarded or revised and new questions were added. A 22-item measure resulted (Crumbaugh and Maholick 1964). For simplicity sake, two-reverse scored items are typically omitted in empirical studies using the PIL, leaving a 20-item measure (Crumbaugh 1968; Crumbaugh and Maholick 1981). This 20-item version of the PIL is a self-report measure of attitudes and beliefs that includes statements such as, "I am usually," with response options that range from "1: completely bored" to "7: exuberant, enthusiastic," and "In life I have, 1: no goals or aims at all—7: very clear goals and aims." The total scale score is obtained by summing item scores. Raw scores of 113 and above are typically interpreted as high purpose, scores of 92–112 reflect moderate levels of purpose, and scores of 92 and below suggest a lack of life purpose (Crumbaugh and Maholick 1964). As expected, the PIL and the Frankl Questionnaire are positively correlated ($r=0.68$; $p<0.05$) (Crumbaugh and Maholick 1967).

The PIL has been administered to a wide range of individuals including women in Junior League (Crumbaugh and Maholick 1964), college students (Crumbaugh 1968; Crumbaugh and Maholick 1964), hospitalized individuals (Crumbaugh 1968), people suffering from alcoholism (Crumbaugh and Maholick 1964; Crumbaugh 1968), psychiatric patients (Crumbaugh and Maholick 1964), business professionals (Bonebright et al. 2000; Crumbaugh 1968), members of religious groups (Crumbaugh 1968), and inmates (Reker 1977). Modified versions of the PIL have also been administered to geriatric (Hutzell 1995), adult (Reker and Peacock 1981), and adolescent populations (Hutzell and Finck 1994; Jeffries 1995). The measure has been translated into a variety of languages, including Chinese (C-PIL; Shek 1993; Shek et al. 1987), Japanese (J-PIL; Okado 1998) and Swedish (Jonsen et al. 2010).

PIL scores correlate with many measures of psychological health. For example, several studies have shown significant negative correlations between the PIL and the Minnesota Multiphasic Personality Inventory—Depression scale ($r=-0.30$ to $-0.65, p<0.01$; Crumbaugh and Maholick 1964, 1981; Crumbaugh 1968), and significant positive correlations have been reported between the PIL and the self-acceptance ($r=0.40$, $p<0.01$), sense of well-being ($r=0.52$, $p<0.01$), achievement via conformance ($r=0.63$, $p<0.01$), and psychological mindedness ($r=0.47$, $p<0.01$) subscales of the California Psychological Inventory (CPI; Bonebright et al. 2000). The PIL is also negatively correlated with the Srole Anomie Scale ($r=-0.48$ for males and $r=-0.32$ for females, $p<0.05$; Srole 1956), suggesting that the concept of the existential vacuum and anomie, or a lack of social norms, may overlap (Crumbaugh 1968).

The PIL has been subjected to more tests than any other measure of purpose. In sum, the measure appears to be a reliable measure of the degree of personal meaning present among both adult (Crumbaugh 1968; Crumbaugh and Maholick 1967; Guttmann 1996; Meier and Edwards 1974; Reker 1977) and adolescent samples (Sink et al. 1998). For example, Sink et al. (1998) administered the 20-item PIL to samples of rural and urban adolescents and reported Cronbach's alpha values of 0.88 and 0.86, respectively. One-week retest reliability coefficients have been found to range from 0.68 to 0.83 ($p<0.01$, Meier and Edwards 1974; Reker 1977). A 6-week retest coefficient of 0.79 ($p<0.001$, Reker and Cousins 1979) and 8-week retest coefficients of 0.66 among rural and 0.78 among urban samples have also been reported (no *p*-values reported; Sink et al. 1998). Reliability estimates among adult samples are similar to those reported with adolescents (Guttmann 1996). Spearman-Brown Corrected split-halt reliability coefficients ranging from 0.76 to 0.85 corrected by the Spearman-Brown formula to 0.87 and 0.92 have been obtained in four different studies with adults (Crumbaugh 1968; Crumbaugh and Maholick 1964; Hutzell 1988; Reker 1977; Reker and Cousins 1979).

Among adult samples, the PIL also appears to be a valid measure of Frankl's will to meaning concept (Chamberlain and Zika 1988; Crumbaugh 1968; Crumbaugh and Henrion 1988; Crumbaugh and Maholick 1967; Hutzell 1988; Reker 1977). Construct validity has been supported by various comparisons of group means of different populations (Crumbaugh and Maholick 1981). Consistent with Frankl's theory, low PIL scores are significantly associated with suicide ideation (Harlowe et al. 1986; Kinnier et al. 1994), psychopathology (Kish and Moody 1989), depression and anxiety (Schulenberg 2004), and drug use (Harlowe et al. 1986; Kinnier et al. 1994; Padelford 1974), while high PIL scores predict positive self-concept, self-esteem, internal locus of control, life satisfaction, and planning (Reker 1977). In fact, because many of the PIL's questions probe happiness, some have argued that the PIL may actually be an indirect measure of life satisfaction (Damon et al. 2003) or an inverse measure of depression (Dyck 1987; Schulenberg 2004; Steger 2006; Yalom 1980). However, positive correlations between purpose and indicators of well-being and negative correlations between purpose and depression are never perfect, suggesting that the PIL is assessing a related but distinct construct.

Questions have also arisen with regards to the dimensionality of the life purpose construct measured by the PIL. Some researchers, using exploratory and confirmatory factor analysis, have concluded that the measure only assesses a single factor when certain items are excluded (Dale 2002; Marsh et al. 2003). Others have argued that it is clearly multidimensional. For instance, based on a qualitative review of the items, Yalom (1980) suggested that the survey assessed six different constructs, including purpose, life satisfaction, freedom, fear of death, suicidal thoughts, and how worthwhile one perceives one's life to be. Others have used factor analytic techniques to identify distinct dimensions. For instance, Shek (1988) concluded that the measure consists of five dimensions, including feelings regarding one's quality of life, goals, death, choices, and retirement. Still others have argued that it features only two dimensions, but they disagree on what those two dimensions are. Using exploratory factor analysis, one team of researchers concluded that the measure assessed an affective (sum of items 3, 4, 13, 17, 18, and 20) and a cognitive dimension (sum of items 1, 2, 5, 6, 8, 9, 11, 12, 16, and 19) (Dufton and Perlman 1986; Shek 1993; Shek et al. 1987), while other researchers concluded it assesses an exciting life (items 2, 5, 7, 10, 17–19) and a purposeful life (items 3, 8, 20; Morgan and Farsides 2009). As a result of these contradictory findings, simply creating a composite score, if they do not assess a single factor, is likely to compromise the reliability and validity of the results and consequently has been cautioned against (Marsh et al. 2003). Additional assessments of the measure with a wider range of participants are clearly needed.

In part as a means of addressing the dimensionality issues raised with the full-length PIL, a shortened version was recently proposed. The Purpose in Life—Short Form (PIL-SF; Schulenberg et al. 2011) includes four of the PIL items that, according to confirmatory factor analytic techniques, fit well together. These four items focus primarily on goal attainment (questions 3, 4, 8, and 20). The internal consistency reliability coefficient alpha for the 20-item PIL was 0.86 and for the independently administered 4-item PIL-SF it was 0.84, suggesting that the short version is as reliable as the long one (Schulenberg et al. 2011). When administered separately, responses to the short form correlated with responses on the full PIL ($r=0.75$, $p<0.01$, one-tailed), and similar to the PIL, scores on the PIL-SF also correlate positively with scores on measures of psychological well-being and negatively with scores on measures of psychological distress. The PIL-SF appears to represent a viable alternative to the full PIL, but it has rarely been used in empirical research.

The PIL, on the other hand, continues to be used regularly with adolescent (Sink et al. 1998) and adult samples (Crumbaugh 1968; Crumbaugh and Maholick 1967; Guttmann 1996; Meier and Edwards 1974; Reker 1977), but it has not frequently been administered to younger individuals. This is likely because some items are inappropriate for early adolescents. For instance, items regarding the clarity of life goals may be too abstract for early adolescents, questions probing the reasons for existence may be beyond the lived experience of early adolescents, and items about death likely represent issues that most early adolescents do not regularly consider. Therefore, researchers interested in assessing purpose among early adolescents selected only the PIL items that were relevant to the lives of youth and created an Existence Subscale of Purpose in Life Test (EPIL; Law 2012). The 7 items of the EPIL focus on enthusiasm and excitement about life, a belief that daily activities are worthwhile, and a conviction that life has meaning. The creators of the measure conducted an assessment of the scale's psychometric properties with 2842 early adolescents (Law 2012). They obtained a Cronbach's alpha value of 0.89. Exploratory factor analysis identified one factor that accounted for 60 % of the variance, and the factor structure was stable across genders. To assess the measures criterion-related validity, it was successfully used to differentiate volunteers from non-volunteers, whereby early adolescent volunteers scored higher on the EPIL than early adolescent youth who were not involved in volunteer activity. Though these findings suggest that the EPIL could be a useful measure of purpose among early adolescents, it has rarely been used in empirical studies. Of course, that may be because the measure is still relatively new.

Similar to the EPIL, the Life Purpose Questionnaire (LPQ; Hablas and Hutzell 1982; Hutzell 1989) represents another variation on the PIL; however, this one has been more widely administered. Because the PIL uses different response anchors for each question, researchers have argued that it may be confusing for some participants (Harlowe et al. 1986; Schulenberg 2004). Therefore, the LPQ was developed as an uncomplicated, easily administered, paper-and-pencil measure of life meaning and purpose. Like the PIL, this measure includes 20 items that assess aspects of purpose and meaning, but unlike the PIL it includes statements, rather than phrases, to which participants respond using a simple dichotomous-choice format (agree—disagree). The LPQ was designed for use with specialized populations of individuals who are likely to be confused by the PIL, including geriatric participants, neuropsychiatric inpatients, alcoholics, and individuals with other special needs (Hablas and Hutzell 1982; Hutzell and Peterson 1986).

Among adults, the LPQ appears to be a psychometrically sound measure of purpose (Hablas and Hutzell 1982). Correlations between the LPQ and the PIL have been found to range from 0.60 to 0.80 (Hutzell 1989; Kish and Moody 1989), and, similar to the PIL, scores on the LPQ correlate positively with life satisfaction and negatively with depression (Hutzell 1989). However, psychometric properties of the LPQ have not been as thoroughly investigated as psychometric properties of the PIL, and additional assessments have been called for (Kish and Moody 1989). In spite of this, the measure does appear to be a useful for assessing purpose among special populations that struggle to understand the more confusing PIL response options (Hutzell 1989). In fact, respondents report that they prefer taking the LPQ to the PIL (Schulenberg 2004).

The Life Purpose Questionnaire has also been adapted for use with adolescents (Hutzell and Finck 1994). The measure omits two items that are not relevant to younger participants (Item 7: "Retirement means a time for me to do some of the exciting things I have always wanted to do." Item 15: "I am not prepared for death.") The remaining 18 items in the Life Purpose Questionnaire—Adolescent version (LPQ-A; Hutzell and Finck 1994) include questions such as the following, "I am often bored," "I have definite ideas of the things I want to do," and "My life is meaningful." Respondents agree or disagree with each of the statements. The measure has been used to assess life purpose among young people undergoing alcohol and drug treatment.

The LPQ-A measure has not been used much in empirical research. As such, its psychometric properties have rarely been investigated beyond the limited assessments conducted by its authors (Hutzell and Finck 1994). As a means of assessing the measure, Hutzell and Finck administered it to two groups of adolescents: one group consisted of youth in a support group for drug and alcohol use ($n=100$) and the other group included more typical youth ($n=100$). Each of the 18 items in the measure was correlated with the total score of the remaining items, and correlations ranged from 0.21 to 0.55 for the support group, averaging 0.37, and from 0.23 to 0.62 for the more typical group, averaging 0.48. Since this measure is based on Frankl's theory regarding the centrality of purpose to human well-being, the authors expected to find that the typical group would score higher than the support group. Results confirmed this hypothesis. The support group mean score was 10.6 (SD=4.1) while the typical group mean score was 12.5 (SD=4.5), and this difference was statistically significant ($t(198)=3.13$; p two-tailed <0.01).

The Purpose In Life Scale (PILS; Robbins and Francis 2000) represents yet another measure of purpose based largely on the PIL. This unidimensional measure consists of 12 items, including the following, "My life seems most worthwhile,"

"I feel my life has a sense of purpose," and "My life has clear goals and aims." Participants respond via a 5-point Likert scale ("1: strongly disagree" to "5: strongly agree.") Psychometric properties of the PILS were assessed among a sample of 517 undergraduate students. A Cronbach's alpha value of 0.90 was obtained, and high scores on the measure were found to be associated with church attendance ($r=0.11$, $p<0.001$), stable extraversion ($r=0.23$, $p<0.001$), and low levels of neuroticism ($r=-0.35$, $p<0.001$) (Robbins and Francis 2000).

In addition to helping develop the PIL, Crumbaugh later developed the Seeking of Noetic Goals Test (SONG) as a complement to the PIL. Just as the PIL assesses the degree to which individuals have found a purpose for their lives, the SONG assesses the degree to which individuals are actively searching for a purpose for their lives (Crumbaugh 1977).

The SONG represents the earliest measure of record to assess the search for purpose. The motivation to find purpose is referred to by Frankl as noetic, or the spiritual, inspirational, aspirational, or non-material aspects of life. Frankl believed people should be motivated to search for a larger meaning for their lives. However, in spite of Frankl's focus on issues beyond-the-self, items in the SONG do not directly assess these kinds of concerns. Instead, items include the following: "I think about the ultimate meaning in life," "I am restless," and "I feel that some element which I cannot quite define is missing from my life." Responses are scaled on a 7 point Likert scale (from "1: never" to "7: constantly").

Several researchers have assessed the psychometric properties of the SONG (e.g., Crumbaugh 1977; Melton and Schulenberg 2008; Reker and Cousins 1979). Reported Cronbach alpha coefficients range from 0.81 to 0.84, and 6 and 8-week retest reliabilities range from 0.66 to 0.78 (no p-values reported in either study; Reker and Cousins 1979; Sink et al. 1998). The SONG appears to distinguish between patient and non-patient groups whereby, as would be expected based on Frankl's will to meaning assumption, psychiatric patients are less motivated to search for purpose than non-patient adults (Crumbaugh 1977).

According to Crumbaugh (1977), scores on the PIL and SONG questionnaires should be inversely related since people with a purpose in their lives should not be motivated to search for one. As Crumbaugh (1977) predicted, SONG scores are significantly negatively correlated with PIL scores ($r=-0.33, p<0.001$; Reker and Cousins 1979). Further, using ten dimensions of life satisfaction, researchers (Reker and Cousins 1979) determined that items loaded on six factors in the PIL and on four factors in the SONG, suggesting again that the PIL and SONG function, as intended, as complementary measures. However, Crumbaugh (1977) proposed that the search for purpose and the presence of purpose were always inversely related, and this does not appear to be the case. Assessments using different measures of purpose have concluded that the search for purpose and the presence of purpose appear to be inversely related among adults, but not among adolescents (Bronk et al. 2009; Steger and Kashdan 2007). To date the PIL and SONG have not been administered together to adolescent samples.

The Life Attitude Profile-Revised (LAP-R; Reker 1992) is yet another survey measure based on Will to Meaning assumption. It is a multidimensional measure designed to assess both current levels of purpose and the motivation to find purpose. The original LAP (Reker and Peacock 1981; Reker et al. 1987) included 56 items, but revisions resulted in a 48-item measure that is conceptually tighter and composed of an equal number of items per dimension (Reker 1992). The LAP-R consists of six dimensions including, purpose, coherence, choice/responsibility, death acceptance, existential vacuum, and goal seeking. Two composite scales are derived from these dimensions: the personal meaning index (purpose + coherence) and existential transcendence (purpose + coherence + choice/responsibility + death acceptance minus existential vacuum + goal setting). The six LAP-R dimensions have been shown to be internally consistent, stable over time, and valid measures of their respective constructs (Reker 1992). Questions in the LAP-R include, "My past achievements have given my life meaning and purpose" and "I feel that some element which I can't quite define is missing from my life." Participants respond to these questions via a 7-point Likert scale ("1: strongly disagree" to "7: strongly agree"), and scores correlate significantly with PIL scores, Life Regard Index-Revised Framework scores, and ratings of meaningfulness (Reker 1992).

Measures such as the LAP-R were designed for use with more typical respondents, but similar measures have also been created for use with more specialized groups of individuals. Frankl believed that challenges and even suffering presented opportunities to discover a purpose in life, and based on this premise, Patricia Starck (1983) created the Meaning in Suffering Test (MIST; Starck 1983, 1985) which assesses levels of meaning in life specifically related to unavoidable suffering. The MIST has two parts. The second part is primarily used for gathering potentially useful information for therapy (Starck 1985), but it is difficult to quantify (Schulenberg 2004) and as such is not frequently used in research. The first part, however, is composed of 20 items including, "I believe suffering causes a person to find new and more worthwhile life goals," and "I believe everyone has a purpose in life; a reason for being on Earth." Responses are scored on a 7-point Likert scale ("1: never" to "7: constantly"). The measure consists of three subscales: subjective characteristics of suffering, personal response to suffering items, and meaning in suffering (Starck 1985). MIST scores among nursing students and hospitalized patients correlate significantly with scores of other measures of purpose and related constructs (Guttmann 1996; Schulenberg 2004; Starck 1985).

The MIST has not been used extensively in empirical studies, but a fairly recent investigation reveals that while total MIST scores demonstrate acceptable internal consistency (Cronbach's alpha = 0.83), two of the measure's three subscales demonstrate low internal consistency (Cronbach's alpha = 0.52 for the 6-item subjective experience of suffering subscale and Cronbach's alpha = 0.53 for the 8-item personal responses to suffering subscale; Schulenberg 2004). As such, when using the MIST in research it is advisable to use the total score rather than the subscale scores (Schulenberg et al. 2006).

Finally, the last measure of purpose based on Frankl's conception of the construct is the Revised Youth Purpose Survey (Bundick et al. 2006). While measures exist that assess both identified purpose and the search for purpose, and measures exist to assess purpose among both adult and adolescent populations, this is the first measure that assesses both identified purpose and the search for purpose among adolescents. In addition to drawing from the PIL, items in this measure are also adapted from other existing measures of purpose (Ryff's Scales of Psychological Well-being; Ryff and Keyes 1995) and meaning (Meaning in Life Questionnaire; Steger et al. 2006). The multidimensional scale was designed to probe the search for purpose, the presence of purpose, active engagement in working toward purpose, and the centrality or significance of purpose. However, repeated use of the survey reveals that these four components can be collapsed into two subscales: an Identified Purpose subscale (15 items; Cronbach's alpha = 0.94) and a Searching for Purpose subscale (5 items; Cronbach's alpha = 0.94; Bronk et al. 2009; Burrow et al. 2010). Participants rate the survey items on a 7-point Likert scale with higher scores indicating greater Identification and more Searching. "I have discovered a satisfying life purpose," is an Identified subscale item and "I am seeking a purpose or mission for my life" is a Searching subscale item.

As previously discussed, scores on the Searching and Identified subscales are positively correlated among adolescents and emerging adults, but not among midlife adults. In other words, adolescents who report having a purpose in life also tend to report searching for one, but consistent with the PIL and SONG relationship, midlife adults who have a purpose in life do not report searching for one (Bronk et al. 2009). Unfortunately, the PIL and SONG have not been administered to adolescent and young adult samples, but the emerging pattern of results suggests that the relationship between searching for and having identified a life purpose may be developmental in nature. The Revised Youth Purpose survey is a relatively new measure, and as a result, it should be subjected to additional tests of psychometric soundness.

Ryff's Purpose in Life Sub-scale

Behind Crumbaugh and Maholick's PIL test, Ryff's Purpose in Life subscale is the second most widely administered measure of purpose (Pinquart 2002). Ryff was an early advocate for empirical research on positive human health. She conceptualizes psychological well-being as consisting of six dimensions: autonomy, environmental mastery, personal growth, positive relations with others, self-acceptance, and life purpose (Ryff and Singer 1998). Called the Scales of Psychological Well-being, her self-report inventory is designed to assess an individual's welfare at a particular moment in time in each of these six areas. Subscales can be administered all together or on their own. The purpose in life subscale includes 20-, 14-, 9-, and 3-item versions. Individuals are asked to respond to questions such as, "I live life one day at a time and don't really think about the future (reverse scored)," and "Some people wander aimlessly through life, but I am not one of them." Responses are scaled from 1 to 6 on a Likert scale, with higher scores indicating the presence of more goals, greater direction in life, and a stronger purpose. Repeated assessments of the 20-item version reveal Cronbach alpha values ranging from 0.88 to 0.90 and a 6-week retest reliability score of 0.82 (Ryff 1989; Ryff et al. 1994, 2003). The 3-item scale was developed for use with telephone surveys, but it is not been found to be internally consistent (Ryff and Keyes 1995).

Antonovsky's Sense of Coherence Survey

Antonovsky's widely administered Sense of Coherence Scale (SOC; 1983) measures a construct similar to purpose. Commonly used in medical research, the SOC was developed to assess "salutogenesis," or the origins of health. More specifically, the SOC gauges the degree to which individuals believe their lives are comprehensible, manageable, and meaningful. Taken together, these beliefs support useful coping mechanisms, and individuals who hold these beliefs are likely to effectively manage stressful situations and stay well. Questions in the SOC include, "How often do you have the feeling that there is little meaning in the things you do in your daily life?"; "Do you have very mixed-up feelings and ideas?"; and "Do you have the feeling that you are in an unfamiliar situation and don't know what to do?" There are at least 15 versions of the SOC (Eriksson and Lindstrom 2005), but the most common versions are the original 29-item version (in which participants respond on a 7-point Likert scale) and a 13-item version (which uses the same response scale and includes a subset of the questions from the longer survey; Jakobsson 2011). While it might be tempting to use the meaning component of the SOC on its own, Antonovsky (1987) warned against this, saying it was intended for use as a measure of dispositional coping comprising all three subscales and its psychometric properties only apply to the full scale.

In 2005, researchers (Eriksson and Lindstrom 2005) conducted a rigorous review of nearly 500 scientific publications featuring the SOC. They determined that in 124 studies using the measure, Cronbach's alpha values ranged from 0.70 to 0.95 and that retest correlations ranged from 0.69 to 0.78 over 1 year, from 0.59 to 0.67 over 5 years, and 0.54 over 10 years. They also concluded that SOC scores typically increase with age. Psychometric problems have arisen with shortened versions of the SOC (e.g., in a study of 1753 participants, the 13-item version failed to show acceptable construct validity; Jakobsson 2011).

Like Antonovsky's "salutogenic" approach (1987), the Life Regard Index (LRI; Battista and Almond 1973) similarly assesses the degree to which life is viewed as meaningful and comprehensible. In particular, it measures the extent to which individuals demonstrate a positive regard for life, which Battista and Almond (1973) define as "an individual's belief that he is fulfilling his life as it is understood in terms of his highly valued life-framework of life-goals" (p. 413). The LRI is a self-report questionnaire composed of two subscales. The Framework subscale (LRI-FR) assesses the degree to which individuals can envision their lives within a meaningful perspective or have derived a set of life-goals, and the Fulfillment subscale (LFR-FU) measures the degree to which individuals see themselves as having fulfilled or as being in the process of fulfilling their framework or life goals.

The LRI includes 28 items. Half of the statements are phrased positively ("I have a clear idea of what I'd like to do with my life") and half are phrased negatively ("I don't really value what I'm doing"). In its original form the survey asked participants to respond on a 5-point Likert scale, but Debats (LRI-R; 1998) suggested a new 3-point Likert scale to avoid extreme responses ("1: I disagree," "2: I have no opinion," or "3: I agree").

The LRI has been subjected to a number of tests of psychometric soundness (e.g., Battista and Almond 1973; Chamberlain and Zika 1988; Debats et al. 1993, 1995). Cronbach's alpha values for the full LRI range from 0.87 to 0.91 depending on the sample (e.g., Cronbach's alpha = 0.87 among typical students; Cronbach's alpha = 0.91 among distressed students; Cronbach's alpha = 0.91 among general population sample). Reported internal consistency scores were similar for the two subscales (Cronbach's alpha LRI-FR = 0.84 among general population sample and Cronbach's alpha LRI-FU = 0.87; Debats et al. 1993). Five-week retest reliabilities for were calculated using Spearman's rho and yielded a coefficient of 0.80 (LRI), 0.73 (LRI-FR), and 0.79 (LRI-FU). Scores do not differ significantly either for the measure as a whole or for the subscales based on educational level or sex. However, married individuals do report significantly higher LRI scores than never married ($t=3.43$, (130), $p<0.001$) and divorced individuals ($t=3.56$, (156), $p<0.001$). To establish the construct validity of the LRI, the measure was correlated with a measure of happiness ($r=0.73$, $p<0.001$), depression ($r=-0.59$, $p<0.001$), anxiety ($r=-0.40$, $p<0.001$), and general psychological distress ($r=-0.52$, $p<0.001$). Lastly, similar to other PIL measures, the LRI differentiates between typical and distressed samples, whereby typical individuals report higher life regard scores than do distressed individuals ($t=10.8$ (269), $p<0.001$, $d=1.36$; Debats et al. 1993).

In a mixed-methods assessment of the LRI, researchers had participants compl te the survey and respond to open-ended questions regarding specific experiences of meaning and meaninglessness. Results suggest that individuals who score high on positive life regard (as measured by the LRI) are more likely to describe experiences of meaningfulness with a variety of people including family, friends, and strangers, in which positive interactions, such as helping, and caring correspond with enjoying life fully and experiencing a sense of well-being (Debats et al. 1995). The authors conclude that meaningfulness, as assessed by the LRI, manifests as a state of positive engagement with others. Given this, and given the lack of goal orientation and beyond-the-self commitment, this measure appears to assess a construct more akin to meaning than purpose.

However, a multidimensional measure of purpose based in part on the LRI was recently proposed. Called the Meaningful Life Measure (MLM; Morgan and Farsides 2009), this survey actually assesses a construct more similar to purpose than meaning since it is composed of select items from the LRI, PIL, and Ryff's Psychological Wellbeing purpose subscale. This 23-item measure includes goal-oriented probes such as the following: "I have a clear idea of what my future goals and aims are," and "I tend to wander aimlessly through life, without much sense of purpose or direction" (reverse scored). Participants respond via a 7-point Likert scale ("1: strongly disagree" to "7: strongly agree"). Exploratory factor analysis reveals that the measure yields five factors, including, the exciting life, the accomplished life, the principled life, the purposeful life, and the valued life. Two of these factors, the purposeful life and the valued life, most closely assess life purpose as it has been conceived of in this book. The principled life measures understanding, the accomplished life gauges responsibility, and the exciting life captures enjoyment.

Preliminary assessments, with a sample composed primarily of college females, suggest that the measure is psychometrically sound. Alpha coefficients for the five subscales range from 0.85 to 0.88, and 6-month retest coefficients range from 0.64 to 0.70 (Morgan and Farsides 2009). However, additional studies are needed to confirm that the measure is reliable with a wider range of participants. Additional tests are also needed to assess the measure's convergent and discriminant validity.

Survey Measures of Meaning and Constructs Related to Purpose

Another cluster of measures assesses constructs closely related to purpose. For example, the Sources of Meaning Profile (SOMP; Reker and Wong 1988) measures the source and degree of personal meaning in one's life at different ages. The SOMP includes 16 items, and participants are asked to indicate on a 7-point Likert scale how important each potential source of meaning is to them. Potential sources of meaning include participating in leisure activities, leaving a legacy for the following generation, and serving others. The 16-item measure has yielded Cronbach alpha values of 0.77 and 0.78 (Reker 1988; Prager 1996) and a 3-month retest reliability coefficient of 0.70 (Reker 1988; Prager 1996).

In contrast to the SOMP, which assesses psychologists' theoretical ideas regarding what should represent individuals' sources of life meaning, the Personal Meaning Profile (PMP; Wong 1998) assesses laypeople's implicit theories of what actually does make their lives meaningful. Originally, this self-report measure consisted of 59 items, but following a revision it was cut down to 57 items that assess seven sources of life meaning, including achievement/striving (16 items), relationships (9 items), religion (9 items), transcendence (8 items), self-acceptance (6 items), intimacy (5 items) and fair treatment (4 items). These factors represent individuals' implicit theories of what makes life meaningful in practice as well as under ideal circumstances. The measure assesses the magnitude or intensity of life meaning (the greater the overall score, the more successful a person is in approximating the ideally meaningful life), the breadth of meaning (individuals who seek meaning from a variety of sources have a broader basis than individuals who derive meaning from only one or two sources), and balance (participants who score roughly equivalent across dimensions of meaning demonstrate a more balanced approach to life meaning). Research finds that self-ratings correlate with prototypical ratings and with criterion scores, suggesting that individuals who score higher on the PMP are closer to approximating an ideally meaningful life. Questions in the PMP include the following, "I have found someone I love deeply," and "I attempt to leave behind a good and lasting legacy." Participants respond to these questions via a 7-point Likert scale ("1: not at all" to "7: a great deal"). While the PMP's conception of meaning shares with purpose a focus on personal significance, it differs in that it lacks both future directedness and a commitment to the broader world.

The Meaning in Life Questionnaire represents another regularly administered measure of meaning (MLQ; Steger et al. 2006). This 10-item survey tool includes two 5-item subscales: a searching for meaning subscale and a presence of meaning subscale. All items are scored on a 7-point Likert scale from "1: absolutely untrue" to "7: absolutely true." A sample Searching item includes, "I am always searching for something that makes my life feel significant," and a sample Presence item includes, "I understand my life's meaning." Recent use of this measure yielded a Cronbach alpha value of 0.80 (Yeagar and Bundick 2009). The measure is valid to the extent that it positively relates to a variety of measures of well-being, including life satisfaction and positive affect, and negatively relates to depression (Steger et al. 2006; Steger and Kashdan 2007).

Whereas the Meaning in Life Questionnaire assesses relatively stable feelings of meaning, a nearly identical measure, the Daily Meaning Scale (DMS; Steger et al. 2008; Stillman et al. 2009) assesses how participants feel "right now." Like the Meaning in Life Questionnaire, the Daily Meaning Scale includes both a Presence subscale (e.g., "Right now, how meaningful does your life feel?" 5-item, Cronbach's alpha = 0.78) and a Searching subscale (e.g., "How much are you searching for meaning in your life?" 5-item, Cronbach's alpha = 0.92), both of which are scored on a 7-point Likert scale, "1: not at all" to "7: absolutely."

Less Commonly Used Survey Measures of Purpose

Another cluster of research tools conflates purpose with other constructs. For example, the Values in Action Inventory of Strengths (VIA) is a self-report survey that assesses a range of potential personal strengths. Designed to help individuals identify their particular combination of character strengths, this survey includes two versions, one for adults 18 years of age and older (VIA—IS; Peterson and Seligman 2004) and one for youth between 10 and 17 years of age (VIA—Youth; Dahlsgaard 2005). Using exploratory factor analysis, the 24 strengths can be collapsed into four groups, including strengths of temperance, wisdom, interpersonal functioning, and transcendence. Transcendent strengths include purpose. However, because purpose is lumped in with other transcendent strengths, including spirituality and gratitude, its scores are not typically reported alone.

The Inventory of Positive Psychological Attitudes (IPPA; Kass et al. 1991) represents another positive psychology scale that includes a purpose in life dimension. This 30-item questionnaire taps two domains, purpose/life satisfaction and self-confidence in potentially stressful situations. The inventory scales were developed using factor analysis and Kass et al. (1991) report Cronbach's alpha values ranging from 0.88 to 0.94 for the total IPPA scale. Positive correlations between the IPPA scale and affect balance ($r=0.66$, $p<0.0001$) and between the IPPA scale and self-esteem ($r=0.79$, $p<0.0001$) and negative correlations between the IPPA scale and loneliness ($r=-0.63, p<0.0001$) have also been obtained. An empirical study using the measure suggests that positive changes in scores on this test correlate with positive changes in the health status of individuals who suffer from chronic pain (Kass et al. 1991). Both of these measures, the VIA and the IPPA, combine purpose with other constructs, and therefore are not useful measures of purpose alone. However, their existence underscores the central role of purpose in assessing physical and psychological well-being.

Other measures of purpose have been administered in professional, rather than research, contexts. For example, the Developing Purposes Inventory (Barrat 1978) is based on Chickering and Reisser's Seven Vectors of Student Development. Created in 1969 (Chickering 1969) and updated in 1993 (Chickering and Reisser 1993), this model of college student growth was designed to assess emerging adults' growth in seven key areas, including: developing competence, managing emotions, moving through autonomy toward interdependence, developing mature interpersonal relationships, establishing identity, developing integrity, and developing purpose (Chickering and Reisser 1993). The "developing purpose" vector assesses students' reasons for attending college and for choosing particular careers. It also measures students' personal aspirations, their commitments to family and other aspects of their lives, and their ability to balance these commitments (Chickering and Reisser 1993).

Barrat (1978) created the Developing Purposes Inventory (DPI) to assess the degree to which students were committed to pursuing a life purpose. His measure consists of three 15-item sub-scales (45 items total) designed to measure each of Chickering and Reisser's (1993) three sub-vectors of developing purpose, including avocational or recreational purpose, vocational or professional purpose, and lifestyle or interpersonal purpose. Sample questions include the following: "I attend special lectures and programs that are about my recreational interests" (avocational purpose); "I read the items that have been suggested or recommended by an instructor for a class but are not required" (professional or career purpose); and "I think about how my personal values relate to my career plans" (lifestyle purpose). Students use a 5-point Likert scale ("1: never true" to "5: always true") to indicate how true each statement is for them.

Another tool designed to assess aspects of Chickering's theory of psychosocial development is the Student Developmental Task and Lifestyle Assessment (SDTLA; Winston 1990; Winston et al. 1999). Similar to the Developing Purposes Inventory, this measure has rarely been used in research, but has more often been used by student affairs professionals to help students understand and reflect upon their growth, to assist them in setting goals and planning for the future, and to guide interventions (Winston 1990). As such, this measure is designed for use with college students between roughly 17 and 24 years of age. It is composed of 140 true–false questions, drawn from six general categories including the following: developing mature interpersonal relations, academic autonomy, salubrious lifestyle, intimacy, establishing and clarifying purpose, and response bias.

The establishing and clarifying purpose dimension is of greatest interest here. Of the 140 total questions, 68 assess this developmental task. Establishing and clarifying purpose consists of five subtasks. The first is Educational Involvement (EI; 16 items), which measures the extent to which students have thoroughly explored and identified well-defined goals for their educational experience and the extent to which they show signs of being self-directed, active learners. The second dimension, Career Planning (CP; 19 items), measures the degree to which students have devised a professional plan that takes into consideration their strengths and weaknesses and their educational background. It also reflects the degree to which students have emotionally committed to a career plan. The third dimension, Lifestyle Planning (LP; 11 items), assesses the extent to which students have identified a personal direction for their lives that takes into account their religious and moral beliefs along with their family and vocational plans. Fourth, this instrument assesses students' Life Management (LM; 16 items) skills, or the degree to which students organize their lives to satisfy their daily needs and to meet their personal and financial responsibilities. Finally, this tool measures students Cultural Participation (CIP; 6 items), or their range of cultural interests and level of participation in cultural activities.

Assessments of the establishing and clarifying purpose measure have been conducted in conjunction with the development of the measurement. Cronbach's alpha values for this 68-item subscale range from 0.45 to 0.90. Two-week retest scores range from 0.80 to 0.87, 4-week retest scores from 0.76 to 0.85, and 20-week retest scores from 0.53 to 0.73 (Winston and Miller 1987; Winston 1988). Investigations into validity reveal that items in the same sub-scale correlate more strongly with each other than with items in any of the other sub-scales; however, items in the academic autonomy sub-scale correlate relatively highly with items in the purpose sub-scale. The purpose sub-scale was also found to correlate positively with measures of study skills, career planning, and career exploration (Winston 1988).

Finally, the last less commonly used measure of purpose is a 1-item survey. This measure asks participants, typically adolescents, to complete the following question, "I feel my life has a sense of purpose," using a 5-point Likert scale ("1: strongly agree" to "5: strongly disagree"; Francis 2000; Francis and Burton 1994; Francis and Evans 1996; Robbins and Francis 2000). This measure has not been administered frequently, given the limitations inherent in a single-item tool.

Taken together, studies utilizing the preceding survey measures of purpose have yielded considerable insight into our growing understanding of the construct both from research and practice perspectives. However, there is one significant problem with existing survey measures. None assesses the "other-oriented" dimension of the construct. None is able to discern whether individuals are motivated to pursue a purpose in life for reasons other than solely self-oriented ones, and this means that none of the existing survey measures is able to assess the full purpose construct. Designing a survey to achieve this task has proven challenging. To assess the illusive but essential beyond-the-self component of purpose, a survey would need to first establish what an individual found purposeful in his or her life and then probe why this aim was particularly meaningful. This multistep task is more easily accomplished using other research tools. In particular, interviews, diary studies, and document reviews have proven to be useful ways of assessing the beyond-the-self dimension of the purpose construct.

Interview Protocols

Interviews are typically used to provide qualitative, "thick descriptions" of an experience (Geertz 1983). They can be used to flesh out quantitative findings and to develop hypotheses that can later be tested in survey research. In the case of purpose, they are particularly useful in shedding light on the motivations behind one's purposeful aims. Unlike surveys, they can be used to better understand individuals' reasons for pursuing personally meaningful aspirations.

In spite of the usefulness of interviews in assessing all the key dimensions of purpose, they are infrequently used. In fact, after a thorough review of the purpose literature, I was only able to identify one interview protocol designed to assess purpose and one designed to assess generativity, a concept related to purpose. The scarcity of interview protocols is likely the result of the time intensive and expensive nature of carrying out interview research.

The Revised Youth Purpose Interview (Andrews et al. 2006) is a semi-structured interview protocol derived from studies of self-understanding and identity development (see, for example, Colby and Damon 1993; Damon and Hart 1988; Hart and Fegley 1995). The protocol consists of two parts. The first part features a line of questioning designed to determine what is particularly important to the individual. Questions in this section include more general, open-ended probes, such as, "What are some of the things you really care about?" and "What matters to you most?" To encourage participants to think about concerns beyond themselves, questions also ask about issues that matter to participants in the broader world. A question along this line includes the following: "Imagine you've been given a magic wand and you can change anything you want in the world, what would you want to be different?" Once interviewees have identified the aim or aims that matter most to them, the interviewer begins the second half of the interview, which focuses on gaining a deeper understanding of the role this potential driver plays in the interviewee's life. So, for example, if the interviewee has said one of the most important aspirations in his or her life is to have a family or help others through a particular career, then the remainder of the interview would focus on understanding just how central this particular aim is, why it is as central as it is, and what steps the interviewee has taken or plans to take in order to make progress toward this aim.

The interview takes about an hour to administer and has typically been used with adolescent and emerging adult samples (Bronk 2005, 2008, 2011, 2012; Bronk et al. 2010; Damon 2008; Moran 2009; Yeagar and Bundick 2009). Findings from studies administering this protocol have revealed much about the prevalence of purpose among different samples of young people (Bronk et al. 2010; Damon 2008; Moran 2009), the role of purpose in healthy identity development (Bronk 2011), and role of meaning in school work and professional plans (Yeagar and Bundick 2009). This protocol has also been used to build a theory of the way purposes develop and change over time (Bronk 2012) and to highlight characteristics of youth with purpose (Bronk 2008). Finally, because the interview protocol is, at present anyway, one of the few reliable ways of determining the motivations behind one's purposeful pursuits, it has also been used to examine the impact of pursuing personal aspirations for self-serving and beyond-the-self reasons. In one such study, characteristics and indicators of youth thriving with self-oriented and other-oriented long-term aims were compared (Bronk and Finch 2010). Results revealed that youth with beyond the-self long term aims reported higher levels of life satisfaction than youth with self-serving aims.

The other relevant interview protocol, the Life Story Interview (McAdams 2008), was designed to gather information about, among other things, generativity among older adults. Generativity represents Erikson's seventh stage of psychosocial development, and it describes adults' level of concern with leaving behind a positive legacy and with making contributions to the broader world that will outlive themselves. For example, parenting or volunteering can be generative acts. In this way, generativity shares with purpose an important focus on beyond-the-self motivations.

The Life Story Interview takes approximately 2 h to administer and is broken into eight sections. The first section focuses on the different chapters in the interviewees' life. The second section asks participants to discuss a variety of key scenes, including high points and low points, in their life story. Third, participants are asked to focus on the future and to discuss their hopes, dreams, and plans. In this section, participants are encouraged to discuss a life project, or "something that you have been working on and plan to work on in the future chapters of your life story. The project might involve your family or your work life, or it might be a hobby, avocation, or pastime" (McAdams 2008). Based on this description, a life project could represent a life purpose. Next, participants are encouraged to reflect on the challenges they have encountered in their lives. The sixth and seventh sections ask participants to reflect on their personal ideology, including their religious, moral, and political beliefs, and their life themes, respectively. Finally, the last section asks participants to reflect on the experience of being interviewed. Themes relevant to purpose and generativity are likely to surface in the life project interview section, but also throughout the interview.

Other Measures of Life Purpose

In addition to survey and interview measures, researchers have also utilized other means of assessing the purpose construct. Early in the study of purpose, Inhelder and Piaget (1958) reviewed the private diaries of a sample of twentieth-century adolescents in Switzerland. The essays, which were not written for public consumption, represent intimate documents. The researchers collected and reviewed them for other purposes, but they noted that the adolescents, without any prompting or encouragement, consistently discussed their hopes, dreams, and aspirations, and in so doing, frequently described various purposes. Despite the interesting and important findings regarding purpose and adolescent development more generally that resulted from this creative study, this approach has some limitations, including the great challenge presented in getting adolescents to share their personal and private musings with researchers. Beyond this, of course, this methodology precludes follow up questions, and does not allow for direct questioning of purpose. Bearing in mind these limitations, diary reviews clearly represent an interesting and potentially underutilized approach to studying the purpose construct.

Another way purpose has been explored is through reviews of historical documents. Mariano and Vaillant (2012) investigated adolescent and emerging adult purposes among the "greatest generation," or individuals who came of age during World War II. They reviewed health documents and interviews conducted with young men who served in World War II with the goal of identifying spontaneous references to purpose and beyond-the-self aspirations. While this approach yielded interesting findings regarding the nature of purpose among this generation, it suffers some of the same limitations as the diary review approach. These robust data sets are rare, expensive to compile, and preclude follow-up and direct questions about purpose.

Finally, DeVogler and Ebersole endeavored to identify the range of inspiring types of purpose or sources of meaning, and they employed a creative means of doing so. First, in the Meaning Essay Document, they asked participants to describe and rank their three most important sources of meaning and to list a concrete experience associated with each one (DeVogler and Ebersole 1980). The investigators had adolescents (DeVogler and Ebersole 1983), college students (DeVogler and Ebersole 1980), and adults (DeVogler and Ebersole 1981) complete this task, and what emerged was a useful classification of sources of meaning.

Subsequent to developing the Meaning Essay Document, Ebersole and Sacco (1983) created the Meaning in Life Depth instrument (MILD). In contrast to their earlier line of inquiry, this measure aims not only to identify different sources of meaning in life, but also to assess the depth of commitment to each source of meaning, partially independent of respondent's self-reports. To complete the MILD, participants rank from most to least personally significant eight commonly identified sources of meaning, derived from DeVogler and Ebersole's earlier studies. Participants are also given the option of selecting "no meaning" for their lives. Next, respondents are asked to write a brief essay about how significant their most important source of meaning is. Judges are then recruited to read the essays and to assign a depth score, relative to the other essays. However, given that a third party ultimately assigns a meaning level, the approach has been criticized as biased (Ebersole and Kobayakawa 1989).

It is clear from this review, that a wide range of tools exists to assess the purpose construct. Of course, no single measure is perfect, but taken together surveys, interviews, and other more creative methodologies are yielding a rapidly emerging picture of purpose—what it is, how it functions, and why it is important. Among other things, empirical studies relying on these measures reveal that purpose plays a central role in optimal human functioning.

Instrument name	Description	Sample question
Survey measures of the presence of purpose and related constructs		
Existence of Purpose in Life subscale (EPIL; Law 2012) for early adolescence	7 items selected from the PIL based on their relevance to the lives of early adolescents	"My life is—(1) *empty (7) running over with good things"*
Life Profile Questionnaire (LPQ; Hablas and Hutzell 1982)	20 items very similar to PIL; agree/disagree format to aid comprehension in geriatric, neuro-psychiatric patient, and other special populations	"I am usually able to think of a usefulness to my life,"—*agree, disagree*
Life Purpose Questionnaire—Adolescent Version (LPQ-A; Hutzell and Finck 1994)	18 items; agree/disagree format to aid comprehension among adolescent participants	"I have discovered many reasons why I was born,"—*agree, disagree*
Meaning in Suffering Test (MIST; Starck 1983)	20 items, 7-point Likert response format; yields a total score and three subscale scores	"I believe my suffering experience has given me a chance to complete my mission in life,"—(1) *never* (7) *constantly*
Purpose in Life Scale (PILS; Robbins and Francis 2000)	12 items with a 5-point Likert response option	"My personal experience is full of direction,"—(1) *disagree strongly* (5) *agree strongly*
Purpose in Life Test (PIL; Crumbaugh 1968; Crumbaugh and Maholick 1964)	20 items, 7-point Likert response format; different anchoring points for each item, with 4 being neutral	"Life to me seems"—(1) *completely routine*—(7) *always exciting*
Purpose in Life Test—Short Form (PIL-SF; Schulenberg et al. 2011)	4 items drawn from the PIL, 7-point Likert response format; different anchoring points for each item, with 4 being neutral	"In life I have"—(1) *no clear goals*—(7) *clear goals and aims*
Ryff's Scales of Psychological Well-being Purpose Subscale (Ryff 1989; Ryff and Keyes 1995)	20, 14, 9, and 3-item versions with a 6-point Likert response option; unidimensional measure of purpose represents one of six dimensions of psychological well-being	"Some people wander aimlessly through life, but I am not one of them"—(1) *strongly disagree*—(6) *strongly agree*
Sense of Coherence Scale (SOC; Antonovsky 1983, 1987)	29 and 13 item versions administered most commonly; 7-point Likert response format	"Until now your life has had"—(1) no clear goals—(7) *very clear goals and purpose*
Survey measures of the motivation to find purpose		
Seeking of Noetic Goals (SONG; Crumbaugh 1977)	20 statements rated on a 7-point Likert response format; unidimensional scale of the motivation to find purpose	"I feel that some element which I cannot quite define is missing from my life"—(1) *never*—(7) *constantly*

(continued)

(continued)

Instrument name	Description	Sample question
Survey measures of purpose and the motivation to find purpose		
Daily Meaning Scale (DMS; Steger et al. 2008)	10 items, 7-point Likert response format; 2 subscales, Presence of meaning (5 items) and Searching for meaning (5 items)	"Right now, how meaningful does your life feel?"—(1) *not at all*—(7) *absolutely*
Life Attitude Profile—Revised (LAP-R; Reker and Peacock 1981; Reker 1992)	48 items, 7-point Likert response format; yields six dimension and two composite scores	"My past achievements have given my life meaning and purpose"—(1) *strongly disagree*—(7) *strongly agree*
Life Regard Index (LRI; Battista and Almond 1973; Debats et al. 1995)	28 items with two subscales; Framework subscale measures existence of life goals and Fulfillment subscale measures progress toward life goals	"I have a clear idea of what I'd like to do with my life"—*I disagree, I have no opinion, I agree*
Meaningful Life Measure (MLM; Morgan and Farsides 2009)	23 items measure composed of items from the LRI, PIL, and Ryff's Psychological Well-being Purpose subscale	"I have a clear idea of what my future goals and aims are"—(1) *strongly disagree*—(7) *strongly agree*
Meaning in Life Questionnaire (MLQ; Steger et al. 2006)	10 items, 7-point Likert response format; 2 subscales, Presence of meaning (5 items) and Searching for meaning (5 items)	"I understand my life's meaning"—(1) *absolutely untrue*—(7) *absolutely true*
Revised Youth Purpose Survey (Bundick et al. 2006)	20 items, 7-point Likert response format; 2 subscales, Identified purpose (15 items) and Searching purpose (5 items)	"My life has a clear sense of purpose" (identified), "I am always looking to find my life's purpose" (searching)—(1) *strongly disagree* to (7) *strongly agree*
Personal Meaning Profile (PMP; Wong 1998)	57 items, 7-point Likert response format; 7 dimensions including achievement, relationships, religion, self-transcendence, self-acceptance, intimacy, and fair treatment	"I am enthusiastic about what I do." "I make a significant contribution to society." (1) *not at all*—(7) *a great deal*
Sense of Meaning Profile (SOMP; Reker 1988; Prager 1996)	16 items, 7-point Likert response format; assesses source and degree of meaning	"Leaving a legacy for the next generation"—(1) *not at all important*—(7) *very important*

Interview measures		
Life Story Interview (McAdams 2008)	Semi-structured interview protocol that guides the participant through a telling of his or her life story, complete with chapters, characters, and themes. Includes a section on life projects	"A life project is something that you have been working on and plan to work on in the future chapters of your life story. The project might involve your family or your work life, or it might be a hobby, avocation, or pastime. Please describe any project that you are currently working on or plan to work on in the future. Tell me what the project is, how you got involved in the project or will get involved in the project, how the project might develop, and why you think this project is important for you and/or for other people."
Revised Youth Purpose Interview Protocol (Andrews et al. 2006)	Semi-structured interview protocol that probes the goals that matter most, the depth of commitment to those aims, the reasons behind these aims, and activity/plans for working toward them	"What are some of the things that really matter to you? Imagine you're 40 years of age, what will you be doing? What will be important to you? Why?"

References

Andrews, M., Bundick, M., Jones, A., Bronk, K. C., Mariano, J. M., & Damon, W. (2006). *Revised youth purpose interview*. Unpublished instrument, Stanford Center on Adolescence, Stanford CA.

Antonovsky, A. (1983). *The sense of coherence scale*. Unpublished instrument, Ben-Gurion University, Israel.

Antonovsky, A. (1987). *Unraveling the mystery of health: How people manage stress and stay well*. San Francisco: Jossey-Bass.

Barrat, W. R. (1978). *Developing purposes inventory*. Iowa City: Hi Tech Press.

Battista, J., & Almond, R. (1973). The development of meaning in life. *Psychiatry, 36*, 409–427.

Bonebright, C. A., Clay, D. L., & Ankenmann, R. D. (2000). The relationship of workaholism with work-life conflict, life-satisfaction, and purpose in life. *Journal of Counseling Psychology, 47*(4), 469–477.

Bronk, K. C. (2005). Portraits of purpose: A grounded theory of the way purpose contributes to positive youth development. *Dissertation Abstracts International*, AAT 3187267.

Bronk, K. C. (2008). Humility among adolescent purpose exemplars. *Journal of Research on Character Education, 6*(1), 35–51.

Bronk, K. C. (2011). Portraits of purpose: The role of purpose in identity formation. A special issue on instructing for and supporting youth purpose. *New Directions in Youth Development, 132*, 31–44.

Bronk, K. C. (2012). A grounded theory of youth purpose. *Journal of Adolescent Research, 27*, 78–109. doi:10.1177/0743558411412958.

Bronk, K. C., & Finch, W. H. (2010). Adolescent characteristics by type of long-term aim in life. *Applied Developmental Science, 14*(1), 1–10.

Bronk, K. C., Finch, W. H., & Talib, T. (2010). The prevalence of a purpose in life among high ability adolescents. *High Ability Studies, 21*(2), 133–145.

Bronk, K. C., Hill, P., Lapsley, D., Talib, T., & Finch, W. H. (2009). Purpose, hope, and life satisfaction in three age groups. *Journal of Positive Psychology, 4*(6), 500–510.

Bundick, M., Andrews, M., Jones, A., Mariano, J. M., Bronk, K. C., & Damon, W. (2006). *Revised youth purpose survey*. Unpublished instrument, Stanford Center on Adolescence, Stanford CA.

Burrow, A. L., O'Dell, A. C., & Hill, P. L. (2010). Profiles of a developmental asset: Youth purpose as a context for hope and well-being. *Journal of Youth and Adolescence, 39*, 1265–1273.

Chamberlain, K., & Zika, S. (1988). Religiosity, life meaning, and well-being: Some relationships in a sample of women. *Journal for the Scientific Study of Religion, 27*, 411–420.

Chickering, A. W. (1969). *Education and identity*. San Francisco: Jossey-Bass.

Chickering, A. W., & Reisser, L. (1993). *Education and identity* (2nd ed.). San Francisco: Jossey-Bass.

Colby, A., & Damon, W. (1993). *Some do care: Contemporary lives of moral commitment*. New York: Free Press.

Crumbaugh, J. C. (1968). Cross-validation of Purpose in Life Test based on Frankl's concepts. *Journal of Individual Psychology, 24*, 74–81.

Crumbaugh, J. C. (1977). The Seeking of Noetic Goals Test (SONG): A complimentary scale to the Purpose in Life Test (PIL). *Journal of Clinical Psychology, 33*(3), 900–907.

Crumbaugh, J. C., & Henrion, R. (1988). The PIL test: Administration, interpretation, uses, theory, and critiques. *The International Forum for Logotherapy, 11*, 76–88.

Crumbaugh, J. C., & Henrion, R. (2001). How to find meaning and purpose in life for the third millenium. *The International Forum for Logotherapy, 24*, 1–9.

Crumbaugh, J. C., & Maholick, L. T. (1964). An experimental study in existentialism: The psychometric approach to Frankl's concept of noogenic neurosis. *Journal of Clinical Psychology, 20*, 200–207.

Crumbaugh, J. C., & Maholick, L. T. (1967). An experimental study in existentialism: The psychometric approach to Frankl's concept of noogenic neurosis. In V. E. Frankl (Ed.), *Psychotherapy and existentialism* (pp. 183–197). New York: Washington Square Press.

Crumbaugh, J. C., & Maholick, L. T. (1981). *Manual of instructions for the Purpose in Life Test*. Murfeesboro, TN: Psychometric Affiliates.

Dahlsgaard, K. (2005). Is virtue more than its own reward? *Dissertation Abstracts International: Section B: The Sciences and Engineering, 66*(6-B). (UMI No. AAI3179723)
Dale, A. (2002). *Do some drug users have less to live for*? Unpublished doctoral dissertation, School of Psychology, Curtin University of Technology, Western Australia.
Damon, W. (2008). *The path to purpose: Helping our children find their calling in life*. New York: The Free Press.
Damon, W., & Hart, D. (1988). *Self-understanding in childhood and adolescence*. Cambridge: Cambridge University Press.
Damon, W., Menon, J., & Bronk, K. C. (2003). The development of purpose during adolescence. *Applied Developmental Science, 7*(3), 119–128.
Debats, D. L. (1998). Measurement of personal meaning: The psychometric properties of the Life Regard Index. In P. T. P. Wong & P. S. Fry (Eds.), *The human quest for meaning: A handbook of psychological research and clinical application* (pp. 237–259). Mahwah: Erlbaum.
Debats, D. L., Drost, J., & Hansen, P. (1995). Experiences if meaning in life: A combined qualitative and quantitative approach. *British Journal of Psychology, 86*, 359–375.
Debats, D. L., Van der Lubbe, P. M., & Wezeman, F. R. A. (1993). On the psychometric properties of the life regard index (LRI): A measure of meaningful life. *Personality and Individual Differences, 14*, 337–345.
DeVogler, K. L., & Ebersole, P. (1980). Categorization of college students' meaning in life. *Psychological Reports, 46*, 387–390.
DeVogler, K. L., & Ebersole, P. (1981). Adults' meaning in life. *Psychological Reports, 49*, 87–90.
DeVogler, K. L., & Ebersole, P. (1983). Young adolescents' meaning in life. *Psychological Reports, 52*, 427–431.
Dufton, B. D., & Perlman, D. (1986). The association between religiosity and the Purpose in Life Test (PIL): Does it reflect purpose or satisfaction? *Journal of Psychology and Theology, 14*, 42–48.
Dyck, M. J. (1987). Assessing logotherapeutic constructs: Conceptual and psychometric status of the Purpose in Life (PIL) and Seeking of Noetic Goals (SONG) tests. *Clinical Psychology Review, 7*(4), 439–447.
Ebersole, P., & Kobayakawa, S. (1989). Bias in meaning in life ratings. *Psychological Reports, 65*, 911–914.
Ebersole, P., & Sacco, J. (1983). Meaning in Life Depth (MILD): Explicit ratings criteria. *Psychological Reports, 56*, 303–310.
Eriksson, M., & Lindstrom, B. (2005). Validity of Antonovsky's sense of coherence scale: A systematic review. *Journal of Epidemiology and Community Health, 59*(6), 460–466.
Francis, L. J. (2000). The relationship between bible reading and purpose in life among 13–15 year olds. *Mental Health, Religion and Culture, 3*, 27–36.
Francis, L. J., & Burton, L. (1994). The influence of personal prayer on purpose in life among Catholic adolescents. *The Journal of Beliefs and Values, 15*(2), 6–9.
Francis, L. J., & Evans, T. E. (1996). The relationships between personal prayer and purpose in life among churchgoing and non-churchgoing 12–15 year olds in the UK. *Religious Education, 91*(1), 9–21.
Frankl, V. E. (1959). *Man's search for meaning*. Boston: Beacon.
Geertz, C. (1983). Thick description: toward an interpretive theory of culture. In R. M. Emerson (Ed.), *Contemporary field research* (pp. 37–59). Boston: Little, Brown.
Guttmann, D. (1996). *Logotherapy for the helping professional: Meaningful social work*. New York: Springer.
Hablas, R., & Hutzell, R. (1982). The life purpose questionnaire: An alternative to the Purpose in Life Test for geriatric, neuropsychiatric patients. In S. A. Wawrytko (Ed.), *Analecta Frankliana: The proceedings of the First World Congress of Logotherapy 1980* (pp. 211–215). Berkeley: Strawberry Hill.
Harlowe, L., Newcomb, M., & Bentler, P. (1986). Depression, self-derogation, substance abuse, and suicide ideation: Lack of purpose in life as a mediational factor. *Journal of Clinical Psychology, 42*, 5–21.

Hart, D., & Fegley, S. (1995). Prosocial behavior and caring in adolescence: Relations to self-understanding and social judgment. *Child Development, 66*, 1346–1359.
Hutzell, R. R. (1988). A review of the Purpose in Life test. *The International Forum for Logotherapy, 11*, 89–101.
Hutzell, R. R. (1989). *Life Purpose Questionnaire overview sheet*. Berkeley: Institute of Logotherapy Press.
Hutzell, R. R. (1995). Life purpose questionnaire. In L. L. Jeffries (Ed.), Adolescence and meaning in life (Doctoral dissertation, University of Houston). *Dissertation Abstracts International*, 56, O8B 4634.
Hutzell, R. R., & Finck, W. C. (1994). Adapting the Life Purpose Questionnaire for use in adolescent populations. *The International Forum for Logotherapy, 17*, 42–46.
Hutzell, R. R., & Peterson, T. J. (1986). Use of the Life Purpose Questionnaire with an alcoholic population. *International Journal of the Addictions, 21*(1), 51–57.
Inhelder, B., & Piaget, J. (1958). *The growth of logical thinking from childhood to adolescence*. New York: Basic Books.
Jakobsson, U. (2011). Testing construct validity of the 13-item Sense of Coherence Scale in a sample of older people. *The Open Geriatric Medicine Journal, 4*, 6–13.
Jeffries, L. L. (1995). Adolescence and meaning in life (Doctoral dissertation, University of Houston). *Dissertation Abstracts International, 56*, O8B 4634.
Jonsen, E., Fagerstrom, L., Lundman, B., Nygren, B., Vahakangas, M., & Strandberg, G. (2010). Psychometric properties of the Swedish version of the Purpose in Life Scale. *Scandinavian Journal of Caring Sciences, 24*(1), 41–48.
Kass, J. D., Friedman, R., Lederman, J., Caudill, M., Zuttermeister, P. C., & Benson, H. (1991). An Inventory of positive psychological attitudes with potential relevance to health outcomes: Validation and preliminary testing. *Behavioral Medicine, 17*(3), 121–129.
Kinnier, R., Mehta, A. D., Keim, J. S., Okey, J. L., Adler-Tabia, R., Berry, M. J., & Mulvenon, S. W. (1994). Depression, meaninglessness, and substance abuse in "normal" and hospitalized adolescents. *Journal of Alcohol and Drug Education, 39*(2), 101–111.
Kish, G. B., & Moody, D. R. (1989). Psychopathology and life purpose. *The International Forum for Logotherapy, 12*, 40–45.
Kotchen, T. A. (1960). Existential mental health: An empirical approach. *Journal of Individual Psychiatry, 16*, 174–181.
Law, B. M. (2012). Psychometric properties of the existence subscale of the Purpose in Life Questionnaire for Chinese adolescents in Hong Kong. *The Scientific World Journal*, Article ID 685741.
Mariano, J. M., & Vaillant, G. E. (2012). Purpose among the "Greatest Generation". *Journal of Positive Psychology*. doi:10.1080/17439760.2012.686624.
Marsh, A., Smith, L., Piek, J., & Saunders, B. (2003). The Purpose in Life Scale: Psychometric properties for social drinkers and drinkers in alcohol treatment. *Educational and Psychological Measurement, 63*(5), 859–871.
McAdams, D. P. (2008). *The life story interview*. Retrieved May 22, 2012, from http://www.sesp.northwestern.edu/docs/LifeStoryInterview.pdf (on 25 September, 2015 from https://www.sesp.northwestern.edu/docs/Interviewrevised95.pdf)
Meier, A., & Edwards, H. (1974). Purpose-in-Life Test: Age and sex differences. *Journal of Clinical Psychology, 30*, 384–386.
Melton, A. M. A., & Schulenberg, S. E. (2008). On the measurement of meaning: Logotherapy's empirical contributions to humanistic psychology. *The Humanistic Psychologist, 36*(1), 31–44.
Moran, S. (2009). Purpose: Giftedness in intrapersonal intelligence. *High Ability Studies, 20*(2), 143–159.
Morgan, J., & Farsides, T. (2009). Measuring meaning in life. *Journal of Happiness Studies, 10*, 197–214.
Okado, T. (1998). *The Japanese version of the Purpose in Life Test*. Tokyo: System Publica.
Padelford, B. (1974). Relationship between drug involvement and purpose in life. *Journal of Clinical Psychology, 30*, 303–305.

Peterson, C., & Seligman, M. E. P. (2004). *Character strengths and virtues: A handbook and classification*. New York: Oxford University Press.
Pinquart, M. (2002). Creating and maintaining purpose in life in old age: A meta-analysis. *Ageing International, 27*(2), 90–114.
Prager, E. (1996). Exploring personal meaning in an age-differentiated Australian sample: Another look at the Sources Of Meaning Profile (SOMP). *Journal of Aging Studies, 10*(2), 117–136.
Reker, G. (1977). The Purpose in Life Test in an inmate population: An empirical investigation. *Journal of Clinical Psychology, 33*(3), 688–693.
Reker, G. (1988). *Sources of personal meaning among middle-aged and other adults: A replication*. Paper presented at the Annual Meeting of the Gerontological Society of America, San Francisco.
Reker, G. (1992). *The Life Attitude Profile—Revised (LAP-R). Procedures manual: Research edition*. Peterborough: Student Psychologists Press.
Reker, G. T., & Cousins, J. B. (1979). Factor structure, construct validity and reliability of the Seeking Of Noetic Goals (SONG) and Purpose In Life (PIL) tests. *Journal of Clinical Psychology, 35*(1), 85–91.
Reker, G. T., & Peacock, E. J. (1981). The Life Attitude Profile (LAP): A multidimensional instrument for assessing attitudes toward life. *Canadian Journal of Behavioral Science, 13*, 64–73.
Reker, G. T., Peacock, E. J., & Wong, P. T. P. (1987). Meaning and purpose in life and well-being: A life-span perspective. *Journal of Gerontology, 42*, 44–49.
Reker, G. T., & Wong, P. T. P. (1988). Aging as an individual process: Toward a theory of personal meaning. In J. E. Birren & V. L. Bengston (Eds.), *Emergent theories of aging* (pp. 214–246). New York: Springer Publishing.
Robbins, M., & Francis, L. J. (2000). Religion, personality and well-being: The relationship between church attendance and purpose in life. *Journal of Research in Christian Education, 9*(2), 223–238.
Ryff, C. D. (1989). Happiness is everything, or is it? Explorations on the meaning of psychological well-being. *Journal of Personality and Social Psychology, 57*, 1069–1081.
Ryff, C. D., & Keyes, C. L. M. (1995). The structure of psychological well-being revisited. *Journal of Personality & Social Psychology, 69*(4), 719–727.
Ryff, C. D., Keyes, C. L. M., & Hughes, D. L. (2003). Status inequalities, perceived discrimination, and eudaimonic well-being: Do the challenges of minority life hone purpose and growth? *Journal of Health and Social Behavior, 44*, 275–291.
Ryff, C. D., Lee, Y. H., Essex, M. J., & Schmutte, P. S. (1994). My children and me: Midlife evaluations of grown children and of self. *Psychology and Aging, 9*(2), 195–205.
Ryff, C. D., & Singer, B. (1998). The contours of positive human health. *Psychological Inquiry, 9*(1), 1–28.
Schulenberg, S. (2004). A psychometric investigation of logotherapy measures and the Outcome Questionnaire (OQ-45.2). *North American Journal of Psychology, 6*(3), 477–492.
Schulenberg, S., Gohm, C., & Anderson, C. (2006). The Meaning In Suffering Test (MIST): A unitary of multidimensional measure? *International Forum for Logotherapy, 29*(2), 103–106.
Schulenberg, S. E., Schnetzer, L. W., & Buchanan, E. M. (2011). The Purpose in Life Test—Short form: Development and psychometric support. *Journal of Happiness Studies, 12*, 861–876.
Shek, D. T. L. (1988). Reliability and factorial structure of the Chinese version of the Purpose in Life Questionnaire. *Journal of Clinical Psychology, 44*(3), 384–392.
Shek, D. T. L. (1993). The Chinese purpose-in-life test and psychological well-being in Chinese college students. *International Forum for Logotherapy, 16*, 35–42.
Shek, D. T. L., Hong, E., & Cheung, M. Y. P. (1987). The Purpose in Life questionnaire in the Chinese context. *Journal of Psychology, 12*, 77–83.
Sink, C. A., van Keppel, J., & Purcell, M. (1998). Reliability estimates of the Purpose in Life and Seeking of Noetic Goals tests with rural and metropolitan-area adolescents. *Perceptual and Motor Skills, 86*, 362.
Srole, L. (1956). Social integration and certain corollaries: An exploratory study. *American Sociological Review, 21*, 709–716.

Starck, P. L. (1983). Patients' perceptions of the meaning of suffering. *International Forum for Logotherapy, 6*, 110–116.

Starck, P. L. (1985). *Guidelines—Meaning in suffering test*. Berkeley: Institute of Logotherapy Press.

Steger, M. F., Frazier, P., Oishi, S., & Kaler, M. (2006). The Meaning in Life Questionnaire: Assessing the presence of and search for meaning in life. *Journal of Counseling Psychology, 53*(1), 80–93.

Steger, M. F., & Kashdan, T. (2007). Stability and specificity of meaning in life and life satisfaction over one year. *Journal of Happiness Studies, 8*, 161–179.

Steger, M. F., Kashdan, T., & Oishi, S. (2008). Being good by doing good: Daily eudaimonic activity and well-being. *Journal of Research in Personality, 42*, 22–42.

Stillman, T. F., Baumeister, R. F., Lambert, N. M., Crescioni, A. W., DeWall, C. N., & Fincham, F. D. (2009). Alone and without purpose: Life loses meaning following social exclusion. *Journal of Experimental Social Psychology, 45*(4), 686–694.

Winston, R. B., Jr. (1988). Tools for assessing students' psychosocial development. *Georgia Journal of College Student Affairs, 3*(2), 15–20.

Winston, R. B., Jr. (1990). The student developmental task and lifestyle inventory: An approach to measuring students' psychosocial development. *Journal of College Student Development, 31*(2), 108–120.

Winston, R. B., Jr., & Miller, T. K. (1987). *Student developmental task and lifestyle inventory manual*. Athens: Student Development Associates.

Winston, R. B., Jr., Miller, T. K., & Cooper, D. L. (1999). *Student developmental task and lifestyle assessment*. Athens: Student Development Associates.

Wong, P. T. P. (1998). Implicit theories of meaningful life and the development of the personal meaning profile. In P. T. P. Wong & P. S. Fry (Eds.), *The human quest for meaning: A handbook of psychological research and clinical applications* (pp. 111–140). Mahwah: Lawrence Erlbaum Associates.

Yalom, I. (1980). *Existential psychotherapy*. New York: Basic Books.

Yeagar, D. S., & Bundick, M. J. (2009). The role of purposeful work goals in promoting meaning in life and school work during adolescence. *Journal of Adolescent Research, 24*(4), 423–452.

The State of Empirical Research on Logotherapy and Existential Analysis

Michael Thir and Alexander Batthyány

Introduction: Psychotherapy and Efficiency Research

Since the formation of psychotherapy as a clinical profession, its development has been accompanied by efforts to provide empirical evidence for its theoretical assumptions and its efficiency. Beginning with Freud's ideas on the use of statistics to document the positive effects of his newly founded psychoanalytic therapy, the paradigms of research on psychotherapy roughly represent two poles until this day: an empirical efficiency-orientated branch and a branch trying to give consideration to the complex processes occurring within psychotherapeutic treatment (Muran et al. 2010). The differentiation and enhancement of research questions and goals of psychotherapeutic research (cf. the summary of national research focuses by Strauss et al. 2015a, b) led to advances in various directions. On the one hand, "empirically supported treatment" (EST; Castelnuovo 2010) aimed at providing empirical findings supporting the respective positions in the form of outcome studies with standardized design (Emmelkamp et al. 2014). On the other hand, a "critical intellectual turn" led to a research approach with a more patient-oriented focus and a supplementation of the research methodology by qualitative and explorative angles (Muran et al. 2010), e.g., systematic case study research (McLeod and Elliott 2011) and

M. Thir (✉)
Viktor Frankl Institute Vienna, Prinz Eugen Str. 18/12, 1040 Vienna, Austria
e-mail: Michael.Thir@gmx.at

A. Batthyány
Viktor Frankl Institute Vienna, Prinz Eugen Str. 18/12, 1040 Vienna, Austria

Viktor Frankl Chair of Philosophy and Psychology, International Academy of Philosophy, Bendern, Principality of Liechtenstein
e-mail: alexander.batthyany@gmail.com

A. Batthyány (ed.), *Logotherapy and Existential Analysis*, Logotherapy and Existential Analysis: Proceedings of the Viktor Frankl Institute Vienna 1,
DOI 10.1007/978-3-319-29424-7_7

practice-oriented initiatives (Castonguay et al. 2015; Strauss et al. 2015a, b). Yet, asides from these research approaches in psychotherapy, and the need for continuous empirical testing, another "client" of equal importance bolsters this demand: the clinical practitioner who works within the framework of a particular health care system and is thus confronted with a permanent, ubiquitous pressure of legitimization both towards other members of multidisciplinary teams of health care professionals and towards public agencies and health insurance companies.

This tenuous position naturally does not only apply to the profession of the psychotherapist as such, but also to the logotherapist. However, while the pressure of legitimization by the presentation of empirical outcome studies providing evidence for the usefulness of psychotherapeutic treatment towards various assessors affects all psychotherapy schools to the same extent, the characteristic basic approach of logotherapy is still to some degree determined by the way Frankl himself dealt with this situation—which fortunately is very well in line with current thinking on the empirical study of psychotherapy. Frankl pointed out that the ongoing demand subjecting any form of psychotherapy and logotherapy in particular to empirical outcome studies should be seen as an opportunity to benefit from: "We have no reason not to admit our need to find our discoveries supported by strictly empirical research" (Frankl in Fabry 1978, 5).

Research on Logotherapy: Past and Present

As much as psychotherapy in general, Viktor E. Frankl's logotherapy and existential analysis has been the subject of empirical behavioral research since its emergence within the field of psychiatry and psychotherapy in the first half of the past century. Frankl's early works do not only document the formation and progression of logotherapy and existential analysis, but also reveal a connection between theoretical development and efficiency research evidently existing from the first hour, thus illustrating the position of logotherapy "in the tension between the 'empirical' and 'existential' camps as a philosophically-grounded psychological model which allows itself, and even demands, to be subjected to empirical scrutiny and clinical outcome studies" (Batthyány 2011, 171).

Frankl's main work was published in the years between 1946 and 1956 (Frankl 1946a, b, 1947, 1948, 1949, 1950, 1956). In contrast to his earliest articles on logotherapy (Frankl 1925, 1938a, b, 1939), these publications are not limited to pointing out the need for a meaning-centered approach towards the rehumanization of psychotherapy, but also describe its structural makeup and report case studies about the application of methods and interventions based on the newly created logotherapy. In the light of this, one article in particular, published together with another paper (Frankl 1959) provides an excellent summary of the main principles of Frankl's theories and thus takes an exceptional position among early reports on the practice of logotherapy: *Results Drawn from the Clinical Application of*

Logotherapy by Kocourek et al. (1959) could be considered the first "modern" research report on logotherapy and existential analysis, i.e., one which is not only listing case studies, but also describes the results of a statistical analysis of the efficiency of the logotherapy treatment applied at the Poliklinik of Vienna.

This outset initiated the development of research on logotherapy, which resulted in a long history up to the present. In their annotated bibliography, Batthyány and Guttmann (2006) present a systematization of the historical progression of research on logotherapy, its initial point marked by the publication in English of *The Doctor and the Soul* in 1955 and *Man's Search for Meaning* in 1959. Batthyány and Guttmann identify three consecutive research periods. The first is primarily based on case histories, with the central research question focusing on the clinical effectiveness of logotherapeutic interventions and lasted until around 1964. Then the focus shifted to questions regarding the operationalization of the main concepts of logotherapy. According to Batthyány and Guttmann (2006), Crumbaugh's and Maholick's Purpose-in-Life Test (1964) marks the beginning of research work concentrating on the development of psychometric tests and measurements, which also implied an advancement towards an objective research methodology as a reaction to critique on its initial, subjective and casuistic approaches. This second period lasted until the middle of the 1980s, and was followed by a third research period focusing on the clinical effectivity of logotherapy within a broad field of operation, covering not only psychotherapy in various settings but also for example industrial and organizational psychology (Levit 1992) and pedagogics (Hirsch 1995; Esping 2012).

In an updated research overview, Batthyány developed a new and advanced system of the historical consistency and development of research on logotherapy and existential analysis which will also serve as the framework for the following review. According to Batthyány's new systematization, during the progress of research on logotherapy in a first period lasting until the year 1975 the foundation for the consecutive development was laid by testing the coherence and relevance of logotherapy's motivation theory (will to meaning). On the basis of a large number of findings supporting the relevance of this motivation theory, two further areas of research emerged: (1) the impact of a sense of meaning on the pathogenesis of and the protection against mental states of suffering, and (2) logotherapy's prediction that a restored sense of meaning may serve as a resource for both healing of and coping with mental health issues (Batthyány 2011). With the findings, which these research areas yielded, in addition to the motivation theory of logotherapy, its personality theory came into the view of empirical research and completed the theoretical foundation of logotherapy by including not only the will to meaning, but also self-transcendence and self-detachment, as "Frankl did not propose a series of mutually independent psychological hypotheses and therapeutic methods, but rather formulated a highly generative overall psychological model, which forms the basis for the development of logotherapeutic methods" (Batthyány 2011, 184).

Previous Reviews

Besides these proposed systematizations of the development of research on logotherapy and existential analysis, several systematic reviews summarizing past and recent findings provide an overview of the state of empirical research on logotherapy. By far the largest register of studies can be found in the bibliography of the *Viktor Frankl Institute Vienna* (Vesely and Fizzotti 2015), which covers a publication range from 1924 up to today and lists more than 1700 empirical and theoretical papers on logotherapy. Reviews focusing on the empirical research on logotherapy are given by Batthyány and Guttmann (2006) for the years of 1975–2005, covering a total number of 620 studies, by Batthyány (2011) for the years of 2005–2012, including 91 studies and by Schulenberg et al. (2008), who cover the publication range of 1972–2006 and include 65 studies. Especially notable is also the work of Hutzell (2000), who gives a commentary on the research findings published in the journal of the American Viktor Frankl Institute of Logotherapy, *The International Forum for Logotherapy*, and reviews 42 studies from the years of 1978–2000. In light of the systematic reviews at hand, the intention of the following review is to serve as a continuation by covering publications published since 2010, with a particular focus on three areas of interest: (1) psychometric instruments operationalizing the theoretical foundations of logotherapy, (2) findings about the impact of the sense of meaning and a purpose in life, especially on pathogenesis and resilience, and (3) clinical outcome research on the efficiency of logotherapeutic treatment.

Psychometric Instruments Measuring Purpose

As stated by Batthyány and Guttmann (2006), the research period between 1964 and the mid-1980s was particularly defined by the development of psychometric tests and measurements to operationalize Frankl's basic concepts, thus introducing logotherapy to the field of academic and clinical psychology. This highly productive period resulted in a broad range of psychometric works with findings well accepted and established at the present day within the research field on the construct of meaning in life. While Brandstätter et al. (2012) register a total of 59 measurement instruments on this topic, the following instruments excel by referring specifically to Frankl's theories: the *Logo Test* (Lukas 1971, 1986), the *Purpose-in-Life Test* (*PIL*; Crumbaugh and Maholick 1964), the *Life-Purpose Questionnaire* (*LPQ*, Hablas and Hutzell 1982), the *Seeking-of-Noetic Goals Test* (*SONG*; Crumbaugh 1977a, b), and the *Meaning-in-Suffering Test* (*MIST*; Starck 1983, 1985). Yet the focus of research on logotherapy tools is by no means limited to this period, although the research questions have been refined in the course of time. At present, the focus lies especially on the examination of the psychometric properties.

Regarding the *Logo Test*, created by Elisabeth Lukas, who is outstanding in her service to logotherapy, a revised version was developed by Konkolÿ Thege et al. (2010). Findings indicating insufficient reliability for the original *Logo Test* were reported by Konkolÿ Thege and Martos (2006), (Cronbach's $\alpha = 0.43$ for the first part, $\alpha = 0.54$ for the second and $\alpha = 0.20$ for the third part, overall reliability: $\alpha = 0.59$ in a sample of $N = 171$ Hungarian adolescents) and Gebler and Maercker (2007) (overall reliability: Cronbach's $\alpha = 0.47$ in a sample of $N = 17$ patients with PTBS). For the revised version *Logo Test-R*, Konkolÿ Thege et al. (2010) found an internal consistency of Cronbach's $\alpha = 0.75$ in a sample of $N = 852$ Hungarian participants, a statistically significant positive correlation with the *Purpose-in-Life Test* ($r = 0.76$, $p < 0.001$), indicating a sufficient convergent validity, and a negative correlation with symptoms of depression, operationalized by the *Beck's Depression Inventory* ($r = -0.80$, $p < 0.001$).

The *Purpose-in-Life Test* (PIL) may be considered as the most popular instrument for the measurement of meaning according to Frankl's logotherapy. Recent findings in terms of the psychometric properties provide satisfactory results: Jonsén et al. (2010) in a Swedish adaption of the *PIL* in five samples with Swedish participants ($N = 499$) found an internal consistency of Cronbach's $\alpha = 0.82$ for a 20-item version and $\alpha = 0.83$ for a 17-item version. A Spanish adaptation was tested by García-Alandete et al. (2011), who report an overall reliability of Cronbach's $\alpha = 0.88$ in a sample of $N = 309$ students. Brunelli et al. (2012) developed an Italian adaptation and found an overall reliability of $\alpha = 0.91$ in a sample of $N = 266$ cancer patients. In addition to the original version of the *PIL*, several revisions and modified versions have emerged over time (e.g., *PIL-R* by Harlow et al. 1987; *PIL-SF* by Schulenberg et al. 2011; *EPIL* by Law 2012; *PIL-10* items by García-Alandete 2014). For the *PIL-SF*, a modification consisting of four items, Schulenberg et al. (2011) reported a reliability of Cronbach's $\alpha = 0.86$ in a sample of $N = 298$ students. For the *EPIL*, a short form consisting of seven items of the original *PIL*, Law (2012) found a reliability of Cronbach's $\alpha = 0.89$ in a sample of $N = 2842$ early adolescents. García-Alandete (2014) created a Spanish ten-item version of the *PIL* and found an internal consistency of Cronbach's $\alpha = 0.85$ in a sample of $N = 180$ students. Furthermore, the internal structure of the *PIL* was investigated by Schulenberg and Melton (2010), who tested ten factor-analytic models for the original version of the *PIL* in a sample of $N = 620$ students and found support for a two-factor model, thus giving an important impetus for future research on the properties of this instrument.

An Italian adaptation of the *Seeking-of-Noetic Goals Test* (*SONG*) was proposed by Brunelli et al. (2012) in a sample of $N = 266$ cancer patients. They found the overall consistency to be highly sufficient with a Cronbach's $\alpha = 0.90$. A factor-analytic evaluation of the original version of the *SONG* was given by Schulenberg et al. (2014) in a sample of $N = 908$ students, the results of which support a two-factor model and provide an important contribution for further research.

The Impact of Sense of Meaning and Purpose in Life

Following the specification of the impact of sense of meaning and purpose in life on pathogenesis and resilience as proposed by Batthyány (2011) as an important area of research at present, recent findings document the continuing empirical evidence verifying the theoretical model of logotherapy. Of interest are especially the following findings, which provide an important impetus for future research.

Park et al. (2010) stressed the correlation between presence of meaning in life, search for meaning in life, life satisfaction, happiness, positive and negative affect, and depression in a sample of $N=731$ adult participants. By conducting a multiple regression analysis the authors were able to give a differentiated view of the correlation between the search for meaning in life and well-being and to point out the interaction between the presence of meaning in life and the search for meaning: they found that participants who scored above 75 % for presence of meaning in life showed a positive correlation between the search for meaning and life satisfaction ($\rho=0.10$), while participants with a score below 75 % meaning in life showed a negative correlation ($\rho=-0.17$ to -0.22). According to Park et al. (2010) these findings indicate that it is easier to discover meaning once meaning is already established, while discovering meaning while having no meaning in life may be experienced more difficult and frustrating.

Steger et al. (2011) studied the relation between meaning in life and life satisfaction, as well as the moderating role of search for meaning on this relation in a sample of $N=151$ undergraduate students. They found the interaction between search for meaning and presence of meaning to be significant, ($\beta=0.18$, $p<0.005$, $\Delta R^2=0.03$, $\Delta F=6.00$, $p<0.05$), and the presence of meaning in life to be more strongly associated with life satisfaction among participants, who were more actively searching for meaning ($\beta=0.59$) compared to those, who were less actively searching for meaning ($\beta=0.29$). Following Steger et al. (2011), these results indicate that the correlation between the presence of meaning in life and life satisfaction is stronger for individuals, who are actively searching for meaning in life.

Similarly, Doğan et al. (2012) found in a sample of $N=232$ university students from Turkey that meaning in life significantly predicted the extent of subjective well-being ($R=0.58$, $R^2=0.34$, $F=59.281$, $p<0.001$). By conducting a regression analysis, the authors found that the presence of meaning in life positively affected subjective well-being ($\beta=0.56$; $p=0.000$), while the search for meaning negatively affected well-being ($\beta=-0.15$; $p<0.007$), and that meaning in life accounted for 34 % of the variance of the subjective well-being of the participants (Doğan et al. 2012).

Within the field of experimental studies on the theoretical assumptions of logotherapy, a notable contribution was made by Joshi et al. (2014), who subjected the complex of the logotherapeutic model to the investigation of the relationship between will to pleasure, will to power, search for meaning in life, presence of meaning in life, existential vacuum, existential frustration, and noogenic neurosis in a sample of $N=750$ college students. By using structural equation modeling, the authors tested four possible models explaining the relationship between these factors, of which two models proposed a frustrated search for meaning to cause noogenic neurosis, and two additional models explained existential frustration by a heightened will to power or will to pleasure (Joshi et al. 2014). An excellent match was found for a model stating will to power and will to pleasure to be affected by a latent variable noogenic neurosis (CFI = 1.00, SRMR = 0.02, ACI = 44.86) and a model hypothesizing existential vacuum to be caused by will to power and will to pleasure (CFI = 1.00, SRMR = 0.02, AIC = 45.87) (Joshi et al. 2014). The best fit was found for a modification of the latter model by including static feedback loops between noogenic neurosis and existential vacuum and existential vacuum and search for meaning (CFI = 1.00, SRMR = 0.01, AIC = 41.13), providing evidence for the theoretical framework of logotherapy and for the assumption that noogenic neurosis could be the result of a persistent cycle of meaninglessness (Joshi et al. 2014).

Several recent studies address the question about the impact of the sense of meaning in different groups specified by demographic and psychological characteristics. Bronk et al. (2010) conducted a study about the role of purpose in life among high ability adolescents in a sample of $n=64$ high ability students and $n=139$ typical students. No significant main effect for type of youth was found regarding the importance of purpose in life ($p=0.9820$), indicating that meaning in life was important both for high ability and typical students. The authors further examined possible development differences, with high ability students committing earlier to purpose in life than typical students and found a significant interaction between type of youth and age ($\chi^2=8.63$, $p=0.035$), which provides an indication for the hypothesized differences in the development of the commitment to a purpose in life.

The relationship between meaning in life, quality of life, and symptoms of anxiety and depression in the elderly was examined by Haugan (2014a) in a sample of $N=202$ nursing-home patients. The author found significant positive correlations ($p<0.01$) between meaning in life and hope ($r=0.586$), overall quality of life ($r=0.457$) and "quality of life: emotional functioning" ($r=0.326$), as well as significant negative correlations between meaning in life and symptoms of depression ($r=-0.555$) and anxiety ($r=-0.285$). The effect of meaning in life on multidimensional well-being (physical, emotional, functional, and social well-being) was further investigated by Haugan (2014b), again in a sample of $N=202$ nursing-home patients. Significant effects were found for meaning in life on emotional well-being (0.56, $p<0.05$) and functional well-being (0.75, $p<0.05$), as well as significant indirect effects of meaning in life on physical (0.33, $p<0.05$) and social well-being (0.20, $p<0.05$). These results indicate the importance of meaning in life for various dimensions of well-being for the elderly (Haugan 2014b).

Recent findings also document the function of meaning in life as a resource for resilience and as a preventive factor. Kalantarkousheh and Hassan (2010) studied the function of meaning in life on marital communication in a sample of $N=57$ spouse students and found a significant correlation between meaning in life and marital communication ($r=0.283$, $p=0.033$). Consequently the authors propose a new model for marital communication based on logotherapy.

The effect of structured meaningful extracurricular activities as protective factor for suicidal ideation was examined by Armstrong and Manion (2013) in a sample of $N=813$ secondary school students. The authors found significant negative correlation between meaningful engagement and suicidal ideation ($r=-0.14$), and risk factors such as depressive symptoms ($r=-0.11$) and risk behavior ($r=-0.09$), as well as significant positive correlations with protective factors such as self-esteem ($r=0.21$), number of supportive persons ($r=0.13$), and satisfaction with support ($r=0.10$). Furthermore, a regression analyses was conducted, which resulted in significant correlations for the meaningful engagement with depressive symptoms ($t=-5.51$, $p<0.001$), risk behaviors ($t=-3.23$, $p=0.001$), self-esteem ($t=4.34$, $p<0.001$), and perceived social support ($t=3.28$, $p=0.001$) in relation to suicidal ideation (Armstrong and Manion 2013). Additionally, breadth of engagement was found to be a significant moderating variable between depressive symptoms ($t=-2.30$, $p=0.02$) and self-esteem ($t=3.34$, $p=0.001$) with suicidal ideation.

Henry et al. (2014) conducted a study on the potential effect of meaning in life on the relation between bullying victimization and suicidal ideation in a sample of $N=2936$ 6th–12th grade US students. The authors hypothesized that meaning in life could serve both as a mediator by explaining why bullying victimization leads to suicidal ideation and as a moderator by buffering the ill effect of bullying. The data analysis suggested a moderation model for the male participants and a mediation model for the female participants: for boys, at low levels of meaning in life bullying victimization was significantly and positively associated with suicidal ideation ($b=0.38$, $SE=0.09$, $p<0.001$), while at high levels of meaning in life victimization was not significantly associated with suicidal ideation ($b=0.07$, $SE=0.10$, NS). Forgirls, no moderation effects were found, but bullying victimization was associated significantly with lower meaning in life and lower meaning in life was associated significantly with suicidal ideation (Henry et al. 2014).

The impact of meaning in life on suicidal tendencies among a population at greater risk was examined by Wilchek-Aviad (2014) in a sample of $N=277$ adolescents, consisting of $n=162$ adolescents of Israeli origin and $n=115$ immigrants with Ethiopian origin. Overall significant negative correlations were found between meaning in life and suicidal tendencies ($r=-0.66$, $p<0.001$), depression ($r=-0.70$, $p<0.001$), and anxiety ($r=-0.49$, $p<0.001$). Further analysis with ANOVA revealed no significant differences in meaning between immigrant and native-born adolescents, $F(1;273)=0.44$, $\eta^2=0.002$, but the immigrants scored higher in suicidal tendencies ($F(1;273)=8.78$, $p<0.01$, $\eta^2=0.032$), depression ($F(1;273)=8.36$, $p<0.01$, $\eta^2=0.031$), and anxiety ($F(1;273)=5.30$, $p<0.05$, $\eta^2=0.02$) than the native-born adolescents.

The mediating effect of reflection on the relationship between the search for meaning, positive affect, negative affect, and positive meaning-finding was investigated by Boyraz et al. (2010) in a sample of $N=380$ bereaved individuals. By conducting a SEM, one model with a good match ($\chi^2=312.411$, $p<0.001$, $CFI=0.96$, $IFI=0.96$, $SRMR=0.054$, $RMSEA=0.063$) revealed significant indirect effects for search for meaning ($b=0.27\times0.22$, $p<0.001$) and positive effect ($b=0.39\times0.22$, $p<0.001$) on the finding of positive meaning, and a significant indirect negative effect for negative effect on positive meaning-finding ($b=-0.16\times0.22$, $p<0.01$) (Boyraz et al. 2010). These results indicate the effect of reflection within the process of finding meaning after loss.

Boyraz et al. (2015) conducted a study on the relationship between three dimensions of death acceptance (neutral, approach, escape) and grief, and meaning in life as a possible mediating factor for the relationship between neutral death acceptance and grief symptoms in a sample of $N=160$ bereaved individuals. Significant negative correlations were found between the presence of meaning and grief symptoms

($r=-0.47$, $p<0.001$) and between the age of the deceased and grief ($r=-0.31$, $p<0.001$), as well as a significant positive correlation between neutral acceptance and presence of meaning ($r=0.23$, $p<0.01$). By conducting a hierarchical regression analysis, the authors found that after controlling for the co-variants (age of the deceased, relationship to the deceased, cause of death, time since loss, previous losses, pre-loss professional psychological help, post-loss professional psychological help), neutral acceptance of death significantly predicted grief ($\beta=-0.19$, $p<0.05$), while the other two dimensions of death acceptance showed no significant results (Boyraz et al. 2015). The inclusion of the variable presence of meaning in life as a mediator and the conduction of a bootstrapping analysis resulted in a significant indirect effect of neutral attitude towards death on grief being mediated by the presence of meaning ($\beta=-0.08$, bootstrap SE$=0.031$), highlighting the role of presence of meaning in life for the negative relationship between a neutral acceptance of death and grief symptoms (Boyraz et al. 2015).

Clinical Outcome Research

An essential subject of research is the outcome efficiency of logotherapeutic interventions in clinical studies. Also in this area there are several recent findings demonstrating the effectiveness of logotherapy for the clinical practice.

In line with the logotherapeutic prediction about both meaning in life as resilience factor in states of mental suffering and mental suffering as challenge for meaning in life, several studies have been conducted recently. Volkert et al. (2014) investigated the relationship of meaning in life to clinical diagnosis and psychotherapy outcome in a pre-, post-, and 6-months-follow-up design. The samples consisted of $n=214$ patients with clinical ICD-10-F-diagnosis and $n=856$ individuals from a nationally representative survey, who were used as a control group. Significantly lower meaning in life was found in patients with mental disorders at admission ($n=209$, $t=21.39$, $p<0.001$, $d=1.65$) and at discharge ($n=141$, $t=13.45$, $p<0.001$, $d=1.22$) compared to the control group (Volkert et al. 2014).

Min et al. (2013) conducted a study to identify characteristics associated with low resilience in a sample of $N=121$ patients diagnosed with depression and/or anxiety. The sample was divided into three groups (high vs. medium vs. low resilience) and a regression analysis was performed. Min et al. (2013) found, apart from spirituality, lower purpose in life to be significantly associated with the low- and medium-resilience group ($p=0.043$), thus indicating the role of meaning as a resilience factor in depression and anxiety disorders.

Mental Disorders and Psychological States of Suffering

In a study on the effectiveness of a 6-week logo-autobiography (guided autobiography based on the philosophy of existentialism and logotherapy) on Korean-American immigrant women ($N=47$) conducted by Bernstein et al. (2012), the treatment group scored significantly lower on depressive symptoms ($F=4.86$, $p=0.002$) and significantly higher on purpose in life ($F=10.93$, $p=0.002$) compared to the control group both in the post-treatment assessment and in a 4-weeks follow-up assessment.

Cho et al. (2013) found similar results for a logo-autobiography treatment in a sample of $N=40$ Korean immigrant women diagnosed with depression in a non-randomized, quasi-experimental study: the treatment groups showed significantly lower scores on depressive symptoms than the control group ($F=6.832$, $p=0.013$; $F=19.800$, $p\leq 0.001$) and a higher score on meaning of life ($F=12.294$, $p=0.001$; $F=12.232$, $p=0.001$) in the post-treatment assessment as well as in the follow-up assessment.

Aguinaldo and de Guzman (2014) conducted a randomized pre-post-design study on the effectiveness of a logotherapy-based bibliotherapy on a sample of Filipino myasthenia gravis patients suffering from depression ($N=30$). Results showed significant differences between the treatment-group and the control-group in terms of depressive symptoms ($d=4.92$ $p=0.00$), regard towards life ($d=19.48$, $p=0.00$), and purpose in life ($d=4.24$, $p=0.00$).

Robatmili et al. (2014) conducted a RCT pre-post-follow-up-design study about the effect of a 10 week group logotherapy-treatment on meaning in life and depression in a sample of $N=20$ Iranian students. Results showed significant differences between the treatment- and the control-group regarding meaning in life both in the post-treatment-assessment ($F=290.48$, $p<0.001$) and in the 1-month follow-up measuring ($F=402.48$, $p<0.001$). Likewise, Robatmili et al. (2014) found significant differences for the depression score ($F=198.69$, $p<0.001$), which also remained significant in the follow-up assessment ($F=262.30$, $p<0.001$).

Moosavi et al. (2012) compared the efficiency of cognitive therapy and logotherapy on a sample of elderly Iranian men with depression ($N=45$) in a randomized pre-post design. Significant differences regarding symptoms of depression appeared both within the cognitive therapy-group (MD$=-3.53$, $p=0.000$) and the logotherapy-group (MD$=-2.47$, $p=0.000$) compared to the control group, while no significant difference was found between CT and logotherapy (MD$=-0.107$, $p=0.025$).

Shoaakazemi et al. (2012) examined the effect of an eight-session logotherapy treatment on the quality of life in a group of $N=24$ female students who survived the earthquake in the city of Bam (Iran) in 2003 and suffered from PTSD in a semi-experimental pre-post design study. Quality of life was measured using a 20-item version of the *WHOQOL* (WHOQOL Group 1998). The authors found significant differences between treatment and control group in physical health ($t=2.13$, $p<0.05$), psychological health ($t=6.58$, $p<0.001$), and life environment ($t=5.07$, $p<0.001$).

Drescher et al. (2012) examined the effect of meaning in life on satisfaction with life in persons suffering from mono-traumatization by measuring perceived effects (financial, social, emotional, and physical) of the disaster, meaning in life, self-efficiency, and satisfaction with life in a sample of $N=361$ individuals affected by the Gulf Oil Spill on the Mississippi Gulf Coast. A hierarchical multiple regression showed a weak model accounting for perceived effects ($R^2=0.027$, ns) as a predictor for satisfaction with life, while an inclusion of the predictors meaning in life and self-efficiency resulted in an additional variance of 26 % ($R^2=0.260$), which appeared to be significant ($F(2;354)=64.522$). Further, a semi-partial correlation to determine the relative importance of these two predictors revealed a greater effect of meaning in life on satisfaction with life (0.302) compared to self-efficiency (0.147), thus indicating the importance to include meaning-orientated approaches in the clinical treatment of persons suffering from the consequences of an ecological disaster.

Substance Abuse

The effect of meaning in life as a predictor for the efficiency of a treatment for cocaine abusers was subjected by Martin et al. (2011) in a sample of $N=154$ adults with cocaine dependence, who participated in a 30 days residential substance use treatment program. The authors found that a lower amount of meaning in life significantly predicted the use of cocaine ($B=-0.04$, $SE=0.016$, $OR=0.96$, $p<0.05$) and alcohol ($B=-0.05$, $SE=0.015$, $OR=0.96$, $p<0.05$), indicating that meaning-orientated interventions could serve as an important addition in the treatment of cocaine abuse.

Kleftaras and Katsogianni (2012) conducted a study on the relationship of meaning, spirituality, alcohol abuse, and depression in a sample of $N=200$ patients with alcohol abuse or alcohol dependence. Significant negative correlations were found between depressive symptoms and meaning in life ($r=-0.39$, $p<0.01$), personal meaning ($r=-0.37$, $p<0.01$), goal seeking ($r=-0.37$, $p<0.01$), and existential transcendence ($r=-0.24$, $p<0.01$). After dividing the sample by the degree of depressive symptoms (high vs. moderate vs. low depression), significant differences ($p<0.001$) were found regarding meaning in life ($\chi^2=42.72$), existential transcendence ($\chi^2=39.92$), personal meaning ($\chi^2=38.97$), and existential vacuum ($\chi^2=25.60$), thus indicating the importance to address the sense of meaning in persons suffering from alcohol dependence.

Schnetzer et al. (2013) examined the effect of depression and meaning in life in alcohol-using college student in a sample of $N=267$ US students. The correlations between meaning and alcohol use ($r=-0.17$, $p=0.006$) and depression ($r=-0.39$, $p<0.001$) appeared to be significant, but no significant correlation was found between depression and alcohol use ($r=0.009$, $p=0.13$). By conducting a hierarchical regression, for female students neither meaning nor depression significantly predicted alcohol use ($F(2;199)=2.42$, $p=0.09$, $R^2=0.02$), and for male students meaning and depression did not serve as individual predictors for alcohol use ($F(2;62)=1.10$, $p=0.34$, $R^2=0.03$), but the interaction between depression and perceived meaning was significant ($\Delta F(1;61)=5.19$, $p=0.03$, $\Delta R^2=0.08$) (Schnetzer et al. 2013). Further examination by comparing a high- vs. low-depression group revealing strong negative relationship between meaning and drinking ($\beta = -2.69$, $t(61) = -2.43$, $p = 0.02$) was found for the low-depression group, while for the high-depression group, a strong positive relationship between meaning and alcohol use ($\beta = 2.28$, $t(61) = 2.10$, $p = 0.04$) appeared (Schnetzer et al. 2013).

The effect of meaning in life as a predictor for changes in smoking status was analyzed by Konkolÿ Thege et al. (2013) in a sample of $N = 4294$ Hungarian participants. Meaning in life was found to be significantly associated with the smoking status at the baseline assessment (OR = 0.51, $z = 3.48$, $p < 0.001$) and at the follow-up assessment (OR = 0.61, $z = 3.60$, $p < 0.001$), indicating that a lower amount of meaning in life is correlated with a higher probability of smoking. While meaning in life did not significantly predict the quitting or uptake of smoking, it differentiated significantly between stable smokers and stable nonsmokers both at the baseline assessment (OR = 0.54, $z = 2.80$, $p = 0.005$) and at the follow-up assessment (OR = 0.64, $z = 2.88$, $p = 0.004$) (Konkolÿ Thege et al. 2013).

Adaptation and Adjustment to Physical States of Suffering

Breitbart et al. (2010) conducted a RCT study using a pre-, post-, and 2-months-follow-up design on the effect of an 8-week *Meaning Centered Group Psychotherapy* (MCGP) treatment based on logotherapy, on spiritual well-being, meaning, hopelessness, desire for death, optimism/pessimism, anxiety, depression, and quality of life in patients with advanced solid tumor cancers (stage III or IV) in a sample of $N = 90$ patients assigned either to MCPG or a supportive group psychotherapy (SGP). A significant difference was found between the MCPG and the SGP group in the compliance of the participants ($t = 5.10$, $p < 0.0001$), as well as significant differences in the MCPG-group regarding the variables "spiritual well-being: total" ($t(36) = 4.38$, $p < 0.0001$), "spiritual well-being: meaning" ($t(36) = 4.51$, $p < 0.0001$), and "spiritual well-being: faith" ($t(36) = 2.44$, $p = 0.02$) for the pre-post-treatment assessment, and even larger improvements for the 2-months-follow-up assessment: "spiritual well-being: total": $t(25) = 4.98$, $p < 0.0001$, "spiritual well-being: meaning": $t(25) = 5.29$, $p < 0.0001$, "spiritual well-being: faith": $t(25) = 2.73$, $p = 0.006$, while no significant differences were found for the SGP-group. A repeated measurement ANOVA was conducted on the group differences and resulted in $F = 5.05$, $p = 0.009$ for interaction and $F = 8.30$, $p < 0.001$ for the main effect. Regarding the variables hopelessness, desire for death and anxiety, the effects were approaching significance in the pre-post-treatment assessment for the MCGP-group (hopelessness: $t(49) = 1.88$, $p = 0.07$; desire for death: $t(50) = 1.76$, $p = 0.09$, anxiety $t(36) = 1.74$, $p = 0.10$) and reached significance at the follow-up assessment for desire for death ($t(25) = 2.09$, $p = 0.04$) and anxiety ($t(25) = 3.00$, $p = 0.02$) (Breitbart et al. 2010). For the SGP-group, significant differences appeared neither for the pre-post assessment nor for the follow-up assessment.

The effect of a group logotherapy treatment on the psychological well-being of infertile women was evaluated by Mosalanejad and Koolee (2013) in a sample of $N=65$ infertile couples, who where randomly assigned to a treatment group ($n=33$) receiving 12 sessions of group logotherapy within 3 months or to a control group ($n=32$). An ANCOVA resulted in significant differences for psychological distress in the treatment group ($t=3.06$, $p=0.004$), while the differences in the control group appeared to be not significant.

The role of meaning in life and depression on the adaptation to physical disabilities was subjected by Psarraa and Kleftaras (2013) in a sample of $N=511$ participants with paraplegia, quadriplegia, amputation, poliomyelitis, multiple sclerosis, or hemiplegia. A significant positive correlation was found between a high depression score and an existential vacuum ($r=0.75$, $p<0.01$), as well as a significantly negative correlation between depression score and meaning in life ($r=-0.84$, $p<0.01$). Furthermore, significant positive correlations were found between a positive adaptation to physical disabilities and meaning in life ($r=0.62$, $p<0.01$), negative adaptation and the presence of existential vacuum ($r=0.75$, $p<0.01$), and significant negative correlations appeared between meaning in life and negative adaptation ($r=-0.79$, $p<0.01$) and between positive adaptation and the presence of existential vacuum ($r=-0.52$, $p<0.01$) (Psarraa and Kleftaras 2013). The authors also found significant differences comparing a low vs. high meaning in life group regarding positive ($t=-7.16$, $p<0.0001$) and negative adaption ($t=6.04$, $p<0.0001$) to physical disabilities.

Julom and de Guzmán (2013) evaluated the effectiveness of a logotherapy treatment by using a pre-post design in a sample of $N=32$ paralyzed inpatients, of whom $n=16$ received the treatment. They found that while the differences within both groups were significant, the differences in the treatment group were higher in the treatment-group for the *Purpose-in-Life Test* (treatment: $t=-15.19$, control: $t=-2.73$, $p<0.05$) and the *Life-Regard-Index* (treatment: $t=-31.65$, control: $t=-4.17$), thus indicating the effectiveness of the logotherapy treatment on paralyzed inpatients (Julom and de Guzmán 2013).

Gebler and Maercker (2014) subjected the effect of the addition of an existential perspective in a cognitive-behavioral group treatment in contrast to a conventional CBT treatment by using a quasi-experimental pre-post-follow-up design (3 and 6 months) in a sample of $N=113$ patients suffering from chronic pain. The authors found the changes of pain-related disability to be significant between the baseline- and the post-treatment assessment ($F(1;111)=30.75$, $p<0.000$), the 3-months follow-up ($F(1;111)=9.53$, $p=0.003$), and the 6-months follow-up assessment ($F(1;111)=3.91$, $p=0.05$). Significant correlation effects appeared for all three assessment periods ($F(1;111)\geq 6.55$, $p\leq 0.012$). While for the existential CBT-treatment medium effect sizes were found for the post-treatment ($d_z=0.77$) and the 3-month follow-up ($d_z=0.52$) and a small effect size at the 6-month follow-up ($d_z=0.43$). A small effect size was found for the conventional CBT treatment for the post-treatment ($d_z=0.28$), and no effects appeared for the follow-up assessments, indicating that the addition of an existential perspective resulted in a greater improvement of pain-related disability in chronic pain patients (Gebler and Maercker 2014).

Hosseinzadeh-Khezri et al. (2014) tested the impact of an eight session group-logotherapy treatment in a sample of $n=35$ patients with colorectal cancer undergoing chemotherapy treatment by using a pre-, post-, and 6-months-follow-up design. In the pre- and post-assessment, significant differences were found between the treatment group and a control group regarding social functioning ($t=2.20, p<0.05$), depression ($t=2.16, p<0.05$), and the total score of general health ($t=2.42, p<0.05$). In the follow-up assessment, no significant differences were found, which according to the authors implies the importance of continued meaning-centered interventions.

The effect of a ten-session group-logotherapy treatment on hope was investigated by Ebrahimi et al. (2014) by using a pre-, post-, and 1-month-follow-up design in a sample of $N=80$ leukemia patients, who were randomly assigned either to the treatment-group or the control-group. A covariance analysis showed significant results for the factors "pathway (goal-oriented) thinking" ($F=236.40$, $p<0.0001$) and "agency thinking" ($F=83.03, p<0.0001$). At the follow-up assessment, the differences remained significant ($F=150.60, p<0.0001$), indicating that the group-logotherapy treatment increased the hope expectancy in leukemia patients.

Scrignaro et al. (2014) investigated the effect of the search for meaning in promoting mental adjustment and eudaimonic well-being in a sample of $N=266$ cancer patients. They found that search for meaning had a significant total ($b=0.072$), direct ($b=0.057$), and indirect effect ($b=0.015$) on anxious preoccupation, a significant total ($b=0.53$) and indirect effect ($b=0.051$) on hopelessness, and a significant total ($b=-0.26$) and indirect effect ($b=-0.17$) on psychological well-being, indicating the effect of meaning on the adjustment towards states of suffering and psychological well-being.

Discussion and Future Perspectives

In an interview about the future of logotherapy conducted by Joseph Fabry (1978), Viktor Frankl commented on the status and attitude of logotherapy towards empirical research at the time by expressing his gladness "… whenever logotherapy is validated by experiments … But we still need more experimentation and empirical validation …" (Fabry 1978, 5–6). The objective of the present chapter is to give an answer to the following question: What is the state of research on logotherapy today, 37 years later? And what does this state imply for the future of research on logotherapy?

Together with the previous systematic reviews of the empirical research on logotherapy, we were able to retrace its progression and take a closer look at the enormous amount of findings providing evidence for the theoretical assumptions of logotherapy, the outcome effectiveness of its applications in various states of suffering, the preventive function of the search for meaning and the presence of meaning in life as an important resilience factor, and the body of assessment instruments operationalizing different aspects of meaning in life according to Frankl's theory, especially their psychometric properties legitimizing their use both for clinical practice and empirical research. The studies included in this chapter document the fact that also for the current decade of the twenty-tens, logotherapy remains a subject of interest for research, and updated findings provide support for logotherapists facing the challenge of validating the position of logotherapy within both the fields of clinical health care practice and psychological research. Considering the spectrum of research (e.g., the proposed logotherapy-based robot interaction with elderly people reported by Masuta et al. 2014), an end of this development is certainly not in sight.

In this regard, a welcome growth of the research community can be observed in recent time, which is both encouraging and promising future contributions to the field of research on logotherapy. Especially notable is both the quantity and quality of recent contributions from South Korea and Iran, demonstrating the performance capacities of these growing research facilities. For example, Kim and Lee (2010) conducted a study on the correlation between social support, meaning in life and suicidal thoughts in cancer patients, Kim et al. (2013) report about the effects of a logotherapy program for early adolescents with cancer, and Kang et al. (2013) investigated the effects of logotherapy on depression for children.

As for Iran, the effectiveness of group logotherapy was examined on the life expectation of cancer patients (Hosseinian et al. 2010), on the increase of life expectancy and health of female teenage Major Thalassemia patients (Golami et al. 2010; see also Nasiri et al. 2014), on patients with Multiple Sclerosis (Rasoli and Borjali 2011), on depression in breast cancer patients (Haghighi et al. 2012), in reducing job burnout (Asadi et al. 2012), on empty nest syndrome (Khaledian et al. 2013) and on reducing the frustration of disabled SCI patients (Esfandiari et al. 2014). The impact of logotherapy was further investigated in other fields, e.g., on marital satisfaction (Kalantarkousheh et al. 2012; Hamidi et al. 2013). A comparative study about the efficiency of logotherapy and guided imagery on depression, anxiety, and hopefulness in female cancer patients was conducted by Abolghasami et al. (2012). Furthermore, Ghodrati et al. (2010) report about interventions to improve the health of Multiple Sclerosis patients, Haditabar et al. (2013) report about increasing the quality of life among female students, and Tayyebi Ramin et al. (2014) about the quality of life of mothers of impaired children. Regarding the role of meaning in life as a predicting factor, recent studies on the relationship between meaning in life and general health (Talebzadeh Shooshtari and Pourshafei 2012), depression, anxiety and stress status among college students (Dehdari et al. 2013), and about purpose in life and identity dimensions as predictors of maladaptive psychological aspects (Rahiminezhad et al. 2011) are also at hand. Further notable work comes, for example, from Malaysia about significant differences in self-esteem in narcotics abuse female prisoners from Sumatra (Maryatun 2013), and from Africa about the efficacy of a sense of meaning intervention amongst managers (Makola 2014).

Nevertheless, it seems important to look ahead by considering the implications of the present findings for future issues and by specifying areas of operation in need of attention.

In terms of the psychological assessments operationalizing the various aspects of logotherapy, Schulenberg et al. (2008) point out the need to examine the psychometric properties of the tools in use. Recent activities to examine these properties by conducting factorial analyses (e.g., *MIST*: Schulenberg et al. 2006; *PIL*: Schulenberg and Melton 2010; *SONG*: Schulenberg et al. 2014) are a positive development, which urgently needs to be perpetuated. The properties of the various translated versions in use and the standardization of the tools by providing representative clinical and normal samples might be considered upcoming topics of interest as well.

In terms of the subjection/subjectivation of the theoretical assumptions of logotherapy, Schulenberg et al. (2008) sum up the substantial operation of empirical research on logotherapy today: testing its theoretical assumptions using increasingly stringent research designs—a call one can only strongly encourage to pursue. The papers included in our review constitute important contributions towards this goal.

However, the importance of using stringent state of the art research designs does not only apply to the testing of the theoretical assumptions, but also to the clinical outcome research on logotherapy. Especially given the growing promotion of evidence-based clinical practice guidelines, an urgent need emerges to present recent empirical outcome studies on the effectiveness of logotherapy treatments in strictly defined psychological disorders and standardized diagnoses, thus enabling the inclusion of logotherapy as an efficient treatment option within evidence-based guidelines. In this regard, the utilization of standardized research designs, well-established within the research on psychotherapy, as well as commonly used psychological assessments (e.g., SCL-90-S, OQ, WHOQOL) is of growing/critical importance. Moreover, the evaluation of integrative treatment approaches, in terms of applying logotherapeutic interventions as an addition to treatment plans of other psychotherapeutic schools, seems to emerge as an important and interesting area of research (Schulenberg et al. 2008)—concordant with Frankl's outlook on the future of logotherapy, according to which "logotherapy is a system open in a twofold sense inasmuch as it is open toward its own evolution as well as toward co-operation with other schools" (Frankl 1982, 3).

Last but not least, regarding prospective systematic reviews, the production of systematic meta-reviews and the calculation of effect sizes seem to be an inevitable and necessary development to catch up with the state of the art in psychotherapy research, to meet the present demands of this field and to prepare logotherapy for the future.

Acknowledgement The authors would like to thank *ABILE* (Austrian Training Institute for Logotherapy and Existential Analysis) and in particular Prof. Dr. Otmar Wiesmeyr for the generous financial support, which made it possible to prepare a preliminary version of the following research report to be submitted to the Austrian Ministry of Health, and for their collaboration in its publication.

References

Abolghasami, S., Saeadi, S., & Morri Najafi, N. (2012). The effect of guided imagery and logotherapy on depression, anxiety, and hopefulness in women with cancer in Ahwaz. *Woman and Culture, 2*(5), 31–47.

Aguinaldo, J. L., & de Guzman, R. (2014). The effectiveness of logo-bibliotherapy on the depression of selected Filipinos suffering from Myasthenia Gravis. *Asian Journal of Natural & Applied Sciences, 3*(2), 31–39.

Armstrong, L. L., & Manion, I. G. (2013). Meaningful youth engagement as a protective factor for youth suicidal ideation. *Journal of Research on Adolescence, 25*(1), 20–27.

Asadi, M., Shafiabadi, A., Panahali, A., & Habibollahzade, H. (2012). The effectiveness of group logotherapy in reducing job burnout. *Andisheh va Raftar (Applied Psychology), 6*(22), 69–78.

Batthyány, A. (2011). Afterword by Alexander Batthyány: Over thirty-five years later—Research in logotherapy since 1975. In V. E. Frankl (Ed.), *Man's search for ultimate meaning* (pp. 169–188). London: Rider.

Batthyány, A., & Guttmann, D. (2006). *Empirical research in logotherapy and meaning orientated psychotherapy*. Phoenix, AZ: Zeig, Tucker & Theisen.

Bernstein, K. S., Cho, S., Cho, S., & Roh, S. (2012). Logo-autobiography and its effectiveness on depressed Korean immigrant women: A replication study. *Journal of Nursing Education and Practice, 3*(6), 51–60.

Boyraz, G., Horne, S. G., & Sayger, T. V. (2010). Finding positive meaning after loss: The mediating role of reflection for bereaved individuals. *Journal of Loss and Trauma: International Perspectives on Stress & Coping, 15*(3), 242–258.

Boyraz, G., Horne, S. G., & Waits, J. B. (2015). Accepting death as part of life: Meaning in life as a means for D=dealing with loss among bereaved individuals. *Death Studies, 39*(1), 1–11.

Brandstätter, M., Baumann, U., Borasio, G. D., & Fegg, M. J. (2012). Systematic review of meaning in life assessment instruments. *Psycho-Oncology, 21*, 1034–1052.

Breitbart, W., Rosenfeld, B., Gibson, C., Pessin, H., Poppito, S., Nelson, C., et al. (2010). Meaning-centered group psychotherapy for patients with advanced cancer: A pilot randomized controlled trial. *Psycho-Oncology, 19*, 21–28.

Bronk, K. C., Finch, W. H., & Talib, T. L. (2010). Purpose in life among high ability adolescents. *High Ability Studies, 21*(2), 133–145.

Brunelli, C., Bianchi, E., Murru, L., Monformoso, P., Bosisio, M., Gangeri, L., et al. (2012). Italian validation of the Purpose in Life (PIL) test and the Seeking of Noetic Goals (SONG) Test in a population of cancer patients. *Support Care Cancer, 20*, 2775–2783.

Castelnuovo, G. (2010). Empirically supported treatments in psychotherapy: Towards an evidence-based or evidence-biased psychology in clinical settings? *Frontiers in Psychology, 1*, 1–10.

Castonguay, L. G., Youn, S. J., Xiao, H., Muran, J. C., & Barber, J. P. (2015). Building clinicians-researchers partnerships: Lessons from diverse natural settings and practice-oriented initiatives. *Psychotherapy Research, 25*(1), 166–184.

Cho, S., Bernstein, K. S., Roh, S., & Chen, D. C. (2013). Logo-Autobiography and its effectiveness on depressed Korean immigrant women. *Journal of Transcultural Nursing, 24*(1), 33–42.

Crumbaugh, J. C. (1977a). *Manual of instructions: The Seeking of Noetic Goals Test (SONG)*. Abilene, TX: Viktor Frankl Institute of Logotherapy.

Crumbaugh, J. C. (1977b). The Seeking of Noetic Goals Test (SONG): A complementary scale to the Purpose in Life Test (PIL). *Journal of Clinical Psychology, 33*, 900–907.

Crumbaugh, J. C., & Maholick, L. T. (1964). An experimental study in existentialism: The psychometric approach to Frankl's concept of noogenic neurosis. *Journal of Clinical Psychology, 20*, 200–207.

Dehdari, T., Yarahmadi, R., Taghdisi, M. H., Daneshvar, R., & Ahmadpoor, J. (2013). The relationship between meaning in life and depression, anxiety, and stress status among college students of Iran University of Medical Sciences in 2013. *Health Education and Health Promotion, 1*(3), 83–92.

Doğan, T., Sapmaz, F., Tel, F. D., Sapmaz, S., & Temizel, S. (2012). Meaning in life and subjective well-being among Turkish university students. *Procedia – Social and Behavioral Sciences, 55*, 612–617.

Drescher, C. F., Baczwaski, B. J., Walters, A. B., Aiena, B. J., Schulenberg, S. E., & Johnson, L. R. (2012). Coping with an ecological disaster: The role of perceived meaning in life and self-efficacy following the Gulf oil spill. *Ecopsychology, 4*(1), 56–63.

Ebrahimi, N., Bahari, F., & Zare-Bahramabadi, M. (2014). The effectiveness of group logo therapy on the hope among the leukemic patients. *Iranian Journal of Cancer Prevention, 7*(1), 9–16.

Emmelkamp, P. M. G., David, D., Beckers, T., Muris, P., Cuijpers, P., Lutz, W., et al. (2014). Advancing psychotherapy and evidence-based psychological interventions. *International Journal of Methods in Psychiatric Research, 23*(1), 58–91.

Esfandiari, D., Refahi, Z., & Shayeghifard, H. (2014). The effect of the existential approach through group practices on reducing the frustration of disabled SCI. *Journal of Novel Applied Sciences, 3*(1), 89–93.

Esping, A. (2012). Logotherapy in educational contexts: A survey of English-language literature. *The International Forum for Logotherapy, 35*(1), 1–11.

Fabry, J. (1978). Aspects and prospects of logotherapy. A dialogue with Viktor Frankl. *The International Forum for Logotherapy, 1*(1), 3–6.

Frankl, V. E. (1925). Psychotherapie und Weltanschauung. Zur grundsätzlichen Kritik ihrer Beziehungen. *Internationale Zeitschrift für Individualpsychologie, III*, 250–252.

Frankl, V. E. (1938a). Zur geistigen Problematik der Psychotherapie. *Zentralblatt für Psychotherapie und ihre Grenzgebiete, 10*, 33–45.

Frankl, V. E. (1938b). Seelenärztliche Selbstbestimmung. *Der christliche Ständestaat, 5*, 72–74.

Frankl, V. E. (1939). Philosophie und Psychotherapie. Zur Grundlegung einer Existenzanalyse. *Schweizerische Medizinische Wochenzeitschrift, 69*, 707–709.

Frankl, V. E. (1946a). *Ärztliche Seelsorge*. Vienna: Deuticke.

Frankl, V. E. (1946b). *Ein Psycholog erlebt das Konzentrationslager*. Vienna: Verlag für Jugend & Volk.

Frankl, V. E. (1947). *Die Psychotherapie in der Praxis. Eine kasuistische Einführung für Ärzte*. Vienna: Deuticke.

Frankl, V. E. (1948). *Der unbewusste Gott*. Vienna: Amandus.

Frankl, V. E. (1949). *Der unbedingte Mensch. Metaklinische Vorlesungen*. Vienna: Deuticke.

Frankl, V. E. (1950). *Homo Patients. Versuch einer Pathodizee*. Vienna: Deuticke.

Frankl, V. E. (1956). *Theorie und Therapie der Neurosen. Einführung in Logotherapie und Existenzanalyse*. Vienna: Urban & Schwarzenberg.

Frankl, V. E. (1959). Grundriss der Existenzanalyse und Logotherapie. In V. E. Frankl, V. E. von Gebsattel, & J. H. Schultz (Eds.), *Handbuch der Neurosenlehre und Psychotherapie Band III: Spezielle Psychotherapie I* (pp. 663–736). Munich: Urban & Schwarzenberg.

Frankl, V. E. (1982). Opening address to the First World Congress: Logotherapy on its way to degurufication. In S. A. Wawrytko (Ed.), *Analecta Frankliana: The Proceedings of the First World Congress of Logotherapy: 1980* (pp. 1–10). San Diego, CA: Institute of Logotherapy Press.

García-Alandete, J. (2014). Análisis factorial de una versión española del Purpose-In-Life Test, en función del género y edad. *Pensamiento Psicológico, 12*(1), 83–98.

García-Alandete, J., Martínez, E. R., Soucase Lozano, B., & Gallego-Pérez, J. F. (2011). Diferencias asociadas al sexo en las puntuaciones total y factoriales del Purpose-In-Life Test en universitarios españoles. *Universitas Psychologica, 10*(3), 681–692.

Gebler, F. A., & Maercker, A. (2007). Expressive writing and existential writing in coping with traumatic experiences. *Trauma & Gewalt, 1*(4), 264–272.

Gebler, F. A., & Maercker, A. (2014). Effects of including an existential perspective in a cognitive-behavioral group program for chronic pain: A clinical trial with 6 months follow-up. *The Humanistic Psychologist, 42*(2), 155–171.

Ghodrati, S., Tabrizi, M., & Esmaeily, M. (2010). The effect of group therapy on the basis of Frankl's theory on general health improvement in patients with multiple sclerosis. *Counseling Research and Development, 9*(34), 7–24.

Golami, M., Pasha, G., & Sodani, M. (2010). To investigate the effectiveness of group logotherapy on the increasement of life expectancy and health on female teenager Major Thalassemia patients of Ahvaz City. *Knowledge & Research in Applied Psychology, 11*(42), 23–42.

Hablas, R., & Hutzell, R. (1982). The life purpose questionnaire: An alternative to the Purpose-in-Life Test for geriatric, neuropsychiatric patients. In S. A. Wawrytko (Ed.), *Analecta Frankliana: The proceedings of the First World Congress of Logotherapy: 1980* (pp. 211–215). San Diego, CA: Institute of Logotherapy Press.

Haditabar, H., Far, N. S., & Amani, Z. (2013). Effectiveness of logotherapy concepts training in increasing the quality of life among students. *International Journal of Psychology and Behavioral Research, 2*(4), 223–230.

Haghighi, F., Khodaei, S., & Sharifzadeh, G. R. (2012). Effect of logotherapy group counseling on depression in breast cancer patients. *Modern Care, 9*(3), 165–172.

Hamidi, E., Manshaee, G. R., & Fard, F. D. (2013). The impact of logotherapy on marital satisfaction. *Procedia – Social and Behavioral Sciences, 84*, 1815–1819.

Harlow, L. L., Newcomb, M. D., & Bentler, P. M. (1987). Purpose in Life Test assessment using latent variable methods. *The British Journal of Clinical Psychology, 26*, 235–236.

Haugan, G. (2014a). Meaning-in-life in nursing-home patients: A correlate with physical and emotional symptoms. *Journal of Clinical Nursing, 23*(7–8), 1030–1043.

Haugan, G. (2014b). Meaning-in-life in nursing-home patients: A valuable approach for enhancing psychological and physical well-being? *Journal of Clinical Nursing, 23*(13–14), 1830–1844.

Henry, K. L., Lovegrove, P. J., Steger, M. F., Chen, P. Y., Cigularov, K. P., & Tomazic, R. G. (2014). The potential role of meaning in life in the relationship between bullying, victimization, and suicidal ideation. *Journal of Youth and Adolescence, 43*, 221–232.

Hirsch, B. Z. (1995). The application of logotherapy in education. *The International Forum for Logotherapy, 18*(1), 32–36.

Hosseinian, E., Soudani, M., & Mehrabizadeh Honarmand, M. (2010). Efficacy of group logotherapy on cancer patient's life expectation. *Journal of Behavioral Sciences, 3*(4), 287–292.

Hosseinzadeh-Khezri, R., Rahbarian, M., Sarichloo, M.-E., Lankarani, K. B., Jahanihashemi, H., & Rezaee, F. (2014). Evaluation effect of logotherapy group on mental health and hope to life of patients with colorectal cancer receiving chemotherapy. *Bulletin of Environment, Pharmacology and Life Sciences, 3*(5), 164–169.

Hutzell, R. R. (2000). Overview of research published in The International Forum for Logotherapy. *The International Forum for Logotherapy, 23*, 111–115.

Jonsén, E., Fagerström, L., Lundman, B., Nygren, B., Vähäkangas, M., & Strandberg, G. (2010). Psychometric properties of the Swedish version of the Purpose in Life scale. *Scandinavian Journal of Caring Sciences, 24*, 41–48.

Joshi, C., Marszalek, J. M., Berkel, L. A., & Hinshaw, A. B. (2014). An empirical investigation of Viktor Frankl's logotherapeutic model. *Journal of Humanistic Psychology, 54*(1), 227–253.

Julom, A. M., & de Guzmán, R. (2013). The effectiveness of logotherapy program in alleviating the sense of meaninglessness of paralyzed in-patients. *International Journal of Psychology & Psychological Therapy, 13*(3), 357–371.

Kalantarkousheh, S. M., & Hassan, S. A. (2010). Function of life meaning and marital communication among Iranian spouses in Universiti Putra Malaysia. *Procedia – Social and Behavioral Sciences, 5*, 1646–1649.

Kalantarkousheh, S. M., Hassan, S. A., Kadir, R. A., & Talib, M. A. (2012). Effects of existential issue training on marital satisfaction among Iranian women. *The New Educational Review, 28*(2), 29–38.

Kang, K. A., Kim, S. J., Song, M. K., & Kim, M. J. (2013). Effects of logotherapy on life respect, meaning of life, and depression of older school-age children. *Journal of Korean Academy of Nursing, 43*(1), 91–101.

Khaledian, M., Parvaz, R., Garosi, M. R., & Habibzade, S. (2013). The effectiveness of logotherapy on the rise of hopefulness in empty-nest syndrome. *International Journal of Basic Sciences & Applied Research, 2*(3), 248–252.

Kim, S. J., Kang, K. A., Park, S. J., Lee, M. N., & Kim, Y. H. (2013). The effects of logotherapy on meaning of life of early adolescents with cancer. *Asian Oncology Nursing, 13*(1), 49–57.

Kim, Y. J., & Lee, K. J. (2010). Relationship of social support and meaning of life to suicidal thoughts in cancer patients. *Journal of Korean Academy of Nursing, 40*(4), 524–532.

Kleftaras, G., & Katsogianni, I. (2012). Spirituality, meaning in life, and depressive symptomatology in individuals with alcohol dependence. *Journal of Spirituality in Mental Health, 14*(4), 268–288.

Kocourek, K., Niebauer, E., & Polak, P. (1959). Ergebnisse der klinischen Anwendung der Logotherapie. In V. E. Frankl, V. E. von Gebsattel, & J. H. Schultz (Eds.), *Handbuch der Neurosenlehre und Psychotherapie Band III: Spezielle Psychotherapie I* (pp. 737–764). Munich: Urban & Schwarzenberg.

Konkolÿ Thege, B., & Martos, T. (2006). Purpose in Life Test—Characteristics of the Hungarian adaption. *Mentálhigiéné és Pszichoszomatika, 7*(3), 153–169.

Konkolÿ Thege, B., Martos, T., Bachner, Y. G., & Kushnir, T. (2010). Development and psychometric evaluation of a revised measure of meaning in life: The Logo-Test-R. *Studia Psychologica, 52*(2), 133–145.

Konkolÿ Thege, B., Urbán, R., & Kopp, M. S. (2013). Four-year prospective evaluation of the relationship between meaning in life and smoking status. *Substance Abuse Treatment, Prevention, and Policy, 8*(8).

Law, B. M. (2012). Psychometric properties of the existence subscale of the Purpose in Life questionnaire for Chinese adolescents in Hong Kong. *The Scientific World Journal*, Article ID 685741.

Levit, R. A. (1992). Meaning, purpose, and leadership. *The International Forum for Logotherapy, 15*(2), 71–75.

Lukas, E. (1971). *Logotherapie als Persönlichkeitstheorie* (Unpublished doctoral dissertation). University of Vienna, Vienna.

Lukas, E. (1986). *LOGO-Test*. Vienna: Deuticke.

Makola, S. (2014). Efficacy of a sense of meaning intervention amongst managers. *Journal of Psychology in Africa, 23*(1), 119–122.

Martin, R. A., MacKinnon, S., Johnson, J., & Rohsenow, D. J. (2011). Purpose in life predicts treatment outcome among adult Cocaine abusers in treatment. *Journal of Substance Abuse Treatment, 40*(2), 183–188.

Maryatun, S. (2013). The effect of logotherapy to changes self esteem of women prisoners with narcotics. *Malaysian Journal of Public Health Medicine, 13*(1), 58–66.

Masuta, H., Matsuo, Y., & Lim, H. (2014). Intelligent interaction of partner robot based on Frankl's psychology. *Journal of Japan Society for Fuzzy Theory and Intelligent Informatics, 26*(1), 549–558.

McLeod, J., & Elliott, R. (2011). Systematic case study research: A practiceoriented introduction to building an evidence base for counselling and psychotherapy. *Counselling and Psychotherapy Research, 11*, 1–10.

Min, J. A., Jung, Y. E., Kim, D. J., Yim, H. W., Kim, J. J., Kim, T. S., et al. (2013). Characteristics associated with low resilience in patients with depression and/or anxiety disorders. *Quality of Life Research, 22*, 231–241.

Moosavi, S., Kafi, S. M., Haghiri, M., Ofoghi, N., Atashkar, S. R., & Abolghasemi, S. (2012). Comparison of efficiency of cognitive therapy and logo therapy on the depression rate of aged men. *International Journal of Psychology and Counselling, 4*(11), 143–149.

Mosalanejad, L., & Koolee, A. K. (2013). Looking at infertility treatment through the lens of the meaning of life: The effect of group logotherapy on psychological distress in infertile women. *International Journal of Fertility and Sterility, 6*(4), 224–231.

Muran, J. C., Castonguay, L. G., & Strauss, B. (2010). A brief introduction to psychotherapy research. In L. G. Castonguay, J. C. Muran, L. Angus, J. A. Hayes, N. Ladany, & T. Anderson

(Eds.), *Bringing psychotherapy research to life. Understanding change through the work of leading clinical researchers* (pp. 3–14). Washington, DC: APA.

Nasiri, M., Hosseini, S. H., & Shahmohammadi, S. (2014). Mental health status in patients with Thalassemia Major in Iran. *Journal of Pediatrics Review, 2*(1), 55–61.

Park, N., Park, M., & Peterson, C. (2010). When is the search for meaning related to life satisfaction? *Applied Psychology: Health and Well-Being, 2*(1), 1–13.

Psarraa, E., & Kleftaras, G. (2013). Adaptation to physical disabilities: The role of meaning in life and depression. *The European Journal of Counselling Psychology, 2*(1), 79–99.

Rahiminezhad, A., Zeynab Kazemi, Z., Farahani, H. A., & Aghamohamadi, S. (2011). Purpose in life and identity dimensions as predictors of maladaptive psychological aspects: A path analysis study. *Procedia - Social and Behavioral Sciences, 30*, 1009–1013.

Rasoli, L., & Borjali, A. (2011). The efficiency of group logo therapy in decreasing anxiety and increasing self-esteem in patients with multiple sclerosis. *Quarterly Clinical Psychology Studies, 1*(3), 43–59.

Robatmili, S., Sohrabi, F., Shahrak, M. A., Talepasand, S., Nokani, M., & Hasani, M. (2014). Theeffect of group logotherapy on meaning in life and depression levels of Iranian students. *International Journal for the Advancement of Counselling*. doi:10.1007/s10447-014-9225-0.

Schnetzer, L. W., Schulenberg, S. E., & Buchanan, E. M. (2013). Differential associations among alcohol use, depression and perceived life meaning in male and female college students. *Journal of Substance Use, 18*, 311–319.

Schulenberg, S. E., Baczwaski, B. J., & Buchanan, E. M. (2014). Measuring search for meaning: A factor-analytic evaluation of the Seeking of Noetic Goals Test (SONG). *Journal of Happiness Studies, 15*, 693–715.

Schulenberg, S. E., Gohm, C. L., & Anderson, C. (2006). The Meaning in Suffering Test (MIST): A unitary or multidimensional measure? *International Forum for Logotherapy, 29*(2), 103–106.

Schulenberg, S. E., Hutzell, R. R., Nassif, C., & Rogina, J. M. (2008). Logotherapy for clinical practice. *Psychotherapy: Theory, Research, Practice, Training, 45*(4), 447–463.

Schulenberg, S. E., & Melton, A. M. A. (2010). A confirmatory factor-analytic evaluation of the Purpose in Life Test: Preliminary psychometric support for a replicable two-factor model. *Journal of Happiness Studies, 11*, 95–111.

Schulenberg, S. E., Schnetzer, L. W., & Buchanan, E. M. (2011). The Purpose in Life Test-Short Form: Development and psychometric support. *Journal of Happiness Studies, 12*, 861–876.

Scrignaro, M., Bianchi, E., Brunelli, C., Miccinesi, G., Ripamonti, C., Magrin, M., & Borreani, C. (2014). Seeking and experiencing meaning: Exploring the role of meaning in promoting mental adjustment and eudaimonic well-being in cancer patients. Palliative and Supportive Care, 1, 1–9.

Shoaakazemi, M., Javid, M. M., Tazekand, F. E., & Khalili, S. (2012). The effect of logo therapy on improving the quality of life in girl students with PTSD. *Life Science Journal, 9*(4), 5692–5698.

Starck, P. L. (1983). Patients' perceptions of the meaning of suffering. *The International Forum for Logotherapy, 6*(2), 110–116.

Starck, P. L. (1985). *Guidelines: Meaning in suffering test*. Abilene, TX: Viktor Frankl Institute of Logotherapy.

Steger, M. F., Oishi, S., & Kesebir, S. (2011). Is a life without meaning satisfying? The moderating role of the search for meaning in satisfaction with life judgments. *The Journal of Positive Posychology, 6*(3), 172–180.

Strauss, B. M., Lutz, W., Steffanowski, A., Wittmann, W. W., Boehnke, J. R., Rubel, J., et al. (2015a). Benefits and challenges in practice-oriented psychotherapy research in Germany: TheTK and the QS-PSY-BAY projects of quality assurance in outpatient psychotherapy. *Psychotherapy Research, 25*(1), 32–51.

Strauss, B. M., Shapiro, D. A., Barkham, M., Parry, G., & Machado, P. P. P. (2015). "The Times They Are a-Changin": 25 years of psychotherapy research—A European and Latin American perspective. *Psychotherapy Research*. Vol 132(6), Nov 2006, 959–992.

Talebzadeh Shooshtari, L., & Pourshafei, H. (2012). The relation between meaning in life and general health among staff of Birjand University (2009–2010). *Journal of Birjand University of Medical Sciences, 18*(1), 55–61.

Tayyebi Ramin, Z., Dadkhah, A., Bahmani, B., & Movallali, G. (2014). Effectiveness of group logo therapy on increasing the quality of the mothers' life of hearing impaired children. *Applied Psychology, 6*, 18–26.

Vesely, F., & Fizzotti, E. (2015). *General bibliography—Logotherapy and existential analysis*. Vienna: Viktor Frankl Institute Vienna. Retrieved January 30, 2015, from http://www.viktorfrankl.org/e/bibE.html.

Volkert, J., Schulz, H., Brütt, A. L., & Andreas, S. (2014). Meaning in life: Relationship to clinical diagnosis and psychotherapy outcome. *Journal of Clinical Psychology, 70*(6), 528–535.

WHOQOL Group. (1998). Development of the World Health Organization quality of life assessment (WHOQOL): Development and general psychometric properties. *Social Science & Medicine, 46*(12), 1569–1585.

Wilchek-Aviad, Y. (2014). Meaning in life and suicidal tendency among immigrant (Ethiopian) youth and native-born Israeli youth. *Journal of Immigrant and Minority Health*. August 2015, 17(1) 4, 1041–1048

The Structural Validity and Internal Consistency of a Spanish Version of the *Purpose in Life Test*

Joaquín García-Alandete, Eva Rosa Martínez, Pilar Sellés Nohales, Gloria Bernabé Valero, and Beatriz Soucase Lozano

The *Purpose in Life Test* (PIL; Crumbaugh and Maholick 1969), in particular Part A (see the appendix), is the most used scale to measure meaning in life according to the assumptions of the logotherapy (Frankl 2010). Many studies have analyzed the psychometric properties of the scale, obtaining usually a high internal consistency (e.g., Jonsén et al. 2010; Melton and Schulenberg 2008), although its structural validity has been questioned because it includes several concepts (meaning in life, fear of death and freedom, among many others), a social desirability bias, and a strong axiological load. Another aspect of the PIL recurrently analyzed, since Crumbaugh and Maholick's (1969) initial study to the present, is its factor structure, which has led to the proposal of different scales, although not all of them have complied with good psychometric assessment criteria (Table 1).

These studies are heterogeneous in the proposed models, as well as in the composition of the samples, the statistical analysis used, and the interpretation criteria. Following Schulenberg and Melton (2010), the high number of PIL models obtained by Exploratory Factor Analysis gives rise to a complicated literature with respect to its factorial validity. The *status quaestionis*, given the relevance of the structural validity of any measuring instrument, suggests analyzing the structure factor of PIL—the most used scale to measure the meaning of life from the theoretical assumptions of logotherapy—with rigorous criteria in order to obtain a robust model.

For this purpose, García-Alandete et al. (2013) carried out a Principal Components Analysis of the PIL using restrictive criteria, obtaining a 2-factor scale with ten items that explained the 57.27 % of the total variance: Satisfaction and Meaning in Life (SML; items 1, 2, 5, 6, 9, 11; 34.17 % of the explained variance), and Goals and

J. García-Alandete (✉) • E.R. Martínez • P.S. Nohales • G.B. Valero • B.S. Lozano
Dpto. de Neuropsicobiología, Metodología y Psicología Social, Universidad Católica de Valencia "San Vicente Mártir", Guillem de Castro, 175, 46008 Valencia, Spain
e-mail: ximo.garcia@ucv.es

A. Batthyány (ed.), *Logotherapy and Existential Analysis*, Logotherapy and Existential Analysis: Proceedings of the Viktor Frankl Institute Vienna 1,
DOI 10.1007/978-3-319-29424-7_8

Table 1 Factor models of the PIL

Number of factors	Model	Factors	Items
1 factor	Crumbaugh and Maholick (1964, 1969)	1: Meaning in life	1–20
	Marsh et al. (2003)	1: Meaning in life	1–6, 8–13, 16–20
	Steger (2006)	1: Meaning in life	1–6, 8–13, 16–17, 19–20
	Schulenberg et al. (2010)	1: Meaning in life	3, 4, 8, 20
	Brunelli et al. (2012)	1: Meaning in life	1–20
2 factors	Walters and Klein (1980)	1: Despair	1, 3–4, 6, 8–9, 11–12, 20
		2: Enthusiasm	2, 5, 17–19
	Dufton and Perlman (1986)	1: Life satisfaction	1–2, 5–6, 9–10, 19
		2: Purpose in life	3–4, 8, 11–12, 17, 20
	Molcar and Stuempfig (1988)	1: General meaning in life	3–4, 7–9, 11, 13, 17, 20
		2: Exciting daily-life	1–2, 5, 10, 12, 14, 18–19
	Shek (1988)	1: Quality of life	1–2, 5–6, 8–9, 11–12, 16, 19
		2: Meaning of existence	3–4, 13, 17–18, 20
	McGregor and Little (1998)	1: Happiness	1–2, 5, 8–9, 19
		2: Meaning	3, 17, 20
	Waisberg and Starr (1999)	1: Life with meaning	3–4, 6, 8–13, 16–17, 20
		2: Interest of the everyday	1–2, 5, 9, 18–19
	Morgan and Farsides (2009)	1: Exciting life	2, 5, 7, 10, 17, 18–19
		2: Life with meaning	3, 8, 20
	García-Alandete et al. (2013)	1: Satisfaction and meaning in life	1–2, 5–6, 9, 11
		2: Goals and purposes in life	3, 7, 17, 20
3 factors	Magaña et al. (2004)	1: Perception of meaning and meaning in life	1–5, 7–10, 13, 17, 19–20
		2: Life satisfaction	6, 11–12, 16, 18
		3: Freedom and control of life	14–15
	Risco (2009)	1: Value of life	1, 4, 6, 9, 10–12
		2: Capacity of meaning	2, 5, 7, 14–15, 17–19
		3: Goals and responsibility	3, 8, 13, 20
	Jonsén et al. (2010)	1: Meaning of existence	1, 3–4, 6, 8–9, 11, 20
		2: Freedom to make meaning in daily life	10, 14–15, 17–19
		3: Will to find meaning before future challenges	2, 5, 7
4 factors	Noblejas (1994)	1: Perception of meaning	4, 6, 9–12, 16–17, 20
		2: Experience of meaning	1–2, 5, 9, 17, 19–20
		3: Goals and tasks	3, 7–8, 13, 17, 19–20
		4: Dialectic fate/freedom	14–15, 18

Purposes in Life (GPL; items 3, 7, 17, 20; 23.1 % of the explained variance). A Confirmatory Factor Analysis (CFA) showed an acceptable fit of the model: Mardia's coefficient = 41.78, $SB\chi^2 = 101.01$, df = 34, $p < 0.01$, NNFI = 0.91, CFI = 0.93, MFI = 0.93, RMSEA = 0.066 [0.051, 0.080]. The scale was named *Purpose In Life Test-10 Ítems* (PIL-10).

Other studies have reported an acceptable adjustment of the PIL-10. In a previously published study that compared the main models proposed for the PIL and in which PIL-10 was used, Rosa et al. (2012), obtained a good fit, GFI = 0.95, AGFI = 0.91, CFI = 0.93, NFI = 0.92, SRMR = 0.041, RMSEA = 0.081. Similar results were obtained by García-Alandete (2014), $SB\chi2(34) = 46.33$, $p = 0.077$, $\chi2/df = 1.36$, CFI = 0.96, IFI = 0.97, RMSEA = 0.045 CI 90 % [0.000, 0.075], as well as a high internal consistency for the scale and for the SML factor, $\alpha = 0.85$ and $\alpha = 0.84$ respectively, and acceptable for the GPL, $\alpha = 0.69$.

The objective of this work is to examine by means of CFA the model for the PIL-10 obtained by García-Alandete et al. (2013), in order to corroborate the fit of its factor structure with new results.

Method

Participants

Participants were 916 Spanish undergraduates (652 females, 71.2 %; 264 males, 28.8 %) of Valencia, Spain, aged from 18 to 42, $M = 22.33$, SD = 4.26, recruited by incidental sampling. Participation was voluntary and anonymous and participants did not receive any compensation for participating in the research. The participants were given appropriate instructions in order to complete the protocol.

Measures

Purpose in Life Test-10 Items (PIL-10; García-Alandete et al. 2013). Spanish version of Crumbaugh and Maholic's (1969) original PIL, a 10-item Likert-type scale, with 7 response categories. Categories 1 and 7 have specific response anchors for each item, and category 4 represents a neutral position. The total score is obtained by adding the value of the response chosen in each item, ranging from 10 to 70, with higher scores denoting greater experience of meaning in life. The scale includes two factors that are: the factor of Satisfaction and Meaning in Life (SML; items 1, 2, 5, 6, 9, 11) and the factor of Goals and Purposes in Life (GPL; items 3, 7, 17, 20).

Procedure and Statistical Analysis

The participants fulfilled a protocol that included the PIL-10, among other scales not used in this study, in the classrooms in which they usually engaged in their academic activities and under the supervision of the authors. The protocol took on average 30 min to complete. Any concerns regarding the completion of the protocol were addressed and the anonymous and confidential nature of the data was emphasized.

To check the fit of the data-model, an AFC was carried out with EQS 6.1 for Windows (Bentler 2006), and the reliability of the scale and the factors (Cronbach's alpha) were estimated with SPSS 15.0 for Windows. To assess the adjustment of the model, the following indexes were considered:

- Non-Normed Fit Index (NNFI): variation of the NFI that includes the degrees of freedom of both the theoretical and independence models (Ullman 1996).
- Comparative Fit Index (CFI): Index widely used and with a good performance (Tanaka 1993): ranges between 0 and 1, 0.90 being the minimum value required to defend the model (Bentler and Bonett 1980).
- McDonald Fit Index (MFI): standard measure of the centrality of the parameter, with recommended values greater than 0.89 to accept the fit of the model (McDonald 1989; McDonald and Marsh 1990).
- Root Mean Square Error of Approximation (RMSEA; Browne and Cudeck 1993; Steiger 1990): considered the best indicator of global adjustment (Marsh et al. 1996), this index measures the total amount of error by degree of freedom of the model (Loehlin 1998). Values below 0.05 are optimal, values between 0.05 and 0.08 are acceptable, and values greater than 0.10 indicate that the model is poor (Browne and Cudeck 1993; Hair et al. 1995).

Results

The Mardia's normalized coefficient, with a value of 66.36, suggested the method of maximum likelihood with robust estimation (Ullman and Bentler 2004), obtaining a good fit of the model: $SB\chi 2 = 142.45$, $df = 34$, $p < 0.01$, NNFI = 0.92, CFI = 0.94, MFI = 0.94, RMSEA = 0.060 CI 90 % [0.050, 0.070] (Hair et al. 1995; Hu and Bentler 1999). All the adjustment indexes showed values greater than 0.90, and the RMSEA index was close to 0.05 (Bentler and Bonett 1980; Browne and Cudeck 1993; Hair et al. 1995). All the parameters of the standard equation were acceptable (Fig. 1).

The reliability coefficient (Cronbach's alpha) was 0.86 for the scale, 0.83 for the SML factor, and 0.71 for the GPL factor. The descriptive statistics were the following: Meaning in Life, $M = 58.04$, SD = 7.63; SML, $M = 33.44$, SD = 5.49; GPL, $M = 24.60$, SD = 2.92.

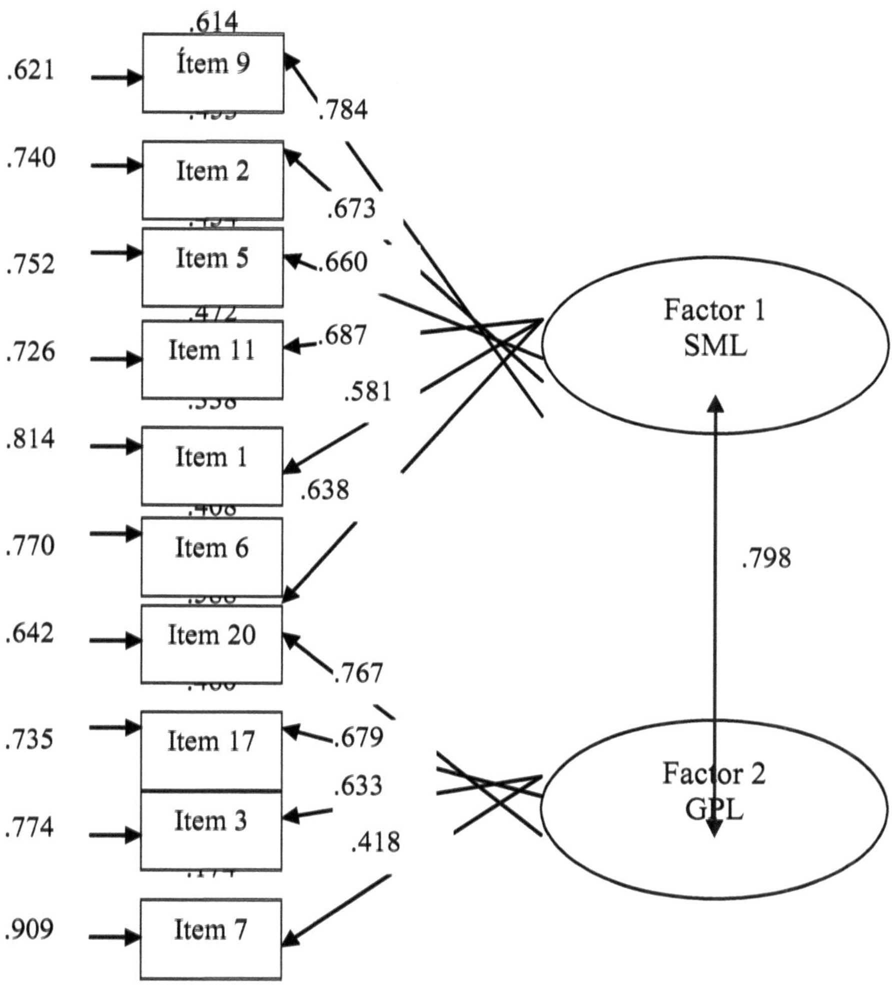

Fig. 1 Standardized solution of the model

Discussion

The objective of this study was to examine the structural validity and to estimate the internal consistency of a Spanish version of Part A of the Purpose in Life Test (PIL; Crumbaugh and Maholick 1969), specifically the 2-factor Spanish version (García-Alandete et al. 2013), the so-called PIL-10, that includes the two factors of Satisfaction and Meaning in Life (SML; items 1, 2, 5, 6, 9, 11) and the Goals and Purposes in Life (GPL; items 3, 7, 17, 20). This factorial structure coincides with some of the main models analyzed by Schulenberg and Melton (2010) that obtained the best settings.

The AFC demonstrated a model)with a good fit which included (1) a cognitive-appreciative component (SML) relating to the perception and general appreciation of meaning in life, and satisfaction with life, and also (2) a motivational component (GPL) relating to the establishment of goals in life, to which activities and personal efforts are oriented (García-Alandete et al. 2013).

Both components are correlated: the more purposes and goals, the greater life satisfaction, and vice versa. The fit of the PIL-10 in this study is concordant with García-Alandete et al. (2013), Rosa et al. (2012), and García-Alandete (2014), and the consistency of these findings can be an indicator of the structural robustness of this model.

The total scale PIL-10 showed a high internal consistency, $\alpha=0.86$, similar to preceding studies (e.g., Jonsén et al. 2010; Melton and Schulenberg 2008), as well as the SML factor, $\alpha=0.83$, while GPL factor consistency was acceptable, $\alpha=0.71$. These results are the same (total scale and GPL) or very close (SML) to those obtained in previous studies (García-Alandete 2014; García-Alandete et al. 2013).

It would be interesting to deepen the structural validity of the PIL test with a clinical population, since some of the original scale items could be maintained (e.g., Brunelli et al. 2012; Haugan and Moknes 2013). For example, item 15 ("With regard to death, I am: unprepared and frightened/prepared and unafraid") as well as item 16 ("Regarding suicide, I have: thought of it seriously as a way out/never given it a second thought") may be clinically relevant in certain populations, such as people with end-stage disease, chronic pain or severe disability, at risk of suicide, the elderly, and those people with personality disorders or depression, among other possible specific situations.

Appendix: *Purpose in Life Test*, Part A (Crumbaugh and Maholick 1969; Spanish translation, Noblejas 1994)

1. **Generalmente me encuentro**: **Completamente aburrido/Exuberante, entusiasmado.**
2. **La vida me parece**: **Completamente rutinaria / Siempre emocionante.**
3. **En la vida tengo: Ninguna meta o anhelo / Muchas metas y anhelos definidos.**
4. Mi existencia personal es: Sin sentido ni propósito / Llena de sentidos y propósitos.
5. **Cada día es: Exactamente igual/Siempre nuevo y diferente.**
6. **Si pudiera elegir: Nunca habría nacido / Tendría otras nueve vidas iguales a ésta.**
7. **Después de retirarme: Holgazanearía el resto de mi vida / Haría las cosas emocionantes que siempre deseé realizar.**
8. En el logro de mis metas vitales: No he conseguido ningún progreso/He llegado a mi realización completa.

9. **Mi vida es: Vacía y llena de desesperación/Un conjunto de cosas buenas y emocionantes.**
10. Si muriera hoy, me parecería que mi vida ha sido: Una completa basura/Muy valiosa.
11. **Al pensar en mi propia vida: Me pregunto a menudo la razón por la que existo / Siempre encuentro razones para vivir.**
12. Tal y como yo lo veo en relación con mi vida, el mundo: Me confunde por completo / Se adapta significativamente a mi vida.
13. Me considero: Una persona irresponsable / Una persona muy responsable.
14. Con respecto a la libertad de que dispone para hacer sus propias elecciones, creo que el hombre es: Completamente esclavo de las limitaciones de la herencia y del ambiente / Absolutamente libre de hacer todas sus elecciones vitales.
15. Con respecto a la muerte, estoy: Falto de preparación y atemorizado / Preparado y sin temor.
16. Con respecto al suicidio: Lo he considerado seriamente como una salida a mi situación / Nunca le he dedicado un segundo pensamiento.
17. **Considero que mi capacidad para encontrar un significado, un propósito o una misión en la vida es: Prácticamente nula / Muy grande.**
18. Mi vida está: Fuera de mis manos y controlada por factores externos / En mis manos y bajo mi control.
19. Enfrentarme a mis tareas cotidianas supone: Una experiencia dolorosa y aburrida / Una fuente de placer y satisfacción.
20. **He descubierto: Ninguna misión o propósito en mi vida / Metas claras y un propósito satisfactorio para mi vida.**

Items and points 1 and 7 anchors (anchor point 4 is Neutral and the rest of points lack anchor).

In bold, the items that compose the PIL-10.

References

Bentler, P. M. (2006). *EQS 6 structural equations program manual.* Encino, CA: Multivariate Software, Inc.

Bentler, P. M., & Bonett, D. G. (1980). Significance tests and goodness of fit in the analysis of covariance structures. *Psychological Bulletin, 88*(3), 588–606. doi:10.1037//0033-2909.88.3.588.

Browne, M. W., & Cudeck, R. (1993). Alternative ways of assessing model fit. In K. A. Bollen & J. S. Long (Eds.), *Testing structural equation models* (pp. 136–162). Newsbury Park, CA: Sage.

Brunelli, C., Bianchi, E., Murru, L., Monformoso, P., Bosisio, M., Gangeri, L., Miccinesi, G., Scrignaro, M., Ripamonti, C., & Borreani, C. (2012). Italian validation of the Purpose In Life (PIL) test and the Seeking Of Noetic Goals (SONG) test in a population of cancer patients. *Supportive Care in Cancer, 2011*, 2775–2783.

Crumbaugh, J. C., & Maholick, L. T. (1964). An experimental study in existentialism: The psychometric approach to Frankl's concept of noogenic neurosis. *Journal of Clinical Psychology*, *20*(2), 200–207. doi:10.1002/1097-4679(196404)20:2<200::AID-JCLP2270200203>3.0.CO;2-U

Crumbaugh, J. C., & Maholick, L. T. (1969). *Manual of instructions for the Purpose in Life Test*. Saratoga, CA: Viktor Frankl Institute of Logotherapy.

Dufton, B. C., & Perlman, D. (1986). The association between religiosity and the Purpose in Life Test: Does it reflect purpose or satisfaction? *Journal of Psychology and Theology, 14*, 42–48.

Frankl, V. E. (2010). *The feeling of meaninglessness. A challenge to psychotherapy and philosophy*. Milwaukee, WI: Marquette University Press.

García-Alandete, J. (2014). Análisis factorial confirmatorio y confiabilidad de una versión española del Purpose in Life Test y diferencias en función del género y la edad [Confirmatory factor analysis and reliability of a Spanish version of the Purpose in Life Test, and gender and age differences]. *Pensamiento Psicológico, 12*(1), 83–98.

García-Alandete, J., Rosa, E., & Sellés, P. (2013). Estructura factorial y consistencia interna de una versión española del Purpose in Life Test [Factorial Structure and Internal Consistency of a Spanish Version of the Purpose in Life Test]. *Universitas Psychologica, 12*(2), 517–530. doi:10.11144/Javeriana. UPSY12-2.efci.

Hair, J. F., Anderson, R. E., Tatham, R. L., & Black, W. C. (1995). *Multivariate data analysis*. Englewood Cliffs, NJ: Prentice Hall.

Haugan, G., & Moknes, U. K. (2013). Meaning-in-Life in nursing home patients: A validation study of the Purpose in Life Test. *Journal of Nursing Measurement, 21*(2), 296–319. doi:10.1891/1061-3749.21.2.296.

Hu, L. T., & Bentler, P. M. (1999). Cutoff criteria for fit indexes in covariance structure analysis: Conventional criteria versus new alternatives. *Structural Equation Modeling, 6*(1), 1–55. doi:10.1080/10705519909540118.

Jonsén, E., Fagerström, L., Lundman, B., Nygren, B., Vähäkangas, M., & Strandberg, G. (2010). Psychometric properties of the Swedish version of the Purpose in Life Scale. *Scandinavian Journal of Caring Sciences, 24*(1), 41–48. doi:10.1111/j.1471-6712.2008.00682.x.

Magaña, L., Zavala, M. A., Ibarra, I., Gómez, M. T., & Gómez, M. M. (2004). El sentido de la vida en estudiantes de primer semestre de la Universidad de La Salle Bajío [The meaning in life among students of first semester of the Universidad de La Salle Bajío]. *Revista del Centro de Investigación, 6*(22), 5–13.

Marsh, H. W., Balla, J. R., & Hau, K. T. (1996). An evaluation of incremental fit indexes: A clarification of mathematical and empirical properties. In G. A. Marcoulides & R. E. Schumacker (Eds.), *Advanced structural equation modeling techniques* (pp. 315–353). Mahwah, NJ: Lawrence Erlbaum.

Marsh, A., Smith, L., Piek, J., & Saunders, B. (2003). The Purpose In Life Scale: Psychometric properties for social drinkers and drinkers in alcohol treatment. *Educational and Psychological Measurement, 63*(5), 859–871. doi:10.1177/0013164402251040.

McDonald, R. P. (1989). An index of goodness-of-fit based on non-centrality. *Journal of Classification, 6*(1), 97–103. doi:10.1007/BF01908590.

McDonald, R. P., & Marsh, H. W. (1990). Choosing a multivariate model: Non-centrality and goodness of fit. *Psychological Bulletin, 107*(2), 247–255. doi:10.1037//0033-2909.107.2.247.

McGregor, I., & Little, B. R. (1998). Personal projects, happiness, and meaning: On doing well and being yourself. *Journal of Personality and Social Psychology, 74*(2), 494–512. doi:10.1037//0022-3514.74.2.494.

Melton, A. M. A., & Schulenberg, S. E. (2008). On the measurement of meaning: Logotherapy's empirical contributions to Humanistic psychology. *The Humanistic Psychologist, 36*(1), 31–44. doi:10.1080/08873260701828870.

Molcar, C. C., & Stuempfig, D. W. (1988). Effects of world view on purpose in life. *The Journal of Psychology, 122*, 365–371. doi:10.1080/00223980.1988.9915523.

Morgan, J. E., & Farsides, T. L. (2009). Measuring meaning in life. *Journal of Happiness Studies, 10*(2), 197–214. doi:10.1007/s10902-007-9075-0.

Noblejas, M. A. (1994). *Logoterapia. Fundamentos, principios y aplicación. Una experiencia de evaluación del "Logro interior de sentido"* [Logotherapy. Foundations, principles, and application. An experience of assessment of the 'internal achievement of meaning'] (Doctoral Dissertation, Universidad Complutense de Madrid, Madrid, Spain). Retrieved from http://eprints.ucm.es/tesis/19911996/S/5/S5005701.pdf

Risco, A. (2009). *Sentido de la vida: Evolución e implicaciones para la Educación Superior* [Meaning in life: Development and implications for Higher Education] (Doctoral Dissertation, Universidad de Salamanca, Salamanca, Spain). Retrieved from: https://www.educacion.gob.es/teseo/imprimirFicheroTesis.do?fichero=12007

Rosa, E., García-Alandete, J., Sellés, P., Bernabé, G., & Soucase, B. (2012). Análisis Factorial Confirmatorio de los principales modelos propuestos para el Purpose in Life Test en una muestra de universitarios españoles [Confirmatory Factor Analysis of the main models proposed for the Purpose in Life Test among Spanish undergraduates]. *Acta Colombiana de Psicología, 15*(1), 67–76.

Schulenberg, S. E., & Melton, A. M. A. (2010). A confirmatory factor-analytic evaluation of the Purpose in Life Test: Preliminary psychometric support for a replicable two-factor model. *Journal of Happiness Studies, 11*(1), 95–111. doi:10.1007/s10902-008-9124-3.

Schulenberg, S. E., Schnetzer, L. W., & Buchanan, E. M. (2010). The Purpose in Life Test-Short Form: Development and psychometric support. *Journal of Happiness Studies, 12*(5), 861–876. doi:10.1007/s10902-010-9231-9.

Shek, D. T. L. (1988). Reliability and factorial structure of the Chinese version of the Purpose in Life Questionnaire. *Journal of Clinical Psychology, 44*, 384–392. doi:10.1002/1097-4679(198805)44:3<384::AID-JCLP2270440312>3.0.CO;2-1.

Steger, M. F. (2006). An illustration of issues in factor extraction and identification of dimensionality in psychological assessment data. *Journal of Personality Assessment, 86*, 263–272.

Steiger, J. H. (1990). Structural model evaluation and modification: An interval estimation approach. *Multivariate Behavioural Research, 25*(2), 173–180. doi:10.1207/s15327906mbr2502_4.

Tanaka, J. S. (1993). Multifaceted conceptions of fit in structural equation models. In K. A. Bollen & J. S. Long (Eds.), *Testing structural equation models*. Newbury Park, CA: Sage.

Ullman, J. B. (1996). Structural equation modeling. In B. G. Tabachnick & L. S. Fidell (Eds.), *Using multivariate statistics* (pp. 709–819). New York, NY: Harper Collins.

Ullman, J., & Bentler, P. (2004). Structural equation modeling. In M. Hardy & A. Bryman (Eds.), *Handbook of data analysis* (pp. 431–459). London: Sage. doi:10.4135/9781848608184.n19.

Waisberg, J. L., & Starr, M. W. (1999). Psychometric properties of the Purpose in Life Test with a sample of substance abusers. *International Forum for Logotherapy, 22*, 22–26.

Walters, L. H., & Klein, A. E. (1980). A cross-validated investigation of the Crumbaugh Purpose in Life Test. *Educational and Psychological Measurement, 40*, 1065–1071. doi:10.1177/001316448004000434.

Factorial Structure of Längle's Existence Scale

André Brouwers and Welko Tomic

Factorial Structure of the Existence Scale

The will to give meaning to life has enjoyed ample attention in psychological research and practice since the 1960s. Frankl's *Man's Search for Meaning* was published in English for the first time in 1959. In it, the author describes how he survived the Nazi concentration camps and developed logotherapy, which is based on the idea that existential meaning is fundamentally important to mental health. According to Frankl (1970), the will to impart meaning is a primary motivation for human beings. Existential meaning is not an extrapolation of personal needs or wishes, but a discovery of something essential that presents itself to man and imparts a purpose and a calling to everyone's life. Man obeys this calling by accepting responsibility for his own life. Without this essential responsibility, man lives in an "existential vacuum." Failure to achieve existential meaning in life may result in psychological distress (Loonstra et al. 2009; Ryff 1989; Steger 2012).

In recent years the construct of existential meaning has received renewed attention. Existential meaning is regarded as an indicator of well-being (Ryff 1989) and promotes adaptive coping (Park and Folkman 1997). Lent (2004) argued for examining and assessing well-being variables such as meaning of existence in order to promote personal growth and recovery. In a review of a large number of studies Steger (2012) demonstrates that people who report greater meaning in their lives

With kind reprint permission from the *Journal of Articles in Support of the Null Hypothesis* (originally published in Vol. 8, No. 2)

A. Brouwers (✉) • W. Tomic
Department of Psychology, The Open University,
P.O. Box 2960, 6401 DL Heerlen, The Netherlands
e-mail: v.tomic@online.nl

A. Batthyány (ed.), *Logotherapy and Existential Analysis*, Logotherapy and Existential Analysis: Proceedings of the Viktor Frankl Institute Vienna 1,
DOI 10.1007/978-3-319-29424-7_9

also report greater well-being, lesser psychopathology, and a more beneficial experience of spirituality. According to Steger (2012) people who say they lead meaningful lives are also quite happy, satisfied with their lives and self, and experience lower levels of psychological suffering, psychopathological complaints, and disruptive behavior. It appears that existential meaning strongly influences human health and well-being. Absence of meaning, on the other hand, is related to psychopathology (Yalom 1980). Consequently, conducting empirical research in this domain is valuable and justified.

The existential scale (ES) developed by Längle and his coworkers (Kundi et al. 2003; Längle 2003a; Längle et al. 2003) is related to the Franklian analysis of a cultural deficit in modern times (Längle 2003b). Social cohesion has been replaced by individualism. A new feeling of uninhibited freedom brings with it cultural isolation and loss of identity. In this situation, people have to find existential motivation and fulfillment.

In the search for meaning, self-transcendence plays a central role. Self-transcendence is embedded in a theory of psychological maturity, in which an individual interacts with his environment in a balanced way. The prerequisite for self-transcendence is self-distance, the ability to distinguish oneself from the surrounding world, to refrain from becoming dependent on other persons or circumstances, and to accept things as they are. Based on this self-distance, one can transcend oneself—that is, enter into relationships with people and other objects and value them—and arrive at a fundamental feeling of harmony between the world and oneself. Self-distance and self-transcendence together form the personality factor of existential meaning. Connected with the personality factor is the existence factor, consisting of freedom and responsibility. Inner freedom is important to make decisions based on one's own conscience and not on fear. Responsibility stands for the inner determination to put one's decisions into practice.

This theoretical foundation has provided the groundwork for the ES, consisting of 46 items rated with a 6-point Likert-type scale, ranging from "fully disagree" to "fully agree." The measure contains 8 items related to self-distance, 14 items related to self-transcendence, 11 items related to freedom, and 13 items related to responsibility. Examples of such items are: "A situation is interesting to me only if it meets my wishes" (self-distance); "After all there is nothing in my life to which I want to devote myself" (self-transcendence); "Without much reflection I try to put off unpleasant decisions" (freedom), and "I take too little time for important things" (responsibility).

Längle's ES has an appealing theoretical basis. The attention is focused on the psychological predisposition required for a sound life orientation. It distinguishes meaning based on self-transcendence from meaning based on self-interest and personal needs, something that other current scales, such as the Purpose in Life Test (Crumbaugh and Maholick 1964), the Life Regard Inventory (Battista and Almond 1973; Debats 1998), and the Sense of Coherence Scale (Antonovsky 1987), fail to do. One can imagine that when meaning is based on self-interest, a person is more vulnerable to circumstances that do harm to his or her interests than when meaning is based on self-transcendence.

The ES can be used to evaluate whether the individual has realized the personal-existential dimension and to what extent it has been incorporated into his or her personality development. We are not aware of any scale that intends to measure human personal-existential dynamics. Längle et al. (2003) tested the ES in a sample of 1028 Austrian adults aged 18–69 years. The resulting 46-item scale included four factors. According to the authors the scale is not only suitable for scientific purposes but also for therapeutic practice. Längle et al. (2003) examined the factorial structure of the scale using exclusively principal components analysis. However, applying this technique does not provide information about the overall fit of factorial models. There is a possibility that the factor model as proposed by Längle et al. (2003) has to be rejected after the models' fit was tested using confirmatory factor analysis. Therefore, the aim of the current study was to test the factorial validity of the ES using confirmatory factor analysis.

The ES questionnaire was not originally developed and tested in the Netherlands. Therefore, before the scale can be applied, it is customary to assess the construct validity of the scale on the basis of a representative sample of Dutch respondents. Delineation of the factor structure of an instrument can contribute substantially to the assessment of construct validity. Confirmatory factor analysis is particularly useful in that respect (Hepner and Sechrest 2002). Because the ES was developed with an a priori hypothesis of the relationship among its items, construct validity investigations should use confirmatory factor analysis (see Atkinson et al. 2011; LaNasa et al. 2009; Taub et al. 2004). Confirmatory factor analysis is an appropriate method to evaluate construct validity (see Thompson and Daniel 1996). Confirmatory factor analysis enables researchers to test explicit hypotheses concerning the factor structure of the data. In addition, confirmatory factor analysis offers a more feasible method for evaluating construct validity in contrast to principal components analysis, conducted by Längle et al. (2003).

The goal of the current inquiry is to examine whether Längle's ES is a valid measure of existential meaning. The focus is on the construct validity. The following hypotheses can be formulated. (1) Construct validity is shown by the four-factor structure of the scale at item level, along the lines of the four assumed subscales. (2) Construct validity is shown by the two-factor structure of the scale at item level, reflecting the theory of the personality factor and the existence factor. (3) Construct validity is shown by a one-factor structure of the scale at item level, in accordance with the assumed mutual dependence between the four subscales.

Method

Participants and Procedure

The studyuses data from four surveys conducted in the Netherlands on the correlation between existential meaning and burnout. The four samples consisted of professionals working in "social occupations" that require frequent and extensive contact with people. With regard to sample 1 we randomly selected 300 teachers of primary schools from a district in the middle of the country and asked them to participate in our study (Tomic et al. 2004). In total 215 surveys were returned, resulting in a response rate of 72 %. The number of male teachers was 44 (20.5 %) and the number of female teachers was 171 (79.5 %). The mean age of our respondents was 39.46 whereas the national mean age of primary school teachers is 40.49. There was no significant difference concerning the variable "age" of the 215 respondents and the total population of teachers: $t(1309)=1.38$, $p=0.09$, $\eta^2=0.002$.

In sample 2 the participants were pastors from orthodox protestant denominations registered as such in the Reformed Church Annual and working in a parish (Loonstra and Tomic 2005). The total population consists of 480 pastors. 266 pastors participated in the study, a response rate of 55 %. The mean age was 45.95 (SD=9.06). There was no significant difference in mean age of respondents (45.95) and the population (46.05): $t(744)=.145$, $p=0.44$, $\eta^2=0.000$.

From a target population of social workers 350 were selected randomly, for sample 3 (Aanraad 2005). The respondents who participated in this study were working for a large city and its surrounding. A total of 192 questionnaires were returned and processed for this study. This is a response rate of 55 %. The sample consisted of 50 men (26 %) and 142 women (74 %). Mean age was 42.44 years with a range of 20–63 years (SD=9.78). Mean age of target population was 43.86 (SD=8.98). Considering mean age the sample of social workers does not differ significantly from the target population [$t(539)=0.82$, $p=0.21$]. $\eta^2=0.001$.

As for sample 4 we randomly selected 1000 school principals across the country (Tomic and Tomic 2008). 514 principal questionnaires were returned resulting in a response rate of 51.4 %; 23.9 % respondents were female and 76.1 % male. The average age of the principals was 50.2 years (SD=6.72), whereas the national mean age of school principals is 50.5 years. There was no significant difference in mean age of the 514 principals and the total population of principals $t(1512)=0.88$, $p=0.19$, $\eta^2=0.001$.

All participants were eligible for the four studies. In the four studies response rates range from approximately 51–72 %, which is not only quite satisfactory for survey research according to Babbie (2006), but also in accordance with the findings of Asch, Jedrziewski, and Christakis (1997).

In the four surveys, participants were asked to perform a self-evaluation by completing a form. In order to increase the response rate, we followed suggestions by Green et al. (1997): We provided respondents with postage-paid envelopes that could be sent anonymously; we sent the questionnaires to the respondents directly; the respondents could contact us at any time if necessary; and we used a fairly brief questionnaire. After 4 weeks, a reminder was sent to all addressees.

Measurement Instrument

The ES has been tested as a measure for existential meaning among more than a 1000 respondents in Austria, but a confirmatory factor analysis has not been performed. The present study used a Dutch translation of the ES. Two researchers and one German teacher translated the original questionnaire from German into Dutch independently of one another and then produced a consensus version. Obviously, the translators emphasized the meaning of the original items and did not follow the wording of the source language very closely, their aim being to produce a good translation. Three other translators with an excellent knowledge of both Dutch and German and blind to the original questionnaire then performed a back-translation. This version was compared with the original German questionnaire.

The method of back-translation was chosen because it can improve the reliability and validity of research in different languages; the quality of the translation is verified by independent translators translating back into the original language. One important benefit of a back-translation is that it allows comparison of the original source language version and the version that was back-translated into the source language. Back-translation is the most highly recommended technique for translation in cross-cultural research (Maneesriwongul and Dixon 2004). The results indicate that the ES was successfully translated for use with Dutch teachers, principals, pastors, and social workers.

Data Analysis

The major task in testing confirmatory factor analytic models is to determine the goodness of fit between the hypothesized model and the sample data (Byrne 1994). The adequacy of model fit was assessed using the chi-square likelihood ratio, the Goodness-of-Fit Index (GFI), the Root Mean Square Residual (RMR), the Adjusted Goodness-of-Fit Index (AGFI), the Normed Comparative Fit Index (CFI; Bentler 1990), the Tucker–Lewis Index (TLI), and the Parsimony Normed Comparative Fit Index (PCFI). Chi-square describes the statistical goodness of fit of the observed matrix compared to the expected matrix predicted by the hypothesized model. A significant chi-square value implies that the hypothesized factor model is not adequate, but it should be mentioned that chi-square is sensitive to sample size. On the one hand, with large samples chi-square values will be inflated and even minor discrepancies can lead to rejection of an in every way adequate model. On the other hand, when samples are small, chi-square value can be non-significant even when the model does not fit adequately (Williams et al. 2010). Due to the sensitivity of chi-square, it is understandable to employ some sensible indices of fit to supplement evaluation of the proposed model, for instance, the normed comparative fit index (CFI) ranging from 0 to 1.00. A value greater than 0.90 indicates an acceptable fit to the data. The normed comparative fit index (CFI) is based on a comparison of the hypothesized model with the null model (i.e., all correlations between the variables are 0) and is oriented towards sample size. According to Byrne (1994) it is recommendable that CFI should be the main index when evaluating model fit.

Results

In order to test the presupposed factorial structure of the ES, confirmatory factor analysis with maximum likelihood estimation was used utilizing the AMOS computer program (Arbuckle 1997). In this confirmatory factor-analytic approach, the fit of five factorial models was tested against the null model (Model 0): Model 1, a one-factor model in which all items of the three subscales were allowed to load on one general existential-meaning factor; Model 2, a two-factor model in which the items of the Self-Distance and Self-Transcendence subscales were allowed to load on one factor, whereas the items of the Responsibility and Freedom subscales were allowed to load on a second factor (the two subscales were allowed to correlate); Model 3, a four-factor model in which the items of the four subscales were allowed to load on their respective factors (the four subscales were allowed to correlate); and Model 4, a higher-order-factor model in which the Self-Distance and Self-Transcendence factors were allowed to load on one second-order factor, whereas the Responsibility and Freedom factors were allowed to load on another second-order factor (the two second-order factors were allowed to correlate).

Evaluation of the model fit was based on the chi-square likelihood ratio, the Root Mean Square Residual (RMR), the Goodness-of-Fit Index (GFI), the Adjusted Goodness-of-Fit Index (AGFI), the Normed Comparative Fit Index (CFI; Bentler 1990), and the Parsimony Normed Comparative Fit Index (PCFI). To assess CFI and PCFI, null models were specified, i.e., models in which the variables are mutually independent (Model 0). Following the recommendations of Bentler and Bonett (1980), the fit of a model was considered to be acceptable when CFI exceeded 0.90. PCFI was used to assess a model's parsimony, which is especially useful when comparing models (Mulaik et al. 1989).

The results of confirmatory factor analysis showed chi-square ratios indicating a poor absolute fit, most likely due to the large sample size. Inspection of the CFI and the Tucker–Lewis Index (TLI), which are relatively insensitive to the sample size (McDonald and Marsh 1990), indicated that the fit of neither model was adequate (see Table 1).

Table 1 Overall goodness-of-fit indices for the Existence Scale (N=1187)

	χ^2	df	RMR	GFI	AGFI	CFI	TLI	PCFI
Model 0	16267.05	1035	0.27	0.30	0.26	0.00	0.00	0.00
Model 1	5046.42	989	0.07	0.81	0.79	0.73	0.72	0.70
Model 2	4938.02	988	0.07	0.82	0.80	0.74	0.73	0.71
Model 3	4799.02	984	0.07	0.82	0.80	0.75	0.74	0.71
Model 4	4789.97	983	0.07	0.82	0.80	0.75	0.74	0.71

Note: RMR root mean square residual, *GFI* goodness-of-fit index, *AGFI* adjusted goodness-of-fit index, *CFI* normed comparative fit index, *TLI* Tucker–Lewis index, *PCFI* parsimony normed comparative fit index

Discussion

The aim of the current study was to test empirically whether the ES developed by Längle et al. (2003) is a valid measure of existential meaning in life. To our knowledge, this was the first study to test the factor structure of this 46-item version of the ES. The results of confirmatory factor analysis indicated that none of the hypothesis can be confirmed. There is no four-factor structure along the lines of the four assumed subscales (Model 3), nor is there a two-factor structure (Model 2) or a higher-order two-factor structure (Model 4) in accordance with the theorized Personality factor and Existence factor. Confirmatory factor analysis does not suggest a one-factor model as the best fit for the data (Model 1).

A comparison with results of previously conducted studies is not feasible, because there are no comparable studies to our knowledge. Längle et al. (2003) applied factor analysis (varimax rotation) to assess the ES. Their results partially confirm that the ES measures a dimension independent of other factors. Factor analysis revealed one factor that is almost exclusively defined by the four sub-scales of the ES. Unlike Längle et al. (2003), our results did not confirm the four-factor structure.

There may be several reasons why the ES did not show an adequate factorial model fit. First, it seems quite likely that the theoretical basis of ES construct is inadequate, and, second, the construct may have been operationalized inaccurately. There are two indications that the latter may be the case. In order to avoid socially desirable answers, most items are phrased negatively, which may confound the factor differences. Moreover, several items are formulated ambiguously. However, at the moment there are no rigorous reasons to reject the theory.

Having found an inadequately fitted factorial model of the ES in the present study, we have concluded that this instrument, in its current state, is not suitable for obtaining precise and valid information about existential meaning in life. Since existential meaning has enjoyed ample attention in psychological research and practice, it is of great importance to modify the ES or to develop a suitable and valid new measurement instrument.

Like most research, the current study has limitations that merit further discussion. First, in spite of a large sample size, all respondents are from four occupational groups or domains, (i.e., clergy, teachers, principals, social workers) which can influence their perceptions due to its practices and other factors. The respondents in the sample were all employed in occupations that require extensive contact with other people. This can be considered to be a restriction for testing the factorial structure of a scale, in particular. Consequently, we need to be cautious when generalizing the results of the current study to the country's population. Further study, for instance, with people in different professions like engineers, scientists, businessmen, laborers is needed to draw a broader conclusion.

Second, the current study's results are based on data gathered in the Netherlands, which was different from the country in which the scale was developed and initially tested. The existential beliefs or cultural differences typical of that country may limit the results to that country or other similar country (i.e., the restriction of the study being conducted in one country makes it difficult to verify results and interpretations with similar studies in other countries). Just as a significant result in one country may or may not generalize beyond its borders, the same goes for nonsignificant results. Therefore, one should proceed with caution when generalizing results found in the current study to populations in other counties without further research.

In spite of its limitations, the current study has several important strengths. First, the current study ventured into a novel domain of measuring existential meaning. Second, the four samples were drawn randomly from the target populations. Third, the total sample size was substantial ($N = 1187$). Fourth, the response rates ranging from 51 to 72 %, have been found to be quite satisfactory for research in these domains (Asch et al. 1997; Babbie 2006; Van Horn and Green 2009). Fifth, the four samples were representative concerning age of the participants. Sixth, we applied an appropriate data-analytic strategy (i.e., confirmatory factor analysis).

Research suggests that existential meaning is strongly related to human health and well-being and that absence of meaning is related to psychopathology (Yalom 1980). Therefore, it is quite understandable that existential meaning has received renewed attention and that conducting empirical research in this domain is valuable and justified. Despite the limitations, the current study contributed to the knowledge of the Existence Scale meant to measure existential meaning in life. This work is only a first step, and future studies are needed in this area.

References

Aanraad, T. (2005). *Existentiële zingeving in relatie tot burnout bij welzijnswerkers.* [Existential meaning and burnout among welfare workers.]. Heerlen: The Open University, unpublished master thesis.

Antonovsky, A. (1987). *Unraveling the mystery of health: How people manage stress and stay well.* San Francisco, NY: Jossey-Bass.

Arbuckle, J. L. (1997). *Amos user's guide version 3.6.*. Chicago, IL: SPSS Inc.

Asch, D. A., Jedrziewski, M. K., & Christakis, N. A. (1997). Response rates to mail surveys published in medical journals. *Journal of Clinical Epidemiology, 50*(10), 1129–1136.

Atkinson, T. M., Rosenfeld, B. D., Sit, L., Mendoza, T. R., Fruscione, M., Lavene, D., Shaw, M., Li, Y., Hay, J., Cleeland, C. S., Scher, H. I., Breitbart, W. S., & Basch, E. (2011). Using confirmatory factor analysis to evaluate construct validity of the Brief Pain Inventory (BPI). *Journal of Pain & Symptom Management, 41*(3), 558–565.

Babbie, E. (2006). *The practice of social research* (11th ed.). Belmont, CA: Wadsworth Publishing Company.

Battista, J., & Almond, R. (1973). The development of meaning in life. *Psychiatry, 36*(4), 409–427.

Bentler, P. M., & Bonett, D. G. (1980). Significance tests and goodness of fit in the analysis of covariance structures. *Psychological Bulletin, 88*(3), 588–606.

Bentler, P. M. (1990). Comparative fit indexes in structural models. *Psychological Bulletin, 107*(2), 238–246.

Byrne, B. M. (1994). *Structural equation modeling with EQS and EQS/Windows: Basic concepts, applications and programming*. Thousand Oaks, CA: Sage.

Crumbaugh, J., & Maholick, L. T. (1964). An experimental study in existentialism: The psychometric approach to Frankl's concept of noogenic neurosis. *Journal of Clinical Psychology, 20*(2), 200–207.
Debats, D. L. (1998). Measurement of personal meaning: The psychometric properties of the Life Regard Index. In P. T. P. Wong & P. S. Fry (Eds.), *The human quest for meaning: A handbook of psychological research and clinical applications*. Mahwah NJ/London: Erlbaum.
Frankl, V. E. (1970). *The will to meaning: Foundations and applications of logotherapy*. New York, NY: New American Library.
Green, K. E., Boser, J. A., & Hutchinson, S. R. (1997). *Effects of population type on mail survey response rates and on the efficacy of response enhancers*. Paper presented at the Annual Meeting of the American Educational Research Association, Chicago, IL, March 24–28 (ERIC Document Reproduction Service No. ED410252).
Hepner, K. A., & Sechrest, L. (2002). Confirmatory factor analysis of the Child Health Questionnaire - Parent Form 50 in a predominantly minority sample. *Quality of Life Research, 11*, 763–773.
Kundi, M., Wurst, E., & Längle, A. (2003). Existential analytical aspects of mental health. *European Psychotherapy, 4*(1), 87–96.
LaNasa, S. M., Cabrera, A. F., & Trangsrud, H. (2009). The construct validity of student engagement: A confirmatory factor analysis approach. *Research in Higher Education, 50*, 315–332.
Längle, A. (2003a). The art of involving the person: Fundamental existential motivations as the structure of the motivational process. *European Psychotherapy, 4*(1), 25–36.
Längle, A. (2003b). Burnout – existential meaning and possibilities of prevention. *European Psychotherapy, 4*(1), 107–121.
Längle, A., Orgler, C., & Kundi, M. (2003). The Existence Scale: A new approach to assess the ability to find personal meaning in life and to reach existential fulfillment. *European Psychotherapy, 4*(1), 135–146.
Lent, R. W. (2004). Toward a unifying theoretical and practical perspective on well-being and psychosocial adjustment. *Journal of Counseling Psychology, 51*, 482–509.
Loonstra, B., Brouwers, A., & Tomic, W. (2009). Feelings of existential fulfillment and burnout among secondary school teachers. *Teaching and Teacher Education, 25*, 752–757.
Loonstra, B., & Tomic, W. (2005). Werkdruk, zingeving en burnout bij predikanten in orthodox gereformeerde kerken. [Work pressure, existential meaning, and burnout among ministers in orthodox reformed denominations.]. *Psyche & Geloof, 16*(2), 66–81.
Maneesriwongul, W., & Dixon, J. K. (2004). Instrument translation process: A methods review. *Journal of Advanced Nursing, 48*(2), 175–186.
McDonald, R. P., & Marsh, H. W. (1990). Choosing a multivariate model: Noncentrality and goodness of fit. *Psychological Bulletin, 107*(2), 247–255.
Mulaik, S. A., James, L. R., van Alstein, J., Bennett, N., Lind, S., & Stilwell, C. D. (1989). Evaluation of goodness-of-fit indices for structural equation models. *Psychological Bulletin, 105*(3), 430–445.
Nunnally, J. C., & Bernstein, I. H. (1994). *Psychometric theory* (3rd ed.). New York, NY: McGraw Hill.
Park, C. L., & Folkman, S. (1997). Meaning in the context of stress and coping. *Review of General Psychology, 30*, 115–144.
Ryff, C. D. (1989). Happiness is everything, or is it? Explorations of the meaning of psychological well-being. *Journal of Personality and Social Psychology, 57*, 1069–1081.
Steger, M. F. (2012). Experiencing meaning in life: Optimal functioning at the nexus of well-being, psychopathology, and spirituality. In: P.T.P. Wong (Ed.), *The human quest for meaning: Theories, research and applications* (2nd edn, pp. 1–19). New York: Routledge. Published in final edited form (2013) in: *Rehabilitation Psychology,* 58(4). doi: 10.1037/a0034393
Taub, G. E., McGrew, K. S., & Witta, E. L. (2004). A confirmatory analysis of the factor structure and cross-age invariance of the Wechsler Adult Intelligence Scale – Third Edition (WAIS-III). *Psychological Assessment, 16*(1), 85–89.
Thompson, B., & Daniel, L. G. (1996). Factor analytic evidence for the construct validity of scores: A historical overview and some guidelines. *Educational and Psychological Measurement, 56*(2), 197–208.

Tomic, W., Evers, W. J. G., & Brouwers, A. (2004). Existential fulfillment and teacher burnout. *European Psychotherapy, 5*(1), 65–73.
Tomic, W., & Tomic, E. N. (2008). Existential fulfillment and burnout among principals and teachers. *Journal of Beliefs & Values, 29*(1), 11–27.
Van Horn, P. S., & Green, K. E. (2009). Survey response rates and survey administration in counseling and clinical psychology. *Educational and Psychological Measurement, 69*(3), 389–403.
Williams, L. J., Hartman, N., & Cavazotte, F. (2010). Method variance and marker variables: A review and comprehensive CFA marker technique. *Organizational Research Methods, 13*(3), 477–514.
Yalom, I. D. (1980). *Existential psychotherapy*. New York, NY: Basic Books.

Meanings of Meaningfulness of Life

Shulamith Kreitler

Introduction

Meaningfulness of Life: Assessment Tools and Theoretical Approaches

In recent years there has been a surge of interest in the construct of meaningfulness of life (MOL), which came to be regarded as a resource for overcoming hardship, moderating the effects of traumata, facilitating coping, and enhancing the ability to enjoy life (Crumbaugh and Maholick 1964; Ryff 1989; Steger et al. 2006). In parallel there has been an increased effort to construct assessment instruments for MOL. Most notable are the Life Regard Index (Battista and Almond 1973), the Life Attitude Profile-Revised (Reker 1992), Meaning in Life Questionnaire (Steger et al. 2006), Sense of Coherence Scale (Antonovsky 1987), Purpose in Life Test (Crumbaugh and Maholick 1964), Purpose in Life Scale (Ryff 1989), and Meaning in Life Questionnaire (Schnell 2009). Many of the scales share several characteristics. The first characteristic is a positive conception of life's meaningfulness. Thus, most scales are based on an explicit or implicit definition of life's meaningfulness as a rich, interesting, authentic, creative, energetic, goal-directed, purposeful, adventurous, or satisfying life. If negative aspects are mentioned, then it is often the positive aspects reflected in acceptance and coping that are emphasized. Second, many of the scales are based on overall evaluations by the person of their life's meaningfulness. Thus, the scales include items concerning the authenticity, richness, degree of fulfillment, self-actualization and overall meaningfulness of one's life. Third, many of the scales are based on an underlying assumption that meaningfulness of life fulfills a basic human need, reflected in the search for meaning. Thus, when

S. Kreitler (✉)
The School of Psychological Sciences, Tel Aviv University, Tel Aviv 69978, Israel
e-mail: krit@post.tau.ac.il

A. Batthyány (ed.), *Logotherapy and Existential Analysis*, Logotherapy and Existential Analysis: Proceedings of the Viktor Frankl Institute Vienna 1,
DOI 10.1007/978-3-319-29424-7_10

it is fulfilled it is reflected in good quality of life, mental health and happiness and when it is unfulfilled then the consequences are crisis of meaning, depression, low quality of life, dissatisfaction, despair and often existential void (Frankl 1963, 1965).

The conceptual framework in which meaningfulness of life has been commonly investigated and assessed up to now is that of personality, positive psychology, and self-actualization with an emphasis on coping with adversity and well-being. This approach is most clearly demonstrated in the major theories of MOL. Thus, Frankl (1963) anchored meaningfulness in finding value—by acts of creativity, by sensory experiences or novel attitudes; Snyder (Feldman and Snyder 2005) emphasized the pivotal role of self-control which allows individuals to feel that they can effectively manage their life so as to attain their goals; Becker (1962) highlighted the role of meaningfulness of life in overcoming death anxiety; and Baumeister (Baumeister and Vohs 2002; Baumeister and Wilson 1996) claimed that meaningfulness is rooted in the four basic needs for meaning: sense of purpose, efficacy, value and a sense of positive self-worth.

There is however another aspect of MOL that is overlooked by the personality theories of MOL: this is the cognitive aspect. Meaningfulness is an adjective that describes meaning. The fact that meaning can have important implications in regard to personality, emotions, and well-being does not justify overlooking the cognitive nature of meaning. Thus, the objective of the present study is to explore the possible contributions of meaning as a cognitive construct to MOL. For this purpose a new meaning-based scale of meaningfulness of life (MMOL) will be presented and tested. This approach could amplify the assessment of MOL and in addition extend Frankl's original approach of defining the "value" of life in terms of the triad of creativity, experience and attitude.

The Theory of Meaning

The cognitive approach to meaning is based on the theory of meaning (Kreitler and Kreitler 1990). It was developed on the basis of the following theoretical considerations: (a) Meaning is a complex phenomenon with a multiplicity of aspects, which implies that it cannot be wholly or adequately reflected in a measure assessing a single aspect, such as actions (as in the behaviorist tradition); (b) Meaning is essentially communicable, because most of the meanings we know have been learned from or through others; (c) Meaning can be expressed or communicated by verbal or different nonverbal means, because not all meanings can be communicated by means of words; (d) There are two types or varieties of meaning—the interpersonally shared meaning and the personal-subjective meaning, because meaning functions both in interpersonal communication and in the private world of individuals. These assumptions led to a new definition of meaning and a new methodology for its assessment. The basic data consisted of responses of thousands of subjects differing in age (2 to over 90 years), gender, cultural-ethnic background and education who were requested to communicate the interpersonally shared and personal meanings of a great variety of verbal and nonverbal stimuli, using any means of expression they considered adequate. Analysis of this data revealed that the meaning communications consisted of semantic molecules referring to a rich variety of contents in a great variety of forms.

Accordingly, meaning was defined as a *referent-centered pattern of meaning values*. In this definition, referent is the input, the carrier of meaning, which can be a word, an object, a situation, an event, a whole period, or any other input, whereas meaning values are cognitive contents assigned to the referent for the purpose of expressing or communicating its meaning. For example, if the referent is "Chair," responses such as "made of wood" or "is in a room" or "a piece of furniture" are three different meaning values. The referent and the meaning value together form a meaning unit (e.g., chair—a piece of furniture).

Five sets of variableswere defined for characterizing the unit of meaning:

(a) *Meaning Dimensions*, which characterize the contents of the meaning values from the point of view of the specific information communicated about the referent, such as the referent's sensory qualities (e.g., grass—green), feelings and emotions it evokes (e.g., storm—scary), range of inclusion (e.g., body—the head and legs).
(b) *Types of Relation*, which characterize the immediacy of the relation between the referent and the cognitive contents, for example, attributive (e.g., summer—warm), comparative (e.g., summer—warmer than spring), exemplifying instance (e.g., country—the U.S.).
(c) *Forms of Relation*, which characterize how the relation between the referent and the cognitive contents is regulated, in terms of its validity (positive or negative; e.g., Yoga—is not a religion), quantification (absolute, partial; apple—sometimes red), and form (factual, desired or desirable; law—should be obeyed, money—I wish I had more).
(d) *Referent Shifts*, which characterize the relation between the referent and the presented input, or—in a chain of responses—the relation between the referent and the previous one, for example, the referent may be identical to the input or the previous referent, it may be its opposite, or a part of it, or even apparently unrelated to it (e.g., when the presented stimulus was "U.S." and the subject responded by saying "I love New York," the subject was responding to a part of the stimulus).
(e) *Forms of Expression*, which characterize the forms of expression of the meaning units (e.g., verbal, denotation, graphic) and its directness (e.g., actual gesture or verbal description of gesture) (Kreitler and Kreitler 1990).

The meaning system may be applied for analyzing any verbal or nonverbal communication or expression of meaning, regardless of whether it has been produced with the intention of expressing meaning or not. In assessing communications of meaning the material is first reduced to meaning units, and then each unit is coded on one meaning dimension, one type of relation, one form of relation, one referent shift and one form of expression. For example, when the referent is "Life" and the meaning value is "is short," the coding on meaning dimensions is Temporal Qualities, on Types of Relation—attributive, on Forms of Relation—positive, on Referent Shifts—identical to input, and on Forms of Expression—verbal.

The meaning system has been used for analyzing meanings of different constructs, such as "Body," "Self," "Health," or "Love." A special kind of closed-format multiple-choice meaning questionnaire has been developed for single constructs. It consists of items referring only to the contents of the meaning dimensions and requests the subject to check how important or adequate the described content is for expressing the meaning of the construct.

Each individual disposes over a certain selected part of the meaning system which represents the specific tendencies of that individual to apply the meaning system in information processing. Thus, each individual tends to use specific meaning variables with higher frequency and other meaning variables with medium or low frequency. The *Meaning Test* was developed for assessing individuals' tendencies to use the different meaning variables. The test includes 11 standard stimuli (e.g., street, ocean) and instructs the subject to communicate the interpersonally shared and personal meaning of these stimuli to someone who does not know the meanings, using any means of expression that seem adequate. Coding the responses in terms of the meaning variables yields the ***subject's meaning profile,*** which summarizes the frequency with which the subject used each of the meaning variables in the test. The subject's meaning profile includes meaning variables from the five sets described above. The coding of the meaning units is done by means of a computer program (Kreitler 2010).

A body of studies has shown that specific clusters of meaning variables are related to the performance of cognitive acts, as well as scores on personality traits, personality dispositions and emotional reactions (Casakin and Kreitler 2011; Kreitler and Kreitler 1987, 1990, 1994). Studies of this kind indicate that the meaning variables represent not only specific domains of contents but also processes. Hence, concerning each meaning variable there is the static point of view, for example, "red" is a meaning value of the meaning dimension Sensory Qualities and "to the right" is a meaning value of the meaning dimension Locational Qualities. But in addition there is the dynamic point of view whereby each meaning variable may be considered as corresponding to a process. For example, the meaning dimension "range of inclusion" corresponds to the process of analyzing some entity or concept into its components; the comparative type of relation corresponds to the process of detecting similarity or difference; the shift of referent to the opposite corresponds to the process of shifting from a given concept to its contrast or opposite. The dynamic aspect becomes manifest when a meaning variable is activated for any function, for example, when exploring the cognitive processes involved in a specific cognitive task.

Thus, the meaning profile of the individual is indicative of the processes that are available to the individual or characterize his or her functioning which involves cognition, including cognitive tasks as well as activation of personality traits or emotions (Kreitler 2003, 2012, 2013a, b).

Objectives of the Study

The purpose of the study was to explore the relations between a new measure of Meaningfulness of Life, the individual's general meaning assignment tendencies as assessed in terms of the Meaning Test and quality of life. The new measure—the meaning-based scale of the Meaningfulness of Life—MMOL)—is based on applying the theory of meaning (Kreitler and Kreitler 1990) to the issue of the meaningfulness of life, thereby testing the feasibility and utility of extending Frankl's (1963, 1965) thesis of "value." The measure included references to meaning domains, such as actions, emotions, functions, thinking, or possessions.

There were three hypotheses , in the study. The first hypothesis was that most of the domains the individual would check on the MOL questionnaire as domains characterizing his or her life (MOL measure 2) would form part of those checked on the MOL questionnaire as contributing to MOL (MOL measure 1). Again, the rationale was that it is likely that the domains an individual would pursue or promote in one's life would correspond to those he or she would consider as contributing to one's MOL.

The second hypothesis was that most of the domains which the individual would check on the MOL questionnaire as contributing to MOL (MOL measure 1) would match the meaning dimensions that score high in the individual's meaning profile. The rationale was that meaning dimensions in the individual's meaning profile affect the kind of contents that the individual uses in other cognitive tasks in general.

The third hypothesis referred to the relation of the number of domains the individual would check on the MOL questionnaire as domains characterizing his or her life (MOL measure 2) (a) to an overall evaluation of the meaningfulness of one's life and (b) to the score on a questionnaire of quality of life (QOL). It was expected that the MOL measure 2 would be correlated positively with both variables. The third hypothesis was designed to provide validation of the MOL questionnaire, both in terms of its relation to the overall evaluation of MOL and in terms of QOL.

Method

Participants

The subjects were 90 university students in different faculties, in the age range 23–29, including an equal number of men and women.

Tools

The Meaning-Based Scale of the MOL (MMOL)

It included 38 items, each of which corresponded to one of the meaning dimensions. Only with regard to two meaning dimensions the contents required more than one item per dimension (i.e., sensory experiences and state). The first and basic set of instructions required the subject to check with regard to each item how much it could contribute to one's MOL. After handing in the responses, the subjects were presented the same questionnaire again and the instructions were to check to what extent the described item existed in their life at present (exists a lot, exists to some extent, does not exist, does not exist at all). Responses to the first set of instructions provided measure 1 of the MOL questionnaire and responses to the second set measure 2 of the MOL questionnaire. MOL 1 was the number of items checked as "contributing a lot" or "moderately," MOL 2 was the number of items checked as "exists a lot" or "exists to some extent."

The Test of Meanings (Kreitler and Kreitler 1990)

The test required the subjects to communicate to another person the interpersonally shared and subjective-personal meanings of eleven presented words (e.g., telephone, street), using any means of expression they found adequate. Coding the responses in terms of the sets of meaning variables (see Table 1) provided the subject's meaning profile, i.e., the frequencies with which each of the meaning variables has been used by the subject in his/her meaning communications.

The Multidimensional Quality of Life Inventory for Adults: Short Version (Kreitler and Kreitler 2006)

The questionnaire included 20 items referring to different domains, such as positive emotions, negative emotions, stress, basic needs, mastery and independence, social functioning, and cognitive functioning. The Cronbach's alpha reliability coefficient was 0.87. The subject was required to check the frequency of occurrence of each item (very often, often, sometimes, rarely). The responses were summed across all items, coded in the direction oriented toward a good QOL.

An Overall Rating of Meaningfulness in Life: On a Single Rating Scale from 1 (None or Very Low) to 7 (Very High)

The question was: Please rate the overall meaningfulness of your life on the following scale from 1 to 7.

Procedure

The four tools were presented to the participants together, in random order. The subjects were asked not to write their names but only their gender and age.

Table 1 Major variables of the meaning system: The meaning variables

Meaning dimensions		Forms of relation	
Dim. 1	Contextual allocation	FR 1	Propositional (1a: Positive; 1b: Negative)
Dim. 2	Range of inclusion (2a: Subclasses; 2b: Parts)	FR 2	Partial (2a: Positive; 2b: Negative)
Dim. 3	Function, purpose, and role	FR 3	Universal (3a: Positive; 3b: Negative)
Dim. 4	Actions and potentialities for actions (4a: by referent; 4b: to referent)	FR 4	Conjunctive (4a: Positive; 4b: Negative)
Dim. 5	Manner of occurrence and operation	FR 5	Disjunctive (5a: Positive; 5b: Negative)
Dim. 6	Antecedents and causes	FR 6	Normative (6a: Positive; 6b: Negative)
Dim. 7	Consequences and results	FR 7	Questioning (7a: Positive; 7b: Negative)
Dim. 8	Domain of application (8a: as subject; 8b: as object)	FR 8	Desired, wished (8a: Positive; 8b: Negative)
Dim. 9	Material	*Shifts in referent*[a]	
Dim. 10	Structure	SR 1	Identical
Dim. 11	State and possible change in it	SR 2	Opposite
Dim. 12	Weight and mass	SR 3	Partial
Dim. 13	Size and dimensionality	SR 4	Modified by addition
Dim. 14	Quantity and mass	SR 5	Previous meaning value
Dim. 15	Locational qualities	SR 6	Association
Dim. 16	Temporal qualities	SR 7	Unrelated
Dim. 17	Possessions (17a) and belongingness (17b)	SR 8	Verbal label
Dim. 18	Development	SR 9	Grammatical variation
Dim. 19	Sensory qualities[b] (19a: of referent; 19b: by referent)	SR 10	Previous meaning values combined
Dim. 20	Feelings and emotions (20a: evoked by referent; 20b: felt by referent)	SR 11	Superordinate
Dim. 21	Judgments and evaluations (21a: about referent; 21b: by referent)	SR 12	Synonym (12a: in original language; 12b: translated in another language; 12c: label in another medium; 12d a different formulation for the same referent on the same level)
Dim. 22	Cognitive qualities (22a: evoked by referent; 22b: of referent)	SR 13	Replacement by implicit meaning value
Types of relation[c]		Forms of expression	
TR 1	Attributive (1a: Qualities to substance; 1b: Actions to agent)	FE 1	Verbal (1a: Actual enactment; 1b: Verbally described; 1c: Using available materials)

(continued)

Table 1 (continued)

Meaning dimensions		Forms of relation	
TR 2	Comparative (2a: Similarity; 2b: Difference; 2c: Complementariness; 2d: Relationality)	FE 2	Graphic (2a: Actual enactment; 2b: Verbally described; 2c: Using available materials)
TR 3	Exemplifying-illustrative (3a: Exemplifying instance; 3b: Exemplifying situation; 3c: Exemplifying scene)	FE 3	Motoric (3a: Actual enactment; 3b: Verbally described; 3c: Using available materials)
TR 4	Metaphoric-symbolic (4a: Interpretation; 4b: Conventional metaphor; 4c: Original metaphor; 4d: Symbol)	FE4	Sounds and Tones (4a: Actual enactment; 4b: Verbally described; 4c: Using available materials)
		FE5	Denotative (5a: Actual enactment; 5b: Verbally described; 5c: Using available materials)

Note. The table does not include the meta-meaning variables

[a]Close SR: 1+3+9+12 Medium SR: 2+4+5+6+10+11 Distant SR: 7+8+13

[b]This meaning dimension includes a listing of subcategories of the different senses/sensations: [for special purposes they may also be grouped into "external sensations" and "internal sensations"] e.g., color, form, taste, sound, smell, pain, humidity, and various internal sensations

[c]Modes of meaning: Lexical mode: TR1+TR2; Personal mode: TR3+TR4

Results

Control analyses were performed to test the relations between the variables of age and gender and the measures used in the study (MOL1, MOL2, Meaningfulness rating, QOL). None of the results was significant. Therefore the whole sample was analyzed together.

The notable finding is that the number of items checked as able to contribute a lot or moderately to one's MOL (MOL 1) is much higher than the number of those checked as existing in one's life a lot or to some extent (MOL 2). The ratio of MOL1 to MOL2 is 2.18. This is not surprising in view of the nature of the measures and the age of the participants.

For testing the first hypothesis, a matching was done between the content of the responses checked as existing in one's life a lot or to some extent (MOL 2) and those checked as contributing a lot or moderately to one's MOL (MOL1). The matching showed that 87 % of the responses to MOL2 coincided with those checked in MOL1. Hence, the majority of MOL2 items (87 %) coincided with MOL1 items. Only 13 % did not.

For testing the second hypothesis a matching was done between the content of the items checked as contributing a lot or moderately to one's MOL (MOL1) and the meaning dimensions that occurred in the individuals' meaning profile (i.e., the frequencies of the meaning dimensions in responding to the Meaning Test). The matching showed that 63 % of the items checked as contributing a lot or moderately to one's MOL (MOL1) matched the meaning dimensions that appeared in the subject's meaning profile. A further check was done by comparing the MOL1 items to the meaning dimensions that occurred in the meaning profile with high frequency (namely, their proportions out of the total of responses were above the median). This matching showed that 71 % of the items in MOL1 turned out to refer to meaning dimensions used by the subject with high frequency.

Finally, only MOL2 was correlated significantly with the rating of the overall meaningfulness of one's life. Hence, the more the domains likely to contribute to one's meaningfulness of life (a lot or moderately) perceived as existing in one's life (a lot or to some extent), the higher the one's overall sense of MOL. However, the overall sense of MOL is unrelated simply to the number of domains one perceives as contributing (a lot or moderately) to one's MOL. Additionally, both measures—MOL1 and MOL2—are related significantly to one's overall QOL.

Further notable results concern the meaning variables that were found to be related to the overall rating of meaningfulness of one's life. The relations were checked by correlating the ratings of meaningfulness of life with the frequencies of the different meaning variables. In order to get a more reliable picture of the findings, in view of the fact that about 5 % of correlation coefficients may turn out to be significant by chance, only significant correlations above the level of 0.40 ($p<0.000$, indicating 16 % of shared variance) were considered. The results show that individuals who scored high on the MOL rating had the following meaning assignment tendencies: high scores on the meaning dimensions of actions, of functions, results, feelings and emotions, and cognitive qualities, but low scores on judgments and evaluations; high scores on the attributive and exemplifying-illustrative types of relation and low scores on the comparative type of relation; high scores on the partial, conjunctive and normative forms of relation and low scores on the negative form of relation; high scores on referent shifts to the medium-range referents; and on the use of graphic media of expression.

Discussion

The findings showed that when individuals are offered a broad range of options as potential contributors to MOL, they check a fairly large number of these options—actually a mean of 37.4 % of those presented—as likely contributors to their MOL. This finding in itself is important both theoretically and practically. Theoretically it supports Frankl's theses that there are domains that provide the possibility for promoting MOL and that each person has the right and duty to determine how to establish and maintain one's MOL. Practically, the fact that there is such a broad range of possibilities guarantees a firm framework for choice and for replacement in case preferred domains for MOL are excluded or difficult to attain. Notably, the range of options considered as potential contributors to MOL is related positively to QOL. This in itself suggests the positive effects of the awareness about a broad range of options for establishing one's MOL. This interpretation is supported also by the finding that the range of domains considered as contributive to MOL is related positively to QOL.

The broad range of domains considered as potentially contributive to MOL constitutes the framework for the domains that the individual chooses to promote and turn into a reality in one's life. In line with the first hypothesis, it was found that the majority of domains checked as existing in one's life a lot or at least to some extent formed part of the larger set checked as likely contributors to MOL. This finding suggests that in order to enhance one's MOL and guarantee its maintenance in view of different possible hardships and difficulties, it is advisable to provide the individual with information and encourage him or her to explore theoretically the possible contributions of a broad range of options to MOL.

Notably, the number of the domains checked as existing a lot or to some extent in one's life is on average 6.5. This number may be considered as fairly high, especially if one expects MOL to rely on 1–3 sources of meaningfulness. Be it as it may, the number is indicative of the tendency to root one's MOL in a variety of domains, both in order to broaden the base of the sources of MOL and guarantee its maintenance.

In line with the second hypothesis, the range of options considered by the individual as possibly contributing to MOL is related significantly to one's meaning profile, namely, to one's meaning assignment tendencies in general. In other words, one thinks about one's MOL in the same terms and with the same tools as one thinks about other issues in one's life and environment. An individual does not seem to have at his or her disposal a special set of constructs for dealing with MOL. Hence, when offered a new conception about MOL, its acceptance and adoption depends primarily on whether the individual has at disposal the cognitive contents and processes to handle this kind of conception. Yet it needs to be mentioned that having the disposal of particular meaning assignment tendencies implies a lot not only about one's thinking and worldview but also about one's personality tendencies and emotional characteristics. Hence, MOL can be considered as rooted deeply in one's personality and lifestyle.

In line with the third hypothesis, both the range of domains considered as contributing to MOL and those viewed as existing in one's life are related to QOL. But only the latter measure—the number of domains considered as existing in one's life—is related to the overall rating of mindfulness. This is an important finding for the validation of the new meaning-based measure of MOL. It indicates first that the new questionnaire provides a measure correlated highly with the overall rating of MOL and hence is valid and in addition it specifies what exactly is the basis for the validity of this new questionnaire of MOL, namely, the number of domains considered as existing in one's life.

The emerging meaning profile of MOL lends further support to the above stated conclusion that MOL may be considered as rooted deeply in one's personality and thinking. MOL appears to be related to a rich variety of cognitive tendencies, suggesting both a tendency to consider the interpersonally shared reality (e.g., TR1) as well as the personally subjective one (e.g., TR3), the more cognitive aspects (e.g., Dim22) as well as the emotional ones (e.g., Dim20). Most notable is the avoidance of the negative form of relation and of the meaning dimension judgments and evaluations.

Finally, concerning the newly presented meaning-based measure of MOL (MMOL) the study showed that it is has validity and that it provides both an overall measure of MOL and specific information about the kinds of domains that constitute its sources and manifestations. Further, it is anchored in a theoretical framework that is firm theoretically and empirically and expands the perspective of MOL into the cognitive level, thus enhancing the innovative approach delineated by Frankl's extraordinary insights into meaningfulness as the antidote of the threatening existential void.

References

Antonovsky, A. (1987). *Unraveling the mystery of health: How people manage stress and stay well*. San Francisco, CA: Jossey-Bass.

Battista, J., & Almond, R. (1973). The development of meaning in life. *Psychiatry, 36*, 409–427.

Baumeister, R. F., & Vohs, K. D. (2002). The pursuit of meaningfulness in life. In C. R. Snyder & S. J. Lopez (Eds.), *Handbook of positive psychology* (pp. 608–618). New York, NY: Oxford University Press.

Baumeister, R. F., & Wilson, B. (1996). Life stories and the four needs for meaning. *Psychological Inquiry, 7*, 322–325.

Becker, E. (1962). *The birth and death of meaning*. New York, NY: Free Press.

Casakin, H., & Kreitler, S. (2011). The cognitive profile of creativity in design. *Thinking Skills and Creativity, 6*(3), 159–168.

Crumbaugh, J. C., & Maholick, L. T. (1964). An experimental study in existentialism: The psychometric approach to Frankl's concept of noogenic neurosis. *Journal of Clinical Psychology, 20*, 200–207.

Feldman, D. B., & Snyder, C. R. (2005). Hope and the meaningful life: Theoretical and empirical associations between goal-directed thinking and life meaning. *Journal of Social and Clinical Psychology, 24*(3), 401–421.

Frankl, V. E. (1963). *Man's search for meaning: An introduction to logotherapy*. New York, NY: Washington Square Press.

Frankl, V. E. (1965). *The doctor and the soul: From psychotherapy to logotherapy*. New York, NY: Vintage Books.

Kreitler, S. (2003). Dynamics of fear and anxiety. In P. L. Gower (Ed.), *Psychology of fear* (pp. 1–17). Hauppauge, NY: Nova.

Kreitler, S. (2010). *Meaning test information system*. http://kreitlermeaningsystem.com/

Kreitler, S. (2012). The psychosemantic approach to logic. In S. Kreitler, L. Ropolyi, D. Eigner & G. Fleck (Eds.), *Systems of logic and the construction of order* (pp. 33–60). Bern, Berlin, Bruxelles, Frankfurt, Oxford, New York, Vienna: Peter Lang Publishing Group [Academic Publisher].

Kreitler, S. (2013a). Consciousness and knowledge: The psychosemantic approach. In S. Kreitler & O. Maimon (Eds.), *Consciousness: Its nature and functions* (pp. 236–264). Hauppauge, NY: Nova Publishers.

Kreitler, S. (2013b). The construction of meaning. In D. Cervone, M. Fajkowska, M. Eysenck, & T. Maruszewski (Eds.), *Personality dynamics: Embodiment, meaning construction, and the social world* (pp. 47–63). Clinton Corners, NY: Eliot Werner Publications.

Kreitler, S., & Kreitler, H. (1987). Psychosemantic aspects of the self. In T. M. Honess & K. M. Yardley (Eds.), *Self and identity: Individual change and development* (pp. 338–358). London: Routledge & Kegan Paul.

Kreitler, S., & Kreitler, H. (1990). *Cognitive foundations of personality traits*. New York: Plenum.
Kreitler, S., & Kreitler, H. (1994). Motivational and cognitive determinants of exploration. In H. Keller, K. Schneider, & B. Henderson (Eds.), *Curiosity and exploration* (pp. 259–284). New York, NY: Springer.
Kreitler, S., & Kreitler, M. M. (2006). Multidimensional quality of life: A new measure of quality of life in adults. *Social Indicators Research, 76*, 5–33.
Reker, G. T. (1992). *Life attitude profile – revised*. Peterborough, Canada: Student Psychologists Press.
Ryff, C. (1989). Happiness is everything, or is it? Explorations on the meaning of psychological well-being. *Journal of Personality and Social Psychology, 57*, 1069–1081.
Schnell, T. (2009). The Sources of Meaning and Meaning in Life Questionnaire (SoMe): Relations to demographics and well-being. *Journal of Positive Psychology, 4*, 483–499.
Steger, M. F., Frazier, P., Oishi, S., & Kaler, M. (2006). The Meaning in Life Questionnaire: Assessing the presence of and search for meaning in life. *Journal of Counseling Psychology, 53*, 80–93.

Meaning and Automatic Stereotyping: Advancing an Agenda for Research

Ivonne A. Florez, Stefan E. Schulenberg, and Tracie L. Stewart

Meaning and Automatic Stereotyping: Advancing an Agenda for Research

Stereotyping (associating members of different groups with particular traits) and prejudice (disliking individuals based on their group membership) are enduring social problems in the United States. These intergroup biases contribute to discrimination against members of disadvantaged out-groups, including widespread disparities in health and education (Orsi et al. 2010; Pewewardy and Severson 2003; Vaught 2009). One recent political economics study revealed that the continuing wage gap between African Americans and White Americans varied systematically across states as a function of levels of individually held racial biases within each state (Charles and Guryan 2008). Adding to the complexities of intergroup bias is the well-documented finding in the social psychological literature that stereotyping and prejudice can occur either at a conscious, or "explicit," level, or at an unconscious "implicit" level. Recent research has found that implicit biases often have more impact than explicit biases on concrete acts of discrimination (e.g., Latu et al. 2011). Given that implicit biases are, by definition, unacknowledged by those who hold these biases, they may be particularly resistant to change. And in fact, many strategies aimed at improving intergroup relations have been found to be ineffective and, in some cases, even counterproductive (e.g., Kalev et al. 2006).

I.A. Florez (✉) • S.E. Schulenberg
Department of Psychology, The University of Mississippi,
205 Peabody, P.O. Box 1848, University, MS 38677, USA
e-mail: psych@olemiss.edu; sschulen@olemiss.edu

T.L. Stewart
Department of Psychology, Kennesaw State University,
Social Sciences (SO 402), Room 5005B, Bartow Ave, Kennesaw, GA 30144, USA
e-mail: tstewa44@kennesaw.edu

A. Batthyány (ed.), *Logotherapy and Existential Analysis*, Logotherapy and Existential Analysis: Proceedings of the Viktor Frankl Institute Vienna 1,
DOI 10.1007/978-3-319-29424-7_11

Given the pervasiveness, consequences, and resistance to change of implicit biases, innovative approaches to understanding and ameliorating this continuing social problem are a pressing need. We propose that one unexplored approach to reducing intergroup biases is the study of perceived meaning. To our knowledge, only one study to date has looked at the role that perceived meaning may play in individuals' manifestation of implicit stereotyping (Florez et al. 2013). In the present chapter, we summarize the literature on the nature of perceived meaning in life and its links to various domains of functioning. We then call for an expansion of meaning research to the study of intergroup biases.

Perceived Meaning in Life

Although meaning in life has been discussed by philosophers for centuries, it was Viktor Frankl who introduced the concept of meaning as a variable of interest for psychology. Frankl developed a psychological model based on the fundamental idea that humans are inherently meaning seekers (Frankl 1959/1984). For Frankl, a will to meaning is the primary driving force in human existence. Frankl's definition of meaning refers to those reasons, tasks, experiences, and acts that are inherent in every situation and that give a person a "why" to existence and, therefore, serve as motivation to complete daily activities as well as to set meaningful goals to fulfill (Frankl 1959/1984, 1994).

Meaning can be actualized in every circumstance and is contingent upon personal values and concrete situations (Frankl 1959/1984, 1994). Thus, meaning is specific and unique for every person and varies across different situations. Closely related to the concept of meaning is Frankl's premise of self-transcendence, the human capacity to intentionally direct attention and efforts to something or someone other than ourselves (e.g., a cause, person/people, or a higher power; Frankl 1959/1984, 1994). According to Frankl, the most effective routes to attain meaning include serving others, cultivating relationships, and engaging in values-directed behavior that goes beyond one's self (Frankl 1959/1984, 1994; Schulenberg et al. 2008).

Since Frankl's introduction of perceived meaning to the field of psychology, numerous theorists and researchers have turned their attention to this concept. As a result, perceived meaning in life is frequently a component of theoretical approaches that highlight the importance of having purpose as a core, fundamental aspect of human existence (Battista and Almond 1973; Reker et al. 1987; Schulenberg et al. 2008; Wong 2012). There is no consensus, however, on the best manner of conceptualizing meaning, and a number of different proposals have been asserted for how meaning may be defined and assessed (e.g., Fjelland et al. 2008; Reker and Fry 2003; Wong 2012).

Shared aspects of the various definitions of meaning include the following: (1) meaning underlies a consistent explanatory framework to evaluate life (Steger and Kashdan 2013); (2) meaning is related to setting future goals, creating a sense of utility and excitement (Battista and Almond 1973; Frankl 1994; Steger 2012); (3) meaning is a subjective perception that motivates the completion of daily activities (Heine et al. 2006; Steger 2012); (4) meaning involves actualization of personal values (Baumeister 1991; Frankl 1994); (5) the lack of meaning in life, or meaninglessness, results in maladaptive thoughts, feelings, and behaviors (Frankl 1994; Maddi 1967; Mascaro and Rosen 2008; Schulenberg et al. 2011, 2014; Vella-Brodrick et al. 2009); and (6) even though it is subjective, meaning has been associated with paths common across people (e.g., relationships, service-oriented behavior) (Emmons 2005; Kashdan and Steger 2007; Schnell 2011; Wong 2012).

In the next section a review is offered on some of the latest research findings on different aspects of meaning in life and its significant association with various domains of human functioning. The goal is to highlight the role that meaning in life plays across these domains prior to discussing automatic stereotyping in greater detail.

Research on Meaning and Human Functioning

The importance of meaning is supported from different perspectives evident in the literature (Proulx 2013; Sheldon 2012). With specific regard to perceived meaning, or meaning making, some researchers have asserted that it is primarily a social process. Meaning is constructed with others and relates to phenomena that are specific to human beings (Proulx 2013; Sheldon 2012; Van Tongeren and Green 2010). From this perspective, culture constitutes the background and framework for meaning, and existential concerns trigger the search for meaning (Proulx 2013; Sheldon 2012).

One theoretical model that attempts to explain the process of meaning making is the meaning maintenance model (MMM; Heine et al. 2006). The meaning maintenance model states that there is a continuous monitoring that occurs in the background of mental activities. This ongoing process assesses the presence of meaning and engages in automatic efforts in order to defend or sustain meaning (Proulx and Heine 2008; Sheldon 2012). Research supporting this model indicates that when individuals perceive a threat to their beliefs or sense of self they engage in active attempts to protect themselves and maintain meaning, such as efforts to bolster self-esteem (Van Tongeren and Green 2010), enhance proximity to others (Williams 2012), and reduce uncertainty (McGregor et al. 2001).

The importance of these studies lies in the idea that individuals are continuously evaluating life events based on their meaning frameworks and that attempts to disrupt their meaning-making systems will lead to efforts to protect or reestablish a sense of meaning (King 2012; Proulx and Heine 2008; Sheldon 2012; Van Tongeren and Green 2010). These findings have important implications for the role of meaning in social processes. Given that threats to the perception of meaning result in psychological counters by individuals is consistent with the idea that meaning-making is a fundamental aspect of the human condition (Sheldon 2012; Van den Bos 2009; Van

Tongeren and Green 2010). Consequently, perceived meaning has garnered major empirical interest across various domains of human functioning (Heine et al. 2006; Proulx and Heine 2008; Schulenberg et al. 2008; Sheldon 2012; Van den Bos 2009; Van Tongeren and Green 2010).

With regard to the role of meaning in mental health and well-being, numerous studies have shown a positive significant relationship between meaning in life and general well-being (Drescher et al. 2012; Ryff and Singer 1998), positive affect (Hicks and King 2007; Pan et al. 2008), resilience (Nygren et al. 2005; Pan et al. 2008), adaptive coping strategies when faced with difficult situations (Farber et al. 2010), perceived social support (Ulmer et al. 1991), posttraumatic growth (Park 2010; Triplett et al. 2012), and physical health (Krause 2009; Park et al. 2008). Furthermore, people with higher levels of perceived meaning have been found to report fewer symptoms of depression (Mascaro and Rosen 2008; Rahiminezhad et al. 2011), anxiety (Rahiminezhad et al. 2011), substance use (Flora and Stalikas 2012; Schnetzer et al. 2013), general distress (Pan et al. 2008), suicidal ideation (Heisel and Flett 2004), and posttraumatic stress (Triplett et al. 2012). Along similar lines, individuals reporting higher levels of meaning also report higher levels of personal growth, autonomy, sense of control, self-acceptance, curiosity, self-esteem, and self-efficacy (DeWitz et al. 2009; Drescher et al. 2012; Steger et al. 2008). Thus, higher perceived meaning is associated with a wide range of positive indicators of mental health and adaptive personal resources.

With specific regard to social interactions, studies of meaning have shown that greater levels of perceived meaning in life positively and significantly correlate with organizational ethical behavior, group achievement (Bligh and Kohles 2009), social skills (Steger et al. 2008; Weinstein et al. 1995; Wrzesniewski et al. 1997), feelings of connection with others (Lambert et al. 2010; Steger and Kashdan 2013; Steger et al. 2008), and interpersonal appeal (Stillman et al. 2011). On the contrary, people with less perceived meaning in life are more likely to report social problems such as alienation and feelings of social inadequacy (Ho et al. 2010), social exclusion (Stillman et al. 2009), loneliness (Stillman et al. 2009; Williams 2012), and social anxiety (Steger and Kashdan 2013). In other words, meaning is associated with better quality of social interactions and feelings of social adequacy and satisfaction.

As for sources of meaning, research findings have pointed towards social relationships, social connectedness, and social roles as important sources of meaning across different populations (Hicks and King 2009; Stillman et al. 2009). Perceived meaning appears to promote and guide interpersonal relationships and consequently has important implications for positive social functioning (Steger and Kashdan 2013), relationships, and the value placed on social affiliation (Stillman et al. 2011). Clearly, on the basis of the aforementioned studies, perceived meaning in life plays an integral role in one's mental health, as well as in one's interpersonal functioning. However, up to this point the literature on meaning has just begun to scratch the surface with respect to the role of meaning in interpersonal processes.

Findings on the relationship between meaning, cognitive processes, and personality traits are also noteworthy because these factors are noted to predispose, to some degree, the way individuals interact with their social environment and how they approach a range of situations (Burrow et al. 2010; Hicks et al. 2010; King 2012; Steger et al. 2008). As for cognitive processes, research on intuitive processing style (solving a problem based on internal cues that indicate a response without a clear explanation of why or how one arrived at a given conclusion) has affirmed that individuals with higher levels of intuition report more feelings of meaning, higher levels of positive explanations when facing a negative event, and a better learning performance and accurate discrimination of stimuli (Hicks et al. 2010; King 2012; King and Hicks 2009). These findings suggest that when ascribing meaning to new situations and recognizing stimuli that we are familiar with, intuition and heuristics play an important role in the evaluation of situations guiding our perception of meaning and helping individuals arrive at accurate interpretations or responses (Hicks et al. 2010; King 2012).

Furthermore, Steger et al. (2008) found that presence of meaning is significantly and positively associated with enjoyment derived from thinking and curiosity. The results of this study suggested that individuals experiencing higher levels of meaning endorse a more active search for information, a greater drive for knowledge, in order to understand how things work. Additionally, other studies have noted that meaning appears to promote goal-directed thinking (Burrow et al. 2010) and greater cognitive flexibility (King 2012), suggesting that perceived meaning facilitates cognitive tasks and decreases cognitive rigidity (Burrow et al. 2010; King 2012; Steger et al. 2008).

Steger et al. (2008) also found that presence of meaning significantly correlates with extraversion (being warm, positive, and active), openness to ideas, agreeableness (specific to altruism and compassion), and conscientiousness (see also Schnell 2011). Alternatively, presence of meaning negatively and significantly correlated with neuroticism (Steger et al. 2008). These and related findings have particular implications for the present chapter, which calls for the examination of meaning in processes of automatic stereotyping, as research affirms that meaning is associated with a higher quality of social relationships (Schnell 2011), values-directed behavior (King et al. 2006), and altruism (Steger et al. 2008).

Continuing to build on this premise, research has systematically demonstrated the importance of perceiving meaning and the positive implications that meaning carries across many different areas of functioning (Fjelland et al. 2008; Reker and Fry 2003; Wong 2012). Research findings among different disciplines and theoretical perspectives have indicated that meaning plays an important role in personal well-being (Peterson et al. 2005; Vella-Brodrick et al. 2009), and it has substantial influence in the way people approach situations (Rosso et al. 2010; Steger et al. 2008) and interact in their relationships (Emmons 2005; Kashdan and Steger 2007; Schnell 2011; Wong 2012). Based on compelling findings that indicate the importance of meaning across many domains of human functioning, it is a logical evolution that research on meaning should be expanded further to address new questions.

In this chapter we assert that meaning is a fundamental variable in terms of increasing our understanding of intergroup biases (consistently benefitting and judging in more positive ways one's group compared to other groups) that are specific to automatic stereotyping. Given our awareness that meaning is associated with prosocial behavior, cognitive flexibility, and better quality of social interactions, it follows that meaning would have applicability in understanding automatic stereotyping. Prior to further discussing the role of meaning (or in this case the lack thereof) as a predictor of automatic stereotyping, a review of the automatic stereotyping literature is offered.

Automatic Stereotyping

Stereotyping is the cognitive process of ascribing traits or other characteristics to individuals based solely on their group membership; it represents a type of heuristic mechanism that people might use to make social judgments quickly, even if not necessarily more accurately (Bodenhausen and Richeson 2010; Jones and Fazio 2010; Kawakami et al. 2000). The information used to form stereotypes can be either positive (e.g., athletic) or negative (e.g., aggressive). Stereotypes are generally shared within the individual's mainstream cultural view and may arise from a number of sources. They may develop from exposure to stereotypic portrayals in the media, from the need to categorize other people quickly due to high cognitive demands, or from an evolved tendency to distinguish one's own group, at the expense of individuating out-groups. Regardless of the origin of stereotypes, once developed, they are highly resistant to change (Bodenhausen and Richeson 2010; Kawakami et al. 2000).

Holding a stereotype specific to an out-group does not necessarily result in discrimination or engaging in negative behaviors towards the out-group (Ashmore and Del Boca 1981; Fiske 2000). However, when stereotypes are negative, they do increase the likelihood that behaviors performed by members of out-groups will be judged in biased, negative ways and that out-group members will be treated in a discriminatory manner (Fiske 2000; Jones and Fazio 2010; Pearson et al. 2007; Stewart and Payne 2008). Negative stereotypes can generate a wide array of behaviors towards a member of an out-group that can vary from subtle changes in attitudes, gestures, and nonverbal behavior, to more salient forms of prejudice such as avoidance or antipathy (Dovidio and Gaertner 2004; Fiske 2000; Jones and Fazio 2010; Pearson et al. 2007; Stewart and Payne 2008).

Decades of social psychological research on intergroup biases have identified two subtypes of stereotyping. Whereas *explicit stereotyping* occurs voluntarily, when an individual intentionally acknowledges holding negative beliefs towards a group, *automatic*, or *implicit*, stereotyping occurs automatically, unintentionally, and outside of conscious awareness (Blair and Banaji 1996; Clow and Esses 2007; Devine 1989; Fiske 2000; Payne et al. 2002; Stewart and Payne 2008). Research findings in the area of automatic stereotyping have revealed that when individuals are unconsciously primed with stereotypical traits, stereotypes are activated in both people reporting higher and lower levels of prejudice (Devine 1989, 2001). Even for individuals that report low levels of prejudice, automatic stereotyping occurs in the presence of an out-group member, impacting the way people respond (Stewart and Payne 2008; Stewart et al. 2003). Furthermore, it has been demonstrated that stereotypes are more likely to occur automatically if individuals are under a high cognitive load or distracted, limiting their ability to intentionally avoid stereotyping (Blair and Banaji 1996). When individuals reporting low levels of prejudice are able to monitor their answers they evidence a less stereotypical response (Devine 1989, 2001).

These findings have had major implications in the study of prejudice because they reveal that even individuals with egalitarian beliefs automatically activate negative stereotypes toward out-group members and are consequently influenced by them (Biernat 2003; Jones and Fazio 2010; Stewart et al. 2003). Everyday interactions with out-group members are biased by automatic activation of stereotyping, and thus multiple contexts are affected through implicit use of negative stereotypes (Biernat 2003; Jones and Fazio 2010; Stewart et al. 2003). Explicit and implicit stereotypes often seem to contradict one another. For example, some people may explicitly hold positive views of women in the workplace but harbor strong biases against women in the workplace at an unconscious, automatic level. Some recent research suggests that outcomes for members of target groups, such as employees' likelihood of receiving a raise or promotion, are better predicted by workplace power-holders' implicit stereotypes than their explicit stereotypes (Latu et al. 2011).

Bearing in mind the pervasiveness of automatic stereotyping and its potential influence on opinions, judgment, decision making, and behavior toward members of stigmatized groups (Biernat 2003; Blair and Banaji 1996; Devine 2001; Fiske 2000), interest in the phenomenon has continued to grow, with calls for research contributing to its understanding and reduction (Fiske 2000; Pearson et al. 2007; Stewart et al. 2012). Studies have suggested that automatic stereotyping can be counteracted by an awareness of the existence of stereotypical information and training to negate existing stereotypes or judge ambiguously stereotype-consistent behaviors in a more neutral way (Kawakami et al. 2000; Stewart et al. 2010). However, there are mixed results on the long-term effectiveness of related interventions (Lambert et al. 2003; Payne et al. 2002; Stewart and Payne 2008).

Several studies have indicated that automatic forms of stereotyping might also be influenced by individual differences (Fiske 2000; Monteith 1993; Moskowitz et al. 1999). Of particular importance for the present study is research on the association between self-esteem and processes of social comparison and intergroup bias. Such theory and investigations have implications for the systematic study of meaning and its relationship to automatic stereotyping (Crocker et al. 1987; Hunter et al. 1996; Lindeman 1997). With specific reference to Terror Management Theory, self-esteem has been considered an important variable that moderates the degree in which an individual holds intergroup biases. Prior to discussing the role of perceived meaning in relation to automatic stereotyping we discuss self-esteem from the Terror Management Theory perspective.

Self-Esteem and Terror Management Theory

The potential importance of self-esteem in understanding stereotyping has been pointed out by theorists and researchers from the perspective of Terror Management Theory (TMT; Solomon et al. 1991). Terror Management Theory asserts that self-esteem is the psychological pathway that directly leads to the reduction of terror associated with death (Routledge et al. 2010; Solomon et al. 1991). For Terror Management Theory, self-esteem "refers to a sense of personal significance and value" (Routledge et al. 2010, p. 900).

Regarding the study of stereotyping, research indicates that when people with low self-esteem are confronted with the possibility of death, they are more vulnerable to experiencing psychological distress from death anxiety (Greenberg et al. 1992; Routledge and Arndt 2008). Moreover, they are more likely to engage in cognitive and behavioral attempts to bolster self-esteem via discriminating against other people and defending their world-views (Greenberg et al. 1992; Routledge and Arndt 2008).

According to Terror Management Theory, people with high self-esteem exhibit a reduced need for prejudice towards other cultures, as their own sense of self-worth provides a buffer for anxiety (Greenberg et al. 2004; Solomon et al. 1991). On the contrary, people with low self-esteem seem to use greater out-group discrimination and engage in more stereotypical beliefs, as a means to compensate for the lack of a sense of self-worth in their own culture (Greenberg et al. 2004; Solomon et al. 1991). Therefore, in order to compensate for low self-esteem, people engage in stereotypical beliefs about other groups (Gonsalkorale et al. 2007). Simply put, one research perspective is that low self-esteem or threats to self-esteem elicit (or evoke) higher levels of stereotyping (Gonsalkorale et al. 2007).

Regarding research on the relationship between automatic stereotyping and self-esteem, however, there are mixed findings. Some researchers of prejudice have found that global self-esteem functions as a moderator of the strength of intergroup bias, where people with higher levels of self-esteem evidence more equanimity and acceptance of out-group members (Baldwin and Wesley 1996; Greenberg et al. 2003; Rudman et al. 2007; Schimel et al. 1999). Individuals with low self-esteem demonstrate increases in negative stereotyping and rigid bias towards out-group members (Baldwin and Wesley 1996; Rudman et al. 2007; Schimel et al. 1999).

In contrast, other studies have indicated that it is high self-esteem (as opposed to low self-esteem) that promotes bias (Aberson et al. 2000; Hunter et al. 2011). Individuals achieve high levels of self-esteem through social identification, and therefore the retention of bias allows them to endorse higher levels of self-esteem (Aberson et al. 2000; Hunter et al. 2011). Thus, overall the results across studies are not uniform with regard to the role of self-esteem in stereotyping; however, it seems apparent that automatic stereotyping varies as a function of the individual's motivation to protect or enhance self-esteem as supported in a number of empirical investigations (Greenwald and Banaji 1995).

As can be seen from this review, self-esteem is considered to play an important role in the process of stereotyping (Greenberg et al. 2003; Rudman et al. 2007; Schimel et al. 1999). Its role is either to protect individuals against holding negative beliefs towards other groups or to promote intergroup biases within a specific group to maintain collective sense of worth. With this in mind, we contend that meaning plays an important part as well. Meaning seems to promote behaviors associated with better quality of social interactions, and meaning is also related to self-esteem (Routledge et al. 2010; Steger and Frazier 2005) and existential anxiety (Vella-Brodrick et al. 2009). Each of these variables appears to moderate processes of automatic stereotyping. Based on this premise we call for the systematic examination of meaning in studies of automatic stereotyping.

Meaning and Automatic Stereotyping

Given that theorists from the perspective of Terror Management Theory support low self-esteem and high death anxiety as mediators of responses of automatic stereotyping, it makes sense to include meaning, a variable that has been found to be related to both self-esteem and death anxiety, in the study of automatic stereotyping. Terror Management Theory proposes that one of the ways that people reduce death anxiety is by perceiving themselves as being valuable parts of a culture that is meaningful, and thus, attaining a sense of personal meaning (Greenberg 2012; Pyszczynski et al. 2010).

As with self-esteem, from the Terror Management Theory perspective meaning is conceptualized as a buffer against existential anxiety, providing a means of achieving symbolic immortality, decreasing death anxiety and life uncertainty (Feldman and Snyder 2005; Greenberg et al. 2004; Vess et al. 2009). Therefore, it follows that perceiving meaning on an individual level could be a critically important method to reducing death anxiety, providing a symbolic sense of self and a means of self-transcendence (Hicks and King 2009; Peterson and Park 2012; Wong 2012).

Meaning is consistently associated with self-transcendence, psychological adjustment, life satisfaction, and well-being (Peterson and Park 2012; Peterson et al. 2005; Vella-Brodrick et al. 2009; Williams 2012). Furthermore, and highly congruent with Terror Management Theory, meaning (or the lack thereof) is also consistently associated with death anxiety. Perceiving meaning is an effective way to cope with existential concerns such as mortality salience as it provides a sense of comprehension and purpose to everyday behavior (Arndt et al. 2013; Proulx 2013; Van den Bos 2009; Vess et al. 2009).

With regard to the relationship between meaning and self-esteem, several studies suggest that high levels of self-esteem are associated with high levels of meaning, and vice versa (Routledge et al. 2010; Steger and Frazier 2005). Research findings have reported significant positive bivariate correlations ranging from 0.38 to 0.76, which support the presence of a strong relationship between the two concepts

(Schlegel et al. 2011; Steger and Frazier 2005). Theoretically, from the meaning maintenance model's point of view, self-esteem is one of the dimensions involved in the perception of meaning. In order for people to perceive life as being meaningful they should also perceive themselves as being people of value (Van Tongeren and Green 2010).

Although the two concepts are associated, meaning involves a wider range of characteristics when compared with self-esteem, relating not only to a sense of personal value, but also to a sense of purpose, an understanding of the world, self-transcendence, and the pursuit of goals (King 2012; Rosso et al. 2010; Proulx and Heine 2008; Schnell 2011; Schulenberg et al. 2008; Sheldon 2012; Steger 2012; Van Tongeren and Green 2010; Williams 2012). Because the concept of meaning encompasses a meaning-making system that guides the evaluation of events and also relates to values-directed behavior and other processes that underlie social interactions, meaning may possess greater utility in explaining a wider array of events, with greater potential to influence physical and emotional well-being. For instance, Lee et al. (2006) implemented a meaning-based intervention in which patients with breast or colorectal cancer received four sessions that explored the meaning of the feelings and thoughts of each individual's experience within the context of past life events and future goals. Compared to the control group and baseline, the experimental group not only endorsed significantly higher levels of meaning, but also significantly higher levels of self-esteem, optimism, and self-efficacy post intervention (Lee et al. 2006). The results suggested that meaning-based interventions indirectly enhance other positive skills and attributes, self-esteem being one example (Lee et al. 2006).

Clearly, as with self-esteem, perceived meaning in life has potential value as a variable that can influence automatic stereotyping. Based on this review of the literature, it follows from Terror Management Theory that if individuals perceive meaning in life, then they would have less need to downgrade members of out-groups as a means of bolstering their symbolic self. Thus, people who report higher levels of meaning should endorse fewer negative stereotypes toward stigmatized groups (i.e., higher levels of perceived meaning should be associated with reduced automatic stereotyping).

With this premise as a foundation, Florez et al. (2013) examined the relationship between meaning in life and automatic stereotyping (defined as the involuntary activation of a set of beliefs towards a target group) in a sample of White college students. They found that higher perceived meaning in life was significantly associated with lower automatic stereotyping towards African-Americans. Moreover, when compared with well-established explicit measures of racial bias and social dominance, the correlational analyses revealed that meaning was more strongly associated with automatic stereotyping (a statistically significant inverse relationship) than were the other measures.

The results from this preliminary study suggested that perceived meaning is an important variable to consider when examining automatic stereotyping, as it may potentially reduce tendencies for people to automatically stereotype members of other racial-ethnic groups. Currently, the authors are extending this research paradigm to expand on the role of meaning, as well as to analyze the unique contributions of meaning and self-esteem as predictors of automatic stereotyping. We are unaware of any published studies examining these variables in a systematic fashion.

Advancing an Agenda for Research

The results of the study by Florez and colleagues (2013) are highly promising, warranting new and increasingly rigorous research on the relationship between meaning and automatic stereotyping, as well as other intergroup biases, in order to better understand the nature of this relationship. Meaning appears to play a role in processes of automatic stereotyping, perhaps fostering cognitive and social processes that buffer individuals against tendencies to unconsciously label people from other groups with negative stereotypes.

Findings on the association between meaning and automatic stereotyping will contribute independently to the respective scientific literatures of meaning and automatic stereotyping, as well as self-esteem, and will promote new lines of research related to the underlying processes of perceiving meaning in association with self-esteem and processes of cognitive bias (e.g., negative stereotyping). Additionally, studies on the positive role of meaning in predicting lower levels of stereotyping increase the understanding of how individual differences can reduce tendencies to automatically stereotype members of vulnerable groups.

A major line of research worth studying is the causal relationship between meaning and automatic stereotyping. Does greater meaning lead to less stereotyping, or could it be that less stereotyping opens the door to finding more meaning? To disentangle this relationship, research on the mechanisms that mediate and moderate the relationship between meaning and automatic stereotyping is needed. First, it is important to further evaluate if meaning in life itself moderates the relationship between automatic stereotyping and self-esteem. Specifically, given the mixed findings on self-esteem and automatic stereotyping it is necessary to determine if individual differences in levels of meaning in life have an impact on the relationship between self-esteem and automatic stereotyping. Then, some variables worth exploring as moderators of the meaning-automatic stereotyping relationship are religious beliefs, values, age, and individual differences such as personal need for structure, egalitarianism, and dogmatism. Regarding variables of mediation, research involving death anxiety (Terror Management Theory), as well as studies of self-transcendence, sources of values, pro-social behavior, and cognitive flexibility, could contribute to the understanding of the active component of meaning that facilitates less automatic stereotyping.

Furthermore, research on the role of meaning in predicting automatic stereotyping could be expanded to include people of different ages, ethnicities, regions, and cultures. Along these lines, it is important to examine processes of meaning and automatic stereotyping towards members of other minority groups commonly affected by negative stereotypes, such as women, gay and lesbian individuals, and members of other racial-ethnic groups. Such research would help us understand how these processes are similar or different across various contexts and in various populations.

Summary and Conclusions

From the perspective of the meaning literature, the relationship between perceived meaning and automatic stereotyping is consistent with research findings on the importance of meaning in human functioning. Meaning guides the evaluation of events and motivates individuals to maintain consistency between personal goals, beliefs, and values (King 2012; Proulx and Heine 2008; Rosso et al. 2010; Schnell 2011; Schulenberg et al. 2008; Sheldon 2012; Steger 2012; Van Tongeren and Green 2010; Williams 2012). Additionally, similar to automatic stereotyping, meaning-making processes (processes in which the individual attempts to maintain meaning) may also occur even at an automatic level, involving intuition and heuristics (Hicks et al. 2010; King 2012). Higher levels of meaning positively correlate with characteristics that will, theoretically, facilitate less automatic stereotyping, such as cognitive flexibility (King 2012), altruism (Steger et al. 2008), self-transcendence (Peterson and Park 2012), and social relatedness (Lambert et al. 2010; Steger and Kashdan 2013; Steger et al. 2008).

Since Frankl declared meaning as a core aspect of human existence, numerous research studies have been conducted that validate his claim, exploring and expanding the complexity of the concept. The growing interest in perceived meaning has led researchers to implement highly rigorous and innovative studies that further inform its applicability in contributing to the establishment and maintenance of meaningful communities and social relationships.

Meaning is an essential concept with significance to the scientific study of automatic stereotyping. This specific avenue of empirical inquiry is vital in furthering our understanding of both perceived meaning and automatic stereotyping. For instance, some meaning-based interventions may have the added benefit of reducing automatic stereotyping, and alternatively, some interventions designed to reduce automatic stereotyping may enhance perceived meaning. Moreover, there are some data to suggest that many interventions designed to reduce intergroup bias do not work and that some might even have the potential to enhance biases and cause reluctance in people to participate in such programs (Kalev et al. 2006). With the idea of meaning functioning potentially as a protective factor against automatic stereotyping, meaning as an intervention tool could be particularly effective, and also elicit less reactance in program participants. For example, if participants are told that they should develop more positive attitudes toward other groups, then they may be reactive, thinking they are being criticized. But if they are guided to experience greater meaning in their lives, they may be more likely to feel they are being helped or supported rather than criticized. Therefore, meaning might be a promising new channel of intervention to reduce intergroup biases.

Future work would benefit from focusing on these and related areas. The incorporation of meaning in the study of automatic stereotyping has significant potential to augment relationships and interactions among people across contexts and populations, ultimately reducing the negative repercussions of automatic stereotyping. This thesis warrants attention and necessitates new, rigorous and systematic research. Finally, this article highlights the significance of meaning across many different areas of human functioning. Based on this premise, we urge researchers in the area of meaning to work toward formulating new empirical questions, conducting novel, well-grounded studies that address the role of meaning in increasingly diverse areas of functioning, such as cognitive processes, social interactions, and positive behaviors.

References

Aberson, C. L., Healy, M., & Romero, V. (2000). Ingroup bias and self-esteem: A meta-analysis. *Personality and Social Psychology Review, 4*(2), 157–173.

Arndt, J., Landau, M. J., Vail, K. E., & Vess, M. (2013). An edifice for enduring personal value: A terror management perspective on the human quest for multilevel meaning. In K. D. Markman, T. Proulx, & M. J. Lindberg (Eds.), *The psychology of meaning* (pp. 49–69). Washington, DC: American Psychological Association.

Ashmore, R. D., & Del Boca, F. K. (1981). Conceptual approaches to stereotyping. In D. L. Hamilton (Ed.), *Cognitive processes in stereotyping and inter-group relations* (pp. 1–35). Hillsdale, NJ: Erlbaum.

Baldwin, M. W., & Wesley, R. (1996). Effects of existential anxiety and self-esteem on the perception of others. *Basic and Applied Social Psychology, 18*(1), 75–95.

Battista, J., & Almond, R. (1973). The development of meaning in life. *Psychiatry, 36*(4), 409–427.

Baumeister, R. F. (1991). *Meanings of life*. New York, NY: Guilford.

Biernat, M. (2003). Toward a broader view of social stereotyping. *American Psychologist, 58*(12), 1019–1027.

Blair, I. V., & Banaji, M. R. (1996). Automatic and controlled processes in stereotype priming. *Journal of Personality and Social Psychology, 70*(6), 1142–1163.

Bligh, M. C., & Kohles, J. C. (2009). The enduring allure of charisma: How Barack Obama won the historic 2008 presidential election. *The Leadership Quarterly, 20*(3), 483–492.

Bodenhausen, G. V., & Richeson, J. A. (2010). Prejudice, stereotyping, and discrimination. In R. F. Baumeister & E. J. Finkel (Eds.), *Advanced social psychology* (pp. 341–384). New York, NY: Oxford University Press.

Burrow, A. L., O'dell, A. C., & Hill, P. L. (2010). Profiles of a developmental asset: Youth purpose as a context for hope and well-being. *Journal of Youth and Adolescence, 39*(11), 1265–1273.

Charles, K. K., & Guryan, J. (2008). Prejudice and wages: An empirical assessment of Becker's The Economics of Discrimination. *Journal of Political Economy, 116*(5), 773–809.

Clow, K. A., & Esses, V. M. (2007). Expectancy effects in social stereotyping: Automatic and controlled processing in the Neely paradigm. *Canadian Journal of Behavioral Science, 39*(3), 161–173.

Crocker, J., Thompson, L. L., McGraw, K. M., & Ingerman, C. (1987). Downward comparison, prejudice, and evaluations of others: Effects of self-esteem and threat. *Journal of Personality and Social Psychology, 52*(5), 907–916.

Devine, P. G. (1989). Stereotypes and prejudice: Their automatic and controlled components. *Journal of Personality and Social Psychology, 56*(1), 5–18.

Devine, P. G. (2001). Implicit prejudice and stereotyping: How automatic are they? Introduction to the special section. *Journal of Personality and Social Psychology, 81*(5), 757–759.

DeWitz, S. J., Woolsey, M. L., & Walsh, W. B. (2009). College student retention: An exploration of the relationship between self-efficacy beliefs and purpose in life among college students. *Journal of College Student Development, 50*(1), 19–34.

Dovidio, J. F., & Gaertner, S. L. (2004). Aversive racism. In M. P. Zanna (Ed.). Advances in experimental social psychology (Vol. 36, pp. 1–52). San Diego, CA: Academic Press.

Drescher, C. F., Baczwaski, B. J., Walters, A. B., Aiena, B. J., Schulenberg, S. E., & Johnson, L. R. (2012). Coping with an ecological disaster: The role of perceived meaning in life and self-efficacy following the Gulf oil spill. *Ecopsychology, 4*(1), 56–63.

Emmons, R. A. (2005). Striving for the sacred: Personal goals, life meaning and religion. *Journal of Social Issues, 61*(4), 731–745.

Farber, E. W., Bhaju, J., Campos, P. E., Hodari, K. E., Motley, V. J., Dennany, B. E., et al. (2010). Psychological well-being in persons receiving HIV-related mental health services: The role of personal meaning in a stress and coping model. *General Hospital Psychiatry, 32*(1), 73–79.

Feldman, D. B., & Snyder, C. R. (2005). Hope and the meaningful life: Theoretical and empirical associations between goal–directed thinking and life meaning. *Journal of Social and Clinical Psychology, 24*(3), 401–421.

Fiske, S. T. (2000). Stereotyping, prejudice, and discrimination at the seam between the centuries: Evolution, culture, mind, and brain. *European Journal of Social Psychology, 30*(3), 299–322.

Fjelland, J. E., Barron, C. R., & Foxall, M. (2008). A review of instruments measuring two aspects of meaning: Search for meaning and meaning in illness. *Journal of Advanced Nursing, 62*(4), 394–406.

Flora, K., & Stalikas, A. (2012). Factors affecting substance abuse treatment in Greece and their course during therapy. *Addictive Behaviors, 37*(12), 1358–1364.

Florez, I. A., Walsh, S. P., Bowden, M. M., Stewart, T. L., & Schulenberg, S. E. (2013). *Examining meaning in life as a predictor of automatic stereotyping*. Poster presented at the Annual meeting of the American Psychological Association, Honolulu, HI.

Frankl, V. E. (1959/1984). *Man's search for meaning*. New York: Washington Square Press.

Frankl, V. E. (1994). *El hombre doliente. Fundamentos Antropológicos de la Psicoterapia.* [The Aching Man. Anthropological Foundation of Psychotherapy]. Barcelona: Herder.

Gonsalkorale, K., Carlisle, K., & Von Hippel, W. (2007). Intergroup threat increases implicit stereotyping. *International Journal of Psychology and Psychological Therapy, 7*(2), 189–200.

Greenberg, J. (2012). Terror management theory: From genesis to revelations. In P. R. Shaver & M. Mikulincer (Eds.), *Meaning, mortality, and choice: The social psychology of existential concerns* (pp. 17–35). Washington, DC: American Psychological Association.

Greenberg, J., Koole, S., & Pyszczynski, T. (2004). *Handbook of experimental existential psychology*. New York, NY: Guilford.

Greenberg, J., Martens, A., Jonas, E., Eisenstadt, D., Pyszczynski, T., & Solomon, S. (2003). Psychological defense in anticipation of anxiety: Eliminating the potential for anxiety eliminates the effect of mortality salience on worldview defense. *Psychological Science, 14*(5), 516–519.

Greenberg, J., Solomon, S., Pyszczynski, T., Rosenblatt, A., Burling, J., Lyon, D., et al. (1992). Why do people need self-esteem? Converging evidence that self-esteem serves an anxiety-buffering function. *Journal of Personality and Social Psychology, 63*(6), 913–922.

Greenwald, A. G., & Banaji, M. R. (1995). Implicit social cognition: Attitudes, self-esteem, and stereotypes. *Psychological Review, 102*(1), 4–27.

Heine, S. J., Proulx, T., & Vohs, K. D. (2006). The meaning maintenance model: On the coherence of social motivations. *Personality and Social Psychology Review, 10*(2), 88–110.

Heisel, M. J., & Flett, G. L. (2004). Purpose in life, satisfaction with life and suicide ideation in a clinical sample. *Journal of Psychopathology and Behavioral Assessment, 26*(2), 127–135.

Hicks, J. A., Cicero, D. C., Trent, J., Burton, C. M., & King, L. A. (2010). Positive affect, intuition and feelings of meaning. *Journal of Personality and Social Psychology, 98*(6), 967–979.

Hicks, J. A., & King, L. A. (2007). Meaning in life and seeing the big picture: Positive affect and global focus. *Cognition and Emotion, 21*(7), 1577–1584.

Hicks, J. A., & King, L. A. (2009). Meaning in life as a subjective judgment and a lived experience. *Social and Personality Psychology Compass, 3*(4), 638–653.

Ho, M. Y., Cheung, F. M., & Cheung, S. F. (2010). The role of meaning in life and optimism in promoting well-being. *Personality and Individual Differences, 48*(5), 658–663.

Hunter, J. A., Banks, M., O'brien, K., Kafka, S., Hayhurst, G., Jephson, D., et al. (2011). Intergroup discrimination involving negative outcomes and self-esteem. *Journal of Applied Social Psychology, 41*(5), 1145–1174.

Hunter, J. A., Platow, M. J., Howard, M. L., & Stringer, M. (1996). Social identity and intergroup evaluative bias: Realistic categories and domain specific self-esteem in a conflict setting. *European Journal of Social Psychology, 26*(4), 631–647.

Jones, C. R., & Fazio, R. H. (2010). Person categorization and automatic racial stereotyping effects on weapon identification. *Personality and Social Psychology Bulletin, 36*(8), 1073–1085.

Kalev, A., Dobbin, F., & Kelly, E. (2006). Best practices or best guesses? Assessing the efficacy of corporate affirmative action and diversity policies. *American Sociological Review, 71*(4), 589–617.

Kashdan, T. B., & Steger, M. F. (2007). Curiosity and pathways to well-being and meaning in life: Traits, states and everyday behaviors. *Motivation and Emotion, 31*(3), 159–173.

Kawakami, K., Dovidio, J. F., Moll, J., Hermsen, S., & Russin, A. (2000). Just say no (to stereotyping): Effects of training in the negation of stereotypic associations on stereotype activation. *Journal of Personality and Social Psychology, 78*(5), 871–888.

King, L. A. (2012). Meaning: Ubiquitous and effortless. In P. R. Shaver & M. Mikulincer (Eds.), *Meaning, mortality and choice: The social psychology of existential concerns* (pp. 129–144). Washington, DC: American Psychological Association.

King, L. A., & Hicks, J. A. (2009). Positive affect, intuition and referential thinking. *Personality and Individual Differences, 46*(7), 719–724.

King, L. A., Hicks, J. A., Krull, J. L., & Del Gaiso, A. K. (2006). Positive affect and the experience of meaning in life. *Journal of Personality and Social Psychology, 90*(1), 179–196.

Krause, N. (2009). Meaning in life and mortality. *The Journals of Gerontology Series B: Psychological Sciences and Social Sciences, 64*(4), 517–527.

Lambert, A. J., Payne, B. K., Jacoby, L. L., Shaffer, L. M., Chasteen, A. L., & Khan, S. R. (2003). Stereotypes as dominant responses: On the "social facilitation" of prejudice in anticipated public contexts. *Journal of Personality and Social Psychology, 84*(2), 277–295.

Lambert, N. M., Stillman, T. F., Baumeister, R. F., Fincham, F. D., Hicks, J. A., & Graham, S. M. (2010). Family as a salient source of meaning in young adulthood. *The Journal of Positive Psychology, 5*(5), 367–376.

Latu, I. M., Stewart, T. L., Myers, A. C., Lisco, C. G., Estes, S. B., & Donahue, D. K. (2011). What we "say" and what we "think" about female managers: Explicit versus implicit associations of women with success. *Psychology of Women Quarterly, 35*(2), 252–266.

Lee, V., Cohen, S. R., Edgar, L., Laizner, A. M., & Gagnon, A. J. (2006). Meaning-making intervention during breast or colorectal cancer treatment improves self-esteem, optimism, and self-efficacy. *Social Science & Medicine, 62*(12), 3133–3145.

Lindeman, M. (1997). Ingroup bias, self-enhancement and group identification. *European Journal of Social Psychology, 27*(3), 337–355.

Maddi, S. R. (1967). The existential neurosis. *Journal of Abnormal Psychology, 72*(4), 311–325.

Mascaro, N., & Rosen, D. H. (2008). Assessment of existential meaning and its longitudinal relations with depressive symptoms. *Journal of Social and Clinical Psychology, 27*(6), 576–599.

McGregor, I., Zanna, M. P., Holmes, J. G., & Spencer, S. J. (2001). Compensatory conviction in the face of personal uncertainty: Going to extremes and being oneself. *Journal of Personality and Social Psychology, 80*(3), 472–488.

Monteith, M. J. (1993). Self-regulation of prejudiced responses: Implications for progress in prejudice-reduction efforts. *Journal of Personality and Social Psychology, 65*, 469–485.

Moskowitz, G. B., Gollwitzer, P. M., Wasel, W., & Schaal, B. (1999). Preconscious control of stereotype activation through chronic egalitarian goals. *Journal of Personality and Social Psychology, 77*(1), 167–184.
Nygren, B., Aléx, L., Jonsén, E., Gustafson, Y., Norberg, A., & Lundman, B. (2005). Resilience, sense of coherence, purpose in life and self-transcendence in relation to perceived physical and mental health among the oldest old. *Aging and Mental Health, 9*(4), 354–362.
Orsi, J. M., Margellos-Anast, H., & Whitman, S. (2010). Black-White health disparities in the United States and Chicago: A 15-year progress analysis. *American Journal of Public Health, 100*(2), 349–356.
Pan, J. Y., Wong, D. F. K., Chan, C. L. W., & Joubert, L. (2008). Meaning of life as a protective factor of positive affect in acculturation: A resilience framework and a cross-cultural comparison. *International Journal of Intercultural Relations, 32*(6), 505–514.
Park, C. L. (2010). Making sense of the meaning literature: An integrative review of meaning making and its effects on adjustment to stressful life events. *Psychological Bulletin, 136*(2), 257–301.
Park, C. L., Malone, M. R., Suresh, D. P., Bliss, D., & Rosen, R. I. (2008). Coping, meaning in life and quality of life in congestive heart failure patients. *Quality of Life Research, 17*(1), 21–26.
Payne, B. K., Lambert, A. J., & Jacoby, L. L. (2002). Best laid plans: Effects of goals on accessibility bias and cognitive control in race-based misperceptions of weapons. *Journal of Experimental Social Psychology, 38*(4), 384–396.
Pearson, A. R., Dovidio, J. F., & Pratto, F. (2007). Racial prejudice, intergroup hate, and blatant and subtle bias of whites toward blacks in legal decision making in the United States. *International Journal of Psychology and Psychological Therapy, 7*(2), 145–158.
Peterson, C., & Park, N. (2012). Character strengths and the life of meaning. In P. T. P. Wong (Ed.), *The human quest for meaning: Theories, research, and applications* (2nd ed., pp. 277–295). New York, NY: Taylor and Francis.
Peterson, C., Park, N., & Seligman, M. E. (2005). Orientations to happiness and life satisfaction: The full life versus the empty life. *Journal of Happiness Studies, 6*(1), 25–41.
Pewewardy, N., & Severson, M. (2003). A threat to liberty: White privilege and disproportionate minority incarceration. *Journal of Progressive Human Services, 14*(2), 53–74.
Proulx, T. (2013). Beyond mortality and the self: Meaning makes a comeback. In K. D. Markman, T. Proulx, & M. J. Lindberg (Eds.), *The psychology of meaning* (pp. 71–114). Washington, DC: American Psychological Association.
Proulx, T., & Heine, S. J. (2008). The case of the transmogrifying experimenter: Affirmation of a moral schema following implicit change detection. *Psychological Science, 19*(12), 1294–1300.
Pyszczynski, T., Greenberg, J., Koole, S., & Solomon, S. (2010). Experimental existential psychology: Coping with the facts of life. In S. Fiske & D. Gilbert (Eds.), *Handbook of social psychology* (8th ed., pp. 724–757). New York, NY: Wiley.
Rahiminezhad, A., Kazemi, Z., Farahani, H. A., & Aghamohamadi, S. (2011). Purpose in life and identity dimensions as predictors of maladaptive psychological aspects: A path analysis study. *Procedia Social and Behavioral Sciences, 30*, 1009–1013.
Reker, G. T., & Fry, P. S. (2003). Factor structure and invariance of personal meaning measures in cohorts of younger and older adults. *Personality and Individual Differences, 35*(5), 977–993.
Reker, G. T., Peacock, E. J., & Wong, P. T. (1987). Meaning and purpose in life and well-being: A life-span perspective. *Journal of Gerontology, 42*(1), 44–49.
Rosso, B. D., Dekas, K. H., & Wrzesniewski, A. (2010). On the meaning of work: A theoretical integration and review. *Research in Organizational Behavior, 30*, 91–127.
Routledge, C., & Arndt, J. (2008). Self-sacrifice as self-defence: Mortality salience increases efforts to affirm a symbolic immortal self at the expense of the physical self. *European Journal of Social Psychology, 38*(3), 531–541.
Routledge, C., Ostafin, B., Juhl, J., Sedikides, C., Cathey, C., & Liao, J. (2010). Adjusting to death: The effects of mortality salience and self-esteem on psychological well-being, growth motivation, and maladaptive behavior. *Journal of Personality and Social Psychology, 99*(6), 897–916.

Rudman, L. A., Dohn, M. C., & Fairchild, K. (2007). Implicit self-esteem compensation: Automatic threat defense. *Journal of Personality and Social Psychology, 93*(5), 798–813.
Ryff, C. D., & Singer, B. (1998). The role of purpose in life and personal growth in positive human health. In P. T. P. Wong & P. S. Fry (Eds.), *The human quest for meaning: A handbook of psychological research and clinical applications* (pp. 237–259). Mahwah, NJ: Erlbaum.
Schimel, J., Simon, L., Greenberg, J., Pyszczynski, T., Solomon, S., Waxmonsky, J., et al. (1999). Stereotypes and terror management: Evidence that mortality salience enhances stereotypic thinking and preferences. *Journal of Personality and Social Psychology, 77*(5), 905–926.
Schlegel, R. J., Hicks, J. A., King, L. A., & Arndt, J. (2011). Feeling like you know who you are: Perceived true self-knowledge and meaning in life. *Personality and Social Psychology Bulletin, 37*, 745–756.
Schnell, T. (2011). Individual differences in meaning-making: Considering the variety of sources of meaning, their density and diversity. *Personality and Individual Differences, 51*(5), 667–673.
Schnetzer, L. W., Schulenberg, S. E., & Buchanan, E. M. (2013). Differential associations among alcohol use, depression and perceived life meaning in male and female college students. *Journal of Substance Use, 18*(4), 311–319.
Schulenberg, S. E., Baczwaski, B. J., & Buchanan, E. M. (2014). Measuring search for meaning: A factor-analytic evaluation of the Seeking Of Noetic Goals (SONG) test. *Journal of Happiness Studies, 15*(3), 693–715.
Schulenberg, S. E., Hutzell, R. R., Nassif, C., & Rogina, J. M. (2008). Logotherapy for clinical practice. *Psychotherapy: Theory, Research, Practice, Training, 45*(4), 447–463.
Schulenberg, S. E., Schnetzer, L. W., & Buchanan, E. M. (2011). The Purpose in Life test – Short Form: Development and psychometric support. *Journal of Happiness Studies, 12*(5), 861–876.
Sheldon, S. (2012). The social psychology of meaning, mortality, and choice: An integrative perspective on existential concern. In P. R. Shaver & M. Mikulincer (Eds.), *Meaning, mortality, and choice: The social psychology of existential concerns* (pp. 401–417). Washington, DC: American Psychological Association.
Solomon, S., Greenberg, J., & Pyszczynski, T. (1991). A terror management theory of social behavior: The psychological functions of self-esteem and cultural worldviews. In M. P. Zanna (Ed.), *Advances in experimental social psychology* (Vol. 24, pp. 93–159). New York, NY: Academic.
Steger, M. F. (2012). Making meaning in life. *Psychological Inquiry, 23*(4), 381–385.
Steger, M. F., & Frazier, P. (2005). Meaning in life: One link in the chain from religiousness to well-being. *Journal of Counseling Psychology, 52*(4), 574–582.
Steger, M. F., & Kashdan, T. B. (2013). The unbearable lightness of meaning: Well-being and unstable meaning in life. *The Journal of Positive Psychology, 8*(2), 103–115.
Steger, M. F., Kashdan, T. B., Sullivan, B. A., & Lorentz, D. (2008). Understanding the search for meaning in life: Personality, cognitive style, and the dynamic between seeking and experiencing meaning. *Journal of Personality, 76*(2), 199–228.
Stewart, B. D., & Payne, B. K. (2008). Bringing automatic stereotyping under control: Implementation intentions as efficient means of thought control. *Personality and Social Psychology Bulletin, 34*(10), 1332–1345.
Stewart, T. L., Latu, I. M., Branscombe, N. R., Phillips, N. L., & Denney, H. T. (2012). White privilege awareness and efficacy to reduce racial inequality improve White Americans' attitudes toward African Americans. *Journal of Social Issues, 68*(1), 11–27.
Stewart, T. L., Latu, I. M., Kawakami, K., & Myers, A. C. (2010). Consider the situation: Reducing automatic stereotyping through situational attribution training. *Journal of Experimental Social Psychology, 46*(1), 221–225.
Stewart, T. L., Weeks, M., & Lupfer, M. B. (2003). Spontaneous stereotyping: A matter of prejudice? *Social Cognition, 21*(4), 263–298.
Stillman, T. F., Baumeister, R. F., Lambert, N. M., Crescioni, A. W., DeWall, C. N., & Fincham, F. D. (2009). Alone and without purpose: Life loses meaning following social exclusion. *Journal of Experimental Social Psychology, 45*(4), 686–694.

Stillman, T. F., Lambert, N. M., Fincham, F. D., & Baumeister, R. F. (2011). Meaning as magnetic force: Evidence that meaning in life promotes interpersonal appeal. *Social Psychological and Personality Science, 2*, 13–20.
Triplett, K. N., Tedeschi, R. G., Cann, A., Calhoun, L. G., & Reeve, C. L. (2012). Posttraumatic growth, meaning in life, and life satisfaction in response to trauma. *Psychological Trauma: Theory, Research, Practice, and Policy, 4*(4), 400–410.
Ulmer, A., Range, L. M., & Smith, P. C. (1991). Purpose in life: A moderator of recovery from bereavement. *Journal of Death and Dying, 23*(4), 279–289.
Van den Bos, K. (2009). Making sense of life: The existential self trying to deal with personal uncertainty. *Psychological Inquiry, 20*(4), 197–217.
Van Tongeren, D. R., & Green, J. D. (2010). Combating meaninglessness: On the automatic defense of meaning. *Personality and Social Psychology Bulletin, 36*(10), 1372–1384.
Vaught, S. (2009). The color of money: School funding and the commodification of black children. *Urban Education*. doi:10.1177/0042085908318776.
Vella-Brodrick, D. A., Park, N., & Peterson, C. (2009). Three ways to be happy: Pleasure, engagement, and meaning. Findings from Australian and US samples. *Social Indicators Research, 90*(2), 165–179.
Vess, M., Routledge, C., Landau, M. J., & Arndt, J. (2009). The dynamics of death and meaning: The effects of death-relevant cognitions and personal need for structure on perceptions of meaning in life. *Journal of Personality and Social Psychology, 97*(4), 728–744.
Weinstein, L., Xie, X., & Cleanthous, C. C. (1995). Purpose in life, boredom, and volunteerism in a group of retirees. *Psychological Reports, 76*(2), 482.
Williams, K. D. (2012). Ostracism: The impact of being rendered meaningless. In P. R. Shaver & M. Mikulincer (Eds.), *Meaning, mortality, and choice: The social psychology of existential concerns* (pp. 309–323). Washington, DC: American Psychological Association.
Wong, P. T. P. (2012). *The human quest for meaning: Theories, research, and applications* (2nd ed.). New York, NY: Taylor and Francis.
Wrzesniewski, A., McCauley, C., Rozin, P., & Schwartz, B. (1997). Jobs, careers, and callings: People's relations to their work. *Journal of Research in Personality, 31*(1), 21–33.

Part III
Applied and Clinical Logotherapy and Existential Analysis

The Pathogenesis of Mental Disorders: An Update of Logotherapy

Elisabeth Lukas

The International Classification for Mental Disorders (ICD 11) will be considerably different from the currently used ICD 10. These changes have become necessary because of multiple research results in genetics and neurobiology. These findings indicate that a number of earlier hypotheses about the development of mental disorders and illnesses are inadequate, or at least incomplete. These new facts have consequences for the doctrinal body of the traditional schools of psychotherapy, among them the concepts of logotherapy.

The most important change concerns the understanding that an unequivocal attribution of certain mental disorders to specific causes is no longer tenable because it has become apparent that the genesis for any mental disorder depends on multiple factors. Traditionally, neuroses have been considered to be psychogenic in origin, while psychoses were thought to be somatogenic. This differentiation is no longer valid as such. It is now a known fact that it is possible to codify and identify genes indicating an increased likelihood for the development of anxiety disorders in patients identified as neurotic, just as is the case in for example patients with manic symptoms.

To these genetic (endogenic) dispositions come epigenetic (exogenic) factors. Both prenatal harmful influences (e.g., exposure to chemicals in the womb) and unsatisfactory childhood attachment experiences or later traumatic life events change genetic expression. It is now known how changes of this kind occur: Changes of the genetic make-up of a person, which occur through harmful influences, mainly con-

Thanks to Dr. Katja Günther, Director of Medical Services and Physician for Public Health in Nürnberg, for details concerning the new International Classification Table for Mental Disorders (ICD 11), which came into effect in May, 2015.

E. Lukas (✉)
Marktplatz 17/4/1, 2380 Perchtoldsdorf, Austria

A. Batthyány (ed.), *Logotherapy and Existential Analysis*, Logotherapy and Existential Analysis: Proceedings of the Viktor Frankl Institute Vienna 1,
DOI 10.1007/978-3-319-29424-7_12

sist of a demethylation of DNA sections that are then "switched off." In other words, they are permanently lost. This leads to a reduction of the margin within which behavioral changes are possible for a person.

It has also been demonstrated that genetics cannot be changed in retrospective; however, the formation of synapses and the density of the interconnectivity of neurons can be altered. This can occur either through attitudinal change or behavioral change. Here lies the physiological foundation and justification of any psychotherapy.

The abandonment of the distinction between neuroses and psychoses leads to two types of differentiation relevant for applied psychotherapy. On the one hand, more attention is now being paid to the degree of severity of a mental disorder, using it as an indication for the application of pharmacotherapy. Here the predominant opinion is that, for example, in the case of severe disorders characterized by fears (formerly termed "neuroses") pharmacological support is necessary by all means, whereas in the case of a light paranoia (formerly termed "psychoses") a mild neuroleptic is prescribed in the course of an acute episode suffices.

The new table in ICD 11 does justice to this criterion by listing descriptive neuropathological medical evidence instead of manifestations of the symptoms of the respective mental disorders. A further criterion of differentiation is the degree of misjudgment of reality in an individual. The more pronounced this is (previously: the more psychotic it is), the more the use of appropriate medication is indicated. A high degree of misjudgment of reality is found in delusions and hallucinations (previously termed "schizophrenia"), a medium degree accompanies borderline and post-traumatic stress disorders, and a mild degree is found in identity and self-worth disorders, irrational fears, and guilt feelings. In order to assess the severity of misjudgment of reality in a patient, it is necessary to conduct a precise anamnesis, interviews, and, if need be, standardized questionnaires and similar measures. In general, it can be concluded that the more severe the degree of a mental disorder and/or the more pronounced the degree of misjudgment of reality, the indication for psychotherapy decreases and the necessity for a medical intervention increases.

To summarize, single-cause hypotheses for the development of mental disorders are no longer considered valid in ICD 11. All mental disorders have physiological correlates (increase or decrease of density of certain receptors for certain neurotransmitters in certain areas of the brain). The specific clinical symptoms that manifest in a patient are dependent on the following factors:

1. The point in time of a damaging influence or an injury; for example, this may be particularly harmful on the embryonic brain or during the first year of life.
2. The localization of the harmful influence in the brain, which may have a particularly harmful effect; for example, on the limbic system, respectively the prefrontal cortex.
3. The extent of the harmful influence.

It is irrelevant whether the noxa is biological or consists of a psychological stress factor (e.g., negligence). In this context, it is of particular interest (and could be empirically tested) that mentally ill persons can relate to themselves and their illnesses in various ways and are thus able to influence themselves and their neuronal processes to a certain degree. However, persons with a considerate cognitive deficit, persistent delusions, and extremely strong misjudgment of reality may be impaired in this process.

Let us now turn to the question what these findings might mean for Viktor Frankl's teachings about neuroses and psychoses.

Frankl was only able to rely on the scientific standards of his own time. However, he was far ahead of his time with his statements about: "psychophysical parallelism"; neuronal correlates in neurotic disorders; "pathoplastic" (specific involvement of the individual) accompanying any "pathogenesis"; and the somato-psychological effects, which play a part even in noogenic crises. The abandonment of clear attributions of causes of psychological disorders has much less impact on logotherapy than on, for example, psychoanalysis, since the latter concentrates its therapeutic approach entirely on the detection of (supposed) psychological causes for illness. Contrary to this the discovery of causes, e.g., in a thorough investigation of a life story, in search of potential risk factors plays a very subordinate role within the logotherapeutic setting. The search for protective factors, however, a characteristic of the logotherapeutic approach, completely corresponds with the modern desideratum to epigenetically evoke improvements of the psychological condition of a patient. That it could be proved in the meantime that changes in attitude can set in motion improvements of this kind, is an excellent confirmation of Frankl's theses.

In my opinion there is only one thing in logotherapy, which needs adjustment with regard to these new insights: the terms *somatogenic*, *psychogenic* and *noögenic* need to be corrected. (I intentionally do not say they need to be abandoned.) For those who are well acquainted with logotherapy, it is clear that Frankl was not creating a final causal explanatory model for different patterns of disorders, but was reaching far beyond causal questions, namely at their *attribution to an ontological dimension*, where life problems manifest and are in need of a solution or an alleviation.

For him "somatogenic" meant that an occurrence became virulent on a physical level of being and needs to be brought to appropriate treatment. "Psychogenic" meant that irregularities in the psychological dimension have reached a critical density and wait for satisfaction. "Noögenic" (which outside of logotherapy does not even get diagnosed!) meant that a person as a spiritual being stumbled during the search for meaning and values and is in need of support.

The entire range of combinations and connections of the above is possible, requiring in turn "therapeutic tongs" (e.g., medication in addition to psychotherapeutic measures or psychotherapeutic measures in addition to conversations about the finding of meaning). Admittedly, the word ending "-genic" suggests an etiological connection, but neither in theory nor in application is the logotherapist focused on etiology, but rather on taking the human being seriously in its ontological manifoldness. In logotherapy, attention is drawn to the fact that to be human is not fully captured in a sum of neuronal processes or in the recording and processing of psychosocial influences.

Frankl himself used the example of crying. A person may cry because the smell of an onion can irritate his eyes. He can also cry because his self-confidence is weak and he is not good at handling criticism. He can cry because he lost a loved one through death. If one would want to abandon all of these differentiations, one would have to claim by abbreviation, that in all cases the activity of the tear glands is responsible for crying, whereby it would be useful to wipe the tears off the crying person. In the case of more intense crying, more handkerchiefs would be indicated. The primitive nature of this approach is self-evident. If one wants to help, one needs to differentiate the origin of the crying. On the physical level, it will be useful to remove the onions. On the psychological level, it will be appropriate to strengthen self-confidence and the ability to tolerate frustration. On the noetic level, consolation only will be helpful, placing the permanent, indestructible validity of the experiential relationship into the foreground of awareness.

My proposal with reference to an adjustment of logotherapeutic nomenclature is therefore to change the word ending "-genic" to a different one in order to clearly define Frankl's position. Perhaps the word ending "-focal" would be an appropriate alternative. *Focal* means "concerning the focus" and, in medical context, even makes reference to the "seat of a disease." Without having to change that much in Frankl's teachings, it would consequently be possible to say "somato-focal"; this would mean that the focus of suffering of a patient and the therapeutic field of intervention would be found on the physical level. "Psycho-focal" would mean that the focus of suffering of the patient and the therapeutic field of intervention, would be found in the psychological field. "Noo-focal" would mean that the focus of the suffering of the patient and the field of therapeutic intervention are to be found in the spiritual field of the person. I cannot claim that I would be happy about this change in terminology, but I yield to the insight that, with progressive understanding, flawed dictions of the past have to be revised.

Concerning the old classification of mental disorders into neuroses and their subdivisions as well as psychoses and their subdivisions, I believe that, in logotherapy, we can move with time and gradually say farewell to these terms. However, we cannot abandon the description of what these terms stood for, because mental illnesses and disorders have not changed since the inception of psychotherapy as a serious science and these disorders have certainly not lessened in frequency in the population.

It will be a little bit tedious to use, instead of short, albeit simplifying, but nevertheless precise special terms, these terms of broader descriptions of variations of mental disorders. But this should not be an obstacle to preserve and pass on to future generations the precious and incredibly helpful wealth of thought of logotherapy.

Relevance and Application of Logotherapy to Enhance Resilience to Stress and Trauma

Steven M. Southwick, Bernadette T. Lowthert, and Ann V. Graber

Logotherapy has been used as a therapeutic intervention for individuals who struggle with a host of medical, behavioral, health, and social problems. For example, logotherapy has been described as helpful for individuals living with schizophrenia, mood disorders, anxiety disorders, posttraumatic stress disorder (PTSD), alcohol use disorders, and personality disorders, as well as cardiac illness, prolonged grief, and chronic pain (Marshall and Marshall 2012).

One reason that logotherapy may have positive effects on such a broad array of problems may be related to its impact on the stress response, and on one's ability to tolerate adversity, to build resilience, and to grow from stressful and traumatic experiences. Chronic stress that is poorly regulated is known to exacerbate a host of medical and psychological conditions and disorders (McEwen 2007).

In this chapter, we discuss how logotherapy can help to regulate chronic stress by fostering resilience and posttraumatic growth. As noted by Ann V. Graber, "Logotherapy attempts to help the client get in touch with his reservoir of strengths within, and to apply the power of the human spirit to overcome the distress which follows in the wake

S.M. Southwick (✉)
VA Connecticut Healthcare System, Yale University School of Medicine,
950 Campbell Avenue, Westhaven, CT 06516, USA
e-mail: steven.southwick@yale.edu

B.T. Lowthert
320 42Nd St, New York, NY 10017, USA

A.V. Graber
Graduate Center for Pastoral Logotherapy, Graduate Theological Foundation,
Dodge House, 415 Lincoln Way East, Mishawaka, IN 46544, USA
e-mail: AnnVGraber@aol.com

A. Batthyány (ed.), *Logotherapy and Existential Analysis*, Logotherapy and Existential Analysis: Proceedings of the Viktor Frankl Institute Vienna 1,
DOI 10.1007/978-3-319-29424-7_13

of human suffering in any category … Logotherapy focuses less on the origin of a given cause of suffering and more on overcoming it (Graber 2004, 130) … and is built to build on client strengths rather than 'pathology'" (Graber 2004, 100).

Definitions

Definition of Resilience

There is no one universally accepted definition of resilience. The American Psychological Association defines resilience as "the process of adapting well in the face of adversity, trauma, tragedy, threats or even significant sources of stress." Other definitions of resilience include the capacity of a dynamic system to adapt successfully to disturbances that threaten the viability, function, or development of that system; the process of harnessing resources to sustain well-being; robust psychobiological capacity to modulate the stress response; and reintegration of self that includes a conscious effort to move forward in an insightful integrated positive manner as a result of an adverse experience (Southwick et al. 2014).

Definition of Logotherapy

Logotherapy may be understood as therapy that seeks to heal through access to meaning and purpose in spiritual terms. In his book, *The Doctor and the Soul*, Viktor Frankl introduced *logotherapy* as "psychotherapy in spiritual terms … Logotherapy must *supplement* psychotherapy; that is, it must fill the void [by inclusion of the spiritual dimension] whose existence we have mentioned. By the use of logotherapy we are equipped to deal with philosophical questions within their own frame of reference, and can embark on objective discussion of the spiritual distress of human beings suffering from psychic disturbances" (Frankl 1986, 17).

To access meaning the logotherapist focuses on the noetic dimension, the dimension that contains our healthy core, where can be found such uniquely human attributes as will to meaning, ideas and ideals, creativity, imagination, faith, love, conscience, self-detachment, self-transcendence, humor, striving toward goals, and taking on commitments and responsibilities. The logotherapist mobilizes these innate human qualities in therapy. As noted by Joseph Fabry, in logotherapy the human being is seen as a unity comprised of body (soma), psyche (intellect and emotions), and spirit (noös). To emphasize this unity or oneness, Frankl speaks of "dimensions of human existence." Our body, psyche, and spirit are three inseparable dimensions, unified. If one is disregarded, we do not get a complete human being but a shadowy two-dimensional projection. Disregard the spirit and you get a shadow, a caricature, an automaton of reflexes, a helpless victim of reactions and instincts, a product of drives, heredity, and environment (Fabry 1975, 20).

Determinants of Resilience

A myriad of genetic, developmental, biological, psychological, social, and spiritual factors have been associated with resilience. For example, from a biological perspective, resilience refers to the capacity to modulate and constructively harness the stress response enabling one to bounce back from adversity (Southwick et al. 2014). As previously described, failure to adequately modulate the stress response can dramatically impact physical and mental health. Stress, if chronic and poorly managed, can contribute to a broad array of illnesses such as diabetes, heart disease, gastric ulcers, asthma, and depression (McEwen 2007). In this discussion we focus on some of the psychosocial factors that have received the greatest support from research as having an effect on the stress response. These include positive emotions and optimism, active problem-focused coping, moral courage and altruism, attention to physical health and fitness, capacity to regulate emotions, cognitive flexibility, religiosity/spirituality, high level of positive social support, and having a meaningful mission (Southwick and Charney 2012b). While many of these psychosocial factors have been linked to reduced symptoms of traumatic stress, as well as positive mental health and resilience, they do not operate in isolation, but, instead, typically interact with other factors.

Optimism

Optimism and Resilience

Optimism refers to the basic belief that the future will be bright and that there is light at the end of the tunnel. A large scientific literature shows that positive emotions and optimism are associated with good physical and mental health. For example, compared to pessimists, optimists have been shown to develop fewer stress-related psychological illnesses (e.g., depression and PTSD) after being exposed to missile attacks (Zeidner and Hammer 1992), better physical health after cardiac surgical procedures (Giltay et al. 2006), and increased immunity from infectious disease (Cohen et al. 2003). There is even evidence that optimists tend to live longer than pessimists (Danner et al. 2001).

Barbara Frederickson, as part of her "Broaden and Build" model of positive emotions, found that positive emotions tend to broaden the scope of one's visual, cognitive and behavioral focus, with a resultant increase in flexibility and creativity, as well as in the ability to integrate information (Fredrickson and Branigan 2005).

Evidence also suggests that compared to pessimists, optimists tend to be more active in their attempts to solve problems and that they tend to experience life as being more meaningful, both of which have been associated with resilience (Ju et al. 2013; King et al. 2006).

A number of researchers have suggested that resilience is most closely associated with optimism that is realistic, rather than blind or "rose colored." As noted by Reivich and Shatté (2003) realistic optimists do not ignore relevant negative information but instead they pay close attention to such information. However, unlike pessimists, realistic optimists tend to disengage rapidly from negative information and can turn their attention to potential solutions.

Optimism and Logotherapy

Viktor Frankl saw optimism as a source of strength and embedded a positive approach to life at the very core of logotherapy. As noted by Frankl, "Rather logotherapy is an optimistic approach to life for it teaches that there is no tragic or negative aspects which could not by the stand one takes be transmuted into positive accomplishments" (Frankl 1988, 73). When discussing the tragic triad, he wrote, "One is and remains optimistic in spite of the "tragic triad" as it is called in logotherapy, a triad which consists of those aspects of human existence which may be circumscribed by: (1) pain (2) guilt (3) death… How is it possible to say yes to life in spite of all that? After all, "saying yes in spite of everything," presupposes that life is potentially meaningful under any conditions, even those, which are most miserable. And this in turn presupposes the human capacity to creatively turn life's negative aspects into something positive and constructive. In other words, what matters is to make the best of a given situation. "The best," however, is that which in Latin is called *optimum*—hence the reasons I speak of tragic optimism, that is, optimism in the face of tragedy…" (Frankl 2006, 136) As noted by Ann Graber (2004), logotherapy takes a pragmatic approach, in that its optimism is realistic in nature and the insights gained through reflection should be applied in the daily tasks of life.

Facing Fear

Facing Fear and Resilience

Fear has an enormous impact on how individuals conduct their lives. While fear is essential for survival, it can also constrict life or even become paralyzing. Learning to face fear is an essential skill for enhancing resilience. This is by no means easy but many techniques have been developed to help people confront and in some cases overcome their fears.

When confronted with danger, humans respond with an increase in hypothalamic pituitary adrenal axis and sympathetic nervous system activity, which assists in fighting or fleeing from the danger. During the fight-flight response, increases in stress hormones and neurotransmitters, such as cortisol, norepinephrine and epinephrine, enhance the individual's capacity to focus on the dangerous stimulus, respond to the danger, and encode and consolidate the experience into memory. Elevation of stress hormones and neurotransmitters, particularly norepinephrine, generally increases consolidation so that memories of dangerous experiences tend to be remembered better than neutral experiences. These "over-consolidated" memories may be especially strong and sometimes unforgettable. While enhanced consolidation of memories for dangerous events has survival value, by making it more likely that the individual will remember what to avoid in the future, it appears that enhanced consolidation also contributes to intrusive traumatic memories that may haunt the survivor for years (for discussion see Southwick and Charney 2012b).

Just as people remember dangerous and traumatic events better than neutral events, they also remember the context in which the dangerous event occurred. Through the process of classical conditioning, sounds, sights, odors, time of day, weather conditions, state of physiological arousal, and other contextual stimuli become linked with the dangerous stimulus. In the future these contextual features, most of which were previously neutral in nature, may provoke feelings of fear by themselves. For example, if someone is almost killed by a shark while swimming in the ocean at sunset, he/she in the future may feel uneasy and afraid in the ocean or at sunset even when no real danger is present.

It is natural for people to avoid situations that make them anxious. However, by avoiding fear-conditioned stimuli, like the ocean in the above example, the individual cannot update or transform their fear-related memories. On the other hand, confronting fear can serve as a catalyst for growth and can potentially expand the range of opportunities in one's life.

Since avoidance is known to perpetuate anxiety disorders and disorders of traumatic stress, the psychotherapies that have proved most effective for treating these disorders (e.g., cognitive behavioral therapies, EMDR, systematic desensitization, and prolonged exposure) all involve some form of exposure to what is feared. Other practical advice for increasing resilience by learning to face fear comes from multiple sources including the US Military. Commonly cited tips for learning to face and deal with fear include viewing fear as a warning or guide rather than as something to avoid, acquiring information about what is feared; learning and practicing skills needed to master the fear, focusing on the ultimate goal or mission rather than the fear itself, viewing the confronting and overcoming of fear as an opportunity for growth; facing fear with friends and colleagues (for discussion see Southwick and Charney 2012b).

Facing Fear and Logotherapy

Logotherapy also addresses fear, particularly as seen in phobias and anxiety neuroses. For example, Frankl referred to the "fear of fear" and the "flight from fear." The phobic or anxious patient generally tries to avoid situations that increase anxiety.

Unfortunately, such avoidance results in “a strengthening of the symptom” or at least prevents the possibility of extinction.

To deal with the patient’s fear, anxiety, and avoidance, logotherapists often take a paradoxical approach. The logotherapist advises the patient to exaggerate and actually wish for that which is feared. For example, if a patient is afraid of stuttering when giving a speech in public, the logotherapist might advise him/her to wish for and intend to stutter as much as possible in an upcoming speech. Frankl found that when a fear is replaced with a wish, “the wind is taken out of the sails of the phobia” (Frankl 1986, 224). In Frankl’s words, “Conversely, if we succeed in bringing the patient to the point where he ceases to flee from or fight his symptoms, but on the contrary, even exaggerates them, then we may observe that the symptoms diminish and that the patient is no longer haunted by them” (Frankl 1986, 224).

As will be discussed later, the use of humor is typically a powerful element of paradoxical intention. With paradoxical intention and humor the individual detaches the self from anxiety and fear. “This procedure, however, must make use of the specifically human capacity for self-detachment inherent in a sense of humor… when paradoxical intention is used, the purpose is to enable the patient to develop a sense of detachment toward his neurosis by laughing at it, to put is simply” (Frankl 1986, 224–225). Paradoxical intention employs what Frankl referred to as “right passivity” because the patient ridicules his symptoms rather than trying to run away from them (i.e., wrong passivity)

Logotherapists can also use “dereflection” to help patients face their fears. With dereflection the patient learns to “ignore” fears or symptoms by focusing on the task at hand. Many individuals who fear a particular situation or encounter tend to focus, or hyper-reflect, on what can go wrong rather than on ways to cope with the feared situation. By focusing on how to meet a particular challenge or overcome a fear, the individual adopts an active problem-oriented approach to coping.

Values

Values and Resilience

For centuries scholars have written about the benefits of articulating and adhering to a core set of moral and ethical values. For example, the stoic philosophers placed great value on virtue and moral character, self-control, discipline, endurance and perseverance, courage, rigorous pursuit of worthy goals, attempting to be the very best, integrity, and dignity in the face of suffering. Many scholars believe that these values and virtues are associated with resilience and strength of character (Sherman 2005). For example, James Stockdale, author and senior commanding officer of the Hanoi Hilton, a notorious North Vietnamese prison that housed many American prisoners of war, had the following to say about integrity, “You can’t buy it or sell it. When supported with education, a person’s integrity can give him something to rely on when his perspective seems to blur, when rules and principles seem to waver, and when he's faced with hard choices of right and wrong. It's something to … keep him afloat when he's drowning." The resilience-enhancing effects of adhering to and defending one's deeply held values and beliefs has been described by many former prisoners of war (Southwick and Charney 2012a). For example, Stockdale's directive to his troops to accept no special favors from the North Vietnamese and to refuse early release, unless all prisoners were released, provided great strength to prisoners who were tempted by their captors.

Perhaps the most admired of the moral and ethical values is moral courage. Rushmore Kidder (2006), director of the Institute of Global Ethics, has defined moral courage as, "standing up for values…the willingness to take a tough stand for right in the face of danger…the courage to do the right thing…the quality of mind and spirit that enables one to face up to ethical challenges firmly and confidently without flinching or retreating (Kidder 2006 72)." As described by Samuel Johnson in the eighteen century, moral courage is "the greatest of all virtues; because unless a man has that virtue, he has no security for preserving any other" (Boswell 1791). For Kidder, moral courage requires committing to a core set of principles and moral values, understanding that one is likely to face hardship or danger by standing up for these values, and being willing to endure the possible loss and hardship that may accompany taking a stand.

Values and Logotherapy

Frankl believed in the power of "universal" or "eternal values." Fabry (1975) referred to these values as "time tested rules of behavior" that reflected the "wisdom of the ages," such as love thy neighbor, honesty is the best policy, and do not commit adultery. Frankl also believed in a hierarchy of values that plays an important role in deciding how to act in situations where two or more universal values conflict with one another. Frankl (2006) himself had to create his own hierarchy of values when he realized that his wife, who was very attractive, might be faced with a choice to save her life by breaking her marital vows, or die at the hands of an SS officer by refusing to do so. He decided to tell his wife to "Stay alive at all costs. Go to any length to survive." In this way he placed the commandment not to kill over the commandment not to commit adultery.

Logotherapy also endorses three basic values as routes to discover meaning. These values have been referred to as the "Meaning Triangle." First: creative values, where the individual gives back to life by using their creativity, unique talents and strengths. One's specific occupation is irrelevant. What matters is how the individual "works, whether he in fact fills the place in which he has happened to have landed. The radius of his activity is not important; important alone is whether he fills the circle of his tasks. The ordinary person, who really masters the concrete tasks with which his occupation and family life present him, is, in spite of his little life, "greater" than and superior to a "great" statesman who may decide the fate of millions with the stroke of a pen, but whose decisions are unscrupulous and evil in their consequences (Frankl 1986, 41)." In other words, meaning can be fulfilled by fully utilizing ones unique talents to engage in life. As Frankl put it, "Our aim is to help our patient to achieve the highest possible activation in life" and "In view of the task quality of life, it logically follows that life becomes all the more meaningful the more difficult it gets…" (Frankl 1986, 54).

The second basic value is experiential where the individual receives from the world and finds meaning through experiences with nature, religion, culture, truth, beauty, and love (Graber 2004). Experiential value is "realized in receptivity toward the world—for example—in surrender to beauty of nature or art." Examples include the intense "shiver of emotion" that one might feel when listening to a moving piece of music, looking at a great work of art, or walking through a forest.

Finally, the third basic category is attitudinal values, which can provide meaning even when one's life "is neither fruitful in creation nor rich in experience. The third group of values lies precisely in a man's attitude toward the limiting factors upon his life. His very response to the restraints upon his potentialities provides him with a new realm of values, which surely belong among the highest values. What is significant is the person's attitude toward his unalterable fate (Frankl 2006, 45)." Thus, in logotherapy the deepest and most noble meaning in life can be found in the attitude the individual takes toward unavoidable suffering. "The way in which he accepts, bears his cross, what courage he manifests in suffering, what dignity he displays in doom, is the measure of his human fulfillment (Frankl 1986, 44)."

In the philosophy of logotherapy, the human spirit is what makes us human, what makes us more than the sole product of biological, social and psychological drives. It is the defiant power of the human spirit, the *noetic* self, that "…has the power to rise above the afflictions of the psychophysical self (Graber 2004, 77)" even when the psychophysical self has become sick.

Altruism

Altruism and Resilience

Altruism, or concern for the welfare of others, has been associated with positive mental health, well-being and resilience. For example, researchers from the University of Massachusetts reported that social interest, a term closely related to altruism, was associated with better physical and mental health, reduced stress, better life adjustment, and less depression and hopelessness. They also found that both the receiving and giving of social support predicted better mental health, but that giving was an even stronger predictor than receiving. A similar finding was reported by Schwartz and colleagues (2003) among over 2000 members of the Presbyterian Church. A number of studies have found the same in children who help others in a meaningful way and/or assume responsibility for someone else, or even a pet (Zimrin 1986). This association between altruism, social interest and better health and well-being may be related to a shift in attention and focus from self to others, enhanced self-esteem, and greater perceived meaning and purpose in life.

Neuroethics is a relatively new field that focuses on "the evolutionary origins of moral sentiments…As a species of social primates, we have evolved a deep sense of right and wrong to reward reciprocity and cooperation and to attenuate selfishness and free riding (Shermer 2011)." For example, among nonhuman primates and humans "reciprocal altruism" appears to have benefits for survival including enhanced power and reputation, greater access to community resources during times of deprivation and even increased opportunities for mating. Researchers are currently investigating potential genetic and brain processes involved in moral thinking and reasoning, social cooperation, and altruism.

Altruism and Logotherapy

Altruism is at the very heart of logotherapy. In *The Doctor and the Soul*, Frankl wrote, "…human existence always points, and is directed, toward something other than oneself; or rather, toward something or someone other than oneself, namely toward meanings to fulfill, or toward other human beings to encounter lovingly. And only to the extent to which a human being lives our his self-transcendence is he really becoming human and actualizing himself (Frankl 1986, 294)." In the language of logotherapy, altruism represents a dereflection away from the self and a reaching out, instead, toward worthy goals, other people and/or meanings to be fulfilled (Graber 2004, 117).

Religion/Spirituality

Religion/Spirituality and Resilience

In *Honor Bound* (Rochester and Kiley 1998), a well-known account of American prisoners in Vietnam, the authors wrote "there is virtually no personal account in the Vietnam POW literature that does not contain some reference to a transforming spiritual episode." For example, the authors quote US Senator John McCain who commented, "To guard against despair in our most dire moments, POWs would make supreme efforts to grasp our faith tightly, to profess it alone in the dark, and to hasten its arrival. Once I was thrown into a cell after a long and difficult interrogation. I discovered scratched into one of the cells walls the creed, "I believe in God the Father Almighty""

A large body of scientific research has found that engaging in positive religious practices is associated with resilience as well emotional and physical well-being, including lower levels of depression, lower blood pressure and possible better immune function (McCullough et al. 2000). The positive health effects of religious practice appear to be related, in part, to attending religious services where parishioners often receive and give support to one another, are encouraged to live a healthy life style, and have access to resilient role models who are accustomed to responding to tragedy, loss of life, and existential questions about meaning of life. Further, Fallot and Heckman (2006) reported that the use of religious coping strategies at the time of a traumatic experience among women with mental health and substance problems was associated with lower post-trauma distress.

Religion/Spirituality and Logotherapy

Frankl viewed logotherapy as a philosophy of life and as a therapy, but not as a religion. He believed that "Fusion of psychotherapy and religion necessarily results in confusion, for such fusion confounds two different dimensions, the dimension of anthropology and theology" (Graber 2004, 45). It is important to keep in mind that the word "spiritual," within the frame of reference of logotherapy, does not mean "religious" but instead it refers to the specifically human dimension of human beings. However, Frankl also understood the power and potential resilience-enhancing effects of religious beliefs: "After all, religion provides man with a spiritual anchor, with a security he can find nowhere else…It is my contention that faith in the ultimate meaning is preceded by trust in the ultimate being, trust in God" (Frankl 1988, 145). While distinct from religion, logotherapy nevertheless is compatible with most religious faiths. Logotherapy is a holistic approach to healing that addresses the mind, the body and the spirit; it finds value in learning from and standing up to unavoidable suffering; and it views religious values as potential sources of strength in the search for meaning and self-transcendence.

For Frankl, religion can serve as a source of strength and resilience when it assists the individual to reach his noetic or spiritual core, which "contains such qualities as our will to meaning, our goal orientation, ideas and ideals, creativity, imagination, faith, love that goes beyond the physical, a conscience beyond the superego, self-transcendence, commitments, responsibility, a sense of humor, and the freedom of choice making" (Fabry 1975, 16).

Flexibility: Acceptance and Cognitive Reappraisal

Flexibility in how one thinks about and behaves in stressful and challenging situations has an enormous impact on resilience. Possessing a repertoire of effective coping mechanisms and being able to shift from one mechanism to the next depending on the requirements of the specific situation gives the individual a strong foundation for responding to a broad array of challenges. A growing body of research has found that resilient individuals tend to use a number of different cognitive and emotional strategies for dealing with stress including accepting that which they cannot change, using emotions such as anger and grief to ignite courage and a sense of meaning, and reframing thoughts and beliefs about adversity through the use of humor and by searching for and finding opportunity in the midst of adversity. (Southwick and Charney 2012b).

Acceptance and Resilience

The ability to accept those things which cannot be controlled, those things beyond free will, has been cited as a source of strength and resilience by both philosophers and psychologists. For example, the stoic philosophers (Sherman 2005) believed in the importance of separating out and focusing on those things within one's power compared to those beyond one's power. While man is not responsible for that which is beyond his power, he is responsible for what is within the grasp of his free will. Acceptance has been associated with better mental health in a variety of different traumatized populations including survivors of extreme environmental hardship (Siebert 1996), and mothers of children undergoing bone transplants for life threatening cancer in their children (Manne et al. 2002). Acceptance has also been incorporated into a number of behavioral health therapies such as mindfulness meditation and Acceptance and Commitment therapy (Orsillo et al. 2005). These two approaches help the practitioner cope with stress by increasing psychological flexibility and accepting the present moment without judging it. Alcoholics Anonymous also emphasize acceptance as evidenced by the well-known Serenity Prayer: "God, grant me the serenity to accept the things I cannot change, the courage to change the things I can, and the wisdom to know the difference."

Acceptance and Logotherapy

Frankl believed in freedom of the human "will." However, he understood that humans are highly influenced and determined by a host of biological, social, historical and psychological forces. Yet, as noted by Joseph Fabry (1975), Frankl did not view man as "pandetermined." Rather, he believed that man always has the capacity to choose his attitude or response toward his fate. As Frankl put it, "Man's freedom is no freedom from conditions but rather freedom to take a stand on whatever conditions might confront him…[and this] capacity to take such a stand is what makes us human beings (Frankl 1988, 16)."

When a negative or tragic situation cannot be changed, Frankl recommended accepting it first, but then transmuting its meaning through the attitude that one adopts toward that fate. He wrote, "Logotherapy teaches that pain must be avoided as long as it is possible to avoid it. But as soon as a painful fate cannot be changed it not only must be accepted but may be transmuted into something meaningful, into an achievement" (Frankl 1988, 72).

Cognitive Reappraisal and Resilience

Cognitive reappraisal involves a reinterpretation of meaning. When cognitive reappraisal is positive, the individual reframes and finds positive meaning in events or situations that were previously viewed as neutral or negative. This capacity to positively reframe, to find opportunity in the midst of adversity, and to extract positive meaning from trauma, and even tragedy, has been associated with resilience. In the 1970s, Norman Finkel (1974) noted that some people use a type of cognitive restructuring to convert stress and trauma into an experience of personal growth. Subsequently, Tedeschi et al. (1998) and others studied what is now called posttraumatic growth. To measure PTG, these researchers developed the Posttraumatic Growth Inventory with five scales: New Possibilities, Relating to Others, Personal Strength, Spiritual Change, and Appreciation of Life. PTG has been described in a number of traumatized populations including war veterans, former prisoners of war, college students, refugees, survivors of assault, and individuals with injuries and a variety of medical diagnoses.

One of the ways that cognitive reappraisal may foster resilience is through its effect on negative emotions. Reappraising the meaning of an event to be more positive alters the emotional and neurobiological reaction to that event. As noted earlier, positive emotions and optimism are related to resilience through multiple psychological and neurobiological mechanisms. For example, recent brain imaging studies have shown that positive cognitive reappraisal of negative situations increases activation in regions of the brain responsible inhibiting areas of the brain that process and respond to emotions such as fear (Ochsner et al. 2012) Thus, in a variety of studies resilience has been associated with the capacity to regulate emotions, particularly the capacity to reframe the meaning of potentially negative or adverse events and situations.

Cognitive Reappraisal and Logotherapy

Positive cognitive reappraisal is a common coping strategy used in logotherapy. For example, logotherapy views stress and tension as necessary for growth and for the fulfillment of meaning, rather than something to consistently avoid. Logotherapy also views past mistakes and failures as opportunities to learn and to self-correct. Frankl had the following to say about mistakes, "We are not to see the future as exclusively determined by the past…The mistakes of the past should serve as fruitful material for shaping a better future…the mistakes should have taught a lesson" (Frankl 1986, 77). Humor, as described in more detail below, is another way to reframe threat, stress, and even tragedy. It does this by creating distance from a difficult situation and gaining a sense of control over it.

Perhaps the most powerful example of cognitive reframing in logotherapy involves its stance toward "inescapable suffering." In logotherapy, inescapable suffering can take on greater meaning than that of painful burden alone. Through a process of cognitive reframing, it is possible for 'inescapable suffering' to become an opportunity for growth. As noted by Ann Graber in *The Journey Home*, "The transformative process—inherent in unavoidable suffering—makes us realize tragedy often contains the seed of grace. We can become more than we were before by facing the challenges life presents to us." And "We can emerge from our trials transformed into stronger and more compassionate human beings" (Graber 2009, 18, 32). In fact, as noted earlier, Frankl believed that one's appraisal of and attitude toward inescapable suffering could provide the deepest and most noble meaning in life.

Humor

Humor and Resilience

Another form of cognitive reappraisal that has been associated with resilience is humor. Like positive emotions, humor is associated with a broadening of attention as well as greater creativity and flexibility of thinking. Studies conducted in multiple populations, including combat veterans as well as cancer and surgical patients, have found that humor is associated with reduced perception of threat, enhanced capacity to tolerate stress, and resilience. (Southwick and Charney 2012b). Using humor, it is often possible to face what is feared by reframing the feared situation into a scenario that is tolerable and over which one has more control. In fact, in some cases, humor creates enough distance from a feared or stressful situation to create a feeling that one has control over the situation by actually making fun of it. Interestingly, brain imaging studies have found that humor is associated with neuronal activation in brain regions known to be involved in cognitive reappraisal, reward, and motivation, each of which have been associated with resilience.

Humor and Logotherapy

Frankl believed that humans are uniquely capable of detaching themselves from painful situations through heroism and through humor. With both heroism and humor, the individual can take a stand toward his fate. As noted by Frankl, "Humor is another of the soul's weapons in the fight for self-preservation. It is well known that humor more than anything else in the human makeup, can afford an aloofness and an ability to rise above any situation, even if only for a few seconds (Frankl 2006, 63)." Thus, humor creates perspective and allows man "to put distance between himself and whatever may confront him. By the same token humor allows man to detach himself from himself and thereby to attain the fullest possible control over himself" (Frankl 1988, 108).

This capacity to detach from the self is at the heart of paradoxical intention, one of the distinct therapeutic techniques in logotherapy, and is often used to help the individual understand that he is not the same as his symptoms. With paradoxical intention, thoughts and sentences are typically formulated in a manner that humorously exaggerates the fear or unwanted behavior. Ann Graber noted that "The moment we laugh at ourselves, some sense of the fear disappears," and Frankl recommended that "paradoxical intention should always be formulated in as humorous a manner as possible" (Graber 2004, 108).

Active Coping

Active Coping and Resilience

A large body of research has found that active problem-focused coping strategies are generally more effective than passive emotion-based coping strategies when dealing with stress, trauma, and adversity (Southwick and Charney 2012b). Typical active coping strategies include gathering information, acquiring skills, problem solving, confronting when necessary, making decisions, seeking social support, and cognitively reappraising negative situations. On the other hand, common passive coping strategies include denying that a problem exists, diverting or distraction attention, avoiding or withdrawing, using substances of abuse, repetitive negative venting, and blaming someone or something else. A positive association between active coping strategies and resilience has been reported in numerous animal studies and in college students, at-risk children, patients with medical illnesses such as cardiac illness, and depressed and traumatized adults among other populations. It is important to note that active problem-focused coping is not always the most effective strategy for dealing with stress and trauma. There are times when pulling back, reflecting, accepting and mindfully observing are most effective.

Active Coping and Logotherapy

Logotherapy advocates an active approach to dealing with challenges in life. While intention and values are of central importance in logotherapy, man's intentions, values, and responsibilities are generally to be realized in the form of concrete tasks. As Frankl noted, "Perhaps the law by which man's responsibilities are revealed only in concrete tasks is more general than we imagine. Objective values become concrete duties, are cast in the form of the demands of each day and in personal tasks. The values lying at the back of these tasks can apparently be reached for only through the tasks" (Frankl 1986, 42). For Frankl, this task quality of life was essential for well-being. One's occupation or station in life did not matter. What mattered was how the individual works, "whether he in fact fills the space in which he happens to have landed. The radius of his activity is not important; important alone is whether he fills the circle of his tasks (Frankl 1986, 43)." Frankl further notes that "nothing is more likely to help a person overcome or endure objective difficulties or subjective troubles than the consciousness of having a task in life (Frankl 1986, 54)."

Classifying coping strategies as active or passive is not always straightforward, and active strategies are not always adaptive while passive strategies are not always maladaptive. For example, Frankl described "wrong passivity" as a behavioral pattern where the individual "flees from fear," and withdraws or avoids situations that he believes will cause anxiety. On the other hand, when the individual ridicules or makes fun of his anxiety through paradoxical intent, this represented an example of what Frankl called "right passivity." Further, Frankl (1986) believed that fighting against obsessions and compulsions constituted "wrong activity" while focusing attention away from the self and away from one's neurosis were examples of "right activity."

Overall, logotherapy takes an active approach to life, where meaning is found, rather than given, and discovered in the individual's day-to-day tasks and responsibilities. As Frankl made clear, "I have said that man should not ask what he may expect of life, but should rather understand that life expects something from him… Life is putting its problems to him, and it is up to him to respond to these questions by being responsible" (Frankl 2006, p. 113). To conclude: Life is the questioner; how we respond to life's challenges is our answer to life.

Stress and Training

Stress, Training, and Resilience

Modern Western society typically views stress as something that is bad for our health and well-being. However, not all stress is harmful: While stress that is overwhelming and beyond our ability to manage tends to be harmful both psychologically and biologically, stress that is manageable can be growth-promoting. On the other hand, too little stress can result in atrophy and weakening. For the purposes of growth, stress inoculation is a useful technique. Stress inoculation involves exposure and adaptation to a gradual but progressive increase in level of stress. For example, when using a stress inoculation approach to training for a marathon, the trainee gradually increases the length and intensity of training sessions until he/she has developed the cardiovascular, muscular and psychological strength and endurance to complete the 26-mile run. As noted in *The US Army Combat Stress Control Handbook*, "To achieve greater tolerance or acclimatization to a physical stressor, a progressively greater exposure is required. The exposure should be sufficient to produce more than the routine stress reflexes. Well-known examples of acclimatization are heat acclimatization, cardiovascular (aerobic) fitness, and muscle strength…you can become aerobically fit only by exerting yourself to progressively greater degrees of physical effort…In other words you must stress the system" (Department of the Army 2003, p. 29). Jim Loehr of the Human Performance Institute describes the process in the following way: "Growth and change won't occur unless you push past your comfort zone, but pushing too hard increases the likelihood that you will give up" (Loehr and Schwartz 2003, 179). A stress inoculation approach to training can be applied to a host of other learning goals such as learning to focus or meditate.

Learning to adapt to and harness stress and tension is an essential component of resilience. Many stress management programs are designed to reduce stress by removing or reducing stressors (e.g., shortening the length of military deployments to combat zones) and by reducing emotional responses to stressors (e.g., meditation, breathing techniques). However, resilience training also focuses on learning to manage and grow from stress. This can be achieved by mindfully focusing on and learning from the routine and unexpected stressors of life and/or by actively seeking out stressful challenges (e.g., running a marathon) with the intention of mastering these challenges.

Stress, Training, and Logotherapy

Like resilience training, logotherapy does not specifically attempt to reduce stress. In fact, Frankl recognized that a certain degree of stress and tension motivates people and that constantly seeking to return to a baseline of minimal stress, as per homeostatic theory, is not the path to living a meaningful life. According to homeostasis theory, man is constantly trying to reduce tension in order to "maintain or restore an inner equilibrium" and "in the final analysis, this is the goal of gratification of drives and the satisfaction of needs." (Frankl 1988, 31). Frankl further writes, "Contrary to homeostasis theory, tension is not something to avoid unconditionally, and peace of mind, or peace of soul, is not anything to avow unconditionally. A sound amount of tension, such as the tension, which is aroused by a meaning to fulfill, is inherent in being human and is indispensable for mental well-being. What man needs first of all is that tension which is created by direction" (Frankl 1988, 48).

Responsibility

Responsibility is at the core of resilience; responsibility to face one's fears, to determine what is and what is not within the grasp of one's free will and power; to foster positive emotions and realistic optimism, to articulate and adhere to a core set of moral and ethical values; to seek support from and to give support to others; to actively solve rather than avoid problems; to cognitively reframe negative, stressful and traumatic experiences in a more positive light and to search for opportunity in adversity; to develop the skills necessary to accomplish one's goals; to embrace challenges; to learn from failure; to accept that meaningful achievement typically requires hard work and perseverance; and to learn how to manage and grow from stress.

Responsibility is also at the very core of logotherapy, which Franklsaw as an education about responsibility. What are some of the responsibilities that logotherapy highlights? The responsibility to use one's free will or freedom to "choose if meaning will be found in the moment to moment circumstances of life"; "to use the passing opportunities to actualize potentialities, to realize values, whether creative, experiential, or attitudinal"; to decide "what to do, whom to love and how to suffer" (Frankl 1988, 74); to "carry out the duties that various roles in life impose upon us, to responsible-ness, that inner mandate of what I ought to do beyond the more obvious what I should do"; to "push toward the concrete meaning of one's own existence;

to seek out what is most meaningful along with the commitment to carry it out;" (Graber 2004, 82); to find the strength, commitment, and resilience that is needed, moment to moment, to live a life of meaning and purpose; to fill "the place in which he [man] happens to have landed" and to "fill out the circle of his tasks" (Frankl 1986, 43).

To embrace the responsibility that constitutes the core of resilience and logotherapy requires courage. Frankl described this beautifully when he wrote, "Responsibility is something we face and something we try to escape…There is something fearful about man's responsibility…It is fearful to know at this moment we bear the responsibility for the next, and that every decision from the smallest to the largest is a decision for all eternity—that at every moment we bring to reality—or miss—a possibility that exists only for the particular moment…But it is glorious to know that the future, our own and therewith the future of people and things around us, is dependent—even if only to a tiny extent—upon our decision at any given moment" (Frankl 1986, 35).

Conclusion

In this chapter we have focused on a handful of well-researched psychosocial and spiritual factors that have been associated with resilience, and discussed how logotherapy might enhance these factors. Our discussion is limited in scope since resilience is a complex construct that can be influenced by a host of biological, psychological, social, and spiritual factors, and since logotherapy likely can affect a substantial number of these factors. Nevertheless, the evidence we have presented suggests that logotherapy, in addition to assisting individuals with a wide range of medical, behavioral health, and social problems can strengthen resilience and facilitate personal growth in the face of adversity and trauma.

References

Boswell, J. (1791). *The life of Samuel Johnson LL.D.* London: J.M Dent & Co.

Cohen, S., Doyle, W. J., Turner, R. B., Alper, C. M., & Skoner, D. P. (2003). Emotional style and susceptibility to the common cold. *Psychosomatic Medicine, 65*, 652–657.

Culver, J. L., Arena, P. L., Antoni, M. H., & Carver, C. S. (November 1, 2002). Coping and distress among women under treatment for early stage breast cancer: comparing African Americans, Hispanics and non-Hispanic Whites. *Psycho-oncology, 11*(6), 495–504.

Danner, D. D., Snowdon, D. A., & Friesen, W. V. (2001). Positive emotions in early life and longevity: Findings from the nun study. *Journal of Personality and Social Psychology, 80*(5), 804–813.

Department of the Army. (2003). *U. S. Army combat stress control handbook.* Guilford, CT: The Lyons Press.

Fabry, J. B. (1975). *The pursuit of meaning: Logotherapy applied to life.* Dublin: Mercier Press.

Fallot, R. D., & Heckman, J. P. (2006). Religious/spiritual coping among women trauma survivors with mental health and substance use disorders. *The Journal of Behavioral Health Services and Research, 32*(2), 215–226.

Finkel, N. J. (1974). Stress and traumas: An attempt at categorization. *American Journal of Community Psychology, 2*(3), 265–273.

Frankl, V. E. (1986). *The doctor and the soul: From psychotherapy to logotherapy: [a new approach to the neurotic personality which emphasizes man's spiritual values and the quest for meaning in life]*. New York, NY: Vintage Books.

Frankl, V. E. (1988). *The will to meaning: Foundations and applications of logotherapy*. New York, NY: Meridian.

Frankl, V. E. (2006). *Man's search for meaning*. Boston, MA: Beacon.

Fredrickson, B., & Branigan, C. (2005). Positive emotions broaden the scope of attention and thought-action repertoires. *Cognition & Emotion, 19*(3), 313–332.

Giltay, E. J., Kamphuis, M. H., Kalmijn, S., Zitman, F. G., & Kromhout, D. (2006). Dispositional optimism and the risk of cardiovascular death: The Zutphen Elderly Study. *Archives of Internal Medicine, 166*, 431–436.

Graber, A. V. (2004). *Viktor Frankl's logotherapy: Method of choice in ecumenical pastoral psychology*. Lima, OH: Wyndham Hall Press.

Graber, A. V. (2009). *The journey home: Preparing for life's ultimate adventure*. Birmingham, AL: LogoLife Press.

Ju, H., Shin, J. W., Kim, C.-W., Hyun, M.-H., & Park, J.-W. (2013). Mediational effect of meaning in life on the relationship between optimism and well-being in community elderly. *Archives of Gerontology and Geriatrics, 56*, 309–313.

Kidder, R. M. (2006). *Moral courage*. Harper Paperbacks.

King, L. A., Hicks, J. A., Krull, J. L., & Del Gaiso, A. K. (2006). Positive affect and the experience of meaning in life. *Journal of Personality and Social Psychology, 90*(1), 179–196.

Loehr, J., & Schwartz, T. (2003). *The power of full engagement: Managing energy, not time, is the key to high performance and personal renewal*. New York, NY: Free Press.

Manne, S., DuHamel, K., Nereo, N., Ostroff, J., Parsons, S., Martini, R., et al. (2002). Predictors of PTSD in mothers of children undergoing bone marrow transplantation: The role of cognitive and social processes. *Journal of Pediatric Psychology, 27*(7), 607–617.

Marshall, M., & Marshall, E. (2012). *Logotherapy revisited: Review of the tenets of Viktor E. Frankl's logotherapy.* CreateSpace Independent Publishing Platform

McCullough, M. E., Hoyt, W. E., Larson, D. B., Koenig, H. G., & Thoresen, C. (2000). Religious involvement and mortality: A meta-analytic review. *Health Psychology, 19*(3), 211–222.

McEwen, B. S. (2007). Physiology and neurobiology of stress and adaptation: Central role of the brain. *Physiological Reviews, 87*, 873–904.

Ochsner, K. N., Silvers, J. A., & Buhle, J. T. (2012). Functional imaging studies of emotion regulation: A synthetic review and evolving model of the cognitive control of emotion. *Annals of the New York Academy of Sciences, 1251*, E1–E24.

Orsillo, S. M., Roemer, L., & Holowka, D. (2005). Acceptance-based behavioral therapies for anxiety: Using acceptance and mindfulness to enhance traditional cognitive-behavioral approaches. In S. M. Orsillo & L. Roemer (Eds.), *Acceptance-and mindfulness-based approaches to anxiety: Conceptualization and treatment*. New York, NY: Springer.

Reivich, K., & Shatté, A. (2003). *The resilience factor: 7 keys to finding your inner strength and overcoming life's hurdles*. New York, NY: Broadway Books.

Rochester, S., & Kiley, F. (1998). *Honor bound: The history of American prisoners of war in Southeast Asia, 1961–1973*. Washington, DC: Historical Office, Office of the Secretary of Defense.

Schwartz, C. E., Meisenhelder, J. B., Ma, Y., & Reed, G. (2003). Altruistic social interest behaviors are associated with better mental health. *Psychosomatic Medicine, 65*, 778–785.

Sherman, N. (2005). *Stoic warriors: The ancient philosophy behind the military mind*. New York, NY: Oxford University Press.

Shermer, M. (2011). The science of right and wrong. *Scientific American,* 304(1), 83

Siebert, A. (1996). *The survivor personality*. New York, NY: Pedigree Books.
Southwick, S. M., Bonanno, G. A., Masten, A. S., Panter-Brick, C., & Yehuda, R. (2014). Resilience definitions, theory, and challenges: Interdisciplinary perspectives. *European Journal of Psychotraumatology, 5*, 10.3402.
Southwick, S. M., & Charney, D. S. (2012a). The science of resilience: Implications for the prevention and treatment of depression. *Science, 338*(6103), 79–82.
Southwick, S. M., & Charney, D. S. (2012b). *Resilience: The science of mastering life's greatest challenges*. New York, NY: Cambridge University Press.
Tedeschi, R. G., Park, C. L., & Calhoun, L. G. (Eds.). (1998). *Posttraumatic growth: Positive changes in the aftermath of crisis*. Mahwah, NJ: Lawrence Erlbaum Associates.
Zeidner, M., & Hammer, A. L. (1992). Coping with missile attack: Resources, strategies, and outcomes. *Journal of Personality, 60*, 709–746.
Zimrin, H. (1986). A profile of survival. *Child Abuse and Neglect, 10*, 339–349.

Meaning-Centered Psychotherapy (MCP) for Advanced Cancer Patients

William S. Breitbart

Introduction

Like many clinical interventions in our field of psycho-oncology, Meaning-Centered Psychotherapy (MCP) arose from a need to deal with a challenging clinical problem, that of despair, hopelessness, and desire for hastened death in advanced cancer patients, who were, in fact, not suffering from a clinical depression, but rather confronting an existential crisis of loss of meaning, value, and purpose in the face of a terminal prognosis. While our group ultimately demonstrated that desire for hastened death in the presence of a clinical depression could be reversed with adequate antidepressant therapy, no effective intervention appeared available for loss of meaning and hopelessness in the absence of clinical depression.

Inspired primarily by the works of Viktor Frankl and further informed by the contributions of Irvin Yalom, our research group adapted Frankl's concepts of the importance of meaning in human existence (and his "logotherapy"), and initially created MCGP (Meaning-Centered Group Psychotherapy), intended primarily for advanced cancer patients. The goal of the intervention was to diminish despair, demoralization, hopelessness, and desire for hastened death by sustaining or enhancing a sense of meaning, even in the face of death.

W.S. Breitbart (✉)
Department of Psychiatry and Behavioral Sciences, Memorial Sloan-Kettering Cancer Center, 641 Lexington Avenue 7th floor, New York, NY 10022, USA
e-mail: breitbaw@mskcc.org

A. Batthyány (ed.), *Logotherapy and Existential Analysis*, Logotherapy and Existential Analysis: Proceedings of the Viktor Frankl Institute Vienna 1,
DOI 10.1007/978-3-319-29424-7_14

Theoretical Conceptual Framework Underlying Meaning-Centered Psychotherapy (Frankl's Concepts of Meaning)

Frankl's logotherapy was not designed for the treatment of cancer patients or those with life-threatening illness. His main contribution to human psychology was to raise awareness of the spiritual component of human experience, and the central importance of meaning (or the will to meaning) as a driving force or human instinct. Basic concepts related to meaning, proposed by Frankl and adapted for MCP in the cancer setting, include:

1. *Meaning of life*—life has and never ceases to have meaning, from the first moment through to the very last. Meaning may change through the years, but it never ceases to exist. When we feel our lives have no meaning, it is because we have become disconnected from such meaning, rather than because it no longer exists.
2. *Will to meaning*—the desire to find meaning in existence is a primary motivating force in our behavior. Human beings are creatures who innately search for and create meaning in their lives.
3. *Freedom of will*—we have the freedom to find meaning in life and to choose our attitude toward suffering. We have the responsibility to discover meaning, direction, and identity. We must respond to the fact of our existence and create the "essence" of what makes us human.
4. *Sources of meaning*—meaning in life has specific and available sources (Table 1). The four main sources of meaning are derived from creativity (work, deeds, dedication to causes), experience (art, nature, humor, love, relationships, roles), attitude (the stance one takes toward suffering and existential problems), and legacy (meaning exists in a historical context, thus legacy—past, present, and future—is a critical element in sustaining or enhancing meaning).

Table 1 Frankl's sources of meaning

Creativity	Engaging in life through work, deeds, causes, artistic endeavors, hobbies, and so on. Examples include our careers/job, volunteer work, involvement with church/synagogue, political and social causes
Experience	Connecting with life through love, relationships, nature, art, and humor. Examples include our family, children, loved ones, the sunset, gardening, beaches, museums, playing with pets, and so on
Attitude	Encountering life's limitations by turning personal tragedy into triumph, things we have achieved despite adversity, rising above, or transcending difficult circumstances. Examples include achieving an education despite personal/financial challenges, overcoming grief/loss, persevering through cancer treatment, and so on
History	Legacy given (past), lived (present), and left (future). Examples include our story, our family history, the history of our name, our accomplishments, and whatever we hope to leave behind

Drawing from these principles, MCGP enhances patients' sense of meaning by helping them to capitalize on the various sources of meaning in their lives. Enhanced meaning is conceptualized as the catalyst for improved quality of life, reduced psychological distress, and despair. Specifically, meaning is viewed as both an intermediary outcome and a mediator of change.

Main Themes and Format of the Therapy

MCGP is an eight-session group intervention, which uses a mix of didactics, discussions, and experiential exercises that are centered around particular themes related to meaning and advanced cancer (Table 2). The intention is to sustain or enhance a sense of meaning and purpose by teaching patients how to use the breadth of possible sources of meaning as coping resources through a combination of:

1. instructed teaching on the concepts of meaning;
2. group experiential exercises to enhance learning;
3. and group leader-facilitated discussion aimed at reinforcing the importance of reconnecting to sources of meaning and using these as resources.

Other existential concepts, such as freedom, responsibility, authenticity, existential guilt, transcendence, and choice, are incorporated into session content as these themes arise. Elements of support and expression of emotion are inevitable in each session (but are limited by the psycho-educational focus of MCGP).

Table 2 Topics covered in MCGP (Meaning-Centered Group Psychotherapy)[a]

Session	MCGP	Content
1	Concepts and sources of meaning	Introductions of group members, introduction of concept of meaning and sources of meaning
2	Cancer and meaning	Identity—before and after cancer diagnosis
3	Historical sources of meaning (Legacy: past)	Life as a legacy that has been given (past)
4	Historical sources of meaning (Legacy: present and future)	Life as a legacy that one lives (present) and gives (future)
5	Attitudinal sources of meaning: Encountering life's limitations	Confronting limitations imposed by cancer, prognosis, and death; introduction to legacy project
6	Creative sources of meaning: Engaging in life fully	Creativity, courage, and responsibility
7	Experiential sources of meaning: Connecting with life	Love, nature, art, and humor
8	Transitions: reflections and hopes for the future	Review of sources of meaning, as resources, reflections on lessons learned in the group, experiential exercise on hopes for the future

[a]Breitbart and Applebaum (2011)

The following is an overview of each session, including the experiential exercises used to facilitate discussion and deepen understanding.

Session 1: Concepts and Sources of Meaning

The first session involves introductions of each group member and an overall explanation of the group's goals. Patient introductions include biographical information, as well as their expectations, hopes, and questions relating to the group. The session concludes with a discussion of what meaning means to each participant, stimulated by an experiential exercise which helps patients discover how they find a sense of meaning and purpose in general, as well as specifically in relation to having been diagnosed with cancer.

Session 1: Experiential Exercise

List one or two experiences or moments when life has felt particularly meaningful to you—whether it sounds powerful or mundane. For example, it could be something that helped get you through a difficult day, or a time when you felt most alive. And say something about it.

Session 2: Cancer and Meaning

The emphasis of session 2 is the linking of identity as a central element of meaning. The session begins as a continuation of sharing meaningful experiences, as well as a detailed explanation of what, or who, made these experiences meaningful. Identity, as a component of meaning, is addressed through the experiential exercise in which patients are asked to respond to the question "who am I?" This exercise provides the opportunity to discuss pre-cancer identity and roles, and then how cancer has affected their identity and what they consider to be meaningful in their lives.

Session 2: Experiential Exercise "Identity and Cancer"

1. Write down four answers to the question, "Who am I?" These can be positive or negative, and include personality characteristics, body image, beliefs, things you do, people you know, and so on… For example, answers might start with, "I am someone who _____," or "I am a ________."
2. How has cancer affected your answers? How has it affected the things that are most meaningful to you?

The following MCGP excerpt exemplifies the type of interaction that occurs between group members and leaders during the Session 2 Experiential Exercise:

PATIENT 1: I am a daughter, a mother, a grandmother, a sister, a friend, and a neighbor. I attempt to respect all people in their views, which sometimes can be difficult. I represent myself honestly and frankly without being offensive, or at least I try. And my philosophy is to do unto others as they would have done unto you. I'm somebody who can be very private and not always share all my needs and concerns. I also have been working on accepting love and affection and other gifts from other people. I'm more of a caregiver than someone who gets care from others, I don't like to receive care, but I'm beginning to, … actually … this may be the one thing that my illness has caused me to mull over. That I'm more accepting of people wanting to do things.

GR*OUP LEADER:* Thank you. That's really interesting. I want to make some comments, but first let's hear from someone else. Patient 2, would you like to go?

PATIENT 2: Well in terms of pre-cancer, I'm my niece's loving aunty whom she currently adores … she's seven, I'm not sure how long that will last, but right now, that's really important to me, and it's brought my brother and me closer. I'm active and am always ready for an adventure. All my friends knew I was a "yes, let's do it, person," enthusiastic, open. I'm a young adult librarian, with a real connection to the teens. I really loved working with them, especially on the advisory council; I really just loved it, and oftentimes would stay very late with them, into the night. I was just, really … connected …. I ran around a lot and I was rarely home before 11 p.m. …. My friends always asked why I wasn't home more. It wasn't that I didn't like home, it's just that I wanted to be out, experiencing life. I also love concerts, and I danced. And I dated. I was the essence of positive, a very good friend, I'm really proud of that.

GROUP LEADER: Thanks. Do you have any questions for each other about the things that you said? Were there any commonalities that you noticed?

PATIENT 1: I guess the commonality that most of us spoke about is, being a member of a unique group, a family and for most of us that was in the top position. That was most important.

PATIENT 2: I have a comment but I don't know if it's what you're asking for. Patient 1 was talking about being a giver, but that it's basically hard for her to receive. I've had friends who are like that and it's frustrating to want to give to a person like you, but you also don't want to take people's wishes lightly … I know I'm probably speaking out of turn for all of your friends who want to be generous back to you.

PATIENT 1: Most of them have been, because they, you know, sit me down and do what they want to do. I guess most of my good friends are very strong-willed people like me and they listen and do for the most part what they want. And I don't get offended for the most part.

GROUP LEADER: It was actually quite striking … that there were many similarities in what you all shared about your identities pre-cancer. For many people, the first, the most important source of your identity, had to do with your love relationships, family relationships, your role in a family, being a daughter, father, an aunt, being a member of immediate family. So it's from these connections that we derive meaning in life, through our connectedness with people we love. And often they are members of our family. And, often, these are our sources of identity, as a member of a family, as a father, an aunt….

PATIENT 1: These roles are also a source of pain.

GROUP LEADER: Yes, that can be true, but they are also clearly a source of meaning. Do you remember which source of meaning? It's the "experiential" source of meaning. Through love, through connectedness with people…. Someone made a comment that Patient 3 didn't mention this source of meaning. Patient 3, you said something interesting. You said you've been alone too long. But you also said that you're a loyal friend, loyal as a puppy, and a good lover. So for you, love is very relevant, too. You derive a sense of meaning through friendship and romantic love. Those are all similar, all love, right? Let me ask you something. Patient 3, did you leave out being a son, or a family member, for a specific reason?

PATIENT 3: Well, I never knew my dad. I didn't really know my mother until I was older. And I have a brother and a sister, but I'm not close to either of them. So, in a way, my job became more of my family, the people I worked with, people in recovery, they were my family because I became more connected to them. But outside of that, no … no real family. So in a sense, family has been a disappointment, pain. So everyone talks about family reunions, I don't have that. That's not a part of my life.

GROUP LEADER: So again this idea comes up that the things that give us meaning, like love and relationships and family, are also potential sources of pain. We have to be aware of that, don't we! The other thing I heard that was common in the responses, besides love and connectedness to other people, is connectedness to other kinds of experiences in life, like dancing, and Patient 4, you were talking about baking, cooking … so it's not just relationships with people, it's relationships to the world, and being in nature, and engaging in pleasurable things, like dancing and eating. And in addition to that, several people talked about their identity coming from what they did for work, being a nurse, a doctor, a lawyer … your work, these are creative sources of meaning because we derive meaning through things we create, the work we do in our lives. And you added something interesting, Patient 1, that had to do with … I think I would used the word compassion … It had to do with caring for other people?

PATIENT 1: Well, you know, you talked about our professions, but I didn't actually talk today about my professional life, I didn't say anything about being a nurse or a health care provider, but I talked about being a caretaker. A caretaker, in general, to the people in my life.

GROUP LEADER: Exactly. So this creative source of meaning doesn't just come from a job you get paid to do, but from the person you create in the world. You've created a person who is loving, giving, and caring. You've created a virtue, a value, compassion is important, caring for others is important. So it's not just the job you do, but the kind of person you become and create in the world, and what values that represents, that is meaningful to you. That's all part of "creative" sources of meaning.

Sessions 3 and 4: Historical Sources of Meaning

Sessions 3 and 4 focus on giving each patient a chance to share their life story with the group, which helps them to better appreciate their inherited legacy and past accomplishments while still elucidating current and future goals. The theme of Session 3 is "Life as a legacy that has been given" via the past, such as legacy given through one's family of origin. The facts of our lives that have been created by our genetics and the circumstances of our past are discussed in terms of how they have shaped us and perhaps motivated us to transcend limitations. Session 4 focuses on "Life as a legacy that one lives and will give," in terms of patients' living legacy and the legacy they hope to leave for others. The Session 3 experiential exercise helps patients to understand the ways in which their pasts have shaped what they find meaningful, and the Session 4 exercise fosters a discussion of future goals, no matter how small.

Session 3: Experiential Exercise: "Life as a Legacy That Has Been Given"

When you look back on your life and upbringing, what are the most significant memories, relationships, traditions, and so on that have made the greatest impact on who you are today? For example: Identify specific memories of how you were raised that have made a lasting impression on your life (e.g., your relationship with parents, siblings, friends, teachers, etc.). What is the origin of your name? What are some past events that have touched your life?

Session 4: Experiential Exercise "Life as a Legacy That You Live and Will Give"

1. As you reflect upon who you are today, what are the meaningful activities, roles, or accomplishments that you are most proud of?
2. As you look toward the future, what are some of the life lessons you have learned along the way that you would want to pass on to others? What is the legacy you hope to live and give?

Session 5: Attitudinal Sources of Meaning

This session examines each patient's confrontation with limitations in life and the ultimate limitation—our mortality and the finiteness of life. The focus is on our freedom to choose our attitudes toward such limitations and find meaning in life, even in the face of death. In discussing the experiential exercise, group leaders emphasize one of Frankl's core theoretical beliefs that by choosing our attitude toward circumstances that are beyond our control (e.g., cancer and death), we may find meaning in life and suffering, which will then help us to rise above or overcome such limitations. One of the more critical elements of this session involves the experiential exercise in which patients are asked to discuss their thoughts, feelings, and concepts of what constitutes a "good" or meaningful death. Common issues that have arisen include where patients prefer to die (e.g., at home in their own bed), how they want to die (e.g., without pain, surrounded by family), and what patients expect takes place after death, funeral fantasies, family issues, and the afterlife. This exercise is designed to detoxify the discussion of death and to allow for a safe examination of the life they have lived and how they may be able to accept that life. Inherent in these discussions are issues of tasks of life completion, forgiveness, and redemption. At the end of session 5, patients are presented with the "Legacy Project," which integrates ideas presented in treatment (e.g., meaning, identity, creativity, and responsibility), in order to facilitate the generation of a sense of meaning in light of cancer. Some examples of Legacy Projects include creating a legacy photo album or video, mending a broken relationship, or undertaking something the patient has always wanted to do but has not yet done.

Session 5: Experiential Exercise "Encountering Life's Limitations"

1. Since your diagnosis, are you still able to find meaning in your daily life despite your awareness of the finiteness of life? (If yes, how? If no, what are the obstacles?)
2. During this time, have you ever lost a sense of meaning in life—that life was not worth living? (If yes, please briefly describe.)
3. What would you consider a "good" or "meaningful" "death?" How can you imagine being remembered by your loved ones? (e.g., what are some of your personal characteristics, the shared memories, or meaningful life events that have made a lasting impression on them?)

Session 6: Creative Sources of Meaning

Session 6 focuses on "Creativity" as a source and resource of meaning in life. One important element of the experiential exercises deals with the issue of "Responsibility" (our ability to respond to the fact of our existence, to answer the question, "what life have we created for ourselves?"). Each patient is asked to discuss what their responsibilities are, as well as for whom they are responsible. Any unfinished business or tasks patients may have is also examined. This discussion invites group members to focus on the task at hand, as opposed to focusing only on their suffering. Additionally, by attending to their responsibility to others, meaning may be enhanced by the realization that their lives transcend themselves and extend to others.

Session 6: Experiential Exercise "Engaging in Life Fully"

1. Living life and being creative requires courage and commitment. Can you think of times in your life when you've been courageous, taken ownership of your life, or made a meaningful commitment to something of value to you?
2. Do you feel you've expressed what is most meaningful to you through your life's work and creative activities (e.g., job, parenting, hobbies, causes)?—If so, how?
3. What are your responsibilities? Who are you responsible to and for?
4. Do you have unfinished business? What tasks have you always wanted to do, but have yet to undertake? What's holding you back from responding to this creative call?

Session 7: Experiential Sources of Meaning

Session 7 focuses on discussing experiential sources of meaning, such as love, beauty, and humor. While creative and attitudinal sources of meaning **require more of an active involvement with life**, experiential sources embody more of **a passive or even sensory engagement with life**. Patients explore moments and experiences when they have felt connected with life through love, beauty, and humor. Often, the discussions highlight how these sources of meaning become particularly important for patients since their cancer diagnosis. Feelings concerning the group's upcoming termination are discussed in preparation for the final session.

Session 7: Experiential Exercise "Connecting with Life"

List three ways in which you "connect with life" and feel most alive through the experiential sources of: LOVE, BEAUTY, HUMOR.

Session 8: Transitions

The final session provides an opportunity to review patients' Legacy Projects, as well as to review individual and group themes. Additionally, the group is asked to discuss topics such as: (1) How has the group been experienced? (2) Have there been changes in attitudes toward your illness or suffering? (3) How do you envision continuing what has been started in the group? The experiential exercise that ends this session focuses on answering the question, "What are your hopes for the future?"

Session 8: Experiential Exercise "Group Reflections and Hopes for the Future"

1. What has it been like for you to go through this learning experience over these last eight sessions? Have there been any changes in the way you view your life and cancer experience having been through this process?
2. Do you feel like you have a better understanding of the sources of meaning in life and are you able to use them in your daily life? If so, how?
3. What are your hopes for the future?

Key Therapist Techniques in the Application of MCGP

Group Process Skills and Techniques

MCGP is essentially a group intervention, and as such, attention to basic tenets of group process and dynamics remains important. Co-facilitators must be cognizant of group etiquette, especially in terms of working together as co-facilitators, attending to and promoting group cohesion and facilitating an atmosphere that is conducive to productive exchanges between patients. While MCGP is not intended to be primarily a supportive group intervention, elements of support are in fact quite inevitable, but are not intentionally promoted or specifically fostered.

Psycho-Educational Approach: Didactics and Experiential Exercises to Enhance Learning

MCGP is also essentially an educational intervention. The goal of MCGP is to have patients understand the concept of meaning, and its importance, particularly as one faces a terminal illness, and the ultimate limitation of death. Additionally, MCGP strives to have patients learn about sources of meaning in order for these to become resources in coping with advanced cancer. This educational process is achieved primarily through a set of brief didactics which introduce each session, followed by an experiential exercise designed to link learning of these abstract concepts with patients' own emotional experiences. Patients each share the content of their experiential exercises, and the process of experiential learning is reinforced through the comments of co-facilitators and patients, as well as through the identification of commonalities among patients' responses.

A Focus on Meaning and Sources of Meaning as Resources

MCGP is designed to have patients learn Frankl's concepts of meaning and to incorporate these sources of meaning as resources in their coping with advanced cancer. In each session, the co-facilitators listen carefully for and highlight content shared by patients that reflect sources of meaning. Co-facilitators identify "meaningful moments" described by patients, and also draw attention to "meaning shifts" when patients begin to incorporate the vocabulary and conceptual framework of meaning into the material they share. An emphasis is also placed on the importance of the patient's ability to shift from one source of meaning to another, as selected sources of meaning become unavailable due to disease progression. A specific technique used to facilitate this process is called "Moving from ways of doing to ways of being." This refers to helping patients to become aware that meaning can be derived in more passive ways. For example, patients can still be good fathers even if they cannot go out to the backyard and play ball with their sons, by being fathers in less action-oriented ways, such as sitting and talking about their son's life goals and fears, and through expressing affection. In MCGP, it is also important for co-facilitators to be aware of the "co-creation of meaning" between group members. All present are "witnesses" or repositories of meaning for each other, and thus part of a meaningful legacy created by the group-as-a-whole.

Incorporating Basic Existential Concepts and Themes

A central concept in MCGP is that human beings are creatures. We create key values and, most importantly, we create our lives. In order to live fully, we must create a life of meaning, identity, and direction. "Detoxifying death" through the therapeutic stance and attitude of the co-facilitators is an important technique utilized throughout MCGP. Co-facilitators speak openly about death as the ultimate limitation that causes suffering and for which meaning can still be derived through the attitude that one takes toward suffering (e.g., transcendence, choice). Another technique, the "existential nudge," occurs when co-facilitators gently challenge the resistance of patients to explore difficult existential realities, such as the ultimate limitation of death or existential guilt.

Key Challenges in Application of MCGP

The key challenge in applying MCGP in an advanced cancer population is related to inflexibility, which is innate to a weekly group intervention that requires regular attendance at a specified day and time. MCGP also has specific themes that are covered weekly, with a logical progression of content as the sessions unfold. Therefore, attending all sessions is desirable. Research with palliative care populations suffers from attrition due to illness, death, conflicts with scheduling chemotherapy, diagnostic tests, other doctor appointments, and brief hospitalizations. Our trials of MCGP have had attrition rates as high as 50 % (interestingly, the rate is the same for Supportive Psychotherapy).

Overview of Evidence on Efficacy

Early research by Yalom, Spiegel, and colleagues demonstrated that a 1-year supportive-expressive group psychotherapy, which included a focus on existential issues, decreased psychological distress, and improved quality of life. More recent studies have described short-term interventions that included a spiritual or existential component, including individual-based approaches. However, results are inconsistent in their effects on depression, anxiety, and desire for death. More importantly, specific aspects of spiritual well-being and meaning were not consistently targeted as outcomes. Thus, despite the seeming importance of enhancing one's sense of meaning and purpose, few clinical interventions have been developed that attempt to address this critical issue.

A randomized controlled trial of MCGP (Breitbart et al. 2010) demonstrated its efficacy in improving spiritual well-being and a sense of meaning, as well as in decreasing anxiety, hopelessness, and desire for death. Ninety patients were randomized to either eight sessions of MCGP or Supportive Group Psychotherapy (SGP). Of the 55 patients who completed the 8-week intervention, 38 completed a follow-up assessment 2 months later (attrition was largely due to death or physical deterioration). Outcome assessments included measures of spiritual well-being, meaning, hopelessness, desire for death, optimism/pessimism, anxiety, depression, and overall quality of life. Results demonstrated significantly greater benefits from MCGP compared to SGP, particularly in enhancing spiritual well-being and a sense of meaning. Treatment effects for MCGP appeared even stronger 2 months after treatment ended, suggesting that benefits not only persist but also may grow over time. Patients who participated in SGP failed to demonstrate any such improvements, either post-treatment or at the 2-month follow-up assessment.

Service Development and Future Directions

While MCGP is effective for patients with advanced cancer, it is demanding, inflexible, and associated with significant attrition. We therefore developed the more flexible individual format, Individual Meaning-Centered Psychotherapy (IMCP) (Table 3). IMCP has proved to be equally effective, but allows for flexibility in time and place (e.g., office, bedside, or chemo suite) for scheduling sessions, and has significantly reduced attrition and enhanced rates of intervention completers. We are currently adapting and testing MCP for other cancer populations, (e.g., early stage cancer, cancer survivors) as well as for oncology care providers. Additionally, we are developing briefer forms of IMCP that can be applied to hospice populations.

Table 3 Topics and goals of IMCP[a]

Session	Weekly topics and goals
1	Concepts and sources of meaning: introduction and overview *Session goals:* Learn patient's cancer story and introduce concepts and sources of meaning
2	Cancer and meaning: identity before and after cancer diagnosis *Session goals:* Develop a general understanding of one's sense of identity and the impact cancer has made upon it
3	Historical sources of meaning: life as a living legacy (past, present, future) *Session goals:* Develop an understanding of one's legacy through exploration of three temporal legacy modes: the legacy that's been given from the past, the legacy that one lives in the present, and finally, the legacy one will leave in the future. Participants also begin developing a Legacy Project
4	Attitudinal sources of meaning: encountering life's limitations *Session goals:* Explore one of Frankl's core therapeutic principals that ultimately we have the freedom and capacity to choose our attitude toward suffering and life's limitations and to derive meaning from that choice
5	Creative sources of meaning: engaging in life via creativity and responsibility *Session goals:* Develop an understanding of the significance of "creativity" and "responsibility" as important sources of meaning in life
6	Experiential sources of meaning: connecting with life via love, nature, and humor *Session goals:* Foster an understanding of the significance of connecting with life through experiential sources of meaning, particularly through experiencing love, beauty, and humor
7	Transitions: reflections and hopes for the future *Session goals:* Review the sources of meaning. Review of the Legacy Project. Reflections on the lessons and impact of the therapy, discussion of hopes for the future, and the transition from being in the therapy to enacting the lessons learned in daily life as the therapy comes to an end

[a]Breitbart et al. (2012)

Summary

MCGP and IMCP have been developed by W. Breitbart and colleagues in the Department of Psychiatry and Behavioral Sciences, Memorial Sloan-Kettering Cancer Center. MCGP is a novel and unique intervention demonstrated to be effective in enhancing meaning and diminishing despair in advanced cancer patients.

References

Breitbart, W., & Applebaum, A. (2011). Meaning-centered group psychotherapy. In M. Watson & D. W. Kissane (Eds.), *Handbook of psychotherapy in cancer care* (pp. 137–148). Chichester, England: Wiley.

Breitbart W et al (2012) Pilot randomized controlled trial of Individual Meaning-Centered Psychotherapy for patients with advanced cancer. Journal of Clinical Oncology 30(12):1304–1309

Breitbart W et al (2010) Meaning-centered group psychotherapy for patients with advanced cancer: a pilot randomized controlled trial. Psycho-Oncology 19:21–28

Enhancing Psychological Resiliency in Older Men Facing Retirement with Meaning-Centered Men's Groups

Marnin J. Heisel and The Meaning-Centered Men's Group project team

There is a clear and pressing need for suicide prevention initiatives targeting older men. Older adults have high suicide rates, engage in violent means of self-injury with a high intent to die, and are more likely than younger adults to succumb to those injuries (Canadian Coalition for Seniors' Mental Health 2006). Men account for over 80 % of the nearly 9400 North Americans over 60 who die by suicide every year (Statistics Canada 2014; WISQARS database; Centers for Disease Control and Prevention [CDC]), and older men have among the highest rates of suicide worldwide (Krug et al. 2002). Few intervention studies have investigated suicide risk reduction among older adults to date (Links et al. 2005) and nearly none have aimed explicitly to reduce risk among older men (Lapierre et al. 2011). This issue poses a substantial challenge to existing healthcare resources given older adults' high healthcare utilization (Canadian Institute for Health Information 2011), the aging of

---

Funding for this study was provided by Movember Canada

The Meaning-Centered Men's Group Project Team additionally includes: **Co-Investigators**: Gordon L. Flett, Ph.D. (York University, Toronto, Ontario, Canada), Paul S. Links, M.D., FRCP(C) (UWO), Ross M.G. Norman, Ph.D., C.Psych. (UWO), Sisira Sarma, Ph.D. (UWO), Sharon L. Moore, Ph.D., R.N., R.Psych. (Athabasca University, Athabasca, Alberta, Canada), Norm O'Rourke, Ph.D., R.Psych. (Simon Fraser University, Vancouver, British Columbia, Canada), and Rahel Eynan, Ph.D. (UWO); **Collaborators**: Kim Wilson, M.S.W., Ph.D. Candidate (University of Guelph, Guelph, Ontario, Canada), and Paul Fairlie, Ph.D. (York University); **Community Partners**: Third Age Outreach-St. Joseph's Health Care, London (Beverly Farrell, R/TRO & Kristan Harris, OT Reg. (Ont.) MHSc CHE), Kiwanis and Hamilton Road Seniors and Community Centre City of London (Michelle Kerr), and the Canadian Coalition for Seniors' Mental Health (Bonnie Schroeder, M.S.W., R.S.W.).

The Meaning-Centered Men's Group project team and M.J. Heisel (✉)
Department of Psychiatry, London Health Sciences Centre-Victoria Hospital,
The University of Western Ontario, 800 Commissioners Rd. E., Office #A2-515,
London, ON, Canada, N6A-5W9
e-mail: Marnin.Heisel@lhsc.on.ca

A. Batthyány (ed.), *Logotherapy and Existential Analysis*, Logotherapy and Existential Analysis: Proceedings of the Viktor Frankl Institute Vienna 1,
DOI 10.1007/978-3-319-29424-7_15

the baby-boomers, a vast birth cohort with a high suicide rate (Mościcki 1996), and the projected population growth of older adults in North America and much of Europe (Cohen 2003; Statistics Canada 2010; United States Census Bureau 2003). Inefficiencies in mental healthcare systems, a reticence among many men to seek mental healthcare, a dearth of provider expertise in suicide prevention, and a paucity of outreach initiatives and proven interventions to reduce suicide risk further contribute to this problem, necessitating effective, feasible, and sustainable interventions (Heisel and Duberstein 2005).

The "gender paradox of suicide" acknowledges that women more frequently engage in suicidal behavior and yet men more frequently die by suicide, suggesting a need to enhance the capacities, among men, to cope with loss, adapt to changing life circumstances, seek help for emotional and health-related difficulties, and nurture supportive interpersonal relationships (Canetto and Lester 1998). North American men's suicide rates increase at retirement age and escalate throughout their later years (CDC; Statistics Canada 2014); retirement may thus be both a key life transition that can trigger increasing suicide risk and a critical period for effective intervention.

The association between retirement and health is complex. Many men who look forward to retirement enjoy health, leisure, and satisfaction in their post-employment years; yet, retirement can also unearth or exacerbate health and mental health problems (Butterworth et al. 2006; Gill et al. 2006; Karpansalo et al. 2005; Pinquart and Schindler 2007; Westerlund et al. 2009). Men tend to have greater difficulty than women in cultivating interests and relationships outside of work, potentially increasing their vulnerability to the psychosocial ramifications of retirement, including marital conflict, loneliness, depression, and substance misuse (Perreira and Sloan 2002; Weingarten 1988). Those who define themselves primarily by their work roles or successes may struggle with retirement, especially if it is too early for them, involuntary, or if they have not planned realistically for meaningful post-retirement pursuits, social relations, or long-term financial needs (Nordenmark and Stattin 2009; Schellenberg and Silver 2004). Early retirement may be reciprocally associated with an increased likelihood of physical and mental health problems. Being laid off, unemployed, or feeling pushed into retirement can also increase men's risk for depression and suicide ideation (Brand et al. 2008; Yen et al. 2005). Empirical findings indicate risk for post-retirement morbidity and mortality, including by suicide, and suggest potential benefit in preventive interventions for vulnerable men facing retirement (Bamia et al. 2008; Brockman et al. 2009; Qin et al. 2003; Schneider et al. 2011). Yet, the intervention literature is nearly silent on this issue. Community outreach interventions have shown promise in reducing suicide risk among depressed older adults via telephone support (DeLeo et al. 2002) and a multicomponent depression care program (Oyama et al. 2005); however, the positive findings of these quasi-experimental studies were largely restricted to older women (Duberstein et al. 2011). Interventions are needed targeting psychological processes causally associated with the onset or exacerbation of suicide risk among older men.

We recently received project funding from Movember Canada, the Canadian branch of the worldwide organization dedicated to raising awareness about men's health problems and raising funds to support men's health research, to implement, finalize, disseminate, and evaluate Meaning-Centered Men's Groups for men facing retirement. Eligible participants for this community-outreach intervention study will include soon-to-be- or newly retired men, 60 years of age or older, who may be vulnerable to the onset of depression and suicide risk by virtue of low perceived Meaning in Life (MIL), a psychological resiliency factor shown to be protective against the presence, intensity, onset, and exacerbation of late-life suicide ideation (Heisel 2009; Heisel and Flett 2006, 2007, 2008, in press). Participants must be cognitively intact, and cannot meet diagnostic criteria for an active mental disorder or endorse severe suicide ideation, and, consistent with the focus of this preventive intervention study, must not be receiving additional forms of psychotherapy.

Participants will be recruited into a 12-session, 90-min, once-weekly session of a meaning-centered men's group. Our intervention will be delivered in community settings in order to enhance participant comfort and access to services, and advertised as a "men's group dealing with adjustment to retirement" rather than a "therapy group" in order to encourage the participation of older men who might be reluctant to seek formal mental health services. Group sessions will focus on intrapersonal and interpersonal transitions associated with retirement in the context of discussions about the meaning of work, retirement, leisure, relationships, and generativity. We have chosen a group format given associated cost and health benefits (Katz et al. 2002; Pinquart et al. 2007), and the advantages of social discourse among men facing a common life transition in enhancing camaraderie and social support (Burke et al. 2010; Gottlieb 2000; Reddin and Sonn 2003), which may further help increase MIL (Krause 2007) and mitigate suicide risk (Purcell et al. 2012; Rowe et al. 2006). A group format can also facilitate healthy self-transcendence. As group members attend to the problems and challenges of fellow participants and provide them with support and assistance, they may focus less on their own difficulties and engage more meaningfully and productively in helping others; such a process of "dereflection" is an important element in effective meaning-centered intervention (Lukas and Zwang-Hirsch 2002).

Middle-age and older men do not typically seek mental healthcare when depressed or suicidal, creating barriers to life-sustaining care (DeLeo 2002). Creative outreach approaches are thus needed that engage vulnerable men in interventions that are empowering, respectful, and delivered in a format that they find acceptable. We have thus developed a multicomponent strategy for participant recruitment. We will convene a "Men's Retirement and Leisure Show," to be hosted by a prominent figure in local media with presentations by a retired male sports, business, healthcare, and/or political figure, who will share personal stories of negotiating the transition to retirement, and project investigators who will give a recruitment presentation. Additional participants will be recruited as needed from health, recreation, and information fairs, local community centers and exercise/wellness facilities and arenas, stores, libraries, and coffee shops, advertisements in local newspapers and newsletters, and by way of outreach through the local Chamber of Commerce, service clubs, Economic Development Council, and financial planners.

This study is predicated on the premise that men low in recognition of MIL and facing retirement may be primed to develop depression and suicide ideation, and that intervening to enhance opportunities to find MIL may promote mental health and well-being and mitigate the onset of depression and risk for suicide. Existential interventions," may be especially relevant for older adults facing important life transitions such as retirement, due to the increasing tendency for self-reflection, increasing capacity for spirituality, and greater potential perception of MIL with age (Guttmann 2008; Hicks et al. 2012; Kimble 2000; Lukas 1986; Neugarten 1996). The proposed study has its origins in our clinical, research, and academic experience in aging and mental health, suicide prevention, and logotherapy. Our focus on MIL is consonant with a growing base of empirical evidence of its fundamental importance in preventing psychopathology and in fomenting health and well-being.

Research findings have indicated positive associations between MIL and adaptive health-related variables including purpose in life (PIL), psychological well-being,," self-transcendence, resiliency, optimism, self-esteem, pain management, and perceived social support, and negative associations between MIL and stress, anxiety, alcoholism, depression, hopelessness, and suicide ideation (Braam et al. 2006; Garcia Pintos 1988; Heisel 2009; Heisel and Flett 2008, in press; Krause 2003, 2009; Krause and Shaw 2003; Reker 1997; Zika and Chamberlain 1992). MIL and PIL have been shown to be associated with longevity; this association may be mediated by physical health and well-being, suggesting merit in incorporating consideration of health challenges and transitions into psychological interventions with older adults (Boyle et al. 2009; Krause 2009; O'Connor and Vallerand 1998). MIL might engender resiliency by encouraging meaningful activity and social interaction, building emotional reserves to mitigate the negative impact of physical, emotional, interpersonal, and situational challenges.

Our group intervention is consistent with Frankl's meaning-centered psychotherapy (Frankl 1971, 1985, 1988), an approach ideally suited to helping enhance resiliency to suicide risk in the context of loss, transition, and suffering. Frankl (1971) theorized that the pursuit of meaning, conceptualized as profound existential significance or purpose, is central to human motivation, and that psychopathology results partly from an existential dilemma typified by a lack of perception of meaning in life situations, and a consequent experience of emptiness or "existential vacuum." The existential vacuum serves as a warning that something is amiss in one's life and ideally promotes meaningful self-examination; ignoring it can lead to frantic efforts to fill the void with risk-taking and other negative health behavior, potentially leading to psychological despair, depression, and suicidality. He advised cultivating multiple sources of MIL to prevent despair associated with loss of a single source of meaning, including *Creative* pursuits, meaningful *Experiences*, healthy *Attitudes* toward both challenges and success, and *Ultimate* questions of one's purpose in life (Frankl 1988). The Experienced Meaning in Life Scale (EMIL; Heisel 2009), a primary outcome measure in this study, was developed to assess these constructs among older adults. Frankl's work with unemployed youth in post-war Vienna supported his theory, helping them find unpaid volunteer activities enhanced their feelings of usefulness and engendered recognition of MIL (Frankl 1997). Encouraging men facing retirement to seek and enhance MIL in their activities, relationships, attitudes, and beliefs may thus similarly enhance well-being and reduce risk for negative health outcomes, including depression and suicidality (Frankl 1992).

Research findings have supported the thesis that meaning-centered interventions can enhance psychological well-being, enhance hope among retirees, and enhance MIL, and reduce the risk to die among individuals with advanced cancer. Breitbart and colleagues (2010) found that their Meaning-Centered Group Psychotherapy significantly enhanced MIL and reduced the wish to hasten death in terminally ill older adults, and proved more efficacious than supportive group therapy. Although not grounded in existential theory, two quasi-experimental intervention studies, of integrated reminiscence and narrative therapies for depressed older adults (Bohlmeijer et al. 2008) and a cognitive-behavioral group designed to train early retirees to set, plan, and pursue meaningful goals (Lapierre et al. 2007), showed post-treatment increases in psychological well-being, yet no between-group increases in MIL or PIL. We recently demonstrated significant reduction in suicide ideation and depressive symptoms and significant improvement in MIL and psychological well-being variables among participants in a focused trial of Interpersonal Psychotherapy adapted for older adults at-risk for suicide incorporating meaning-focused discourse (Heisel et al. 2009; in press). These findings together suggest that developmentally relevant psychological interventions can enhance well-being and decrease psychopathology in later life, and yet suggest benefit in theoretically grounded existential interventions when aiming to enhance MIL. Encouraging men facing retirement to seek and enhance MIL in their activities, relationships, attitudes, and beliefs may thus help enhance well-being and reduce risk for negative health outcomes, including depression, hopelessness, and suicide ideation.

Our iterative, 3-year, multistage preventive intervention study will initially involve the implementation, refinement, and evaluation of Meaning-Centered Men's Groups in London, Ontario, Canada, and will be followed by the delivery of one group each in the Canadian provinces of Alberta and British Columbia. We will deliver an initial group intervention in order to refine, finalize, and begin evaluating our intervention, drawing heavily on participant feedback and input and the observations of the group facilitators. We will then conduct a second course of our group, aiming to evaluate pre- to post-intervention reduction in the presence and severity of depressive symptoms, hopelessness, and suicide ideation, and improvement in MIL, social support, and life satisfaction. A nonrandomized controlled trial will follow, comparing outcomes for Meaning-Centered Men's Group participants with those of participants in a current events discussion group. Knowledge translation will involve training group facilitators to deliver Meaning-Centered Men's Groups in sites outside Ontario, delivering training workshops to providers working with men facing retirement, and dissemination of study updates and empirical findings to researchers, policy personnel, consumers, and service providers via list serves, newsletters, best practice websites, presentations at conferences, knowledge exchanges, information fairs, and journal publications. We also plan to publish our study intervention manual.

This project responds to a critical need to translate research findings on healthy aging into innovative interventions for potentially vulnerable groups. Our objective is to evaluate whether Meaning-Centered Men's Groups are cost-effective, tolerable, acceptable, and effective at enhancing MIL, mental health, and well-being, and mitigating the onset or exacerbation of depression and suicide ideation. Findings are expected to have relevance for program and policy development regarding outreach interventions for community-residing older adults, and may have commercial applications in terms of enhancing health and well-being among older workers and forming the basis for interventions to enhance employee post-retirement health and well-being. Future applications of this intervention could include adaptations for men with chronic health conditions, heightened risk for suicide, Internet-based groups for socially—or geographically—isolated men, and may include groups for women struggling in the face of retirement or other transitions.

References

Bamia, C., Trichopoulou, A., & Trichopoulos, D. (2008). Age at retirement and mortality in a general population sample: The Greek EPIC Study. *American Journal of Epidemiology, 167*, 561–569.

Bohlmeijer, E. T., Westerhof, G. J., & Emmerik-de Jong, M. (2008). The effects of integrative reminiscence on meaning in life: Results of a quasi-experimental study. *Aging & Mental Health, 12*, 639–646.

Boyle, P. A., Barnes, L. L., Buchman, A. S., & Bennett, D. A. (2009). Purpose in life is associated with mortality among community-dwelling older persons. *Psychosomatic Medicine, 71*, 574–579.

Braam, A. W., Bramsen, I., van Tilburg, T. G., van der Ploeg, H. M., & Deeg, D. J. H. (2006). Cosmic transcendence and framework of meaning in life: Patterns among older adults in the Netherlands. *Journal of Gerontology: Social Sciences, 61B*, S121–S128.

Brand, J. E., Levy, B. R., & Gallo, W. T. (2008). Effects of layoffs and plant closings on subsequent depression among older workers. *Research on Aging, 30*, 701–721.

Breitbart, W., Rosenfeld, B., Gibson, C., et al. (2010). Meaning-centered group psychotherapy for patients with advanced cancer: A pilot randomized controlled trial. *Psychooncology, 19*, 21–28.

Brockman, H., Müller, R., & Helmert, U. (2009). Time to retire - time to die? A prospective cohort study of the effects of early retirement on long-term survival. *Social Science & Medicine, 69*, 160–164.

Burke, C. K., Maton, K. I., Mankowski, E. S., & Anderson, C. (2010). Healing men and community: Predictors of outcome in a men's initiatory and support organization. *American Journal of Community Psychology, 45*, 186–200.

Butterworth, P., Gill, S. C., Rodgers, B., et al. (2006). Retirement and mental health: Analysis of the Australian national survey of mental health and well-being. *Social Science & Medicine, 62*, 1179–1191.

Canadian Coalition for Seniors' Mental Health. (2006). *National guidelines for seniors' mental health: The assessment of suicide risk and prevention of suicide*. Toronto: Canadian Coalition for Seniors' Mental Health.

Canadian Institute for Health Information. (2011). *National Health Expenditure Trends, 1975 to 2011*. Ottawa, ON: Canadian Institute for Health Information.

Canetto, S. S., & Lester, D. (1998). Gender, culture, and suicidal behavior. *Transcultural Psychiatry, 35*, 163–190.

Centers for Disease Control and Prevention, National Center for Injury Prevention and Control. *WISQARS (Web-based Injury Statistics Query and Reporting System) Fatal Injury Reports National and Regional, 1999-2009. Data file*. Retrieved from http://webappa.cdc.gov/sasweb/ncipc/mortrate10_us.html.

Cohen, J. E. (2003). Human population: The next half century. *Science, 302*, 1172–1175.
DeLeo, D. (2002). Struggling against suicide: The need for an integrative approach. *Crisis, 23*, 23–31.
DeLeo, D., Dello Buono, M., & Dwyer, J. (2002). Suicide among the elderly: The long-term impact of a telephone support and assessment intervention in northern Italy. *British Journal of Psychiatry, 181*, 226–229.
Duberstein, P. R., Heisel, M. J., & Conwell, Y. (2011). Suicide in older adults. In M. E. Agronin & G. Maletta (Eds.), *Principles and practice of geriatric psychiatry* (2nd ed.). Philadelphia, PA: Lippincott Williams & Wilkins.
Frankl, V. E. (1971). *The doctor and the soul: From psychotherapy to logotherapy (trans. R. Winston)*. New York, NY: Bantam.
Frankl, V. E. (1985). *Man's search for meaning*. New York, NY: Washington Square Press. Originally published 1946.
Frankl, V. E. (1988). *The will to meaning: Foundations and applications of Logotherapy*. New York, NY: Penguin.
Frankl, V. E. (1992). Meaning in industrial society. *The International Forum for Logotherapy, 15*, 66–70.
Frankl, V. E. (1997). *Recollections: An autobiography*. New York, NY: Plenum Press.
Garcia Pintos, C. C. (1988). Depression and the will to meaning: A comparison of the GDS and PIL in an Argentine population. *Clinical Gerontologist, 7*, 3–9.
Gill, S. C., Butterworth, P., Rodgers, B., et al. (2006). Mental health and the timing of men's retirement. *Social Psychiatry and Psychiatric Epidemiology, 41*, 515–522.
Gottlieb, B. H. (2000). Self-help, mutual aid, and support groups among older adults. *Canadian Journal of Aging, 19*, 58–74.
Guttmann, D. (2008). *Finding meaning in life, at midlife and beyond: Wisdom and spirit from Logotherapy*. Westport, CT: Praeger Publishers.
Heisel, M. J. (2009). Assessing experienced meaning in life among older adults: The development and initial validation of the EMIL. *International Psychogeriatrics, 21*, S172–S173.
Heisel, M. J., & Duberstein, P. R. (2005). Suicide prevention in older adults. *Clinical Psychology: Science and Practice, 12*, 242–259.
Heisel, M. J., Duberstein, P. R., Talbot, N. L., King, D. A., & Tu, X. M. (2009). Adapting interpersonal psychotherapy for older adults at risk for suicide: Preliminary findings. *Professional Psychology: Research and Practice, 40*, 156–164.
Heisel, M. J., & Flett, G. L. (2006). The development and initial validation of the Geriatric Suicide Ideation Scale. *The American Journal of Geriatric Psychiatry, 14*, 742–751.
Heisel, M. J., & Flett, G. L. (2007). Meaning in life and resilience to suicidal thoughts among older adults. In P. T. P. Wong, L. C. J. Wong, M. McDonald, & D. Klaassen (Eds.), *The positive psychology of meaning and spirituality* (pp. 183–196). Abbotsford, BC: INPM Press.
Heisel, M. J., & Flett, G. L. (2008). Psychological resilience to suicide ideation among older adults. *Clinical Gerontology, 31*, 51–70.
Heisel, M. J., & Flett, G. L. (in press). Do meaning in life and purpose in life protect against suicide ideation among community-residing older adults? In Batthyany & P. Russo-Netzer (Eds.), *Meaning in existential and positive psychology*. New York, NY: Springer.
Heisel, M. J., Talbot, N. L., King, D. A., Tu, X. M., & Duberstein, P. R. (in press). Adapting interpersonal psychotherapy for older adults at risk for suicide. *The American Journal of Geriatric Psychiatry*.
Hicks, J. A., Trent, J., Davis, W. E., & King, L. A. (2012). Positive affect, meaning in life, and future time perspective: An application of socioemotional selectivity theory. *Psychology and Aging, 27*, 181–189.
Karpansalo, M., Kauhanen, J., Lakka, T. A., et al. (2005). Depression and early retirement: Prospective population based study in middle-aged men. *Journal of Epidemiology and Community Health, 59*, 70–74.
Katz, D., Kappie, T. M., Wu, D., et al. (2002). Sociodemographic characteristics and health related quality of life in men attending prostate cancer support groups. *The Journal of Urology, 168*, 2092–2096.

Kimble, M. A. (2000). *Viktor Frankl's contribution to spirituality and aging*. Binghamton, NY: The Haworth Pastoral Press.
Krause, N. (2003). Religious meaning and subjective well-being in late life. *Journal of Gerontology: Social Science, 58B*, S160–S170.
Krause, N. (2007). Longitudinal study of social support and meaning in life. *Psychology and Aging, 22*, 459–469.
Krause, N. (2009). Meaning in life and mortality. *Journal of Gerontology: Social Sciences, 64B*, 517–527.
Krause, N., & Shaw, B. A. (2003). Role-specific control, personal meaning, and health in late life. *Research on Aging, 25*, 559–586.
Krug, E. G., Dahlberg, L. L., Mercy, J. A., Zwi, A. B., & Lozano, R. (Eds.). (2002). *World report on violence and health*. Geneva: World Health Organization.
Lapierre, S., Dubé, M., Bouffard, L., & Alain, M. (2007). Addressing suicidal ideations through the realization of meaningful personal goals. *Crisis, 28*, 16–25.
Lapierre, S., Erlangsen, A., Waern, M., et al. (2011). A systematic review of elderly suicide prevention programs. *Crisis, 32*, 88–98.
Links, P. S., Heisel, M. J., & Quastel, A. (2005). Is suicide ideation a surrogate endpoint for geriatric suicide? *Suicide and Life-Threatening Behavior, 35*, 193–205.
Lukas, E. (1986). *Meaning in suffering: Comfort in crisis through Logotherapy*. Berkeley, CA: Institute of Logotherapy Press. Trans. J.B. Fabry.
Lukas, E., & Zwang-Hirsch, B. (2002). Logotherapy (Chapter 14). In R. F. Massey & S. D. Massey (Eds.), *Comprehensive handbook of psychotherapy. Volume 3: Interpersonal/humanistic/existential*. Hoboken, NJ: Wiley. Series Editor: F.W. Kaslow.
Mościcki, E. K. (1996). Epidemiology of suicide. In J. L. Pearson & Y. Conwell (Eds.), *Suicide and aging: International perspectives* (pp. 3–14). New York, NY: Springer.
Neugarten, B. L. (1996). *The meanings of age: Selected papers of Bernice L. Neugarten*. Chicago, IL: University of Chicago Press.
Nordenmark, M., & Stattin, M. (2009). Psychosocial wellbeing and reasons for retirement in Sweden. *Aging & Society, 29*, 413–430.
O'Connor, B. P., & Vallerand, R. J. (1998). Psychological adjustment variables as predictors of mortality among nursing home residents. *Psychology and Aging, 13*, 368–374.
Oyama, H., Watanabe, N., Ono, Y., et al. (2005). Community-based suicide prevention through group activity for the elderly successfully reduced the high suicide rate for females. *Psychiatry and Clinical Neurosciences, 59*, 337–344.
Perreira, K. M., & Sloan, F. A. (2002). Excess alcohol consumption and health outcomes: A 6-year follow-up of men over age 50 from the health and retirement study. *Addiction, 97*, 301–310.
Pinquart, M., Duberstein, P. R., & Lyness, J. M. (2007). Effects of psychotherapy and other behavioral interventions on clinically depressed older adults: A meta-analysis. *Aging & Mental Health, 11*, 645–657.
Pinquart, M., & Schindler, I. (2007). Changes in life satisfaction in the transition to retirement: A latent-class approach. *Psychology and Aging, 22*, 442–455.
Purcell, B., Heisel, M. J., Speice, J., et al. (2012). Family connectedness moderates the association between living alone and suicide ideation in a clinical sample of adults 50 years and older. *The American Journal of Geriatric Psychiatry, 20*, 717–723.
Qin, P., Agerbo, E., & Mortensen, P. B. (2003). Suicide risk in relation to socioeconomic, demographic, psychiatric, and familial factors: A national register-based study of all suicides in Denmark, 1981-1997. *The American Journal of Psychiatry, 160*, 765–772.
Reddin, J. A., & Sonn, C. C. (2003). Masculinity, social support, and sense of community: The men's group experience in Western Australia. *Journal of Men's Studies, 11*, 207–223.
Reker, G. T. (1997). Personal meaning, optimism, and choice: Existential predictors of depression in community and institutional elderly. *The Gerontologist, 37*, 709–716.
Rowe, J. L., Conwell, Y., Schulberg, H. C., et al. (2006). Social support and suicidal ideation in older adults using home healthcare services. *American Journal of Geriatric Psychiatry, 14*, 758–766.

Schellenberg, G., & Silver, C. (2004). You can't always get what you want: Retirement preferences and experiences. *Canadian Social Trends, 75*, 2–7.
Schneider, B., Grebner, K., Schnabel, A., et al. (2011). Impact of employment status and work-related factors on risk of completed suicide: A case-control psychological autopsy study. *Psychiatry Research, 190*, 265–270.
Statistics Canada. (2010). *Population projections for Canada, provinces, and territories: 2009-2036. Catalogue no. 91-520-X (ISBN: 0-660-19525-9)*. Ottawa: Statistics Canada.
Statistics Canada. (2014). *CANSIM, table 102-0551:Deaths and mortality rate, by selected grouped causes, age and sex, Canada*. Retrieved from http://www.statcan.gc.ca/tables-tableaux/sum-som/l01/cst01/hlth66a-eng.htm.
United States Census Bureau. (2003). *National population projections*. Retrieved from http://www.census.gov/prod/2001pubs/c2kbr01-10.pdf
Weingarten, H. R. (1988). Late life divorce and the life review. *Journal of Gerontological Social Work, 12*, 83–97.
Westerlund, H., Kivimaki, M., Singh-Manoux, A., et al. (2009). Self-rated health before and after retirement in France (GAZEL): A cohort study. *Lancet, 374*, 1889–1896.
Yen, Y. C., Yang, M. J., Yang, M. S., et al. (2005). Suicidal ideation and associated factors among community-dwelling elders in Taiwan. *Psychiatry and Clinical Neurosciences, 59*, 365–371.
Zika, S., & Chamberlain, K. (1992). On the relation between meaning in life and psychological well-being. *British Journal of Psychology, 83*, 133–145.

Amelioration of Obsessive-Compulsive Disorder Using Paradoxical Intention

Marshall H. Lewis

Introduction

Paradoxical intention is a technique of logotherapy in which the patient is encouraged to do or to wish that which is feared (Frankl 1969). It has long been recognized as a brief form of therapy for those suffering from specific symptoms of Obsessive-Compulsive Disorder. It has also been recognized that paradoxical intention can be combined with other forms of therapy to achieve long-lasting clinical results in a short amount of time (Frankl 1969). Moreover, a specific manner of presenting paradoxical intention has been developed by Frankl to apply to those experiencing intrusive thoughts of blasphemy during religious practices (Frankl 1955).

The evidence base for paradoxical intention is sound. The most recent review of outcome studies in paradoxical intention reveals that the procedure yielded positive results in all but one of 19 published articles. No adverse effects are reported in any study. The review includes articles on paradoxical intention published between 1966 and 2009. The number of clients treated per study range from 5 to 88 with treatment plans that range from 1 to 17 weeks of treatment. The lone study that did not produce a positive finding used paradoxical intention to treat insomnia and did not find the procedure more effective than placebo. The authors of that article note with surprise, however, the relative effectiveness of the placebo condition (Fabry 2010).

An additional review of the literature from the American Psychological Association (APA) PsycINFO database as compiled by Batthyány and Guttmann (2006) reveals 37 published studies on paradoxical intentional. Of these 37 studies, 25 report clinical outcomes. Other types of studies involve technical aspects of the

M.H. Lewis (✉)
LogoTalk, P. O. Box 632, Ulysses, KS 67880, USA
e-mail: logotalk@pld.com

A. Batthyány (ed.), *Logotherapy and Existential Analysis*, Logotherapy and Existential Analysis: Proceedings of the Viktor Frankl Institute Vienna 1,
DOI 10.1007/978-3-319-29424-7_16

procedure itself, such as varying the ways in which paradoxical intention instructions may be given, or are of a theoretical nature, or are themselves reviews of previous literature. Of the 25 studies that report clinical outcomes, 21 studies show clinical efficacy for the procedure while four produce inconclusive results.

Fabry (2010) and Batthyány (2012) note that paradoxical intention has been incorporated into a variety of psychotherapeutic models including cognitive behavior therapy. Consequently, it has been tested and validated outside of the field of logotherapy (Batthyány 2012). A helpful overview is provided by Ascher (2005). The APA recognizes cognitive therapy as an evidence-based treatment for Obsessive-Compulsive Disorder that "aims to help the person identify, challenge, and modify… dysfunctional ideas." Such therapy is identified by the APA as having strong research support (APA 2011).

Method of Treatment

The patient is diagnosed with Obsessive-Compulsive Disorder using DSM-IV-TR criteria (APA 2000) through two clinical interviews—one by a psychiatrist and the other by a master-level psychotherapist. The patient's symptoms are exclusively obsessions; compulsive behaviors are absent. The patient began thinking of obscene words during both personal and corporate prayer along with unbidden mental images of sexual acts. This meets DSM-IV-TR criterion A, namely, "recurrent and persistent thoughts, impulses, or images that are experienced… as intrusive and inappropriate and that cause marked anxiety or distress" (APA 2000, 462). The patient has good insight and, fulfilling criterion B, realizes that the intrusive thoughts are "excessive or unreasonable" (APA 2000, 462). Because of social withdrawal, these thoughts meet criterion C, cause "marked distress," and interfere with the patient's "usual social activities or relationships" (APA 2000, 463). Additional assessment demonstrates that no other mental disorder is present, no general medical condition is present, and no relevant psychoactive substances are being ingested (see APA 2000). The patient received an initial score of 58 on the DSM-IV-TR "Global Assessment of Functioning" (GAF) Scale reflecting a moderate degree of impairment in social functioning. The GAF Scale is a 100-point measure of psychological, social, and occupational functioning included in the DSM-IV-TR system of diagnosis (APA 2000). Other outcome measures were not in use in the clinic at the time.

Paradoxical intention emerges as the treatment of choice during a multidisciplinary clinical staffing. The treatment team familiar with the patient's history recognizes that other approaches to elicit responses incompatible with anxiety have produced only temporary results with this patient. Moreover, the patient reports increased anxiety at the thought of stimulus exposure, such as in exposure and response prevention, rending the procedure unacceptable to the patient. The patient provides informed consent for the procedure given by Frankl, because it describes a procedure specific to intrusive thoughts experienced as blasphemous and because the patient has interest in attempting a different approach. Protected health information has been altered or removed in accordance with ethical principles on the use of case material (APA 2000).

The patient received three, 1-h sessions of paradoxical intention (Frankl 1955, 2004). In the first session, the patient was told of a similar case (Frankl 2004) and this especially fascinated the patient. Following Frankl's special procedure on dealing with obsessive blasphemy (Frankl 1955), the patient was engaged in dialogue such that the patient endorsed the proposition that God would know the difference between true blasphemy (blasphemy deriving from the inner spirit) and blasphemous thoughts resulting from a psychiatric disorder. The patient was asked to describe the thoughts that disturbed the patient after the patient agreed that the therapy office was a protected space in which the thoughts could be clinically examined without fear of the thoughts being defined as blasphemous. Based on the patient's description of the thoughts, the patient and therapist then worked together to devise some humorously blasphemous and risqué thoughts involving the saints meeting one another for sexual liaisons that the patient could paradoxically will.

In the second session the patient reported that the paradoxical thoughts devised in the first session had not been used. Symptoms were unchanged and the patient's GAF score remained stable at 58. Treatment was then supplemented with relaxation techniques based on Wolpe (1969). Frankl reports that combining paradoxical intention with relaxation has been successful (Frankl 1969, 2004); this is further documented in Lazarus (1972). The therapist demonstrated relaxation techniques to the patient and then verbally guided the patient through in vivo practice of the techniques. The patient was instructed to practice the relaxation techniques daily prior to willfully thinking of the risqué thoughts devised in the first session. In the third session the patient reported use of both relaxation and paradoxical intention as suggested. The symptoms had completely remitted per the patient report. The patient was engaging in personal and corporate prayer, as before, and interacting socially without distress. The patient received a GAF score of 71 reflecting transient and expected reactions to psychosocial stressors.

Results and Discussion

A follow-up appointment was given to the patient six weeks after the third session. The patient was found to remain in remission at that time with no intrusive blasphemous thoughts and no impairment in social or occupational functioning. The GAF score remained unchanged at 71.

Frankl explains that paradoxical intention is effective by drawing upon the uniquely human ability to distance oneself from one's symptoms. Moreover, Frankl asserts that this ability is inherent in humor (Frankl 1955). Hutzell (1990) notes that humor in paradoxical intention requires the patient to achieve a perspective that puts distance between the patient and the symptom. This allows the patient to realize that other aspects of life have greater significance than the symptom, leading to symptom reduction. In other words, the processes of thought identification, challenge, and modification recognized by the APA (2011) as clinically effective are all included in the technique.

This case study demonstrates the effectiveness of paradoxical intention in a contemporary outpatient community mental health center. Results are similar to those reported by Frankl and others in that symptoms are reduced or eliminated with a small number of sessions and that symptoms remain in remission for an extended period of time after treatment. Moreover, the procedure includes all of the general elements of a recognized evidence-based treatment with which it has been closely associated for more than two decades.

References

American Psychiatric Association. (2000). *Diagnostic and statistical manual of mental disorders (4th edition, text revision)*. Washington, DC: American Psychiatric Association.

American Psychological Association. (2011). *Cognitive therapy for obsessive-compulsive disorder*. Retrieved Oct 3, 2011, from http://www.div12.org/PsychologicalTreatments/treatments/ocd_cognitive.html.

Ascher, L. M. (2005). Paradoxical intention and related techniques. In A. Freeman, S. H. Felgoise, C. Nezu, A. M. Nezu, & M. A. Reinecke (Eds.), *Encyclopedia of cognitive behavior therapy*. New York, NY: Springer-Verlag.

Batthyány, A. (2012). New afterword to man's search for ultimate meaning. In V. E. Frankl (Ed.), *Man's search for ultimate meaning*. London: Rider. Paperback Edition.

Batthyány, A., Guttman, D., & In collaboration with PsycINFO, a department of the American Psychological Association. (1887–present, APA). (2006). *Empirical research on logotherapy and meaning-oriented psychotherapy: An annotated bibliography*. Phoenix: Zeig, Tucker and Theisen, Inc.

Fabry, D. D. S. (2010). Evidence base for paradoxical intention: Reviewing clinical outcome studies. *The International Forum for Logotherapy, 33*, 21–29.

Frankl, V. E. (1955). *The doctor and the soul: From psychotherapy to logotherapy*. New York: Vintage Books. Editon years 1965, 1980, 1986; Transl. R. and C. Winston.

Frankl, V. E. (1969). *The will to meaning*. New York, NY: World Publishing.

Frankl, V. E. (2004). *On the theory and therapy of mental disorders*. New York, NY: Brunner-Routledge. Transl. J. M. Dubois.

Hutzell, R. R. (1990). An introduction to logotherapy. In P. A. Keller & S. R. Heyman (Eds.), *Innovations in clinical practice: A source book* (9th ed., pp. 145–152). Sarasota: Professional Resource Exchange.

Lazarus, A. (1972). *Clinical behavior therapy*. New York, NY: Brunner-Mazel Publishers.

Wolpe, J. (1969). *The practice of behavioral therapy*. New York, NY: Pergamon Press.

Family Adaptation in Families with Children with Autism Spectrum Disorder (ASD)

Maria Ángeles Noblejas, Pilar Maseda, Isabel Pérez, and Pilar Pozo

Introduction

Families with a child diagnosed with an autistic spectrum disorder (ASD) are known to be exposed to stress; (Bristol 1984, 1987; Honey et al. 2005; Konstantareas and Papageorgiou 2006; Pozo et al. 2006; Sivberg 2002a). Parents often report more parenting stress than either parents of children without disabilities or parents of children with other disabilities such as Down's syndrome (e.g., Schieve et al. 2007). Mothers and fathers of children with ASD face great challenges and demands associated with the uneven developmental progress of their child and are at increased risk of developing psychological problems (Hastings 2003; Hastings et al. 2005a, b).

However, family care involving children with disabilities is not necessarily a negative experience (Floyd et al 1996; Singer and Irvin 1989). It has become apparent that family outcomes of stress are the result of multiple interacting factors

M.Á. Noblejas (✉)
Asociación Española de Logoterapia, Equipo Específico de Alteraciones Graves de Desarrollo, Comunidad de Madrid, C/Ribadavia 10, 6°J, 28029 Madrid, Spain
e-mail: ma_aeslo@yahoo.es

P. Maseda
C.E.S. Don Bosco, Universidad Complutense de Madrid,
Calle de María Auxiliadora, 9, 28040 Madrid, Spain

I. Pérez
Colegio Concertado de Educación Especial CEPRI,
CEPRI (Asociación para la investigación y el estudio de la deficiencia mental),
Dirección: c/San Sebastián n° 25, 28220 Majadahonda, Madrid, Spain

P. Pozo
Facultad de Psicología, Universidad Nacional de Educación a Distancia,
Juan del Rosal, n° 10 (Ciudad Universitaria), 28040 Madrid, Spain
e-mail: ppozo@bec.uned.es

A. Batthyány (ed.), *Logotherapy and Existential Analysis*, Logotherapy and Existential Analysis: Proceedings of the Viktor Frankl Institute Vienna 1,
DOI 10.1007/978-3-319-29424-7_17

(McCubbin and Patterson 1983; Singer and Irvin 1989). One consistent framework that has been used to understand family adjustment to stressors associated with having a child with)ASD is the double ABCX model (McCubbin and Patterson 1983). It was derived from the classic ABCX model of Hill (1949). The expanded model added the factor of time to Hill's original model, extending it to also comprise a post-crisis adjustment. In the double ABCX model, the stressor element (aA) consists of the severity of the initial stressor, the pileup of demands, and additional life stressors. The model also contains mediating variables: existing and expanding family resources applied by families in order to face and manage demands and needs (bB), and the grasp and meaning the family finds in their situation (cC). Coping is a bridging concept in the model and is understood as an attempt to restore balance in family functioning (BC). Family crisis and post-crisis adaptation (xX) is the outcome factor. The resulting adaptation is seen as a continuum of outcomes ranging from balanced "bonadaptation" to negative maladaptation, which is characterized by a continuous imbalance in family functioning.

One line of research has focused on causal modeling and the sorting of variables, whereas other studies have concentrated on the predictive capacity of the elements of the model. Some of them have dealt specifically with autism (e.g., Bristol 1984, 1987), Asperger Syndrome (e.g., Pakenham et al. 2005) or ASD (e.g., Konstantareas and Papageorgiou 2006; Pozo et al. 2006). These studies showed that the double ABCX model was an effective way of predicting adjustment and pointing out specific predictable measures of family adaptation. In this way, Bristol's study (1987) demonstrated that the severity of the child's disability contributed significantly to prediction of adaptation, but in some instances, the direction of effect was unexpected. Other family stressors and perceptions of social support adequacy were related to better maternal adjustment. The mother's subjective definition of the child's disability was one of the best predictors of both her parenting quality and marital adjustment and her level of depressive symptoms. Likewise the research of Pakenham et al. (2005) supported that better maternal adjustment was related to higher levels of qualitative social support and emotional coping, and lower levels of child behavioral problems, pileup of demands, stress appraisals, and passive avoidance coping. Unexpectedly, quantitative social support and problem-focused coping were unrelated to adjustment. On the same line, Pozo et al. (2006) analyzed maternal stress in mothers of children wit ASD and showed that the empirical model fitted the double ABCX model. The authors also obtained a direct and positive relationship between stressors and stress. Besides, social support and perception of stress—in their study, sense of coherence—had a direct and negative influence on stress and functioned as modulating variables.

In the last few years there has been an increasing body of research literature related to the BC and cC variables that demonstrates the relevance of coping strategies and grasp of the situation as mediating variables of family adjustment in parents with children with ASD. Vermeulen (1997) pointed out the influence that attributions, cognitive dissonance, personal appraisal and beliefs, hopes, etc. had on the coping with stress in families with children with pervasive developmental disorders. Similarly, findings of Dale et al. (2006) suggested that participating mothers made a diverse and complex range of attributions that were consistent with Weiner's dimensions of locus of cause, stability, and controllability. The nature of their attributions reflected particular difficulties associated with their child's diagnosis of ASD, such as uncertainties regarding cause and prognosis.

Hastings et al. (2005a, b) found connections between coping strategies and parental stress and mental health in parents of children with autism. They showed that active avoidance coping for both mothers and fathers was associated with more stress, more anxiety and symptoms of depression. Religious/denial coping was also associated with depression in mothers and both depression and anxiety in fathers. On the other hand, Sivberg's (2002a, b) studies dealt with variables such as meaning in life and sense of coherence to evaluate their influence on family relations and parental attitudes towards their child with autism (loving care, worry, stress, and guilty feelings).

Meaning in life is a concept developed in the framework of a particular existential therapy—logotherapy (Frankl 1946/1986). This construct refers to the human need to find meaning and purpose in personal existence. The "will to meaning" is a motivational resource that encourages and helps persons to face and overcome adverse situations. Meaning in life can be found in all life experiences. An adverse experience stands as a challenge to find meaning. The life-meaning construct (Noblejas 2009) influenced psychological models of stress and coping (Zika and Chamberlain 1992). Relatively stable patterns of commitment affect the way situational events are appraised in terms of their possible impact on wellbeing, as well as influencing the way these events are managed. Life-encounters, which challenge important commitments, are likely to be appraised as a threat, increasing the person's vulnerability to stress. However, this vulnerability may also serve a positive function by driving a person towards an action, which alleviates the threat, and thus secures coping. Patterns of commitment are viewed as necessary, since their absence would lead to a pervasive state of meaninglessness.

On the other hand, the construct of hardiness is conceptualized as a buffer or mediating factor in mitigating the effects of stressors and demands. Hardiness is characterized by a sense of control over the outcomes of life events and hardships.

The growing number of studies that include cognitive-existential variables has been reflected in another descriptive works. The study directed by Belinchón (2001) noticed the relevance for parents of both their relational expectations and their experiences with a child with ASD and personal values and the question of meaning in life with their child.

Family adaptation has been measured in different ways. Not many studies have applied family-level measures (e.g., quality of parenting, marital satisfaction, family functioning) as dependent variables (Bristol 1987; Higgins et al. 2005). In general, family adaptation has been measured through psychosomatic symptoms such as anxiety or depression or through stress experienced by parents.

The Double ABCX Model treats the family as a unit, but most variables have been typically operationalized and measured on an individual basis. This has made it possible to assess differences in adaptation between mothers and fathers. Differences have been reported in the most significant predictors of parenting stress. Hastings et al. (2005a; b) found gender differences in several coping strategies in families with children with autism. Mothers reported more frequent use of active avoidance and problem-focused coping than fathers. Hastings et al. (2005a; b) informed about more depression symptoms and higher levels of positive perception of the child's impact on the family in mothers. Neil's results (2002) indicated that females used social diversion coping more than males.

The aim of the present study was to examine relations between family adaptation (evaluated as family satisfaction and personal depression) and the double ABCX predictors looking for differences between mothers and fathers. Furthermore, the authors' purpose was to add to the growing body of research on family stress by examining the predictive capacity of cognitive-existential variables (measured as family hardiness and meaning in life).

Method

Participants

A total of 57 families collaborated on this study. Final data reflect findings among 89 parents (54 mothers and 35 fathers) of children with autism spectrum disorder aged between 9 and 38 years (children's mean age was 15 years).

Participants were recruited through their children's educational centers and day-time services from March to June of 2004. All settings were public, officially approved facilities and located in Madrid (Spain). Eligibility criteria included having a child with a proved psychological or medical diagnosis of ASD. Mothers and fathers of all children were informed about the study and later were asked to participate in it. They could leave the study whenever they liked. The characteristics of the sample are summarized in Table 1.

Measures

To test correlations between family adjustment and the double ABCX predictors, the present authors gathered selected measures. The choice of variables measured does not by any means exhaust the dimensions of the model. Those measured, however, do represent variables shown by previous research to influence stress or coping in families with children with ASD. Separate forms obtained mothers' and fathers' measures.

Severity of the Stressors

Included were measures of child characteristics suspected to increase parental stress: physical incapacitation, social obtrusiveness, difficult personality characteristics, adaptive behavior, and intellectual level of the child. The answers of fathers and

Table 1 Characteristics of the participants

	Age						
	28–39	**40–49**	**50–59**	**60+**	**NS/NC**		
Fathers	5	16	11	3			
Mothers	12	24	12	5	1		
	Marital status						
	Married couple		**Separated**	**Divorced widow/er**		**Single**	**NS/NC**
Fathers	35						
Mothers	49		2	1			1
	Education level						
	NO		**Elementary**	**Secondary**	**University (3 years)**	**University (5 years)**	
Fathers	0		7	13	2	13	
Mothers	2		11	18	6	17	
	Work						
	Home	**External**	**Unemployed**				
Fathers	0	31	4				
Mothers	12	24	18				

mothers to selected scales from the Holroyd (1974) Questionnaire on Resources and Stress (QRS) were used as measurements for the three first variables. These subscales were the same as the ones used by Bristol (1987): Physical Incapacitation (QRS11), Social Obtrusiveness (QRS14), and Difficult Personality Characteristics (QRS15).

Psychologists of the educational and adult day care centers provided data of adaptive behavior and intellectual level. Data of the adaptive behavior were obtained using the Spanish version of the Inventory for Client and Agency Planning (ICAP, Bruininks, et al. 1986). The ICAP is an instrument that has 77 adaptive behavior items divided into four areas: motor skills, social and communications skills, personal living skills, and community living skills. It also evaluates behavioral problems, and includes scores for independence, adaptive behavior and a service score that indicates overall level of care, supervision, or training required. For all scales, higher scores indicate better personal level functioning. Reliability studies show a good internal consistence (generally higher than 0.80) with several samples.

Professionals also collected Intellectual level data from the child's updated school or clinic history. In data analysis, the age of the child was considered too.

Pileup of Demands

The pileup of other stress factors unrelated to the child was measured using the Holroyd QRS Limits on Family Opportunity (Subscale 9). This subscale assesses the extent to which a family has to pass up educational, vocational, or other self-development opportunities because of the child. In addition, all parents completed a modified Schedule of Recent Experience (SRE, Holmes and Rahe 1967), which measures the number of major personal, family, occupational, and financial events signifying changes in the preceding 2 years. This modified schedule was used by Bristol (1987) and Pakenham et al. (2005). It has been validated across cultures, races, religious groups, and class.

Social Support

Bristol's (1987) modified version of the Carolina Parent Support Scale for the Handicapped (CSPH) was used to assess parental perceptions of the availability and helpfulness of sources of support. This scale is brief and considers both formal and informal sources of support. Informal sources of support were defined as those that do not require exchange of money or participation in formal organizations. These included spouse, wife's relatives, husband's relatives, the family's own children, other unrelated children, friends, neighbors, and other parents of children with special needs. Formal support sources include persons and services ranging from paid babysitters to ministers and respite-care programs.

Coping Strategies

The Coping Health Inventory for Parents (CHIP, McCubbin et al. 1991a, b), originally designed for measuring parental response to management of family life with a seriously and/or chronically ill child, was adapted for use in this study of children with ASD. The CHIP is a 45-items instrument with three subscales developed through factor analysis: maintaining family integration, cooperation, and an optimistic definition of the situation (Factor I), maintaining social support, self-esteem and psychological stability (Factor II); understanding the problem through communication with other parents and consultation with professional staff (Factor III). The CHIP has good internal consistency with alphas of 0.79 for the first two factors and 0.71 for Factor III.

The CHIP was also adapted to be used in other studies (e.g., Higgins et al. 2005) to assess coping strategies in parents of children with ASD.

Grasp of the Situation

The Family Hardiness Index (FHI) of McCubbin et al. (1991a; b) was used to measure the characteristic of hardiness as a stress-resistance and adaptation resource in families. Hardiness refers to the internal strength and durability of the family. The FHI has four subscales: co-oriented commitment, confidence, challenge, and control. However, the overall score seems the best indicator of hardiness. This instrument has a good internal consistency with an alpha of 0.82.

In addition, the Purpose In Life Test (PIL) of Crumbaugh and Maholick (1969) was used in its Spanish adaptation (Noblejas 2000) as another measure of the appraisal of the situation. The aim of the PIL test is to detect existential vacuum (as the opposite concept to meaning in life). The Spanish adaptation of PIL identified four factors: meaning perception, experienced meaning, aims and tasks, destiny-freedom dialectic. The PIL test was used in previous research (Sivberg 2002a, b) with parents with children with ASD. The split-half reliability of the PIL test was determined by Crumbaugh and Maholic (1969) as 0.82. The Spanish adaptation of PIL test also has good internal consistency with an alpha of 0.89 (Noblejas 2000).

Family Adaptation

As measurements for adaptation, depression and family satisfaction were assessed both in mothers and fathers. Two tests were used: Depression Questionnaire (Sandín and Valiente 1998) and Family Satisfaction by Adjectives Scale (Barraca and López-Yarto 1999). The first is a 16-item questionnaire designed for rapid assessment of clinical depression as opposed to mere depressive mood. The questionnaire was constructed on the basis of symptoms required in the DSM-IV for the diagnosis of major depression. It has an alpha of 0.88. The second instrument is a scale of bipolar adjectives consisting of 27 items designed to measure family satisfaction, mainly related to affective connotation derived from family interaction. It has a good internal consistency with an alpha of 0.97.

Statistical Methodology

Factor analysis was carried out to reduce the severity of the stressor variables to few uncorrelated ones. The analysis was made on 14 variables in a sample of 89 parents, so the cases ratio was 1:6 and sample was near 100, meeting basic criteria for the analysis. The method used was principal components extraction and varimax rotation with Kaiser normalization. The factor selection criteria were eigenvalue greater than one.

Correlation and hierarchical regression analysis was performed to examine relationships between family adaptation and predictor variables.

Hierarchical regression was implemented using the SPSS (version 9, SPSS Inc.) "Linear Regression Block" procedure. The correlation matrix and factorial analysis were obtained with the same statistical package.

Results

Four factors were extracted accounting for 78 % of variance of stressors, and their factor loadings are displayed in Table 2. Factor 1 included most of the ICAP variables, (except lack of behavioral problems) so we can refer to it as "level of performance" of the child. Factor 2 included difficulties in personality, physical incapacitation, and the intellectual level (negative loading: the smaller the child's intellectual level, the more care difficulties), so this factor seemed to reflect "care difficulties." Factor 3 included age (positive loading), social obtrusiveness (negative loading), and intellectual level (negative loading), and we could refer to it as "lack of social obtrusiveness." Factor 4 included lack of behavioral problems and social obtrusiveness (negative loading), so it was named "lack of behavioral problems."

The results for correlations between family adaptation and independent variables are shown in Table 3.

Five variables appeared significantly correlated with depression in mothers. The highest correlation coefficients were obtained for the appraisal of the situation variables (meaning in life and family hardiness) being inversely related with depression. Enhancing depression were other recent stress experiences. Furthermore, coping strategies were inversely related with depression, significantly so for the family component (CHIP factor 1). The last variable with a significant correlation coefficient was "limits on family opportunity."

Table 2 Factor loadings for severity of stressors variables

	Factor1	Factor2	Factor3	Factor4
Independence	**0.953**	−0.245	0.019	0.056
Motor skills	**0.911**	−0.222	−0.028	0.039
Social and communications skills	**0.889**	−0.290	−0.047	−0.024
Personal living skills	**0.868**	−0.168	0.161	0.030
Community living skills	**0.853**	−0.315	−0.045	0.108
Service score	**0.794**	0.243	−0.098	0.100
Adaptative behaviour	**0.567**	−0.082	0.377	0.208
Difficult personality characteristics	−0.111	**0.852**	0.148	−0.050
Physical incapacitation	−0.264	**0.840**	−0.114	0.012
Intellectual level	0.369	**−0.582**	**−0.569**	0.094
Age	0.184	0.118	**0.844**	−0.099
Social obtrusiveness	0.159	0.185	**−0.510**	**−0.510**
Lack of behaviour problems	0.234	0.027	−0.114	**0.860**

Table 3 Correlations between family adaptation variables and predictors

	Mothers		Fathers	
	Depression	Family satisfaction	Depression	Family satisfaction
Independent variables	Coef.	Coef.	Coef.	Coef.
AF1 Level of performance	0.169	0.009	0.276	−0.154
AF2 Care difficulties	0.082	**−0.365****	−0.003	0.033
AF3 Lack of social obtrusiveness	0.018	−0.051	−0.013	0.113
AF4 Lack of behaviour problems	−0.223	0.182	0.011	−0.075
Limits on family opportunity	**0.243***	**−0.381****	0.281	**−0.323***
Schedule of recent experience	**0.430*****	−0.189	**0.284***	−0.235
Support	−0.020	0.099	0.044	0.042
CHIP1 Coping strategies—Family	**−0.251***	**0.307***	−0.166	**0.375***
CHIP2 Coping strategies—Social and individual	−0.170	0.219	−0.055	**0.289***
CHIP3 Coping strategies—Medical	−0.172	**0.239***	0.205	0.114
Family hardiness	**−0.490*****	**0.520*****	**−0.428****	**0.532*****
Meaning in life	**−0.688*****	**0.532*****	**−0.633*****	**0.425****

*$p<0.05$; **$p<0.01$; ***$p\leq 0.001$

For depression in fathers three variables showed significant correlation coefficients: meaning in life and family hardiness with negative coefficients, and recent stress experiences.

Family satisfaction was positively correlated with grasp of the situation variables and with coping strategies for both mothers and fathers. Nevertheless, the family and medical components of coping are more important for mothers, while family and social and individual components are significant for fathers. In the case of mothers, negative correlations were also found with care difficulties.

For implementing hierarchical regression models, the ABCX model determined the order of entry of predictor variables. Severity of the stressor variables was entered on step 1, pileup of demands on step 2, support on step 3, variables of coping on step 4, and appraisal of the situation variables on step 5. Tolerance to multicollinearity is especially low in the paternal depression model. In this model, family hardiness appeared with a significant positive coefficient, while in the correlation matrix the relationship between family hardiness and depression of the father had a coherent negative sign. This multicollinearity was motivated by a high correlation between meaning in life and family hardiness. To resolve this problem, family hardiness was eliminated from analysis and meaning in life was maintained because the correlation coefficients obtained for the models using this variable instead of family hardiness were higher. With this change, the cognitive and existential variables block was reduced to one distinct variable (meaning in life) and the model's tolerance to multicollinearity do not approach zero.

Hierarchical regression model results are showed in Table 4.

Three of the obtained models explain a significant amount of variance (41–67 %), but the explained variance (40 %) for family satisfaction in fathers was not significant.

Child stressors severity accounted for 17 % of the variance (significant at the 93 % level) of family satisfaction in mothers. In the other models the amount of variance explained by child stressors was smaller and not significant. Despite of this, the standardized coefficient of child level of performance (Factor 1 of child stressors) was significant, in depression of the father.

Pileup of demands accounted for a significant increment in the variance in maternal depression (20 %), and in paternal family satisfaction (19 %). For paternal depression the variance increment was significant at the 93 % level.

Support was unrelated to all measures of adaptation both for mothers and fathers.

Coping strategies accounted for a significant amount (22 %) of variance only for paternal depression.

After controlling the effects of all other predictors, meaning in life explained a significant amount of variance (7–26 %) for depression (of both mothers and fathers) and family satisfaction of mothers. The amount of variance of this block was not significant for family satisfaction in fathers.

Discussion

Our findings present new data to analyze the applicability of the double ABCX model in explaining the process of adaptation in parents with a child diagnosed with ASD. As expected, better parental adaptation is related to higher levels of grasp of the situation variables and, to some extent, higher coping strategies, and lower levels of child needs and pileup of demands.

Table 4 Results of hierarchical regression analysis

	Mothers				**Fathers**			
	Depression		**Family satisfaction**		**Depression**		**Family satisfaction**	
Independent variables	**ΔR²**	**β**	**ΔR²**	**β**	**ΔR²**	**β**	**ΔR²**	**β**
AF1 Level of performance		0.111		0.143		0.382*		–0.155
AF2 Care difficulties		–0.107		–0.282		–0.011		0.169
AF3 Lack of social obtrusiveness		0.065		–0.051		–0.128		0.144
AF4 Lack of behaviour problems		–0.061		0.040		0.160		–0.289
Child Stressors block	0.085		0.172 [a]		0.118		0.063	
Limits on family opportunity		–0.047		–0.103		0.090		–0.308
Schedule of recent experience		0.190		–0.106		0.161		–0.116
Pileup of demands	0.202**		0.070		0.155 [a]		0.189*	
Support	0.003	0.064	0.000	–0.061	0.007	0.171	0.000	–0.138
CHIP1 Coping strategies—Family		–0.114		–0.037		–0.317		0.392
CHIP2 Coping strategies—Social and individual		–0.084		0.164		0.255		–0.019

(continued)

Table 4 (continued)

	Mothers				Fathers			
	Depression		Family satisfaction		Depression		Family satisfaction	
Independent variables	**ΔR²**	**β**	**ΔR²**	**β**	**ΔR²**	**β**	**ΔR²**	**β**
CHIP3 Coping strategies—Medical		0.204		0.113		0.356		–0.164
Coping block	0.036		0.100		0.220*		0.125	
Meaning in life	0.256***	–0.699***	0.067*	0.358*	0.170**	–0.587**	0.020	0.202
Total R-Square (adjusted)	0.582 (0.473)		0.409 (0.254)		0.670 (0.513)		0.398 (0.109)	
Total F	5.317***		2.646*		4.252**		1.380	

$^{*}p<0.05$; $^{**}p<0.01$; $^{***}p<0.001$ $^{a}p<0.07$

Our models explained 58 % (mothers) and 67 % (fathers) of variance for depression. These percentages are similar to the 58 % explained by Pakenham et al. (2005) and higher than the 38 % explained by Bristol (1987).

For family satisfaction the explained variances by models are lower than the ones obtained for depression models, especially for fathers.

Correlation coefficients are higher for C variables than for A and BC variables. Likewise, hierarchical regression models are mainly based on C variables. These results indicate that parental way to perceive, define, and assess the meaning of the situation is more important in the prediction of family adaptation than characteristics of the child, as discussed by Saloviita et al. (2003).

In spite of low stressors influence in family adaptation, this influence exists and must be discussed. There is a significant amount of variance to explain family adaptation through pileup of demands and child's level of performance.

Child stressors block approaches to a significant amount of variance only for maternal family satisfaction, with standardized beta coefficients greater for the child's level of performance (positive coefficient) and care difficulties (negative coefficient). This fact indicates a bigger influence of the child's exigencies on mothers than on fathers, as also pointed out by an earlier study (e.g., Hastings 2003; Hastings et al. 2005a, b).

However, for depression of the father the level of performance of the child shows a direct significant correlation, that is to say, when child performance increases, father's depression scores are higher. This could be explained by parental difficulty to come to terms with a diagnosis of autism or a related condition when the child did not apparently show an altered functioning in a range of situations. We also ought to point out that child level of performance relies on ICAP scores, that this instrument tries to evaluate the characteristics of the child rather than its impact on family life, and that it was carried out by professional staff and not by parents.

On the other hand, the pileup of demands variable explains, as expected (in fathers only significant at the 97 % level) a significant amount of variance for depression. In this block the greater influence is due to recent stress experiences (see their higher beta coefficients). In family satisfaction models pileup of demands seems to stand out only for fathers and more importantly for limits on family opportunities.

With regard to social support, it does not present significant amounts of variance, nor significant beta coefficients as in the study of Pakenham et al. (2005). As these authors point out, this issue could be explained by limitations on social support scales or because social support is related to adjustment only if the social support is responsive to the needs elicited by the stressor.

On another hand, some of the coping measurements (CHIP factors) have significant correlation coefficients with family adaptation measurements except for depression in fathers. Nevertheless, the paternal depression model is the only one with a significant amount of variance for coping block. Hastings et al. (2005a; b) indicate a different coping approach between fathers and mothers facing depression and our results show different performance for paternal depression too.

It is important to point out that appraisal of the situation variable (meaning in life) has great importance in all significant models with a high number of explained variances. This fact corroborates the findings of Sivberg (2002a, b) for meaning. Family hardiness was eliminated from analysis because multicollinearity and less variance explained, but results were similar to those obtained with meaning in life.

Only for the family satisfaction model in fathers there is no significant explained variance. It is important to notice that the amount of variance corresponding to meaning in life is not significant when model variance is not significant either.

Summarizing briefly, in our study, the variables that contribute more to explain family adaptation are grasp of the situation, as mediating variable, and pileup of demands, as stressor. Coping strategies and child stressors are less influential. The support variable does not significantly explain variance in any model. Parental depression can be better explained than family satisfaction. Mothers and fathers show similar models but with some differences that would be interesting to consider in more depth in future works.

Implications for the Future and Practical Application

From a methodological point of view, more works including cognitive-existential parameters are needed to assess deeply their influence on family adaptation. Likewise, the analysis of the factorial scores of other test factors, which have factorial structure, (e.g., the PIL test) can be useful to go more deeply into the data.

The present study suffers several limitations. A greater sample is desirable. The generalizability of its findings may be limited by the nonrandom sample recruitment. The correlational method does not make it possible to assert firm conclusions regarding causality. Despite of these limitations, the present study uses multiple measures in accordance with a widely accepted theoretical model, a classical statistical methodology, and it includes a novel approach to the appraisal of the situation variables (meaning in life and family hardiness).

Weighing up variables related to the appraisal of the situation (meaning in life and family hardiness) when parental support programs are developed, could improve the quality of personal and family, life helping parents to find meaning in the family situation. This recommendation does not want to forget support in dealing with the child's and the caregivers' needs and to enhance coping strategies.

Conclusions

Our results explained 58 % (mothers) and 67 % (fathers) of variance for depression. For family satisfaction the explained variances by models are lower than the ones obtained for depression models, especially for fathers.

Correlation coefficients are higher for C variables than for A and B variables. Likewise, hierarchical regression models are mainly based on C variables. These results indicate that the parents' way to perceive, define, and assess the meaning of the situation is more important in the prediction of family adaptation than characteristics of the child.

It is important to point out that the meaning in life has great importance in all significant models with a high amount of explained variances. Family hardiness was eliminated from analysis because multicollinearity and less variance explained, but results were similar to those obtained with meaning in life.

Weighing up variables related to the appraisal of the situation (meaning in life and family hardiness) in the development of parental support programs could improve the quality of personal and family life, helping parents to find meaning in the family situation without forgetting the support to deal with the child's and the caregivers' needs and to enhance coping strategies.

Acknowledgements The authors wish to express their gratitude to the parents and education professionals who participated to make this work possible.

References

Barraca, J., & López-Yarto, L. (1999). *ESFA. Escala de satisfacción familiar por adjetivo* (2nd ed.). Madrid: Publicaciones de Psicología Aplicada.

Belinchón, M. (2001). *Situación y necesidades de las personas con trastornos del espectro autista en la Comunidad de Madrid.* Madrid: Caja Madrid.

Bristol, M. M. (1984). Family resources and successful adaptation to autistic children. In E. Schopler & G. Mesibov (Eds.), *The effects of autism on the family* (pp. 289–310). New York, NY: Plenum.

Bristol, M. M. (1987). The home care of children with developmental disabilities: Empirical support for a model of successful family coping with stress. In S. Landesman & P. Vietz (Eds.), *Living environments and mental retardation* (pp. 401–422). Washington, DC: American Association on Mental Retardation.

Bruininks, R.H., Hill, B.K., Weatherman, R.F., Woodcock, R.W. (1986). *Inventory for client and agency planning.* Allen, TX: DLM Teaching Resources. (Spanish version: Montero Centeno, D. (1993). *Evaluación de la conducta adaptativa en personas con discapacidades.* Adaptación y validación del ICAP. Bilbao: ICE, Universidad de Deusto, Mensajero.)

Crumbaugh, J. C., & Maholick, L. T. (1969). *Manual of instructions for the Purpose In Life test.* Saratoga: Viktor Frankl Institute for Logotherapy.

Dale, E., Jahoda, A., & Knot, F. (2006). Mothers' attributions following their child's diagnosis of autistic spectrum disorder. Exploring links with maternal levels of stress, depression and expectations about their child's future. *Autism, 10*(5), 463–479.

Frankl, V. (1986). *The doctor and the soul: From psychotherapy to logotherapy.* New York, NY: Vintage Books. first publ. 1946.

Frankl, V. E. (1946). Ärztliche Seelsorge. Grundlagen der Logotherapie und Existenzanalyse. Vienna: Deuticke.

Floyd, J. F., Singer, G. H. S., Powers, L. E., & Costigan, C. (1996). Families coping with mental retardation: Assessment and therapy. In J. W. Jacobson & J. A. Mulick (Eds.), *Manual of diagnosis and professional practice in mental retardation* (pp. 277–288). Washington, DC: American Psychological Association.

Hastings, R. P. (2003). Child behavior problems and partner mental health as correlates of stress in mothers and fathers of children with autism. *Journal of Intellectual Disability Research, 47*(4), 231–237.

Hastings, R. P., Kovshoff, H., Brown, T., Ward, N. J., Espinosa, F., & Remington, B. (2005). Coping strategies in mothers and fathers of preschool and school-age children with autism. *Autism, 9*(4), 377–391.

Hastings, R. P., Kovshoff, H., Ward, N. J., Espinosa, F., Brown, T., & Remington, B. (2005). Systems analysis of stress and positive perceptions in mothers and fathers of pre-school children with autism. *Journal of Autism and Developmental Disorders, 35*(5), 635–644.

Higgins, D. J., Bailey, S. R., & Pearce, J. C. (2005). Factors associated with functioning style and coping strategies of families with a child with an autism spectrum disorder. *Autism, 9*(2), 125–137.

Holmes, T., & Rahe, R. (1967). The social readjustment rating scale. *Journal of Psychosomatic Research, 11*, 213.

Holroyd, J. (1974). The Questionnaire on Resources and Stress (QRS-F): an instrument to measure family response to a handicapped member. *Journal of Community Psychology, 2*, 92–94.

Hill, R. T. (1949). *Families under stress: Adjustment to the crisis of war separation and reunion.* New York, NY: Harper.

Honey, E., Hastings, R. P., & Mcconachie, H. (2005). Use of the Questionnaire on Resources and Stress (QRS-F) with parents of young children with autism. *Autism, 9*(3), 246–255.

Konstantareas, M. M., & Papageorgiou, V. (2006). Effects of temperament, symptom severity and level of functioning on maternal stress in Greek children and youth with ASD. *Autism, 10*(6), 593–607.

McCubbin, H. I., McCubbin, M. A., Nevin, R. S., & Cauble. E. (1991). Coping Health Inventory for Parents (CHIP). In K. Corcoran, J. Fischer (Eds., 2000), *Measures for clinical practice: A Sourcebook.* (3rd Ed., 2 vols. Vol. 1, pp. 226–231). New York: Free Press.

McCubbin, M. A., McCubbin, H. I., Thompson, A. I. (1991). Family hardiness index ('FHI'). In K. Corcoran, J. Fischer (Eds., 2000), *Measures for clinical practice: A Sourcebook.* (3rd Ed., 2 vols, Vol. 1, 312–314). New York: Free Press.

McCubbin, H. I., & Patterson, J. M. (1983). The family stress process project: The double ABCX model of adjustment and adaptation. In H. I. McCubbin, M. B. Sussman, & J. M. Patterson (Eds.), *Social stress and the family: Advances and developments in family's stress theory and research* (pp. 7–37). New York, NY: Haworth.

Neil, T. L. (2002). Coping strategies and stress levels of parents of children with autism. *Dissertation Abstracts. International Section A: Humanities & Social Sciences, 63*(4-A), 1302.

Noblejas, M. A. (2000). Fiabilidad de los tests PIL y Logotest. *Noûs, 4*, 81–90.

Noblejas, M. A. (2009). Dimensiones del concepto de sentido. Una aproximación empírica desde la logoterapia. *Noûs, 13*, 11–44.

Pakenham, K. I., Samios, C., & Sofronoff, K. (2005). Adjustment in mothers of children with Asperger Syndrome: An application of the double ABCX model of family adjustment. *Autism, 9*(2), 191–212.

Pozo, P., Sarriá, E., & Méndez, L. (2006). Estrés en madres de personas con Trastornos del Espectro Autista (TEA). *Psicothema, 18*(3), 342–347.

Saloviita, T., Itälinna, M., & Leinonen, E. (2003). Explaining the parental stress of fathers and mothers caring for a child with intellectual disability: a Double ABCX Model. *Journal of Intellectual Disability Research, 47*(4), 300–312.

Sandín, B., & Valiente, R. M. (1998). Cuestionario de Depresión (CD). In B. Sandín (1999), *Estrés psicosocial*, (pp. 269–270). Madrid: Klinik.

Schieve, L. A., Blumberg, S. J., Rice, C., Visser, S. N., & Boyle, C. (2007). The relationship between autism and parenting stress. *Pediatrics, 119*(Suppl. 1), 114–121.

Singer, G. H. S., & Irvin, L. K. (1989). Family caregiving, stress, and support. In G. H. S. Singer & L. K. Irvin (Eds.), *Support for caregiving families. Enabling positive adaptation to disability* (pp. 9–25). Baltimore, MD: Paul H. Brookes Publishing.

Sivberg, B. (2002a). Family system and coping behaviors. A comparison between parents of children with autistic spectrum disorders and parents with non-autistic children. *Autism, 6*(4), 397–409.

Sivberg, B. (2002b). Coping strategies and parental attitudes: A comparison of parents with children with autistic spectrum disorders and parents with non-autistic children. *International Journal of Circumpolar Health, 61*(Suppl.2), 36–50.

Vermeulen, P. (1997). *Sólo pensamientos... los padres de niños con TGD y sus cogniciones.* In Actas del V Congreso Internacional Autismo Europa (pp. 1085–1102). Barcelona: Escuela Libre Editorial.

Zika, S., & Chamberlain, K. (1992). On the relation between meaning in life and psychological well-being. *British Journal of Psychology, 83*, 133–145.

Integrating Logotherapy with Cognitive Behavior Therapy: A Worthy Challenge

Matti Ameli

Introduction

Logotherapy, developed by Victor Frankl in the 1930s, and cognitive behavior therapy (CBT), pioneered by Aaron Beck in the 1960s, present many similarities. Ameli and Dattilio (2013) offered practical ideas of how logotherapeutic techniques could be integrated into Beck's model of CBT. The goal of this article is to expand those ideas and highlight the benefits of a logotherapy-enhanced CBT. After a detailed overview of logotherapy and CBT, their similarities and differences are discussed, along with the benefits of integrating them.

Overview of Logotherapy

Logotherapy was pioneered by the Austrian neurologist and psychiatrist Viktor Frankl (1905–1997) during the 1930s. The Viktor-Frankl-Institute in Vienna defines logotherapy as: "an internationally acknowledged and empirically based meaning-centered approach to psychotherapy." It has been called the "third Viennese School of Psychotherapy" (the first one being Freud's psychoanalysis and the second Adler's individual psychology). Frankl (1995) viewed logotherapy as an open, collaborative approach that could be combined with other psychotherapeutic orientations. He presented logotherapy as a complement to psychotherapy, not a substitute.

M. Ameli (✉)
Calle de Ribera, 4, 46002 Valencia, Spain
e-mail: matti_ameli@yahoo.com

A. Batthyány (ed.), *Logotherapy and Existential Analysis*, Logotherapy and Existential Analysis: Proceedings of the Viktor Frankl Institute Vienna 1,
DOI 10.1007/978-3-319-29424-7_18

Fundamental Tenets of Logotherapy

Tridimensional View of the Human Being: Intentionality

Logotherapy envisions man in three overlapping dimensions: somatic, psychological, and spiritual. Frankl defines the human spirit as "uniquely human" or what distinguishes human beings from other animals. He refers to the spiritual dimension as "noetic" to avoid religious connotations.

The noetic dimension is the site of authentically human phenomena such as humor, love, or gratitude. Frankl points out that in contrast with the first two dimensions where our reactions are often automatic, in the third dimension *we can choose how to behave* (Lukas 1998). Intentionality is the key factor in this case. For example, one can decide to express love or avoid hatred in spite of the situation. This is what makes human beings unpredictable. As Lewis (2011a, b) explains, Frankl calls this unpredictable quality "the defiant power of the human spirit."

Frankl (1959/1984) illustrates this concept that he was able to observe even in the concentration camp: "…there was always choices to make. Every day, every hour, offered the opportunity to make a decision, a decision which determined whether you would or would not submit to those powers which threatened to rob you of your very self, your inner freedom; which determined whether or not you would become the plaything of circumstance, renouncing freedom and dignity to become molded into the form of the typical inmate." In summary, the human person makes an intentional decision of who he/she is and who he/she wants to become every minute of his life.

Meaning and Freedom of Choice

In contrast with Freud's "will to pleasure" and Adler's "will to power," Frankl's theory is based on the premise that human beings are motivated by a "will to meaning," an inner pull to discover meaning in life. According to Frankl (1969) and as described by Ameli and Dattilio (2013), the three main principles of logotherapy are:

Freedom of will: human beings are not fully determined because they have the freedom to choose their response within the limits of given possibilities, under all life circumstances. They are not "free from" their biological, psychological, or sociological conditions but they are "free to" take a stand toward those conditions. There is always an "area of freedom" and the option of choosing one's attitude remains available.

Will to meaning: the main motivation of human beings is to search the meaning and purpose of their lives. Human beings are capable of sacrificing pleasure and supporting pain for the sake of a meaningful cause or person.

Meaning in life: life has meaning under all circumstances, even in unavoidable suffering and misery. Meaning in life is unconditional and human beings have to discover it "in the world" and not to invent it. Frankl (1959/1984) insists that life has meaning in spite of suffering but only if that suffering is unavoidable. If it were avoidable, then removing its cause would be the meaningful thing to do.

As described by Ameli and Dattilio (2013), we can discover meaning in life in three different ways known as the categorical values: creative, experiential, and attitudinal. The creative value consists of what we give to the world like accomplishing a task, creating a work, or doing a good deed. The experiential value is what we take from the world like the experience of truth, beauty, and love toward another human being. It could be actualized through nature, culture, art, music and literature, and through loving relationships. The attitudinal value reflects the stand we take toward an unchangeable situation or unavoidable suffering. As Lewis (2011a, b) describes, the attitudinal value is actualized when "one chooses bravery over cowardice, mercy over revenge, or justice over appeasement."

Actualizing the attitudinal value is key to face adversity or bear with an unchangeable destiny and as Frankl (1959/1984) points out: "to turn a predicament into a human achievement or personal triumph." A meaningful life is a life where the three categories of values are actualized to the highest possible degree (Lewis 2011a, b).

The following statement perfectly illustrates the main logotherapeutic principles and values described previously:

> "We who lived in concentration camps can remember the men who walked through the huts comforting others, giving away their last piece of bread. They may have been few in number, but they offer sufficient proof that everything can be taken away from a man but one thing: the last of the human freedoms—to choose one's attitude in any given set of circumstances, one's own way" (Frankl 1959/1984).

When the will to meaning is frustrated or blocked and a person is incapable of finding meaning or purpose in his/her life, he/she will experience a sensation of emptiness, hopelessness, or despair that Frankl (2003) calls *existential vacuum*. Some of the symptoms of that condition include apathy and boredom, and it may lead to aggression, addiction, depression, and possibly *noogenic neurosis*. Frankl (2004) defines *noogenic neurosis* as a clinical condition where the psychological symptoms are a result of existential or spiritual conflicts. Since in this case the root of the neurotic problem is in the third "noetic dimension," Frankl proposes logotherapy as the specific therapy for the treatment of that category of neurosis.

Responsibility

In logotherapy, responsibility is considered the essence of human existence. Being human means taking responsibility to deal with life's challenges through our actions and behaviors. Frankl (1959/1984) explains that we are not the ones who should ask something from life; we are questioned by life on a daily and hourly basis and "our answer must consist, not in talk or meditation, but in right action and in right conduct."

Applying the concept of responsibility in clinical practice consists of:

- Helping the client to become fully aware of his/her sense of responsibility. He/she is the one who has to decide for what, to what, or to whom he/she is responsible, based on his/her own understanding. The therapist should not impose value judgments or act as a "preacher" (Frankl 1959/1984).
- Taking into account that the client is not a "victim" but the "coauthor" of his/her destiny (Lukas 1998). Therefore, he/she is also responsible for his/her own recovery through the therapy process. One of the principals of the logotherapeutic process is: you have to bring help but without taking away responsibility (Lukas 1998).

Self-transcendence

In contrast with Maslow's theory, defining self-actualization as man's ultimate need, Frankl proposes the concept of self-transcendence. He declares: "being human always points, and is directed, to something, or someone, other than oneself—be it a meaning to fulfill or another human being to encounter. The more one forgets himself—by giving himself to a cause to serve or another person to love—the more human he is and the more he actualizes himself. What is called self-actualization is not an attainable aim at all, for the simple reason that the more one would strive for it, the more he would miss it. In other words, self-actualization is possible only as a side-effect of self-transcendence" (Frankl 1959/1984). In summary happiness can't be pursued; it's a buy-product of self-transcendence. Interestingly, Maslow arrived at a similar conclusion: "Self-actualization is not the highest human need; self-transcendence is the ultimate need of the human soul" (Pattakos 2004).

Use of Healthy Inner Resources

According to logotherapy, every person has a healthy core and the goal of the therapist is to help the client discover his/her intact, healthy forces and strengths, and use them in order to overcome his/her problems. Logotherapy focuses both on the client's "current positives" (assets and strengths) and "future potentials" or possibilities for expansion (Lukas 1998). Frankl believes in "overestimating" the person so he/she can achieve his/her highest potential. He says with Goethe: "if we take man as he is, we make him worse, but if we take man as he should be, we make him capable of becoming what he can be." He considers the above maxim as crucial for all psychotherapeutic intervention.

The two healthy resources mainly used by logotherapy are: self-distancing (ability to detach from oneself and set a distance between self and the symptoms) and self-transcendence (Lukas 1998). Sense of humor is another important human asset appealed to by logotherapy.

Tragic Optimism

According to Frankl (1959/1984) “tragic optimism” is the ability to remain optimistic in spite of the “tragic triad” of pain, guilt, and death. This is based on the principle that life is meaningful under any circumstance and the human capacity to make the best of any given situation by creatively turning negative aspects into positive and constructive ones. Optimism including the triad of hope, faith, and love could be used to face tragedy by: “(1) turning suffering into a human achievement and accomplishment; (2) deriving from guilt the opportunity to change oneself for the better; and (3) deriving from life’s transitoriness an incentive to take responsible action” (Frankl 1959/1984). Frankl insists that optimism cannot be commanded; one needs to discover a reason for optimism, a meaning.

Goals and Therapeutic Process

Frankl (1959/1984) declares that logotherapy is “neither teaching nor preaching.” He compares the role of the logotherapist to an ophthalmologist who enables the person to see the world as it is, thus considering logotherapy as an objective therapy. He explains: “the logotherapist’s goal consists of widening and broadening the visual field of the patient so that the whole spectrum of potential meaning becomes conscious and visible to him” (Frankl 1959/1984). Frankl (1959/1984) quotes Lukas, saying “throughout the history of psychotherapy, there has never been a school as undogmatic as logotherapy.”

Frankl proposed logotherapy as the “specific” therapy for noogenic (or existential) neurosis and as a “nonspecific” or collaborative therapy for other types of neuroses. Referring to that second category Frankl (1995) explains that logotherapy is a real therapy for attitudinal change; rather than focusing on symptoms, it facilitates the change of posture of a patient in regards to his/her symptoms.

Considering the main tenets of logotherapy, the goal of the logotherapist would be to tap into the unique human capacities such as intentionality, responsibility, and freedom of choice to help the client discover and actualize the meaning potentials in his/her life. In summary, logotherapy is an objective, active, collaborative, and action-oriented form of therapy, where the client (as long as his/her noetic dimension remains open) is held responsible for his/her recovery process in therapy as well as for his/her life, through his/her personally meaningful attitudes, decisions, behaviors, and actions. The client is always free to decide no matter what his/her circumstances are and in spite of his/her biological or psychological limitations; therefore he/she is not considered a “victim” nor is he/she exempt from responsibility.

Techniques of Logotherapy

The three main techniques used in logotherapy are: paradoxical intention, dereflection, and attitude modification.

Paradoxical Intention

Description and Use

Paradoxical intention was first used by Frankl in 1929. This technique is based on self-distancing through the use of humor. The client is asked to expose himself/herself to his/her worst fear by wishing with humorous exaggeration the very thing that provokes his/her greatest fear or anxiety. For example, in the case of a person who has panic attacks and fears a heart attack: "I am going to have five heart attacks today." Paradoxical intention counteracts anticipatory anxiety (it's not possible to fear something and wish strongly for it to happen) and thus breaks the anxiety vicious circle. It is illustrated in detail by Dattilio (1987, 1994). Paradoxical intention has been used mostly in cases of panic disorder and agoraphobia, and also in the framework of family therapy (Ameli and Dattilio 2013).

The central components of paradoxical intention include: "(a) a nonmanipulative therapist-client partnership, (b) ruling out biological etiology, (c) educating clients about paradoxical intention with regard to what it is and how it works, (d) tailoring the technique to the individual's presenting complaints, (e) participating in the fear state, while (f) simultaneously incorporating humor to counteract anxiety" (Schulenberg et al. 2008).

Lukas (1981) describes the first step of paradoxical intention as self-distancing from the symptoms through humor followed by a change of attitude and symptom reduction.

Frankl points out many of the similarities between paradoxical intention and behavioral techniques such as exposure, flooding, or satiation. He refers to behavior therapists such as Dilling, Rosefeldt, Kockott, and Heyse, who argue that although not developed in the frame of the learning theory, paradoxical intention is possibly based on similar mechanisms underlying behavior modification techniques such as exposure therapy techniques (cf. Frankl 1995, 44). According to Ascher (1989) some of the behavioral techniques, mainly implosion and satiation, are simply "the translation of paradoxical intention."

The use of humor is the essence of paradoxical intention and what distinguishes it from behavior modification techniques. This inclusion of the sense of humor as an intrinsically human characteristic in logotherapy adds a substantial advantage compared to many of the techniques in behavior therapy (Frankl 2004). Humor is a healthy human resource directed only toward the symptom, not the client. Hutzell (Fabry 2010) points out that humor allows the individual to distance himself from his behavior and become aware that other aspects of one's life are more significant than the symptom behavior. This intervention helps to reduce anticipatory anxiety, as well.

Research

The first attempt to validate paradoxical intention was conducted by behavior therapists. Ascher (1978–1979) points to the first pilot study conducted by Solyom, Garza-Pérez, and Ledwige (1972) studying ten patients who complained of recurrent compulsive thoughts. Applying the technique of paradoxical intention helped to reduce or eliminate the target symptom for five of the subjects. For the remaining subjects studied, three presented with unchanged symptoms and two failed to apply the technique appropriately (cf. Ascher 1978–1979, 18).

Ascher and Efran (1978) employed paradoxical intention to five cases of onset sleep insomnia were resistant to behavioral treatments. The results indicated that all five cases "experienced the immediate reduction of sleep onset latency and further attention to this problem was terminated after 2 or 3 weeks" (Ascher 1978–1979). Further studies by Asher and associates confirm that paradoxical intention is a clinically effective technique for clients presenting with sleep disruption (Ascher 1978–1979).

Levinson (1979) also reports a case of insomnia that was successfully treated with paradoxical intention.

A recent review of 19 clinical outcome studies on paradoxical intention was conducted by Fabry (2010). The studies were selected among articles published between 1966 and 2009 using the following criteria: publication in a scholarly journal, quantitative research methodologies, presence of pre- and post-intervention, and enrollment of participants in a paradoxical intention program. The author concluded: "positive results were yielded for all but 1 out of 19 outcome studies with no adverse effects reported. It can be seen that paradoxical intention is supported by the empirical research data as a therapeutic method" (Fabry 2010, 24). The author further points out that paradoxical intention was integrated successfully into the cognitive behavioral protocol two decades previously (Fabry 2010).

Paradoxical intention has been validated empirically for sleep disorders, agoraphobia, and public speaking anxiety, mainly in the presence of recursive anxiety (Schulenberg 2003).

In terms of clinical intervention, Frankl has presented various cases of clients suffering from obsessive–compulsive disorder and agoraphobia that were treated successfully and in a short period of time, using paradoxical intention (Frankl 1995, 2004). Dattilio has integrated behavioral techniques with paradoxical intention. He proposed paradoxical intention as an alternative to symptom induction and relaxation, especially in cases where there is a risk of undiagnosed cardiac disease or seizure disorder and in patients who might be prone to experiencing relaxation-induced anxiety (Dattilio 1987, 1994).

Marshall Lewis, a logotherapist and clinician trained in CBT, describes the case of a patient diagnosed with obsessive compulsive disorder who was suffering from intrusive thoughts of blasphemy and received 3, 1-h sessions of paradoxical intention (Lewis 2011a, b). In the third session, the patient received a combination of the specific strategy that Frankl had developed to apply paradoxical intention to patients presenting intrusive thoughts of blasphemy, and relaxation training based on Wolpe's techniques (Lewis refers to Frankl explaining that combining paradoxical intention with relaxation has been successful). The results show that "when combined with relaxation training, the symptoms remit by the end of the third session. The patient remains symptom-free at a 6-week follow-up appointment" Lewis (2011a, b). He concludes that the result obtained using paradoxical intention in a clinical setting is consistent with the research literature.

In conclusion, paradoxical intention appears to be a valid and effective technique that can be integrated well into a CBT framework. Its complimentary component serves to broaden the scope of treatment.

Dereflection

Description and Use

The technique of dereflection was developed by Frankl shortly after World War II. It is based on self-transcendence, described above. As highlighted by Ameli and Dattilio (2013): “The dereflection technique counteracts hyperreflection which could be defined as an over-focus or dwelling on a problem or a symptom that makes it worse or a compulsive tendency toward self-observation. Dereflection shifts the client’s attention away from the symptom and reorients it towards another person or a motivating/meaningful area.”

Frankl (2004) explains that while paradoxical intention trains the client to “make fun” of his neurosis, dereflection helps a client ignore his symptoms. Lukas (1998) defines dereflection as disregarding something that may possibly become worse through reflection. She insists that dereflection is more than a distracting strategy; it’s reaching beyond oneself and rebuilding self-transcendence. She refers to this as a “recipe against egocentricity” (Lukas 1998).

The dereflection technique was originally developed for sexual disorders. The client is instructed to ignore the ruminative thoughts (this breaks the hyperreflection) and focus on meaning (Lukas 1998). For example, in the case of impotence due to excessive self-observation, there is a recommendation for abstinence during a period of time, and the client is asked to focus on giving love, attention and tenderness through caresses, and understanding to his partner. As a result, the patient’s sexual capacity regenerates and he eventually breaks the abstinence rule.

According to Lukas (1981), the four steps in the dereflection process are: (1) self-transcendence, (2) finding meaningful tasks and goals, (3) symptom reduction, and (4) change in attitude. She highlights that in dereflection, discovering meaningful goals and tasks serves as therapeutic itself because the client’s attention is focused away from “what’s wrong with me” to “what’s right with me.”

Dereflection has been applied to a variety of problems such as insomnia, swallowing and speech disorders, depression, rumination, fear of failure, and narcissism (Frankl 2004; Lukas 1991, 1998; Rogina 2004). It has also been used successfully in couple therapy (Schulenberg et al. 2010). Ameli and Dattilio (2013) provide an example of how dereflection could be incorporated in the CBT protocol for depression.

Research

The dereflection technique is an important part of the sexual therapy model proposed by Frankl in 1947. His model predated Masters and Johnson’s sexual therapy model, developed in 1970 (Ameli and Dattilio 2013). William S. Sahakian and

Barbara Jacquelyn Sahakian share the opinion that Masters and Johnson's investigations validated Frankl's treatment protocol and results for sexual disorders (cf. Frankl 1995, 65).

Ascher (1980) notes that, before Frankl's focus on the use of dereflection for certain sexual dysfunctions, the treatment plan for those disorders lacked direction and a consistent positive outcome. He points out that although many components of the Masters and Johnson sexual therapy model were based on data derived from their own research, significant aspects of their therapeutic programs did not originate with them, but had previously appeared in the professional literature; among them "dereflection" and Wolpe's desensitization techniques. He adds: "It does not seem unreasonable that these therapeutic components were responsible for much of the clinical success reported by Masters and Johnson." (Ascher 1980, 13).

In terms of clinical intervention, Frankl reports specific cases of clients who were treated successfully with dereflection, in a brief period of time, mainly for sexual and sleep disorders and also for autonomic psychomotor dysfunctions such as swallowing and speech problems: the attention is redirected to "what" to eat or to say instead of "how" to do it, the autonomic part (Frankl 1995, 2004). Lukas reports successful results using this technique with problems such as depression, rumination, and fear of failure (Lukas 1991, 1998).

At a metacognitive level, it is worth noting the resemblance between dereflection and some of the attention techniques included within the frame of Metacognitive Therapy (MCT), developed by Adrian Wells (Wells 2009). According to MCT, psychological disorders are maintained because of the individual's unhelpful) thinking style referred to as CAS (Cognitive Attention Syndrome). Wells (2009) defines CAS as a "toxic" style of thinking, found in all disorders, "consisting of worry/rumination, threat monitoring, unhelpful thought control strategies, and other forms of behavior (e.g., avoidance) that prevent adaptive learning." The CAS locks the person into prolonged and intense periods of negative emotional experience. It is mainly characterized by self-focused attention and self-related topics. The Attention Training Technique (ATT) is used to redirect the attention away from excessive and persistent self-focused activity, a key element in worry and rumination, and to strengthen the client's control over the focus of his/her attention. It is important to note that ATT is not a distraction or avoidance technique that involves shifting the client's attention to neutral or positive events. Rather, it is based on the use of auditory stimuli within a specific procedure. Clients are asked to direct their attention, as instructed, to the auditory stimuli while regarding the unwanted thoughts and feelings as additional noise. They should not block or resist them, but rather follow the procedure and let those intrusive thoughts take care of themselves (Wells 2009).

The concepts of hyperreflection and CAS are comparable since they both are characterized by an excessive self-focused attention. Although there are theoretical and practical differences between ATT and dereflection, the main goal of both types of techniques is to counteract excessive self-focus and remove dwelling and rumination, by ignoring the unwanted thoughts and feelings. One idea would be to combine both techniques: redirect the client's attention away using ATT and then refocus and "lock" it into a personal meaningful aspect (tasks, goals, people, etc.,), using dereflection. This could be accomplished by incorporating personally meaningful words (related to tasks, goals, projects, or other people) or sounds (nature, music, animals, etc.,) within the ATT protocol, in addition to neutral auditory stimuli.

Attitude Modification

Description and Use

The term of "attitude modification" was proposed in 1980 Elisabeth Lukas, student of Frankl's (Lukas 1998). Through Socratic dialogue, the client explores personally meaningful values, motivations, perspectives, areas of freedom, choices, and available meaningful options or actions. It is essentially a guided discovery process.

Unlike behavior modification, logotherapy's focus is to first modify the attitude because modifying an internal attitude leads effortlessly to a modified behavior (Lukas 1998). The goal of attitude modification is to help the client improve his/her attitude in regard to "something" and activate the will to meaning. In order to deal with the existential vacuum (the client is unable to perceive value and meaning in life) and to train the client in "meaning sensitization," Lukas (1998) proposes the following steps: (1) define clearly the problematic behavior (what is my problem?), (2) define the areas of freedom for action in spite of apathy, boredom etc. (where is my area of freedom?), (3) draw upon the client's imagination to list all possible options (what are my options?), (4) select the most meaningful options based not on pleasure but on the imagined consequences for all parties involved (which option is the most meaningful?), (5) ask the client to implement the most meaningful option that he has chosen in spite of his/her condition (lack of motivation, fear etc.).

Lukas (1980) explains that to modify negative or destructive attitudes, common sense is often used as a guideline. When the client displays an unhealthy attitude, the therapist questions it and helps the client discover all of his/her available choices. The goal is to help the client to become aware of his/her personally meaningful values hierarchy so that he/she can actualize those values. The therapist doesn't "prescribe" attitudes and doesn't decide if an attitude is "correct" or "moral," but rather facilitates a reflection for the client.

When faced with unavoidable suffering or unchangeable and negative external factors (the "tragic triad": suffering, guilt and death) the client still has the choice to adopt a new attitude toward his/her situation. To help the client actualize the attitudinal values, consistent with Frankl's "tragic optimism," Lukas (1998) describes the following procedure based Frankl's guidelines:

(1) Show the value: this consists of showing that maintaining a positive attitude in a tragic situation is commendable because it reflects the capacity of the human spirit to resist and to turn suffering into personal triumph; (2) show the meaning: help clients realize that there is some positive aspect to their situations in spite of the suffering. Lukas recommends some caution with this strategy because the "positive in spite

of the suffering" could be discovered more easily by the non-affected than the affected person; (3) show the rest: indicate the available positive opportunities that are not affected by suffering and should not be affected by it. It's "saving the rest" without substituting the loss; (4) show perspectives: tactfully offer perspectives that could help "soften" the situation, based on "logophilosophy." For example, all suffering is a process of growth, a maturing opportunity through which one comes to see more value in life's luxuries and people whom he/she loves. Guilt is an opportunity to learn, compensate and actualize forgiveness. Finally, death is a reminder that life is finite. Therefore, it is important to take advantage of the meaningful opportunities that it offers us every day and to implement our projects without procrastinating.

In summary, the goal of the attitude modification technique is to correct negative attitudes by transforming them into meaningful actions, experiences and attitudes. This technique could be used for issues such as guilt, loss, grief, suffering, serious diseases or terminal illnesses, neurosis, and depression.

Lukas (1998) explains that with anxiety disorders such as phobia, although the somatic symptoms cannot always be controlled or regulated, the client is free to decide how to react and respond: taking it seriously, ignoring it, escaping, or persevering in the situation in spite of his/her fear. The therapist can motivate clients to go through the exposure process by exploring their "free areas" or choices (tapping into that third human dimension) in order to facilitate a shift from: "I am a slave to anxiety or fear" to "I am the master and I choose to not allow fear to paralyze me." Ameli and Dattilio (2013) describe an example of attitude modification with a client suffering from generalized anxiety.

In summary, Lukas describes the three techniques listed above as a change of how the client responds to the external world (by changing his internal view): paradoxical intention corrects the anxious expectation, dereflection corrects the focus of attention, and attitude modification corrects the negative attitude.

Another interesting technique to consider is *the Values Awareness Technique* (VAT) developed by Hutzell and Eggert (1989/2009). It's a pen and pencil format and the goal is to help people discover their personally meaningful values hierarchy (based on Frankl's categorical values), define meaningful goals for short, intermediate and long term, and align them with their values. It could be used to facilitate dereflection and define meaningful goals at the end of the CBT depression protocol (Ameli and Dattilio 2013).

Research Data on Logotherapy

Background

Frankl was aware of the importance of quantitative, evidence-based studies and encouraged researchers to conduct scientific research on logotherapy. As a neurologist, he was very interested in empirical research and validation. He expressed it specifically (Batthyany and Guttmann 2006):

> You cannot turn the wheel back and you won't get a hearing unless you try to satisfy the preferences of present-time Western thinking, which means the scientific orientation or, to put it in more concrete terms, our test and statistics mindedness […]. That's why I welcome all sober and solid empirical research in logotherapy, however dry its outcome may sound (Fabry 1978/1979, 5–6).

A large number of research studies have been conducted to validate the main concepts, constructs, and tools used in logotherapy as is evident by more than 600 studies listed by Batthyany and Guttmann (2006).

Although there is still a need for further assessment and refinement of research tools to evaluate the therapeutic value of logotherapy, the authors conclude: "we may say with all due respect and modesty, that Frankl would have been very pleased to find that the research in logotherapy has far surpassed his dream" (Batthyany and Guttmann 2006).

Psychometric Assessment

A variety of psychometric tools have been created to quantify the life-meaning-construct. The earliest and most investigated one is the PIL (Purpose In Life Test) developed by Crumbaugh and Maholick in 1964. It contains 20 items with a seven-point likert-type response format and measures the degree to which a person experiences a sense of personal meaning (Schulenberg and Melton 2008).

In terms of validity, based on a number of studies and reviews, the PIL shows positive correlations with constructs such as self-control, life satisfaction, extroversion, self-acceptance, and emotional stability, and correlated negatively with anxiety, depression, and boredom proneness. Those results are consistent with logotherapy's postulate and research studies showing the association between life meaning and well-being (Schulenberg and Melton 2008).

In terms of PIL's reliability, the alpha-coefficient is ranging from 0.86 to 0.97. It can be concluded that the PIL is a relevant research tool in the area of meaning. Schulenberg envisions the PIL as a potential instrument that could be included in a battery of psychological measurement tools to "highlight clients' strengths" (Schulenberg and Melton 2008).

It has also been shown that meaning in life has discriminative power: it can distinguish between clinically distressed and not distressed subjects and also between clinical population and those with no mental illness (Schulenberg and Melton 2008).

A recent study (García-Alandete et al. 2009) using the PIL and the hopelessness scale (Beck et al. 1979) shows a statistically significant negative correlation between life meaning and hopelessness, confirming the hypothesis that existential vacuum is associated with high levels of despair. Taking into account that hopelessness is a powerful suicide risk predictor, the authors suggest that the concept of existential vacuum could be considered a significant predictor of moderate to high suicide risk. In contrast the sense of purpose and life meaning indicates a minimum suicide risk.

Those findings support the mathematical equation that Frankl proposed to illustrate the concept of despair: D (despair) = S (suffering) − M (meaning).

In addition to PIL, other existing tools for the measurement of meaning and meaning-related concepts are: The Life Purpose Questionnaire (LPQ), the Seeking of Noetic Goals Test (SONG), the Meaning In Suffering Test (MIST), and the Life Attitude Profile-Revised (LAP-R).

Theoretical Base of Logotherapy

Frankl defines logotherapy as both "existential" and "phenomenological." One of the major influences on the development of logotherapy is the phenomenology of Max Scheler (Lewis 2011a, b). Other influential philosophers are Karl Jaspers and Martin Heidegger, emphasizing the concepts of responsibility and freedom of action (Lukas 2008).

It is also important to highlight that Frankl's personal experience in the Nazi concentration camps has influenced the concepts of his logotherapy. He was able to validate some of them by observing in a real and extreme setting the behavior of human beings. The concentration camp was his "natural" laboratory. One of his conclusions is that meaning has survival value: those prisoners who were oriented toward the future, toward a task or a meaning to fulfill had a higher chance of survival (Frankl 2003). These results were confirmed by American psychiatrists based on data from the wars with Japan, Vietnam, and Korea (Frankl 2003).

One aspect that makes the foundation of Logotherapy unique in comparison with other types of therapies is the fact that its founder validated the main concepts of his approach through his real-life experiences, in some of the most extreme, tragic, and cruel circumstances in the history of humanity. Frankl remained the authentic model of his theory and teachings until his death (Klingberg 2001; Ryan 2008).

Overview of CBT

Cognitive therapy was developed by the psychiatrist Aaron T. Beck in the early 1960s. While conducting experiments to validate the fundamental psychoanalytic concepts of depression, he was surprised to find the opposite. As a result of those findings, Beck et al. (1979) proposed a new clinical approach to depression based on the concept of "automatic thoughts" about oneself, the world, and/or the future. He called this new approach "Cognitive Therapy" and it has also become known as "Cognitive Behavior Therapy" (CBT).

The Beck Institute defines cognitive therapy as: "a comprehensive system of psychotherapy and treatment based on an elaborated and empirically supported theory of psychopathology and personality." Since its introduction, Beck's model has been expanded by researchers and several variants of cognitive therapy have been proposed.

CBT is empirically based and has been proven effective by hundreds of outcome studies for a wide variety of psychiatric disorders such as: depression, the full range of anxiety disorders, substance abuse, eating disorders, personality disorders, and bipolar disorder and schizophrenia (in combination with medication). It is also used for problems such as: low self-esteem, anger management, relationship difficulties, and grief/loss. CBT has broad applications and is used effectively with children, adults, couples, families, and groups.

The Cognitive Behavior Model

Cognitive therapy is based on a cognitive theory of psychopathology and the importance of information processing. According to that model, people's perceptions or thoughts about situations (cognitions) largely determine their emotional and behavioral reactions.

When an individual is distressed, his/her perceptions and thoughts become distorted and this leads to dysfunctional behaviors and emotions. In addition, according to Beck et al. (1979), the beliefs or assumptions an individual has of himself/herself, the world and others are based on previous experiences and if they are distorted, they could also give rise to dysfunctional thoughts. Through CBT, clients learn to identify, evaluate (against objective data and facts), and modify their "automatic thoughts" (spontaneous cognitions), assumptions, and beliefs so their thinking becomes more realistic and adaptive. The therapeutic change occurs at three interactive levels: cognitive, behavioral, and affective. The cognitive change facilitates behavioral change by allowing the client to adopt a risk taking perspective and in turn putting into practice the new behaviors helps to validate that perspective. Emotions can be moderated by considering alternative interpretations of the situation (based on objective evidence and facts) and in turn emotions influence cognitive change, given that learning is more prominent when emotions are triggered (Beck and Weishaar 1989). CBT puts emphasis on thoughts in both initiating and maintaining therapeutic change.

Cognitive change happens at three levels and the therapist works with the client at those three levels (Dattilio and Padesky 1990). (1) *Automatic thoughts* are the most accessible surface thoughts. They are images or beliefs that are situations specific (e.g., "my wife is late, she doesn't care about my feelings" or the image of her having a good time with her friends). (2) *Underlying assumptions* are more generalized and conditional rules that help us structure our perceptions. They are at a deeper level and underlie automatic thoughts (e.g., "you can't count on women for support"). (3) *Schemas* are inflexible unconditional core beliefs (e.g., "I will always be alone"). Those three levels are interconnected and the goal is to produce change at all three levels.

It is important to highlight that although thoughts are emphasized, CBT is an interactive model where thoughts, emotions, behaviors, environment, and biology can each influence the others (Dattilio and Padesky 1990).

Goals and Therapeutic Process

According to Beck and Weishaar (1989), "the goalsof cognitive therapy are to correct faulty information and to modify dysfunctional beliefs and assumptions that maintain maladaptive behaviors and emotions." Besides achieving the remission of the disorder, relapse prevention is also emphasized in the frame of CBT.

Both cognitive and behavioral techniques are utilized in CBT and the client is taught the following throughout the treatment process: (1) to monitor his/her negative automatic thoughts (cognitions); (2) to recognize the connections between cognition, affect, and behavior; (3) to examine the evidence for and against his/her distorted automatic thoughts; (4) to substitute more reality-oriented interpretations for these biased cognitions; and (5) to learn to identify and alter the dysfunctional beliefs which predispose him/her to distort his/her experiences. (Beck et al. 1979).

A strong therapeutic alliance is a key element of CBT. The therapist and the client collaborate as a team and set the goals for therapy and the agenda for each session together.

The two main strategies used are collaborative empiricism and guided discovery (Beck and Weishaar 1989). Through collaborative empiricism, the client takes up the role of a "scientist" and tests the validity of his/her thoughts and beliefs against objective data and evidence (gathered by both himself/herself and the therapist). Through the process of guided discovery, the therapist serves as a guide to help the client clarify his/her problematic thoughts and behaviors and setup behavioral experiments to test hypothesis based on those thoughts and behaviors.

In terms of dialogue, a gentle Socratic questioning style is usually used to help clients identify, evaluate, and respond to their automatic thoughts and beliefs.

CBT is an active, structured, action-oriented, and time-limited approach. Homework assignments play a key role: clients are taught to become their "own therapist" through the acquisition and practice of cognitive, behavioral, and emotional regulation skill.

According to the Beck Institute, CBT is generally short term and the structure of a session includes the following: "a mood check, a bridge between sessions, prioritizing an agenda, discussing specific problems and teaching skills in the context of solving these problems, setting of self-help assignments, summary, and feedback."

It is also important to note that CBT is present oriented: although an evaluation of the past origin of the problem is conducted, the main focus is to eliminate the present maintaining factors.

Theoretical Base of CBT

CBT has been mainly influenced by three sources (Beck and Weishaar 1989):

- The phenomenological approach rooted in Greek Stoic philosophy, Kant's work (conscious subjective experience), and the writings of Adler, Alexander, Horney, and Sullivan;

- The structural theory: mainly Freud's conceptualization of cognitions into primary and secondary processes; and
- Cognitive psychology: primarily based on the model of "personal constructs" of Kelly and the work of Richard Lazarus on the role of cognitions in behavioral and emotional change.

Behavior therapist such as Bandura, Mahoney, and Meichenbaum have also made important theoretical contributions. It is also important to note that the work of Albert Ellis in Rational Emotive Behavior Therapy (REBT) has provided impetus to the development of CBT (Beck et al. 1979).

Comparing CBT with Logotherapy

As seen earlier, there are similarities between behavior modification techniques and logotherapeutic techniques such as paradoxical intention and research has validated paradoxical intention, and deflection within the model of sexual therapy. Frankl (2004) points out that logotherapy anticipated many features that were validated later on through solid experimental research by behavior therapy.

Frankl (2000) describes the emergence of behavior therapy as a "healthy and reasonable" trend in comparison to psychoanalysis that has made a valuable contribution to psychotherapy by demystifying neurosis. Comparing both approaches, he conceives behaviorism as a therapy of "reactions" and logotherapy as a therapy focused on "action" that goes beyond behaviorism, without contradicting it (Frankl 1969). He uses the example of an airplane: the fact that an airplane can fly doesn't contradict its capacity to move on the ground like a car (Lewis 2011a, b). It's important, however, to point out that Frankl refers to behaviorism (first wave) in his writing and not to CBT (second wave) as used today.

Lukas (2006) refers to the cognitive element that has allowed behavior therapy to move beyond conditioning. She believes that CBT has an exact and scientifically objective foundation and is efficient and valid in the psychological dimension. In the same way, she points out, that logotherapy is efficient and valid in the noetic dimension. She highlights that since there isn't a rigid line that separates the psychological and noetic dimensions, there shouldn't be one either between CBT and logotherapy; but rather a "fruitful symbiosis" between these two important orientations (Lukas 2006). She points out that the future of CBT and logotherapy depends on the motivation of their respective representatives to complement each other and combine the two orientations.

Similarities and Differences Between CBT and Logotherapy

CBT and logotherapy present many similarities:

- They have both been influenced by phenomenology.

- They both emphasize that modifying internal maladaptive "attitudes" (Beck refers to attitudes or schema) leads to behavioral change.
- Both are active, participative, action-oriented, and collaborative approaches (between the client and the therapist) and use a process of "guided discovery" without the therapist imposing his/her personal concepts of reason or meaning.
- The therapeutic alliance is important in both approaches.
- The Socratic dialogue is the main conversation tool and both make use of imagination.
- Both approaches are sound, brief, and solutions focused. The use of common sense is a key factor.
- Their main goal is to resolve the present issue, not explore the past.
- Both approaches take into account empirical research and use valid tools and pragmatic techniques.

There are also major differences:

- Logotherapy goes beyond learning principals, reinforcement, and cognition. It takes into account the "unique" human dimension where authentic human phenomena such as self-distancing and self-transcendence reside.
- Referring to that third noetic dimension, the concepts of intentionality, freedom of choice, meaning, and responsibility are central to logotherapy but absent in CBT. In that dimension, a person can choose how to behave.
- Humor (defined as intrinsically human) is an integral part of the exposure methodology in logotherapy (paradoxical intention).
- The main focus of logotherapy is to discover life meaning and purpose (which would lead to the "correct" attitude) versus modifying only erroneous thinking patterns in CBT.
- Logotherapy is value based and puts emphasis on personal meaning in a broad sense and not in purely intellectual or rational terms.
- Logotherapy taps into the healthy, intact part of the client, the positive, and helps him/her discover and use his/her strengths.
- Logotherapy is a positive form of psychotherapy and CBT is a "coping" model: the goal of logotherapy is to increase well-being and not only to overcome a disorder like in CBT.

In summary, logotherapy and CBT have a similar therapeutic process. Logotherapy doesn't dispute the empirical results and procedures used in CBT; however, it goes beyond by taking into account the third, noetic, dimension.

Benefits for Combining CBT and Logotherapy

CBT and logotherapy compliment each other: CBT as a psychotherapy is very much a "coping" model. In this respect, the CBT model compliments the principles of logotherapy. As a positive therapy, logotherapy in turn adds the noetic dimension and focuses on well-being, going beyond rationality and disorder resolution.

Ameli and Dattilio (2013) have presented through specific examples the benefits of integrating the concepts and techniques of logotherapy with CBT at the clinical level. Those benefits are presented below along with additional ones:

- The concept of freedom of choice could be valuable at several levels: (1) in the exposure procedure it could motivate the client to face anxiety or fear by making him/her see it as an option; he/she can't control his anxiety level but can choose how to react: run away or stay in spite of the fear; (2) it could facilitate perceptual shifts and action by eliminating excuses rooted in the past: one is free to choose new behaviors in spite of his/her past learning history and conditionings; (3) in case of unavoidable suffering (terminal or incurable illness, grief, loss, etc.,), integrating the attitudinal choice (one is free to take a stand, including the discovery of meaning in suffering) into the cognitive protocol could help the client to better accept and bear with pain and suffering, minimizing the risk for depression, despair, and suicide (Ameli and Dattilio 2013).
- The use of humor in the exposure procedure helps in reducing anticipatory anxiety (Ameli and Dattilio 2013).
- Combining the PIL and VAT with cognitive behavior instruments could help assess the risk for suicide and help clients take steps toward building a meaningful life at the end of therapy (Ameli and Dattilio 2013).
- Using the concept of "intentionality" helps differentiate between the cause and the reason, which in some cases get mixed up in CBT. Frankl uses the example of love and hate as "human phenomena" because they are intentionally directed toward a person or an object. Human beings have always motives to love or hate and their behavior is rooted in a reason and not only a biological or psychological cause that urges or pushes them to act aggressively. At the human level, one can choose, for example, to avoid or overcome aggression.
- Integrating the concept of responsibility has multiple benefits: (1) it can motivate the client to take the CBT process seriously and own their progress and results; he/she is responsible for his cure as the decision maker of his/her life; (2) using the logotherapeutic principle that one is not a victim but the "cocreator" of his/her destiny could better counteract the "victim" or the "martyr" schema; (3) it could stimulate the client to better analyze his/her choices and take responsibility for his/her errors in order to adopt new interpretations and behaviors.
- Adding the concepts of personal values and meaning could make the therapy process more individualized and effective, and allows working with a broader range of clients.
- Increasing well-being through hope and optimism leads to a proactive and resilient attitude that could improve relapse prevention.
- A few authors have pointed out the value of enhancing cognitive behavior therapies with logotherapy and existential–phenomenological therapies:

- Corrie and Milton (2000) insist on a strong case for connecting existential and cognitive models and suggests that adding the concept of value to the cognitive model offers a "framework through which it is possible to explore the choices we make about who we are and who we want to become."
- Lukas (2006) points out the benefit of combining both approaches at the therapeutic level so that therapists could work with the complete tridimensional (somatic, psychological, and noetic) representation of the human being.
- Hutchinson and Chapman (2005) highlight the "remarkable similarities" between Rational Emotive Behavior Therapy (REBT) and logotherapy. They point out that: "logotherapy-enhanced REBT can facilitate reciprocal and comprehensive alterations of both rational processes and core existential schema."
- Along the same lines, Lewis (2009) promotes a meaning-centered REBT approach, generating both rational and meaningful cognitions and attitudes that would lead to self-transcendence. He also points out that adding the concept of personal meaning could increase the client's motivation in completing the homework assignments in cognitive behavior therapy (Lewis 2009).
- Losa Grau (2009) reports the benefits of combining cognitive behavior therapy with logotherapy through her research with support groups dealing with the loss of a close relative: the process of meaning recreation and discovery helped participants to reflect on the positive meaning that the death of their loved one had for them and value what really mattered in their life.
- Hutzell (2009) points out that logotherapy complements cognitive behavior therapy on several powerful and validated variables such as: "client variables, therapist variables, and technique variables."

Conclusion

Integrating logotherapy with CBT is a worthy challenge because it could add value at all levels: client's motivation and well-being, therapeutic process efficiency, effectiveness, and relapse prevention. Logotherapy opens that third "human" dimension and broadens the scope of treatment: not only are the dysfunctional reactions and thoughts modified but intentional, responsible, and meaningful actions are promoted and the client is capable of creating purposeful goals which will increase his/her well-being and resilience at the end of therapy. Suffering is minimized while well-being is maximized.

Moving toward a logotherapy-enhanced CBT or a meaning-based CBT would be beneficial for both approaches: CBT could take advantage of valid tools and techniques in the noetic dimension and logotherapy could benefit from a valid and empirically based model in the psychological dimension.

It would be desirable for experts in CBT and logotherapy to collaborate in order to design integrative protocols that would provide the most efficient and effective treatment plans.

References

Ameli, M., & Dattilio, F. M. (2013). Enhancing cognitive behavior therapy with logotherapy: Techniques for clinical practice. *Psychotherapy, 50*(3), 387–391.

Ascher, L. M. (1978–1979). Paradoxical intention: A review of preliminary research. *The International Forum for Logotherapy, 1*, 18–21.

Ascher, L. M. (1980). Paradoxical intention viewed by a behavior therapist. *The International Forum for Logotherapy, 3*, 13–16.

Ascher, L. M. (Ed.). (1989). *The therapeutic paradox*. New York, NY: Guilford.

Ascher, L. M., & Efran, J. S. (1978). The use of paradoxical intention in a behavioral program for sleep onset insomnia. *Journal of Consulting and Clinical Psychology, 46*, 547–550.

Batthyany, A., & Guttmann, D. (2006). *Empirical research on logotherapy and meaning-oriented psychotherapy. An Annotated Bibliography*. Phoenix, AZ: Zeig Tucker.

Beck, A. T., Rush, A. J., Shaw, B. F., & Emery, G. (1979). *Cognitive therapy of depression*. New York, NY: Guilford Press.

Beck, A. T., & Weishaar, M. (1989). Cognitive Therapy. In A. Freeman, K. M. Simon, L. E. Beutler, & H. Arkowitz (Eds.), *Comprehensive handbook of Cognitive Therapy*. New York, NY: Plenum Press.

Corrie, S., & Milton, M. (2000). The relationship between existential-phenomenological and cognitive-behaviour therapies. *The European Journal of Psychotherapy, Counseling & Health, 3*, 7–24.

Dattilio, F. M. (1987). The use of Paradoxical Intention in the treatment of Panic Attacks. *Journal of Counseling and Development, 66*, 102–103.

Dattilio, F. M. (1994). Paradoxical Intention as a proposed alternative in the treatment of panic disorder. *Journal of Cognitive Psychotherapy, 8*, 33–40.

Dattilio, F. M., & Padesky, C. A. (1990). *Cognitive therapy with couples*. Florida: Professional Resource Exchange, Inc.

Fabry, D. D. S. (2010). Evidence base for Paradoxical Intention: Reviewing clinical outcome studies. *The International Forum for Logotherapy, 33*, 21–29.

Frankl, V. E. (1959/1984). *Man's search for meaning*. Boston, MA: Beacon Press.

Frankl, V. E. (1969). *The will to meaning: Foundations and applications of logotherapy*. New York, NY: World Publishing.

Frankl, V. E. (1995). *La psicoterapia en la práctica médica*. Buenos Aires: San Pablo.

Frankl, V. E. (2000). *Man's search for ultimate meaning*. New York, NY: Perseus Books.

Frankl, V. E. (2003). *Ante el vacío existencial*. Barcelona: Herder.

Frankl, V. E. (2004). *On the theory and therapy of mental disorders*. New York, NY: Runner-Routledge.

García-Alandete, J., Gallego-Pérez, J. F., & Pérez-Delgado, E. (2009). Sentido de la vida y desesperanza: Un estudio empírico. *Universitas Psychologica, 8*(2), 447–451.

Hutchinson, G. T., & Chapman, B. P. (2005). Logotherapy-enhanced REBT: An integration of discovery and reason. *Journal of Contemporary Psychotherapy, 35*, 145–159.

Hutzell, R. R. (2009). Why cognitive psychotherapists in the USA benefit from learning logotherapy. In A. Batthyany & J. Levinson (Eds.), *Existential psychotherapy of meaning: Handbook of logotherapy and existential analysis*. Phoenix, AZ: Zeig Tucker & Theissen.

Hutzell, R. R., & Eggert, M. D. (1989/1995/2009). *A workbook to increase your meaningful and purposeful goals (2009 PDF Edition)*. Retrieved January 1, 2012 from http://www.viktorfrankl.org/source/hutzell_workbook_2009.pdf.

Klingberg, H. (2001). *When life calls out to us: The love and lifework of Viktor and Elly Frankl*. New York, NY: Doubleday.

Levinson, J. (1979). A combination of paradoxical intention and dereflection. *The International Forum for Logotherapy, 2*, 40–41.

Lewis, M. H. (2009). *Logotalk, episode 8: Meaning Centered Cognitive Therapy*. An online podcast at http://www.logotalk.net.

Lewis, M. H. (2011). *Defiant power: An overview of Viktor Frankl's logotherapy and existential analysis*. pdf version. Retrieved August 3rd, 2011 from http://defiantpower.blogspot.nl/p/ebook.html

Lewis, M. H. (2011). *Amelioration of obsessive-compulsive disorder using paradoxical intention*. Paper presented at the Eighteenth World Congress of Logotherapy, Dallas, TX.

Losa Grau, A. M. (2009). Elaborando juntos el duelo: Los grupos de ayuda mutua. In J. Garcia Alandete & J. F. Gallego-Pérez (Eds.), *Adversidad, sentido y resiliencia*. Valencia: EDICEP.

Lukas, E. (1980). Modification of attitudes. *The International Forum for Logotherapy, 3*, 25–35.

Lukas, E. (1981). New ways for dereflection. *The International Forum for Logotherapy, 4*, 13–28.

Lukas, Elisabeth (1991). Die magische Frage "Wozu". München: Herder.

Lukas, E. (1998). *Logotherapy textbook: Meaning-centered psychotherapy*. Toronto, ON: Liberty Press.

Lukas, E. (2006). *También tu vida tiene sentido*. Mexico: Ediciones LAG.

Lukas, E. (2008). *Viktor E. Frankl: El sentido de la vida*. Barcelona: Plataforma Editorial.

Pattakos, A. (2004). *Prisoners of our thoughts*. San Francisco, CA: Berrett Koehler.

Rogina, J. M. (2004). Treatment and interventions for narcissistic personality. *The International Forum for Logotherapy, 27*, 28–33.

Ryan, M. F. (2008). *The last freedom*. Bloomington: Universe, Inc.

Schulenberg, S. E. (2003). Empirical research and logotherapy. *Psychological Reports, 93*, 307–319.

Schulenberg, S. E., & Melton, A. M. A. (2008). On the measure of meaning: Logotherapy's empirical contributions to humanistic psychology. *The Humanistic Psychologist, 36*, 21–44.

Schulenberg, S. E., Nassif, C., Hutzell, R. R., & Rogina, J. M. (2008). Logotherapy for clinical practice. *Psychotherapy Theory, Research, Practice, Training, 45*(4), 447–463.

Schulenberg, S. E., Schnetzer, L. W., Winters, M. R., & Hutzell, R. R. (2010). Meaning-centered couples therapy: Logotherapy and intimate relationships. *Journal of Contemporary Psychotherapy, 40*, 95–102.

Solyom, L., J. Garza-Perez, B. L. Ledwige, and C. Solyom: "Paradoxical Intention in the Treatment of Obsessive Thoughts: A Pilot Study." *Comprehensive Psychiatry*, Vol. 13, No. 3 (May 1972), 291–297.

Wells, A. (2009). *Metacognitive therapy for anxiety and depression*. New York, NY: Guilford Press.

Workload, Existential Fulfillment, and Work Engagement Among City Council Members

Marinka Tomic

Introduction

If there is a group that is supposed to be highly inspired and engaged, than we do expressly think of politicians. They are assumed to be people with a particular vocation and are attracted to serve the public interest. In general, one must have a vocation for politics.

In his famous lecture at Munich University in 1921 entitled "Politics as vocation", Max Weber asserts, that "politics may be a man's avocation or his vocation" (1921, 5). Weber posits that there are two ways of making politics one's vocation: "Either one lives *for* politics or one lives *off* politics" (1921, 6). In the present chapter, we focus on council members and share Weber's first way.

In the Netherlands, 71 % of all council members have a regular paid job. They spend an average of 38 h a week on their paid job (De Jager-De Lange et al. 2010). Despite the fact that a council member spends an average of 14 h per week on council-related activities, this work is not considered a normal job. Council member activities are often performed alongside a regular job. In their spare time, they are willing to promote public interest in spite of the fact that they do not receive appreciable financial incentives. Membership of a city council is an additional function. As a council member it is hardly possible to live off politics.

Much psychological research focused on unhealthiness and being indisposed (Schaufeli and Bakker 2001). Since the beginning of this century, however, researchers have shown an increasing interest in positive aspects of personal functioning in organizations and institutions (Schaufeli and Bakker 2007). This turn is likely due to a new movement called positive psychology, "the scientific study of positive experiences and positive individual traits, and the institutions that facilitate their development" (Duckworth et al. 2005, 629).

M. Tomic (✉)
Van Hövell tot Westerflierhof 31a, 6431 DG Hoensbroek, Netherlands

A. Batthyány (ed.), *Logotherapy and Existential Analysis*, Logotherapy and Existential Analysis: Proceedings of the Viktor Frankl Institute Vienna 1,
DOI 10.1007/978-3-319-29424-7_19

Workload

Workload is the perceived pressure due to amount of work and task heaviness. Employees experience a heavy workload when they are not able to meet the task requirements decreed by the employer. Perceived workload is a dynamic concept. It is related to the individual work situation and the subjective perception of the employee. Workload indicates the degree to which the job is taxing in terms of mental effort, complexity of work, and speed of work (De Jonge et al. 1995; Van Veldhoven and Broersen 1999). Workload seems to be related to health. Research suggests that those with higher workloads report more health problems (Tummers et al. 2000).

Existential Fulfillment

In addition to workload, existential fulfillment is an important factor in the current study. It refers to a way of life that is full of meaning and purpose and reveals an existential psychological approach to life (Längle et al. 2003). Independence is bounded by the limitations of our own competence, the environment, and the fact that life is finite (Pyszczynski et al. 1999). To obtain a fulfilled existence, humans must overcome the psychological conflicts evoked by these boundaries. One who accepts the self-accepts his or her potentialities and intrinsic limitations. One who actualizes the self-explores and develops his or her possibilities and potentialities for the sake of personal growth in understanding and abilities. One who transcends the self-recognizes the otherness of the reality beyond the self, searches for respectful relationships with this reality, derives life-meaning from these relationships, feels responsible for them, feels part of a larger whole, distinguishes interests that surpass self-interests, and is able to see the self in perspective of the outer reality (Loonstra et al. 2007; Tomic and Tomic 2008, 2011). Self-transcendence is considered by Frankl (2004) to be the essence of human existence. This spiritual ability, not necessarily religious, enables the individual to make intentional contacts with the world beyond the self, which provides ultimate meaning to life.

In fulfilling these existential tasks, people find life-meaning and a fulfilled existence. The notions of self-acceptance, self-actualization, and self-transcendence can be interpreted as basic attitudes in pursuing existential fulfillment and overcoming the psychological conflicts caused by human limitedness. The inability to achieve existential goals may lead to burnout (Pines and Aronson 1988), whereas the achievement of these goals may result in work engagement (Schaufeli and Bakker 2001).

Work Engagement

Positive psychology focuses on health and well-being. One of the dimensions is the concept of work engagement, which is a positive, fulfilling, work-related state of mind. It is a positive, affective-cognitive state of supreme satisfaction (Schaufeli and Bakker

2001). The concept has three components: vigor, dedication, and absorption. *Vigor* is characterized by high levels of energy and mental flexibility while working, the willingness to invest effort in one's work, and perseverance in the face of difficulties. *Dedication* refers to a commitment to work and is characterized by a sense of significance. Dedication is a useful and meaningful experience, inspiring, and challenging; it evokes feelings of pride and enthusiasm. *Absorption*, the final dimension of engagement, refers to the full concentration on and deep engrossment in one's work.

Employees who display a high level of engagement work especially hard and diligently because they enjoy their work, not because of a strong, compelling inner motivation alone (Schaufeli and Bakker 2007). When they experience fatigue, such individuals describe the feeling as quite pleasant because of its association with positive achievements rather than failures (Schaufeli and Salanova 2008).

The outcomes of work engagement primarily include positive attitudes toward work and the organization, such as job satisfaction, commitment to the organization, and a lack of desire to turnover (Demerouti et al. 2001; Schaufeli and Bakker 2004). Likewise, engagement leads to positive organizational behavior, such as displaying personal initiative, a strong motivation to learn (Sonnentag 2003), and proactive conduct (Salanova et al. 2003).

When employees are engaged with their work, there is congruence between the employees' priorities and the organizations' goals. There are indications that the degree of work engagement is positively associated with job performance (Schaufeli and Bakker 2007). Schaufeli and Salanova (2007) conclude that engaged individuals have a well-developed ability to adequately respond to change, quickly adapt to a new environment, and easily switch from one activity to another. Engaged employees continue to seek new challenges in their work and perform at a high quality level, resulting in positive feedback from both managers and clients. Work engagement is contagious and thus is transferable from one person to another (Schaufeli and Salanova 2007). Research also indicates that work engagement is positively related to health, i.e., fewer depressed, stress-related and psychosomatic symptoms were found (Schaufeli and Bakker 2004; Demerouti et al. 2001). Finally, a study by Fullagar, Culbertson, and Mills (2009) shows that invigorated and dedicated employees carry over their positive work experiences for a happier home life, i.e., generating high levels of engagement among people has a positive impact on the work–family interface. There are indications that work engagement has many advantages for both employees, employers, and home life. However, the level of work engagement varies for each profession. Nevertheless, to our knowledge, work engagement among council members has never been systematically assessed in published articles, to date. This article makes a modest contribution toward remedying that omission.

City Council Members

Encouraging research among specific professional groups that may be expected to have higher levels of work engagement and to be highly inspired by their work is very much recommended (Schaufeli and Bakker 2001). Council members, even though they are no employees in the narrow sense of the word, are assumed to be particularly engaged and inspired in their work. The importance of research on work engagement among local politicians is strongly emphasized. For example, it is interesting to determine why some council members walk out of the council early, or no longer offer themselves for reelection while other council members, working under the same conditions, continue to work in a highly engaged manner.

A councilor is a member of a city council, the legislative body that governs a city. According to Troost (2000), representation of the people is the primary function of an elected council member. He/she represents the citizens and makes judgments on behalf of them. A council member also strongly influences what will appear on the political agenda and is closely associated with policy preparation. He/she determines the political line in an early stage and translates it into political commissions to the bench of mayor and aldermen. Finally, the city council checks afterwards whether mayor and aldermen have implemented the policy within the frameworks outlined by the city council.

It is important to expand upon the theory of work engagement through research on potential predictor variables. Existential fulfillment may contribute to the theory of work engagement among council members.

The above discussion provides sufficient grounds for further investigation among council members. In order to design conceivable effective, targeted interventions, at a later stage for instance, that promote work engagement among council members, research on the relationships between workload and existential fulfillment on the one hand and work engagement on the other hand is necessary. Promoting and maintaining work engagement may result in working with pleasure and enthusiasm as well as in the prevention of (health) problems, sickness absence, and turnover. This could be of benefit to the quality of local politics.

The present study is the first to assess workload, existential fulfillment, and work engagement among council members. We hope that this research will contribute to the theory in the field of workload and existential fulfillment in relation to work engagement. The study addressed the following research questions: To what extent do workload, existential fulfillment, and work engagement influence well-being among council members? In addition, it was investigated to which extent the first two independent variables influence work engagement.

Method

A survey methodology was used in the current study. An online survey was developed and utilized. The sample of respondents received an e-mail containing a hyperlink to a survey website and they replied with their answers. The survey was mailed to a large random sample of 420 council members.

The findings of Tolstikova and Chartier (2009), for instance, suggest that internet-based methods can be a suitable and valid alternative to more traditional paper-and-pencil methods.

Participants

The participants were council members in the Netherlands. First, we selected council members from all provincial capitals (12 in total). In addition, we selected per province 12 other municipalities. The number of council members depends on the number of municipality residents. The council members were selected at random. Per provincial capital a random sample of 25 council members was drawn, per other municipality 10, respectively. The council members were approached via their e-mail addresses. All council members were eligible for the study. In total, 247 questionnaires were returned, resulting in a response rate of 59 %. This response rate is very good for survey research (Babbie 2004; Van Horn and Green 2009).

Of the 247 respondents who completed the questionnaire, the average age was 53.5 (SD = 10.9), ranging from 20 to 75 years of age. 64 % was male. For the record, the average council member age in 2006 was 50.0 years (Post and De Lange 2008). Their average age increased from 50.0 in 2006 to 53.5 years in 2009. It should be mentioned that the city council as a whole is getting on in years every year. In most municipalities a new term of 4 years started in 2006. Consequently, an increase of 3.5 years is obvious. Therefore, the sample was representative for council age. Regarding council member age and gender the sample in the current study is in line with the real situation in the Netherlands, i.e., external validity is guaranteed (representativeness and generalizability).

Measurements

Perceived Workload. These items were measured on a six-point scale using a "strongly disagree" to "strongly agree" response format. An example of an item is: "Work will be left to me that should have been finished." The items are partly based on the questionnaire of Van Veldhoven and Broersen (1999). The maximum score is 42. The internal consistency coefficient is 0.74. High scores on this scale indicate more perceived workload.

Existential Fulfillment. Existential fulfillment, composed of the three dimensions of self-acceptance, self-actualization, and self-transcendence, was measured by means of the Existential Fulfillment Scale (EFS) (Loonstra et al. 2007). The EFS consists of 15 items (five items for each dimension) measured on a five-point Likert scale, ranging from 0 ("not at all" relevant to me) to 4 ("fully" relevant to me). The maximum score per dimension is 20. The five items on self-acceptance refer to the urge to prove oneself to others, rejection of the self, inner uncertainty, and psychological reliance (e.g., "Often I do things more because I have to than because I want to"). The self-actualization items deal with intrinsic motivation, the passion of one's own ideals, and feeling free to calmly pursue one's goals (e.g., "I remain motivated to go on, even when things are going against me"). The self-transcendence items focus on feeling part of a larger, meaningful totality, conceiving a sense of life that transcends personal interests, and being convinced that life is good for something (e.g., "I think my life has such a deep meaning that it surpasses my personal interests"). In a study of 812 students, the factorial structure of the EFS showed an acceptable fit (Loonstra et al. 2007). The internal consistency coefficients are 0.79, 0.76, and 0.82, respectively.

Work Engagement. Work engagement was measured with the Utrecht Work Engagement Scale (UWES) (Schaufeli and Bakker 2001). The UWES has been found to be a reliable and valid self-report questionnaire (Schaufeli et al. 2006). There are three subscales with five items each: vigor, dedication, and absorption. Participants responded on a seven-point Likert scale, ranging from 0 (*never*) to 6 (*always*, *daily*), with a maximum score per subscale of 30. Examples of items are: "At work I bubble over with energy" (vigor), "Work inspires me" (dedication), and "I am totally absorbed in my work" (absorption). High scores on these scales indicate greater work engagement (vigor, dedication, and absorption). Internal consistency coefficients are 0.84, 0.86, and 0.72, respectively.

Procedure

The council members received an e-mail at their workplace containing a hyperlink to a survey website. The survey addressed topics in the following order: perceived workload scale, existential fulfillment scale, work engagement, and demographic characteristics (age, gender, years of council member experience, weekly spent time on their council work, number of residents, council members' political convictions, and denomination). The accompanying cover letter stated that the purpose of the study was to better understand council members' feelings of existential fulfillment, workload, and well-being. The letter also explained that participation in the survey was completely voluntary, answers to the survey questions would be kept in the strictest confidence, and the researchers would not know the source of specific responses. Specific hypotheses were not revealed. After the survey was received by all participants, one reminder was sent by e-mail 14 days later. In addition, in order to raise the response rate, we followed suggestions from Fox, Crask, and Jonghoon (1988) and Green, Boser, and Hutchinson (1997): prenotification by attached letter, university sponsorship of the survey, forwarding of questionnaires directly to the respondents via e-mail, the provision of contact information (to be used at any time if necessary), a fairly brief questionnaire, and electronic follow-up.

Statistical Analysis

Descriptive statistics were calculated to summarize the sample characteristics. Correlations between demographic and independent variables (workload and existential fulfillment) and the study's outcome variables (dimensions of work engagement) were calculated before the main analysis. All p-values were two-tailed and p-values < 0.05 were considered statistically significant. Hierarchical regression analysis was performed to identify the independent variables associated with work engagement.

Results

Sample Description

Personal characteristics of the sample are detailed in Table 1. The majority of the participants were male (64 %). Age of the subjects varied across all age ranges. The largest percentage of participants was 45–64 years of age (64 %). Over 13 % of the participants were older than 65 years of age.

Council member characteristics of the sample are also portrayed in Table 1. Approximately 70 % of the respondents had worked as a council member for between 1 and 8 years. Another 29 % had between 9 and more than 17 years council member experience. The majority of the sample worked 9–24 h weekly. Over 32 % of the participants were members of the Labor Party, followed by 22.6 % of the Christian Democratic Appeal. Over 12 % were members of the People's Party for Freedom and Democracy. The majority of the participants were adherents of the Christian Faith (57.2 %), while 41.5 % of the participants described themselves as currently having no faith.

There were no differences between female and male mean scores on the dependent and independent variables. The older one is, the more years of experience one had as a council member $\chi^2(20) = 47.58$, $p < 0.001$ and $r = 0.36$, $p < 0.001$. Men had more experience in years as a council member than women [$t(245) = 2.36$, $p < 0.05$]. Female council members spent more hours per week on council-related matters than their male counterparts [$t(245) = 3.62$, $p < 0.001$].

Results show that the average score of council members 65 years of age or older on workload was higher than the average council member score $t(278) = 2.56$, $p < 0.01$. Likewise, the highest score on perceived workload is observed from council members who spent between 30 and 36 h per week on council membership.

The Table 1 shows that 86 % of council members resided in municipalities ranging in size from less than 50,000 to 150,000 residents. In 2009, 11 out of 441 municipalities (2.5 %) had more than 150,000 inhabitants (Census Bureau 2010).

The Green Left council members [$t(236) = 2.87$, $p < 0.001$] and the Socialist Party group [$t(226) = 3.31$, $p < 0.001$] experienced a higher workload compared to the average workload of council members. The Socialist Party group had the lowest scores on self-acceptance [$t(226) = -3.80$, $p < 0.001$]. The Christian Union group had the highest score on self-transcendence [$t(236) = 3.92$, $p < 0.001$].

Council members who adhered not to be religious had a higher perceived workload level compared to their religious counterparts [$t(322) = 2.33$, $p < 0.05$]. The Evangelical Christian group in the council had the highest scores on vigor [$t(237) = 1.91$, $p < 0.05$]

Table 1 Demographic statistics of council member sample ($N=247$)

N (%)	Mean	SD
Gender:		
Female	89	36.0
Male	158	64.0
Age (years)	53.5	10.9
≤25	1	0.4
26–35	12	4.9
36–44	44	17.8
45–54	77	31.2
55–64	80	32.4
>65	33	13.4
Political party membership		
Labor Party (PvdA)	70	32.3
Christian Democratic Appeal (CDA)	49	22.6
People's Party for Freedom and Democracy (VVD)	27	12.4
Christian Union (CU)	21	9.7
Green Left (Groen Links)	21	9.7
Socialist Party (SP)	11	5.1
Local	18	8.3
Religious conviction		
Christian Faith	131	57.2
Not Religious	95	41.5
Jewish	1	0.4
Islamic	2	0.9
Experience in years	*8.2*	*4.6*
≤4	102	41.3
5–8	73	29.6
9–12	44	17.8
13–16	14	5.7
>17	14	5.7
Weekly number of hours	*22.3*	*7.8*
≤8	13	5.3
9–16	93	37.7
17–24	86	34.8
25–30	32	13.0
31–36	13	5.3
>37	10	4.0
Number of city residents		
≤50,000	88	35.6
51,000–100,000	58	23.5
01.000–150,000	56	22.7
151,000–200,000	18	7.3

(continued)

Table 1 (continued)

N (%)	Mean	SD
201,000–250,000	2	0.8
>251,000	25	10.1

and self-acceptance [$t(237) = 2.13, p < 0.05$]. Participants who described themselves as having no faith scored below the average self-transcendent score of the sample [$t(321) = 4.21, p < 0.001$].

Research question 1 addressed the level of workload, existential fulfillment, and work engagement among council members. Table 2 shows the mean scores and standard deviations of the study variables mentioned. The table also shows that alpha coefficients for the instruments were found to be 0.70 or higher, except for self-actualization. This is a reasonable level of acceptance for the group of items (Nunnally and Bernstein 1994). The internal consistencies were also sufficient values according to the British Psychological Society Steering Committee on Test Standards (1995) for this kind of research. Skewness and kurtosis analysis indicated that the data on the research variables were distributed normally.

The second question addressed the relationships between workload and existential fulfillment on the one hand and work engagement on the other. The results are displayed in Table 2 (survey of correlation and internal consistency coefficients) and Table 3 (regression analysis).

The older participants were, the more years of council member experience they had. There was an inverse relationship between council member age and perceived workload. Council members who reported higher scores on self-acceptance were older. There was also an inverse relationship between the number of council member years and perceived workload: the more years participants acted as council members, the lower their scores on workload. Results show that the more weekly hours spent on council activities, the higher the scores on perceived workload. The lower the scores on self-acceptance, the more hours per week they spent on council-related activities. Higher levels of perceived workload correlated significantly with lower levels of work engagement and existential fulfillment. Perceived workload correlated significantly negative with the three dimensions of work engagement, i.e., vigor, dedication, and absorption. The higher the scores on workload, the lower the scores on work engagement. Self-acceptance and self-actualization correlated negatively with workload. The three dimensions of existential fulfillment correlated significantly positive with the three work engagement dimensions. High levels on self-actualization, self-acceptance, and self-transcendence corresponded with high levels on work engagement dimensions.

A hierarchical regression analysis was carried out in order to examine the extent to which the dimensions of work engagement could be explained by the independent variables workload and existential fulfillment. To this end, the regression analysis was carried out three times, once for each of the dimensions: vigor, dedication, and absorption (see Table 3). With each work engagement dimension as a dependent variable, the control variable "gender" was first added to the regression

Table 2 Summary of means, standard deviations, correlations between variables, and internal consistency coefficients (on diagonal), $N=247$

	Variables	*M*	SD	1	2	3	4	5	6	7	8	9	10	11	
1	Gender (male 158, 64 %)														
2	Age	53.5	10.9	0.16*											
3	Experience in years	8.2	4.6	0.15*	0.36**										
4	Weekly number of hrs.	22.3	7.8	–0.23**	12	0.08									
5	Number of residents			–0.24**	–0.14*	–0.07	0.39**								
6	Workload	27.1	6.6	–0.06	–0.26**	–0.14*	0.15*	0.13*	(0.82)						
7	Vigor	27.4	4.9	–0.07	0.08	0.02	0.06	–0.02	–0.33**	(0.85)					
8	Absorption	25.7	5.3	–0.11	0.07	0.00	0.03	–0.08	–0.21**	0.79**	(0.83)				
9	Dedication	28.9	4.8	–0.07	0.08	–0.03	0.09	–0.04	–0.33**	0.79**	0.77**	(0.90)			
10	Self-actualization	18.5	3.0	–0.07	0.05	–0.01	0.05	–0.01	–0.36**	0.57**	0.55**	0.50**	(0.66)		
11	Self-acceptance	10.8	3.1	0.08	0.11	0.01	–0.03	–0.01	–0.47**	0.39**	0.19**	0.33**	0.26**	(0.75)	
12	Self-transcendence	17.3	4.5	0.04	0.09	–0.05	–0.02	–0.11	–0.18**	0.36**	0.38**	0.33**	0.54**	0.04	(0.83)

*$p<0.05$; **$p<0.001$

Maximum scores for workload (42); for vigor, absorption, and dedication (30); for self-actualization, self-acceptance, and self-transcendence (20)

Table 3 Summary of hierarchical regression analyses for variables predicting work engagement dimensions among council members ($N=247$)

		Vigor		Dedication		Absorption	
	Variables	β	ΔR^2	β	ΔR^2	β	ΔR^2
	Step	−0.06	0.00	−0.06	0.00	−0.11	0.00
1	Gender	0.01	0.01	0.01	0.01	0.04	0.01
2	Age	0.02	0.00	0.05	0.00	0.01	0.00
3	Experience in years	−0.02	0.00	−0.05	0.00	0.01	0.00
4	Hours per week	0.05	0.00	0.12	0.00	0.01	0.00
5	Number of city residents	−0.02	0.00	−0.07	0.01	−0.09	0.01
6	Workload	−0.05	0.12**	−0.12	0.12**	0.03	0.04*
7	Self-actualization	0.43**	0.22**	0.33**	0.15**	0.45**	0.24**
8	Self-acceptance	0.25**	0.04**	0.19**	0.02*	0.08	0.00
9	Self-transcendence	0.11	0.01	0.11	0.01	0.14*	0.01*
	Multiple R	0.64		0.57		0.57	
	R^2 Total	0.40		0.33		0.32	
	Overall regression f-test	17.79**		12.45**		12.756**	

*$p<0.05$; **$p<0.01$

equation (step 1), followed by the control variable "age" (step 2), the independent variables "number of years council member experience" (step 3), "number of council member hours weekly" (step 4), "number of city residents" (5), "workload" (step 6), "self-actualization" (step 7), "self-acceptance" (step 8), and "self-transcendence" (step 9), according to Aiken and West (1991) and Tabachnik and Fidell (2001).

On the basis of the hierarchical regression analysis, the following results are reported. The Table 3 shows the best predictors of vigor, dedication, and absorption. Workload correlated significantly negative with dedication, and explained 12 % of the variance, i.e., the more perceived workload, the less dedication. The correlations between the dimensions of existential fulfillment and work engagement were as follows. First, there were positive significant correlations between self-actualization and vigor ($\beta=0.42$, $p<0.001$), dedication ($\beta=0.34$, $p<0.01$), and absorption ($\beta=0.45$, $p<0.001$). Self-actualization explained 22 % of the variance in vigor, 15 % of the variance in dedication and 24 % in absorption. We concluded that the higher the score on self-actualization, the higher the scores on vigor, dedication, and absorption.

There appeared to be a significant positive correlation between self-acceptance and one dimension of work engagement, i.e., vigor ($\beta=0.19$, $p<0.01$). The explained variance was 2 %. The higher the score on self-acceptance, the higher the score obtained on vigor. Self-transcendence correlated significantly positive with one dimension of work engagement, namely absorption ($\beta=0.14$, $p<0.05$) and explained 1 % of the variance. The higher the score on self-transcendence, the higher the score on absorption. These results indicate that self-actualization alone had a positive and significant correlation with all dimensions of work engagement.

Discussion

The current study represents an initial attempt to examine the levels of workload, existential fulfillment, and work engagement among council members and the association between the variables mentioned. In addition, the extent to which the first two independent variables influence work engagement was investigated. To the best of our knowledge, there is no published empirical data on the relationships between these concepts among council members. Therefore, a comparison with results of previously conducted studies among politicians is hardly feasible. On the other hand, a comparison between council members and nurses can be made as the latter professionals are also assumed to be highly inspired and particularly engaged in their work. Although the results must be interpreted with care due to the cross-sectional design of the study, they nonetheless suggest important, previously unexamined associations.

With regard to personal characteristics the study shows that female council members spend more hours per week on council-related matters than their male counterparts. These results are in accordance with De Jager-De Lange, Flos, and Snijder (2010).

Results show that council members 65 years of age or older score higher on workload than their younger colleagues. Since retirement age of 65 is official, we may assume that council members who reached retirement age can spend more time on council-related matters and, therefore, experience a higher workload.

One Christian political party (The Christian Union group) has the highest score on self-transcendence. This is not an unexpected outcome, since self-transcendence measures spirituality (Kirk et al. 1999). In addition, research reveals a strong relationship between spirituality and religiosity (Freiheit et al. 2006).

Council members who described themselves as having no faith score below the average on self-transcendence. This outcome supports the findings of Kirk et al. (1999) and Freiheit et al. (2006).

Correlational analysis revealed that workload was strongly negatively associated with the three dimensions of work engagement. A higher workload level experienced by council members resulted in lower scores on engagement. This finding is consistent with Van Rhenen's (2008) study, in which he advises that people concentrate on work pleasure because enthusiastic staff members are a positive contribution to an organization. A higher degree of perceived workload may result in decreased work engagement, including mental resilience and perseverance. Regression analysis shows that workload contributed significantly to explaining the variance of one dimension of work engagement, i.e., dedication. Dedication, a particularly strong work involvement, diminishes, and the question is to what extent council members experience their work as meaningful and inspiring. It is likely that council members with a higher perceived workload would not be fully concentrated and deeply engrossed in their work (absorption). Workload partly affects work engagement in this specific population. A few studies (on ministers, mine industry managers, telecom managers, nurses) have shown that workload affects both work engagement and the opposite pole, i.e., burnout dimensions (Loonstra and Tomic

2005; Rothmann and Joubert 2007; Schaufeli et al. 2009; Tomic and Tomic 2011). In this specific population, it is not appropriate to speak of employers and employees. Consequently, individual employment contracts do not exist. In addition, we may interpret this finding as a predominant vocation for political activity.

A positive relationship between existential fulfillment and work engagement was confirmed for the dimension of self-actualization. The results show that self-actualization contributed significantly to explaining the variance of vigor, dedication, and absorption. These results parallel the findings from a study by Tomic and Tomic (2011). Self-actualization is motivated by internal drives instead of external obligations. It refers to motivation to realize own maximum potential and possibilities and is considered to be the master motive. Maslow's hierarchy of needs demonstrates that the need for self-actualization is the final need that manifests when lower level needs have been satisfied (Maslow 1943).

On the other hand, in terms of explained variance, it is important to note that in this sample, self-acceptance and self-transcendence hardly explained variance in work engagement dimensions. With regard to self-transcendence, this is consistent with the results reported by Loonstra et al. (2009) and Tomic and Tomic (2011).

Several limitations may have influenced the results of the current study. First, our study was limited by its cross-sectional design, i.e., data were all collected at one time period. This feature precludes any definite conclusion about causality. The relationships shown do not reveal the causal direction. The results indicate that self-actualization influences work engagement, but one can also imagine influences moving in the opposite direction: a low level of work engagement leads to diminished self-actualization. When a council member is subjected to strict demands from his/her party leaders and the work environment does not offer opportunities for personal development and growth, self-actualization may be diminished.

Second, the direction of causation requires further investigation. Further research using a longitudinal design is needed to clarify this issue, i.e., to evaluate the possibility of causal relationships between workload, existential fulfillment, and work engagement. A longitudinal research design would shed light on the effects of workload and existential fulfillment on work engagement. Likewise, by applying a longitudinal design, the possible common method bias can be reduced. This methodological artifact occurs when the instruments employed affect the scores that are being collected (Doty and Glick 1998; Podsakoff et al. 2003).

Third, the measurements in our study were based on self-reports. Consequently, we do not know the extent to which these self-reports accurately reflect perceived workload, existential fulfillment, and work engagement. Naturally, the results of the present study for the association between workload, existential fulfillment, and work engagement should be interpreted with caution, but there are no indications that these findings solely reflect biased respondent reporting. Combining self-report data with data obtained in a more objective manner is recommended for further research so that powerful statistical techniques can be applied for hypothesis testing. The findings of the present survey could be used to generate hypotheses for future research.

In spite of its limitations, our study has several important strengths. (1) The current study ventured into a novel domain of workload, existential fulfillment, and work engagement. (2) Measurement error was contained since the study employed established instruments with known psychometric properties. Reliability analysis shows that the measurements satisfy psychometric standards. In the study validated, metrics were used to measure workload, existential fulfillment, and work engagement, allowing for the comparison of findings with the general population and across studies. Both internal and external validity was guaranteed. (3) The sample size was substantial and the response rate of 59 % has been found to be quite high for research in this domain (Babbie 2004; Van Horn and Green 2009). Moreover, the sample was representative concerning age of the population of council members. (4) Since our study took into account geographical spread or the various working environments of council members, we don't need to be cautious when generalizing the results of our study to all council members in the country. Although our study was limited to one group of politicians, i.e., council members, it is possible that the results could also be applied to other politicians, for instance provincial council members, members of the Senate and members of the House of Representatives. (5) We applied an appropriate multivariate data-analytic strategy, i.e., hierarchical regression. (6) We adopted a theoretical framework that may help to organize research findings across investigations. (7) The observed association between workload, existential fulfillment dimensions, and work engagement were not only statistically significant, but also interesting and meaningful.

Despite the limitations, the current study contributed to the knowledge of this particular political profession with regard to workload and existential fulfillment in relation to work engagement. However, speculations about the practical relevance of the study are premature. This work is only a first step and future studies are needed in this area.

Because the aim of the present study was to generate empirical knowledge about positive behaviors in political organizations, we may conclude that this study fits into the research context of positive psychology. New studies should be initiated to increase our understanding of the predictors of work engagement in politicians. This study could be replicated in a sample of the provincial council members, for instance, to identify factors that may influence the relationships studied in this research. Our findings led us to conclude that existential fulfillment appears to be a determinant of work engagement. This study further illustrates the usefulness of a theory-based approach to examine the association between workload and existential fulfillment on the one hand and work engagement on the other hand among council members.

References

Aiken, L. S., & West, S. G. (1991). *Multiple regression: Testing and interpreting interactions*. Newbury Park, CA: Sage.

Babbie, E. (2004). *The practice of social research* (Tenthth ed.). Belmont, CA: Wadsworth Publishing Company.

British Psychological Society Steering Committee on Test Standards. (1995). *Psychological testing: A user's guide*. Leicester, UK: British Psychological Society.
Centraal Bureau voor de Statistiek. (2010). *Gemeentelijke indeling op januari 2010*. Den Haag: CBS. Census Bureau. [Municipal classification on January 2010.]
De Jager-De Lange, G., Flos, B. J., & Snijder, E. J. (2010). *Nationaal Raadsledenonderzoek 2009*. Nijmegen: Daadkracht. National Council Membership Investigation 2009.
De Jonge, J., Boumans, N., Langdeweerd, A. B., & Nijhuis, F. (1995). Werkkenmerken en Werkbeleving. [Work characteristics and work perception]. *Tijdschrift voor Verpleegkundigen, 6*, 186–189.
Demerouti, E., Bakker, A. B., de Jonge, J., Janssen, P. P. M., & Schaufeli, W. B. (2001). Burnout and engagement at work as a function of demands and control. *Scandinavian Journal for Work and Environmental Health, 27*, 279–286.
Doty, D. H., & Glick, W. H. (1998). Common methods bias: Does common methods variance really bias results? *Organizational Research Methods, 1*, 374–406.
Duckworth, A. L., Steen, T. A., & Seligman, M. E. P. (2005). Positive psychology in clinical practice. *Annual Review of Clinical Psychology, 1*, 629–651.
Fox, R. J., Crask, M. R., & Jonghoon, K. (1988). Mail survey response rate. A meta-analysis of selected techniques for inducing response. *Public Opinion Quarterly, 52*, 467–491.
Frankl, V. E. (2004). *An introduction to logotherapy*. London: Random House/Rider. Man's search for meaning.
Freiheit, S. R., Sonstegard, K., Schmitt, A., & Vye, C. (2006). Religiosity and spirituality: A psychometric evaluation of the Santa Clara Strength of Religious Faith Questionnaire. *Pastoral Psychology, 55*, 27–33.
Fullagar, C., Culbertson, S., Mills, M. (2009). *Employees who are engaged in their work have happier home life*. Paper for The annual conference for Society for Industrial and Organizational Psychology. New Orleans, April.
Green, K. A., Boser, J. A., Hutchinson, S. R. (1997). *Effects of population type on mail survey response rates and on the efficacy of response enhancers*. Paper presented at the annual meeting of the American Educational Research Association, Chicago, March. (ERIC Document Reproduction Service No. ED 410252).
Kirk, K. M., Eaves, L. J., & Martin, N. G. (1999). Self-transcendence as a measure of spirituality in a sample of older Australian twins. *Twin Research, 2*, 81–87.
Längle, A., Orgler, C., & Kundi, M. (2003). The existence scale. A new approach to assess the ability to find personal meaning in life and to reach existential fulfillment. *European Psychotherapy, 4*, 135–151.
Loonstra, B., Brouwers, A., & Tomic, W. (2009). Feelings of existential fulfillment and burnout among secondary school teachers. *Teaching and Teacher Education, 25*, 752–757.
Loonstra, B., & Tomic, W. (2005). Werkdruk, zingeving en burnout bij predikanten in orthodox gereformeerde kerken. [Workload, existential fulfillment and burnout among ministers in orthodox reformed churches]. *Geloof & Psyche, 2*, 66–81.
Maslow, A. H. (1943). A theory of human motivation. *Psychological Review, 50*(4), 370–396.
Nunnally, J. C., & Bernstein, I. H. (1994). *Psychometric theory* (3rd ed.). New York, NY: McGraw-Hill.
Pines, A. M., & Aronson, E. (1988). *Career burnout: Causes and cures*. New York, NY: Free Press.
Podsakoff, P. M., MacKenzie, S. B., Lee, J. Y., & Podsakoff, N. P. (2003). Common method biases in behavioral research: A critical review of the literature and recommended remedies. *Journal of Applied Psychology, 88*, 879–903.
Post, W. E. J., & De Lange, G. (2008). *Het gemeenteraadslid. Onderzoek naar de tijdsbesteding en werkzaamheden van gemeenteraadsleden. [Council member. A study of time spending and activities of council members]*. Nijmegen: Daadkracht.

Pyszczynski, T., Greenberg, J., & Solomon, S. (1999). A dual process model of defense against conscious and unconscious death-related thoughts: An extension of terror management theory. *Psychological Review, 106*, 835–845.

Rothmann, S., & Joubert, J. H. M. (2007). Job demands, job resources, burnout and work engagement of managers at a platinum mine in the North West Province. *South African Journal of Business Management, 38*(3), 49–61.

Salanova, M., Llorens, S., Cifre, E., Martínez, I., & Schaufeli, W. B. (2003). Perceived collective efficacy, subjective well-being and task performance among electronic work groups: An experimental study. *Small Group Research, 34*, 43–73.

Schaufeli, W. B., & Bakker, A. B. (2001). Werk en welbevinden. Naar een positieve benadering in de arbeids- en gezondheidspsychologie. [Towards a positive approach in work and organizational psychology.]. *Gedrag en Organisatie, 14*, 229–253.

Schaufeli, W. B., & Bakker, A. B. (2004). Bevlogenheid: een begrip gemeten. [Work engagement: a concept measured]. *Gedrag en Organisatie, 17*, 89–112.

Schaufeli, W. B., & Bakker, A. B. (Eds.).(2007). *De psychologie van arbeid en gezondheid.* Tweede druk. [Psychology of work and health. Second Edition.] Houten: Bohn, Stafleu en Van Loghum.

Schaufeli, W. B., Bakker, A. B., & Salanova, M. (2006). The measurement of work engagement with a short questionnaire. A Cross-National Study. *Educational and Psychological Measurement, 66*, 701–716.

Schaufeli, W. B., Bakker, A. B., & Van Rhenen, W. (2009). How changes in job demands and resources predict burnout, work engagement, and sickness absenteeism. *Journal of Organizational Behavior, 30*(7), 893–917.

Schaufeli, W. B., & Salanova, M. (2007). Work engagement: An Emerging Psychological Concept and Its Implications for Organizations. In S. W. Gilliland, D. D. Steiner, & D. P. Skarlicke (Eds.), *Research in social issues in management: Managing social and ethical issues in organizations* (pp. 135–177). Greenwich, UK: Information Age Publishers.

Schaufeli, W. B., & Salanova, M. (2008). Enhancing work engagement through the management of human resources. In K. Näswall, M. Sverke, & J. Hellgren (Eds.), *The individual in the changing working life* (pp. 380–404). Cambridge, UK: Cambridge University Press.

Sonnentag, S. (2003). Recovery, work engagement, and proactive behaviour: A new look at the interface between non-work and work. *Journal of Applied Psychology, 88*, 518–528.

Tabachnik, B. G., & Fidell, L. S. (2001). *Using multivariate statistics* (4th ed.). Boston, MA: Allyn and Bacon.

Tolstikova, K., & Chartier, B. (2009). Internet method in bereavement research: Comparison of online and offline surveys. *Omega: Journal of Death & Dying, 60*(4), 327–349.

Tomic, W., & Tomic, E. N. (2008). Existential fulfillment and burnout among principals and teachers. *Journal of Beliefs and Values, 29*, 11–27.

Tomic, M. A., & Tomic, E. N. (2011). Existential fulfillment, workload and work engagement among nurses. *Journal of Research in Nursing, 16*, 1–12.

Troost, C. (2000). *Notitie volksvertegenwoordigende, kaderstellende en controlerende functie van de raad.* Goirle: Gemeente Goirle. [Memorandum representative, framework adjusting activity and monitoring function of the city council.]

Tummers, G. E. R., Landeweerd, J. A., & Van Merode, G. G. (2000). Organisatieaspecten, ervaren werkkenmerken en werkreacties in de verpleging. [Organizational aspects, perceived work characteristics and work reactions in nursing]. *Verpleegkunde, 15*, 132–141.

Van Horn, P. S., & Green, K. E. (2009). Survey response rates and survey administration in counseling and clinical psychology. *Educational and Psychological Measurement, 69*(3), 389–403.

Van Rhenen, W. (2008). *From stress to engagement.* Amsterdam: Universiteit van Amsterdam. Academisch proefschrift. [University of Amsterdam: Unpublished doctoral dissertation.]

Van Veldhoven, M., & Broersen, J. P. J. (1999). *Psychosociale arbeidsbelasting en werkstress in Nederland. Een verkenning gebaseerd op gegevens verzameld door arbodiensten met de Vragenlijst Beleving en Beoordeling van de Arbeid (VBBA) in de periode 1995 t/m 1998.* [Psychosocial work load and work stress in the Netherlands. An investigation based on data gathered by Health and Safety Executive during the period 1995 until 1998 with the Work Experience and Evaluation questionnaire.] Amsterdam: Stichting Kwaliteitsbevordering Bedrijfsgezondheidszorg. [Foundation for Quality Promotion in Organizational Healthcare.]
Weber, M. (1921). Politik als Beruf. In M. Weber (Ed.), *Gesammelte Politische Schriften* (pp. 396–450). München: Originally a speech at Munich University. Duncker & Humblodt.

Meaning and Trauma. From Psychosocial Recovery to Existential Affirmation. A Note on V. Frankl's Contribution to the Treatment of Psychological Trauma

Georges-Elia Sarfati

Introduction

This chapter proposes considering the contributions of logotherapy and existential analysis to the treatment of psychological trauma. This involves reflecting on the manner by which psychotraumatology deals with the problem of meaning within the context of the traumatic experience on the one hand, compared with the manner by which logotherapy envisages the stimulation of redefinition of the existential dynamic after a traumatic event on the other hand.

The hypothesis, which orients this reflection, is the following: We think that *traumatic neurosis is accompanied in most cases by what V. Frankl calls a noogenic neurosis.*

The question, which arises in this context, is which concept of meaning is implied by the traditional therapeutic models, in view of the logotherapeutic concept of meaning.

The response to this question supposes a second hypothesis that we will formulate in the following manner: *while classic forms of psychotherapy take for their objective the psychosocial recovery of the subject, logotherapy intends to lead the subject to the definition of a fundamental existential project, beyond psychosocial functioning* (Sarfati 2013).

The two perspectives articulate two absolutely complementary concepts of meaning, both of them, however, situated respectively on distinct structural levels of the personality. Both are involved with a phenomenology of meaning, each starting from different priorities. This contribution aims to show how these two perspectives complement each other, for the benefit of a broadened conception of psychotraumatology.

G.-E. Sarfati (✉)
French School for Existential Analysis and Therapy (Logotherapy) V. Frankl – EFRATE (EFRATE), 23, rue de Valmy, 94220 Charenton-le-Pont, France
e-mail: georgesarfati@gmail.com

A. Batthyány (ed.), *Logotherapy and Existential Analysis*, Logotherapy and Existential Analysis: Proceedings of the Viktor Frankl Institute Vienna 1,
DOI 10.1007/978-3-319-29424-7_20

Phenomenology of the Traumatic Experience

Psychological trauma causes a breach in the existential project. The suffering, which is linked to it, contributes to isolating the subject, who has become a prisoner of his traumatic memory. Traumatic neurosis coincides with a loss of meaning.

The Traumatic Event and the Crisis of Meaning

Trauma is truly a psychological wound (Crocq 2012), incapacitating to the highest degree for the subject who has undergone its impact. From the historical viewpoint, understanding trauma is linked to the analysis of war neuroses by the pioneers of psychoanalysis during the First World War. In *Psychologie collective et analyse du moi* (1919–1920), S. Freud defines traumatic breakdown as the "perception of the reality of death," to which the self is powerless to be able to resist in the least. The effects of the traumatic impact develop like a foreign body attaching to the core of the psyche. In his notes on trauma, recorded in his *Clinical Diary* (1995) S. Ferenczi describes trauma as a shock, which is at the origin of the fragmentation of the self. The resulting symptoms define a semiology, which confers on trauma the meaning of a desperate effort by the psyche to keep itself alive. Otto Fenichel, in his work *The Psychoanalytic Theory of Neurosis* (1945) supplies a precise description of the symptoms of traumatic neurosis. First of all, he distinguishes what he calls the "blockage of the functions of the self," that is: the functions of perception of the environment, the higher, cognitive functions, and the sexual functions. Added to these three are the emotional crises, such as anger and anxiety, and sleep disturbances (insomnia, nightmares). According to Fenichel, blockage of the functions of the self constitutes a "passive-receptive form of integration of the outer world," aimed at urgently mobilizing "the archaic non-specific mastery" of a brutal situation. These different contributions have enabled us to identify the principal symptoms of PTSD.

In the DSM-V, the *American Psychiatric Association* (Grohol 2013) now lists four clusters for PTSD: (1). Reexperiencing the event (spontaneous memories of the traumatic event, recurrent dreams related to it, flashbacks or other intense or prolonged psychological distress); (2) Heightened arousal (aggressive, reckless, or self-destructive behavior or related problems); (3) Avoidance (distressing memories, thoughts, feelings or external reminders of the event); (4) Negative thoughts and moods or feelings (feelings may vary from a persistent and distorted sense of blame of self or others, to estrangement from others or markedly diminished interest in activities, to an inability to remember key aspects of the event).

Certain orientations of research put more stress on the modifications, which take place in the subject's vision of the world, subsequent to a traumatic event. R. Janoff-Bulman, who favors a cognitive approach, states that "at the core of our assumptive world are abstract beliefs about ourselves, the external world, and the relationship between the two (Janoff-Bulman 2002, p. 6). According to the author, the "three fundamental assumptions" are the following: "The world is benevolent," "the world is meaningful," and "the self is worthy."

But the impact of trauma destroys the stability of these fundamental beliefs, which are distinct modalities of what Erik Erikson (1950) calls "the basic trust" in the world and others, which is normally acquired and developed during childhood.

It is reasonable to suppose that the destruction of these "fundamental beliefs," subsequent to a traumatic event, is conceived, from the standpoint of the subjective experience, as a radical challenge to the *existential evidence*. The "fundamental assumptions" identified by R. Janoff-Bulman define the whole grouping of the cognitive links which connect us with what Husserl calls the "Life-World" (*Lebenswelt*). They make up an integral part of what A. Schutz, following Husserl, has described as the "structures of the life-world." In other words, they are the entirety of the propositions that characterize the knowledge of common meaning.

Common meaning is spontaneously understood as a set of horizons of expectation: One's beliefs have a daily hermeneutic value, since they allow us to anticipate typical situations, and consequently to orient ourselves within the world; they even give us the possibility of interpreting these situations pertinently. These beliefs depend in turn on two strongly interiorized principles: on one hand the conviction that I can do certain things ("I can do it"), on the other hand the conviction that what has already happened will happen again ("it will happen again"). This logic of common meaning defines in sum the spontaneous philosophy, which allows us to project ourselves into a familiar universe, made up, in part, of reassuring habits and foreseeable situations. This state of affairs cannot be dissociated from the sentiment that our experience unfolds as something taken for granted, beyond any questioning.

In this perspective, the traumatic shock provokes a crisis of the structures of the world of life, which corresponds to a crisis of the evidence of common meaning. In sum, it is because the traumatic impact destroys the "fundamental assumptions" that it affects the subject's good psychosomatic and psychosocial functioning in the first place.

The Traumatic Event and the Loss of Meaning

V. Frankl's thought is pioneering both concerning the analysis of traumatic symptoms and concerning the understanding of the traumatic experience. The postulates of *existential analysis* make up a very accurate definition of the principal characteristics of the human condition: suffering, guilt, and finitude distinguish the "tragic triad." From a strictly philosophical point of view, we can obviously consider that these three terms give a very abstract definition of the inevitable horizon of every existence. Nevertheless, in a traumatic situation, these three terms refer in fact to an experience that is among the most concrete, and at the same time of infinite complexity.

Indeed, the term "finitude" no longer designates a metaphysical concept, but a challenge at every moment, one associated with the intuitive and quite real perception of death, or of its very possibility. "Guilt" too designates the quite real ordeal of the devaluation of the self, the sentiment of not having been "up to" the situation (lack of reaction in a situation of aggression, or of any victimization whatsoever). As to "suffering," it also consists of the manifestation of an ordeal which is often related to the experience of violence, of destruction and of cruelty.

The practical combination of these subjective experiences is very much among the effects of traumatic shock, which most often results in the traumatized subject having the impression of having lost all reason for living.

On the other hand, in addition to a clinical profile specific to traumatic impact (PTSD being its most typical expression), the victim sets up coping strategies, which can turn out to be as destructive as the evil, which they are meant to remedy. V. Frankl also perceived that. When describing the threats of our times, he indicates that the crisis of meaning is at the origin of new pathologies: addictions, new forms of depression, and the manifestations of violence. Now, it is quite remarkable that this pathological triad corresponds, word for word, to the most typical kinds of dysfunctioning of posttraumatic comorbidity: addictive behaviors are attempts at self-medication; auto-aggressive or hetero-aggressive attitudes attest to the violence of the malaise as much as the loss of points of reference. As to depression, it attests to the entry into lasting crisis of a mode of healthy psychosocial functioning. The pathogenic manifestations noticed at the moment are serious indicators of traumatic neurosis: They determine the defeat of the feeling of evidence of "being in the world," and also make themselves felt as very concrete expressions of the loss of meaning.

As we know, for Viktor Frankl, the feeling of understanding goes hand in hand with a healthy spiritual dynamic—or a "noodynamics," dedicated to the pursuit of strongly affirmed goals. Now, what clinical experience teaches us about psychotraumatology is that a traumatic neurosis is accompanied most often by a noogenic neurosis. In other words, added to the specific suffering of PTSD is the feeling of an existential vacuum. Thus, it is reasonable to consider that the violence of traumatic shock, and the psychosomatic and psychosocial disorders that they entail for the subject constitute, simultaneously, a rupture of the existential dynamics. According to this point of view, the entry into crisis of the beliefs of common sense/common meaning is prefigured and doubled by a crisis of personal meaning, in other words, of a failure of the feeling of existential coherence and completeness. The loss of the "fundamental assumptions" implies, at the same time, the collapse of subjective values which underlie what is unique in the project of life.

The Restoration of Meaning

The preceding exposition has enabled us to show that the traumatic impact not only destroys the subject's psychosomatic and psychosocial equilibrium, but most often interrupts his existential dynamics. The most effective models of psychotherapy for treating psychotrauma generally succeed in gradually reducing the symptoms, by helping the subject to resume a relationship with the world, which ceases being problematic, at least as far as the phenomenology of common meaning is concerned (Herman 1992). Nevertheless, as most therapists—including the most committed theoreticians (Cloître et al. 2006)—observe, the question of meaning, that is, of once again displaying an existential project, remains most of the time one of the most delicate concerns, one for which no solution exists in protocol form. To be sure, traditional forms of psychotherapy (the psychodynamic, or those inspired by cognitive or behavioral theories) succeed in stimulating cognitive and emotional skills as well as stimulating enfeebled practices, but they are not generally capable of responding to the question of meaning of life that the patient continues to ask himself, even after having recorded the traumatic event in his biography. The reason for what one must indeed call partial success probably comes from the fact that the classic forms of psychotherapy do not set as a hypothesis the existence of a spiritual dimension in the human being. The implicit anthropology of the classic forms of therapy remains dependent on the psychosomatic model, and for that reason, those forms limit themselves to certain types of treatment, while excluding others.

However, it is to the great merit of certain therapeutic initiatives that they have taken into account V. Frankl's dimensional ontology, in order to enrich the palette of classic psychotraumatology, by seeking to address the spiritual dimension of the subjects. The therapeutic programs put into practice at the hospital center for Vietnam War veterans have shown the extraordinary effectiveness of the use of logotherapy, and of the concepts of *existential analysis*, as a complement for the treatment methods of psychotherapy and pharmacotherapy (Southwick et al. 2006).

Patients suffering from PTSD, who have agreed to follow this new therapeutic strategy, show rates of remission and of feeling better that are unquestionably quite higher than those whose therapeutic framework does not incorporate the dimension of the concept of meaning defined by V. Frankl.

The veterans are treated according to this mixed approach, which combines the methods of classic psychotherapy and of pharmacotherapy (when necessary) with the perspectives of logotherapy. The application of Frankl's ideas shows that the "psychoeducation" that precedes the reappropriation of lost skills, goes hand in hand with "noetic (spiritual) education" necessary for a good understanding of the clinical practice of the "avenues of meaning." "Psychoeducation" consists in explaining the nature and manifestations of traumatic pathology to the subject in distress. This knowledge enables him to understand its development, which in a certain way contributes to relativizing it, if not to relativizing his own disquiet. By analogy, "noetic education" consists in, and should consist in, expounding Frankl's principal ideas about the subject in distress: the independence of the noetic (spiritual) dimension, psycho-noetic (psycho-spiritual) antagonism, and especially the attributes of self-transcendence and self-distancing, the tragic triad, and the avenues of meaning. These two forms of education are complementary, just as the underlying forms of anthropology are complementary: psychosomatic anthropology and dimensional ontology, with their respective notions of "meaning."

In effect, beyond psychosocial recovery, it is essential that the patient knows not only that he also has the internal capacity to resume an existential project (starting from the values of ethos, eros, or pathos), but that he can moreover depend on the contributions of logotherapy to overcome traumatic shock in a lasting manner.

Posttraumatic recovery defines, as we see, a continuum, where the issue is one of reappropriating for oneself, in stages, the value of two concepts of "meaning" that are indispensable to each other. The first stage, directly connected with traditional forms of psychotherapy, aims at recovering the structure of common sense/common meaning, whereas the second stage seeks the reconstruction and restructuring of a personal meaning beyond the gradual reduction of the most severe symptoms. Trauma therapy can be considered as successful from the moment when it has enabled the patient in distress to overcome his symptoms and to resume a specific life project, that is, an existential affirmation endowed with meaning for himself.

But, in order for the therapist to be able to claim such a good result, and in order for the patient to be able to vouch for it by the quality of his experience, it is still necessary for the therapy to have enabled the subject to pursue a process of repair to the end, followed or accompanied by a process of taking back his own existence. From this viewpoint, the therapeutic work coincides with a process of restoration of meaning, which presupposes two quite distinct stages, as indicated by the following table:

Therapeutic continuum	Psychotherapy (psychoeducation)	Logotherapy (noetic education)
Level of treatment	Psychosomatic and psychosocial	Noetic and existential
Purpose	Restructuring of fundamental beliefs	Reconstruction of the life project
Theoretical paradigm	Phenomenology of the structures of the world of life	Phenomenology of the avenues of meaning
Level of structuring	Level of common meaning	Level of personal meaning

Thus understood, assuming care of a trauma patient defines a continuum, which includes the work of psychotherapy, notably aimed at resolving the symptoms, as well as the work of logotherapy, aiming to identify one or more perspectives of meaning. Between psychotherapy properly speaking and the time of logotherapy, there exists an implicit hierarchy. Psychotherapy is first in that it tends to socialize the subject again; while logotherapy directs itself to his individuality itself.

- Psychotherapy consists in reestablishing the fundamental beliefs that have been uprooted due to traumatic shock: Its precondition is "psychoeducation" aimed at informing the patient about the nature of his symptoms, how they presented and how they developed; also by drawing his attention to the possible elements of comorbidity (addictions, depression, anxiety disorders). This stage is indispensable for it allows therapists to establish a distance between the patient and his suffering, thanks to which he learns to not identify himself with the pathologies connected with his trauma.

- Logotherapy, concerned with stimulating the patient's existential dynamics, can in a first stage rely on a phase of "noetic education."
- The latter consists precisely in dispensing to the patient the most significant notions of Franklian anthropology: dimensional ontology, distinction of the psychosomatic level from the noetic level, spiritual faculties of self-distancing and self-surpassing, and the notion of avenues of meaning.

Once the above have been performed, the two forms of transmission (psychoeducation and noetic education) can advantageously come together to utilize the notion of "tragic triad," in order to bring the patient to a realization of the universal—and not merely individual=character, of the latter, to a recognition of the existential orientations which seem to him to be felt when emerging from the trauma. It is in that manner that the phenomenology of common meaning—concerned with restoring psychosomatic and psychosocial equilibrium—gives up its place to a phenomenology of the personally felt, characterized by the rediscovery of a reasonable life project. A true therapeutic strategy of psychotrauma cannot do without either one of these two stages.

References

Cloître, M., Cohen, L. R., & Koenen, K. C. (2006). *Treating survivors of childhood abuse. Psychotherapy for the interrupted life*. New York: Guilford Publications.

Crocq, L. (2012). *Seize leçons sur le trauma*. Paris: Odile Jacob.

Erikson, E. H. (1950). *Childhood and society*. New York: Norton.

Fenichel, O. (1945). *The psychoanalytic theory of neurosis*. New York: Norton (3 vols).

Ferenczi, S. (1995). *The clinical diary*. London: Harvard University Press (Ed. J. Dupont, transl. M. Balint, N. Zarda. N. Jackson).

Herman, J. (1992). *Trauma and recovery*. New York: Basic Books.

Grohol, J. M. (2013). DSM-5 Changes: PTSD, trauma and stress-related disorders. *Psych Central Professional*, article online on 26 September 2015 at: http://pro.psychcentral.com/dsm-5-changes-ptsd-trauma-stress-related-disorders/004406.html

Janoff-Bulman, R. (2002). *Shattered assumptions. Towards a new psychology of trauma*. New York: Free Press.

Sarfati, G. E. (2013). V. Frankl: l'Analyse existentielle et la logotherapy. In M. A. Kédia & A. Sabouraud-Seguin (Eds.), *Aide-mémoire de psychotraumatologie* (2nd ed., pp. 26–39). Paris: Dunod.

Southwick, S. M., Gilmartin, R., McDonough, P., & Moussey, P. (2006). Logotherapy as an adjunctive treatment for chronic combat-related PTSD: A meaning-based intervention. *American Journal of Psychology, 60*(2), 161–174.

Logotherapy and Post-Traumatic Stress Disorder (PTSD): A Case Study of a Kidnapping in Guatemala

Lucrecia Mollinedo de Moklebust

Introduction

The following is a case study of a patient referred with chronic Post-Traumatic Stress Disorder, of late onset, six months after surviving a kidnapping. This study will cover a logotherapeutic approach to diagnosis and treatment of presenting problems, long-term goals, objectives, strategies, techniques or interventions, estimated length of treatment, and measure of outcome.

Descriptive Narrative

The patient, "Maria," is a practicing Catholic and has a good relationship with her family. She owns a small convenience neighborhood store near her home, has a limited income, but enough for her basic needs. She stated that in January 2012, two men and one woman, whom she thought were customers, came into the store, and at gunpoint took the cash and forced her into a pickup truck with tinted windows. She was blindfolded and taken to an unknown location, outside of the city. There, she was kept for almost 2 weeks locked in a small room with a window covered with paper. She stated that of the two women, who guarded her, one was indifferent to her and the other woman was very kind. On the final day of captivity, she was abruptly blindfolded and driven to another location, then instructed to wait for 2 h

L.M. de Moklebust (✉)
Instituto de Ciencias de la Familia (ICF), Guatemala/Asociación Guatemalteca de Logoterapia, 1a. avenida 10-20 zona 3 Mixco Colonia el Rosario, Guatemala, C.A. C.P. 01057, Guatemala
e-mail: lucreciamoklebust@gmail.com

A. Batthyány (ed.), *Logotherapy and Existential Analysis*, Logotherapy and Existential Analysis: Proceedings of the Viktor Frankl Institute Vienna 1,
DOI 10.1007/978-3-319-29424-7_21

before looking for assistance, or they would go after her family. She found herself in a remote rural area and after a 1-h walk she found help. She was taken by emergency responders to a hospital and was eventually reunited with her family.

Maria reports that she did not experience any of her symptoms immediately after the event. During captivity, she had strong religious feelings and felt cared for by her family during her ordeal. After her release, she was worried about what her daughters went through and the economic toll to both their households, and the suffering that she caused to her family. She did not return to live in her house, but went to live with her eldest daughter, and her Catholic community visited often. She has not opened her store since the incident, and her two daughters support her.

PTSD Background

The diagnostic criteria for PTSD were revised in 2000, in the Fourth Edition of the Diagnostic and Statistical Manual of Mental Disorders (DSM-IV). (Only in 1980, the APA formally recognized it as a disorder and classified and codified it.)

Diagnosis

309.81 DSM-IV Criteria for Post-Traumatic Stress Disorder (The symptoms of "Maria" are given in Italics and marked*)

The criteria below are the ones listed in the Diagnostic and Statistical Manual of Mental Disorders, Fourth Edition of the American Psychiatric Association (DSM-IV).

A The person has been exposed to a traumatic event in which both of the following have been present:

1 *Actual or threatened death or serious injury or a threat to the physical integrity of self or others.* *
2 *The person's response involved intense fear, helplessness, or horror.* *

B The traumatic event is persistently re-experienced in one (or more) of the following ways:

1 *Recurrent and intrusive distressing recollections of the event, including images, thoughts, or perceptions.* *
2 *Recurrent distressing dreams of the event.* *
3 Acting or feeling as if the traumatic event were recurring (includes a sense of reliving the experience, illusions, hallucinations, and dissociative flashback episodes, including those that occur upon awakening or when intoxicated).
4 Intense psychological distress at exposure to internal or external cues that symbolize or resemble an aspect of the traumatic event.*

5 *Physiological reactivity on exposure to internal or external cues that symbolize or resemble an aspect of the traumatic event.**

C Persistent avoidance of stimuli associated with the trauma and numbing of general responsiveness (not present before the trauma), as indicated by three (or more) of the following:

1 *Efforts to avoid thoughts, feelings, or conversations associated with the trauma.*
2 *Efforts to avoid activities, places, or people that arouse recollections of the trauma.**
3 Inability to recall an important aspect of the trauma.
4 *Markedly diminished interest or participation in significant activities.**
5 *Feeling of detachment or estrangement from others.**
6 Restricted range of affect (e.g., unable to have loving feelings).
7 Sense of a foreshortened future (e.g., does not expect to have a career, marriage, children, or a normal life span).

D Persistent symptoms of increased arousal (not present before the trauma), as indicated by two (or more) of the following:

1 *Difficulty falling or staying asleep.**
2 *Irritability or outbursts of anger.**
3 *Difficulty concentrating.**
4 *Hyper vigilance.**
5 *Exaggerated startle response.**

E Duration of the disturbance (symptoms in Criteria B, C, and D) is more than 1 month.*
F The disturbance causes clinically significant distress or impairment in social, occupational, or other important areas of functioning.*

Specify if

Acute: If duration of symptoms is less than 3 months.
*Chronic: If duration of symptoms is 3 months or more**.

Specify if

*With delayed onset: if onset of symptoms is at least 6 months after the stressor.**
(Table 1)

Multiaxial Diagnosis for "Maria": (On Referral)

Axis I: 309.81 Post-Traumatic Stress Disorder.
Axis II: none.
Axis III: gastric problems, back soreness, skin rash.

Table 1 Patient "Maria"—Concurrence with DSM-IV diagnostic criteria

			Present
A.		The person has been exposed to a traumatic event in which both of the following have been present:	
	A.1.	The person experienced, witnessed, or was confronted with an event or events that involved actual or threatened death or serious injury, or a threat to the physical integrity of self or others	*
	A.2.	The person's response involved intense fear, helplessness, or horror	*
B.		The traumatic event is persistently re-experienced in one (or more) of the following ways:	
	B.1	Recurrent and intrusive distressing recollections of the event, including images, thoughts, or perceptions	*
	B.2.	Recurrent distressing dreams of the event	*
	B.3.	Acting or feeling as if the traumatic event were recurring (includes a sense of reliving the experience, illusions, hallucinations, and dissociative flashback episodes, including those that occur upon awakening or when intoxicated)	–
	B.4.	Intense psychological distress at exposure to internal or external cues that symbolize or resemble an aspect of the traumatic event	*
	B.5.	Physiological reactivity on exposure to internal or external cues that symbolize or resemble an aspect of the traumatic event	*
C.		Persistent avoidance of stimuli associated with the trauma and numbing of general responsiveness (not present before the trauma), as indicated by three (or more) of the following:	
	C.1.	Efforts to avoid thoughts, feelings, or conversations associated with the trauma	*
	C.2.	Efforts to avoid activities, places, or people that arouse recollections of the trauma	*
	C.3.	Inability to recall an important aspect of the trauma	–
	C.4.	Markedly diminished interest or participation in significant activities	*
	C.5.	Feeling of detachment or estrangement from others	*
	C.6.	Restricted range of affect (e.g., unable to have loving feelings)	–
	C.7.	Sense of a foreshortened future (e.g., does not expect to have a career, marriage, children, or a normal life span)	–
D.			
	D.1.	Difficulty falling or staying asleep	*
	D.2.	Irritability or outbursts of anger	*
	D.3.	Difficulty concentrating	*
	D.4.	Hyper vigilance	*
	D.5.	Exaggerated startle response	*
E.		Duration of the disturbance (symptoms in Criteria B, C, and D) is more than 1 month	*
F.		The disturbance causes clinically significant distress or impairment in social, occupational, or other important areas of functioning	*
		Chronic: Duration of symptoms is 3 months or more	*
		With delayed onset: At least 6 months after the stressor	*

Table 2 Patient "Maria" Purpose in Life Test comparative scores

PIL test initial score (Part A)		PIL retest score (Part B)	
Item	Answer	Item	Answer
1.	3	1.	5
2.	3	2.	5
3.	2	3.	5
4.	4	4.	6
5.	1	5.	5
6.	4	6.	4
7.	4	7.	5
8.	2	8.	5
9.	3	9.	6
10.	3	10.	5
11.	3	11.	5
12.	3	12.	5
13.	5	13.	7
14.	4	14.	6
15.	3	15.	5
16.	6	16.	6
17.	3	17.	6
18.	3	18.	5
19.	1	19.	5
20.	3	20.	6
Total	62	Total	106

Axis IV: detachment from supportive family; unable to go back to work after stressor (Table 2).
Axis V: EEAG = 69 (upon referral).

Patient Maria´s initial score of the PIL Test (Part A) suggests a lack of clear meaning in life. After a 7-months logotherapeutic treatment, 20 sessions, once a week, a retest of the PIL (Part B), Maria´s score of 106 indicates a significant increase in the notions of perceived meaning/purpose in life.

The logotherapeutic assessment

Soma	Insomnia	Paradoxical intention
Psyche	Anxiety, painful memories, sense of danger	Dereflection
Nous	Lack of clear meaning in life	Socratic dialogue, VAT, modification of attitudes, mountain-range technique, guided autobiography (existential diary)

Table 3

Table 3 Noetic axial assessment (meaning indicators) Lucrecia de Moklebust, Guatemala), Patient "Maria"

Noetic axial assessment (Moklebust/ICF Guatemala)	Satisfactory	Regular	Unsatisfactory	None
	Not presenting problems, adequate functioning	A moderate absence or dysfunction but not significantly affecting the person	Absence of or dysfunction significantly affects the person	Severe dysfunction. Total absence of noogenic or spiritual ability (i.e., total absence of meaning in life)
Values Awareness: Consciousness of what is important in his/her life, being aware of values and practicing them Creative values (meaning in work, what the person gives to the world) Experiential values (meaning in friendship and love, what the person receives from the world); Attitudinal values (healthy attitude toward diverse circumstances of existence, what the person shares with the world)			*	
Meaning in life: Level of awareness of purpose/meaning in life, in both Ultimate meaning (the level of the meaning of life) Meaning of the moment (short-term goals)			*	
Freedom Assessment of external conditioning factors affecting behavior or decision-making (i.e., something blocking the person's decision-making, such as chronic disease)			*	
Responsibility **Awareness of consequence of his/her actions on his/herself and on others**		*		
Choice **A clear perception of options to solve problems/assume the difficulty**			*	
Adaptability **Ability to deal with the problem/cope the difficulty, and how it has affected his/her functioning.**				*

Presenting Problems

PTSD-related: insomnia, anxiety, constant sense of danger, nightmares, and painful memories. Meaning-related: lack of clear meaning in life

Patient information

The patient, who we named "Maria" to protect her identity, is a 58-year-old single mother with two married daughters, has five grandchildren, three from the eldest daughter and two from the youngest. Before the event, she was living on her own in Guatemala City and owned a small neighborhood convenience store near her residence. Her financial resources were quite limited, but she managed with her expenses. She indicates that her religious beliefs helped her get through her captivity, and feels guilty of feeling sad or afraid because that goes against her Christian beliefs. Occasionally, she attends a religious support group where everyone praises her strength and faith. She now lives with her married daughter and family. No history of substance abuse or addiction. She spends most of her time at home.

Previous Treatments

Six months after the stressor event, she presents" anxiety, the inability to fall and remain asleep, and an increased startle response, especially from loud noises. She was referred to a psychiatrist for evaluation and pharmacological treatment, and cognitive behavioral therapy. The first line of treatment was prescription medications for anxiety to reduce her startle response, constant fear, and difficulty to fall/remain asleep.

Pharmacological treatment: prescription medication for anxiety

Prescription meds	Amount	Reported side effects
Selective serotonin re uptake inhibitors (SSRI) Paxil	Daily dose of 30 mg (initial 20 mg)	Nausea, dry mouth, constipation

CBT: To improve her anxiety and help her to fall asleep, Maria was referred to a cognitive behavioral therapy treatment for cognitive restructuring, consisting of 13 weeks, one session every week. After 6 weeks of treatment, she has difficulty to adhere both to the pharmacological and CBT therapies.

Logotherapeutic Treatment Plan

Choice of Treatment

Maria was diagnosed with chronic PTSD ”of late onset, was having difficulty to adhere to her prescription treatment, and abandoned her CBT treatment. Although medications are helpful in minimizing symptoms of PTSD, most of the time they are best used in conjunction with psychotherapy. Logotherapy was offered as an adjunct treatment for PTSD, but evolved to first-line treatment.

According to Viktor Frankl, there is no mental disorder with one exclusive somatic, psychological, or noetic origin, but it is always a combination. Frankl´s logotherapy relies on two core concepts: (a) that there is an intuitive consciousness in man about the existence of a meaning in life, that man has a basic will to finding this meaning because this meaning is the main motivational force in his behavior, and that man possesses the freedom and the ability to find that meaning; and (b) that man is a totality of three dimensions: his somatic or physical, his psychological or emotional, and his noetic or spiritual self (Guttmann 1998).

Logotherapy is oriented to the future and focuses on enhancing and discovering personal strengths and makes the person responsible for his attitudes and change. A logotherapeutic treatment helps the patients to remember the details of the stressor event, self-transcend to transform their suffering into human accomplishment, and guilt into a meaningful contribution to the world.

After evaluation, it was determined that a logotherapeutic treatment for increasing Maria’s perception of a clear meaning in life would improve her quality of life, satisfaction, happiness, emotional stability, and improve her overall social functioning.

To reduce her anxiety and improve her ability to go to sleep, unspecific logotherapy in the form of paradoxical intention was applied.

Therapeutic Goals

I PTSD related.

- A Increase ”ability to fall/remain asleep.
- B Reduce anxiety.
- C Reduce painful memories.

II Meaning related.

- A Improve values awareness.
- B Increase perception of meaning in life.

C Resolve factors blocking freedom of functioning.
D Enhance awareness of consequences of his/her actions on his/herself and on others.
E Stimulate a clear perception of options to solve the problem/accept the difficulty.
F Raise the ability to adapt and deal with the problem/cope with the difficulty, and how it has affected her functioning.

Logotherapeutic Techniques (Nonspecific Logotherapy)

Presenting problem:	Inability to fall/remain asleep
Choice of treatment:	Paradoxical intention

Example of Intervention with Paradoxical Intention: Maria

First Week

Maria: I'm desperate because I cannot sleep at all, I do not tell my family but since I'm living now with my youngest daughter, I can´t sleep at all. If I continue like this, I'm gonna be sick so more and more.

Therapist: I think you should not worry so much about that. Look, there are many things about us that we do not know, for example, the fact that the body accumulates hours of sleep, from past occasions where we may have slept more than we actually need.

Maria: That I did not know.

Therapist: Before the event, did you sleep well?

Maria: Yeah, ok, I went to bed at 10 pm and get up at 5 always.

Therapist: And after that, when you went to live with your eldest daughter, could you fall asleep and remain asleep?

Maria: Yes, looked not as easy as when I lived alone because at my daughter's, I sleep in the room with her daughters and it took a little longer to fall asleep, but I had no problem.

Therapist: Or we can say that until recently, you never had problems falling asleep.

Maria: Aha.

Therapist: How many hours of sleep would you say are enough for you?

Maria: Well, 5 or 6 h is more than enough.

Therapist: So we can say that you have in your favor several hours of cumulative sleep from when you had no problems with sleeping.

Maria: Aha.

Therapist: This is what we will do: I do not want you to fight against your insomnia. Since we established that you have many hours in your sleep reserve, there will be no problem. What I want you to do is to try to stay up all night.

Maria: What are you saying? Hm, that, I cannot believe. What?

Therapist: But you wont't be doing nothing. You told me you like to pray. Tell me, what is the longest and most difficult prayer you know?

Maria: That's the rosary, but the whole crown, that is all the mysteries, not just praying the mysteries of 1 day, but the five mysteries for the 5 days altogether.

Therapist: Do you know it well?

Maria: Oh yes, since I was a child

Therapist: Well, then do not fight your insomnia, but try to stay up all night. To pass the time you will pray the entire rosary, as you say, all the mysteries, of all the days.

Maria: And with all the litanies?

Therapist: With all the litanies.

Maria: Well, ok, it's ok.

Observations on the use of the technique:

- Know the context of the patient: Maria has a strong religious background, lives with her daughter with a schedule (staying awake could harm the family functioning).
- Use the complementary relationship to give the paradoxical statement: at the moment of the therapeutic process, the logotherapist generates an expectation to be met by the patient.
- Confidently stating: "I know this works" and explain the rationale behind it (cumulative hours).

Second Week

Maria: I could not pass beyond the second mystery, nor complete it.

Therapist: Well, now for this week the same, try to stay up all night, you will pray the five mysteries of the rosary. That should keep you awake.

Third Week

Maria: Now I failed you badly, I could not pass the second mystery, even though that I sat straight on the bed.

Therapist: For this week, you will begin earlier with your prayers, and will pray two complete rosaries complete, that is, two complete rosaries. I want you to stay up all night.

Maria: That is not necessary, now I only see the beads and fall right asleep! I have already accumulated more sleep for another lot of sleepless nights! I think I have no trouble sleeping, haha! Now I have debt prayers! Haha!

Therapist: For that, you certainly also have backup!

Logotherapeutic Treatment Patient Maria

	Clinical goals	Techniques used	Content
Self-distancing	Improve adherence to treatment	Psycho-education	Provide information on the reality of PTSD, symptoms, and attitude toward medications
Self-distancing	Improve ability to fall/remain asleep	Paradoxical intention	Assignment: stay awake, don´t fight insomnia
Self-distancing	Reduce anxiety, constant fear	Dereflection	Explaining the relationship between anticipatory anxiety and reflection. Developing a plan to reduce hyper-reflection. Develop an alternative list of activities that would enrich life instead of reflecting on the symptom
Self-distancing	Reduce painful memories	Socratic dialogue	Naïve questioning, addressing unnecessary suffering
Self-distancing	Finding meaning in guilt	Socratic dialogue	Questioning on religious views, world view, unnecessary suffering, and guilt
Self-discovery	Reduce painful memories	Guided autobiography (to be developed for the length of the treatment)	Give structure for the nine stages of life: My parents, my early childhood, my school years, my early adulthood, my present, my near future, my distant future, my dying, the traces I want to leave on earth
Self-discovery	Increase awareness of values	Mountain-range technique	View life like a mountain-range with its peaks and low lands, and discover recurring values (own and from others)
Self-discovery	Increase perception of meaning in life	Socratic dialogue	Questions regarding "clues" on patient's noetic core (through interests, concerns, topics)
Self-discovery	Reduce anxiety	Logo-anchor technique	Past experiences, events that filled the patient with wonder and sense of uniqueness

	Clinical goals	Techniques used	Content
	Find new meaning to stressor event	Attitude modification (toward unavoidable suffering)	Once negative symptoms are reduced, help her accept positive attitudes toward life
Self-transcendence	Assess meaning in stressor event	Attitude modification (toward unavoidable suffering)	Discover what was meaningful and helped her through captivity
Self-transcendence	Participate in positive activities		Develop a schedule to reopen her store and help with family income
Self-transcendence	Enhance awareness of consequence of actions		Develop a plan to helping her grand daughters in the afternoons
Self-transcendence	Find new meaning to stressor event		She wishes to volunteer in a victims-of-violence group

Outcomes of Treatment

Purpose in Life retest results: Patient Maria's initial score of the PIL Test (Part A) suggests a lack of clear meaning in life. After a 7-month logotherapeutic treatment, 20 sessions, once a week, a retest of the PIL was administered. Maria's score of 106 indicates a significant increase in the notions of perceived meaning and purpose in life.

Therapist Report

Besides the reduction of PTSD-related symptoms, such as insomnia and fear, during therapeutic treatment, different aspects emerged to be dealt with. The avoidance of painful events was approached from logotherapy and she was able to identify the noetic resources that helped her in captivity. Adherence to pharmacological treatment improved due to education on PTSD, and logotherapy replaced CBT treatment. Guilt resulting from her interpretation of faith was oriented toward discovering spiritual, nonreligious resources, such as helping with caring for her granddaughters and volunteer work.

Self-Report

Maria reports that now she feels happy again, she feels responsible for her granddaughters, she knows her family needs her and that motivated her to work again in the mornings, with her youngest daughter, and take care of her granddaughters in the afternoons. She volunteers on Saturdays at a victim-of-violence women's group. She reports her sense of fear has reduced considerably. She is in the follow-up stage of treatment.

Conclusions

In the quest for a better treatment of patients suffering with PTSD, a thorough assessment of meaning-related issues will enable therapists to better guide patients through traumatic experiences, and to then help them in recognizing their noetic core and to find meaning in their existence.

Although logotherapy does not focus on PTSD symptoms, these may be reduced as a by-product of a successful meaning-oriented treatment. The effectiveness of logotherapy, measured by the Purpose in Life Test, shows a significant increase in the perceptions of purpose and meaning in the patient's life.

Reference

Guttmann, D. (1998). *Logoterapia para Profesionales. [Logotherapy for the helping professional: Meaningful social work]*. Bilbao: Desclée de Brouwer.

Unimaginable Pain: Dealing with Suicide in the Workplace

Beate von Devivere

Dealing with Sudden, Unnatural Deaths in the Workplace: Ten Reasons for "Managing The Unmanageable"

A Shattering Loss

Each sudden unnatural death[1] is an absolutely extreme, tragic, and shattering reality that brings a singular and unique person's life to an untimely and ultimate end. It is the sudden end of a life-long process, drawing from all aspects of this individual's personal, social, family, professional, private and work place experiences, their individual personalities, their aspirations, their resources, their relations, their culture, their values, their hopes and fears, their communities near and far.

The extreme event of a suicide or a sudden, unnatural death does bear high emotional risks for members of the deceased person's family and for his/her colleagues in the workplace and potentially triggers very personal traumatic recollections.

[1] The article is referring either to suicide or to "sudden, unnatural deaths" or "*external causes of death.*" These terms are used by coroners, investigators, and statistics experts in the classification of human deaths not properly describable as deaths by natural causes. Both categories include deaths resulting from intentional self-harm, mainly suicide, transport accidents, and homicide. Dealing with sudden, unnatural deaths in the workplace mainly refers to (potential) suicides, keeping in mind that in many cases questions on the ultimate cause remain unresolved.

B. von Devivere (✉)
Hansaallee 22, D-60322 Frankfurt am Main, Germany
e-mail: devivere@bvd-consult.de

A. Batthyány (ed.), *Logotherapy and Existential Analysis*, Logotherapy and Existential Analysis: Proceedings of the Viktor Frankl Institute Vienna 1,
DOI 10.1007/978-3-319-29424-7_22

Ever-Rising Urgency

There are few families, communities, and workplaces that have not been affected and tragically touched by sudden, unnatural death, either directly or indirectly. Depression, the major cause of suicide, is on the rise in all industrialized countries. Joint actions in all areas and on all levels are showing positive results in reducing the suffering and pain.

Raising Awareness and Prevention

Each of these deaths is the result of a complex set of circumstances rather than an isolated event. There are many contributing factors and few simple answers to the questions that arise in the context of such a tragic loss.[2]

Awareness for individual risk and protective factors, overcoming the stigma with information, and sharing effective prevention activities are marking the road map of shared responsibilities.

A Call for Best Workplace Health Management

For all these reasons, proactively and visibly integrating mental health issues into organizational work place health management is a main task for the twenty first century. There is no one-fits-all approach. Each organization needs to tailor their best-fit health management system.

Learning from Best Practices

Each community, each organization, each employer, and individual staff members can play an important part, compassionate and informed, in helping to reduce the pain that comes after a sudden unnatural death, and can make a contribution to general health and welfare.

The Bereaved Community

According to the WHO, the aftermath of suicide or "sudden unnatural death, including potential suicide, are affecting at least six other persons, having severe and far-reaching effects on family, friends, colleagues and communities". Being confronted

[2] Breaking the Silence in the Workplace (2012). The Irish Hospice Foundation and Console, Dublin.

with the shattering information of the sudden unnatural death of a colleague triggers very personal experiences of loss and bereavement, of individual hopes and fears, of perceptions and beliefs. The reality is that in most workplaces these issues would remain silent, invisible, unspoken, "the last taboo" (Kinder 2006).

Inevitable Questions

No one can be expected to know how to respond to sudden unnatural death in the workplace. There is advice, information, knowledge, and help from many professionals in the workplace and beyond in dealing with this tragic event.

When dealing with the aftermath of this loss, employees and management may be deeply concerned with questions: What is right? What is wrong? What is enough? What is too much? What is my responsibility in my role? What is our individual, team, and organizational responsibility? There are no quick, no single answers, sometimes no answers at all.

Managing Extreme Emotions and Feelings

"No man is an island," John Donne pointedly formulated: A sudden, unnatural death or suicide immediately and inevitably leads to basic existential questions and triggers ultimate issues like the inevitability of death, freedom and responsibility, suffering, despair, fear, meaning of life, and isolation. The incident can have a huge emotional impact on those left behind. Feelings of guilt, shame, of grief, and depression may arise.

The emotional response is highly individual, drawing from the individual staff member's coping mechanisms, situational and personal background, convictions and beliefs.

Guiding Through the Storm

Managing human resources sensitively and compassionately includes taking these basic emotions into sensitive account. Denial would rather raise additional despair, fears, and anger.

Managers play exceptionally critical roles in guiding staff through these difficult times.

There are many ways to make a difference, to deal with this extreme, existential situation in a supportive and compassionate way, helping those left behind in their natural grieving and bereavement.

Everyone can share the load of overcoming suffering in times of crisis and in building a healthy workplace environment.

Crisis Management

When confronted with a sudden, unnatural death, employers are challenged with managing the crisis, guiding staff, and keeping the balance between a sensitive and a factual approach, bridging the gap of emotional acceptance and letting go on the one side and managing business needs efficiently on the other side. There cannot be an either or.

Facts and Figures: An Urgent Call for Joint Action

Mental disorders and substance abuse combined were the leading cause of nonfatal illness worldwide in 2010, contributing nearly 23 % of the total global disease burden. Depressive disorders are the most common mental health disorders, followed by anxiety disorders, drug use disorders, and schizophrenia. Mental health problems are rising in the European Union. Diagnosed depression and anxieties make up for the majority of cases.[3]

- About 1/3 of all depression cases have attempted or will attempt suicide.
- More than 90 % of all suicides have had a depression history.

Depression: The Situation in Europe

- 25 % of the EU population has been suffering or will suffer from depression at some point in life.
- In any given year, 9 % of the EU population suffers from depressive disorders.
- This corresponds to 20.8 million women and men suffering from depression each year.
- Depression is generally under-recognized and undertreated in health care systems:
- In all countries, treatment rates are low. At best about 50 % of depression cases receive any professional attention.
- Diagnosed depression rates are increasing—particularly among the young population.
- Depression ranks as No. 1 among the most disabling diseases.

[3] SUPPORT Project, Mental Health Indicators and Data in EU Member States, Preventing Suicide and Depression. www.supportproject.eu.

There is a massive direct and indirect burden of depression on all:

- Effects on the individual: e.g., high distress, disruption of social roles, of capability to work, productivity, sickness days, disability, premature mortality).
- Effects on the family: e.g., high emotional distress, economic consequences, malignant effects on dependent family members, friends, and colleagues.
- Effects on society: direct and indirect health and social costs.

Suicide: The Global Situation (Wasserman and Rihmer 2009)

- From 1950 to 1995, the global rates of suicide have increased by 60 %.
- In 2000, suicide claimed an estimated 815,000 lives worldwide.
- Suicide rates among adolescents and young adults have increased considerably over the last few decades in a number of industrialized countries.
- The magnitude of the problem is even more significant when the number of attempted but uncompleted suicides—20 times more common—is included. Registered suicides are equivalent in magnitude to deaths from road traffic accidents.
- In Germany, deaths by suicide exceed deaths by traffic accidents, homicide, and AIDS together.
- In a 10-year period, over 630,000 people will die by suicide in the EU 27. This is equivalent to the extinction of the entire population of Frankfurt, Germany.
- Premature death from suicide is a significant cause of mortality in the EU 27.
- The rate of actual suicides may often be double that of official suicide rates.
- On average, there were 9.4 deaths per 100,000 inhabitants resulting from suicide in the EU 27 in 2010. Each year 63,000 people die by suicide in the EU 27.
- The rate of hidden suicides is considerably higher.
- Since 1995, suicide rates have decreased in many countries.
- Some countries have experienced a noticeable rise in suicide rates in young males. Suicide has become a leading cause of death in the young, and in some countries (e.g., Sweden) it is now the most common cause of death in 15–24 year-olds.
- A continuous dramatic rise of suicides is being reported in Greece connected to the economic crisis: from 677 reported suicides in 2009 to 830 cases in 2010, 927 cases in 2011, and above 1000 cases in the past 2 years.
- Suicide is heavily stigmatized and only a portion of actual suicides is recorded as such (Fig. 1).[4]

---

[4] Available data either refer to suicide or to deaths not properly describable as suicide with the term "unnatural, sudden and unexpected deaths" including mainly potential suicide, homicide and intentional self-harm. Investigation and classification is strictly limited to official bodies, post-mortem medical examiners, police investigation and/or forensic pathologists. All official statistics available for both categories are based on their assessment.

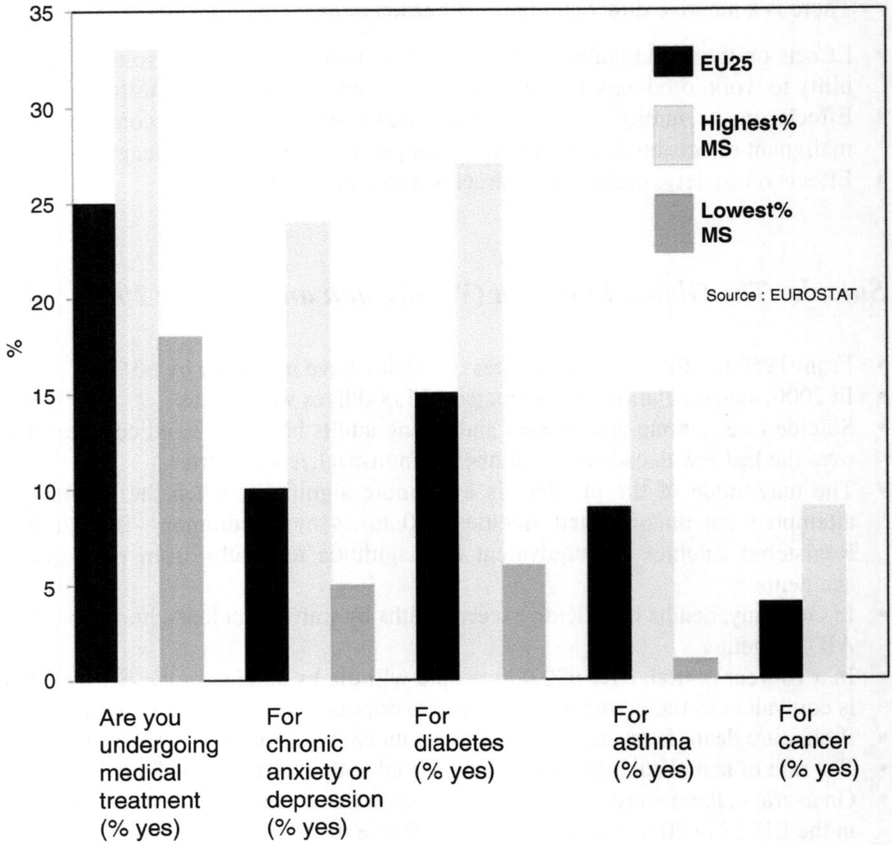

Fig. 1 Comparison of chronic anxiety or depression with three other reasons for currently received medical treatment for a long-term condition (EU 25 compared with highest/lowest member state data) Source: Mental Health in the EU Key Facts, Figures, and Activities. A Background Paper, European Communities, 2008

References

Kinder, Andrew (2006). In: Counselling at work. *BACP*, Winter 2006.

Wasserman, D., Rihmer, Z.(2009). *Suicide. What policy can do about it.* Presentation at a Conference on Prevention of Depression and Suicide, under the European Pact for Mental Health and Well-being.

Part IV
Existential Psychology and the Humanities

Acceptance Speech (Honorary Professorship, Bestowed from the Institute of Psychoanalysis, Moscow)

Elisabeth Lukas

My dear Ladies and Gentlemen,

After more than seven decades of experience in life, I dare say that life is full of surprises. But not only good ones, I must admit. Sometimes, life surprises us with unexpected blows of fate and rough provocations. Often, though, and not always we give life the credit it deserves for it, it surprises us with fascinating offers and totally unexpected gifts.

The fact that I stand here today is one of these gifts. I have given lectures, seminars, workshops, etc. at 53 universities, but never at the University of Moscow. My books have been published in 17 languages, but none of them in Russian. That the fame of my humble work in the area of logotherapy has reached Russia is truly a big surprise life granted me.

If I may, I would like to add the following to the subject of "Life's Surprises": one should keep an open mind for them well into old age. It is known that fear of the new and the unusual, among others, is a sign of a neurotic existence. What we are used to, the familiar and the everyday things suggest some security, which in fact never exists. We are able to navigate the familiar, what we are used to and think to known, and thus believe to be able to master life. However, the more we tend to trust in the manageability of the known, the more shocking are experiences of abrupt changes and new situations. To stay open for the changes of time, which also require letting go and changing direction will, provide more flexibility to react to the surprises of life, when they hit us in the face.

Editorial Note: Elisabeth Lukas on occasion of the conferment ceremony of her honorary professorship delivered the following speech on May 18, 2014 at the Billroth Library of the Vienna Medical Society during the 2014 "The Future of Logotherapy II" Congress in Vienna, organized by the Viktor Frankl Institute Vienna.

The speech has been published in: Lukas, E. (2015). Das Schicksal waltet - der Mensch gestaltet - mit Versöhnung und Frieden. Perchtoldsdorf: Plattform Martikenek Verlag.

E. Lukas (✉)
Marktplatz 17/4/1, 2380 Perchtoldsdorf, Austria

A. Batthyány (ed.), *Logotherapy and Existential Analysis*, Logotherapy and Existential Analysis: Proceedings of the Viktor Frankl Institute Vienna 1,
DOI 10.1007/978-3-319-29424-7_23

One of the many supportive strategies of logotherapy is that it trains us preventively not to freeze or to feel completely overwhelmed when faced with life's surprises, but to tackle them with a degree of serenity. Where do I get this from? Well, Frankl's philosophy enters so intensely into the full spectrum of human existence that the more we penetrate into it the more we start to engage with all possible surprises of life. In our realm of thought, we already start to move along tracks, for which the future alone can build these tracks and switches. If, for example, we study Frankl's assertions about the tragic triad in life, we definitely encounter our own suffering, our own guilt, our own death so that in our imagination there is hardly a rift between what we have suffered and what we are still to suffer. Or if we study the Franklian triad of values, we experience a happy balance between creative accomplishments, the bliss of love, the pride of courage, and again the gap between what was and what is yet to come shrinks. "Everything we see is harvest, even if it is still in the fields, or maybe already stored in the barn." This is just to cite one of Frankl's famous parables. Logotherapy indeed is able to equip us for the process of continuous harvest, come what may, to enable us to deal with pain as well as to foster the boundless estimation of grace.

So today I stand before all of you, before the audience but in a special way before those who have invited me to this beautiful celebration, trying to express my thanks and appreciation. At my age, of course, I am well aware of the passing nature of all worldly splendors, I know that possessions, power, prestige, and honor are extremely relative and quickly go up in smoke. But this celebration today is very special for me because it is tied to people that mean a lot to me. To be precise, I must first thank my writings and second, my students, for the honor of being here. Without my writings and without my loyal and talented former students, such as Prof. Batthyany, nobody in Moscow would ever have noticed me. But to whom do I owe my writings, and to whom do I owe my students?

I owe my literary activity to Prof. Frankl, who in 1978 urged me to write a book about my experiences of the practical applications of logotherapy. Personally, I would not have had the confidence to write the book, but my first work emerged due to his insistence and literally because of my esteem for him. The ice was broken… How did I get my wonderful students? These I owe to my husband, who in 1985 took the initiative to smoothen the difficult path for the foundation of our Institute of Logotherapy in southern Germany, in Fürstenfeldbruck near Munich. I myself did not have the confidence to head a scientific institute with an outpatient psychotherapy clinic, but he had faith in me, and so a place of training was established, in cooperation, where over the years more than a thousand experts graduated in logotherapy. This is why today I wish to dedicate this tribute to me, to Prof. Frankl, and to my husband. They both have contributed decisively to my entire personal evolution. Both were like beacons in a stormy sea for me, making sure that my boat of life did not capsize, sink, or get lost somewhere in the dark.

I am extremely sorry that my husband is now in hospital and cannot be with us. But I feel him close in thought, and as if he were on my side as he has always been. I just want to share with you one of his innumerable small gestures: When I lectured in the United States or Canada, my husband was given the rare opportunity to fly an aircraft. He held an American pilot license and fuel back then was much more affordable there than in Germany. But he, the passionate pilot, remained by my side in the auditorium. Prof. Frankl wrote famous essays on spiritual "being with" (Bei-Sein), "to be with the things that interest us" (Bei-den Dingen-unseres-Interesses-sein), "being with the people we love" (Bei-den-Menschen-unserer-Liebe-sein) a "being with," which certainly longs for a physical expression, but does not depend on physical presence per se, so I can well imagine that he is right now present among us.

Based on the understanding of the importance of encouragement at the right time, I personally would like to encourage the officials of the University of Moscow not to be irritated by any obstacles or psychological countercurrents and to continue the teaching task that has been started to integrate Frankl's thought into their curriculum. It will be of much benefit to them and their students.

I guess I am not mistaken when I say that in recent decades there have been many changes in Russia. People are moving on from a troubled past. In Central Europe, too, there have been massive changes. The Greek phrase "panta rhei" (everything is in flow) holds a deep truth. Frankl's phrase "every age has its neuroses and every age needs its therapy" is also very true. Throughout my life alone, I have been able to observe a great variety of stages this country has gone through. I would like to briefly describe, what I have experienced, even though I can only refer to the situation in my own country:

- First, there was postwar poverty. I was only a child and we had—like most—barely enough to live. There were no toys, no winter heating, etc. I remember my grandfather crossing Vienna with a backpack to reach the potato fields north of the Danube River because of a rumor that there were potatoes for sale there. When he came back at night, tired and with an empty backpack because he had come too late, I heard my mother cry. And yet, I experienced that part of my life with a profound sense of security. We were together; everybody helped each other, and values still existed.
- Then came the growing prosperity of the 1950s, and with it, great joy. I have never again perceived so much joy in my social circles. I was in high school and I was happy. One could buy a book, afford a new dress, and... oh God... get a bicycle. It was like intoxication and it ended like one.
- The economic miracle (*Wirtschaftswunder*) of the 1960s overwhelmed us and let all traditional values crumble. The wave of sexual debauchery flooded us, authorities were toppled, and people went beside themselves. Suddenly everyone wanted to be his or her true self, no matter at whose expense. All this happened while I was at University and I was pulled in by the trends of this rebellious period. If I had not met Prof. Frankl, who knows what psychological labyrinth, I would have lost myself in.
- Well, economic well-being expanded and joy faded away. A new generation grew up in the late 1970s. The "no-future-generation" as they called themselves sarcastically. Their label was "*Null Bock auf Nichts*" (I can't be bothered about anything). Since I was already familiar with logotherapy, I recognized the symptoms of the "existential vacuum," which took hold of people and swallowed

them alive. There were cars and housing for all, there was enough work, there were all kinds of liberties people could wish for, there were opportunities for adventurous travel, and…depression, suicide, freaky young people, drug addicts, and crimes of meaningless violence and destruction increased. I already worked as a psychologist and through my patients I got to know unnecessary self-inflicted suffering and pain that affected them and those around them, a result of their own discontent, displeasure, boredom, indifference, and selfishness. From the known saying: "*primum vivere, deinde philosophari*" (first food, then philosophy) I learned: after too much food, there is no more moral. Frankl had already predicted, prophetically, even before World War II, when there was no idea of luxury and excessive pleasures, that it is not good for the psyche of man when he is too well off outwardly and materialistically.

- Progress moved on worldwide, and at a dizzying pace. With electronic computing and globalization, a new era dawned. Suddenly everything was connected via networks and the world's problems began rattling the prosperity of the pampered nations. The end of the previous millennium brought the realization that resources started to dwindle. Work and money started to become scarce. But as little as many people in my country had appreciated their prosperity, as little they were and are ready to do without it. Their mentality began to develop into the direction of our current society. People work hard to maintain a high standard of living, but stress charges a high price. Mobbing, envy, competitive infighting, panic attacks, physical exhaustion, burnout, and symptoms of strain are psychological issues of the day. To this add the addiction to drifting off in front of the screen, which is allowed to progressively absorb the soul of the viewer. Economic crisis, energy crisis, and crisis in the family are today's positions. Amidst all this, there is an immense yearning for tranquility, peace, and well-being, for a simple life instead of constant struggles in the workplace, and in the complicated relationships of human interaction as we see them all around us. I myself am past the stress now. I no longer work. I have been living in a happy marriage for 44 years, and have a good relationship with our children. But I feel a great degree of compassion for the younger people.

The spiritual question is "present in all the stages I have listed above. It raises its head in poverty and wealth alike, in need and in abundance. If one observes carefully the development of the processes I described, we can see a trend that Frankl had already sensed for some time and explained with the increasing loss of tradition and instinct in mankind; that is, that in our digital age we are left alone more and more in our search for answers to our spiritual questions. It has become disturbingly difficult to simply form an opinion that makes sense in any way. Does it make sense to grow genetically modified wheat? Does it make sense to entrust children to life partners of the same gender? Does it make sense to give loans to foreign companies? Does it make sense to enter personal information on the Internet? Every day, we are presented with an endless questionnaire, which no individual can answer objectively or reasonably, because the pro- and counter-arguments appear to be in balance. The media are the opinion makers. Depending on economical, political, or religious positions, they bombard the individual with selective pseudo-arguments, for which a person has barely any defenses. Each TV "spot" tells of a hidden "meaning" of the actions of its protagonists and great strength of character—or even better—continence is required, in order to escape these subtle manipulations. It is possible that this situation varies in Russia or in other continents. However, there, too, the stage is set more and more by the gripping attempt of each individual to find meaning in life in the light of its manifold contradictions and influences and to shape one's own actions in a meaningful way. According to psychological studies, we are currently living a "renaissance of the question of meaning" because meaning has become so doubtful, almost fragile.

So what can Viktor Frankl offer us, whose teachings have been at the tracks of this phenomenon of meaning for almost a hundred years already, in the light of these extreme transformations of the Post-Modern era? As you can see, I am reversing the theme of the conference a little bit. I am not worried about the "Future of Logotherapy." Logotherapy will constantly gain in importance, but the "future itself" gives reason to worries, so I would like to pursue the question, what perspectives logotherapy has prepared for us for the future? Well, I will tell you: In the building of Frankl's teaching, there are profound aspects of hope that are highly relevant. Let me mention four of them because they appear particularly important to me.

First, the aspect of conscience—the human "organ of sense": Although terribly slow, it is being refined with the progress of culture. We are beings with such a short life to live, so we do not get this impression. "But Frankl, with his broad vision, observed that beyond the pathologies of each respective Zeitgeist, there are and have been throughout history, so to speak, mutations of sentiment on a grand scale that push into a positive direction. He made it evident with the example of slavery, which was once considered legal but is now proscribed worldwide. Similarly, today different thoughts and opinions emerge around the globe and especially among the young. Supported by the means of modern communication, making everything infinitely more transparent than before, more and more nations rise against dictatorship, corruption, terror, and tyranny. Unfortunately, these mass protests rarely occur without the employment of arms, which is certainly not consistent with a collective revolution of awareness. Anyway, it is a glimmer of hope on the horizon that brutal tyrants find it increasingly hard to gag their subjects and rob them because the resistance and self-confidence of nations grow, enabling them to struggle for freedom, self-determination, and the safeguard of their human rights.

Joseph Fabry, a longtime friend of Prof. Frankl," once commented on a discussion in which Frankl described conscience not only as the most intimate pathfinder of the individual but also as a tool of human evolution. Frankl believed—and I quote, "In a society tolerating and proclaiming cannibalism, only the man with a highly developed conscience could muster the strength to oppose the commonly used standards which had also been imposed on him. Obeying his conscience in this regard—a conscience that dared to reject cannibalism—made him a rebel. He might have lost his life; but he had awakened the conscience of others. I believe that this is the way human evolution progresses..."

This is an excellent example because it does not imply that he, who was not a cannibal, attacked or exterminated his partners, who still were. The "rebel" in

Frankl's picture is a pacifist; he refuses to harm human dignity and if necessary, abides by the consequences. If today the increase of protests of nations against prevailing injustices, against the impoverishment of many and the enrichment beyond measure of a few and similar things would go hand in hand with the amazing accomplishments of peaceful resistance by conviction, indeed a progress of humaneness would be within reach.

The **second** aspect of hope I am detecting is the widespread longing for a break from the daily turmoil. Twenty years ago already, the slogan "to be ripe for the island" produced a smile, but also a remarkable echo. Since then, the dream of a "time off," if at all affordable, is alive in the heads of many people, as long as one can afford it. Not always is the urge to escape the impetus for it. A feeling of wanting to leave the infamous "hamster wheel" has formed, that there should be an opportunity to escape the constant sensory overload and to live a simpler life with more awareness and authenticity. Although this is frequently not feasible, a vision forms in that regard in the hearts of many people, a strong vision, which could become increasingly more fertile in its intensity.

Prof. Frankl once argued on a radio show, and here I quote, that "…man should learn again to go into the desert for a while, for a weekend perhaps,—and there are deserts nearby, they are everywhere; be it a hike to a mountain hut, be it a secluded bay on a shore. There at least one can finish thinking one's own thoughts…," so Frankl, who already in his youth was identified as a "thinker who thinks things through" (Zu-Ende-Denker).

Yes, our thoughts—Consider this: there are not only two kinds of feelings: the purely basic feelings of hunger, fear, anger, greed, etc., and the specifically human feelings of sense of value, friendship, enthusiasm, artistic or scientific fascination, etc., as described by Frankl in his book: "*Der unbewusste Gott*" (The Unconscious God). There are also two modes of thinking: intelligence, logic, memory, etc. on the one side, and the specifically humane level of wisdom, understanding, insight, and acceptance. The former is based on cortical performance; the latter goes beyond mere physiology; it is spiritual.

Frankl was right, of course: only in silence, in a withdrawal of stimulation, that is, in our personal "desert" are we able to think something to the end in peace; can we feel what we really want or must do, can we clearly see what "makes sense just now," what can receive our wholehearted Yes. However, most people are no longer used to this way of thinking.

I would like to give you a simple example. I wrote my first ten books still on my typewriter. This was tiring because every page had to be typed several times, from draft to final text. As it was very difficult to correct mistakes on the typewriter, it was necessary to develop the ability to formulate entire paragraphs in one's head and to write them down print-ready in one throw. The following principle prevailed: "think first—then act"—in my example, think through a phrase first and then write it down. When computers arrived, it became incomparably more convenient, and no one could do without word processing nowadays. But the principle changed. As you can correct, change, delete, and conceptualize again, today the principle is: "act first act—then think"; in this example, write a half-baked phrase and then correct or delete it. When writing a book, this may not be that serious, but in life, "act first—then think" is not at all a principle I recommended because a poor thought process can no longer be corrected and could easily become a boomerang.

In life, today's generation, too, should stick to, or rather return" to "think first—then act" and this will be much easier if there is a general habit of making excursions into the private desert, where one can think in silence and "think things through"; where we encounter our true inner self; where we can hear the spiritual calling of the hour. This regenerative step into the desert, however, requires a sacrifice: self-restraint and humility. Those who fill their free time with events and entertainment, shopping, surfing, talking on the phone, and other pastimes will have the same experience as those who stuff their homes with things they do not need: they drown in the clutter. Clearing things out, slowing down, and a new frugality would be the liberating elements, which would place the innermost longings of the human being, at least in our Western society—that is, longings completely different from those the constant propaganda promises to fulfill—within our reach. Let us hope for a new culture of reflection—it could help to change the face of the earth for the better.

The computer leads "us to **another** aspect of hope, crystallizing, despite all prophecies of doom from the turmoil of our time. Mankind has created a third brain. In addition to its archaic brainstem, with its automatic and homeostatic regulation of performance, and its amazingly integrative associative layer, the neo-cortex, homo sapiens now also has high-performance computers available, capable to deliver almost instantly information extracted from huge data files, which human analyzing and research alone could never have been able to produce. Aside from this, the information provided by the computer is not affected by emotions and assumptions, as is the case in the process of human thought.

Of course everything can be abused, as bad experiences with the Internet have shown. How wise was Frankl, when he stated that things never depend on a certain technology but on the spirit in which they are handled. But apart from any abuse, the "third brain" opens opportunities we never guessed at to access the real secrets of being, which surround and include us, and to get to know and better understand reality.

Anyone who has worked therapeutically with those seeking advice knows how much depends on an adequate assessment of reality. Not only does misjudgment of reality dramatically impair the lives of psychotically ill patients. Patients with neurotic disturbances also suffer from unrealistic fears and imaginary drowning of one's self. Even people that can be considered psychologically healthy, sometimes act against their realistic situation, by getting into debt, which they cannot afford, eating foods that are harmful to them, or hastily agreeing to do things they cannot face. Failure to accept reality is a process of self-punishment, which usually has bad consequences, both in big and in small things. Historians, for example, have demonstrated that both world wars of the previous century started by mere flawed assessment of reality and not just among those in charge inside the political machinery, but also among the broad population. The more ideologies are set, the more they slip away from reality.

The "third brain" of humanity" can, if used properly, help to assess reality correctly. With its help, a vehicle could be landed on Mars—just to mention one detail among millions. To achieve such a success, immense precision and the analysis of many physical relations were necessary. The slightest error, for example in the calculation of the trajectory, would have ruined the whole project. Anyhow, the computers cannot determine whether it makes any sense at all to land on Mars. But when we, humans beings, believe something makes sense, they might be able to inform us whether it is possible or not and how.

We started with the problem that due to the complexity of our time it has become more difficult to distinguish between what makes sense and what does not. But nobody can take this task from us; it remains the responsibility par excellence of the human being. However, faced with these difficulties, more and more sophisticated machines are able to provide detailed information for the feasibility of our plans, for the prediction of the consequences of our actions, for the realistic effects of grave interventions in nature, and so on. They can be placed at the service of the search for and the finding of meaning, as they filter out illusions and join ideals with feasibility. The condition is that they are "put to service," that is, they serve, and that humans control them and not the other way around. This needs to be worked on and I believe it is the biggest task for the youth of our days: to turn computers on and off, to use them for meaning-oriented purposes without succumbing to them and their seductions. If they succeed, we will be able to conquer" fabulously promising options for the future with the help of our "third brain."

I still want to address a **fourth** aspect of hope, the controversial topic of globalization," which stirs the minds and certainly cannot be turned back. To the contrary, everything in this world starts to mix and everything that happens has effects on everything else. Single nations can no longer "cook their own soup"; other nations throw alien ingredients into their pot, if they like it or not. We can complain about it, rage against it, but we know from psychotherapy that counter positions per se are not constructive. Constructivism can always be found in a creative acceptance, in this case: an acceptance of the world worth to be lived in. Frankl's saying that "the world is not healthy, but it can be healed," is still and especially valid in our days. What then could contribute to healing in this age of unstoppable and unavoidable moving closer together?

Let's think about this: Why is there so much friction between neighbors near and far? The answer is: because they are so different. Different races, different world views, different parties, different desires and worries, different capacities, different age-old adjustments to different environments ...endless differences...how, then, can they possibly understand each other? Nevertheless, they share in a great, a splendid common denominator, and we truly owe it to Prof. Frankl: that we do not just have a clue, but the weight of his decisive words: each human being of every nation is a spiritual, noëtic person. This is the only fundamental bond between us all. This is what unites us: the spiritual, and with it, freedom, responsibility, creative potential, and boundless and inalienable personal dignity.

Although it sounds astonishing, it is just this phenomenon ,"of globalization that might become helpful when we consider the common ground. From the understanding that our well-being and suffering are united, that nobody can get out any more of looming disasters, such as climate threats, and that in the future we will either all be well or all be miserable, there is a chance for a single credo to arise in unison, roughly equivalent to what Frankl had already claimed decades ago: *a monanthropism*: faith in our common humanity we are all part of—a faith, which would be able to bridge all the differences, which today confuses us so desperately.

As one of the first students of Frankl, allow me to say, then, what Frankl would most likely have offered to man on his path of search for meaning at the beginning of the Twenty first Century. He would, I should think, say: "Get up! Rise against the permanent causation of suffering that surrounds you; open your subtle sense for true values and fight for tolerance and mutual respect—but renounce counter-aggression and any other angry fighting." Frankl taught us that bad means desecrate the best cause. In his forcefully moving play "Synchronization in Buchenwald," he has left us a calling: "We do no longer want to pay injustice with injustice, reply to hatred with hatred, and to power with power! The chain—the chain...must finally be broken!", a heritage that could not be more convincing.

He would continue like this: "Be frugal. Do not get lured by the siren calls of consumerism and take a little break in your personal desert. Listen to the voice of transcendence!" He has advised us, in a time when then 10 commandments seem to lose their validity, to observe the 10,000 rules hiding in the 10,000 situations in our complicated lives. But, how can anyone perceive 10,000 rules? It is simple, they manifest themselves to us in silence, piece by piece, but not as strict commands from "above," but as loving whispers of the truest friend we have: our conscience.

Frankl probably would continue by saying: "Meanwhile, you, have accumulated an amazing technical repertoire, which provides you with enormous opportunities, but be careful with it! Any technological feature needs to be controlled by something meta-technical, so as not to turn against its own inventors." Frankl elucidated, based on psychotherapeutic techniques, that even art and wisdom are not enough if they are not paired with the human aspect—the human aspect which gives technology its adequate place and sets its limits.

And a final assumption: Frankl would say, "Don't ever forget, you are the being that always decides. Decides, what you will be in the next moment. You, due to your spiritual facilities, are the active collaborator of your fate. United in one mankind, you are the active contributor to human history. With your actions you are writing in a book of history from which nothing can be erased, not the glorious and not the awful, but which still has an unknown number of pages, white, blank pages, which at the end will testify on your behalf. Turn this into a communal epic worthy of you." I remember an anecdote Frankl used to tell about some students who were not talking to each other, until the day their bus got stuck in the mud. Suddenly, they were working shoulder to shoulder to free the bus, and any disagreements between them vanished. Frankl emphasized that there was nothing as placating as a common meaningful task. Therefore he would probably close with these words: "Take these children as an example! There are enough treasures in the world that can be released from the mud with joined forces. Work with confidence, shoulder to shoulder, each person with its own," talents so that the 'tragic optimism,' which I have upheld all *my* life, will in *your* lives gradually turn to 'a justified optimism'".

One cannot express it more beautifully than Prof. Frankl; let us thank him for his inspiration and example. And I thank you for listening.

Logotherapy Beyond Psychotherapy: Dealing with the Spiritual Dimension

Dmitry Leontiev

When something new is being invented, it is often very difficult to overcome the natural tendency of seeing this new thing as an improved variant of an old thing, even by the inventor him/herself, not to mention the public. But the new thing may be something hardly fitting the old categories.

What is logotherapy? It depends. When saying, for example "psychoanalysis," we may ,have in mind at least three different things. First, the word denotes the theory and metatheory, worldview and view of the human being elaborated by Sigmund Freud and shared by a large community of his followers. Second, it denotes a know-how, the methodology of interpretation, that is of uncovering hidden contents—that is what we have in mind, saying "psychoanalysis of dreams" or "psychoanalysis of religions." Third, we may have in mind another know-how, the therapeutic methodology of healing, of producing some cathartic or other effects that help the client move along the way of healthier self-awareness and increased well-being (see Freud 1923). In fact, psychoanalysis embraces all three components, but usually only one of them is meant. However, the second meaning seems to be the key one, due to the initial meaning of the word "analysis" as "investigation."

While saying "logotherapy," we may have in mind either the system of anthropological and psychological views, or a form of psychotherapy. The latter meaning is imposed by the root word "therapy." This twofold image of logotherapy seems to become rather stable by now: logotherapy as philosophy and psychological theory, on the one hand, and, on the other, logotherapy as practice, the "Third Viennese School of Psychoanalysis."

D. Leontiev (✉)
Department of Psychology, Moscow State University,
Mokhovaya str. 11-5, Moscow 125009, Russia
e-mail: dleon@smysl.ru

A. Batthyány (ed.), *Logotherapy and Existential Analysis*, Logotherapy and Existential Analysis: Proceedings of the Viktor Frankl Institute Vienna 1,
DOI 10.1007/978-3-319-29424-7_24

The main argument of this chapter goes somewhat contrary to this established view: *the most important, powerful, valuable, and new ideas in the practice of logotherapy do not belong to the realm of psychotherapy. Logotherapy constitutes a self-sufficient form of psychological help, other than psychotherapy* per se *and having a very broad field of application both within and beyond psychotherapy.*

Irvin Yalom (1980) criticized the methodological side of logotherapy for not fitting well enough into the present-day methodological requirements for psychotherapy, in particular for not providing the client with enough autonomy in the search for meaning. Even within the framework of these requirements he was not entirely correct—E. Lukas (1983) described the process of logotherapy as one gradually moving from distorted autonomy of the client to increased autonomy, rather than presuming her/his full autonomy from the beginning. But there is one more reason why Yalom's criticism is hardly relevant. True, logotherapy claimed to be a psychotherapy, inviting its evaluation from the traditional psychotherapeutic viewpoint. I believe, however, that this claim is not fully correct. *The point is not that logotherapy would not fit the standard criteria of effective psychotherapy*; *the point is that these criteria do not fit logotherapy*! In the period since it was created there was no option for its positioning other than as a school of psychotherapy. Now, however, multiple insights in various branches of psychology shed some new light on the issue and suggest a new vision of what logotherapy is about. How much of psychotherapy do we find in logotherapy (and in other versions of existential psychotherapy)?

Psychotherapy is more than Psychotherapy

As early as 1965, James Bugental described in his book, "The Search for Authenticity" (rev. ed. 1981) two stages of any psychotherapeutic process. He called the first one the analytical stage, when the focus of the therapist's work is the client's complaints, his or her inner blocks that psychologically invalidate him or her, preventing them from achieving full awareness and hindering their living. The therapist must unfold, elaborate, and remove resistances existing in the client, namely the ways he or she strives to get rid of existential anxiety. The methodology applied at this stage has no radical divergences from the methodology of psychoanalysis or other in-depth approaches. When this stage is over, the second stage must start, which Bugental called "ontogogy" (from "ontos," being, and "pedagogy"), meaning by this "a leading out into being" (Bugental 1981, 318). The therapist's work at this stage is aimed at helping the client to get in touch with his or her life, to discover and fulfill the potential of living.

The latter task seems to exceed the competence of psychotherapy. Indeed, "ontogogy is not a therapeutic procedure as such" (Bugental 1981, 317). What do psychotherapists do with their clients? The answer that immediately comes to mind is that they do psychotherapy. In fact, psychotherapists do different kinds of work, besides psychotherapy. They sometimes inform clients, sometimes consult them, sometimes teach them, sometimes train them, sometimes enlighten them, etc. A good psychotherapist would use different forms of interaction with their client, but should we call psychotherapy everything that takes place in the therapist's office? Indeed, we are tempted to do so—in the twentieth century everything is called psychotherapy, because in the West psychotherapy has become a general cultural model for any kind of work with individuals, referring to any kind of dialogue, of interaction, or of influence. This word seems to be used in somewhat broader senses than its exact meaning. Psychotherapy as a culturally accepted and socially constructed form of human practice now embraces a multitude of forms of psychological help and support, and fulfills religious, educational, informational, and other functions, just like pastoral guidance in earlier ages also embraced the functions of teaching, psychotherapy, family counseling, etc., besides pastoral guidance *per se*.

Psychotherapy as the entire professional activity fulfilled by psychotherapists thus appears, from the methodological standpoint, to be rather heterogeneous. Therapists not only do therapy, they also do another kind of work, more educational in nature. Bugental repeatedly and unambiguously stated that psychotherapy is an educational effort rather than a medical procedure (Bugental 1991, 8). The role of the psychotherapist as a teacher has been strongly emphasized in *Reality Therapy* (Glasser 1975). James Hillman (1965), a prominent therapist of the Jungian tradition, noted that the word "doctor" originates from the Latin "*docere*," to teach; "document" originally meant "the lesson" and the verb "to educate" is also from this root.

The shift or extension of the function of psychotherapy from healing to teaching can be treated as a historical trend. "Once clinical psychologists had patients. Over the years, the discipline grew concerned that "patient" implied illness, which in turn implied a conception of health, a conception of the goal of therapy that the field did not really have. Thus, patients became clients.... Clients define their goals in a way that patients do not.... What will psychologists call the recipients of their services if and when a positive psychology comes to fruition? ... The right term, I think, is students." (Schwartz 2000, 87).

Thus at least one of the tasks fulfilled by psychotherapists, especially existentially oriented ones, is the kind of life guidance labeled "ontogogy" by James Bugental (1981); later he spoke of "life coaching" (Bugental 1999). It is not absolutely identical to education; rather, it is a common component of the work of a good existential psychotherapist and a good teacher, or pastor, or social worker, or any person who is not indifferent to his or her fellows.

Not only can some aspects similar to educational practice be found in psychotherapy, but inversely, some therapy-like processes are detected in higher education. Making a special comparison of college teaching with psychotherapy, A. Tolor pointed at some notable similarities between them in goals, methodology, interaction systems, outcomes, common pitfalls, and personal requirements: "It is the professor's task to assist students in attaining their human potential, in structuring themselves and the world in a more differentiated manner, in coming to terms with values and ethical dilemmas, in fashioning methods useful in searching for the truth, regardless of the conceptual and emotional dislocations which such an effort entails, and in making judgments that balance and integrate personal responsibility with the data base available" (Tolor 1984, 711). No wonder that "certain college professors with no specific training in psychotherapy can become good psychotherapists" (ibid. 716). This conclusion strongly resonates with my experience of university teaching for over 30 years, smoothly transformed into practical groupwork during the last 10 years (see Leontiev in press). In some other relatively new approaches to child education and upbringing this similarity to psychotherapy can also be seen very clearly (e.g., Snyder et al. 1985).

Education, however, must be understood in a broader meaning than just didactics, "downloading" the information about reality, knowledge about what is right and what is wrong. There have been numerous attempts, mostly within the cognitive-behavioral tradition, to construe the therapy process as replacing the false, or misleading, or destructive beliefs by right, or constructive ones (Ellis 1994; Glasser 1975 a.o.).

A similar point is made in philosophical counseling—a practice of helping people by means of philosophical discussions, elaborated in the 1980s by the German philosopher Gerd Achenbach (see, e.g., Schuster 2002). It is being practiced by professional philosophers (an M.A. in Philosophy is a minimal requirement). Like logotherapy, philosophical counseling explicitly points at Socrates as the prototype. Socrates' metaphor of majeutics—birth assistance—is the guiding image of philosophical counseling: the counselor serves as a spiritual midwife who helps the clients "to give birth to philosophical insights into the problematic and complex issues of life" (ibid. 257). The dialogue is about the ultimate issues of being, and it is hardly likely that you meet a psychotherapist able and ready to discuss such issues. Achenbach views philosophical counseling as something different from therapy, an alternative practice (ibid. 259). To some degree philosophical counseling recalls a much older practice of pastoral counseling; in the latter, however, the underlying values guiding both the counselor and the counselee are much more definite, while the former provides a wider spectrum of "philosophical narratives."

Finally, a reference should be made to Abraham Maslow, who spoke on the special methods directed at heightening the presence-of-being-values in everyone. "Such an approach might be called *metacounseling*, combining the roles of regular counselors, psychotherapists and educators" (Maslow 1966/1996, 92, italics by Maslow).

In a broader sense, education means enlightenment, making sense of the world in which one lives, giving due acknowledgment to the incompleteness of information, the uncertainty of existence, and the variety of interpretations of reality. Personal meanings, activity structures and skills, tolerance of ambiguity and risk, and relationships of dignity and support are equally important aspects of such an education (see Leontiev 2013, 32; Krasko 2004). The point made here is not that psychotherapy is or should be a kind of education but rather that there are shared aspects of psychological dynamics common for psychotherapy and education (both broadly conceived), and not only for them, and these aspects belong to the existential dimension of human existence. Indeed, there have been some convincing attempts to explicate the educational, rather than therapeutic, potential of logotherapy (Krasko 2004; Wolicki 2009).

Living Existence vs. Determined Behavior: The Specific Challenge for Existential Psychotherapy

Existential psychotherapy, unlike other schools, is the one where this nontherapeutic, ontogogic aspect comes to the fore. This is characteristic for all the schools and versions of existential psychotherapy, including Frankl's logotherapy. Usually therapists identifying themselves as existential ones use, flexibly, a broad spectrum of devices, and approaches in their work. It is stressed that existential psychotherapy creates an additional layer or level of work, above the more traditional layers, and the tools of existential analysis are added to, rather than substitute, the methods elaborated in other schools and approaches (e.g., May 1967; Bugental 1981).

An institutional view may help us to draw a distinction based both on the institutional regulations associated with these forms of psychological practices and on underlying philosophical assumptions. Today, many forms of psychotherapy are included in health insurance programs, assuming that their positive effect can be somehow warranted. They are also legally regulated in some countries, on the assumption that they can be abused, at least on the part of the psychotherapist (the regulations in different countries are not the same; what I am writing about here is a general trend and these statements may not apply to some countries). Both these facts suggest that these forms of psychotherapy are legally treated as effective intervention tools. Using these tools, a skilled therapist can provide a definite result. Both social institutions—insurance and legal regulation—suggest that in these forms of psychotherapy the therapist has some power over a client to provide the effect in line with the client's demand but largely independent of the client's individual peculiarities and behavior. It is assumed that the human mind is based on a system of objective mechanisms that can sometimes malfunction beyond the awareness and volition of their owner. A psychotherapist (like a physician) is a master of fixing and tuning these mechanisms; their professional certificate certifies that they are appropriately skilled in this work. One is healthy if these mechanisms are (again) functioning well. This assumption is inherent in traditional mainstream psychology and psychotherapy.

In my view (Leontiev 2004a, b, 2014), the critical distinction between traditional mainstream psychology and existential psychology is related to the issue of determinism. Traditional psychology describes the human being as a determined being—and that turns out to be true in most cases—when the conditions are stable, and the individual is satisfied with what they have and does not strive to anything beyond successful adjustment. Quite often, traditional deterministic explanations work perfectly and existential views seems redundant. But there are at least two kinds of situations in which this kind of explanation just does not work. First: the moments of crises, losses, or disasters, when the life-world is suddenly shattered and crushed and no "factors" can rule the decisions—the individual is facing the unknown world. Second: when the individual is not satisfied with successful adjustment and well-being, and strives for more, beyond any apparent necessity. The existentialist view is relevant not only for these two types of situations, but its validity is most evident in them. It says that your actual choices determine your life.

The point is that a human being may function at different levels—either at a subhuman level, where everything may be accurately deduced from the constellation of internal and external independent variables (dispositions, drives, stimuli, social expectations, reinforcements etc.; Bugental (1991) called these variables "tapes" that may reproduce only what had been recorded on them), or at a human level in which one mediates the influences through the "pause" (May 1981) and fills this pause with new types of self-created determinants (Bugental (1991) referred to this as true life). A human being is both determined and self-determined—at different levels and in different moments. Determination never stops, but it defines the outcomes in less than 100 % of cases—we all fly in airplanes despite gravity. Existential psychology gives an adequate account of a human being as a self-determined being (at least potentially) and thus complements traditional psychology, which deals with a human being as a totally determined being. Certainly none of us are free from being determined, but at some point we may oppose some other regularities to this determination, like an airplane that may sometimes overcome gravity while still being governed by it. Thus, existential psychology may be treated as a psychology of self-determination, that becomes possible as soon as we start mediating our behavior by our reflective consciousness (Vygotsky 1997), by symbolization, imagination, and judgment (Maddi 1971), and by our relations to the life-world at large. Self-determination is a special optional level of human functioning, qualitatively distinct from the level of determined functioning.

This statement is close to Rollo May's statement that existential psychotherapy opens a new level of analysis in addition to the ones revealed in more traditional schools of psychotherapy. Existential psychotherapy is thus a supplement to, rather than a substitute of, other approaches in psychotherapy (May 1967). In line with this, May kept labeling himself a psychoanalyst till the end of his life, though all his writings presented views quite different from psychoanalytic ones, addressing the level of human functioning that classical psychoanalysis never reaches (and deems illusory).

Frankl and the Challenge of the Noetic Dimension

Viktor Frankl was probably the first author to draw the attention of psychologists to the spiritual level of human functioning. "Man is more than psyche: man is spirit" (Frankl 1967, 63). Focusing on the mind alone, we miss a very important dimension of human functioning; it does not play an important role in all cases, but when it does it totally changes the whole picture. Frankl never ceased to emphasize that the spiritual, noetic dimension of human existence[1] and its functioning differ from the psychological, mental dimension no less than the latter differs from the bodily,

[1] Klingberg (2009, pp. 205–209) provided a very precise analysis of relationship between noetic, spiritual and religious in Frankl's works and mainstream psychology of his and our days.

material dimension; reducing the first to the second would be no more reasonable than to reduce the second to the third. Frankl called the unavoidable distance in us between the psychological and the spiritual *psychonoetic antagonism* (Frankl 1984); it is this distance that gives birth to many person-related phenomena. "The spiritual, however, is ignored by the 'psychologism'. From this follows also the insufficiency of all the psychotherapy in the narrow, traditional psychological meaning: it does not see the spiritual" (Frankl 1984, 169). Defining logotherapy as a spiritually based therapy, Frankl clearly states that though logotherapy stays "in a didactic contradiction to the previous psychotherapy, psychotherapy in the narrow meaning of the word, it should not be conceived as its substitute. It is not possible to substitute psychotherapy by logotherapy; it is, however, necessary to supplement psychotherapy with logotherapy" (ibid. 172; see also Frankl 1973, 17).

In fact, logotherapy deals with the processes of human understanding and experience processing through reflective self-awareness, with mental practices which are much more ancient than psychotherapy. "On my tours in Asia, in India and Japan,"—recollected Frankl—"people pointed out to me that what I was saying were old truths one might find in the ancient Vedas, in Zen, or in the writings of Laotse" (quoted after Fabry 1968, 188). As A. Längle noted, the practice of logotherapy was associated for Frankl with the work of persuasion based on arguments to be consciously accepted (Überzeugungsarbeit), rather than with the work of transference (Übertragungsarbeit) (Längle 1998, 146).

The focus of attention and the object of therapeutic elaboration here seem to be something different than the person him/herself, something in the world at which the person is intentionally directed, in line with Frankl's concept of self-transcendence. He used the clever metaphor of a boomerang for human intentionality: "Only the boomerang that has missed the goal, returns back to the point from which it has been thrown; its initial function is to hit a prey, rather than to return to the hunter" (Frankl 1987, 104). Meanings and values there in the world are our prey; only having missed them, can we turn back to focus on our own Self. "If one wants to approach one's Self, oneself, the way goes through the world" (ibid. 103). It resonates also with the recent version of existential psychotherapy explicated by Ernesto Spinelli (2007). The latter is based on two key concepts: "worldling" (by this Spinelli understands relatedness, or being-in-the-world in its more processual–dynamic, rather than static, aspects), and the worldview that refers to the structure imposed on the process of experience. Existential psychotherapy "is principally concerned with the investigation of the dissonances and distortions imposed upon the process-like experience of worldling by the structural worldview" (p. 32).

Frankl's dimensional model has also found strong support in the four-dimensional model of the life-world elaborated by Emmy van Deurzen. To the three aspects of the life-world conceptualized by Ludwig Binswanger (1946/1958)—the surrounding outer world (Umwelt), the private inner world (Eigenwelt), and the public conversational world (Mitwelt)—she has added a fourth, the ideal transcendent world, "the absolute world of values" (van Deurzen 2002). In fact, what has been added by van Deurzen to Binswanger's model is just Frankl's noetic dimension.

It follows from the above that psychological work in the existential dimension is *sensu stricto* something different than psychotherapy: where an existential approach starts in the work of a therapist, it ceases to be psychotherapy, and where pure psychotherapy starts, all the peculiarity of the existential approach dissolves. *What is existential in existential psychotherapy is not exactly psychotherapy*; *what is therapeutic in it is not unique for existential therapy alone*. Existential psychotherapy deals with the general issues of human life in a unique fashion through counseling and life coaching, ontogogy, addressing the client's reflexive consciousness rather than through psychotherapy addressing the client's emotional ties. We see this division again in the writings of James Bugental. His highly appreciated and widely acknowledged textbook *The Art of the Psychotherapist* (Bugental 1987) presents a brilliant microanalysis of the psychotherapeutic process, but the stamp of the author's existential way of thinking is not too evident—the book would be extremely helpful for almost any therapist, independent of his or her theoretical background. Its sequel, Bugental's last book, "Psychotherapy Isn't What You Think" (Bugental 1999), is, in contrast, markedly existential, but even the provocative title, as well as the whole book, challenges the traditional image of what psychotherapy is about.

This brings us to the conclusion that existential psychotherapy in its pure, special form does not exist. There is psychotherapy as art, or craft, or science, or all three, and there is an existential worldview, an existential approach that may be added to the therapeutic work, lifting the therapist to a higher level of expertise, or to other forms of psychological practice as well. *The special form of practice following from the existential approach is counseling, or other interventions addressing the client's awareness, reasoning, and self-detachment rather than a therapeutic alliance and emotionally loaded transferences*. It fulfills the client's needs to comprehend, to make sense, to reconstruct the general vision of the world, to have an orientation, to realize their potential, to reach authentic living. "But small is the gate and narrow the road that leads to life, and only a few find it" (Matt 7:14). People look for this in a church, at school, in books, in psychotherapy, to mention only a few places. Viktor Frankl organized special places fulfilling this function in Vienna at the late 1920s, at the early stage of his professional career—consultations for middle school graduates (see Frankl 2005). By the end of his career, public lecturing had become the dominant form of practical work he performed. Both practices are highly representative of Frankl's logotherapy. Both have nothing to do with psychotherapy (except for the metaphoric use of the word).

The same is true for the three methods of logotherapy elaborated by Viktor Frankl: paradoxical intention, dereflection, and Socratic dialogue, recently being described as attitude modulation (Lukas 1991). The first two techniques are definitely psychotherapeutic; they have found a broad application within quite different psychotherapeutic approaches, besides logotherapy and other existential methods of treatment. Irvin Yalom (1980) has put into question the essential link of these two methods to an existential context, especially logotherapy. Elisabeth Lukas (1983) argued that they are fundamentally linked to it. Her argument makes sense; however, in fact the wide use of both techniques outside logotherapy suggests that they completely maintain their power in a different context as well. Socratic dialogue is, on the contrary, an inalienable element of existential work, but is it psychotherapy? Socrates was no therapist, he only tried to evoke some comprehension in his neighbors. This is a technique of applied philosophizing—guiding the person toward answering one's life questions, finding and reposing the questions themselves, meaning construction in a dialogue, enlightenment facilitation, to use the most general label. To call it attitude modulation, as E. Lukas (1991) does, seems to me a kind of psychologization of spiritual issues in psychotherapy, so strongly criticized by Frankl (1984, 169), though in a more general perspective Lukas (1983) explicitly described logotherapy as a developmental process, a movement toward maturation.

In my own practical work I have distilled an existential practice labeled Life Enhancement, defined as a positively grounded and consciousness-based practice of facilitating the capacity of working through one's life experiences. It is an ontogogic practice of solving life problems, which can be applied both as part of a psychotherapist's work and apart from psychotherapeutic settings. In a sense, life enhancement may be treated as a refined, completely psychotherapy-free logotherapy. This practice embodies the above considerations; it has been described in a special publication (Leontiev in press). In the second part of this chapter, I will speculate on some psychological mechanisms, which underlie transformations at the noetic level.

Worldview and the Acquisition of the Noetic Experience

The differences between psychotherapy and logopractice (let me use this new term to stress these differences) can be best highlighted through the analysis of relationships between being-in-the-world (worldling in E. Spinelli's terms, see above) and worldview. Their dissonance (see Spinelli 2007), indeed, seems to be the focus of this practice.

Our experience of the world is more than just information, or biographical events; it is rather an event or information processed and integrated into a worldview. This processing may go smoothly and without awareness, but often it proceeds as a complicated inner activity. Acquiring new experience allows us to direct and correct our actions in the world.

Correcting one's behavior as a function of the feedback on the outcomes of previous activities is called self-regulation, or autoregulation (see Carver and Scheier 1998; Leontiev 2012). Let's take a brief look at the evolution of this mechanism (Leontiev 2008).

The simplest autoregulation mechanism is trial and error: successful (positively reinforced) attempts get inprinted, unsuccessful (not reinforced or negatively reinforced) attempts are inhibited. This outline gets more complicated when an individual, instead of repeating trials every time, recollects the previous results and trusts these memories. These memories possess less credibility as compared to actual trials, because something might have changed during the time interval; however, this addition provides gains in efficacy, making repeated trials redundant.

At the next step one may lean on others' memories, communicated interpersonally, instead of one's own ones. They are still less trustworthy, they increase the distance between the individual and the world; however, they allow one's orientation and activity to spread into much broader situations and domains of experience. They broaden one's picture of the world, though this picture is less credible as compared to what one experienced in an immediate contact. This picture gets still more complicated when humans start using and applying cognitive maps borrowed from the storage of human culture. These manifold maps, often contradicting each other, provide comprehensive systems of orientation in the world, though their credibility is still more questionable.

The worldview thus serves as a source of information believed to be trustworthy and complementary to the immediate feedback on the outcomes of our existence. This information is made of generalizations of collective and cultural experience, rather than the individual one.

In my own conceptualization of the worldview (Leontiev 2004a, b, 2007, 2008), it is defined as the core of the person's picture of the world, a more or less coherent system of general understandings about how human beings, society, and the world at large exist and function. A worldview also includes ideals of the desirable or "perfect" human being, society, and world. Though acquired knowledge, cultural stereotypes and schemes and group ideologies are responsible for much of the content of an individual's world view, the latter is nevertheless a highly individuated structure. Knowledge is alloyed in it with firm beliefs, fuzzy ideas and unconscious schemes and prejudices. In this view, *the core* of an individual's worldview is construed as a system of *generalizations*. These elements of a worldview are beliefs that pertain to generalities rather than single objects or single subjects. For example, a belief like "This minister is a liar" does not belong to a worldview concept, but "Most ministers are liars" does belong. The belief that "Music is what I love most of all" does not belong, but "Every educated person loves music" does. Individual worldviews always claim to reflect and/or express general truths.

Being of individual character and belonging to the core of a person's identity, the content of a worldview subjectively appears as knowledge of "how things are." In fact, shared knowledge is intertwined in it with subjective interpretations and prejudices. This makes worldview generalizations, in a sense, highly projective. They look like purely cognitive statements; however, when we ask a person about people at large and the world at large, we can expect that these generalizations will be loaded by plenty of subjective meanings emerging from the deep layers of personality dynamics. Transforming one's personal meanings into worldview generalizations, a person thus presents them as objective cognitions, or general truths. There are two principal ways of coming to such generalizations: inductive processing of one's life experiences (worldview as inner work), or introjection and uncritical acceptance, "downloading" of ready-made explanatory structures from external sources (worldview as inner myth). In the second case. worldview structures are more rigid, less malleable.

Psychotherapy vs. Life Enhancement; Rehabilitation vs. Understanding

The human being is thus facing a fundamental uncertainty. The feedback information from our actions is trustworthy, but narrowly localized. The information that originates from worldviews is comprehensive but its credibility is questionable. Hence, if you want to get the most trustworthy information about your life and the world, you should narrow the context and focus on the feedback of what you are doing. This is what a psychotherapist does, locating his or her work with a client in an invariant and narrow space of one-to-one interaction limited by the borders of the therapeutic hour and the terms of the therapeutic contract. This narrow "chronotope" (M. Bakhtin) allows maximizing the credibility of what is going on in this interaction, providing the optimal possibility for the client to face the truth of his/her life. This complementarity can also be rephrased as the complementarity of truth and meaning as regards the strategy of psychological help. Striving to maximize truth, I have to narrow the context, thus restricting meaning. Striving to maximize meaning, I have to extend the context, thus moving away from the immediately experienced reality, from the credibility of my immediate experience.

Helping the client to face and assimilate the truth about their life beyond all the defenses and resistances is a universal task of any in-depth psychotherapy, from psychoanalysis to existential therapy. It is a universal challenge every human being is facing. There is another challenge, complementary to the first one: facing the perspectives, the meaningful possibilities of one's living beyond its facticity. It is not about the truth of living, it is about the comprehensiveness of the worldview; its meaningfulness is more important than trustworthiness. Helping a person finding such perspectives in the broad context is usually the task of an educator, a pastor, a politician, sometimes a counseling psychologist, or even a psychotherapist, especially an existential one. However, this is not psychotherapy *sensu stricto*, this is just what I call life enhancement, and Bugental called ontogogy, or life coaching. Psychotherapy works with the truth of the way the patient is living here and now; life enhancement with the perspective of meaning-making beyond the facticity of this living. Both objectives cannot be pursued simultaneously, but both strategies are open for the psychologist to choose and to switch from one to another.

This poses a methodological problem of the possibility and mechanisms of deep personality transformations through the insights in world understanding. I prefer not to label them "cognitive" in order to escape oversimplification implied by the misleading rigid polar dichotomy "cognitive vs. emotional" that fails to embrace the unique reality of personal meaning. Understanding is thus about meaning-making, about the integration into a comprehensive personal context, rather than about knowledge acquisition. The relationship between the progress in understanding the world and the progress in personality development seems to be much more intimate than has ever been recognized within the psychotherapy context. How do we perceive our own personality development? What do we feel when an outside observer, armed with multiple tests, says that our personality development has been registered? What corresponds to it in our subjective representation? My hypothesis is that the progress in understanding is *the* introspective correlate of personality development, the only form in which our own development is given to us. It can be articulated as a variant of the complementarity principle: *progress in understanding is the subjective side of personality development, and personality development is the objective side of progress in understanding* (Leontiev 2002). We change for an outside observer, but cannot detect the changes in ourselves. For us the world changes, the picture of the world changes its shape and structure, so that we have a better, a more differentiated and integrated picture of the world, or "self-and-world construct system" (Bugental 1999). This seems to be also the basic mechanism explaining the effects of logotherapy.

Conclusion

The aim of this chapter was to propose a nontraditional answer to the question of what Viktor Frankl's logotherapy is about. The chapter questions the stereotyped vision of logotherapy as a form of psychotherapy; it seems to be more helpful to treat it as a special form of psychological (not just purely psychological) practice other than psychotherapy in the strict meaning of the word. The presence of this work at the noetic level in a psychotherapist's work (ontogogy) allows us to speak of psychotherapy as an educational, rather than medical, enterprise; this especially refers to existential psychotherapy including logotherapy.

Acknowledgment The study was supported by the Russian Scientific Foundation, project No. 14-18-03401.

References

Binswanger, L. (1946/1958). The existential analysis school of thought. In R. May, E. Angel, & H. F. Ellenberger (Eds.), *Existence* (pp. 191–213). New York, NY: Basic Books.
Bugental, J. F. T. (1981). *The search for authenticity: An existential-analytic approach to psychotherapy* (2nd ed.). New York, NY: Irvingston Publishers. Enlarged edition.
Bugental, J. F. T. (1987). *The art of the psychotherapist*. New York, NY: Norton.
Bugental, J. F. T. (1991). Outcomes of an existential-humanistic psychotherapy: A tribute to Rollo May. *The Humanistic Psychologist, 19*(1), 2–9.
Bugental, J. F. T. (1999). *Psychotherapy isn't what you think*. Phoenix, AZ: Zeig, Tucker & Co.
Carver, C., & Scheier, M. (1998). *On the self-regulation of behavior*. New York, NY: Cambridge University Press.
Ellis, A. (1994). *Reason and emotion in psychotherapy: Comprehensive method of treating human disturbances: Revised and updated*. New York, NY: Citadel Press.
Fabry, J. B. (1968). *The pursuit of meaning: Logotherapy applied to life*. Boston, MA: Beacon.
Frankl, V. E. (1967). *Psychotherapy and existentialism*. New York, NY: Simon and Schuster.
Frankl, V. E. (1973). *The Doctor and the soul: From psychotherapy to logotherapy*. New York, NY: Vintage Books.
Frankl, V. E. (1984). *Der leidende Mensch: Anthropologische Grundlagen der Psychotherapie*. Bern: Huber.

Frankl, V. E. (1987). *Logotherapie und Existenzanalyse*. München/Zürich: Piper.
Frankl, V. E. (2005). *Frühe Schriften. 1923–1942.*. Wien: Verlag Wilhelm Maudrich.
Freud, S. (1923). Psychoanalyse und Libidotheorie. *Gesammelte Werke. 13*, 209–233. Frankfurt am Main: S. Fischer Verlag, 1976.
Glasser, W. (1975). *Reality therapy*. New York, NY: Harper & Row.
Hillman, J. (1965). *Suicide and the soul*. New York, NY: Harper Colophon.
Klingberg, H. (2009). Logotherapy, Frankl, and positive psychology. In A. Batthyany & J. Levinson (Eds.), *Existential psychotherapy of meaning: A handbook of logotherapy and existential analysis* (pp. 197–223). Phoenix, AZ: Zeig, Tucker, & Theisen, Inc.
Krasko, G. L. (2004). *This unbearable boredom of being: A Crisis of meaning in America*. New York, NY: iUniverse Inc.
Längle, A. (1998). *Viktor Frankl: Ein Porträt*. München: Piper.
Leontiev, D. A. (2002). Simbioz I adaptatsiya ili avtonomiya I transtsendentsiya: vybor lichnosti v nepredskazuemom mire (Symbiosis and adaptation vs. autonomy and transcendence: the choice for the person in the unpredictable world). In E. Yatsuta (Ed.), *Lichnost v sovremennom mire: ot strategii vyzhivaniya k strategii zhiznetvorchestva (The person in the contemporary world: from the strategy of survival to the strategy of life enhancement)* (pp. 3–34). Kemerovo, RU: Graphika.
Leontiev, D. A. (2004a). Existential psychology as a response to the challenges of the 21st Century. *International Journal of Existential Psychology & Psychotherapy, 1*(1), 103–105.
Leontiev, D. A. (2004b). Mirovozzrenie kak mif I mirovozzrenie kak deyatelnost' (Worldview as a myth and worldview as an activity). In V. Kabrin & O. Muravieva (Eds.), *Mentalitet I kommunikativnaya sreda v tranzitivnom obschestve (Mentality and communicative environment in a transitional society)* (pp. 11–29). Tomsk, RU: Tomsk State University Press.
Leontiev, D. A. (2007). Approaching worldview structure with ultimate meanings technique. *Journal of Humanistic Psychology, 47*(2), 243–266.
Leontiev, D. A. (2008). Mirovozzrenie i bytie-v-mire kak osnovaniya regulatsii (Worldview and being-in-the-world as bases of regulation). *Ekzistentsialnaya traditsiya: filosofiya, psikhologiya, psikhoterapiya (Existential Tradition: Philosophy, Psychology, Psychotherapy), 2*(13), 72–77.
Leontiev, D. A. (2012). Why we do what we do: The variety of human regulations. In D. Leontiev (Ed.), *Motivation, consciousness, and self-regulation* (pp. 93–103). New York, NY: Nova Science Publishers.
Leontiev, D. A. (2013). Emerging contexts and meanings of human education. In O. Kovbasyuk & P. Blessinger (Eds.), *Meaning-centered education* (pp. 24–34). New York/London: Routledge.
Leontiev, D. A. (2014). Extending the contexts of existence: Benefits of meaning-guided living. In A. Batthyany & P. Russo-Netzer (Eds.), *Meaning in positive and existential psychology* (pp. 97–114). New York, NY: Springer.
Leontiev, D. A. (2015). Experience processing as an aspect of existential psychotherapy: Life enhancement methodology. *Journal of Contemporary Psychotherapy*. Volume 45 Issue 1, pp 49–58
Lukas, E. (1983). *Höhenpsychologie: Die andere Sicht vom Menschen*. Freiburg, DE: Herder.
Lukas, E. (1991). *Auch dein Leben hat Sinn*. Freiburg, DE: Herder.
Maddi, S. (1971). The search for meaning. In W. J. Arnold & M. M. Page (Eds.), *Nebraska symposium on motivation, 1970* (pp. 137–186). Lincoln, NE: University of Nebraska Press.
Maslow, A. H. (1966). Higher motivation and the new psychology. In E. Hoffman (Ed.), *Future visions: The unpublished papers of Abraham Maslow*. (pp 88–98) Thousand Oaks: Sage, 1996.
May, R. (1967). *Psychology and the human dilemma*. Princeton, NJ: Van Nostrand.
May, R. (1981). *Freedom and destiny*. New York, NY: Norton.
Schuster, S. C. (2002). Philosophical narratives and philosophical counseling. In S. DuPlock (Ed.), *Further existential challenges to psychotherapeutic theory and practice* (pp. 250–267). London, UK: The Society for Existential Analysis.

Schwartz, B. (2000). Self-determination: The tyranny of freedom. *American Psychologist, 55*, 79–88.

Snyder, M., Snyder, R., & Snyder, R., Jr. (1985). *The young child as person*. New York, NY: Human Sciences Press.

Spinelli, E. (2007). *Practicing existential psychotherapy: The relational world*. Los Angeles, CA: Sage.

Tolor, A. (1984). How similar is college teaching to psychotherapy? *Psychological Reports, 55*, 711–718.

van Deurzen, E. (2002). *Existential counseling and psychotherapy in practice*. London, UK: Sage.

Vygotsky, L. S. (1997). *The history of development of higher mental functions. The collected works of L.S. Vygotsky, Vol. 3.*. New York, NY: Plenum.

Wolicki, M. (2009). The pedagogical implications of the logotheoric concept of self-transcendence. In A. Batthyany & J. Levinson (Eds.), *Existential psychotherapy of meaning: A handbook of logotherapy and existential analysis* (pp. 307–319). Phoenix, AZ: Zeig, Tucker, & Theisen, Inc.

Yalom, I. (1980). *Existential psychotherapy*. New York, NY: Basic Books.

The World Still Cries for Meaning: Are We Still Listening?

William F. Evans

Introduction

My first encounter with the life and work of Dr. Viktor E. Frankl occurred while participating in a Holocaust Remembrance week during the spring semester of 1977 when I was a graduate student at Duke University. I was introduced to his book, *Man's Search for Meaning* (Frankl 1984), which I read that week for the first time. It was a timely encounter for me, personally, for my father had just been diagnosed with terminal cancer, my mother, who had struggled with bipolar disorder most of her adult life, had just been hospitalized for severe depression, my career path seemed suddenly uncertain, my relationship with my girlfriend seemed tenuous, and my entire worldview felt extremely fragile. I desperately needed meaning in my life, and this introduction to logotherapy, and the life and work of Dr. Frankl, came just in the nick of time. Thankfully, I was able to regain my bearings, and the truths of logotherapy gave me a strong foundation upon which I was able to grow and develop, both personally and professionally. I was starving for a solid sense of meaning in my life, and logotherapy provided the structure: freedom of will—will to meaning—meaning in life; "deeds done—loves loved—learning to suffer with courage and dignity" suddenly became for me a solid foundation for rebuilding my life.

I have read and reread *Man's Search for Meaning* at least once every year since the spring of 1977, and some years three or four times. It always provides me with a clearer perspective on what is really important in life, and I am reminded time and again of the need for, and the ability to pursue and find, meaning in life. I have read all of Dr. Frankl's books that have been translated into English, but this book remains foundational for me. In 1977, as surely as before and after, I was crying out for mean-

W.F. Evans (✉)
Department of Psychology, James Madison University,
1173 Miller Hall—MSC 7704, Harrisonburg, VA 22807, USA
e-mail: evanswf@jmu.edu

A. Batthyány (ed.), *Logotherapy and Existential Analysis*, Logotherapy and Existential Analysis: Proceedings of the Viktor Frankl Institute Vienna 1,
DOI 10.1007/978-3-319-29424-7_25

ing in my life. In logotherapy, and in the life and work of Dr. Viktor Frankl, I discovered many profound truths, simply and clearly stated, that I desperately needed to live meaningfully and well. The truths of logotherapy as lived and taught by Dr. Frankl are as needed and as timely today as they were during the Holocaust for him and for me in 1977 and since. The world still cries for meaning! Are we still listening?

The Search for Meaning as a Universal Human Quest

Every human being desires to live a meaningful life. I find support for this idea in Viktor Frankl's statement: "Man's search for meaning is the primary motivation in his life." (Frankl 1984, 105); and in Bjorklund and Bee's writing: "The quest for meaning is a basic human characteristic… the search for meaning is an integral part of the human experience." (Bjorklund and Bee 2008, 268).

The real essence of this quest for meaning as the ultimate concern of human beings is called self-transcendence (Frankl 1984, 1997). This is clearly more than simply fulfilling the need for self-actualization as constructed by Abraham Maslow. By self-transcendence I refer to a longing for something or someone beyond ourselves that we desire to give ourselves to. Viktor Frankl defined self-transcendence this way in *Man's Search for Ultimate Meaning* (1997): "Human existence is always directed to something, or someone, other than itself, be it a meaning to fulfill or another human being to encounter lovingly. I have termed this constitutive characteristic of human existence "self-transcendence." What is called self-actualization is ultimately an effect, the unintentional by-product, of self-transcendence." (Frankl 1997, 84) "A human being is actualizing itself precisely to the extent to which he is forgetting himself and he is forgetting himself by giving himself, be it through serving a cause higher than himself or loving a person other than himself. Truly, self-transcendence is the essence of human existence." (Frankl 1997, 138).

Key Issues

So, then, how does the study of psychology and psychotherapy relate to the human quest for meaning? Originally, the field of psychology was defined as the study of the human soul or psyche. This meant studying that, which appeared to be uniquely human: consciousness, reason, love, will. However, as Erich Fromm noted in his classic book, *Psychoanalysis and Religion*, that practice was soon discarded for other goals, especially the desire for respect in the world of science:

> "The tradition in which psychology was a study of the soul, concerned with man's virtue and happiness, was abandoned. Academic psychology, trying to imitate the natural sciences and laboratory methods of weighing and counting, dealt with everything but the soul… Psychology thus became a science lacking its main subject matter, the soul, it was concerned with mechanism, reaction formations, instincts, but not with the most specifically human phenomena: love, reason, conscience, values." (Fromm 1950, 6).

Therefore, as Viktor Frankl also noted, "A psychology that a priori shuts out meaning and reason cannot recognize the self-transcendent quality of the human reality and instead must resort to drives and instincts." (Frankl 1997, 132) Psychology became the study of naturalistic biochemical machines. "Whereas behaviorism, championed by such advocates as John Watson, stressed the mechanistic and overt aspects of human functioning, Freud and his followers developed a theory premised on covert intrapsychic determinism." (Corsini and Weddington 2008, 301).

In the process of seeking to understand this biochemical human machine, psychologists have often admitted that something appears broken within human beings, something that definitely needs repairing. Yet I've often wondered how one flawed biochemical machine can somehow fix itself in such a way that it is then capable of fixing another flawed biochemical machine? It always seemed much like the blind leading the blind to me, which, of course, would result in both stumbling and falling.

However, the existential approach to psychology, espoused by Frankl, Fromm, May, Yalom, and others, "rejects the deterministic view of human nature espoused by orthodox psychoanalysis and radical behaviorism. [Whereas] psychoanalysis sees freedom as restricted by unconscious forces, irrational drives, and past events; behaviorists see freedom as restricted by socio-cultural conditioning... Existential therapists... emphasize our freedom to choose what to make of our circumstances. This approach is grounded in the assumption that we are free and therefore responsible for our choices and actions... We are not victims of our circumstances; we are what we choose to be... Existential therapy is a process of searching for the value and meaning of life. The therapists' basic task is to encourage clients to explore their options for creating a meaningful existence." (Corey 2001, 143).

The school of existential psychotherapy called logotherapy by its founder, Dr. Viktor Frankl, sought to rehumanize psychology and turn it back to the study of the human soul. Frankl believed that the essence of being human lies in searching for meaning and purpose. His life was an illustration of his theory, for he lived what his theory espoused. (Corey 2001, 141) "Logotherapy aims to unlock the will to meaning and to assist the patient in seeing a meaning in his life." (Frankl 1997, 128) Logotherapy is "height psychology" as opposed to "depth psychology" (Frankl 1997; 1984) Frankl often wondered, "If meanings and values really are 'nothing but' defense mechanisms and reaction formations, is life really worth living?" (Frankl 1997, 105).

Now, regarding religion and its relationship to existential psychology, and more specifically, logotherapy, Frankl stated: "We have seen that there is not only a repressed and unconscious libido, but also repressed and unconscious religio" (Frankl 1997, 55), and "A religious sense is existent and present in each and every person, albeit buried, not to say repressed, in the unconscious." (Frankl 1997, 151). Furthermore, Frankl acknowledged, "Religion provides man with more than psychotherapy ever could—but it also demands more of him." (Frankl 1997, 80) By this "more" he meant ultimate meaning, or what he termed, "self-transcendence." (Frankl 1997).

As a practicing psychiatrist, Magdalena Naylor wrote, "The purpose of psychotherapy is to help us become free to be aware of and experience our possibilities... Ultimately, the mission of the psychotherapist differs little from the priest – to teach us (1) how to be, (2) how to care for our soul, and (3) how to die." (Naylor et al. 1994, 186–187) This is true to a point, with one main exception… the priest, pastor, rabbi, or religious leader almost always will bring into focus one's relationship with God, or should, I think, whereas the psychiatrist is free to leave God out, and often does. How one can study the human soul without addressing a person's spiritual world view would seem to me, at best, a daunting task.

Philosophical Foundations for Life Meaning

Frankl espoused three philosophical foundations: (1) freedom of will, (2) will to meaning, and (3) meaning in life. As to freedom of will—Frankl often stated that human beings had the ability to choose at any moment who we will be, and that we needed to take responsibility for our lives. "Between stimulus and response, there is a space, and in that space is our ability to choose our response." (Vesely 2010). As for the will to meaning, Frankl believed this to be the primary motivation and the deepest longing of every human being, as stated earlier. Regarding meaning in life, he believed that meaning could be found, and that it was the responsibility of every human being to seek this meaning. He did not believe the psychotherapist could give meaning to any individual, but the therapist could, and should, convince the client that there is a meaning to be found. Please note that while Frankl believed these maxims to be absolute truths about human life, he also saw the fulfillment of each as relative to a person's unique discoveries, creations, and experiences (Frankl 1984, 1997).

The Necessary Conditions for Meaning in Life

In addition to these three philosophical foundations, Frankl also believed there are three necessary conditions for meaning in life. According to logotherapy, human beings "discover this meaning in life in three different ways: (1) by creating a work or doing a deed, (2) by experiencing something or encountering someone, and (3) by the attitude we take toward unavoidable suffering" (Frankl 1984, 115), in other words, by "the deeds done, the loves loved, and last but not least, the sufferings they have gone through with courage and dignity." (Frankl 1984, 151).

As to love, is it possible to live a meaningful life without at least one genuine loving relationship with another person? I cannot imagine it. "Love is the ultimate and highest goal to which man can aspire," wrote Frankl (Frankl 1984, 49). "Life without love would be nothing." (Naylor et al. 1994, 99). "To have only ourselves to love, to have no greater project in life than ourselves, is surely the very depths of meaninglessness." (Naylor et al. 1994, 101).

As for work—it appears to me that the giving of ourselves to some cause or project that utilizes our best skills and abilities to make some positive difference in the world is certainly a great human need. And yet, "The number of people who enjoy their work and find it truly meaningful are a minority in the population." (Naylor et al. 1994, 158).

I consider myself a very fortunate person to work in an academic environment where the mission statement reads, "We are a community committed to preparing students to be educated and enlightened citizens who lead productive and meaningful lives" (JMU Mission Statement 2010). This mission gives me the freedom and the responsibility to create and facilitate a learning environment that enables me to work meaningfully. I genuinely love my work as a professor of psychology, and my goal is to influence people in this learning community in such a way that, together, we fulfill the mission statement of our university.

As for suffering with courage and dignity, I believe it is taking an unalterable fate and allowing it to make us a stronger, wiser, and more compassionate human being. No one needs to invite suffering, as it seems to be a commonality among all human beings—more for some, of course, than for others. "If there is a meaning in life at all, then there must be a meaning in suffering. Suffering is an ineradicable part of life, even as fate and death" (Frankl 1984, 76). "No one can relieve him of his suffering or suffer in his place. His unique opportunity lies in the way in which he bears his burden" (Frankl 1984, 86). "It is possible to say 'yes to life' in spite of all the tragic aspects of human existence" (Frankl 1984, 13). Each person, then, will have the choice as to what to make of his or her unique suffering. One may become a bitter person, a victim, or one may become a better person, a victor, more capable than ever before of compassionate understanding toward other people in their times of pain and suffering.

The Effects of Low Meaning

Regarding the state of the human quest for meaning, Frankl stated, "Today, man's will to meaning is frustrated on a worldwide scale. Ever more people are haunted by a feeling of meaninglessness which is often accompanied by a feeling of emptiness – as I am used to calling it, an existential vacuum. It mainly manifests itself in boredom and apathy. While boredom is indicative of a loss of interest in the world, apathy betrays a lack of initiative to do something in the world, to change something in the world." (Frankl 1997, 139).

Erich Fromm once stated, "we are a society of notoriously unhappy people: lonely, anxious, depressed, destructive, dependent—people who are glad when we have killed the time we are trying so hard to save." (Fromm 1996, 5–6). "Man is a being in search of meaning," wrote Frankl, and… "Today his search is unsatisfied and this constitutes the pathology of our age." (Frankl 1997, 112). So, what are the effects of this lack of meaning? Frankl called this the "existential vacuum," defined as "a feeling of emptiness or meaninglessness" which has three facets: depression, aggression, and addiction (Frankl 1984, 143).

Regarding depression, many studies have demonstrated a significant negative correlation between life meaning and depression (Batthyany and Guttmann 2005), including my own research, which has shown a significant negative correlation between the Purpose in Life (PIL) scale and the Beck Depression Inventory, $r(184)=-.61, p<.001$ (Evans et al. 2010a). Frankl noted that "depression often results in suicide." (Frankl 1997, 99) For youth in America between the ages of 10 and 24, suicide is the third leading cause of death (Center for Disease Control 2010). In my research, I have also discovered a clear negative correlation between purpose in life, as measured by the PIL, with both "suicidal thoughts," $r(183)=-.25, p<.01$ and "suicidal attempts," $r(180)=-.21, p<.01$ (Evans et al. 2010a). Without a clear reason to live, it seems many cannot cope with all the difficulties and pain life can inflict.

As to addiction, empirical research has also noted the prevalence of alcohol and drug abuse among those who measure low on life meaning (Batthyany and Guttmann 2005). I have recently conducted research among university students supporting these claims, measuring substantial negative correlations between Purpose in Life and the consequences of excessive alcohol use, measured by an adapted CORE Alcohol Survey, such as "being arrested while under the influence of alcohol," $r(184)=-.23, p<.01$; "being taken advantage of sexually," $r(184)=-.20, p<.01$; and "poor academic performance," $r(184)=-.21, p<.01$ (Evans et al. 2010a). Frankl observed that in one study, "90 % of alcoholics looked upon their existence as meaningless and without purpose." (Frankl 1997, 102) According to a recent Alcohol-Related Disease Impact tool, "from 2001–2005, there were approximately 79,000 deaths annually attributable to excessive alcohol use. In fact, excessive alcohol use is the third leading lifestyle-related cause of death for people in the United States each year." (Center for Disease Control 2010).

Here are some recent statistics related to alcohol use among college students in America:

- Deaths: 1700 college students die each year from alcohol-related injuries, including motor vehicle crashes.
- Drunk Driving: 2.1 million students drove while under the influence of alcohol last year.
- Injury: 599,000 students are unintentionally injured while under the influence of alcohol.
- Assault: more than 696,000 students are assaulted each year by another student who has been drinking.
- Sexual Abuse: more than 97,000 students are victims of alcohol-related sexual assault or date rape each year.
- Unsafe Sex: 400,000 students report having unprotected sex while more than 100,000 report being intoxicated while consenting to have sex.
- Academic Problems: about 25 % report academic problems related to their drinking habits, including missing classes, falling behind, poor performance on exams, and receiving lower grades as a consequence (Hingson et al. 2002, 2003a, b, 2005, 2009).

As Naylor et al. recognized, "People take drugs because they are alienated and powerless and have no sense of meaning in their lives." (Naylor et al. 1994, 65)

As for aggression, Frankl wrote, "people are most likely to become aggressive when they are caught in this feeling of emptiness and meaninglessness." (Frankl 1997, 104). "Drug abuse and violent crime are among the most destructive ways in which Americans deal with alienation and separation." Naylor and associates report, "Homicide is the 6th leading cause of premature death in the United States, occurring at a rate of 4.4 times higher than in the next most violent Western industrialized nation." (Naylor et al. 1994, 63) According to the Center for Disease Control, "Violence is a serious public health problem in the United States. In 2006, more than 18,000 people were victims of homicide and more than 33,000 took their own life" (Center for Disease Control 2010).

Without a revealed life meaning, it appears that many individuals may lapse into bitterness and victimization, resulting in depression, addiction, and aggression as a consequence of the existential vacuum. This is no less true today than it was in 1938, 1946, or 1977; indeed, the existential vacuum and the unheard cry for meaning may be more pronounced in the twenty-first century than ever before in human history!

May I be so bold as to add anxiety as another aspect of the human condition in the twenty-first century? Anxiety, it appears to me, is a pervasive attitude among the students I teach and relate to, stemming, I believe, from a lack of meaning and purpose in life. I my research conducted during the 2010–2011 academic year, I discovered that there was a highly significant negative correlation between anxiety and life meaning, as measured by the Beck Anxiety Inventory and the PIL, $r(116) = -.475$, $p < .001$. I also discovered that there was a significant negative correlation between death anxiety and life meaning, as measured by the Collett-Lester Fear of Death scale and the PIL, $r(117) = -.300$, $p < .001$.

After conducting separate *t*-tests on death anxiety for both the experimental and control groups, for the experimental group, at pretest ($M = 94.59$, $SD = 20.95$), participants reported significantly more death anxiety than at posttest ($M = 82.47$, $SD = 21.23$), $t(60) = 2.263$, $p = .027$. For the control group, at pretest ($M = 84.72$, $SD = 23.69$), participants did not significantly differ in death anxiety than at posttest ($M = 81.97$, $SD = 26.14$), $t(56) = .421$, $p = .675$.

The experimental group consisted of my death-and-dying classes compared to all my other classes, which served as the control group. In my death-and-dying class, reading, discussing, and writing a reflection paper on Dr. Frankl's *Man's Search for Meaning* is required of all students. They are challenged to think deeply about the sources of meaning in their lives, or the lack thereof. They are also encouraged to construct a life mission statement and their "bucket list" of goals they want to achieve in their lives.

The pretest occurred during the first week of the semester and the posttest during the last week. I honestly believe that it is the encounter with Dr. Frankl's life and legacy that made the meaningful difference for these students. So, I now share his life and work in all of my classes, and in most of them, I also require a component of service for the community in order to promote self-transcendence (Olivieri et al. 2012). In my research project conducted last semester, I discovered that a "motivation to serve others" is clearly related to Purpose in Life (PIL): $r(245) = .295$, $p < .01$; also, "civic action" demonstrated a strong positive association with Purpose in Life (PIL): $r(245) = .363$, $p < .01$ (Langridge et al. 2012).

Conclusion

In conclusion, please allow me to restate some key points. First, every human being aspires to live well and meaningfully. Second, I sincerely believe that we need to pursue holistic health in our study of psychology and psychotherapy and our quest to understand the nature of human nature. By this I mean that we need to ask ourselves constantly and consistently, "will this enhance life; will it empower one to make a positive difference in the world; will this foster healthy human relationships; and will it enable one to suffer with courage and dignity?" Third, logotherapy, in all its aspects of inquiry, teaching, and therapy, can help us understand the nature of human nature, including the human need for meaning in life and the possibility to discover and create this meaning in life that is so desperately needed in our world. Fourth, let us learn to honor the human quest for truth, a pursuit of the best we can know that leads us to the highest aspirations of humankind, i.e., height psychology, or self-transcendence.

Charles Darwin, after a lifetime devoted to his work, wrote that if he had his life to live over again, he would read a little poetry every day and listen to music at least weekly. He stated, "My mind seems to have become a machine for grinding general laws out of large collections of facts… the loss of these emotional tastes is a loss of happiness… the erosion of higher sensibilities may possibly be injurious to the intellect, and more possibly to the moral character, by enfeebling the emotional part of our nature." (Darwin 1897, 81–82).

Darwin appeared to realize a human longing for something more in life. Albert Einstein also seemed to recognize a human need for meaning in life when he wrote, "The man who regards his own life and that of his fellow creatures as meaningless is not merely unfortunate but almost disqualified for life." (Einstein 1984, 3).

We have the freedom to choose how we will view life and how we will live. Will we define life as Shakespeare did in Macbeth, act 5, scene 4:

> "Life's but a walking shadow, a poor player That struts and frets his hour upon the stage,
> And then is heard of no more;
> It is a tale, told by an idiot, full of sound and fury,
> Signifying nothing." (Shakespeare 2005)

This option, of course, is pure nihilism. Or, will we define life more meaningfully, as Frederick Buechner did it in his autobiography:

> "Listen to your life; see it for the fathomless mystery that it is:
> In the boredom and pain of it no less than the excitement and gladness.
> Touch, taste, smell your way to the holy and hidden heart of it, For in the last analysis, all moments are key moments,
> And life itself is grace." (Buechner 1992, 2)

My sincerest hope is that, with the best and highest that can be known through the study and practice of logotherapy, we will all grow to see that life, lived well and meaningfully, is a precious, fragile gift, meant to be treasured. The world still cries for meaning! Are we still listening? How will we respond?

Bibliography

Abdel-Khalek, A. (2005). Death anxiety in clinical and non-clinical groups. *Death Studies, 29*, 251–259.

Abdel-Khalek, A., & Al-Sabwah, M. N. (2005). Satisfaction with life and death distress. *Psychological Reports, 97*(3), 790–792.

Abdel-Khalek, A., & Lester, D. (2009a). Death anxiety as related to somatic symptoms in two cultures. *Psychological Reports, 105*(2), 409–410.

Abdel-Khalek, A., & Lester, D. (2009b). Religiosity and death anxiety: no association in Kuwait. *Psychological Reports, 104*, 770–772.

Allport, G. W. (1956). *The individual and his religion*. New York, NY: Macmillan.

Arehart-Treichel, J. (2002). Mental illness on rise on college campuses. *Psychiatric News. American Psychiatric Association, 37*(6), 6.

Batthyany, A., & Guttmann, D. (2005). *Empirical research on logotherapy and meaning- oriented psychotherapy*. Phoenix, AZ: Zeig, Tucker & Theisen, Inc.

Batthyany, A., & Levinson, J. I. (2009). *Existential psychotherapy of meaning: A handbook of logotherapy and existential analysis*. Phoenix, AZ: Zeig, Tucker, & Theisen Inc.

Beck, A. T. (2006). *Depression: Causes and treatment*. Philadelphia, PA: University of Pennsylvania Press.

Beck, A. T., Epstein, N., Brown, G., & Steer, R. A. (1988). An inventory for measuring clinical anxiety: psychometric properties. *Journal of Consulting and Clinical Psychology, 56*(6), 893–897.

Bjorklund, B. R., & Bee, H. L. (2008). *The journey of adulthood* (6th ed.). Upper Saddle River, NJ: Pearson/Prentice Hall.

Buechner, F. (1992). *Listen to your life*. New York, NY: Harper Collins.

Center for Disease Control. (2010). Accessed from www.cdc.gov.

Collett, L. J., & Lester, D. (1969). The fear of death and the fear of dying. *Journal of Psychology, 72*, 179–181.

Corey, G. (2001). *Theory and practice of counseling and psychotherapy*. Belmont, CA: Wadsworth/ Thomson Learning.

Corsini, R. J., & Weddington, D. (2008). *Current psychotherapies*. Belmont, CA: Thomson-Brooks/Cole.

Crumbaugh, J. C. (1968). Cross validation of Purpose in Life Test. *Journal of Individual Psychology, 24*, 74–81.

Crumbaugh, J. C., & Maholick, L. T. (1964). An experimental study in existentialism: The psychometric approach to Frankl's concept of noogenic neurosis. *Journal of Clinical Psychology, 20*, 200–207.

Crumbaugh, J. C., & Maholick, L. T. (1969). *Manual of instructions for the Purpose-in-Life Test*. Munster, IN: Psychometric Affiliates.

Darwin, C. (1897). *The life and letters of Charles Darwin*. New York, NY: Appleton & Co.

Daughtry, D., & Runkel, M. A. (1993). Experience of depression in college students: A concept map. *Journal of Counseling Psychology, 40*(3), 316–323.

Echterling, L., Evans, W., Cowan, E., Staton, R., Stewart, A., Presbury, J., et al. (2007). *Thriving! A manual for the helping professions* (2nd ed.). Boston, MA: Lahaska/Houghton Mifflin Publishing, Inc.

Einstein, A. (1984). *The world as I see it*. New York, NY: Kensington Publishing.

Evans, W. F. (1997). *Attitudes toward religious values in counseling among counselor educators and counselors-in-training*. Columbia, SC: University of South Carolina Doctoral Dissertation.

Evans, W. F. (2005). A holistic-integrative method of assessment and intervention. *The Virginia Counselors Journal, 28*, 56–58.

Evans, W. F., Forde, E., Atwood, K., Edwards, C. (2010b/In process). Meaning, religiosity and death anxiety. Article submitted to the Journal of *Death Studies*.

Evans, W. F., Kibler, E. J., Jenkins, J., Garafalo, A., Girard, J., Moon, M., Goodpasture, A. (2010a/In process). Alcohol use and life meaning among college students. Submitted to *Journal of American College Health.*

Fowler, J. W. (1981). *Stages of faith: The psychology of human development and the quest for meaning*. San Francisco, CA: Harper Collins Publishers.

Frankl, V. E. (1978). *The unheard cry for meaning*. New York, NY: Simon & Schuster.

Frankl, V. E. (1984). *Man's search for meaning*. New York, NY: Simon & Schuster.

Frankl, V. E. (1997). *Man's search for ultimate meaning*. New York, NY: Harper Collins.

Frankl, V. E. (2000). *Recollections: An autobiography*. New York, NY: Basic Books.

Freud, S. (1989). *The future of an illusion*. New York, NY: W.W. Norton & Company.

Fromm, E. (1950). *Psychoanalysis and religion*. New Haven, CT: Yale University Press.

Fromm, E. (1996). *To have or to be*. New York, NY: Continuum Press.

Geiger, J. F. (2004). Differences in meaning in life in students: The effect of nontraditional status and region of country. *College Student Journal*. v 38 n 4 p 569–574.

Hingson, R., Heeren, T., Winter, M. R., & Wechsler, H. (2003a).). Early age of first drunkenness as a factor in college students' unplanned and unprotected sex attributable to drinking. *Pediatrics, 111*, 34–41.

Hingson, R., Heeren, T., Winter, M., & Wechsler, H. (2005). Magnitude of alcohol-related mortality and morbidity among U.S. college students ages 18-24: Changes from 1998 to 2001. *Annual Review of Public Health, 26*, 259–279.

Hingson, R., Heeren, T., Zackos, R., Winter, M., & Wechsler, H. (2003b). Age of first intoxication, heavy drinking, driving after drinking, and risk of unintentional injury among U.S. college students. *Journal of Studies on Alcohol and Drugs, 64*, 23–31.

Hingson, R., Heeren, T., Zakocs, R. C., Kopstein, A., & Wechsler, H. (2002). Magnitude of alcohol-related mortality and morbidity among U.S. college students ages 18–24. *Journal of Studies on Alcohol and Drugs, 63*, 136–144.

Hingson, R. W., Zha, W., Weitzman, E. R. (2009). Magnitude of and trends in alcohol-related mortality and morbidity among U.S. college students ages 18–24, 1998-2005. *Journal of Studies on Alcohol and Drugs*. 2009 Jul; (16): 12–20.

Holahan, C. J., Moos, R. H., Holahan, C. K., Cronkite, R. C., & Randall, P. K. (2003). Drinking to cope with alcohol use and abuse in unipolar depression: A 10 year model. *Journal of Abnormal Psychology, 112*(1), 159–165.

Ishida, R., & Okada, M. (2005). Effects of a firm purpose in life on anxiety and sympathetic nervous activity caused by emotional stress: assessment by psycho-physiological method. *Stress and Health, 22*, 275–285.

James, W. (1936). *The varieties of religious experience*. New York, NY: Modern Library.

JMU Mission Statement. (2010). Retrieved from http://www.jmu.edu/planning/mission

Johnson, D. (2006). Finding wholeness: Students' search for meaning and purpose in college. *Journal of College & Character, 7*(1), 1–6.

Koenig, H. (1999). *The healing power of faith*. New York, NY: Simon & Schuster.

Kubler-Ross, E. (1986). *Death: The final stage of growth*. New York, NY: Simon and Schuster.

Langridge, N., Evans, W., Dixon, A., Janser, S. (2012/In process). Meaning in life – is this the greatest ROI of the college experience? Submitted to the *Journal of College & Character.*

Lester, D., & Abdel-Khalek, A. (2003). The Collett-Lester fear of death scale: A correction. *Death Studies, 27*, 81–85.

Lester, D., & Kam, E. G. (1971). Effect of a friend dying upon attitudes toward death. *Journal of Social Psychology, 83*(1), 149–150.

Lester, D., & Templer, D. (1992–1993). Death anxiety scales: A dialogue. *Omega: Journal of Death & Dying, 26*(4), 239–253.

Lester, D., Templer, D. I., & Abdel-Khalek, A. (2006). A cross-cultural comparison of death anxiety: A brief note. *Omega: Journal of Death & Dying, 54*(3), 255–260.

Lewis, C. S. (1970). *God in the dock*. Grand Rapids, MI: Eerdmans Publishing.

Lewis, C. S. (1996). *The abolition of man*. New York, NY: Simon & Schuster.

Martino-McAllister, J. (2010). *Alcohol and drug use among James Madison University students*. Harrisonburg, VA: James Madison University, Office of Substance Abuse Research.

McCullough, M. E., Hoyt, W. T., Larson, D. B., Koenig, H. G., & Thoresen, C. E. (2000). Religious involvement and mortality: A meta-analytic review. *Health Psychology, 19*, 211–222.
Molasso, W. R. (2006). Exploring Frankl's purpose in life with college students. *Journal of College & Character, 7*(1), 1–10.
Murphy, J. G., McDevitt-Murphy, M. E., & Barnett, N. P. (2005). Drink and be merry? Gender, life satisfaction, and alcohol consumption among college students. *Psychology of Addictive Behaviors, 19*(2), 184–191.
Naylor, T., Willimon, W., & Naylor, M. (1994). *The search for meaning*. Nashville, TN: Abingdon.
Okasaka, Y., Morita, N., Nakatani, Y., & Fujisawa, K. (2008). Correlation between addictive behaviors and mental health in university students. *Psychiatry and Clinical Neurosciences, 62*, 84–92.
Olivieri, A., Evans, W., & Apple, K. (2012). *Death education effects on levels of meaning, anxiety, death anxiety and religiosity* (p. 25). Omega: Journal of Death & Dying.
Pruyser, P. W. (1976). *A dynamic psychology of religion*. New York, NY: Harper & Row.
Sartre, J. P. (1965). Questions about the meaning of life. *Religious Studies, 1*, 125–140.
Schneider, K. J. (2004). *Rediscovery of awe*. St. Paul, MN: Paragon Press.
Schneider, K. J. (2007). *Existential-integrative psychotherapy: Guideposts to the core of practice*. New York, NY: Routledge.
Shakespeare, W. (2005). *The Oxford Shakespeare: The complete works*. Oxford, UK: Oxford University Press.
Smith, H. (2001). *Why religion matters*. San Francisco, CA: Harper Collins.
Staton, R., Benson, J., Briggs, M., Cowan, E., Echterling, L., Evans, W., et al. (2007). *Becoming a community counselor: Personal and professional explorations*. Boston, MA: Lahaska Press/ Houghton Mifflin.
Substance Abuse and Mental Health Services [SAMHSA], (2009). *Results from the 2008 national survey on drug use and health: National findings*. Washington, D.C.: SAMHSA.
Tillich, P. (1948). *The shaking of the foundations*. New York, NY: Charles Scribner's Sons.
Tillich, P. (1957). *Dynamics of faith*. New York, NY: Harper & Row.
Tillich, P. (2000). *The courage to be*. New Haven, CT: Yale University Press.
Vesely, A. (2010). *Viktor Frankl Institute Video Archive*. http://logotherapy.univie.ac.at/e/clipgallery.html.
Warner, M. J., & Evans, W. F. (2006). *Inspiring leadership: It's not about the power*. Boston, MA: Pearson Publishing.
Wechsler, H., Lee, J. E., Kuo, M., & Lee, H. (2000). College binge drinking in the 1990s: A continuing problem: Results of the Harvard School of Public Health 1999 College Alcohol Study. *Journal of American College Health, 48*, 199–210.
Wittgenstein, L. (1960). *Tagebücher.* 1914–1916. Frankfurt a. M.
Yalom, I. D. (1980). *Existential psychotherapy*. New York, NY: Basic Books.
Young, J. E., Rygh, J. L., Weinberger, A. D., & Beck, A. T. (2008). Cognitive therapy for depression. In D. H. Barlow (Ed.), *Clinical handbook of psychological disorders: A step- by-step treatment manual* (4th ed., pp. 492–546). New York, NY: Guilford Press.
Zaje, A. T. H., & Karim, N. M. (2007). Is gender relevant only for problem alcohol behaviors? An examination of correlates of alcohol use among college students. *Addictive Behaviors, 33*(2), 359–365.

The Importance of Meaning in Positive Psychology and Logotherapy

Leo Michel Abrami

Meaning in Positive Psychology

Professor Martin Seligman, chairman of the Psychology Department at the University of Pennsylvania and founder of the school of positive psychology, defines positive psychology as "the scientific study of the strengths and virtues that enable individuals and communities to thrive. It is founded on the belief that people want to lead meaningful and fulfilling lives, to cultivate what is best within themselves and to enhance their experiences of love, work, and play." He also wrote "… just as well-being needs to be anchored in strengths and virtues, these in turn must be anchored in something larger, just as the good life is something beyond the pleasant life, the meaningful life is beyond the good life." (Seligman 2002, 14).

Pursuing this approach, he concluded the last chapter of his book *Authentic Happiness* with these poignant words:

> "The best we can do as individuals is to choose to be a small part of furthering this progress. This is the door through which the meaning that transcends us can enter our lives. A meaningful life is one that joins with something larger than we are—and the larger that something is, the more meaning our lives have… The good life consists in deriving happiness by using your signature strengths every day in the main realms of living.
>
> The meaningful life adds one more component: using these same strengths to forward knowledge, power or goodness. A life that does this is pregnant with meaning, and if God comes at the end, such a life is sacred." (Seligman 2002, 206).

And again, three pages further, at the end of the appendix, the author restates the same affirmation in almost similar terms:

L.M. Abrami (✉)
Arizona Institute of Logotherapy, 13315 W. Aleppo Drive,
85375 Sun City, West Arizona, USA
e-mail: abrami@cox.net

A. Batthyány (ed.), *Logotherapy and Existential Analysis*, Logotherapy and Existential Analysis: Proceedings of the Viktor Frankl Institute Vienna 1,
DOI 10.1007/978-3-319-29424-7_26

> "A meaningful life adds one more component to the good life—the attachment of your signature strengths to something larger. So beyond happiness, this book is meant as a preface to the meaningful life…
>
> Finally, a full life consists in experiencing positive emotions about the past and the future, savoring positive feelings from the pleasures, deriving abundant gratification from your signature strengths, and using these strengths in the service of something larger in order to obtain meaning." (Seligman 2002, 263).

Nine years after he published *Authentic Happiness*, Seligman published a new book entitled *Flourish*: *A Visionary New Understanding of Happiness and Well-Being* in which he includes a summary of the original theory developed in his first book, in the following terms:

We often choose what makes us feel good, but it is very important to realize that often our choices are not made for the sake of how we will feel. I chose to listen to my 6-year-old's excruciating piano recital last night, not because it made me feel good, but because it is my parental duty and part of what gives my life meaning (Seligman 2011, 11). Martin Seligman then enumerates the three elements that we choose for their own sakes: positive emotion, engagement, and meaning. Positive emotion, he explains, is what we feel: pleasure, rapture, ecstasy, warmth, comfort, and the like. An entire life led successfully around this element, would be a "pleasant life." Engagement is about flow: being one with the music, time stopping, and the loss of self-consciousness during an absorbing activity. A life lived with these aims could be referred to as an "engaged life."

The third element of happiness is *meaning*. Indeed, "the pursuit of engagement and the pursuit of pleasure are often solitary, solipsistic endeavors. Human beings, ineluctably, want meaning and purpose in life. The Meaningful Life consists in belonging to and serving something that you believe is bigger than the self, and humanity creates all the positive institutions to allow this: religion, political party, being Green, the Boy Scouts, or the family." (Seligman 2011, 11–12). As we examine this definition of the meaningful life, we soon realize that it coincides with the approach of logotherapy which states that meaning in life can be discovered in three different ways: (1) by creating a work or doing a deed, that is creativity; (2) by experiencing something (such as goodness, truth and beauty, nature, or culture) or encountering another human being and by loving him/her; and (3) by the attitude we take toward unavoidable suffering (Frankl 1984, 133).

Frankl goes even beyond the existential meaning to the notion of what he calls a *super-meaning* or an ultimate meaning. The latter, he asserts, has its origin in the transcendental realm, in the world of spirituality and religion. (Frankl 2000, 138). We must also note that these characteristics of meaning are virtually identical to the elements of meaning enumerated by Seligman, if we allow for some minor variations in the terminology used by these authors: Belonging to and serving something bigger than the self, religion, family… is indeed expressions of transcendence, or emanating from a realm that is beyond the self. Seligman prefers to call these "something that is bigger than the self" which is a way of staying clear of the use of the term "transcendence" which often has an ethereal connotation.

As for the need to reach out to another person or persons, Frankl and Seligman both agree on the importance of the inter-human relationship. Both of them use the term *love* to describe the most sublime aspect of this exchange between two human beings. Seligman rightfully states that "the pursuit of engagement and the pursuit of pleasure are often…solipsistic endeavors. Human beings, ineluctably, want meaning and purpose in life" because meaning and purpose in life supersede in importance the elements of engagement and pleasure. For sure, the motivation of the engagement may well be found in the meaning and purpose of the task that is eliciting it. We are engaged because we are captivated by the profound significance of the project we are pursuing. The engagement is therefore a consequence of meaning and not a motivation in itself. As for the experience of pleasure, it is ephemeral and cannot be an end in itself, albeit it is a pleasant experience. It would thus seem that Martin Seligman is aware of the fact that only meaning and purpose can ultimately validate the value of the fleeting moment of pleasure we experience.

It would seem that the main difference between the conception of Martin Seligman and that of Viktor Frankl resides essentially in the realm of semantics and the choice of the terms we use to designate certain personal experiences. Both agree that certain emotions referred to as "positive" in Seligman's writings and as "meaningful" in Frankl's descriptions, are conducive to experiencing a profound sense of satisfaction, leading to a sense of happiness. This feeling can be derived from an authentic relationship with a person whom we love, or from the realization of a project which embodies a unique meaning and which is usually prompted by some form of engagement. Both, Frankl and Seligman, emphasize the realization of these unique projects, which are imbued with a particular noetic significance. In all of them, there is no question that meaning is the primary motivation. The various aspects of these projects may be described in a different order, but in reality, they are all experienced simultaneously and one would be hard pressed to state which element came first and which one was the effect or the cause of the other one.

Meaning in Logotherapy

We find basically the same etiology of happiness in the writings of Viktor Frankl. In his seminal book *Man's Search for Meaning*, Frankl clearly states that man's search for meaning is the primary motivation in his life and not a "secondary rationalization" of instinctual drives. This meaning is unique and specific in that it must and can be fulfilled by him alone; only then does it achieve a significance, which will satisfy his own will to meaning (Frankl 1984, 121).

This fundamental principle contains a double affirmation. It asserts that our life decisions are not only motivated by a search for meaning but by an inner need, a will to fulfill the meaningful projects that are prompted by our inner self. In other terms, it is not just a matter of choice, but of acquiescing to a higher instance, which calls us to realize the meaning(s) we have discovered in ourselves.

Even though it does not single out this notion, positive psychology seems to imply it in almost the same way as logotherapy. That is probably the reason why the author of "*Authentic Happiness*," wrote, "this book is a preface to the meaningful life." We might thus be inclined to believe that logotherapy and positive psychology are based on some of the same premises.

However, what is regarded as a consequence in logotherapy is regarded as a constitutive element of happiness in positive psychology. Whereas logotherapy asserts that the person who fulfills a *meaningful purpose* derives a genuine satisfaction from it [which may lead to a feeling of happiness], positive psychology states that *positive emotions* (often inspired by meaning) will surely lead to happiness. We cannot, however, put the horse before the cart. Emotions are often preceded by strong expectations, though felt as we experience love for a person or admiration for a human accomplishment. The anticipation may help create the happy mood but the actual experience is still necessary in most cases.

We may also note that while positive psychology uses the term *happiness* to designate the goal of its endeavors, logotherapy uses the term *meaning* (logos) as the original motivation and the consequence or "by-product" to describe the feeling—or emotion—of deep fulfillment which is experienced by the individual who realizes one of his dreams or ideals. It would thus seem that in spite of different modes of exposition and a slightly different terminology, positive psychology has many similarities to logotherapy.

Mihaly Csikszentmihaly

In a volume entitled *The Evolving Self, a Psychology for the Third Millennium*, Mihaly Csikszentmihaly, professor of psychology at the University of Chicago, uses concepts that are very similar to those of Viktor Frankl. Summing up the content of his book in the very last two pages, he states,

> "Strange as it may seem, life becomes serene and enjoyable precisely when selfish pleasure and personal success are no longer the guiding goals. When the self loses itself in a transcendent purpose—be it to write great poetry, craft a beautiful piece of furniture, understand the movement of galaxies, or help children be happier—it becomes largely invulnerable to the fears and setbacks of ordinary existence. Psychic energy becomes focused on goals that are meaningful, that advance order and complexity, that will continue to have an effect in the consciousness of new generations, long after our departure from this world." (Csikszentmihaly 1993, 292)

One may easily recognize several key notions that are similar to the ones used by Frankl: *goals that are meaningful* and *transcendent purpose*. Csikszentmihaly and Frankl fully agree on the transcendental nature of the higher purpose, which motivates the individual. Reading this paragraph of *Evolving Self* cited above, one might have been hard put to identify the author of the paragraph as Csikszentmihaly or Viktor Frankl. He also emphasizes the concept of *flow* which according to him, is characterized by a strong motivation and a complete immersion into an experience which produces intense positive emotions, hallowed with feelings of great joy and even rapture. As Csikszentmihaly remarks, however, "having goals, having a clear sense of purpose, is necessary to attain flow." (Ben Shahar 2007, 86) Such a statement is indeed very similar to the principle on which Frankl based his entire psychotherapeutic method.

Tal ben Shahar

One of the most popular professors at Harvard University, Tal ben Shahar, a disciple of Martin Seligman, published a best-seller book *Happier* some four years ago, in which he refers extensively to Viktor Frankl. He actually devotes almost an entire chapter to Frankl's Man's Search for Meaning and acknowledges his enormous debt of gratitude to Frankl's teachings:

> "... we need the experience of meaning and the experience of positive emotions; we need present and future benefit. My theory of happiness draws on the works of Freud as well as Frankl. Freud's pleasure principle says that we are fundamentally driven by the instinctual need for pleasure. Frankl argues that we are motivated by a will to meaning rather than by a will to pleasure—he says, "striving to find meaning in one's life is the primary motivational force in man." In the context of finding happiness, there is some truth in both Freud's and Frankl's theories. We need to gratify both the will for pleasure and the will for meaning if we are to lead a fulfilling happy life..."

Ben Shahar then stresses the notion that people must be able to recognize and acknowledge the meaning they have fulfilled in order to derive the full satisfaction that will result from it. Being grateful in this way can *itself* be a source of real meaning and pleasure. When we derive a sense of purpose from what we do, our experience of pleasure is intensified; and taking pleasure in an activity can make our experience of it all the more meaningful. (Ben Shahar 2007, 42–43).

Ben Shahar probably meant that we derive a sense of satisfaction and gratification from having done that, which was purposeful, and meaningful in our eyes and not that "we derive a sense of purpose from what we do." The sense of purpose is the motivation and not the result of our actions. He thus acknowledges the significant contribution made by Viktor Frankl who stressed the importance of meaning and purpose as the *conditio sine qua non* to our attainment of happiness.

In a subchapter entitled "The Meaning, Pleasure, Strengths (MPS) Process", Ben Shahar is quite explicit on this matter:

> "Finding the right work... can be challenging. We can begin the process by asking these three crucial questions: "What gives me meaning? What gives me pleasure? What are my strengths?" and noting the trend that emerges... We may need to spend time reflecting, thinking deeply to recall those moments in our lives when we felt a sense of true purpose." (Ben Shahar 2007, 103).

The basic notion that meaning and purpose are essential to the attainment of happiness has been accepted by many psychologists and philosophers in our generation. Though we may not be able to measure the degree of happiness a person experiences—because it is essentially a subjective state of mind—we may still be able to measure some of the consequences of happiness such as joy, hope, optimism, and a sense of satisfaction with life. For the authors we have mentioned above, meaning, purpose, flow, and engagement are some of the key factors leading to happiness.

The Authentic Happiness Center

The Authentic Happiness Center, which was created by Prof. Martin Seligman may help one get a more concrete idea of the way positive psychology can affect our life. It has a fine website and one may follow the developments of this new approach by becoming a member. The Authentic Happiness Center welcomes the visitor with these words:

> "Authentic Happiness is the homepage of Dr. Martin Seligman, Director of the Positive Psychology Center at the University of Pennsylvania and founder of positive psychology, a branch of psychology, which focuses on the empirical study of such things as positive emotions, strengths-based character, and healthy institutions. This website has more than two million users from around the world, and you are welcome to use all of the resources available here for free."

Dr Seligman then suggests that "the best place to start to learn more about the latest theory and initiatives in positive psychology, is by checking out recent presentations" and taking some questionnaires on well-being. One of them was developed by M. F. Steger, P. Frazier, and S. Oishi and is entitled "Meaning in Life Questionnaire (MLQ-10)." In it, we find some 10 questions formulated in the first person like "I am looking for something that makes my life feel meaningful" or "I am seeking a purpose or mission in my life."

A first reading of the MLQ-10 questionnaire might give the impression that it is fairly similar to the "Purpose in Life (PIL)" questionnaire of Crumbaugh and Maholick, which is widely used in the practice of logotherapy. A further examination, however, indicates that it is quite different from it because it attempts to assess not only the awareness of the importance of meaning in life but also the engagement and willingness of the patient to find that meaning ("I am looking for something meaningful or am seeking my mission in life.") The quality and intensity of this aspiration is indeed as important as the awareness of the presence or absence of meaning in life.

Martin Seligman goes on to enumerate the theoretical and practical principles involved in the *Positive Psychology Initiatives, which* he has developed. In one of the essays entitled *Introducing a New Theory of Well-Being*, he introduces the formula of **PERMA**, formed with the initials **P**ositive emotions, **E**ngagement, **R**elationships, **M**eaning and Purpose, and **A**ccomplishment of which happiness and life satisfaction are all necessary components (Seligman 2011, 16). Interested people are invited to participate in the research to help develop the **PERMA** questionnaire. This approach has the merit of involving the members of the Authentic Happiness Center and enabling them to participate in a valuable initiative in cooperation with the leaders of the movement.

A fascinating question has been raised by Dr. Laura A. King who teaches at the University of Missouri, Columbia, on the subject of meaning: Does the awareness of meaning lead to happiness or does the experience of happiness creates meaning? In the conclusion of one of her many articles on meaning, she writes:

> "Our research on the detection of meaning and the experience of meaning in life lead to the conclusion that in thinking about meaning, meaning in life, and happiness, psychologists have often confused causes and effects. Faced with traumatic life events, a meaning-maker might note that, "If I could just make sense of this, I would feel better." Our research suggests that the situation may be more accurately expressed, "If I could just feel better, this would make sense." In thinking about meaning in life and happiness, the self-help literature seems to convey the message that "If life had meaning, I could be happy." Our work suggests a different conclusion: "If I were happy, life would have meaning…" (King 2011).

King then sums up her reflection with this concluding sentence: "Meaning is often not a problem to be solved but an aspect of experience that is simply and intuitively present."

As Dr King acknowledges it, meaning is indeed part of the experience and "intuitively present" but the person still has to become aware of it, in order to derive the satisfaction, which will come with it. There is, however, a problem that remains unsolved and it concerns the persons who do not feel happy, as for example those who are faced with suffering or death; can we say that there is no meaning to their experience? Not at all, says Frankl, a person may still find a certain peace of mind, realizing that their suffering may have a meaning [on a spiritual level] in spite of the total absence of a physical pleasure. The conclusion of Laura King may therefore be premature and may require further inquiry.

Conclusion

At the term of this brief comparison between the attitudes of positive psychology and logotherapy on the role played by meaning in their respective theoretical approaches, we have found that there exist many similarities between them. They both agree that meaning is "intuitively present" even when the individual still has to become aware of it. Freud would have suggested that all people are guided by an unconscious intuition or desire to fulfill [*accomplish*] certain tasks or projects that may prove to be important and meaningful to them. The true motivation of our actions, whether conscious or unconscious, may have comprised a meaningful purpose. Whether we call it the desire to *engage* or the "*will to meaning*" may just be a matter of semantics.

At a time when so many people are searching for ways of attaining happiness and finding the meaning(s) of their lives, it is fortunate that both positive psychology and logotherapy are there to provide the help and guidance that is most needed. From a theoretical point of view, we must agree that more research is needed to ascertain the various interactions that exist between pleasure, happiness and meaning.

References

Authentic Happiness Center. Retrieved from www.authentichappiness.sas.upenn.edu/.
Ben Shahar, T. (2007). *Happier*. New York, NY: McGraw-Hill.
Csikszentmihaly, M. (1993). *The evolving self, a psychology for the third millennium*. New York, NY: Harper Collins.
Frankl, V. (1984). *Man's search for meaning*. New York, NY: Washington Square Press.
Frankl, V.E. (2000). *The Unheard Cry for Meaning*. New York: Perseus.
King, L. (2011). *Meaning: Ubiquitous and effortless*. Accessed 26 September 2015 at: http://portal.idc.ac.il/en/symposium/hspsp/2011/documents/cking11.
Seligman, M. E. P. (2002). *Authentic happiness*. New York, NY: Free Press.
Seligman, M. E. P. (2011). *Flourish: A visionary new understanding of happiness and well-being*. New York, NY: Free Press.

Meaning-Seeking, Self-Transcendence, and Well-being

Paul T.P. Wong

Introduction

By declaring that man is responsible and must actualize the potential meaning of his life, I wish to stress that the true meaning of life is to be discovered in the world rather than within man or his own psyche, as though it were a closed system. I have termed this constitutive characteristic "the self-transcendence of human existence." It denotes the fact that being human always points, and is directed, to something or someone, other than oneself—be it a meaning to fulfill or another human being to encounter. The more one forgets himself—by giving himself to a cause to serve or another person to love—the more human he is and the more he actualizes himself. What is called self-actualization is not an attainable aim at all, for the simple reason that the more one would strive for it, the more he would miss it. In other words, self-actualization is possible only as a side-effect of self-transcendence (Frankl 1985, 133).

A man struggling for existence will naturally look for something of value. There are two ways of looking… if he looks in the right direction, he recognizes the true nature of sickness, old age, and death, and then he searches for meaning in that which transcends all human suffering. In my life of pleasures, I seem to be looking in the wrong way (Buddha 1966, 8).

What is the best way to prepare people for all the suffering in life, such as sickness, old age, and death? What is the best way to equip people to realize their potentials and live a fulfilling and worthy life? The answer to both questions is meaning-seeking and self-transcendence, as illustrated by the above two quotes from two very different sources—one from Western psychology, another from Eastern religion.

P.T.P. Wong (✉)
International Network on Personal Meaning (INPM),
Pos13 Ballyconnor Court, Toronto, ON, Canada M2M 4C5
e-mail: drpaulwong@gmail.com

A. Batthyány (ed.), *Logotherapy and Existential Analysis*, Logotherapy and Existential Analysis: Proceedings of the Viktor Frankl Institute Vienna 1,
DOI 10.1007/978-3-319-29424-7_27

The main purpose of this paper is to develop a conceptual framework based on Viktor Frankl's (1985) concepts of meaning-seeking and self-transcendence for achieving well-being for individuals and society (Wong 2014). Such a conceptual framework may contribute to a meaning-centered curriculum for Life and Death Education that emphasizes the importance of personal responsibility to develop the spiritual values of will to meaning and serving the greater good.

I also want to emphasize that this meaning framework is particularly relevant for people working in hospital and hospice settings. In such situations, the health workers not only have to wrestle with their own suffering and death anxiety, they also have to confront on a daily basis the suffering of their patients. Sometimes they may feel overwhelmed by the huge demand for relief of suffering, but there is no effective medical treatment to cure human suffering and fear of death. Frankl's (1986) logotherapy, as a medical ministry, offers patients the choice to relate to suffering in such a way that they still can have the freedom and responsibility to live meaningfully.

Spiritual Nature of Meaning-Seeking and Self-Transcendence

In recent years, meaning-seeking and meaning-making have received much attention from researchers (Hicks and Routledge 2013; Shaver and Mikulincer 2012). Most of them recognize Viktor Frankl's contribution, but very few of them bother to investigate what Viktor Frankl actually said. Typically, these researchers take a cognitive and mechanistic approach to studying meaning, in contrast to Frankl's focus on existential meaning and spirituality.

Frankl's major contribution to human psychology is his concept of *will to meaning*, which represents the deepest and universal human need to reach beyond oneself and serve something greater. Interestingly, there is almost a consensus among research psychologists that meaning is experienced when people serve something greater than themselves (Baumeister et al. 2013; Seligman 2011). These psychologists simply presented this as an empirical fact, without offering a compelling and comprehensive theoretical explanation. Frankl, on the other hand, started with a theoretical framework about the anthropology of human nature and attributed self-transcendence to the spiritual nature of human beings. This theoretical framework has profound implications for how we understand ourselves, and the human phenomena of religion and spirituality. Frankl is almost unique in elevating self-transcendence as the hallmark of spirituality and as the end state of becoming fully human.

Frankl emphasized that spirituality is the part of human nature that separates us from other animals. Humans are by nature meaning-seeking and meaning-making creatures. We are motivated by both the need to understand the world in which we live, and the yearning to search for something of value and significance that makes life worth living in the midst of suffering.

This emphasis on spirituality as inherent in human nature has a long and venerable tradition in psychology, going back to William James (1902/1997). His book, *The Varieties of Religious Experience*, continues to impact psychology. In philosophy, interest in spirituality can be traced back even earlier (e.g., Kierkegaard, Pascal).

The essence of Viktor Frankl's logotherapy is to awaken people's sense of responsibility to live a meaningful life based on self-transcendence. It is through recognition of the basic human need for meaning and transcendence that we are able to fully appreciate what is right and noble about human beings. It is through pursuance of the path of self-transcendence that we become fully human. In other words, only by fully developing our spiritual nature can we become optimally functioning human beings.

The construct of self-transcendence as developed by Viktor Frankl serves as a useful conceptual framework for both theistic and non-theistic spirituality. More importantly, it provides a spiritual vision for the future of humanity based on awakening and harnessing of our spiritual values of sacrificial love and serving others.

Three Levels of Self-Transcendence

But how do we practice self-transcendence? How do we translate it into daily living? How does self-transcendence contribute to meaningful living and well-being? Based on my research on Viktor Frankl, I propose that there are three levels of self-transcendence, which can be summarized as following:

1. Seeking ultimate meaning—To reach beyond our physical limitations within the confines of time and space and gain a glimpse of the invisible glory of the transcendental realm. For non-theistic seekers, seeking ultimate meaning means seeking the ultimate ideals of goodness, truth, and beauty.
2. Seeking situational meaning—To reach beyond our mental and situational constraints and connect with our spiritual values. This involves being mindful of the present moment with an attitude of openness, curiosity, and compassion.
3. Seeking one's calling—To reach beyond self-actualization and pursue a higher purpose for the greater good. This involves engagement and striving to achieve a concrete meaning in life, a life goal of contributing something of value to others.

At all three levels, we are motivated by the intrinsic need for spiritual values. If we can cultivate all three levels of transcendence, we will develop a spiritual lifestyle that is good and healthy for individuals and society. We will explain how we can practice these three kinds of self-transcendence.

Seeking Ultimate Meaning

Frankl differentiates between ultimate meaning and situational meaning. He refers to ultimate meaning as Supra-meaning or God; it is something that we can vaguely understand but never truly comprehend. Ultimate meaning reflects our intuitive knowledge and presuppositions, which are beyond rational analysis. We typically seek ultimate meaning through self-reflection and philosophical or spiritual inquiries.

This level of meaning is metaphysical and transcendental; it has to do with a person's philosophical assumptions, worldviews, religious beliefs, and global beliefs. It may also include myths and metanarratives about the spiritual, transcendental world. At this level, meaning-seeking is a continuous process because ultimate meaning is by definition unreachable.

The global belief in ultimate meaning has many functional values. For example, it reassures victims of crime of ultimate justice, even if the perpetrators were able to get away within the human justice system. Faith in ultimate meaning also gives hope and consolation that physical death is not the end of everything and there is some form of immortality.

The belief in ultimate meaning also provides a conceptual framework to make sense of the chaotic, unpredictable nature of life. It affirms that everything happens for a purpose, even when people feel confused and overwhelmed. To a scientist, such beliefs might seem primitive, but their prevalence and enduring popularity indicate that they serve some adaptive functions and that religious beliefs and practices will always remain a human phenomenon.

An important derivative from belief in ultimate meaning is the affirmation of the intrinsic meaning and value of every individual life. Frankl (1985, 1986) often appealed for the intrinsic value of life in order to rescue patients from their suicidal ideation. Often when patients learn about their prognosis of being a terminal case or the verdict that they are paralyzed for life, the typical reaction is to declare that there is no more meaning in their lives and that there is no point in living an undignified existence without hope for recovery. Frankl had to convince them that their suffering actually gave them a rare opportunity for human achievement. Frankl argued that, in spite of their physical limitations and their need to depend on others to take care of them, they can still live with dignity as long as they take a heroic stance and maintain an attitude of freedom and responsibility for their own happiness.

Seeking Situational Meaning

Frankl puts more emphasis on situational meaning than on ultimate meaning, because we can never fully understand the ultimate meaning, but we can discover the meaning potential of each situation. His phenomenological approach is very similar to the Buddhist practice of mindful awareness. Frankl suggests that we not only pay deliberate attention to all the details of our inner experience and external circumstances from moment to moment, but that we also need to relate to our immediate experience in an open, curious, and responsible way. In each situation, we need to ask "what is the right thing to do?"

At this level, self-transcendence is achieved by being detached from self-interest, social conditioning, and all kinds of preconceptions and biases that may distort our perception of what is actually happening at the present. Self-detachment or self-distancing not only enables us to have a more accurate observation of our experiences, but also allows us the spaciousness to access our spiritual values such as conscience, compassion, will to meaning, and responsibility.

Self-detachment is a unique human capacity to distance oneself and take on the perspective of looking at our situations and ourselves from "the outside". This is not splitting from oneself, because one is totally aware of one's own psychological integrity at all times. It is more like perspective-taking and detaching oneself from all kinds of anxieties related to self-interest. This capacity to step away from ourselves allows some space and time to choose to respond with the right attitude in accordance with our spiritual values.

Seeking One's Calling

In between ultimate meaning and situational meaning, there is also the existential meaning of one's sense of calling for a mission or vocation. A sense of calling straddles between ultimate meaning and situational meaning. If you believe that the world is organized according to some higher purpose and grand design, it is easier for you to believe that you have a special calling to fill a unique niche in the larger scheme of things. Secondly, a particular event may trigger one's desire to pursue a certain mission consistent with one's values and passion. For example, a person may have the desire to serve the poor and disadvantaged. When he learns about the opportunity to serve in a leper colony, he may accept this mission as his calling.

At the third level, one attains self-transcendence by pursuing an achievable life goal that is greater than oneself. Calling is not just about work and career—it is also about how one responds to life's demand of the self. It is about not what I can get from life, but what life wants from me. Calling comes to those who are not only aware of their strengths, the need of the hour, and the opportunities available, but also who have a sense of responsibility to serve the common good. One's life is meaningful to the extent that one has discovered one's purpose in life or raison d'être based on calling.

Dik and Duffy (2009) define calling as: "A transcendent summon, originating beyond the self, to approach a particular life role in a manner oriented toward demonstrating or deriving a sense of purpose or meaningfulness and that holds other-oriented values and goals as primary motivation." (p. 427)

This definition echoes Frankl's emphasis on self-transcendence. A general sense of calling, regardless of one's occupation, is the call to devote one's life to serving others and to improving oneself in order to fulfill one's potential. A specific sense of calling is to discover a special niche or life role that makes use of one's unique talents, temperament, and experiences. This calling may change according to an individual's stage of development, station in life, and the demands of each situation.

A sense of calling endows one's life with a sense of meaning, responsibility, and dignity. Calling necessarily needs to entail some sense of societal contribution above and beyond personal happiness and success. There is near-consensus that calling is linked to meaning and purpose, as well as the betterment of society (Dik et al. 2013; Dik and Duffy 2009; Hardy 1990). From Frankl's perspective, pursuing a sense of calling as a concrete meaning in life entails both the global belief in ultimate meaning and the mindful awareness of situational meaning.

Empirical Findings in Support of the Role of Meaning in Well-Being

Ultimate Meaning and Religious/Spiritual Beliefs

All three levels of self-transcendence contribute to well-being. I want to discuss some of the empirical findings relating self-transcendence to well-being.

Regarding ultimate meaning, there is a huge literature on the adaptive benefits of religious beliefs and spiritual practices (e.g., Koenig et al. 2001; Pargament 1997; Wong et al. 2012). In addition to the commonly mentioned benefit of contributing to a sense of coherence and community, Fredrickson's (2002) research findings suggest that some of the health benefits of religious beliefs might be mediated by positive emotions.

Research on death acceptance (Wong 2008; Wong and Tomer 2011) is another fertile area that has demonstrated how religious and spiritual beliefs help prepare people to embrace and celebrate death and new possibilities. Recently, I developed the Life Orientation Scale (LOS; Wong 2012a, 2012b, 2012c) to measure global belief in ultimate meaning. This is a new scale with important implications. Future research with this scale will determine whether many of Frankl's ideas about ultimate meaning can be confirmed.

Situational Meaning and Mindfulness

Research on mindful meditation or mindful awareness has clearly demonstrated the health benefits of such practices (e.g., Kabat-Zinn 2005; Siegel 2010). There are also research findings suggesting that mindfulness is related to meaning in life and well-being (Brown et al. 2007; Wong 2012c). Another line of relevant research is the flow experience (Csikszentmihalyi 1990). When one is engaged in work or play, one can reach the flow state when the perceived challenge stretches personal skill and when there are clear proximal goals. The third line of research has to do with discovering and remembering meaningful moments.

My research on adaptive types of reminiscence (Wong and Watt 1991) showed that both instrumental and integrative memories are beneficial to the elderly. In instrumental reminiscence, the seniors remembered an incident or a moment when they were able to overcome a difficulty or resolve a problem. In integrative reminiscence, they remembered cases in which they were able to achieve reconciliation with an alienated loved one or gain a spiritual insight about an unresolved issue. Recalling such memories at the end of each day may also have the same adaptive function.

Recently, I encouraged people to write down meaningful moments at the end of every day, rather than toward the end of their lives. Meaningful moments are defined as moments that are full of emotional significance, both negative and positive, and have considerable impact on their lives. Future research will determine whether simply writing about meaningful moments can improve one's well-being.

Life's Calling and Goal Striving

There is increasing research evidence that personal meaning is often linked to a sense of mission and pursuit of calling (Baumeister 1991; Dobrow 2006; Hall and Chandler 2005; Wrzesniewski and Dutton 2001). Positive psychology research provides evidence that one experiences life as meaningful when one's calling is to serve some greater good (Hunter et al. 2010; Seligman 2002; Steger et al. 2009). There is also a vast literature on the benefits of goal striving (Emmons 2005) and personal projects (Little 1998), providing further support to the importance of pursuing a worthy life goal.

The biological imperative of having a purpose has been well documented (Wong 2012b; Wong and Fry 1998). The present self-transcendence hypothesis states that all purposes are not equal. Misguided life purposes, such as pursuing pleasure and power with total disregard for ethical and legal issues, eventually will result in self-destruction. However, when we strive to serve a higher purpose and greater good, then each step of the journey is rewarding and inspiring, even when we do not receive recognition or reward (Wong 2012a).

Self-Transcendence, Aging and Well-Being

Logotherapy or meaning therapy is uniquely designed to meet the spiritual and existential needs of the aging population. In the areas of aging and spiritual care, self-transcendence is a central issue. As our capacities decline with advancing age, and as our familiar world recedes because of disabilities and chronic illnesses, our spiritual capacity to transcend our physical limitations becomes a promising source of well-being. Research has clearly shown that self-transcendence has become an important topic for spiritual care, especially for the very old (e.g., Coward and Reed 1996; Nygren et al. 2005; Reed 1991).

For the elderly, the adaptive functions of self-transcendence can be found in increased well-being (e.g., Coward 1996; Ellermann and Reed 2001; Runquist and Reed 2007) and spirituality (e.g., Emmons 2005, 2006; Grouzet et al. 2005). Self-transcendence is especially important for the elderly and patients with terminal illnesses (e.g., Burr et al. 2011; Coward and Reed 1996; Haugan et al. 2013; Iwamoto et al. 2011; Matthews and Cook 2008; McCarthy and Bockweb 2013; Reker and Woo 2011). Some researchers have even applied logotherapy or meaning therapy to increase the well-being of cancer patients (Breitbart 2002; Noguchi et al. 2006). Much research needs to be done to discover how each level of self-transcendence can enhance the well-being of the elderly and the terminally ill.

Conclusion

In conclusion, I propose that the perspective of meaning-seeking and self-transcendence may be helpful in developing a curriculum for Life and Death Education. At present, there is a great deal of interest in positive education (Seligman et al. 2009) at the public schools, but advocates of positive education mostly emphasize the science of happiness and the signs of character strengths as championed by Seligman (2002, 2011). In contrast, I advocate a meaning orientation for the following two reasons: (1) To focus on the pursuit of personal happiness and success may lead to egotism, disappointment, and psychological disorders. In the present climate of low employment and little opportunity for fulfilling personal happiness and ambitions, too much emphasis on positivity may lead to negative results for individuals and society (Coyne 2013). (2) History has shown both the pros and cons of capitalism. A materialistic culture based on overproduction and overconsumption is not sustainable given the limited resources on our planet. The world will not have enough resources to support China when its population is able to consume at the same rate as Americans (O'Leary 2006).

In view of the above two concerns, I am proposing the meaning framework, which emphasizes the importance of **personal responsibility** towards fellow human beings, the environment, and the Creator. The trumpet call from Viktor Frankl is to awaken people on their responsibility of fulfilling their spiritual destiny of serving a higher purpose and the greater good.

A little-known logic related to self-transcendence is that it demands continual self-improvement if we are to realize our full potential. There is no limit to personal growth, at least in the spiritual realm. Therefore, when one is motivated to transcend both external and internal limitations and realize one's full potential, one is expressing self-transcendence. Almost the entire literature on personal improvement focuses on the self, such as self-esteem, self-efficacy, and self-actualization. In contrast, Frankl's self-transcendence construct emphasizes that the path towards fulfillment of one's potential is not through constant self-referral, but rather serving others as a reference point. We are able to fully develop our potential only when we devote our time and energy towards a mission greater than ourselves.

In sum, self-transcendence offers a vision of the best possible future, not only for individuals, but also for humanity. In a paradoxical way, self-transcendence points out that we have to redirect our focus from self-interest to others, in order to live the good life. It is in awakening and cultivating our spiritual values of will to meaning and self-transcendence that we find a sense of fulfillment and significance. If we continue to expand our interest beyond ourselves to include an ever growing circle of influence, we will eventually lose our "small selves" in finding our "larger selves."

References

Baumeister, R. F. (1991). *Meanings of life*. New York, NY: Guilford.

Baumeister, R. F., Vohs, K. D., Aaker, J. L., & Garbinsky, E. N. (2013). Some key differences between a happy life and a meaningful life. *Journal of Positive Psychology*. Retrieved from http://faculty-gsb.stanford.edu/aaker/pages/documents/SomeKeyDifferencesHappyLifeMeaningfulLife_2012.pd.

Breitbart, W. (2002). Spirituality and meaning in supportive care: spirituality-and meaning-centered group psychotherapy interventions in advanced cancer. *Support Care Cancer, 10*(4), 272–280.

Brown, K. W., Ryan, R. M., & Creswell, J. D. (2007). Mindfulness: Theoretical foundations and evidence for its salutary effects. *Psychological Inquiry, 18*(4), 211–237.

Buddha, S. (1966). *The teaching of Buddha*. Tokyo: Society for the Promotion of Buddhism, Japan. BDK Canada c/o Toronto Buddhist Organization.

Burr, A., Santo, J. B., & Pushkar, D. (2011). Affective well-being in retirement: The influence of values, money, and health across three years. *Journal of Happiness Studies, 12*, 17–40.

Coward, D. D. (1996). Self-transcendence and correlates in a healthy population. *Nursing Research, 45*(2), 116–121.

Coward, D. D., & Reed, P. G. (1996). Self-transcendence: A resource for healing at the end of life. *Issues in Mental Health Nursing, 17*(3), 275–288.

Coyne, J. (2013). *Self-help for the affluent: positive psychology's bourgie bias*. [Web log post]; Accessed Sept 5, 2013: http://www.tricycle.com/blog/positive-psychologys-bourgie-bias-how-positive-thinking-blinds-us-injustice.

Csikszentmihalyi, M. (1990). *Flow: The psychology of optimal experience*. New York, NY: Harper & Row.

Dik, B. J., Byrne, Z. S., & Steger, M. F. (Eds.). (2013). *Purpose and meaning in the workplace*. Washington, DC: American Psychological Association.

Dik, B. J., & Duffy, R. D. (2009). Calling and vocation at work definitions and prospects for research and practice. *The Counseling Psychologist, 37*(3), 424–450.

Dobrow, S. R. (2006). *Having a calling: A longitudinal study of young musicians*. Cambridge, MA: Harvard University.

Ellermann, C. R., & Reed, P. G. (2001). Self-transcendence and depression in middle-aged adults. *Western Journal of Nursing Research, 23*, 698–713.

Emmons, R. A. (2005). Striving for the sacred: Personal goals, life meaning, and religion. *Journal of Social Issues, 61*, 731–746.

Emmons, R. A. (2006). Spirituality: Recent progress. In M. Csikszentmihalyi (Ed.), *A life worth living: Contributions to positive psychology* (pp. 62–84). New York, NY: Oxford University Press.

Frankl, V. E. (1985). *Man's search for meaning (Revised and updated)*. New York, NY: Washington Square Press.

Frankl, V. E. (1986). *The doctor and the soul: From psychotherapy to logotherapy (Revised and expanded)*. New York, NY: Vintage Books.

Fredrickson, B. L. (2002). How does religion benefit health and well-being? Are positive emotions active ingredients? *Psychological Inquiry, 13*(3), 209–213.

Grouzet, F. M., Kasser, T., Ahuvia, A., et al. (2005). The structure of goal contents across 15 cultures. *Journal of Personality and Social Psychology, 89*(5), 800–816.

Hall, D. T., & Chandler, D. E. (2005). Psychological success: When the career is a calling. *Journal of Organizational Behavior, 26*(2), 155–176.

Hardy, L. (1990). *The fabric of this world: Inquiries into calling, career choice, and the design of human work*. Grand Rapids, MI: Eerdmans Publishing.

Haugan, G., Rannestad, T., Hammervold, R., Garåsen, H., & Espnes, G. A. (2013). Self-transcendence in cognitively intact nursing-home patients: A resource for well-being. *Journal of Advanced Nursing, 69*, 1147–1160.

Hicks, J. A., & Routledge, C. (Eds.). (2013). *The experience of meaning in life: Classical perspectives, emerging themes, and controversies*. New York, NY: Springer.

Hunter, I., Dik, B. J., & Banning, J. H. (2010). College students' perceptions of calling in work and life: A qualitative analysis. *Journal of Vocational Behavior, 76*(2), 178–186.

Iwamoto, R., Yamawaki, N., & Sato, T. (2011). Increased self-transcendence in patients with intractable diseases. *Psychiatry and Clinical Neurosciences, 65*(7), 638–647.

James, W. (1997). *The varieties of religious experience* (First Touchstoneth ed.). New York, NY: Touchstone. Original work published 1902.

Kabat-Zinn, J. (2005). *Full catastrophe living: Using the wisdom of your body and mind to face stress, pain, and illness (15th anniversary*. New York, NY: Delta Trade Paperback/Bantam Dell.

Koenig, H. G., McCullough, M., & Larson, D. B. (Eds.). (2001). *Handbook of religion and health*. New York, NY: Oxford University Press.
Little, B. R. (1998). Personal project pursuit: Dimensions and dynamics of personal meaning. In P. T. P. Wong & P. S. Fry (Eds.), *The human quest for meaning: A handbook of psychological research and clinical applications* (pp. 193–212). Mahwah, NJ: Lawrence Erlbaum Associates Publishers.
Matthews, E. E., & Cook, P. F. (2008). Relationships among optimism, well-being, self-transcendence, coping, and social support in women during treatment for breast cancer. *Psycho-Oncology, 18*(7), 716–726.
McCarthy, V. L., & Bockweb, A. (2013). The role of transcendence in a holistic view of successful aging: A concept analysis and model of transcendence in maturation and aging. *Journal of Holistic Nursing, 31*, 93–94.
Noguchi, W., Morita, S., Ohno, T., et al. (2006). Spiritual needs in cancer patients and spiritual care based on logotherapy. *Support Care Cancer, 14*(1), 65–70.
Nygren, B., Aléx, L., Jonsén, E., et al. (2005). Resilience, sense of coherence, purpose in life and self-transcendence in relation to perceived physical and mental health among the oldest old. *Aging & Mental Health, 9*(4), 354–362.
O'Leary, D. B. (2006). *Escaping the progress trap*. Westmount, QC: Geozone Communications.
Pargament, K. I. (1997). *The psychology of religion and coping: Theory, research, practice*. New York, NY: Guilford Press.
Reed, P. G. (1991). Self-transcendence and mental health in oldest-old adults. *Nursing Research, 40*(1), 5–11.
Reker, G. T., & Woo, L. C. (2011). Personal meaning orientations and psychosocial adaptation in older adults. *SAGE Open, 1*(1), 1–10.
Runquist, J. J., & Reed, P. G. (2007). Self-transcendence and well-being in homeless adults. *Journal of Holistic Nursing, 25*, 1–13.
Seligman, M. E. P. (2002). *Authentic happiness: Using the new positive psychology to realize your potential for lasting fulfillment*. New York, NY: Free Press/Simon and Schuster.
Seligman, M. E. P. (2011). *Flourish: A visionary new understanding of happiness and well-being*. New York, NY: Free Press.
Seligman, M. E., Ernst, R. M., Gillham, J., Reivich, K., & Linkins, M. (2009). Positive education: Positive psychology and classroom interventions. *Oxford Review of Education, 35*(3), 293–311.
Shaver, P. R., & Mikulincer, M. (Eds.). (2012). *Meaning, mortality, and choice: The social psychology of existential concerns*. Washington, DC: American Psychological Association.
Siegel, R. D. (2010). *The mindfulness solution: Everyday practices for everyday problems*. New York, NY: Guilford Press.
Steger, M. F., Oishi, S., & Kashdan, T. B. (2009). Meaning in life across the life span: Levels and correlates of meaning in life from emerging adulthood to older adulthood. *Journal of Positive Psychology, 4*, 43–52.
Wong, P. T. P. (2008). Meaning management theory and death acceptance. In A. Tomer, G. T. Eliason, & P. T. P. Wong (Eds.), *Existential and spiritual issues in death attitudes* (pp. 65–87). New York, NY: Lawrence Erlbaum Associates.
Wong, P. T. P. (2012a). What is the meaning mindset? *International Journal of Existential Psychology and Psychotherapy, 4*(1), 1–3.
Wong, P. T. P. (Ed.). (2012b). *The human quest for meaning: Theories, research, and applications* (2nd ed.). New York, NY: Routledge.
Wong, P. T. P. (2012c). Toward a dual-systems model of what makes life worth living. In P. T. P. Wong (Ed.), *The human quest for meaning: Theories, research, and applications* (2nd ed., pp. 3–22). New York, NY: Routledge.
Wong, P. T. P. (2014). Viktor Frankl's meaning seeking model and positive psychology. In A. Batthyany & P. Russo-Netzer (Eds.), *Meaning in existential and positive psychology*. New York, NY: Springer.

Wong, P. T. P., & Fry, P. S. (Eds.). (1998). *The human quest for meaning: A handbook of psychological research and clinical applications*. Mahwah, NJ: Lawrence Erlbaum Associates.
Wong, P. T. P., & Tomer, A. (2011). Beyond terror and denial: The positive psychology of death acceptance. *Death Studies, 35*(2), 99–106.
Wong, P. T. P., & Watt, L. (1991). What types of reminiscence are associated with successful aging? *Psychology and Aging, 6*, 272–279.
Wong, P. T. P., Wong, L. C. J., McDonald, M. J., & Klaassen, D. W. (Eds.). (2012). *The positive psychology of meaning and spirituality (Proceedings of Meaning Conferences)*. Birmingham, AL: Purpose Research.
Wrzesniewski, A., & Dutton, J. E. (2001). Crafting a job: Revisioning employees as active crafters of their work. *Academy of Management Review, 26*, 179–201.

Laudatio for Eleonore Frankl

Dmitry Leontiev

Dear friends,

I don't remember ever having a more difficult task to fulfill than tonight. Frankly speaking, I don't know what an honorary doctorate is, so I will just share some fragmented considerations about what is going on now and how I understand the event that has collected us here tonight. I cannot just say some simple formal words because Elly Frankl is one of the persons of whom you can never speak formal words; it's a kind of testing of your openness, sincerity, and integrity. You just cannot say anything that would not come from your heart. So saying these words is a very responsible task for me.

Today we are here to celebrate the honorary doctorate awarded to Elly Frankl by the Moscow Institute of Psychoanalysis. I hope that Rector Lev Surat will forgive me, but it is probably a greater honor for the Institute of Psychoanalysis than for Elly. She was granted Viktor Frankl as her greatest award, and he was granted her as his. I don't think there can be an award of comparable value to either of them. When I was trying to prepare this talk I found a wonderful quotation from Abraham Maslow that perfectly describes the relationships between Viktor and Elly as I understand them: "Only as men become strong enough, self-confident enough, and integrated enough can they tolerate and finally enjoy self-actualizing women, women who are full human beings. But no man fulfills himself without such a woman, in principle. Therefore strong men and strong women are the condition of

---

Editorial NoteThe following speech was given in honor of Eleonore Frankl on May 18, 2014 at the Dome Hall of the Natural History Museum, Vienna, on the occasion of the conferment ceremony of an honorary doctoral degree to Eleonore Frankl at the 2014 "The Future of Logotherapy II" Congress.

D. Leontiev (✉)
Department of Psychology, Moscow State University,
Mokhovaya str. 11-5, Moscow 125009, Russia
e-mail: dleon@smysl.ru

A. Batthyány (ed.), *Logotherapy and Existential Analysis*, Logotherapy and Existential Analysis: Proceedings of the Viktor Frankl Institute Vienna 1,
DOI 10.1007/978-3-319-29424-7_28

each other, for neither can exist without the other. They are also the cause of the other because women grow men and men grow women. And finally of course, they are the reward of each other. If you are a good enough man, that's the kind of woman you'll get and that's the kind of woman you'll deserve" (Maslow 1968, 87).

I have been thinking what can be said about this prominent person. I've known Elly from her brief visits to Moscow with Viktor in 1986 and 1992 and my brief visits to Vienna in 1991 and 2005. On those occasions she was somewhat in Victor's shade, and our personal communication was limited. However, I also read the inspirational book *When Life Calls Out to Us* by Haddon Klingberg, based on long interviews with the Frankls. It gave me a lot of insights and I don't know what to add to his glowing description. I don't feel it appropriate to narrate Elly's entire biography, nor is it a complex story on its surface. A regular, rather poor child had survived in wartime and then started working in the Viennese Poliklinik as a deputy nurse. There she met Viktor, fell into a relationship and stayed with him the rest of his life and the rest of her life till now.

The most important thing we can get from extraordinary people is learning the lessons they teach us. I don't mean they preach to us; on the contrary, they do it only by their personal example and the best thing we can do is to learn this personal example, to learn these personal lessons without direct instructions. I saw a brilliant saying on the net about educating children. "Your children will be like you anyway. Don't educate them—educate yourself." What can we learn from Elly? What can we follow, or take from the example she provides for us?

The first lesson is the lesson of vitality. Erich Fromm would call it "biophily," a love of life. It is not that easy. It can be formulated like this: let the life reside within you. There are many people (surely not among those who are present here), who exchange their livelihood for some conformist comfort or extrinsic goods. This never repays itself. We existential psychotherapists spend a lot of effort to bring them back to life, to do the job of psychological reanimation. Our human responsibility is mostly maintaining these sparks of unpredictable ever-changing life in ourselves, and this we can learn from Elly as her first important lesson.

I was trying to guess what might have attracted Viktor to this girl. In Klingberg's book there is a cue: after first meeting Elly, Viktor asked one of his colleagues standing nearby: "Did you see those eyes?" (Klingberg 2001, 207). Once I was at a conference where the organizers presented an amazing slideshow. They collected some 70 or so Rembrandt self-portraits. They adjusted the size and focus of the slides and placed them in such a way that if you change the slides quickly you see one changing face. It starts with the youngest periods of his work of self-portraits and as the painter grows old the portraits naturally change. There was, however, one thing that never changed and stayed the same in all the portraits, from the youngest ones to the oldest: Rembrandt's eyes. They were absolutely the same in the 20-year-old Rembrandt and in the 70-year-old Rembrandt. All of us who are here in this room are so happy because we can look at Elly's eyes and see in them the spring of life that Viktor saw many years ago—they have not changed.

The second lesson is about resilience. Despite all the things that mass culture tries to impose on us, existentialists know well that life is not easy. Life requires effort, resilience, hardiness, the ability to withstand many hardships—Frankl called this attitude *Trotzmacht des Geistes*, defiant power of spirit. Life requires a capacity to oppose everything that may try to transform us without losing our own spirit and optimism, even sometimes a tragic optimism. We have to withstand many things in this life. The role of women is especially important in facing the challenges. The role of an outstanding woman is not so much a kind of direct assistance to the man but rather creating a space where the man can totally relax and gain strength again; there is no other way of getting it. Sometimes tolerating pathetic events, fame and glory, is as difficult as tolerating real hardships. And the most important thing is just being able to tolerate all the aspects of your life. You must have this as your inner position, your inner existential center, to be able to relate to all those things that come from outside. And this is the second lesson: to be yourself, to stay yourself, you must have your own inner position and point of support from which you can take the attitude to anything and freedom from anything, from which you can implement attitudinal values and transform anything you wish to transform.

The third lesson is positive attitude, the belief for the better that does not need some cognitive or rational justification; the capacity of saying "Yes" to life whenever possible. Bad things happen due to some uncontrollable forces or natural spontaneous regularities; entropy is something that comes about itself. All the evil things have the nature of entropy. Good things have the nature of negentropy. They never happen spontaneously, they must be effortfully created. The third lesson we learn from Elly is the necessity to invest ourselves in making good things, otherwise they will never happen and the bad things will prevail. Frankl called it "tragic optimism": good things come about only through our choice and efforts (1985a, 84–85). And that's what love is about. Love is about effort; it's not just a feeling, it's self-investment. Elly mentioned that she was a kind of background for Viktor, but you know that figure and background relationships can switch. Today it would be absolutely correct to say that they were both the background for each other. Viktor Frankl defined meaning as a possibility on the background of reality (1985b, 260). I feel that Elly was this background reality, who created a possibility of Viktor Frankl being Viktor Frankl. This is what we honor tonight. We are really happy that Elly gained the appreciation she deserves and that her name will be forever linked together with the name of Viktor Frankl.

References

Frankl, V. E. (1985a). *The unconscious God*. New York, NY: Washington Square Press.

Frankl, V. E. (1985b). Logos, paradox and the search for meaning. In M. J. Mahoney & A. Freeman (Eds.), *Cognition and psychotherapy* (pp. 259–275). New York, NY: Plenum Press.

Klingberg, H. (2001). *When life calls out to us: The love and lifework of Viktor and Elly Frankl*. New York, NY: Doubleday.

Maslow, A. H. (1968). *Toward a psychology of being* (2nd ed.). New York, NY: Van Nostrand Reinhold.

Part V
Philosophy

What Are Minds For?

John Beloff

I shall introduce my problem with the help of that well-tried philosopher's device, the imaginary world. Let us suppose that we have two parallel coexisting universes. Universe A is our actual familiar universe and so, for the moment, we need say no more about it. Universe A′ is an exact physical replica of A such that for every physical object that exists in A there is a corresponding object in A′ and for every physical event that occurs in A there is a corresponding physical event in A′. The one and only feature which serves to distinguish between A and A′, apart from their spatial separation, is the fact that in A′ there are no mental entities or conscious

Editorial Note: The following article was written by the late John Beloff (1920–2006), eminent psychologist and senior lecturer at the Department of Psychology at Edinburgh University, mentor and academic role model to several generations of psychologists and clinical researchers. He was an accomplished teacher, doing everything he possibly could to support, encourage, nurture and inspire his students, many of whom have gone on to have successful academic careers themselves. His voice is sorely missed. All the more we are honored to be able to rescue the following paper from being left unpublished, especially given its relevance to logotherapy's model of dimensional ontology and free will.
For the greater part of his academic life, Beloff researched the relationship of mind, brain, and psyche, arguing for a non-reductionist (i.e. interactionist) model of mind and brain. While Beloff was sympathetic to the perspective of, he was not grounded in existential psychology (or, for that matter, logotherapy); rather, his argument for non-reductionism rests on the case of the functions of consciousness. Arguments of this kind are currently only rarely discussed by existential psychologists, yet fare relatively prominently in contemporary debates on mind, mental causation, and free will. As readers will soon recognize, the questions addressed by Beloff are closely related to the model of personhood proposed by Frankl; what makes his case especially striking and compelling, however, is the fact that support for some of the core tenets of logotherapy's model of personhood can be developed from a naturalistic starting point.
This is the first time this article appears in print. We wish to thank Prof. Beloff's daughter Zoe Beloff for granting us permission to publish it in this volume.

J. Beloff (deceased)

A. Batthyány (ed.), *Logotherapy and Existential Analysis*, Logotherapy and Existential Analysis: Proceedings of the Viktor Frankl Institute Vienna 1,
DOI 10.1007/978-3-319-29424-7_29

experiences. Thus, although the whole of evolution and the whole of history unfolds in A′ exactly as it does in A, so as to be indistinguishable to an observer, there are no observers in A′, no one indeed who is aware of anything that happens there, if to be aware is to have a conscious experience.

I am here assuming that being conscious entails having a mind although having a mind does not necessarily imply being conscious, there is, I would say, nothing self-contradictory in the idea of unconscious mental events. However, consciousness is, by common consent, the most distinctive attribute of mind and it would be hard to make sense of a mind that never at any time became conscious. At all events Universe A′ is, ex hypothesi, a purely physical or totally mindless universe.

Given this hypothetical situation we can now state our problem as follows:

Why should our actual world correspond with Universe A rather than with Universe A′? If this is a valid question, it admits only two answers. Either there is no reason at all, it is just a God-given or contingent fact that that is how things actually are, like the fact that anything at 11 should exist rather than nothing, or else there is some reason, for example we might suppose that the world we know could not have evolved as it has done had it not been for the intervention of mind.

The first answer, that from an a priori standpoint A and A′ are equally probable candidates for actualization, presupposes that mind plays no part in the determination of physical events. The second answer which asserts that A′ is no more than a logical possibility and could never be actualized implies that mind has some degree of autonomy in determining the course of events. Materialism is a name that has been given to a variety of doctrines but, as I shall use the word here, a materialist is one who is logically committed to giving the first answer. Similarly, what I shall call interactionism will here be taken to mean the doctrine, which logically commits one to giving the second answer. The purpose of the present paper is to examine these two doctrines and assess their relative merits. I shall try to show that there are no insuperable or logical objections to either of them, whatever may have been said to the contrary, and that there are manifold advantages and disadvantages whichever one we adopt. Accordingly in present circumstances it must remain a matter of one's personal philosophical predilections which of them one chooses (my own happens to be for the second but I shall try not to let that influence the argument). However, with the growth of knowledge, circumstances may change and I will end by discussing what would need to be the case before it became more rational to prefer one or other given alternative.

Before I can even embark on this plan, however, we must first consider very carefully whether the hypothetical situation we took as our point of departure is indeed a legitimate one and is not perchance vitiated by some internal inconsistency or conceptual incoherence as many might protest. It is after all only too easy to think up situations, which, on examination, turn out to be logical absurdities. We have only to think of that favorite device of the science-fiction writer, time-travel. This seems innocuous enough when it is first introduced into the narrative but very soon we are beset by all kinds of insoluble paradoxes. Could it be that our imaginary world, Universe A′, was in fact just such another flawed fantasy?

Like time-travel, one must admit that it has some very bizarre consequences. Consider the following thought-experiment.

We take an individual P, let him be a family man, from Universe A and suddenly and instantaneously we exchange him with his counterpart P′ from Universe A′.

The first thing we may note about this thought-experiment is that it produces absolutely no observable differences to indicate that anything whatever has changed. P′s wife and children will never know P′ is not the husband or father whom they knew and cherished, that indeed he is not a person at all but an insentient automaton. For, ex hypothesi, nothing in the appearance or behavior of P′, no far-away look in his eyes or anything of that sort can ever betrays the secret to which we are privy. Likewise, if we follow the adventures of P flow transposed to A′, we know that he can never discover his solipsistic predicament; he will continue to believe that the beings which he takes to be his wife and children have minds like his own. But while this is certainly bizarre, it generates no paradox of a logically objectionable kind. It is absurd only because A′ is an absurd universe, our thought-experiment has done no more than make explicit the well known truism that no object however life-like and no behavior however mind-like can ever entail the presence of consciousness. It is true that, on any positivist criterion of meaning, our thought-experiment must be dismissed as meaningless since it is in principle impossible to verify that it has been carried out. And yet, provided we can understand the distinction between A and A′, P and P′, the supposition that such an exchange has been made is perfectly intelligible. Indeed the intelligibility of such a thought-experiment could well be advanced as a conclusive refutation of the positivist theory of meaning.

In view of what has just been said, it is surprising to find how large a slice of the recent literature on the philosophy of mind would, in defiance of the truism, which we have just enunciated, disallow the distinction we have made. I suppose the two most important doctrines in this connection are (1) Logical Behaviorism (Ryle 1949) and (2) Central State Materialism (Armstrong 1968). If, therefore, we can deal with the objections from these sources we may feel reasonably confident that we stand on firm ground.

Now, according to the former, what it means for an organism to be conscious or sentient is nothing over and above its being disposed to react to situations in an appropriate or discriminating way. The elimination of any existential element from consciousness by means of this stipulative redefinition of the concept derives such plausibility as it may possess from the ambiguity of the word consciousness as used in everyday discourse when it is seldom necessary to distinguish between the behavioral criteria for the ascription of consciousness and consciousness as such. Thus, when the doctor is called in to pronounce whether the victim of the accident is conscious or not we are normally quite content to accept his verdict as final. And yet, logically, it is perfectly permissible to surmise that even when the most refined physiological tests known to medicine show that the patient is comatose, that is behaviorally unconscious, he may nevertheless be experiencing some vivid hallucination or out-of-body experience and hence be conscious in the basic sense. It is, of course, exclusively in the basic sense, not in the derived behavioral sense, that the inhabitants of our Universe A′ are said to be unconscious.

We should note, at this point, that it is only in its derived sense that we can define or explicate what we mean by consciousness. In its basic sense it can no more be defined than any other primitive concept. With any primitive concept, either one understands what is intended or one fails to understand. A logical behaviorist may be defined as someone who has failed to grasp what consciousness means in this sense. Confronted with a logical behaviorist, various strategies may be adopted in order to get him to understand what we mean. A nice example is that suggested by Kirk (1974) who asks us to imagine ourselves converted step by step into a "Zombie" (his name for our counterpart in A′) by losing one sense-modality after another while continuing to behave in a normal fashion. However, if all such strategies fail and our logical behaviorist persists in denying that he understands what we are talking about, the dialog can go no further; all that we can then do is to echo Dr. Johnson when he declared that while he could give his opponent an argument he could not give him an understanding.

But, if we reject Logical Behaviorism, then, by the same token we must also reject Central State Materialism, which equally refuses to recognize the primary connotation of consciousness. Indeed, the latter doctrine differs from the former only in that it literally identifies the mental states and processes with the relevant brain states and processes. Mentalistic talk, we are told, is essentially "topic-neutral", by itself it tells us nothing about its ontological reference, however science gives us the authority to go beyond this neutrality and construe it as referring to the activities of the brain. But if that were so there would be absolutely nothing that we could say about the inhabitants of A that we could not equally say about the inhabitants of A′ since, ex hypothesi, they have identical brains. As it is, however, we have said that the former have conscious experiences while the latter do not. For those to whom this statement is intelligible both of these proffered solutions of the mind–body problem are non-starters.

The two viable forms which materialism may take are, first, the old-fashioned epiphenomenalism which regards the mind-brain relationship as a causal relationship but one in which the causation works in one direction only so that mental events figure only as effects, never as causes, and, secondly, the more recent double-aspect or double-attribute theory, as it is variously known, according to which the mind–brain relationship is one of actual identity, that is to say mental events are conceived of as brain events but as such events are apprehended by the brain itself as opposed to the way in which they are apprehended by an external observer (i.e. by another brain). This latter theory differs from the Central State version of the identity theory in that it treats consciousness as an irreducible fact, not as something needing to be analyzed in dispositional terms. Various conceptual advantages have been claimed for it over the earlier epiphenomenalist theory but whether, in the last resort, anything more is involved than a mere verbal shift or, indeed, whether it even makes sense to talk about an identity in this context is still very much open to question. These are not questions, however, which we need pursue here for, whether we say that the mind is a function of the brain or whether we say that it is the brain in one of its aspects, the explanatory weight rests wholly upon the physical processes involved. Hence both forms of materialism carry the same implication, namely that even if, per impossibile, the brain did not generate conscious experiences or even if it had no other aspect than the physical one, even so everything else would go on exactly as before.

Despite repeated attempts by philosophers to discover some knock-down argument, which would show, once for all, that materialism or interactionism, as the case may be, was an untenable position, the persistence of both suggests that such attempts have been less than successful. The problem to which we must now address ourselves is which position has the greater claim on our allegiance, all things considered?

The immediate difficulty is that, traditionally, materialism takes its stand on, and draws its strength from, science whereas, traditionally, interactionism appeals to our common sense or moral intuitions. It is true that interactionism as a doctrine was first formulated by Descartes who was also one of the chief architects of the scientific revolution but he may have been swayed by his religious commitments, certainly his doctrine held little attraction for his successors. At all events, by the late Nineteenth Century, at a time when science had reached a peak of self-assurance and was pressing its right to be considered the final arbiter on the nature of man, epiphenomenalism had become the orthodox scientific position on the mind–body issue and, in effect, it has remained so ever since.

Meanwhile those philosophers who could not embrace materialism gravitated for the most part to one or other form of Idealism. From this lofty vantage point science itself could be viewed, not as the one objective authority which alone can legitimate our beliefs, but as just one of the creative manifestations of the human intellect and imagination which, however great its practical importance, could not take precedence over other equally valid belief-systems. In our own day, when Idealism ceased to be fashionable, philosophers have argued in a similar vein that science is no more than a specialized activity, which cannot, in the nature of the case, overturn the view of mind sanctioned by ordinary language. Interactionism was kept alive in the meantime by those few who took scientific materialism seriously enough to try and refute it on its own grounds. They numbered among their ranks philosophers, psychologists, physiologists and, of course, psychical researchers, but, despite the eminence of some of the names one could cite, theirs was a minority position which continued to bear a somewhat heretical or, at least, deviant taint.

In what sense can it be said that science lends support to materialism? The answer, I suggest, is twofold.

First, in the theory of evolution, materialism finds at least a plausible cosmology; secondly, the science of neurophysiology presents us with some striking demonstrations of the one-sided dependence of mind on brain.

From our point of view what was important in Darwinism was not so much that it explained the origin of species with recourse to supernatural intervention but that the one simple principle of the survival of the fittest—perhaps the most fertile principle in the whole history of ideas—could be applied quite generally to explain any semblance of design or purpose in nature wherever there is random variation and natural selection. Thus evolution is by no means restricted to phylogenesis. We talk of the evolution of galaxies out of the primeval inter-stellar dust or the evolution of organic and macro-molecules out of the elements just as appositely as we talk of the evolution of intelligent life from simpler organisms. In the face of this smooth cosmological sequence it is not easy for the interactionist to gain a foothold. For, if inanimate nature evolved of its own accord as a result of exclusively physio-chemical processes; if, furthermore, the whole of the plant kingdom in all its prodigious diversity evolved without the benefit of mind, as presumably did much of the animal kingdom as well in its lower echelons, is it plausible to suppose, as the interactionist must, that somewhere there is some definite point beyond which further development would not have been possible had not mind providentially supervened? Nor is it only in the phylogenetic sequence that continuity must be breached in this unlikely way for the same question arises with respect to the ontogenetic sequence of individual growth and development.

Does mind cohere with matter at conception? At birth? At some point intermediate between these two events? And, if the latter, is the union automatic and invariable? Or, if not, does a mindless embryo fail to develop and so perish?

One has only to pose such questions to realize how difficult it is to reconcile an interactionist metaphysic with modern biological knowledge or to appreciate why a latter day Darwinian, like Monod (1971), should champion materialism. Moreover there exists no credible cosmology that would account for the origins of mind or provide a reason for the intrusion of mind into a mindless universe in the first instance, at best we have the various mythical, religious or occult systems of a pre-scientific vintage to fall back upon. In desperation some anti-materialists have opted for a pan-psychism according to which mind inheres in all matter everywhere even though its presence is somehow made more manifest in the brain. However, while this restores a measure of continuity, it is an extravagant solution with its implication that we are potentially conscious in every atom of our body!

The argument from brain-science has perhaps an even more direct bearing on our problem than the cosmological argument we have just considered. The critical evidence in this connection comes from the study of brain damage, whether due to injury, disease, or deliberate surgical intervention. The point here is that, if the interactionist is right to attribute some degree of autonomy to mind, we would expect that we would be able to circumvent to some extent such localized disruption, perhaps by using other parts of the brain, whereas the evidence suggests, on the contrary, that, in the adult brain at least, quite small lesions may suffice to cause the loss of vital cognitive and motor functions or even, in some cases, drastic deterioration in the personality of the afflicted individual. Even when, by a heroic effort, the individual learns to adopt strategies to compensate for his disabilities, as with LuriA's patient, the deficit remains (Luria 1972). Sadly we must admit that, in this context, the triumph of mind over matter is, at best, no more than a figure of speech.

One special type of brain damage that has already provoked a certain amount of philosophical controversy is that resulting from the so-called split-brain operation, or commissurotomy, an operation that is carried out only in certain very severe cases of epilepsy as a means of restricting its scope. A patient whose corpus callosum has been severed is without the normal physical means whereby information received at one cerebral hemisphere is transferred to the other. Although such a person is able to function more or less normally in daily life—so much so, indeed, that it was many years before it was realized that the operation had these consequences—when tested in special situations that can be contrived in the laboratory it could be shown that the two hemispheres were functioning autonomously and even, in certain circumstances, at cross-purposes with one another!

Such a demonstration was possible because, with the cutting of the optic chasm visual stimuli from one half of the visual field would go only to the contralateral hemisphere while tactile stimuli from one side of the body would go only to the ipsilateral hemisphere. As a result of the pioneering investigations of Sperry in the 1960s and of the work of his successors we now know that a set task can be successfully accomplished under the control of one hemisphere alone without the other hemisphere evincing any sign of knowing what has happened. Since it is the left hemisphere that contains the speech centers, this means, in particular, that the split-brain subject will deny any knowledge of an object that has been presented exclusively to his right hemisphere even when, by the appropriate response of his right hand, he has just indicated his recognition of it! (Sperry 1965; Trevarthen 1974).

The philosophical problem, which arises out of these facts, is how we should best describe such a paradoxical situation? Are we to say that the subject's mind, like his brain, has now been split in to two yielding two parallel streams of consciousness insulated from one another? Or should we say, for example, that the subject's mind is now associated exclusively with his dominant left hemisphere leaving the mute right hemisphere to function purely automatically and unconsciously? Nagel (1971) has drawn attention to paradoxical consequences of any attempt to interpret the situation in terms of our familiar concept of the self. Zangwill (1976), on the other hand, has voiced a strong plea for adopting our first suggestion and acknowledging frankly the duplication of consciousness. At the same time he rebukes Eccles for adopting our second suggestion stigmatizing it as a desperate rear guard bid to preserve the integrity of the soul. As Zangwill very aptly points out, by all the criteria we normally apply when ascribing consciousness, with the exception of speech, the activities associated with the right hemisphere in the split-brain cases merit the attribution of consciousness and to withhold it must incur the suspicion of special pleading. Moreover he mentions at least one instance where the patient's entire left hemisphere was removed and yet this patient did not thereafter appear to be any the less of a conscious human being.

From the standpoint of the interactionist, these discoveries are undeniably disconcerting precisely because they bring out so dramatically the dependence of mind on brain. Indeed long before commissurotomy was a practical possibility its hypothetical implications were being discussed by thinkers of rival persuasions (Zangwill 1974).

The dominant view, represented by Fashioner who believed in mind and matter as parallel realities, was that the mind like the brain would become divided and in course of time two distinct personalities would emerge depending on which hemisphere was engaged. The minority view, represented by McDougall who was a staunch interactionist, insisted that the unity of consciousness and of the self would be preserved and that its preservation might afford the most convincing proof for the existence of the soul! What, then are we to say now that we know what transpires? We cannot say that either party has been completely vindicated. Except under the highly artificial conditions of the laboratory the personality of the split-brain patient survives intact. What happens, it seems, is that the dominant or conversant left hemisphere takes charge and represents the individual to the outside world. At the same time the subject's behavior in the experimental situation is hard to reconcile with a McDougallian or Cartesian unity of consciousness. However, this unity had already been severely undermined by the increasing evidence that came to light during the late Nineteenth Century of dissociated states and automatisms. Such bizarre phenomena as automatic writing, secondary, alternating ,and even co-conscious personalities, fugue states, amnesic episodes and suchlike—all of which were well known to McDougall who had to do his best to grapple with them (Boden 1972, Chap. 7)—raised questions about the unity of mind no different in principle from those presented by Sperry's evidence.

When the concept of the unconscious was still a novelty there was a division of opinion, which anticipates that between Zangwill and Eccles about what was involved in unconscious activity. Some, like Zangwill, wanted to postulate a secondary center of consciousness to go with it, which remained inaccessible to the subject's primary consciousness. Others, à la Eccles, wished to deny it the title of mental activity and regard it as the routine workings of the cerebral machinery, no different in principle from the autonomic and reflex activity of the nervous system that likewise takes place outside our conscious awareness or control. The long Empiricist tradition in philosophy which equated mind and consciousness made it seem inevitable that, when confronted with clear evidence of intelligent or adaptive behavior that was not accessible to introspection, either one had to posit an extra center of awareness or else regard such behavior as the activity of a sophisticated natural computer. A third possibility, namely that mind might manifest itself unconsciously, although a commonplace among psychical researchers, was rarely entertained.

Even the depth psychologists who followed Freud, who were so preoccupied with the unconscious, were, for the most part, content to adopt a non-committal attitude regarding its ontological status provided they were allowed complete freedom to develop their theories independently of current physiological knowledge. We, however, who have liberated ourselves from the positivist dogmas of Empiricism, should have no trouble acknowledging that our unconscious actions may be no less under the control of mind than our conscious behavior.

Consciousness may well be the most distinctive sign of mentality but there is no reason why we should regard them as synonymous. In the case of the severed right hemisphere discussed by Zangwill I have no doubt that its activities were controlled by some sort of a mind but, whether that mind is conscious or not and what relationship it has to the mind which governs the subject's dominant left hemisphere are questions about which I must profess myself agnostic. I will merely point out, before we leave the topic, that it would be unwise to make so much of these rare anomalous cases, however intriguing or important they may be, as to overlook the truly astonishing degree of unity and coherence which obtains in our normal waking consciousness. To quote Eccles: "Our brain is a democracy of ten thousand million nerve cells, yet it provides us with a unified experience". (Eccles 1965, 36)

We have now covered at least some of the ground where materialism could be expected to make most of the running. It is time to turn to a different realm where the roles are reversed and it is materialism that is on the defensive.

No philosopher, however partial to materialism, would deny that the way in which we think about one another's behavior in reality or the way, in which this is reflected in all our ordinary discourse, is, in its presuppositions and in its implications, overwhelmingly interactionist. For example, in real life it is universally assumed that the fact that we consciously choose to do something is causally relevant to the fact that we do it. To the materialist, on the contrary, both our conscious choice and the subsequent movement of our limbs are alike the effects of the particular brain state we happen to be in at the time or, more specifically, perhaps, of the particular distribution of electric charges in the cortex which determine which nerve cells will fire and in what order. No amount of philosophical double-talk (and there has been plenty) can disguise the fact that we have here a massive contradiction, which cries out for a resolution one way or the other.

The demand is even more insistent in the case of our moral discourse. The language of praise and blame, of pride and remorse, are meaningful only if the ultimate responsibility for the action resides in the agent. If a computer makes an error we do not hold it morally responsible for deceiving us, yet it is hard to see why, if we are indeed just conscious automata, as the materialist supposes, we should be held morally responsible for anything that we do.

Even those philosophers, the so-called "soft determinists" who maintain that, in principle, there is no incompatibility between physical determinism and the existence of free will, now usually concede that, in practice, we cannot at one and the same time conceive of ourselves as physical objects and as moral agents. There is, it seems, a fundamental antagonism between these two conceptions, to pass from one to the other demands a gestalt switch of a kind that can be achieved only with exceptional mental agility.

The materialist can, of course, dismiss free will as an illusion and moral judgments as nonsense, as do the "hard determinists", but, while many philosophers from Spinoza onwards have adopted this course, none, I think, has successfully transferred it from the study to the market-place for the simple reason that, in practice, it is virtually impossible to abstain from moral judgment. Hence the hard determinist lays himself open to the charge of bad faith. None of this, of course, disproves materialism or determinism because our moral intuitions may just be confused but it does expose the strong counter-intuitive element in these doctrines.

What, in the end, makes materialism irretrievably implausible (though not necessarily false!) is precisely that which makes our imaginary universe A′ so unbelievable. If the interactionist is right in supposing that the presence of mind is necessary in order to produce mind-like behavior, then it is perfectly understandable why there should never be a state of affairs like that represented by our universe A′. But, if, on the other hand, the materialist is right and there is no reason at all why we ourselves should be conscious rather than non-conscious, then there is nothing even improbable about the situation that obtains in A′. Indeed, if we one day encounter intelligent life elsewhere in the universe, where evolution may be presumed to have taken a different course, we would have no grounds whatever for assuming that these alien beings were sentient creatures like ourselves. Worse still, the materialist is peculiarly vulnerable to solipsistic doubts even when among his own kind.

The fluke, which made our species conscious, might, perhaps, have occurred only in his own unique case, he might be a complete sport in that respect. He cannot invoke the traditional analogical argument for rejecting solipsism, namely that behavioral similarities between ourselves and others justify the ascription of consciousness to them no less than to ourselves. For, by his own admission, mind plays no part in the determination of behavior. The ultimate paradox of materialism is that the one feature of the universe, which alone gives meaning to all the rest is the one feature, which has to be declared redundant! Nothing can account for its emergence; nothing follows from its existence.

Such considerations, however, are too abstract and metaphysical to count for much with the materialist. For the truth is that the strength of materialism has never been its logical cogency but rather its pragmatic or heuristic value for science. By this I mean that if we adopt a materialist approach to the phenomena of life or mind we open up the prospect of a reductive explanation and even if this is never attained at any rate we have not upset the unity of the sciences; nowhere are we forced to introduce some new entity or principle that has no equivalent elsewhere in science. Now, contrary to what some philosophers have written, reductive explanations are by no means the only valid type of explanations but they are, undoubtedly, the most powerful, perhaps for the same reason that physics is the most powerful and universal of the sciences.

It is true that when we come to the behavioral sciences there is precious little that admits of a reductive explanation but even if what we have is no more than an abstract theoretical model it provides a challenge to the neurophysiologist to explain how it might be embodied in the brain, thereby completing the conceptual bridge linking behavior at one end to physics at the other.

It is now generally recognized that explanation in psychology is a two-stage affair. This is best illustrated, I think, in the cognitive sphere.

We start by asking how is it possible for us to acquire skills or solve problems; how, for example, do we contrive to recognize a melody? Ride a bicycle? Put our thoughts into words etc.? At this stage someone comes along with a theory. No reference is yet involved to the brain but if the theory is at all rigorous it should be possible to program a computer to simulate the activity in question. At this stage, which we might call the stage of "theoretical psychology", our concern is much the same as that of the cyberneticist or exponent of artificial intelligence. Only when further evidence from the direction of brain-science is forthcoming is the second stage complete when we are in a position to say that our theory tells us how the brain actually operates in these circumstances as opposed merely to how it might operate.

Lest we lose our sense of perspective at this point we should take note that this second stage has not yet been completed even with the most basic cognitive functions such as memory although, of course, there are scores of abstract theories as to how particular kinds of remembering might be mediated. It is no less important to recognize that all the dominant schools of psychology are reductionist in the a foregoing sense. This applies equally to those who now call themselves "mentalists" or "cognitive theorists" who use concepts like "internalized grammars" etc. as it does to the hardened behaviorist who prefers to talk in terms of conditioning and to concentrate on overt performance. Chomskyans and Skinnerians alike share the assumption that the brain, as a physical system, possesses all the properties and structures necessary to actualize their theoretical suppositions.

Granted that the whole enterprise of a scientific psychology makes sense, it is hardly surprising that interactionism (often scornfully, if inaccurately, referred to as the homunculus theory of mind) should be viewed as a gross betrayal. For, if one starts from the assumption that how a person behaves depends, in part at least, on his having a mind that is endowed with certain unique properties and powers over and above those that belong to a conceivable physical system such as the brain, then one tends to end up explaining the behavior in terms of those very powers of mind that one has invented, on an ad hoc basis, precisely to account for the behavior.

This type of circular explanation, notorious in psychology, takes us back to the armchair theorists and faculty psychologists of the Nineteenth Century. The only escape from this is to have an independent theory of mind, analogous to physics as a theory of matter, but this has so far eluded us, and mind as such remains the densest of mysteries. The history of psychology has been largely, therefore, a revolt against interactionism which was identified with common sense psychology.

Fear of the homunculus has kept academic psychology firmly tied to the apron strings of materialism. Perhaps the one important school of psychology—if indeed one can describe it as a school—which acknowledged the autonomy of mind, was Functionalism, which flourished around the turn of the century. Its most illustrious spokesman, William James, took issue with the epiphenomenalism of Wundtian psychology or Kraepelinian psychiatry and argued that mind, like everything else in nature, must have a biological function. But his championship was not enough to turn the tide.

We have, it seems, reached a stalemate. Materialism, we may concede, is more in tune with scientific thinking and more conducive to scientific research but, in all that concerns our humanity, there seemed little doubt that interactionism makes better sense. Unless, therefore, some fresh arguments were to make materialism intuitively more plausible or, alternatively, unless fresh evidence were forthcoming that would make interactionism scientifically more acceptable, which of the two commands our allegiance may depend on whether our outlook is more influenced by scientific or humanistic considerations. While it is clearly impossible to anticipate what ingenious new arguments may yet be cast into the arena, there is already a body of evidence, which, if it carried more weight, would seriously weaken the scientific plausibility of materialism. For there is one empirical implication, which we have not, so far mentioned which does distinguish between the two opposed positions. If mind is something distinct from the brain with which it normally interacts, then it is at least conceivable that it could, in certain circumstances, interact with other physical objects or systems. If, on the contrary, there is no distinction between mind and brain, inasmuch as mental processes are just a function of brain processes, then, clearly it makes nonsense to talk of the mind functioning independently of the brain.

Now it so happens that there is already what one can only describe as a vast amount of evidence, which, if taken at its face value, would suggest that mind interacts on occasion, with external physical objects. I refer, of course, to parapsychology (Beloff 1974, 1977).

Although, in our present state of ignorance, parapsychology has to be defined in purely negative terms, i.e. as the study of those phenomena that cannot be explained in terms of accepted scientific principles, that is to say in materialist terms, conceptually, it could be thought of as concerned with those powers of mind that are irreducibly mental or non-physical.

According to this positive conception parapsychology could be defined as that part of psychology which deals with the mind-matter interface. At a more concrete operational level parapsychology is concerned with two particular phenomena:

(a) where an organism obtains information about events remote in space and/or time without such information being conveyed via any known physical channels, as is the case with normal perception
    and:
(b) where an organism influences events remote in space and/or time again without such an effect being transmitted via any known physical channels as is the case with normal motor activity.

(a) is known technically as ESP and (b) is known technically as PK and, collectively, the phenomena are known technically as PSI.

Although, as I have said, the evidence for PSI is extensive, much of it is of an inferior quality, some of it is definitely suspect and none of it is decisive. It is not decisive for one very good reason: there is as yet no PSI effect that can be demonstrated on demand.

Science cannot afford to relax the rule, which demands that any new claim must be confirmable by those competent to test it. Whether PSI phenomena are peculiarly elusive or non-existent or whether we simply do not yet know enough about the conditions under which they occur to ensure their reproducibility, the fact remains that they cannot qualify as yet for inclusion into the body of accepted scientific knowledge. Nevertheless, when this has been said, the fact remains that one would need to be either very ignorant or very prejudiced or, better still, both to argue that the evidence is so derisory that it can safely be ignored in this context.

What the materialist must ask, therefore, is, assuming that the evidence is valid, does it necessitate an interactionist interpretation or could it in the last resort be reconciled with materialism? It is true that nothing so far known to brain-science would have led us to suspect that the brain, as a physical system, could communicate with objects remote in space, let alone in time, nevertheless one can never say that one is never in a position to say that all the physical possibilities have been exhaustively considered. Hence, however tempting it may be to describe PSI phenomena in terms of mind-matter interactions, alternative conceptualizations cannot be excluded.

Two developments within parapsychology would, I believe, upset the case for claiming this field as affording empirical grounds for the interactionist thesis. If it were possible to demonstrate ESP or PK using only computers or other appropriate artifacts or using only living tissue in vitro or even plants in lieu of a human or animal subject, in other words systems to which we would not normally attribute a mind, there would be little temptation left to think of such phenomena as a manifestation of mind. The state would be set for their eventual incorporation into an extended and revised physics and materialism and, with it, the unity of science would be vindicated. But if this does not happen and if, nevertheless, parapsychological claims become increasingly hard to ignore, then the case for interactionism would become more than just a metaphysical choice.

To avoid misunderstanding at this point, it should not be thought that the interactionist will have to propose certain paraphysical forces or energies to make up for the missing physical connections, as one often finds in the more naive parapsychological theories. It is much more plausible to suppose that the way in which mind and matter interact is different in kind from the way matter interacts with matter. There is a strong suggestion, which I cannot enlarge upon here, that, in PK for example, the effect is produced not by feeding additional energy into the target-system but rather by feeding in pure information so as to alter the probabilities of events at the microphysical level while leaving the overall energy of the system invariant. There is likewise a strong suggestion that PSI processes may be irreducibly teleological in their mode of action by which I mean that the end somehow dictates the specific means, which bring about its fulfillment. But this takes us into the realm of speculation, critics might even say into the realm of magic.

For the present, and in all probability for a very long time to come, it must remain a matter of philosophical opinion whether mind is for anything, and if so, what precisely it is for, or whether mind is merely an aspect of matter which, by the grace of nature as it were, happens to be associated with the workings of our brain. Psychology as we have known it so far could teach us only about the behavior and experience of the unified psychophysical organism; it might be, however, that the mind-science of tomorrow, when paranormal as well as normal phenomena have been taken into account, will be able to return an unequivocal answer to the question of why we have minds at all.

References

Armstrong, D. M. (1968). *A materialist theory of mind*. London: RKP.

Beloff, J. (Ed.). (1974). *New directions in parapsychology*. London: Elek.

Beloff, J. (1977). Historical overview. In B. B. Woiman (Ed.), *Handbook of parapsychology*. New York, NY: Van Nostrand.

Boden, M. A. (1972). *Purposive explanation in psychology*. Cambridge, MA: Harvard University Press.

Eccles, J. C. (1965). *The brain and the unity of conscious experience. 19th Eddington Memorial Lecture*. Cambridge: Cambridge University Press.
Kirk, R. (1974). Sentience and behavior. *Mind, 83*, 43–60.
Luria, A. R. (1972). *The man with a shattered world.* Harmondsworth: Penguin.
Monod, J. (1971). *Chance and necessity*. New York, NY: Knopf.
Nagel, T. (1971). Brain bisection and the unity of consciousness. Synthese, 22, 396-413 Reprinted in J. Glover (Ed.) (1976). *The philosophy of mind.* Oxford: Oxford University Press
Ryle, G. (1949). *The concept of mind*. London: Hutchinson.
Sperry, R. W. (1965). Brain bisection and mechanisms of consciousness. In J. C. Eccles (Ed.), *Brain and conscious experience*. Berlin: Springer.
Trevarthen, C. (1974). Analysis of central activities that generate and regulate consciousness in commissurotomy patients. In S. J. Dimond & J. G. Beaumont (Eds.), *Hemisphere function in the human brain*. London: Elek Science.
Zangwill, O. L. (1974). Consciousness and the cerebral hemispheres. In S. J. Dimond & J. Graham Beaumont (eds.), *Heremisphere Function in the Human Brain*. Hobiken, NJ: Wiley.
Zangwill, O. L. (1976). Thought and the brain. *British Journal of Psychology, 67*, 301–314.

Towards a Tri-Dimensional Model of Happiness: A Logo-Philosophical Perspective

Stephen J. Costello

Happiness Must Not be Pursued

Every follower of Frankl knows that happiness must not be pursued, that it must ensue; happiness happens. For Frankl, happiness is a by-product, a side effect of man's search for meaning as the primary motivating factor. This article addresses the dialectic between happiness and meaning by showing parallels between Frankl's approach to the subject and the work of some contemporary philosophers. The hermeneutics of Paul Ricoeur, the French phenomenologist, seeks meaning "in spite of" meaninglessness, misery and failure; the equivalent in Frankl would be the hope that the "triumphant triad" (of healing, forgiveness and meaning) would overcome the "tragic triad" (of suffering/pain, guilt and death). Charles Taylor, a contemporary Canadian philosopher, in his, *A Secular Age*, argues that finding meaning in fulfillment, what he labels "fullness" and which he relates to transcendence (Frankl's "supra-meaning"), is superior to immanentistic flourishing (*eudaimonia*). As such, the philosophical positions adopted by Frankl, Taylor and others represent implicit critiques of an Aristotelian eudaimonistic ethic, which has been so prevalent in the Western philosophical tradition. Aristotle explicitly argued in his *Nicomachean Ethics* that every pursuit aims at some good (teleology) and the good or happiness is that at which all things *aim* (see Aristotle 1978, 63). It will be shown, by reference to some logotherapeutic techniques, that Frankl's phenomenological

Dr Stephen J. Costello is a philosopher, logotherapist, and existential analyst, director of the Viktor Frankl Institute of Ireland and author of over ten books, the most recent being: *Philosophy and the Flow of Presence* and *The Truth about Lying*.

S.J. Costello (✉)
Viktor Frankl Institute of Ireland, Dartmouth Terrace, Ranelagh, Dublin 6, Ireland
e-mail: stephenjcostello@eircom.net

A. Batthyány (ed.), *Logotherapy and Existential Analysis*, Logotherapy and Existential Analysis: Proceedings of the Viktor Frankl Institute Vienna 1,
DOI 10.1007/978-3-319-29424-7_30

psychology, lacking in the purely philosophical perspectives, is the empirical linchpin that consolidates the thesis that, (1) happiness should not be aimed at directly contra Aristotle, and (2) rather, finding or locating meaning in life is paramount, both philosophically and psychologically.

A Hermeneutics of Happiness

Nietzsche had proclaimed that life itself is interpretation; if this is true then philosophy is the interpretation of interpretations, i.e., hermeneutics. For Ricoeur, there is interpretation where there is multiple meaning. There are diverse hermeneutics; a Freud sees everything in terms of a semantics of desire; a Nietzsche and an Adler see everything in terms of will to power, a Marx sees everything in terms of capital and class consciousness. If we could put all the hermeneutic readings together we may catch a glimpse of the Promised Land of ultimate understanding; it would be, in Ricoeur's felicitous phrase, a 'hermeneutics of God's coming, of the approach of his Kingdom' (Ricoeur 2004, 20). Due to equivocal expressions being endemic in language, hermeneutics remains unsurpassable. No one reading of anything can give us an exhaustive explanation; our viewpoints are restricted and limited, our perspectives partial but that doesn't mean they need to be reductionistic. All contributions are modest and myopic. We see only small sections of reality. Philosophers, as well as everyone else, grasp things generally from one point of view. So, in this piece, I would like to explore a hermeneutics of happiness in relation to meaning. My thesis is Franklian: rather than speaking of "the meaning of happiness" we should speak instead of "the happiness of meaning". Similarly, the meaning of life is a life of meaning.

Happiness, Duty and Desire

Freud

At the end of *The Future of an Illusion*, Freud exclaims., that he can offer us no consolation, no happiness, only harshness and resignation to *Ananke*, to the blows of fate and fortune, to what in "Beyond the Pleasure Principle", he calls "sublime" Necessity (Freud 1920, 317). And at the end of his *Studies on Hysteria* Freud informs us that his aim is to replace neurotic suffering with common human *unhappiness*. For Freud, tragic knowledge is reconciliation with the inevitable and self-understanding comes slowly through suffering. Ricoeur sums up the Freudian position thus: "In this terrible battle for meaning, nothing and no one comes out unscathed. The 'timid' hope must cross the desert of the path of mourning" (Ricoeur 2004, 172). We work towards meaning which for Freud merely represents our infantile consolation. Freud strips the ego of its omnipotence; he wounds us well and forces desire to accept its own death. However, the reductive hermeneutics of Marx, Nietzsche, and Freud are welcomed by Ricoeur (which doesn't mean that they are accepted). Because it is from a moment of destruction that we can find inspiration and instruction and on surer foundations than before. All three offer their deconstructive critiques of religion; for Marx, to believe in God is a form of alienation; God is a projection for Freud (and for Feuerbach) and based on an infantile illusion. Nietzsche had proclaimed God dead. But none of them really ever speak of God, only the Gods of men and these we will always have with us. According to the hermeneutic hypothesis of these three "masters of suspicion", as Ricoeur calls them, "man is a being sick with the sublime" (Ricoeur 2004, 335). However, for Ricoeur, the Protestant, the sacred calls upon man confronting him with the ethical task of moving from slavery and sin to sanctity and sense. We are urged toward hope and happiness while realizing that "happiness is not our accomplishment: it is achieved by superaddition, by surplus" (Ricoeur 2004, 412). If it comes, it comes as a gift, as grace.

For Kant, whom Frankl controversially calls "the greatest philosopher of all times" (Frankl 1988, 122), we have an indirect duty to seek our own happiness, in so far as this is compatible with the moral law but we need to make ourselves *worthy* of happiness. Furthermore, happiness is one thing, being good is something else.

Kant

In the *Groundwork of the Metaphysic of Morals*, Kant .,writes: "To assure one's own happiness is a duty (at least, indirectly); for discontent with one's state, in a press of cares and amidst unsatisfied wants, might easily become a great *temptation to the transgression of duty*" (Kant 1985, 64). He goes on to say that we all have the strongest inclination towards happiness but the "prescription for happiness is, however, often so constituted as greatly to interfere with some inclinations, and yet men cannot form under the name of 'happiness' any determinate and assured conception of satisfaction of all inclinations as a sum" (Kant 1985, ibid.). For Kant, happiness is ethical if seeking to further it is done, not from inclination, but from duty, then such conduct has "real moral worth" (Kant 1985, 65). There is one end that may be supposed as actual in all rational beings, to whom imperatives apply and there is one purpose, happiness. It is a hypothetical imperative (see Kant 1985, 79). Moreover, happiness is a nebulous or "indeterminate concept", that "although every man wants to attain … he can never say definitely and in unison with himself what it really is that he wants and wills" (Kant 1985, 81). What is required for the "Idea" of happiness as a whole is maximum wellbeing in my present and future state. But this is difficult, contends Kant. He asks:

> Is it riches that he wants? How much anxiety, envy, and pestering might he not bring in this way on his own head! Is it knowledge and insight? This might perhaps merely give him an eye so sharp that it would make evils at present hidden from him and yet unavoidable seem all the more frightful, or would add a load of still further needs to the desires which already give him trouble enough. Is it long life? Who will guarantee that it would not be a long misery? Is it at least health? How often has infirmity of body kept a man from excesses into which perfect health would have let him fall! – and so on. In short, he has no principle by

> which he is able to decide with complete certainty what will make him truly happy, since for this he would require omniscience …. What action will promote the happiness of a rational being is completely insoluble; and consequently that in regard to this there is no imperative possible which in the strictest sense could command us to do what will make us happy, since happiness is an Ideal, not of reason, but of imagination (Kant 1985, 81–2).

What he is saying here is that the categorical imperative (duty) cannot be based on any interest (desire).

Ricoeur

For Ricoeur, who was much influenced by Kant, .,and following the lead of St. Paul, in spite of death and misery and meaninglessness, we hope and wager in ultimate meaning. This "in spite of" sin and death, is the inverse, the shadow side, of the joyous "how much more than" which pertains to the logic of superabundance and surplus. Hope works towards the Kingdom of God despite evil and totalitarianism, which constitute the pathology of hope. For Kant, virtue is the obedience to pure duty and happiness is the satisfaction of desire. But perhaps, to venture a Hegelian synthesis here, duty is not incompatible with desire, or hope and happiness and meaning with sin, death, and despair? To put it in Franklian terms, to retain the pessimistic perspective of the tragic triad without permitting the triumphant triad into the frame of reference is lopsided. As such, to Freud's "cheerful pessimism", we may oppose Frankl's "tragic optimism". The glass, to take the clichéd example, is always half full and half empty at the same time. To put it another way, when the glass is half full it is also half empty. By focusing on the part that is full alone or empty alone one is incorporating a limited understanding of reality. Isn't wisdom the cognitive ability to discern both realities simultaneously and not one at the expense of the other, to have, as James Joyce put it, two thinks at a time? Blake had summarized such dialectical thinking thus: "There is no progress without contraries". So to the question: "would you like a cup of coffee or tea?" the only dialectical answer is "yes please"!

We should, therefore, not be in too much of a rush to leave the tragic in favor of the triumphant but to retain both perspectives in a delicate dialectical and dynamic tension; in Hegel's memorable phrase, we need to spend some time "looking the negative in the face, and tarrying with it. This tarrying with the negative…" (Hegel 1997, § 32, 19) is one side of the dialectic and an important one lest we become humanistic hopefuls or positive psychologists who toe the Dalai Lama line: "The purpose of life is to be happy" as he puts it (Cutler and His Holiness the Dalai Lama 1998, xiii). The other extreme is Schopenhauerian pessimism. Frankl's shorthand is "D = S-M" (the DSM!): "*despair is suffering without meaning*" (Frankl 2000, 132). In such a situation we are prone to experience with Shakespeare's Hamlet the feelings he describes thus: "How weary, stale, flat and unprofitable seem to me all the uses of the world. Fie on it!" (Act I, Scene II). But suffering need not be an obstacle to happiness—often it is a means to it, less a pathology than a path.

The modern-day moral injunction is: "*happiness as the supreme duty*", as Slavoj Žižek, the Lacanian Slovenian philosopher, puts it in his *In Defense of Lost Causes*

(Žižek 2008, 44). But, against this tradition that Žižek is also critiquing, Frankl contends that meaning rather than happiness is the objective—what Ricoeur calls "a hermeneutics of meaning" (Ricoeur 2004, 139). Meaning is embodied in human intersubjectivity, "in art, in symbols, in language, and in the lives and deeds of persons" as Bernard Lonergan, S. J., puts it in his *Method in Theology* (Lonergan 1971, 57). In his discussion on what constitutes meaning, Lonergan cites three works of Frankl: *The Doctor and the Soul*, *Man's Search for Meaning*, *The Will to Meaning* and, with others, *Psychotherapy and Existentialism* (see Lonergan 1971, 70). For Lonergan, it is incarnate meaning that combines many of the carriers of meaning: *Cor ad cor loquitur*. It can be intersubjective, artistic, symbolic, linguistic; it is "the meaning of a person, of his way of life, of his words, or of his deeds" (Lonergan 1971, 73). He notes: "Meaning enters into the very fabric of human living" (Lonergan 1971, 81). (Meaning is communicative, constitutive, efficient and cognitive). We move from an infant's world of immediacy into a world mediated by meaning (see Lonergan 1971, 89) and in this world man discovers mind; he discovers logos which, as Frankl says, is deeper than logic (see Frankl 2004a, b, 122). Lonergan observes: "There is an intelligence, a *logos*, that steers through all things. It is found in God and man and beast, the same in all though in different degrees. To know it, is wisdom" (Lonergan 1971, 91). As Heraclitus, the Pre-Socratic, said: "When you have listened not to me but to the logos it is wise to agree that all is one". Philosophically, it is hermeneutics which "studies the varying relations of acts of meaning to terms of meaning" (Lonergan 1971, 92) and which, in terms of a hermeneutics of religion, interprets this Logos that was in the beginning. The Logos as Word is "the bearer of all grace and of all reality", in Karl Rahner, S.J.'s beautiful words (Rahner 1941, 41).

Logotherapy

The *three* basic foundations of Frankl's existential analysis are: (1) the freedom of the will—we are free to search for meaning, (2) the will to meaning—we have a will to find meaning, and (3) the meaning of life—that life is always worth living. Hence, his redeployment of the ancient symbol *logos* in his "logotherapy", where *logos* is intended to signify "the spiritual" and denote "meaning". By contrast, "logophobia" is a term we may use, following Eric Voegelin's lead, to describe a fear and hatred of philosophy, of a refusal to engage in the search for meaning and the truth of existence. Voegelin, Lonergan, and Frankl would hold that our *nous* is capable of comprehending eternal being, that *Geist* is the core of the human person. Man is a "psycho–physico–spiritual entity" in Frankl's words (Frankl 2009, 28). Voegelin acknowledges Frankl's work in existential psychology and expresses his gratitude to him for rediscovering what Schelling called "'pneumopathology', Frankl's 'noological dimension' of man, as well as the treatment of its diseases by 'logotherapy'. It would not be surprising if sooner or later psychologists and social scientists were to find out about the classic analysis of noetic existence as the proper theoretical basis for the psychopathology of the 'age'". (Voegelin 1990a, b, 278–9; Commenting on both Frankl and Voegelin, Prof. David Walsh, a Voegelin expert, writes thus, in a private communication with the author: “Frankl is essentially a parallel figure to Voegelin, who appreciated him as doing something similar. The core convergence seems to be on the need for spiritual order, an order of the soul, as the basis for the life of reason”. Fr. Brendan Purcell, an expert on Voegelin and Lonergan, wrote to me that: “Voegelin admired Frankl and felt he had rediscovered Platonic ‘therapy’)”. Rahner similarly writes that the human person is spirit (see Rahner 1941, 9). He notes: “To be human is to be spirit [*Der Mensch ist Geist*], i.e., to live life while reaching ceaselessly for the absolute, in openness toward God …. We are forever the infinite openness of the finite for God” (Rahner 1941, 53). Spirit is the intellectual soul in man. And the spirit can never be sick (Frankl’s psychiatric credo).

So we are enjoined to find (spiritual) meaning in life, to seize the “meaning of the moment” and to fulfill ultimate meaning through noetic existence. Frankl believes that “the greatness of a life can be measured by the greatness of a moment …. a single moment can retroactively flood an entire life with meaning” (Frankl 2009, 58). We do not know what life has still in store for us, or what “magnificent hour may still await” us (Frankl 2009, 69).

Frankl sets out *three* ways as to how we can find meaning: (1) by being creative, (2) by experiencing something (especially experiencing the True, the Good, and the Beautiful) or encountering someone, and (3) by changing one’s attitude to unavoidable suffering or unchangeable situations. The last one—attitudinal values—entails facing one’s fate without flinching; the ancient Stoics gave prominence to this the last of human freedoms in their philosophical *therapeia*. It testifies to the enduring and “defiant power of the human spirit”. As Plutarch puts it: “The measure of a man is the way he bears up under misfortune”.

Lack of meaning or the impossibility to fulfill meaning potential is the main reason for the “existential vacuum” of *ennui* and apathy, of doubt, despair, hopelessness, and spiritual *acedia*. Such is the *taedium vitae*. Yes, Frankl says, “things are bad” (Frankl 2000, 89) but unless we seek to ameliorate them, everything will become worse! To live is to suffer but to survive is to find some meaning in suffering. Frankl often asked his patients why they didn’t commit suicide, thus recognizing with Albert Camus, that the only philosophical question is whether we should commit suicide out of disgust with life. *If* there is meaning, it is unconditional and neither suffering nor dying can detract from it (see Frankl 2000, 156). To trust there is transcendental in the Kantian sense. Indeed, it is tempting to read Frankl as a transcendental Thomist. Religion is the fulfillment of this will to ultimate meaning (see Frankl 2000, 153) and to this end, Frankl cites: “To be religious is to have found an answer to the question, What is the meaning of life?”: “To believe in God is to see that life has a meaning” (see Frankl 2000, 153).

Happiness Versus Meaning

Franklian psychology teaches that *life does not owe us happiness, it offers us meaning*. Happiness, like success and satisfaction, are by-products of our pursuit of meaning. And all meaning converges in the highest meaning, that is to say, in transcendent reality. As such, our search for meaning is implicitly, if construed theistically, (and it doesn't have to be so construed) a search for God, for the intelligent Ground of being, for the divine Logos. Ultimate meaning may be approached, it is never appropriated; by contrast, the meaning of the moment can be found and fulfilled. This involves being mindful of the moment as we tend and attend to, as well as profit from, the present instant and the call of the hour.

Franklian psychology and philosophy deny *three* attitudes: nihilism, which is the denial of meaning; reductionism, which is the denial of the will to meaning; and pandeterminism, which is the denial of our freedom to find meaning. Isn't neurosis an illness of the soul that has not found meaning in life, as Jung hypothesized? The most fruitful arena wherein meaning can be found is self-transcendence, that is, the human ability or capacity to reach or stretch out beyond ourselves. For Bernard Lonergan, "Man achieves authenticity in self-transcendence" (Lonergan 1971, 104). The pursuit of happiness, by contrast, is the pursuit of self-fulfillment; it ignores the Other. We are driven to gain things for ourselves instead of doing things for others. For Frankl, this is the paradox of pleasure. For example, the more we seek pleasure or happiness, the less we find it. Why? Because pleasure is a by-product of having done something meaningful like happiness. At the heart of the pursuit of pleasure and happiness is ultimate failure and paradox. Happiness must not be aimed at directly; this is Frankl's constant refrain. We have to let it happen by not caring about it, or giving it our energy. The surest way to be unhappy is to fixate on happiness, to demand or desire it, to hyper-reflect on it. We need to surrender to it happening, to let go and forget about it. Self-transcendence is the ultimate ethical and spiritual "beyond" of self-actualization. Hyperintention is the excessive striving for a goal such as happiness or pleasure. Frankl encourages us to dereflect from this egotistical pursuit of happiness. As such, we need to *find meaning* and *forget about happiness*! It is the noetic dimension of the human spirit that contains the core of our vast spiritual resources, amongst which is our human capacity for self-transcendence. We are not self-enclosed Leibnitzian monads; we open out to the Other. Self-transcendence is, in Rahner's words, a "reaching for more" (Rahner 1994, 47). We "continually transcend everything toward pure being" (Rahner 1994, 53), which is the fullness of absolute, supramundane, infinite Being. For Rahner, being is luminous, being is light; being is lucidity. The human person is a spirit reaching out into the divine domain that "only the fullness of God's absolute being can fill" (Rahner 1994, 54). For the theist, "God is the meaning of humanity" (Rahner 1994, 19), not happiness.

In the Preface to the 1992 edition of *Man's Search for Meaning*, Frankl tells us that the following was the advice he gave to his students:

> Don't aim at success – the more you aim at it and make it a target, the more you are going to miss it. For success, like happiness, cannot be pursued; it must ensue, and it only does so as the unintended side effect of one's dedication to a cause greater than oneself or as the by-product of one's surrender to a person other than oneself. Happiness must happen, and the same holds for success: you have to let it happen by not caring about it. I want you to listen to what your conscience commands you to do and go on to carry it out to the best of your knowledge. Then you will live to see that in the long run – in the long run, I say! – success will follow you precisely because you had *forgotten* to think of it (Frankl 2004a, b, 12–3).

According to Frankl, man lives and moves in his everyday life in a dimension whose positive pole is success and whose negative pole is failure. However, the *Homo patiens* (the suffering man) who, by virtue of his humanness is capable of rising above his suffering moves in a dimension whose positive pole is fulfillment and whose negative pole is despair. A human being strives for success but that doesn't depend on his fate. By the very attitude he chooses, man is capable of finding and fulfilling meaning even in hopeless situations. For Frankl, there can be as much meaning in suffering as in success. As he states: "*Lack of success does not signify lack of meaning*" (Frankl 2004a, b, 110). This philosophical position is only comprehensible through Frankl's dimensional approach, his construal of man as being body, mind, and spirit, which form a biopsychospiritual unity—there is, of course, also the social dimension. Frankl allots to the attitudinal values a higher dimension that to creative and experiential values. One can have a successful career and yet feel that one's life is meaningless and feel caught or trapped in the existential vacuum ("ev"), below "success" and at the right side of "despair", in the diagram below (see Frankl 1988, 75), in which case, we may speak, as Frankl does, of *despair despite success*. On the other hand, there is a phenomenon which can be described as *fulfillment despite failure*, localized in the upper left angle, marked by "SQ" (San Quentin).

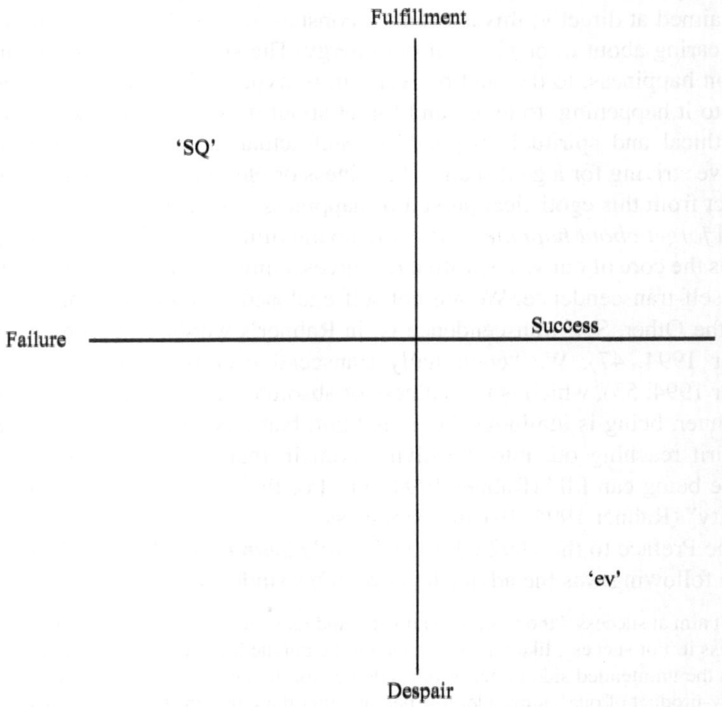

In the light of Frankl's dimensional anthropology and ontology, despair is compatible with success, just as fulfillment of meaning is compatible with suffering and dying (see Frankl 1988). As Goethe once remarked: "There is no predicament that we cannot ennoble either by doing or enduring".

Happiness and success and pleasure have one thing in common: they are substitutes for fulfillment, derivatives of the will to meaning, in this Franklian logo-philosophical, tri-dimensional perspective. Interestingly, it was John Stuart Mill who first counseled caution in relation to the direct aiming at happiness. In his *Autobiography* Mill muses: "But I now thought that this end [one's happiness] was only to be attained by not making it the direct end. Those only are happy (I thought) who have their minds fixed on some object other than their own happiness …. Aiming thus at something else, they find happiness along the way …. Ask yourself whether you are happy, and you cease to be so" (Mill 1909, 94). Henry Sidgwick, the English utilitarian philosopher and follower of Mill, made the same point in his *The Methods of Ethics*, that we should put happiness "out of sight and not directly aim at it" (Sidgwick 1963, 3). Pascal, for his part, tells us "All men seek happiness. There are no exceptions" (Pascal 1995, no. 148, 74–5). But this demand for happiness can wait; it must be postponed. The ancient Stoics taught us to withdraw into ourselves to find peace whereas others advise us to look outside ourselves. Pascal asserts: "Happiness is neither outside nor inside us: it is in God, both outside and inside us" (Pascal 1995, 407).

Let us repeat: the essence of existence is self-transcendence. Existence is both intentional and transcendent. Self-actualization is possible only as a side effect of self-transcendence (see Frankl 2004a, b, 115). For Frankl, our whole therapeutic culture stresses the idea that we ought to be happy, that we have a *right* to be happy, "that unhappiness is a symptom of maladjustment" (Frankl 2004a, b, 118). But paradoxically, our burden is increased by unhappiness about being unhappy! Frankl continues:

> One must have a reason "to be happy". Once the reason is found, however, one becomes happy automatically. As we see, a human being is not one in pursuit of happiness but rather in search of a reason to become happy, last not least, through actualizing the potential meaning inherent and dormant in a given situation …. Once an individual's search for a meaning is successful, it not only renders him happy but also gives him the capability to cope with suffering (Frankl 2004a, b, 140–1).

Pleasure

Frankl is critical of Freud's emphasis on pleasure being the goal of life (the pleasure principle or what Frankl calls the "will-to-pleasure"). Pleasure, far from being the goal of our endeavors and aspirations, is the consequence of attaining them, as Kant had pointed out. In *The Doctor and the Soul*, Frankl opines: "Commenting on the hedonist ethics, eudemonism, Scheler has remarked that pleasure does not loom up before us as the goal of an ethical act; rather, an ethical act carries pleasure on its back" (Frankl 2009, 51–2). According to Frankl, life teaches most people that we are not here to enjoy ourselves (see Frankl 2009, 53); we experience more unpleasurable sensations than pleasurable ones. People don't necessarily want pleasure; they want what they want. If we set up pleasure as the whole meaning of life, in the final analysis, life will seem meaningless. "Pleasure cannot possibly lend meaning to life" (Frankl 2009, ibid.). Now the man who first stated the supremacy of pleasure was Eudoxus (406–355 BC), a pupil of Plato's.

For Eudoxus and Epicurus later, pleasure is the supreme Good (see Aristotle 1978, 86). Aristotle, in his *Ethics*, summarizes the main philosophical positions on pleasure as: (1) some say that no pleasure is a good, (2) others say that some pleasures are good but that most are bad; and (3) even if all pleasures are good, pleasure itself cannot be the supreme good (see Aristotle 1978, 250). For Aristotle, pleasure is necessary up to a point but excessive or insufficient enjoyment of pleasure is not. Pleasure is a constituent of happiness; it is not itself happiness however. According to Aristotle, (see Aristotle 1978, 256) when people feel excessive pain in life they tend to pursue excessive pleasure, especially bodily pleasure as a cure for their suffering (Frankl makes a similar point when he says that when people are in the existential vacuum they usually fill it up with libidinal dynamics). But Aristotle advises us not to become slaves to self-indulgence, to avoid licentiousness and lead lives of temperateness and moderation instead. We ought "to put on immortality" (Aristotle 1978, 331) while realizing that "pleasure and pain permeate the whole of life" (Aristotle 1978, 312). He observes: "The best and most pleasant life is the life of the intellect, since the intellect is in the fullest sense the man. So this life will also be the happiest" (Aristotle 1978, 331). Happiness, for Aristotle, is co-extensive with contemplation.

As early as 1911 in "Formulations on the Two Principles of Mental Functioning", Freud had written that the human organism strives "towards gaining pleasure" (Freud 1911, 36). The "reality principle" does not negate the dominance of the pleasure principle; it merely postpones satisfactions, according to the Freudian formulation. The "pleasure-ego" works for a yield of pleasure and attempts to avoid unpleasure. Of course, for Lacan, unpleasure can itself be a source of pleasure, an experience he labels *jouissance*. In 1920, in "Beyond the Pleasure Principle", Freud announced, in his second theory of the instincts, that there was something "beyond pleasure" and that is pain or the death drive (*Thanatos*). However, even the first sentence of this work suggests no abandonment of his previous perspective of 9 years earlier: "In the theory of psychoanalysis we have no hesitation in assuming that the course taken by mental events is automatically regulated by the pleasure principle" (Freud 1920, p. 275). He says he is not concerned what philosophical system his hypothesis of the pleasure principle may be placed in; actually, it may be described as philosophical materialism. He still states his belief in "the dominance of the pleasure principle in mental life" (Freud 1920, 277). Of course, there are other principles, such as the reality principle but for Freud this doesn't negate the pleasure principle, as we have said. Freud wonders, "if there is a 'beyond the pleasure principle'" (Freud 1920, 305). Even the death drive, for Freud, is pleasurable in that "*the aim of all life is death*" (Freud 1920, 311). Life is a circuitous path to death, death, which the ego-instincts *desire*. The tendency of mental life is towards constancy, the removal of internal tension, what Freud calls (borrowing this phrase from Barbara Low) the *Nirvana principle* (see Freud 1920, 329), a tendency, he writes, which "finds expression in the pleasure principle" (Freud 1920, ibid.). He concludes by opining that there are many processes in the mental life of man, "matters over which the pleasure principle has as yet no control; but it does not follow that any of them are necessarily opposed to it" (Freud 1920, 336). The search for pleasure is intense. In relation to the paradox of pleasure, Freud observes: "Hence arises the paradoxical situation that the living organism struggles most energetically against events (dangers, in fact) which might help it to attain its life's aim rapidly—by a kind of short-circuit" (Freud 1920, 312).

This "pleasure paradox" is known in ethics too; pleasure and happiness, it is said, are strange phenomena; they do not obey normal principles. The paradox of hedonism points out that pleasure cannot be acquired directly, only indirectly, which is the Franklian position too. Somewhere in *Either/Or* Kierkegaard says: "most men pursue pleasure with such breathless haste that they hurry past it". To secure it, we need to shun it. Abstain in order to obtain. To get, forget. To give an example: suppose my best friend Darren likes martial arts. According to utilitarianism and most socio-psychological models of human behavior, it is believed that Darren likes martial arts because he gets a pleasure from this activity. However, if you tell Darren this, he is likely to disagree. He does get pleasure from martial arts but this is not the process that explains *why* he does martial arts. He is not saying to himself: "I must do martial arts in order to obtain pleasure". Martial arts are not just a means towards pleasure. Darren just likes martial arts. Pleasure and happiness cannot be reverse engineered. If you heard that martial arts or philately, just to give another example, was very pleasurable and started a stamp collection as a means towards happiness or pleasure, it would inevitably be in vain. To achieve happiness or pleasure, you must not seek it directly but motivate yourself towards things unrelated to pleasure or happiness, like the collection of stamps. The pleasure paradox means that if one sets oneself a goal to please oneself too highly (hyperintention) then the mechanism jams itself. To attain pleasure or happiness (and they are often mistakenly equated) we must put them out of sight. Aristotle had alerted us to the futility of purely pursuing pleasure because pleasure is not continuous. Furthermore, sooner or later finite beings will be unable to acquire and expend the resources necessary to maintain their sought-after goals of pleasure and ultimately we all find ourselves in the company of misery and miss out on the experience of joy.

Pleasure, Happiness, Joy

At the bodily level we thirst for pleasure and sense experience—these come from the world; at the soul level we seek happiness and knowledge—these come from ourselves; but joy and wisdom pertain to the level of spirit, which is the deepest level; they come from God. One philosopher opines: "Happiness is to pleasure what knowledge of truth is to awareness of sense data: a deeper level" (Kreeft 1989, 126). Spirit is dynamic just as joy is infinite. Self-transcendence means that joy lies outside the self. Self-forgetfulness is the secret of joy. Pleasure is agitated aliveness, happiness "has peace in place of agitation, but sleepy satisfaction in place of aliveness. Only joy has both peace and aliveness, aliveness without agitation and peace without sleepiness" (Kreeft 1989, 142). Joy is not homeostasis; it does not obey the Freudian "constancy principle". Joy is pure affirmation. The same philosopher goes on:

> Pleasure is the restless mind moving along a line, never reaching the end. Happiness is the mind resting at the end. Joy is the mind eternally moving *at* the end, motion at a point …. Pleasure is moving; happiness is still; joy is moving while still. Pleasure is like work, happiness is like sleep, joy is like play. Pleasure is like action, happiness is like rest, joy is like contemplation (Kreeft 1989, 143).

So these three: pleasure, happiness, and joy. The higher dimensions include but transcend the lower. Thus, one can have pleasure without happiness and happiness without joy but one can't have happiness without pleasure or joy without both happiness and pleasure.

Desire is not an obstacle to joy as it is in Buddhism, where desire is seen as the cause of suffering. Christianity asks us instead to purify our desires, from selfish to unselfish and attach them to right objects (God rather than idols). "For joy is always directed towards an object", Frankl writes (2009, 55). Joy is an intentional emotion. Frankl observes:

> How well Kierkegaard expressed this in his maxim that the door to happiness opens outward. Anyone who tries to push this door open thereby causes it to close still more. The man who is desperately anxious to be happy thereby cuts off his own path to happiness. Thus in the end all striving for happiness – for the supposed 'ultimate' in human life – proves to be in itself impossible (Frankl 2009, 55).

Further on in the same book Frankl repeats, in a Kantian vein:

> we see how misguided all striving for happiness is, how the desperate attempt to achieve happiness, to achieve pleasure as such, is condemned to miscarry. … the striving for happiness is not one of man's basic drives; that in general, life is not directed towards pleasure at all. Kant has remarked that man wants to be happy, but that what he ought to want is to be worthy of happiness. We hold, however, that man does not want to be happy. Rather, he wants to have a reason for being happy. Which is to say that all deflection of his desire from the object to the desire itself, from the aim (the reason for being happy) to the pleasure (the consequence of attaining the aim), represents a derivative mode of human striving (Frankl 2009, 155).

In *Man's Search for Ultimate Meaning*, Frankl maintains that happiness is the side effect of living out the self-transcendence of existence. "Once one has served a cause or is involved in loving another human being, happiness occurs by itself. The will-to-pleasure, however, contradicts the self-transcendent quality of human reality. And it also defeats itself, for pleasure and happiness are by-products. Happiness must ensue. It cannot be pursued. It is the very pursuit of happiness that thwarts happiness. The more one makes happiness an aim, the more he misses the aim". (Frankl 2000, 89–90; see also Frankl 1988, 33).

To this end, Frankl quotes Albert Schweitzer: "The only ones among you who will be really happy are those who have sought and found how to serve" (Frankl 2000, 157). What is behind the emphasis on power or sexual pleasure, according to Frankl, is the frustrated "will to meaning". Self-transcendence, by contrast, involves living with intentionality, oriented towards values and meaning. If there is a *reason* for happiness, happiness ensues, automatically and spontaneously. Frankl observes:

> And that is why one need not pursue happiness, one need not care for it once there is a reason for it. But even more, one cannot pursue it. To the extent to which one makes happiness the

> objective of his motivation, he necessarily makes it the object of his attention. But precisely by so doing he loses sight of the reason for happiness, and happiness itself must fade away (Frankl 1988, 34).

The very pursuit of pleasure and happiness is what thwarts it. Hyper-intention and hyper-reflection are likely to cause or create neurotic patterns of behavior. Pleasure, no more than happiness, is not the goal of human strivings, rather, it is the side effect of attaining a goal; it is this attaining of a goal that constitutes a reason for being happy. If there is a *reason* for being happy, happiness ensues. Frankl (1988, 34) depicts this philosophy in a diagram thus:

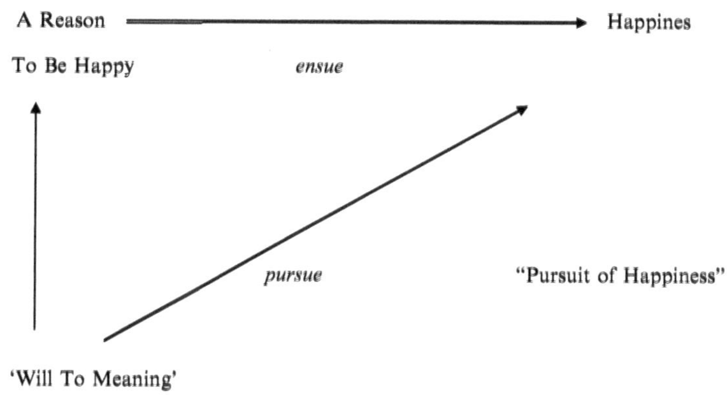

And what is true for happiness is also true for peak-experiences, in Maslow's sense: they too must ensue. Maslow himself said that "hunting peaks is a little like hunting happiness" (cited by Frankl 1988, 39). Thus, there is a self-defeating quality inherent in the pursuit of pleasure, peak-experiences, power, happiness, health and self-actualization, too. In *The Doctor and the Soul*, Frankl notes: "This very 'pursuit of happiness', however, again is foredoomed to fail" (Frankl 2009, 237). The hysterical hunt for happiness needs to be forgotten.

In *On the Theory and Therapy of Mental Disorders*, Frankl observes: "The path to pleasure and self-actualization leads over the path of self-giving and self-forgetting" (Frankl 2004a, b, 32). Later in the same work, he continues: "the more he seeks his own pleasure, the more it escapes him, and finally the pleasure is completely lost" (Frankl 2004a, b, 123). We may liken it to insomnia. Sleep, as Dubois says in his introduction to Frankl's book, is a dove that flies away as soon as you make a grab for it. Or, to take another example, from the American conservative politician, William Bennett: "Happiness is like a cat, if you try to coax or call it, it will avoid you; it will never come. But if you pay no attention to it and go about your business, you'll find it rubbing against your legs and jumping into your lap". The striving and straining after happiness is, for Frankl, "misguided" and "neurotic" (Frankl 2009, 155 and 139, respectively). As Frankl puts it: "Once one has served a cause or is involved in loving another human being, happiness occurs by itself" (Frankl 2000, 89).

Elisabeth Lukas observes that at the level of psyche, we are pleasure-oriented but at the noetic level we are meaning-oriented (see Lukas 2000, 14). Frankl explains a bit repetitively, it has to be said: "Pleasure is also an effect that does not allow itself to be 'grabbed at'. Kierkegaard speaks analogously when he notes that the door to happiness opens outwards; it closes itself the more tightly as we try to push our way into happiness. We could say that the hunt for happiness scares it away—the fight for pleasure chases it away" (Frankl 2000, 126; see also 192 where he writes: "The hunt for happiness scares it away, the fight for pleasure drives it away"). Lukas elucidates the difference thus: she holds that logotherapy "calls the popular 'philosophy of happiness' of psychology into question. According to this philosophy, happiness is the fulfillment of needs. Taking the noetic dimension of human beings into consideration, happiness, however, means inner meaning fulfillment" (Lukas 2000, 30) and later in the same book she opines: "One is happy when one is good for something" (Lukas 2000, 168). And lest we are inclined to think that only logotherapists hold these views, it is worth citing the well-known American psychologist, Steven Pinker. In *How the Mind Works*, drawing on the work of the evolutionary psychologist, Donald Campbell, who described humans as beings on a "hedonistic treadmill" (cited by Pinker 1997, 393), Pinker, commenting on the psychology of pleasure, notes that, "the study of happiness often sounds like a sermon for traditional values. The numbers show that it is not the rich, privileged, robust, or good-looking who are happy, it is those who have spouses, friends, religion, and challenging, meaningful work" (Pinker 1997, ibid.). Campbell sums up his research thus: "The direct pursuit of happiness is a recipe for an unhappy life" (Pinker 1997, ibid.).

Dereflection

Frankl is explicit: the focus instead should be directed outward away from the pleasure-ego. "In the final analysis, dereflection means ignoring one's self" (Frankl 2004a, b, 207). It is the logotherapeutic technique of dereflection that promotes such self-forgetfulness. Putting it another way: self-transcendence is the basis of dereflection (just as paradoxical intention is the basis of self-detachment). Dereflection counters hyperintention and hypereflection by directing attention outward away from the ego. As Dubois observes: "Dereflection mobilizes the human capacity for self-transcendence" (Frankl 2004a, b, xxiii). A story is told about a man who was promised a 100 dollars if he would not think about a chameleon and although he had not, before that, thought about the lizard, now he couldn't stop thinking about it! But as soon as he was told to think about an elephant he stopped thinking about the chameleon! So dereflection puts the brakes on (pathological) hyperintention and acts as a guidepost that turns the mind to other thoughts that are more meaning-centered rather than ego-encased. The Irish philosopher and novelist, Iris Murdoch, gives an example in her *The Sovereignty of Good*. Murdoch relates:

I am looking out of my window in an anxious and resentful state of mind, oblivious of my surroundings, brooding perhaps on some damage done to my prestige. Then suddenly I observe a hovering kestrel. In a moment everything is altered. The brooding self with its hurt vanity has disappeared. There is nothing now but kestrel. And when I return to thinking of the other matter it seems less important. And of course this is something, which we may also do deliberately: give attention to nature in order to clear our minds of selfish care (Murdoch 1970, 84).

In this example, dereflection ushered in self-transcendence and an alteration, therefore, in moral vision. Frankl likes the line from Bernano's *Diary of a Country Priest*: 'It is easier than one believes to hate oneself; grace consists in forgetting the self'. Frankl expounds: "Persons do not exist for the sake of observing themselves and contemplating their own egos, rather, they exist in order to give themselves up, to give themselves away, to knowingly and lovingly devote themselves" (Frankl 2004a, b, 208). "And only to the degree that persons transcend themselves in this manner do they also fulfill themselves, in the service of a thing, or in the love of another person! In other words, human persons are wholly human only when they are absorbed in some things or are completely devoted to another person. And only those who forget themselves are completely themselves" (Frankl 2004a, b, 233). We must "let go" but this "letting go" is a surrendering to "more" rather than to "less". Frankl calls it "dereflection", as we have said; Assagioli, the founder of psychosynthesis, (see Assagioli 1965, 58, 197, 302; he mentions Frankl as a parallel figure to his own work. He says that Frankl, whom he calls a "spiritual existentialist" on p. 113 has emphasized the ethical element and religious tendencies in human nature on p. 36, and affirms the reality of spiritual experience, "of the 'noetic' or 'noological' dimension (as Frankl aptly calls it)", p.195; see also p. 197), calls it "disidentification"; Iris Murdoch calls it "unselfing"; Simone Weil calls it "décreation"; and Meister Eckhart calls it "detachment". A story illustrates the point nicely: it is the famous Zen story of the two monks, which is illustrative of our attachments and detachments and the problems we have in letting go.

Two monks were making a pilgrimage to venerate the relics of a great saint. During the course of their journey they came to a river where they met a beautiful young woman—an apparently worldly creature, dressed in expensive finery and with her hair done up in the latest fashion. She was afraid of the current and afraid of ruining her lovely clothing, so she asked the brothers if they would carry her across the river. The younger and more exacting of the brothers was offended at the very idea and turned away with an attitude of disgust. The older brother didn't hesitate and quickly put the woman upon his shoulders, carried her across the river and set her down on the other side. She thanked him and went on her way, and the brother waded back through the waters. The monks resumed their walk, the older one in perfect equanimity and enjoying the beautiful countryside while the younger one grew more and more brooding and distracted, so much so that he could keep silence no longer and suddenly burst out: 'Brother, we are taught to avoid contact with women and there you were not just touching a woman but carrying her on your shoulders!' The older monk looked at the younger one with a loving, pitiful smile and said: 'Brother, I set her down on the other side of the river; you are still carrying her.'

The younger monk was unable to dereflect; he was tormented and preoccupied by his own ego-projections. Through dereflection the spiritual resources of self-transcendence are employed. For Frankl, love and conscience are two manifestations of self-transcendence. Conscience, according to the Franklian formulation, is creative and intuitive and irreducible to the Freudian superego. It is also fallible—because it is human it can err. It may pit us against the customs and conventions and moral mores of society. It has the power to "discover unique meanings that contradict accepted values" (Frankl 1988, 63); indeed, it is the organ of meaning and comes as a "hint from Heaven". Love, for its part, "is that capacity which enables him [man] to grasp the other human being in his very uniqueness. Conscience is that capacity which empowers him to seize the meaning of a situation in its very uniqueness, and in the final analysis meaning is something unique" (Frankl 1988, 19). Meaning is also objective whereas pleasure is subjective satisfaction.

Meaning is more than being; indeed, it sets the pace for being (see Frankl 1988, 128). Our Augustinian hearts are indeed restless until they have found and fulfilled meaning outside our egos. "Human existence is not authentic unless it is lived in terms of self-transcendence" (Frankl 1988, 52). Frankl is adamant: "Self-transcendence is the essence of existence" (Frankl 1988, 50). It is the model of the spiritual or noetic unconscious and discloses "the essential transcendence of the spiritual unconscious", as Frankl puts it in *Man's Search for Ultimate Meaning* (Frankl 2000, 61). Conscience is transcendent. Frankl exhorts us to be the master of our will but servants of our conscience; in this respect, he speaks of "the transcendent quality of conscience" (Frankl 2000, 59), as it whispers ultimate meaning. The task of conscience is to disclose to man the *unum necesse*—the one thing necessary. Conscience reaches down into unconscious depths and stems from an unconscious ground; it is the premoral understanding of meaning (see Frankl 2000, 39). We need to listen to the still, small, silent voice of conscience and of grace in existence itself.

Meaning, however, cannot be bestowed; it must be found (by oneself). Meaning is not universal—values are, and humanity is (Voegelin speaks of "universal humanity" just as Frankl speaks of "monanthropism"). Meanings are unique to the individual. And we find such meanings creatively, experientially, and attitudinally. And for Frankl, we have the capacity to wrest and win meaning from life even up to our last breath. In *Psychotherapy and Existentialism*, Frankl notes: "To look for the general meaning of man's life would be comparable to asking a chess player: 'What is the best move?' There is no such thing as 'the best move' apart from the one that is best within the context of a particular situation of a particular game" (Frankl 1985, 67).

For Frankl, either life has meaning and if so it retains it or life has no meaning (see Frankl 2000, 129). He quotes Albert Einstein: "The man who regards his life as meaningless is not merely unhappy but hardly fit for life" (Frankl 2000, 134). For Frankl, we don't really care for happiness as such but rather for that which *causes* happiness (see Frankl 1988, 42). This is most noticeable in the case of unhappiness. Let us suppose someone is mourning the death of his beloved friend and he is offered some pills to tranquilize him and bring him relief from his depression. He may not actually want to anesthetize his grief. The drugs won't change anything; they won't revive his friend. In other words, the reason for being depressed remains. For Frankl, he will be concerned not with the *removal of* his depression but with the *reason for* his depression (see Frankl 1988, ibid).

For Lonergan, too, life has meaning and the human subject is self-transcending (see Lonergan 1971, 286). Such self-transcendence is achieved primarily in loving; love has the quality of self-surrender and brings a "deep set joy" (Lonergan 1971, 105). Further on, Lonergan notes: "For a man is his true self in as much as he is self-transcending. Conversion is the way to self-transcendence" (Lonergan 1971, 357). Conversion, be it moral, intellectual or religious, is a modality of self-transcendence. Man reaches fulfillment and joy by living a life of meaning and by moving outside himself (only after he has come to rest in himself, from a position of self-esteem) beyond the realms of finite goods and into the transcendental realm in which God is known and loved (see Lonergan 1971, 84). As Lonergan writes: "Holiness abounds in truth and moral goodness, but it has a distinct dimension of its own. It is other-worldly fulfillment, joy, peace, bliss" (Lonergan 1971, 242).

The Greeks understood it as a state of spiritual health, of *eudaimonia*, which literally translates as "good-spirit-ness"—it is not about feelings or subjective satisfaction; it is wholly objective. If it is objective, then perhaps it is not in us; rather, we are in it. Suffering, as the Greek tragedians taught, is an occasion of wisdom and wisdom is an important ingredient in happiness. We can talk, therefore, of the objective happiness of subjective unhappiness. Our humanity is divine discontent. The American Declaration of Independence has as one of its promises the right to pursue happiness. Commenting on this, C. S. Lewis states: "We Have No 'Right to Happiness'" (Lewis 1963 10–12; see also Lewis 1970, 317–322). It was Freud who asked in *Civilization and Its Discontents*: why aren't we happy, despite the fact that we have fulfilled most of our desires in our technological age. He answers that he doesn't know. But to suggest that happiness is one of our inalienable rights is the surest way to unhappiness. Children aren't even happy, no one is really. Malcolm Muggeridge, the British author and convert to Catholicism, in a section entitled "Happiness" in his book *Jesus Rediscovered*, writes:

> The sister-in-law of a friend of Samuel Johnson was imprudent enough once to claim in his presence that she was happy. He pounced on her hard, remarking in a loud, emphatic voice that if she was indeed the contented being she professed herself to be then her life gave the lie to every research of humanity .... The pursuit of happiness, included along with life and liberty in the American Declaration of Independence as an inalienable right, is without any question the most fatuous that could possibly be undertaken. This lamentable phrase – the pursuit of happiness – is responsible for a good part of the ills and miseries of the modern world (Muggeridge 1979, 179).

Pleasure, Happiness, Joy

Throughout this paper we have been touching on the difference between pleasure, happiness, and joy, it is now time to make this more explicit with reference to Frankl's tri-dimensional ontology. In terms of the relationship between pleasure, happiness, and joy and relating them to Frankl's dimensional ontology, I would like to advance the notion that pleasure pertains to the somatic, happiness to the psychical and joy to the noetic. Somatic "happiness" is pleasure, psychic "happiness" is happiness, while noetic "happiness" is joy.

Physical happiness (somatic):	Pleasure
Psychological happiness (psychical):	Happiness
Spiritual happiness (noetic):	Joy

We have been speaking a lot about pleasure and happiness, now let us say something about joy. Joy is the ultimate gift from God, according to theism. It resides in the spirit, the noetic core or realm. And conscience is the voice of spirit. Joy has an air of eternity about it and opens us up to the Other. "Enter into the joy of the Lord" (Matthew 25:21), we are told. Joy is ek-stasis not homeostasis, which Frankl rightly critiques. Joy is ecstatic because it is a standing outside of oneself, as in self-transcendence. Joy is the ek-static experience of self-forgetfulness. In a Franklian vein, C. S. Lewis, in *Surprised by Joy*, notes: "Only when your whole attention and desire are fixed on something else … does the 'thrill' arise. It is a by-product" (Lewis 1955, 168; 220–1). Commenting on the final joy, in his *City of God*, St. Augustine shows that our own happiness cannot be properly located anywhere else but in contemplation and love of the inner life of God. Augustine relativizes all the alternative descriptions of human happiness; for him all good points to the Good. But recalling Frankl's "tragic optimism" let us say: we can be fairly happy, reasonably happy here! Josef Pieper, the great German Thomist philosopher, like Frankl, maintains that we cannot set out to obtain joy as if it were the direct object of our search. It is, he writes, in complete agreement with Frankl, a "by-product" (Pieper 1989, 32–9), the result of knowing and "doing" the truth. Joy follows on from truth and right.

Henri de Lubac, S.J., the French Catholic theologian, has some interesting and similar observations to Frankl and the other philosophers we have been considering in his small book of aphorisms entitled *Paradoxes of Faith* (see De Lubac 1987). He too is of the opinion that suffering is part and parcel of the fabric of life and doesn't preclude joy. "Suffering is the thread from which the stuff of joy is woven. Never will the optimist know joy" (De Lubac 1987, 39). No, but the tragic optimist might! Suffering can be redemptive; it can bring blessings. Prayer, love, and suffering are three ways, which free us from sentimentality. "Under the species of pain, the substance of joy is there, already …. There is only one way of being happy: not to be ignorant of suffering, and not to run away from it; but to accept the transfiguration it brings. *Tristitia vestra vertetut in gaudium*" (De Lubac 1987, 173). ["But your distress shall be turned to joy" as in John xvi, 20). True happiness is the result of an alchemy, of an openness and orientation of the soul to the depths of the divine Ground of being. Real radiance is a centripetal force. "I shall draw everything to me". In relation to happiness, and on a Franklian note, de Lubac observes: "We only find it by not looking for it" (De Lubac 1987, 113). Many promises of happiness, he contends, are "swindles or childish dreams" (De Lubac 1987, 182). The difference between joy and happiness is brought out in the following assertion: "God has made us for Beatitude—and we meanly look for happiness. Happiness is what we conceive and desire spontaneously. It is a thing unworthy of us, and which the deepest part of our nature rejects. Beatitude is God" (De Lubac 1987, 210–2). So there it is: real joy is faith and found in the Father. Joy is the very life of Heaven. Joy is self-transcendence: joy points to its ultimate beyond, to God. Joy is not a feeling; it is one of the fruits of the Spirit. The road to joy: "Thy will be done". De Lubac summarizes the relationship the Christian has to happiness, thus:

> The Christian does not ask for happiness. Jesus teaches him to ask for the Father's Name to be hallowed, for his kingdom to come, for his Will to be done. The Christian does not expect happiness. He expects the new heavens and the new earth, 'which Justice inhabits'. The Christian does not desire happiness. He hungers and thirsts after Justice. He is athirst for eternal life. The Christian does not hope for happiness. He hopes to see the glory of God. *Satiabor cum apparuerit gloria tua.* ... Happiness is all that and can be but that (De Lubac 1987, 202).

Self-Transcendence

Frankl writes about his spiritual self-transcendence thus:

> In a last violent protest against the hopelessness of imminent death, I sensed my spirit piercing through the enveloping gloom. I felt it transcend that hopeless, meaningless world, and from somewhere I heard a victorious 'Yes' in answer to my question of the existence of an ultimate purpose. At that moment a light was lit in a distant farmhouse, which stood on the horizon as if painted there, in the midst of the miserable grey of a dawning morning in Bavaria. "*Et lux in tenebris lucet*" – and the light shineth in the darkness (Frankl 2004a, 2004b, 51–2).

Love: this is the ultimate. Writing about such other-worldly fulfillment, Frankl, further on in the same work, writes that a thought transfixed him and it was this: that for the first time in his life he saw the truth that had been expounded by the poets and philosophers of all times, that love is the ultimate goal to which the human spirit can aspire, that life is about meaning and not happiness, that man's salvation is in and through love. He writes movingly:

> I understood how a man who has nothing left in this world still may know bliss, be it only for a brief moment, in the contemplation of his beloved. In a position of utter desolation, when man cannot express himself in positive action, when his only achievement may consist in enduring his sufferings in the right way – an honorable way – in such a position man can, through loving contemplation of the image he carries of his beloved, achieve fulfillment. For the first time in my life I was able to understand the meaning of the words, "The angels are lost in perpetual contemplation of an infinite glory." (Frankl 2004a, b, 49).

Any and every therapy worthy of the name ought to attempt to mobilize the vast spiritual resources of the noetic core of the human subject, which permits him to live a life of love and reason.

Conclusion

To conclude, in Franklian fashion, let our thoughts turn away from the ego, that monumental construct of our narcissism, and become oriented, instead, to the true, the good, and the beautiful and attend to these three transcendental categories of being, to whatever and whomsoever lifts us beyond ourselves even if only momentarily. Plato insists that our souls be ordered to the *Agathon*; Aristotle advises us to indulge in divine thoughts; and in terms of the Christian differentiation of consciousness, there is no more moving an account of dereflection than the advice given in *Philippians*:

> …Whatsoever things are true, whatsoever things are honest, whatsoever things are just, whatsoever things are pure, whatsoever things are lovely, whatsoever things are of good report, if there be any virtue, and if there be any praise, think on these things (Philippians 4:8).

The transcendentals of the true, the good, and the beautiful, beckon. They call, pointing to the transcendent Ground of all being, the Eternal Logos, source of all ultimate meaning, hope, purpose, and joy—source and final solace.

References

Aristotle. (1986). *The ethics of Aristotle*. London: Penguin Books. Trans. J.A.K. Thomson.

Assagioli, Roberto. (1965). Psychosynthesis: A Manual of Principles and Techniques. London: mandala.

Cutler, H., & His holiness the Dalai Lama. (1998). *The art of happiness: A handbook for living*. Philadelphia, PA: Coronet.

De Lubac, H. (1987). *Paradoxes of faith*. San Francisco, CA: Ignatius.

Frankl, V. E. (1985). *Psychotherapy and existentialism: Selected papers in logotherapy*. New York, NY: Washington Square Press.

Frankl, V. E. (1988). *The will to meaning: Foundations and applications of logotherapy*. New York, NY: Meridian.

Frankl, V. E. (2000). *Man's search for ultimate meaning*. New York, NY: Basic Books.

Frankl, V. E. (2004a). *Man's search for meaning*. London-Sydney-Auckland-Johannesburg: Rider.

Frankl, V. E. (2004b). *On the theory and therapy of mental disorders: An introduction to logotherapy and existential analysis*. New York and Hove: Brunner-Routledge. Trans. J. Dubois.

Frankl, V. E. (2009). *The doctor and the soul*. London: Souvenir Press. Trans. R. and C. Winston.

Freud, S. (1911). *Formulations on the two principles of mental functioning* (On metapsychology: The theory of psychoanalysis). London: Penguin.

Freud, S. (1920). *Beyond the pleasure principle* (On metapsychology: The theory of psychoanalysis, Vol. 11). London: Penguin.

Hegel, G. W. (1977). Phenomenology of Spirit. Trans. A. V. Miller. Oxford-New York-Toronto-Melbourne: Oxford University Press.

Kant, I. (1985). Groundwork of the metaphysic of morals. In H. J. Paton (Trans. & Ed.), *The moral law*. London: Hutchinson.

Kreeft, P. (1989). *Heaven: The heart's deepest longing*. San Francisco, CA: Ignatius Press.

Lewis, C. S. (1955). Surprised by Joy. London: Harper Collins.

Lewis, C. S. (1963). Saturday Evening Post. Vol. 236, December.

Lewis, C. S. (1970). God in the Dock. Grand Rapids, Mich.: Eermann.

Lonergan, B. (1971). *Method in theology*. Toronto: University of Toronto Press.
Lukas, E. (2000). *Logotherapy textbook*. Toronto: Liberty Press.
Mill, J. S. (1909). *Autobiography (Ed. C.E. Norton)* (Harvard classics, Vol. 25). New York, NY: P.F. Collier & Son.
Muggeridge, M. (1979). Jesus Rediscovered. New York: Doubleday.
Murdoch, I. (1970). *The sovereignty of good*. London and Henley: Routledge and Kegan Paul.
Pascal, B. (1995). *Pensées*. New York, NY: Penguin Books. Trans. A.J. Krailsheimer.
Pieper, J. (1989). Josef Pieper - An Anthology. San Francisco: Ignatius Press.
Pinker, S. (1997). How the Mind Works. London: Penguin Books.
Rahner, K. (1941/1994). *Hearer of the word*. New York, NY: Continuum. Trans. J. Donceel.
Ricoeur, P. (2004). *The conflict of interpretations: Essays in hermeneutics*. London and New York: Continuum.
Sidgwick, H. (1874/1963/2001). *The methods of ethics*. London: MacMillan and Co. Savage Publishing.
Voegelin, E. (1990a). What is history? And other late unpublished writings. In T. Hollweck & P. Carigella (Eds.), *The collected works of Eric Voegelin* (Vol. 28). Baton Rouge & London: Louisiana State University Press.
Voegelin, E. (1990b). Published essays 1966–1985. In E. Sandoz (Ed.), *The collected works of Eric Voegelin* (Vol. 12). Baton Rouge & London: Louisiana State University Press.
Žižek, S. (2008). *In defense of lost causes*. London and New York: Verso.

"Meaning Until the Last Breath": Practical Applications of Logotherapy in the Ethical Consideration of Coma, Brain Death, and Persistent Vegetative States

Charles McLafferty Jr.

In the United States, the PBS News Hour (September 30, 2014) reported that, in California, more than 4000 individuals are being kept alive in subacute facilities; these patients have long-term conditions requiring at least a feeding tube and trach (Faryon and Faryon and Racino, B. (Producer) 2014). The average length of stay is more than 10 years; rarely does the patient improve before death. How can logotherapy help in a meaningful decision-making process in such difficult, taxing circumstances? As will be demonstrated, these questions cannot be addressed without considering the profound advances in medical technology.

As a meaning-centered existentialist philosopher and psychiatrist, Viktor Frankl tested his ideas and theories in the darkest crucibles of human existence. He emphasized that "life has meaning under every circumstance" and that this meaning was available "until the last breath." This is one of Frankl's most unequivocal positions and is widely considered a foundational tenet of logotherapy.

Viktor Frankl (1984) entered Auschwitz with the manuscript of a book sewn into his jacket. It was his life's work—his only possession of value. Though he had already developed many of the foundational elements of logotherapy, the life of survival in the cruelty and inhumanity of four concentration camps gave Frankl the opportunity to test these ideas. The manuscript was quickly lost, but Frankl survived typhus by reconstructing key ideas and fragments on scraps of paper. The book was later rewritten and published, and we know it today as *The Doctor and the Soul* [*Ärztliche Seelsorge*] (Frankl 1986).

Frankl (1984) emerged from one of the most horrific environments designed by mankind to declare that "human life, under any circumstances, never ceases to have a meaning, and that this infinite meaning of life includes suffering and dying, privation and death" (p. 104). This idea has become a center point of logotherapy and

C. McLafferty Jr. (✉)
Purpose Research, LLC, 803 Greensprings Hwy #19051, Birmingham, AL 35219, USA
e-mail: charles@purposeresearch.com

A. Batthyány (ed.), *Logotherapy and Existential Analysis*, Logotherapy and Existential Analysis: Proceedings of the Viktor Frankl Institute Vienna 1,
DOI 10.1007/978-3-319-29424-7_31

serves as a permanent inoculation against the genocide and unspeakable cruelty of the concentration camps.

In the concentration camps, Frankl (1984) was careful to remind his fellow prisoners that, regardless of their circumstances, there remained before them a choice. Even though all other freedoms had been removed from them, each prisoner could still choose an attitude toward this fate. Human dignity can only be maintained in light of this choice:

The way in which a man accepts his fate and all the suffering it entails, the way in which he takes up his cross, gives him ample opportunity—even under the most difficult circumstances—to add a deeper meaning to his life. It may remain brave, dignified, and unselfish. Or in the bitter fight for self-preservation he may forget his human dignity and become no more than an animal. Here lies the chance for a man either to make use of or to forgo the opportunities of attaining the moral values that a difficult situation may afford him. And this decides whether he is worthy of his sufferings or not (p. 88).

Thus human existence affords a choice—in every circumstance. This choice—part of our humanness—has to do with the fact that human experience is rooted in multiple, interrelated dimensions. The *soma* (physical world) and the *psyche* (emotions and intellect) are mechanical parts of ourselves that we share with the animal kingdom. It is in the *noëtic* (human spirit) that the person has an arena of choice. This noëtic dimension, by definition, differentiates us from the animal kingdom; it is in this dimension that we are able to choose an attitude towards our unalterable fate (Frankl 1986).

In fact, Frankl (1967) noted that logotherapy always involves *action*; it is not a passive, theoretical position, but one of *choice in action*. It is not the holding of lofty values, but the living of them—the active choosing of these values in our daily lives—that constitutes logotherapy lived. It is in actualizing our choice from the range of possibilities available in each moment that we harvest potentials into actualities; in this manner does the choice become rescued from the future into the past for all time.

The choosing of these values today is not as simple as it was when Frankl formulated these ideas in the last century. We are at a transition point in human history, in which Frankl's genius is more needed than ever. Many argue that "traditional values" are being lost in an era of overwhelming materialism and self-interest. Frankl rightly anticipated this trend, as he called for each person to become responsible to an intuitive, though imperfect, inner compass he called *conscience*. On the one hand, the loss of imposed, authoritarian values may result in a mad, selfish scramble for selfish pursuits. On the other, the emergence of human *response-ability* requires this transitional period in human history, as the imposition of external authority is subsumed by awareness and unfolding of the individual conscience (Fabry 2013).

New Technologies Bring New Questions

In this transition, technological developments have far surpassed our human capability to understand their implications. For the first time in human history, most individuals on our planet have the ability to take an idea and post it on the Internet, where it can potentially spread worldwide in days, if not hours. Control of ideas is passing from the moneyed powerful—and those with assumed authority—to the individual. This has forced each person to take responsibility for both the focus of their attention and the discernment of that, which is true, beautiful, and good. Opportunities for the discovery of meaning—and growth of responsibility—are unparalleled in human history.

Another technology has changed our lives: Scientists have developed techniques and technologies to save and sustain life that border on the miraculous. The ventilator, the feeding tube, as well as dialysis, and heart-lung machines replace vital functions whose disruptions a century ago would have assured cessation of bodily function (death). The feeding tube seems most innocuous of all, as the person can survive without food for weeks. The body's design places the mouth, teeth, and throat as close to the brain stem as possible to maximize chances for survival. In the past, damage to brain functioning, such that the feeding and/or breathing mechanisms were impaired, was a built-in barometer of mortality.

The current use of invasive medical techniques causes two effects: it greatly increases the odds of survival in those cases where healing is possible, and it allows survival of cell life when there is "nobody home." In the latter case, is it possible that modern medicine has demonstrated the existence and necessity of a human soul, by showing us what limited existence is available in its absence or inaccessibility? Practitioners of medicine cannot distinguish between those who should and should not be saved—medical treatments are used on all who are injured and have access to modern care.

Thus a dark cloud hovers on the horizon. As I write this, for example, in the United States two patients have been declared "brain dead" but their bodies remain on life support. There does not seem to be a clear answer in either situation—in one case, the family hoped for divine intervention and wanted their teenage daughter's body to be kept on life support even after a coroner issued a death certificate; in the other, a pregnant woman was kept alive against the wishes of the family in order to serve as an incubator for her deformed fetus because a state law forbade the removal of life support in pregnant women.

These are difficult, wrenching decisions for those involved. Traditional answers seem incomplete. If we are called to live—and help others to live—logotherapy *uniquely*, then predetermined answers are not enough. Those who live in a meaning orientation have a decreasing reliance on others for authoritative answers as they cultivate their active, intuitive compasses of conscience. Those who practice logotherapy have as a touchstone the "unconditional dignity" of each person:

Whoever is cognizant of the dignity, the unconditional dignity of every individual person, likewise has the unconditional respect for the human person, for the ill person, as well as for the incurably ill person, and indeed for the incurably ill person of the spirit. In truth, there can be no illnesses of the spirit at all (Frankl 1996, cited in Lukas 2000, 25).

Lukas (2000) noted that a person, who presents with symptoms of dementia or psychosis (as in Alzheimer's disease) "still possesses an intact portion of the noëtic dimension, even though it may be partially or occasionally blocked or not available for reasons of psychophysical disease processes" (p. 25). Lukas added that the noëtic dimension is present, even though the person is becoming physically feeble, is addicted to drugs, or has a psychosis caused by chemical imbalance in the brain. At such times, she noted that the application of logotherapy to the patient is contra-indicated. However, articles have been written about the use of logotherapy in care-givers of those who are thus affected (Graca and Archer 1991; Harris 1997; Wade and Shantall 2005).

Logotherapists informally note that conditions of such blockage allow the care-giver to find meaning. This suggestion, when given to the caregiver, offers the opportunity for the caregiver to resonate with the meaning-opportunities presented. But such a meaning orientation may leave out the possibility that the patient whose noös is blocked from expression may have the greatest suffering. It is important that the logotherapist consider his or her own values, such as religious beliefs and the idea that the only help the logotherapist can offer is to the caregiver and not the patient; this reflection is necessary so that the helper does not impose values in the process of helping. To be sure, the helper's own values cannot be discredited nor dishonored, but the unconditional dignity called for by Frankl requires that we honor the values of *all* involved.

It is necessary to make two points here: first, there is a fine line here to be discerned regarding the inherent dignity of the person and the resulting need for each person to be able to take responsibility for these decisions. Second, this manuscript does not address cases of so-called "mercy killing" or euthanasia, in which a person's life is artificially terminated. Nor is this manuscript intended to address the situations of "blockage" of the spirit as found in persons displaying symptoms of dementia, psychoses, or addictions; these have already been explored in depth (Frankl 1967, 1986, 2004; Lukas 1995, 2000). This paper is limited to the ethical question of the repeated or chronic usage of medical inter-ventions to prolong cellular life (a) in the absence of a patient's desire to endure such treatments and (b) without hope for the resumption of the physical body as the "container" and means of expression of the spirit, as noted by Lukas (1995). In particular, the use of medical interventions has opened a new spectrum of issues regarding the indefinite maintenance of the physical body in cases where there is little hope for healing.

The Case of Kevin

I admit that these issues Case of are deeply personal for me (McLafferty Jr 2006) and I must be careful not to impose my answers on others, but rather to use my experiences to enhance meaning-potential for others. About 35 years ago, an event forced these issues into my awareness. In his second year of college, my brother, Kevin, was involved in a car accident. He was comatose for 9 months, 6 of them in an ICU. He underwent numerous emergency interventions during that period. As he gradually regained awareness of the world around him, it became apparent that he was a functional quadriplegic. It would be many more months before the impact of his injury could be assessed, as he had marked difficulty talking (aphasia). My parents never gave up on Kevin— from the Greenville, South Carolina, General Hospital, he went to the Braintree Neurological Hospital in Boston for 9 months. Next was the Woodrow Wilson Rehabilitation Center in Fishersville, Virginia. My dad would commute from his workplaces in South Carolina and Stamford, Connecticut to visit and help my mother on weekends.

After several years of recovery and rehabilitation in several facilities, Kevin lived with my parents at their home. Three to four times a year they drove him to the Cleveland Clinic, where he was evaluated and given updated prescriptions, exercises, and rehab. They procured a live-in stint for Kevin for several months at a new rehab facility in Florida, which gave them a lengthy and much-needed break (the only respite they would have for the rest of Kevin's life). They researched all they could find about head injury (this was in the 1970s), and became charter members of the National Head Injury Association. They founded the South Carolina Head Injury Association and advocated for research and treatment of those with head injuries.

Kevin's condition was fairly stable for many years, though he had profound memory, emotional, attentional, and physical impairments. One experience brought it home to me. It was May 1997, and my parents were visiting Virginia to attend my graduation. We were preparing to leave the house. Kevin was in his wheelchair, making his way down the bumpy slope that was our front yard. He suddenly stopped and looked up at my dad.

"How long… have I been… here?" Kevin asked in his halting voice.

"In Charlottesville? We've been in Charlottesville for three days," Dad replied. "No." Kevin pointed to his wheelchair. "I mean… like this…."

"Oh. You've been in your wheelchair for about 17 years."

"Ooooooooh." Kevin's eyes opened wide. There was a long pause as he furrowed his brow, as if he was processing the answer. He leaned forward, and motioned to my dad to move closer. He spoke very quietly, as if it were a secret. "How long… do I have to stay… like this?"

My dad looked down at the grass. "I don't know. I don't know."

Soon after, Kevin had another fit of rage. These were his lucid moments, when he glimpsed the reality of his situation. His anger soon passed, and eventually he put his chin on his palm with a resigned look.

A few months later, Kevin had a massive stroke. After a week of surgeries to relieve pressure on his brain and minimize the damage, the surgeons said they could do no more.

He was placed in the neurological ward with a daytime attendant paid for by the hospital. The CAT scan showed that roughly a baseball-sized portion in the center of his brain was gone. Though now paralyzed on one side, Kevin pulled out his feeding tube numerous times; each time, it was surgically re-implanted and carefully taped out of reach of his functioning arm.

To be sure, even now, Kevin was not brain dead; nor will I argue that he was in a persistent vegetative state, though he was diagnosed as in a mild coma using the

Glasgow Coma Scale (Teasdale and Jennett 1974) repeatedly over these later years. Kevin was still there, hidden behind veils, though I could not communicate with him. My experiences with Kevin and his rage at being trapped in a nonfunctioning mechanism for so long have given me much to ponder over the years. He was hospitalized for 3½ more years, with assisted breathing and a hydration/nutrition tube, before he died in June 2001.

How to Apply Principles of Logotheory?

How does a logotherapist resolve these issues? Is there a way to resolve the ethics of these difficult, even wrenching, decisions? Is there a way that Frankl's theory can give us a greater perspective?

Perhaps we can begin by asking: "What is life?" Frankl (1967) gave us a clue, that life requires us to act on our values; having values or beliefs is not enough:

Man cannot avoid decisions.... Man not only behaves according to what he is, he also becomes what he is according to how he behaves.... It is time that this decision quality of human existence be included in our definition of man (pp. 47–48).

As mentioned, it is through the choices we activate that we "rescue" a potentiality into an actuality for eternity (Frankl 1967, 92). It is because of the choices before us, for which we are responsible (*able to respond*) that meaning is present in potential. When we are unable to act on our values... unable even to make the simplest choice, even to choose the attitude we take toward our fate, then is it possible that Frankl's values (creative, experiential, attitudinal) are no longer relevant, as they cannot be activated? If we are literally *unable to respond*, then we cannot be *responsible*. The decisions required in cases of brain death or persistent vegetative state are concerned with situations in which the individual involved *lacks free will of any kind* and whose body would not be alive except for medical intervention. This is consistent with Frankl (1984): "Logotherapy sees *in responsibleness the very essence of human existence*" (p. 131, italics added). If we consider that *essence* is the root of the word *essential*, it is possible to consider that, without responsibleness, existence is possible... but is it human?

So perhaps Frankl has given us a differentiating line here for thinking about life. The phrase "under every circumstance" is used in the context of *human* life—and he defined the noëtic dimension as that which makes us "uniquely human," the dimension of free will in which we make and activate our choices. He further argued that "decision quality" should be part of the *definition* of the person. The noëtic is defined as that which makes us greater than the animal; is it possible that the physical body that has been declared "brain dead" and arguably no longer has even a rudimentary intellect is now "less than the animals"?

Perhaps it is also noteworthy that Frankl sometimes used words with multiple meanings; translation from German to English compounds the problem. Because logotherapy is concerned with *meaning* this is not without implications. In this case, Frankl spoke of "life" throughout his writings and speeches. There is "human life" that has meaning under every circumstance, and there is a higher "life" that calls to each person:

Man should not ask what the meaning of his life is, but rather he must recognize that it is *he* who is asked.... He can only answer to life by *answering for* his own life; to life he can only respond by being responsible (Frankl 1984, 131, italics in original).

Thus the logotherapist must carefully consider and clarify use of the word "life" in each dimension.

Not so long ago, when a person was found to be "brain dead"—had no brain activity—and there was no hope for healing, that person's body stopped working. We saw it as a natural process, a fact of life. It is only relatively recently that medical technology has been able to sustain cellular activity indefinitely, even in the absence of human response-ability.

Emergent Value Conflicts can be Addressed

Some would argue, using Frankl's words, that "life has meaning until the last breath." Others conclude that all life is sacred. In such a case, it is important to ask—would we administer similar prolonged life support to an animal, such as our favorite pet? If so, under what conditions? Each of us may have a different answer; in fact, if the answer is derived with an inner compass rather than an external authority, we must come to the conclusion in the silence of our hearts, in our own time. Even Frankl's answer, and those of other logotherapists, cannot assume authority for each unique person and situation. Otherwise, for example, if all life has meaning, profound implications ensue—even the vegetarian must take life to survive. Resolution of these value conflicts is deeply personal; there are no easy answers.

In the practical application of logotherapy in our daily lives, and in helping others to apply logotherapy, we begin with the uniqueness of each person in each situation. Can we then assume there are universal answers? How do we avoid imposing our own values on our patients, even if we have seen a similar situation? How can we help *them* to clarify and to choose those values with which *they* resonate most strongly, while not imposing our own? Frankl (1984) noted that he did not judge anyone for the good or bad decisions they made in the concentration camps: "The best of us did not return" (p. 24).

Kevin's Last "Words": A Unique Experience

Late in Kevin's life, I had a unique, unexpected, experience. From the time of his accident onward, I found it was difficult to visit him. No matter how hard I tried, I had noticed that I would become angry in his presence. I often walked away from the hospital with resentment and anger. I could not understand it; in fact, I felt profoundly guilty that I was unable to control my emotions around him, as my intention was to offer love and support. Years passed and the pattern repeated without fail. As mentioned, Kevin spent the last three and a half years of his life in the neurological ward of a hospital after a stroke. After repeated surgeries, the surgeons did not replace the top of his skull, simply covering his brain with his scalp. It was a macabre picture. Kevin had a feeding tube and ventilator, and was unable to speak. In fact, he tore out the feeding tube that was implanted in his abdomen several times, whereon it was dutifully reinstalled.

In November 2000, I was on a family trip to Florida when we decided to take a detour to see my parents. It was a sudden decision, and we arrived at Kevin's hospital room with only a few hours' notice. It had been over 3 years since Kevin had been hospitalized after a massive stroke. While my wife and daughter visited with my parents at the foot of the bed, I sat beside my brother to greet him. He did not move or turn his head. I said hello and just visited quietly. Soon I noticed a sense of anger descending on me. I was in a calm state when I entered, and nothing had happened in my thinking to change my inner state. For the first time, it dawned on me that this feeling—identical each time—was not mine.

I became quiet inside, and focused my thoughts. Without speaking outwardly, I said to my brother, "Kevin, is that you?"

His response was immediate and clear. "Who the hell do you think it is?" I didn't hear it; I'm not sure how it registered. But it was unmistakably Kevin—he had a wry sense of humor even when angry. Though the emotions were high, I simultaneously realized a sense of relief that the anger was not mine, that it had a source outside of myself. I fought to remain quiet and still, despite the turbulence. I silently asked him another question: "What is it that you want from me?" "TELL THEM TO LET ME GO!" I remember it vividly, even a decade later. The emotion became a flood, so strong as to be overwhelming—I felt it as pure rage, decades of pent-up anger.

I found my inner stillness and replied, "Kevin, you know how they are. I have tried many times, but they won't listen to me. But, for you, I will try again." I looked over at my parents and family, still talking and catching up. It was like they were in another world, just a few feet away.

There was no direct response. But within a few seconds I noticed a change, a lifting. Within a minute the rage and resentment were completely gone, replaced with a peace and stillness that were like the sun and blue skies breaking through the clouds after a storm. The peace became complete, and there was a new calmness in Kevin's face. I kept my promise just a few minutes later when we went to dinner, to no avail.

Though Kevin lived another 6 months and I came to see him several times, I never again experienced the anger or rage. Nor was I ever able to "hear" his "voice" again. In sharing this experience with a family member, it was interpreted as "reading Kevin's mind." I pointed out that this wasn't mind reading, as I had never been able (or wanted) to do that. Besides, I wasn't very good at "mind reading" if it took me 20 years to get the message! Rather, it was something I was enabled to experience once, perhaps a gift of grace.

Questions for Consideration: By the Helper and Those Being Helped

Several steps may be helpful for clarifying the ,issues involved. These are relevant for both healers and those being helped. In general, it is helpful for a helper to begin with his or her own values before attempting to serve in a helping role.

1. It is important to note that these decisions are deeply personal. As such, the healer must also recognize and respect the intensity and intimacy with which these matters are shared with another. There are few issues that penetrate as deeply into the core of life.
2. The healer should realize that there are no easy, universal answers to these medical developments. For example, to assume that medical interventions should be used to prolong life in every case invites exploration of exactly that situation. For example, Fine (2005) acknowledged the official allocution of Pope Paul II regarding the moral obligation to use artificial nutrition and hydration universally; the Pope noted the slippery slope of arbitrarily withholding or ending these modes of support. In contrast, Pope Pius XII (1957, cited in Fine 2005) noted earlier that "life, health, all temporal activities are in fact subordinated to spiritual ends" (p. 309). Father Richard McCormick (2004, cited in Fine 2005), asked us to imagine all 300 beds of a Catholic hospital filled with patients who are in a persistent vegetative state, maintained for months and years: "An observer of the scenario would eventually be led to ask: Is it true that those who operate this facility actually believe in life after death?" (p. 309). Such questions encourage us to examine our values by extending our answers as if they are universals. Over the past 20 years, I have received several well-intended suggestions from logotherapists that Kevin's injury, both at the time of the car accident and after his massive stroke, were meant by Life as a meaning-opportunity for my parents in their caregiving. Certainly the commitment of my parents to head injury causes is congruent with this idea. But my brother's outbursts of rage (which happened several times a day before his stroke) were likely indications of his wishes. My overriding interest was not about me (or the caregivers), it was about Kevin. We cannot know what other commitments my parents would have been able to take on had they not needed to spend every day taking care of Kevin; before his accident, they had already been active in the community and with civic organizations.
3. This leads us to the consideration of the soul (noös, noëtic, uniquely human dimension) of the person who is impaired. As noted earlier, the spirit is still there, even if it is blocked. It is important to remember, however, that "spirit" has two discrete dimensions in logotherapy. Several authors (McLafferty Jr 2009, 2012; Shantall 2009) have pointed out that Frankl (2000) clearly stated the existence of two spiritual dimensions. While the noëtic is the dimension of the *human* spirit, what Shantall (2009) and McLafferty Jr (2012) termed the "transcendent" dimension is that of the *divine* spirit, or Ultimate Meaning (Frankl 2000). What is notable about this clarification (or extension) of logotheory is that

statements about the spirit as perfect and existing outside of time and space refer to the divine spirit; the human spirit is that noëtic capacity that is able to exercise free will, to make choices through the mechanism of the physical/psychic human body in time and space. The diagnosis of "brain death" or "persistent vegetative state" does not eliminate either dimension from the person but indicates the existence of a more or less permanent blockage. The noëtic dimension, the human capacity for some arena of choice, is faced with but one decision—whether to wait for the physical body to repair itself (if that is possible) or to move on to another realm. The presence of medical support removes the capacity of choice from the noëtic dimension of the person; in other words, the soul (noös) *can no longer choose* to place the weight of its being on the side of "energizing" or "withdrawing from" the soma and psyche.

4. Is it possible that this removal of choice robs such an individual of human dignity?

   Preservation of the physical body (somatic dimension) is elevated to the highest value, to the exclusion of values on any other dimension; for Terri Schiavo, who was in a persistent vegetative state for years, some family members described removal of artificial medical support as "murder" (McLafferty Jr 2006). The helper may have to give attention to exploring values as they apply to each dimension. For example, one question that came to mind with my experience with Kevin's injury and prolonged illness was "Is Kevin the same as his physical body?" A deeper question also emerged: "Where is Kevin, now that he is in a coma?" Next, "When I consider Kevin in all of his dimensions, what is possible for the essence of Kevin, given the condition of his physical body (and in particular his extensive brain damage)?"
5. Directly from this questioning process, it is possible to begin to ask questions regarding personal meaning and values. If no cases emerge in a helper's own introspection, it is possible to use news reports of cases like these: "If you were in this situation, what would you like to have done for you?" The perceived potential for healing and growth is an important topic for consideration. A less personal approach might be, "Do you think [your loved one] would want to live like this?" If yes, "For how long?" and "For what purpose?" can be explored. Borrowing from other traditions, the empty chair technique (e.g., see Gladding 1992) can be used, with the comatose patient "present" in the empty chair. The caregiver might be directed to ask the patient questions, as if the patient is in the chair. Later, the caregiver can be asked to sit in the empty chair and take the role of the patient, and thus allowed to answer those questions "as if" speaking for the patient.
6. In helping relatives to answer these difficult ethical questions in real-life situations, sometimes it is helpful to ask them to describe how they think their loved one is feeling right now (i.e., in a persistent vegetative state). A physical body that is diagnosed as brain dead may show no feeling or emotion, but patients in a coma or persistent vegetative state may appear to demonstrate anguish, anger, and despair. Sometimes this is congruent with medical complications. For example, for months after my brother's accident, his face was contorted as if to show

anguish; consistent with that, he developed ulcers that became so acute they required multiple surgeries, eventuating in the severing of his vagus nerve.

7. As the tools of medical intervention continue to develop they become at once more pervasive and more subtle. As mentioned earlier, the dilemma of a hospital with every bed taken by a patient in a persistent vegetative state for months or years can be used as a thought experiment. What resources would be required? Is there a better, higher use for these resources? One possible value to be explored might be the concept of "what is the greatest good for the greatest number?" On the other hand, how do we balance this with the "slippery slope" of euthanasia of Nazi Germany? And in these uniquely personal and intimate situations, who should (and must) decide?
8. If human life has meaning until the last breath, what does this mean? When Frankl formulated this phrase, human life had a more definite ending point; medical technologies were not available to sustain life, and death was a natural, beneficent process. Perhaps a clue is contained in the metaphor "until the last breath." The word "in-spire" means literally "to breathe in," so the idea of "the last breath" has a multidimensional relationship—our breathing is intimately connected with our spirit. It is not by accident that the word "expire" has as one of its meanings "to die." There is therefore a subtle dimensional conflict between the respiration of our physical bodies, and the breathing in, or inspiring, of the noëtic and transcendent dimensions.

The emergence of medical technologies to sustain physical life requires a parallel concern for the meaning potentials and life values that undergird our existence. Logotherapy offers a framework for consideration of these values in helping us to consider "What is life?" from a multidimensional perspective. Further, the idea that there is one answer to the question in all cases should be carefully evaluated in light of the uniqueness of each individual and the meaning potential presented by each situation.

References

Fabry, J. B. (2013). *The pursuit of meaning: Viktor Frankl, logotherapy, and life*. Birmingham, AL: Purpose Research.

Faryon, J., Racino, B. (Producer). (2014). *An impossible choice* [Documentary]. Retrieved from http://www.pbs.org/newshour/bb/let-go-families-patients-life-support-face-painful-choice/. PBS documentary (with inewsource) available at http://impossiblechoice.org

Fine, R.L. (2005). From Quinlan to Schiavo: Medical, ethical, and legal issues in severe brain injury. *Proceedings (Baylor University. Medical Center), 18*(4), 303.

Frankl, V. E. (1967). *Psychotherapy and existentialism*. New York, NY: Washington Square Press.

Frankl, V. E. (1984). *Man's search for meaning* (3rd ed.). New York, NY: Pocket Books.

Frankl, V. E. (1986). *The doctor and the soul (Original work published 1946 as Ärztliche Seelsorge; Vienna: Franz Deuticke.) (transl. R. Winston and C. Winston)*. New York, NY: Knopf.

Frankl, V. E. (2000). *Man's search for ultimate meaning*. Cambridge: Perseus.

Frankl, V. E. (2004). *On the theory and therapy of mental disorders: An introduction to logotherapy and existential analysis (transl. J. DuBois)*. New York, NY: Brunner-Routledge.

Gladding, S. T. (1992). *Counseling: A comprehensive profession*. New York, NY: Merrill.

Graca, J., & Archer, D. (1991). Assisting caregivers of Alzheimer's victims. *The International Forum for Logotherapy, 14*(2), 53–57.

Harris, W. M. (1997). Meaning in grief. *The International Forum for Logotherapy, 20*, 120–122.

Lukas, E. (1995). *Psychotherapy with dignity: Ten reflections on Viktor E. Frankl's psychotherapy. (transl. J.B. Fabry, H.T. Smith & J. O'Meara)*. Fürstenfeldbruck, Germany: Süddeutsches Institut für Logotherapie und Existenzanalyse.

Lukas, E. (2000). *Logotherapy textbook: Meaning-centered psychotherapy (transl. T. Brugger)*. Don Mills, ON: Canada Liberty Press.

McLafferty, C. L., Jr. (2006). *Schiavo case shows that human life is about choices*. Paper presented at the XV World Congress of Logotherapy, Dallas, Texas. Retrieved from http://mclafferty.net/Schiavo.

McLafferty, C. L., Jr. (2009). *Living in Frankl's four dimensions: Meaning as a mediator and counterbalance to reductionism in teaching and healing professions*. Paper presented at the 17th World Congress of Logotherapy, Dallas, Texas.

McLafferty, C. L., Jr. (2012). The future of logotherapy: Frankl's greatest omissions. Paper presented at the International Network on Personal Meaning, Toronto, Ontario.

Shantall, T. (2009). Relation of logotherapy and religion: A synopsis. *The International Forum for Logotherapy, 32*(1), 28–30.

Teasdale, G., & Jennett, B. (1974). Assessment of coma and impaired consciousness. A practice scale. *The Lancet, 304*(7872), 81–84. doi:10.1016/S0140-6736(74)91639-0.

Wade, B. L., & Shantall, T. (2005). Finding meaning in caring for people with Alzheimer's disease. *The International Forum for Logotherapy, 28*(2), 72–77.

Part VI
Book Reviews

Before Prozac. The Troubled History of Mood Disorders in Psychiatry: By Edward Shorter. Oxford University Press, 2008 Reviewed by S. Nassir Ghaemi

S. Nassir Ghaemi

The field of history of medicine, prior to the mid-twentieth century, was largely an antiquarian's delight, devoted mostly to showing the inevitable progress of medicine. In that sense, it was a reflection of the meliorist, evolutionary ideology of the late nineteenth century. Two world wars shook that confidence, and, especially in post-war France, history of medicine was reborn as part and parcel of the postmodernist movement, an approach to culture that involved a deep rejection of the Enlightenment tradition. Ironically, a founding tome of the postmodernist movement was a book on the history of psychiatry (Foucault's famed work *Madness and Civilization*). It followed that history of medicine (and history of psychiatry more specifically) became a largely postmodernist discipline: where there had been order, there was now Brownian motion; where progress, regression; where logic, power; where reason, money. The new histories of medicine, especially from the 1960s onward, reflected this revisionism, and the corresponding academic journals today, like *History of Psychiatry*, would automatically reject, with disdain, any paper that dared breathe the word "progress." The old catechism has become the new heresy; the old heresy now excommunication-worthy doctrine.

Into this modern era of postmodernist extremism, we find the occasional historian, often also a physician, who seeks to bridge the two approaches. In this vein, one might place such worthies as Owsei Temkin, Roy Porter, and the current author, Edward Shorter. But if they err in any direction, it seems to me, it is where the current climate is most forgiving—toward the postmodern faith.

Shorter's work over decades has been a great benefit to psychiatry, in my view. His *History of Psychiatry* is, I think, the best single volume to read on that topic. In

---

Editorial Note: Reprinted with kind permission from *Metapsychology* (metapsychology.mentalhelp.net). Acknowledgments go to Christian Perring for his kind support.

S.N. Ghaemi (✉)
Sackler School of Biomedical Sciences, Tufts University, Campus: Boston, Office: Pratt 303, 145 Harrison Avenue, Boston, MA 02111, USA
e-mail: nghaemi@tuftsmedicalcenter.org

A. Batthyány (ed.), *Logotherapy and Existential Analysis*, Logotherapy and Existential Analysis: Proceedings of the Viktor Frankl Institute Vienna 1,
DOI 10.1007/978-3-319-29424-7_32

that work in particular, he received some fire from postmodernists who thought he gave too much credit to the biological in psychiatry, and was too critical of psychoanalysis. I think Shorter hit the balance just right, criticizing all sides, but also recognizing merit in biology.

In this book, Shorter turns to a more extended critique of the biological approach in psychiatry, especially as directed to the DSM-III diagnostic system, and the subsequent rise of antidepressant medications. His overall critique is sound, I think, and his historical work is solid; but his clinical beliefs are, in my view, one-sided and detract from the other merits of the book.

Shorter has gone to the American Psychiatric Association (APA) archives and dug up entertaining and informative minutes of many of the DSM-III task force proceedings in the 1970s; he also returned to interview Robert Spitzer and others involved in the process. He also read up on the FDA committee notes about the various studies on the new generation antidepressants in the 1980s and 1990s, as well as earlier FDA records in the 1960s when the new rules requiring randomized clinical trial (RCT) evidence for drug approval were instituted. His historical sleuthing is first rate.

For instance, he nicely reconstructs the whole debate about whether to include the concept of "neurotic depression" in DSM-III; how the term "minor" depression was rejected as implying that the illness was, well, minor; how the term "major" depression was created in the end to capture some of these milder kinds of depressions as well as the more severe melancholic version that had originally been intended; how the psychoanalysts rebelled at the last second to preserve their livelihoods based on insurance reimbursement for neurotic depression; and how a "neurotic peace treaty" was devised whereby dysthymia and generalized anxiety disorder were invented to allow the psychotherapists something to bill.

Shorter seems more personally explicit in this book than in the past; after documenting all the politics behind DSM-III, he concludes that there is a "complete bankruptcy of the mood disorders."

He then follows with a description of the subsequent exploitation of DSM-III by the pharmaceutical industry in marketing the SRIs. The stage was set by the FDA's new rules, which legitimized evidence-based medicine (EBM) methods, in the 1960s and 1970s. Using FDA meeting archives, he describes how the FDA moved from being hostile to the pharmaceutical industry in the 1960s and 70s to being compliant with it in the 1980s and 90s. He concludes that the FDA's later obsession with "the average effects" seen in RCTs produced a "regulatory nihilism" whereby all negative studies were discounted, and small positive effects were exaggerated in importance. For instance, having required two positive studies versus placebo for approval, the FDA ignored all negative studies. With Prozac, for instance, 6/8 studies were negative. With Zoloft, all inpatient studies were negative; the drug was solely approved based on a few positive outpatient studies, the FDA knowing full well that it would also be used in hospitals, despite proof it did not work in those patients. Worse, such negative studies usually went unpublished, and thus clinicians did not know that they were using disproven agents in certain settings. (I will add that a recent analysis of the FDA database indeed found that published RCTs with new antidepressants produced about a 95 % positive–5 %

negative ratio; but once unpublished RCTs available at the FDA are included, the actual ratio is 51 % positive—49 % negative).

Shorter is refreshingly catholic in his criticisms; he does not aim solely, or even mostly, at the pharmaceutical companies (everyone's favorite bugaboo these days), but also at the FDA, at the APA, and at the average psychiatrist. (I might also have added the average patient, who so often demands drugs for symptoms.)

I could go on at length about the meat of this history, which is important and useful, but I will leave it to readers to see it for themselves. Despite my approbation of most of the book, I will spend more space on my critique of what I think is its major flaw, a flaw which comes across throughout the book in asides and clinical assumptions, and is reflected in its, at times, overly critical tone.

As a non-clinician, Shorter's clinical views are based to some extent on his clinical consultants, and the ones he uses represent a specific ideology in psychiatry, which though not without merit, are not, in my view, wholly supportable. These clinicians support ECT as the most effective treatment in psychiatry, and they are quite suspicious of the pharmaceutical industry (Shorter and one of this group, David Healy, have written a laudatory history of ECT). They are critical of most psychiatric diagnoses as now used, especially depression and bipolar disorder, as well of the evidence-based medicine (EBM) movement of recent years, with its emphasis on clinical, rather than biological, research. They think that such socially constructed concepts should be replaced by more biologically solid notions, like the old syndrome of "melancholia," a severe condition of depression with physical stereotyped symptoms (especially psychomotor retardation), biological correlates (marked over-activity of the adrenal gland reflected in a positive dexamethasone suppression test, DST), and perhaps most importantly, exquisite responsiveness to ECT but poor response to the Prozac prototypes.

There are scientific and historical problems with these beliefs.

Scientifically, I am not a DST expert, and perhaps I am mistaken, but my reading of this literature is that DST is not specific, being positive in non-melancholia syndromes (in most psychotic conditions, like psychotic depression and psychotic mania and schizophrenic psychosis; and even in nonpsychotic conditions with elevated psychological and physiological stress, like PTSD).

Perhaps more importantly, to privilege biological over clinical research is a Galenic move that itself has been disproven by the history of medicine; Galenic theory, based on the best biology of its time, held back medical progress (one must insist on the word) for two millennia. It led to bleeding and purging and much more harm than good, until it was disproven by... clinical research, statistics, Pierre Louis' numerical method, all of what later led to randomized clinical trials and clinical epidemiology—the foundation of what is now called EBM. There is no doubt there is a case to be made against EBM, but there is also a strong case for it, both scientifically and historically.

It may turn out, further, that melancholia as a syndrome is not, contrary to this group's beliefs, diagnostically important. It was the view of Kraepelin (presaged by Pinel) that recurrence was the hallmark of a condition like MDI, not the specific poles of melancholia and mania. This concept has some biological support as well (e.g., circadian rhythm research), and it is completely ignored in much of the writing of this group of clinicians and historians (e.g., Healy's book on the history of bipolar disorder). If recurrence is the key aspect of this condition, then the diagnosis of MDI would be more clinically and scientifically valid than the pathological state of melancholia (or mania for that matter).

Finally, regarding ECT, the matter is much more complex than simply viewing it as the most superior treatment for almost any psychiatric condition, including melancholia and mania. ECT is only a superior treatment short-term; it has never been shown to be better than anything else long-term (and rarely with randomized data; recently, the largest RCT of maintenance ECT found it was equal to drugs, without a placebo control for us to know if either treatments were really effective at all, given that one-half relapsed in a year, the same result by the way as the largest RCTs of antidepressants). My understanding is that in earlier days (1960s–1970s), ECT specialists used ECT only acutely, and they used lithium for long-term prophylaxis (not just for depressive but also of manic episodes, in the Kraepelinian view that they were preventing recurrence, with polarity being unimportant). That is how ECT was useful: to generate acute euthymia wherein one could then institute lithium prophylaxis. (I have been told this by some of the former students of the same ECT specialists consulted in Shorter's book.)

In contrast, ECT in recent years has been more widely used for ideological and economic reasons: Ideologically, doctors have become lazy about diagnosis, or .believe perhaps post-modernistically that clinical diagnoses do not matter; this faith in the unimportance of clinical diagnosis is then used to justify the nonspecific use and benefit of ECT for everything (depression, mania, psychosis). Economically, managed care insurance companies do not question weeks of hospitalization for ECT, whereas they breathe down doctors' necks when patients are only receiving medications. Thus, patients get discharged without careful diagnosis, without any thought-through long-term drug prophylaxis, and end up either re-hospitalized once ECT wears off, or are committed to maintenance ECT largely by default. I have no problem with the acute use of ECT, if combined with careful clinical diagnosis, and good long-term drug prophylaxis, especially with mood stabilizers. This is how it is practiced by Italian mood disorder specialists, like Athanasios Koukopoulos in Rome and his group, who see themselves as inheritors of the mantle of the founder of ECT, Lucio Bini. But by demeaning drugs to mere artifacts of EBM + pharmaceutical marketing, as is the drift in this book and in others by its consultants, ECT is left as only a short-term fix which guarantees long-term relapse.

It is good to be critical about the history of our clinical diagnoses and our clinical research on its treatments; it is harmful to be cynical about both, to deny the clinical value of even our most historically and scientifically solid diagnoses. One might share much of the critique of depression and antidepressants—though even there it can go too far in the direction of either postmodernist nihilism or biologist biases—but it is truly a veering off in the direction of Foucaultian fantasy to deny, as some in this group do (though not Shorter so far) the clinical validity of most of the presentations of most mental illnesses, even the best established, like manic-depressive illness, and to deny the utility of even our most scientifically proven treatments, like lithium.

Shorter's book is best as history and critique, weakest as science and solution. There is much that is wrong with DSM-III and its depressive nosology, and much that is mistaken in our use of new antidepressants. The concept of neurosis needs to be reconsidered and rehabilitated; the notion of melancholic depression is important; our antidepressant treatments are less effective in many ways than claimed. This history well documents those claims. But ECT is not the cure-all, biological research is not more sound than clinical, and replacing disease nosology with psychopathology, like melancholia, will not entail our mellifluous manumission from all this mistaken misery.

Philosophical Issues in Psychiatry II. Nosology: By Kenneth S. Kendler and Josef Parnas (Editors), Oxford University Press, 2012

Jacob Stegenga

Controversy about psychiatric disease categories is ubiquitous. Do fidgety young boys have a disease that goes by the name "Attention Deficit Hyperactivity Disorder"? Should a person who grieves the death of a spouse be excluded from a diagnosis of depression? Are psychiatric disease categories coextensive with specific abnormalities of brain physiology? This book—a collection of fifteen chapters written by prominent figures in psychiatry and philosophy of psychiatry—addresses such questions of psychiatric nosology: the logic of psychiatric diseases.

The book seems to have arisen out of a conference dedicated to psychiatric nosology (I infer this based on several comments of the authors throughout the book). This lends a colloquial and accessible language to the chapters, and affords conversation between some of the authors. The structure of the book itself fosters such engagement: each chapter has three parts written by separate authors—an introduction, the main text, and a commentary—and the introduction and commentary engage directly with the main text of each chapter. The fact that the book arose out of a conference perhaps explains some of its repetitiveness—many of the authors address the same core themes, in similar ways, using similar tropes. These themes include the question of nosological realism (do psychiatric categories represent real diseases?), the historical shifts in thinking about the basis of classifying psychiatric illnesses (from an etiological approach in the early twentieth century, to an "atheoretical" approach with the development of the DSM-III in the 1970s, to an "axiological" approach in the DSM-IV, and now to a "dimensional" approach with

Reprinted with kind permission from *Metapsychology* (metapsychology.mentalhelp.net). Acknowledgments go to Christian Perring for his kind support.

J. Stegenga (✉)
Department of Philosophy, University of Utah, Salt Lake City, UT 84112, USA
e-mail: jacob.stegenga@utah.edu

A. Batthyány (ed.), *Logotherapy and Existential Analysis*, Logotherapy and Existential Analysis: Proceedings of the Viktor Frankl Institute Vienna 1,
DOI 10.1007/978-3-319-29424-7_33

the advent of the DSM-V), and the criteria of adequacy that ought to be employed when evaluating psychiatric nosology (for example, diagnostic reliability versus some form of validity). Given the structure of this book, with its many contributors and several themes about an enormously complex subject, what follows is at best a cursory review.

One of the most interesting aspects of the book is the diversity of views expressed regarding diagnostic criteria. For instance, Kendler seems to favor operationalized criteria (125), Ghaemi argues that diagnosis should be based on causal etiology (47), and Krueger favors dimensional models of psychopathological impairment (300). In contrast to all of these views, Bolton argues that psychiatry is too concerned with classification, and should focus more on prediction, including predictions of patient outcomes based on medical interventions (7). As first notes, the non-specific nature of most psychiatric treatments renders predictions of patient outcomes little more reliable given one diagnosis compared with another (12).

Another interesting aspect of the book is the discussion of the historical shifts in psychiatric thinking and how such shifts became codified into the various revisions of the DSM. For instance, Berrios boldly asserts that since the nineteenth century little has changed in the epistemological basis of the classificatory models of psychiatry (101). Writing about more recent psychiatry, a chapter by Pincus, provides some detail to the development of the DSM-IV (154). One must look past some intellectual chest thumping. For example, Pincus, who was a central contributor to the development of the DSM-IV, is careful to note that the development of the DSM-IV was "evidence-based" and depended on a "hierarchy of evidence." In several places Pincus takes parting shots at the DSM-V—he claims that "the continued revision of a descriptive classification has little utility … changes in future descriptive classifications should be infrequent and guided by a highly conservative process" (157–8). We got it right (the fourth time)—such thinking goes—and so there is no need to change it.

Parnas has a lovely phrase in his chapter, which captures a central concern of this book: "the ontology of the psychiatric object" (230). What *is* the ontology of the psychiatric object? Here too the diversity of views expressed throughout the book is fascinating. Parnas says: the patient's experience. Ghaemi says: microphysiological entities or processes that cause disease (44). Contemporary diagnostic manuals say: syndromes, or sets of symptoms. McHugh says: the localization and pathogenesis of problems of consciousness (271). That this fundamental question remains unresolved is both intriguing and worrying. Worrying, of course, because the stakes are so high. Regier, one of the central contributors to the forthcoming new edition of the DSM, writes that one of his motivations in his career has been a concern about "false positives and the medicalization of normal human experiences." Several contributors to the book note the expansive momentum of psychiatry, which increases the number of subjects within its pharmacological jurisdiction.

Kendler's previous books in this series have displayed more appreciation for rigorous philosophy—past contributors include many of today's leading philosophers of science. Despite its title, the present volume is, on the whole, philosophically lightweight. There are few contributions from professional philosophers (I count three of sixteen authors). More salient, only several of the contributions engage with serious contemporary philosophical work on the subject, and many of the contributions smack of philosophical amateurism.

For instance, in the third chapter Ghaemi argues that "we don't need a general definition of mental illness to identify specific psychiatric diseases" (43)—not only does this neglect the rich philosophical literature on disease and illness (none of which is cited), it ignores the foundational motive for such literature, namely, that identifying a condition *as a disease* requires at least some sort of theory of disease. Ghaemi writes that specific diseases are identifiable simply as abnormalities of the body, and that this condition (bodily abnormality) is sufficient for disease attribution (44). However, there is near-consensus among scholars who have thought deeply about this question that this condition is in fact insufficient. I am sympathetic, though, with Ghaemi's view that it is a *necessary* condition: he argues with good motivation for resuscitating an etiological approach to psychiatric nosology, on the grounds that knowing the causes of diseases will contribute to developing more effective treatments. A corollary to this, says Ghaemi, is therapeutic conservatism, which he associates historically with Osler, and suggests that we ought to have more of in present-day psychiatry. To use a phrase from McHugh's chapter (270), such therapeutic conservatism might be better than present therapeutic regimes, which have "haphazard outcomes."

We also witness philosophical breeze in a few passing remarks from several of the contributors regarding the question of whether or not our psychiatric categories represent *real* diseases in nature. Kendler invokes a staple argument for scientific realism, usually referred to as the "no-miracles argument": although psychiatry is in its infancy and its categories are only "highly flawed first approximations," he claims that psychiatry has made plenty of advances, and asks "would these advances have been possible if all of our attempts at psychiatric classification were, at a fundamental level, deeply flawed?" (100). His desired answer, I suppose, is "no." But are they flawed or aren't they? (He says both, after all.) The no-miracles argument is convincing when applied to those areas of science, which are, well, seemingly miraculous, such as Jean Perrin's measurement of Avogadro's number, to take a famous example from the history of science. Perrin was able to measure Avogadro's number using 13 distinct methods, and these methods all closely agreed in their measurements. It would be a miracle if these measurements all agreed so closely and yet molecules were not real, and since science does not accept miracles as explanations (hence the argument's name), molecules *must* be real. I risk stating the obvious for the sake of being thorough: the science and practice of psychiatry is hardly miraculous.

Kendler calls his invocation of the no-miracles argument "positivistic," a cute foible the irony of which will not be lost on the philosophically initiated. A better attempt at defending his optimism is found in his full chapter, in which he borrows the idea of "epistemic iteration" from the historian of science Hasok Chang (305). Kendler seems to understand the notion of iteration as something like gradual progress toward a true description of reality. However, as Schaffner notes in his commentary, Chang's original use of epistemic iteration was quite different—Chang held that "truth is a destination that is only created by the approach itself" (325). Kendler maintains the modest view that epistemic iteration does not necessarily warrant thinking that psychiatric categories represent real diseases in nature; one might be optimistic that some of our disease categories are iteratively becoming better descriptions of real diseases, while be pessimistic about other disease categories (317, 320).

The converse of the no-miracles argument is usually referred to as the "pessimistic induction": since many or all of our past theories have turned out to be false, our present theories also will likely turn out to be false. Cooper invokes this argument in a rather confusing manner: "getting a version of the pessimistic induction to work for psychiatry is hard—there isn't much history, and there's even less past success" (38). This is odd for several reasons. Psychiatry has a history at least as long as, say, modern physics (arguably psychiatry is older than even classical physics!). It's just that, as Cooper says, this history has so few successes. That fact, though, provides *warrant* to a version of the pessimistic induction for psychiatry, contrary to Cooper's claim. A long history of nosological and therapeutic failures in psychiatry ought to make us at least a little suspicious of present psychiatric categories and treatments.

In the end, should we be optimists or pessimists about our psychiatric categories? The beauty of this book is the range of reasoned answers to this question. On the whole, though, it appears that our best research psychiatrists hold humble views regarding psychiatric nosology. Krueger expresses pessimism when he writes "most mental disorders are probably not categories in nature" (298). Kendler, one of the most cited psychiatrists today, calls his own discipline an "immature science" (318). McHugh puts the point politely: psychiatry has yet to come of age (269).

The dearth of careful philosophical analysis in this book should not turn many readers away. It is, as I hope to have indicated, a rich read. Professional psychiatrists and students will find it interesting, as will cultural commentators who discuss and debate the developments of the DSM, and similarly, perhaps, will the growing number of unfortunate people who are diagnosed with psychiatric diseases. These authors give us an insider's view of psychiatric nosology, and the sight seen is unsettling. This book is promising, though, precisely because it is the result of continued concern among professional psychiatrists regarding the philosophical foundations of their discipline. Such concern might—someday, one hopes—help psychiatry to come of age.

The Healing Companion: Stories for Courage, Comfort, and Strength—By The Healing Project, LaChance Publishing, 2009

Christian Perring

This is a collection of about 45 stories on 250 pages, each by a person describing how alcohol abuse has affected their lives. They are from a variety of perspectives: drinkers, spouses, parents, and children of drinkers; while most contributors are white, some of them belong to minority groups, although none of them gay or lesbian. Some declare religious faith, while others do not. The majority are sympathetic to the idea that alcoholism is a disease and that Alcoholics Anonymous is a good approach to dealing with alcohol problems, but not all of them are. The goal of the book is to provide stories that will help others with similar problems.

I had a grandparent who was by all accounts a chronic alcoholic who died in an asylum before I was born. His children were all affected by his drinking and his violence. I have other family members with a chronic history of overdrinking which has affected their ability to function. I suspect that the drinking was and continues to be a method of coping with the difficulties of the world ("self-medicating" as the lingo goes). I myself enjoy alcohol and sometimes use it to relieve tension. I've seen the damage that long-term alcohol use can do to a person's brain. Furthermore, I've experienced the frustration of trying to get someone with an alcohol problem to stop damaging themselves and those around them.

Although I know that alcohol use can cause brain damage, I am skeptical of claims that alcoholism is just a disease like any other, because it obscures the alcoholic's moral responsibility for the harm that he or she causes to others. So this is an especially interesting collection because people write about how alcoholism has

Reprinted with kind permission from *Metapsychology* (metapsychology.mentalhelp.net). Acknowledgments go to Christian Perring for his kind support.

C. Perring (✉)
Department of Philosophy, Dowling College,
Idle Hour Boulevard, Oakdale, NY 11769, USA
e-mail: perringc@dowling.edu

A. Batthyány (ed.), *Logotherapy and Existential Analysis*, Logotherapy and Existential Analysis: Proceedings of the Viktor Frankl Institute Vienna 1,
DOI 10.1007/978-3-319-29424-7_34

affected their personal lives and the relationships of people who drink too much and those around them.

Donna Veneto describes her father as loving, caring, and fun to be around, but then she spends most of her contribution talking about "Daddy Hyde," her father under the influence of drink. Daddy Hyde had a violent temper and spent much of his time away from home in local bars. Once in her teens, she got into many fights with him. She is similarly ambivalent in her judgments, saying that she is unsure. Sometimes she feels sorry for him, and at other times believing that he could have tried harder.

Tracey Alverson describes her father with some anger. She ends her piece with a dramatic statement. "I am starting a life of my own, and he doesn't want help. He knows he drinks too much but he has justified all the times he's stolen from us, threatened my mother, come close to physically harming one of his children. I choose instead to live with the pleasant memories I have. It's not my fault my father wants to die and is slowly killing himself with the bottle" (34). Similarly, Gloria Raskin talks about the resentment she felt toward her brother Arthur at the time of his death from cirrhosis of the liver, at his poor choices in life. He refused help and when their mother gave him some money at a difficult point in his life, he spent some of it on more alcohol. She describes his son Paul as responsible, hard-working, caring and a good father and laments that Arthur lost all those traits. So while she never explicitly says it, she implies that he became irresponsible, lazy, uncaring, and a bad father.

Lisa Dordal also describes her alcoholic parent as a sort of split personality in her piece "Two Mothers." Her daytime mother was a ,lively and charming person. Her evening mother drank, so she was sluggish and slurred her words. On retirement, her drinking got considerably worse, starting in the morning. Dordal describes her own drinking too, and recognizes how it became a problem for her. Yet when her first marriage ended, she quit drinking and turned to God. Mridu Kullar is another contributor who highlights the contrast between the public face of her father as a good family man and his behavior at home when he would get intoxicated and difficult. She struggles with the question whether he is really an alcoholic although the rest of her family denies it.

The difficulty of distinguishing between the good loveable qualities of a person and the way that person acts as a result of drinking is a common theme of the contributions. Allison Jones puts it succinctly when she writes about her husband, "Trying to control Brian's drinking made me insane. I was no longer able to separate the disease from the man" (95). He was attending A.A. meetings, yet he was still drinking, which made him a very difficult person to be with. She says that eventually they repaired their marriage, and part of the healing process was coming to see that she was powerless over his drinking, so that she was able to forgive herself and her husband. This sort of view that she gained from Al Anon helped her cope with her feelings about him. What stands out here is the idea of forgiveness: Brian hurt her and was accountable for what he did, and eventually she came to put her anger and resentment past her. It is not that her feelings were unjustified, but that they were able to move on from them.

Some heavy drinkers ,also blame themselves and report shame at the things they do when drunk. Karen Waggoner writes, "My disease, my condition, my chemical makeup, maybe even my character make it impossible for me to resist the ease and comfort that alcohol brings to me. We who suffer from alcoholism love the effect of drinking more than we love ourselves, our jobs, our families or our integrity" (53). While she describes her problem as a disease, she also describes it as a problem of love and identity. She became utterly selfish and withdrew from her relationships with her children and grandchildren. She ascribes her realization of her problem to an act of divine providence.

The ability to take control, of one's life and conversely, the inability to do so (i.e., powerlessness) feature prominently in the stories. Many contributors say that alcoholics are powerless over alcohol, and yet many of the same people then describe how they took control of their lives. Sometimes they resolve this contradiction by invoking an external power such as God. Yet the idea of powerlessness can be used for other purposes. Sheri Ables writes about her alcoholic husband, and justifies her leaving him by saying he is unable to reform himself, so what she is doing is best for her and their children, and may even be best for him. Other contributors write about hitting bottom, the AA way of describing the event that led them to recognize that they needed external help. In some cases, the families of alcoholics held interventions to get them to go into rehabilitation programs. Yet the truth is that it is very difficult to know what enables a heavy drinker to turn their life around. There are some data that suggest that AA can be helpful, but it is certainly not the most helpful mental health treatment available, and even the best treatments have a low success rate. There are some biological forms of treatment available and more in development, but ultimately it is all about getting a person to change their own behavior, drawing on their own resources of self-control. So the notion of powerlessness is very hard to make coherent, which is presumably why so many of the descriptions combine it with the idea of some external power or even a miracle that comes to set the alcoholic on the right path. If we are going to understand a person's recovery without appeal to supernatural powers, then we have to admit that people do have some power over their own lives, and under the right circumstances, they will be able to use that power, even if they are not able to do so in other situations. Many of the stories make clear how difficult that is; they describe the many attempts that alcoholics make before achieving some relatively permanent ability to avoid returning to heavy drinking, and make clear how it continues to be an ongoing struggle against temptation. It is occasionally possible to sort through the confusing language of powerlessness to find descriptions of people's power to control their lives.

Yet the writings in this book make very clear how much people's thinking and self-description when it comes to alcohol use has become infused with the rhetoric of AA, Al Anon, popular psychology, popular biology, and religion. Many different ideas and theories get thrown together and enter our language in a jumble, to the extent that it almost becomes impossible to write about alcohol use in any neutral way. *Voices of Alcoholism* gives a very American mix, and is, interesting as a representation of how we do think about alcohol use. Maybe it will be useful to people trying to make sense of their own lives, because there are enough different views in it to have something for everyone. The editing of the book has been done well, and all the writing is of a high standard. Most of the stories are interesting. So this is a collection with a great deal to offer, even for readers who don't accept all the assumptions of the contributors.

Mind and Its Place in the World: By Alexander Batthyány and Avshalom Elitzur (Editors), Ontos, 2008. Irreducibly Conscious: By Alexander Batthyány and Avshalom Elitzur (Editors), Winter Universitätsverlag, 2009

Marshall H. Lewis

One key task of contemporary logotherapists and existential analysts is to confront reductionism when applied to the identity of the human person. Viktor Frankl's body of work does this with respect to the major theories and movements of his day. It falls to us, however, to continue this work with respect to the major theories and movements of our own day. Chief among these movements is neuropsychiatry when it asserts that human consciousness is nothing more than the mechanical-like workings of our neural apparatus. An excellent way for the contemporary logotherapist to become familiar with the contours and positions in the current debate over the nature of human consciousness is by reading the pair of books herein reviewed: *Mind and Its Place in the World: Non-Reductionistic Approaches to the Ontology of Consciousness*, edited by Alexander Batthyány and Avshalom Elitzur (2006, Ontos Verlag) and *Irreducibly Conscious: Selected Papers on Consciousness*, edited by Alexander Batthyány and Avshalom Elitzur (2009, Universitätsverlag Winter). Both books offer a treasure trove of insight.

Mind and Its Place in the World is Volume 7 of a larger series on Phenomenology and Mind edited by Arkadiusz Chrudzimski and Wolfgang Huemer. Batthyány and Elitzur's volume consists of 12 articles and essays on the problem of consciousness. In it they seek to bring the non-reductionist tradition up to date by providing analysis and perspectives on the most recent trends in consciousness research. Unlike earlier works in the tradition that focussed exclusively on a dualistic model of consciousness, *Mind and Its Place in the World* is eclectic. Its contributors represent a range of non-reductionist approaches and opinions that the editors hope will stimulate debate.

Batthyány explains the context: "Most of our authors follow Chalmers' suggestion to divide the problem of consciousness into two categories, which he marks as the 'easy problem' and the 'hard problem'. The first category yields to conventional

M.H. Lewis (✉)
LogoTalk, P. O. Box 632, Ulysses, KS 67880, USA
e-mail: logotalk@pld.com

A. Batthyány (ed.), *Logotherapy and Existential Analysis*, Logotherapy and Existential Analysis: Proceedings of the Viktor Frankl Institute Vienna 1,
DOI 10.1007/978-3-319-29424-7_35

scientific methods and is usually researched in the context of psychology, the neurosciences and cognitive science. The hard problem fundamentally differs from the easy problems to the same extent as content differs from quality. Here the question is not about what we experience and by which information processes we navigate through the world, but more fundamentally: why and how it is that we do have subjective experiences and inner awareness at all?" (Batthyány 2006, 8). A logotherapist and existential analyst cannot help but hear the echo of Frankl's sharp division between the psychophysical organism and the noetic in the frame of this debate.

With backgrounds ranging from physics to philosophy and from mathematics to psychology, the volume's contributors include J. Kenneth Arnette, Alexander Batthyány, Hoyt L. Edge, Avshalom C. Elitzur, Peter J. King, Gershon Kurizki, Steven Lehar, Peter B. Lloyd, Paul Løvland, Riccardo Manzotti, Donald P. Merrifield, SJ, Russell Pannier, Howard Robinson, Fiona Steinkamp, and Thomas D. Sullivan.

The work of the editors and contributors is further extended in the more recent title on this topic, *Irreducibly Conscious*. *Irreducibly Conscious* clearly asserts the view that a few voices in the field of consciousness studies have been drowning out the rest—specifically, voices that seek to reduce consciousness to a physical phenomenon, manifested by either the brain or the behavior of the organism. *Irreducibly Conscious* provides a corrective by bringing together another group of distinguished, international researchers to highlight the limits of the reductionist approach and to advance alternative approaches and unexamined paths of research related to the phenomenal or experiential aspects of consciousness.

In the words of the editors, "This book is about science and consciousness. More precisely, it is about science's most powerful method, namely, reduction, and consciousness' most salient feature, namely, qualia. It is qualia that seems to be irreducible, hence the tension out of which this book was born. None other than the staunch reductionist Emil du Bois-Reymond confessed: 'Ignoramus et ignorabimus (We do not know, and we shall never know)', when referring to consciousness. While all the contributors to this collection agree with the first part of this unhappy statement, most of them seem to take exception to its end" (Elitzur and Batthyány 2009, 7).

This exception fuels debate throughout the remainder of the book. By using tools and methods from multiple fields including philosophy, logic, empiricism, and mathematics, *Irreducibly Conscious* contains twelve articles that reflect on what we know and that argue for positions and directions to advance our knowledge. Contributors include Alexander Batthyány, John F. G. Eastmond, Avshalom C. Elitzur, Stewart Goetz, W. D. Hart, William Hasker, Michael Lipkind, Paul Løvland, Bruce MacLennan, Charles Taliaferro, and Daniel von Wachter.

There can be no doubt that non-reductionist approaches to consciousness follow the arc of Frankl's thought and contributions through logotherapy and existential analysis. In fact, it is the question that life poses to the field today; it is the question with which the field must grapple if it is to remain a vibrant participant in the scholarship that forms the basis of its own ontology. Through the 24 articles in these two volumes, the contributors set forth scholarly arguments that represent the current best thinking in the non-reductionist tradition. As such, *Mind and Its Place in the World* and *Irreducibly Conscious* are volumes that belong on the desk of every logotherapist.

Identity: Complex or Simple? Georg Gasser and Matthias Stefan (Editors), Cambridge University Press, 2013

Robert Zaborowski

The collection is made up of contributions supporting either simple or complex approaches to the question of personal identity. While the latter approach (also sometimes referred to as reductionism) is about explicating the notion of personal identity by pointing to other phenomena, the former (called also non-reductionism) is based on the premise that personal identity cannot be explicated by any other term for it is simple and unanalyzable. Yet, in both cases, there is no room for doubt about personal identity as such because it is taken for granted. No position denying it is discussed in the volume (which explains why Hume, for example, is seldom referred to).

The collection is divided into three sections, each consisting of four essays. Those of the first section outline the framework of the discussion on personal identity; the next four (plus one reply) contain arguments for one or another of the approaches (simple or complex); the last set of essays focuses more specifically on elaborating the simple view. This is a deliberate step, since, as we are informed from the very beginning, "the simple view is poorly understood, and therefore deserves more attention than it has received so far" (an opinion already voiced in 2010 by Olson) (1).

In the introduction, the editors clarify, first, that the so-called problem of personal identity can in fact embrace four distinct questions (i.e., biographical ,or narrative identity, personhood, metaphysical nature, and, finally, diachronic identity) and, secondly, that epistemic criteria of personal identity are not to be confused with

Reprinted with kind permission from *Metapsychology* (metapsychology.mentalhelp.net). Acknowledgements go to Christian Perring for his kind support.

R. Zaborowski (✉)
Department of Philosophy, University of Warmia and Mazury,
Michała Oczapowskiego 2, Olsztyn, Poland
e-mail: thymos2001@yahoo.fr

A. Batthyány (ed.), *Logotherapy and Existential Analysis*, Logotherapy and Existential Analysis: Proceedings of the Viktor Frankl Institute Vienna 1,
DOI 10.1007/978-3-319-29424-7_36

ontic criteria. In other words, finding out if there is an identity between two persons is a different issue from whether they actually are one and the same person. A person can still be the same even if she is no longer recognizable. For example, "[b]iological and psychological continuity may be regarded as epistemic criteria for diachronic identity, but they are neither necessary nor sufficient conditions for personal identity" (3). As it is stated clearly, the book is a consideration of personal identity in its ontic dimension. The introduction in itself is a useful account of what the debate on personal identity currently is about and not just—as it is often the case—a mere summary of the essays included in the volume. The editors present the main issues, tenets and arguments, as well as the problems raised by the complex (both in its biological and psychological versions) and the simple approaches.

Chapter 1 ("Chitchat on Personal Identity" by D. Barnett) is modeled on Plato's dialogue form (consequently with no bibliography at all). Two twin brothers are trying to find out which of them is the person on the photo they find in their attic. From this they engage into asking more and more questions about how to determine personal identity. They tackle the role of the brain, sensory experience (past and present), body, sensations, feelings, beliefs, memories, intellect as well as other features of a conscious being or personality traits. In order to grasp the core of personal identity they proceed by progressive elimination. The outcome is quite Platonic because we arrive at the following aporia: "'[…] How in the world could I be a squad?'—'In some sense it seems possible; in some sense it doesn't […]'" (42). With ,this dictum it seems that there would be no possible clear-cut response since, as it emerges from the dialogue, the complex as well as simple view has each its own descriptive advantages and flaws.

"In Search of the Simple View" by Eric T. Olson is an attempt at both determining the common denominator of the complex and simple views and finding a distinction between the two positions (for example while it could seem that a denial that our identity can be indeterminate is common to all advocates of the simple view, it appears that also some supporters of the complex view say the same). The main distinction would be to accept or reject such a thing as a criterion of identity, hence the complex view amounts to criterialism and the simple view to anti-criterialism. Olson spells out why for example Cartesianism is wrongly considered as a paradigm case of a simple view, while in fact it is a version of criterialism and, consequently, of the complex view (unless, as he states, Cartesianism would claim that although "personal identity consists in identity of soul, identity of soul insists in nothing" (56)—yet this position, called *bruteness*, is denied by some Cartesians). Next Olson discusses the confusion between evidential and constitutive criteria of personal identity. This happens when conditions used for making judgments about personal identity are taken to be constitutive for it. In conclusion Olson appeals to the fact that philosophers disagree about explanatory demands as well as about questions to be answered. Since "some philosophers expect more facts to be explained than others do, and there is probably some correlation between this and whether one holds a view classified as complex or one classified as simple" (62), it is hard to elucidate satisfactorily a criterion ,distinguishing both kinds of view and, as he concludes, "[t]he simple view remains elusive" (62). It could, however, be asked if the complex view is not elusive as well, not to speak about the divide itself between both views.

In "Personal identity, Indeterminacy and Obligation" Ryan Wasserman ,examines the indeterminacy argument as it is stated by Parfit ("it is possible for questions about personal identity to lack determinate answers" (63). Opponents argue that since personal identity cannot be indeterminate, complex view must be wrong. But the premise itself, i.e., that personal identity cannot be indeterminate, is rarely discussed. At first glance, it seems that it cannot be indeterminate and, as Wasserman says, "something deep inside of me says that there must *be* an answer" (64). Even if only intuitive, this conviction is so strong that it should be examined. There are several versions of the complex view (depending on what is referred to as the basis of the identity), but all of them are referring to the continuity or connectedness—which, in turn, is a vague criterion ("[h]ow continuous does a series need to be to be continuous?" 65). Wasserman appeals to the notion of obligation, especially moral obligation in order to show that if identity is indeterminate, obligation would be indeterminate too, and this cannot be accepted. Yet again he relies on intuition claiming that questions of obligations must be determinately answered. Otherwise many issues in moral matters turn out to be indeterminate, too. Wasserman falsifies the complex view by refuting the indeterminacy obligation which results from the indeterminacy of personal identity which, in turn, results from the complex view (this is what he calls the indeterminacy argument). Although the indeterminacy argument is subject to both epistemicist and subjectivist response these two in turn are subject to objections presented by Wasserman. His conclusion is, however, a bit disappointing or, at least, too poetical, as he ends with the following paragraph: "If personal identity is genuinely indeterminate, then that is all we can ask for. Perhaps that is all we need." (81).

Another attempt at clarifying the distinction between the complex and the simple view is presented in "Personal Identity and its Perplexities" by Harold W. Noonan. After reformulating the question about personal identity into one, about the necessary condition for being person Noonan sets the distinction between the simple and the complex view of identity as considered diachronically. The main part of the paper is centered on the indexicality of the concept of a person, that is that personal identity is one's own: it is mine, yours, his, etc. In the course of his discussion he declares himself a psychological continuer theorist. Finally Noonan argues against indeterminacy—a theme touched upon already in Wasserman's paper—that could be involved in personal identity. He underlines the difference between questions about personal identity and questions about the conditions of personhood, and he distinguishes indeterminacy as related to the "person," into epistemic indeterminacy and ontic indeterminacy. Although he applies his conceptual distinctions throughout the analysis in the last part of the paper I do not see where, if at all, he concludes.

In part II Richard Swinburne ("How to Determine which is the True Theory of Personal Identity"), by analyzing what is metaphysically, possible and particularly logically possible, wants to determine which, of the two—simple or complex—theories of personal identity is true. And so he starts with a clarification on logical necessity, the possibility and impossibility of sentences. From there he tries to solve the disagreement between the complex and simple theorists by way of determining if either of them accepts the logical impossibility of personal identity as understood by them. He therefore analyses the expression "is the same person as" applying it to both theories. Swinburne—unlike complex theorists who focus on continuity of body, memory and character—points to "direct awareness of personal identity" which is linked to a sort of "overlapping conscious events [that] are experiences of the same person, from which it follows that any stream of such events are also experiences of the same person" (114). That kind of awareness is, so to speak, undeniable and "can only be described as an awareness of himself as a continuing subject of experience" (114). I could therefore think that identity is a logical consequence of the notion of subject. By virtue of being a subject a person is "immune to error though (sic!) misidentification" (119). In a word, he who uses the word "I" when referring to his experiences knows the essence of that word because he is the subject of the experiences that happen to him. And yet his knowledge of how to use "I" is not determined by "any continuity of brain, memory of character" (119). Finally, Swinburne, if I understand him correctly, associates the "I" with all the experiences, establishing it as the human soul. As he concludes, "the only essential properties necessary for a person to exist are the essential properties of any soul, which—I suggest—are simply the one property of having (in some sense) a capacity to be conscious" (122). One might ask, however, whether or not these essential properties are to be identified in their content with the above-mentioned existential experiences. But this is a point that Swinburne does not address.

Sydney Shoemaker ("Against Simplicity") first, argues for complex identity of other things than, persons, trees in his case. He arrives at the Lockean claim that "[t] emporally proximate instantiations of the property must belong to the same tree, since otherwise we would have different trees, occupying the same place at the same time" (127), and, thereby, tree must exist as spatio-temporally continuous. This is why, Shoemaker suggests, "[t]he diachronic unity relation cannot be simple and unanalyzable if it's obtaining requires spatio-temporal continuity or causal connectedness" (129). From there on, Shoemaker applies his argument to personal identity. He claims that in this case, too, its persistence over time "consists in phenomena occurring over a period of time and depends on successive stages of the behaviour being manifested by one and the same person" (130) or else we would be led to extreme skepticism in judging other minds. (I wonder if he is not confusing the epistemic and ontic requirements here.) Shoemaker goes on claiming that "[a]ny state, psychological or not, necessarily belongs to the thing of which it is a subject, and so gets its identity from the identity of its subject" (132)—now I wonder what remains of the subject of, for instance, memory, if the subject is devoid of it on and in what sense memory is direct (see 130), if it is just a state that belongs to its subject. The former need not entail the latter as *directness* and *belonging* seem to be different categories. Moreover, this is all the more intriguing because later on Shoemaker avoids or reformulates circularity by the notion of holism [1]: but, as far as I understand holism and apparently Shoemaker, too, ("[t]he nature of the properties and the nature of the persistence conditions of the things that have them cannot be explained independently of one another," 135), what is included under that label is one and indivisible, hence simple, and it is separable only conceptually. Similarly, if "in the most cases our concept of a property is far from including a full specification of its causal profile" (135) [2], it should be shown that the relation between "the *nature* of the trans-temporal identity and the *nature* of the causal profiles of the properties" (135) is ontic and not only epistemic. If the former is the case—as Shoemaker would have us believe ("a conceptual holism"[3])—it would rather give more strength to the simple than the complex view of identity.

E. J. Lowe's ("The Probable Simplicity of Personal Identity") two main points are that (1) the simple view of identity is more probable than the complex, and as ,such the simple view is nothing more than the most plausible, option, and (2) diachronic and synchronic identity are not different sorts of identity. According to Lowe anyone who wants to avoid epistemic presuppositions about identity or difference between two persons is in serious need of a criterion of personal identity. Yet, Lowe is careful in making assumptions whether or not such criterion can successfully be found. Sections on logical identity (especially with reference to Frege's two-level identity criteria) are followed by remarks on what a person is. Since the essence of a person has been understood differently by different philosophers, this has given rise to different conceptions of a person's identity. Persons—apart from being "or at least capable of being, aware of" (145) themselves—"are not really a single *kind* of thing" (145). In what follows, Lowe discusses Locke's criterion of personal identity together with Reid's and Butler's charges of circularity made against it, along with the criticism which, as he says, applies to any psychological account of personal identity, namely: if personal identity is based on experiences and experiences are properties of a person, then the criterion is circular because "we cannot *both* individuate persons in terms of their experiences [...] *and* individuate personal experiences in terms of the persons having them" (150). Lowe's view is that a person is an entity, with distinctive properties such as thought and feeling, rather than a mere property or feature of some other thing, for example of his brain. If therefore "persons really are *fundamental* in our ontological scheme [...], then we simply should not expect to be able to appeal to other entities of suitable kinds in their case" (152). Accordingly, even if this is hard to prove, a negative thesis like the simplicity thesis, skepticism about the reality of persons is not to be recommended by any means. But given that complex accounts are proven flawed, the simple theory of personal identity seems to be the better option. The last section of the paper is devoted to an objection made to Lowe's argument against a neo-Lockean criterion by Shoemaker. Chapter 8 in turn, is a one-page reply to Lowe by Shoemaker.

Martine Nida-Rümelin in "The Non-Descriptive Individual Nature of Conscious Beings" starts by distinguishing conscious (also called *experiencing*), individuals from other kinds), of individuals (such as material objects) in virtue of the former's having a non-descriptive individual nature. Having a non-descriptive individual nature means that "the constitutional basis of [a conscious beings'] existence is non-descriptive" (160), which amounts to saying that such constitutional basis "can only be described using a rigid designator which directly or indirectly refers to" (161) it.

While in the case of material (i.e., non-conscious) individuals there is no hidden feature of their existence, in the case of conscious individuals "every formulation of the constitutional basis of [their] existence requires rigid reference to" (165) them themselves. In other words, while there may exist a perfect counterpart for a material object, in the case of a conscious being its only perfect counterpart is that very being itself. The being of a person consists in "living that person's life [...] experienc[ing] the world from that person's perspective [...] hav[ing] that person's body, and [...] enjoy[ing] that person's pleasures" (168). However, "from one's perspective" is not to be taken psychologically, e.g., imagining to be like someone in some important respect or imagining to be in someone's situation. It rather refers to the fact of being the very subject of experiencing, i.e., that subject that exists rather than non-exists, especially because, for that particular subject, it is fundamentally different whether he exists or not. Similarly, the mental activity of a person is non-descriptive because the only way to grasp it is to refer to that person's mental activity. And referring to her own being itself means referring to what is her personal identity. As she puts it, "[t]he difference lies in nothing but *who* is experiencing that life" (173) with the manifest corollary that "according to our understanding of what it is to be an experiencing subject, it is essential for being an experiencing subject that one's individual nature is non-descriptive" (173). In the final part of her paper Nida-Rümelin refers to elements of her more general position wherein, it seems to me, she is close to a Heideggerian approach. For she writes: "the nature of what it is to be an experiencing subject is revealed to us by being a subject of experience" (176), and even more explicitly: "[i]n order to find out what it is to be an experiencing subject, we need not wait for any scientific discovery: we simply have to uncover what we implicitly knew all along" (176), which could also be compared with C. G. Jung's claim that "one understands nothing psychological unless one has experienced it oneself".

In "Personal Identity: a Not-So-Simple Simple View" Lynne Rudder Baker starts from the claim that being essentially a person means being a person at), any time she exists (we cannot think about still existing without being person). She takes the simple view, yet in a way different from the standard case, according to which persons are immaterial. For Baker person is embodied with the ability to think of herself as herself. The body is her support for person-level activities with the unique feature that they are first-personal (not-persons share only third-personal persistence conditions). As she writes, "[...] first-person perspective is a property instance that cannot be divided or duplicated. So, a molecule-for-molecule replica of [one's] body would not have [his] first-person perspective" (182). What she calls her not-so-simple simple view is this: "a person is a being with a first-person perspective essentially and persists as long as her first-person perspective is exemplified" (182) with the qualification that she must possess mechanism supporting her first-person reference to herself as herself. One of the differences between her and other simple views is that Baker admits a degree of identity, because human persons come into existence gradually. Another one is that she admits parts of persons although they should be understood only as ordinary—and not mereological—parts. The fact that there are no informative criteria of personal identity (because personhood is a basic property and because it is not susceptible to a non-personal or sub-personal account) should not be a concern. This is the very fact that so far as human beings are irreducible persons, any informative persistence conditions must be avoided. Baker ends by listing six of several uniquely human features (e.g., having self-narratives, having war crimes, international courts and human rights) that emerge from those shared with non-human animals. They are meant to be the evidence of "an ontological difference between human and animals" (191). I wonder, however, to what extent she adopted a similar approach to that of Nicolai Hartmann, who insisted in his work on strata of reality by referring to their ontological features.

Christian Kanzian ("Is 'Person' a Sortal Term?") explores to what extent "person" can be understood as a sortal term in the analysis of personal identity),and once again addresses the opposition),between the complex and the simple views. Although he is concerned more with semantics, he remarks in his introduction that "[a]n absolute complex view is impossible" (193), because—here Kanzian could have referred to Aristotle—we cannot go back *in infinitum*. Since one must stop at some point, its supporters, so Kanzian claims, "might start with a complex view, but end as supporters of simple, non-analyzable units, whatever they are" (193). After discussing arguments in favour of person-not-being-a-sortal-term claim (its ancestor being Gilbert of Poitiers who claimed that personhood is something added to the human being, hence personhood is accidental) which is flawed because an accidental term has no identification function and for this reason cannot be the ground one refers to, then in favour of person-being-a-sortal-term claim (its ancestor being Boethius for whom person is a substance-kind), also flawed because it switches to dualism, and finally "the don't care" view (which is flawed by being semantically inconsistent; this is the case of Peter Singer), Kanzian passes on to setting "person" as a semantically unique term. Although there are no empirical criteria connected with "person," it is dependent on other terms, which means that "person" is an incomplete one. Being dependent on something else does not amount, however, to being reducible to something else. In other words, while "person" can be dependent conceptually it does not mean that person is reducible ontologically. Hence Kanzian's conclusion: "diachronic personal identity [...] must be simple [...] but dependent in a unique way on something which is not simple: for example on *human* identity. It is incomplete in nature, because of its essential dependence on something complex." (203)

Dean Zimmerman in "Materialism, Dualism, and 'Simple' Theories of Personal Identity," the longest paper of the volume, after presenting a detailed background of), the complex/simple theory [J1] controversy (e.g., he discusses Parfit's mentioning of Chisholm as non-reductionist), and setting a new definition of reductionism, puts forward a thesis about "the supervenience of personal identity upon microphysical facts, or upon microphysical facts supplemented only by 'impersonal' psychological facts" (212). This thesis is next analyzed in two versions: physicalist and non-physicalist reductionism with a separate paragraph in which Zimmerman offers thought experiments to test whether materialism is a better option than dualism. This is yet another paper that concludes with an aporia ("loose ends and confessions" in Zimmerman's wording), since while some arguments are inconclusive as to providing "reasons for believing in a dualism of persons and bodies [...], other considerations push [...] toward dualism" (234).

Hud Hudson ("The Morphing Block and Diachronic Personal Identity") looks for the best criterion of diachronic personal identity and such that would),be understood as),constitutive rather than epistemic. He examines the issue from the materialist position ("a human person is identical to a certain, highly organized, material object," (237) and more particularly by analyzing perdurantism (object is extending in four dimensions and composed of temporal as well as spatial parts) and endurantism (object is an entity extending in three spatial dimensions) approaches. Hudson presents then a conception of time because the concept of diachronic personal identity is strongly determined by how time is understood. For instance, to assume that only present and past things exist (growing block theory) is largely different from assuming that only present and future things exist (shrinking block theory). Hudson carries on his analysis from a substantivalist position, i.e., identifying "times hyperplanes,), and incorporat[ing] a certain independence or recombination principle for space-time points," taking "space-time to be a concrete particular with an ontological status not reducible to relations between material objects" and "identif[ying] space-time and its extended sub-regions with either pluralities or else fusions of uncountably many, simple, unextended, space-time points" (240). Such a morphing block theory is the most promising alternative for "the theories of personal identity that share the causal dependence requirement" (248). Although Hudson presents a series of charges against that position, the morphing block option makes possible a simple view of identity without resort to the causal dependence requirement.

Taken as a whole this is an amazing collection of papers. It mirrors the intricacy of the topic and, since both parties are similarly convincing, a reader can feel lost which of two views to adopt. One can have—at least I had—the same impression as after reading one of Plato's early dialogues: *now* I know no more what personal identity is [4]. The fact that there is little, if at all, dogmatism on either side is to be praised because this makes the book philosophically fruitful. For example after having read it an impression can be that the divide between simple and complex view is not as straightforward as it would be expected: in the diversity of viewpoints there is much more than a clear-cut dichotomy. Moreover, some papers are only sketches or investigations of sort with no ambition of reaching a strict conclusion. We find a good deal of provisional solutions (not to speak about papers with no solution at all), hesitations, queries, confessions and so on. In this sense the book is aporetical in its very character. This is not surprising given the nature and essence of personal identity. Whether simple or complex it seems that there is a thing such as personal identity [5]. Alternatively one could say that either view can be accurate, depending on what perspective is taken. For instance, Plato, similarly to some extent, hesitates whether the soul is simple (*monoeides*) or composite (*polueides*). Apparently the former is more useful in explaining the persistence of the soul, while the second fits better in spelling out the internal conflict. Finally, one could also wonder if the entire question about personal identity being simple or complex is not erroneously formulated.

My main concern is to see that feelings, or if you will, the whole of the affective life, i.e., affectivity, is used so little, if at all, throughout the chapters of the book. This is all the more surprising because some authors refer to what they call experience, yet without explicating what they understand by that term. I would be inclined to think that the notion of experience includes affectivity but this does not go without saying and therefore should be elucidated. Some remarks made by supporters),of both the simple as well as—and this is extremely interesting—the complex view relating to experience give the impression that affectivity could be conceived of as their common denominator. Affectivity—unless I am mistaken, in which case I would say experience—emerges as a crucial element in revealing the essence of personal identity. For example Shoemaker does not use that category, yet he claims that, for instance, "identity judgment appears to be one I know to be true without the use of any criterion of identity. My knowledge of it seems to be direct and not grounded on evidence of identity of any sort." (130) I am willing to believe that knowledge mentioned here is not only of intellectual character but has also an experiential component which, in turn, is not entirely devoid of an affective side.

Last not least, the issue of personal identity with a couple of points discussed in the volume has been interestingly presented—though in a literary form—for example by Thomas Mann in his novel *Transposed Heads*. For a reader of it several passages of the volume may seem repetitive, especially when one thinks about examples of thought experiments of removing and transplanting one's brain/head into/onto another's body.

As it is, the volume is rich and offers much food for thought. It is impressive how the contributors argue in different ways for either of two views discussed. Yet since the arguments are often fine-grained, this book is not easy to read. I would rather recommend),it as a starting-point or inspiring stimulation for a further inquiry into personal identity.

[1]. For a similar procedure of reshaping what is believed to be a vicious circle by means of holism—though in a different realm—see B. W. Helm, *Emotions and Motivation: Reconsidering Neo-Jamesian Accounts* in: Peter Goldie (ed.), *The Oxford Handbook of Philosophy of Emotion*, Oxford 2010, p. 313: "[t]he circularity of the account is therefore a normal part of such holism and is not at all vicious".

[2]. A similar concern is expressed by M. Evans, *A Partisan's Guide to Socratic Intellectualism* in: S. Tenenbaum (ed.). *Desire, practical reason, and the good*, Oxford 2010, p. 22: "each of us has an infinite number of beliefs, most of which are so complex that no mortal creature could ever succeed in expressing them".

[3]. For a similar mutual causal relationship between),character and emotions see Aristotle: earlier emotions determine later character which, in turn, determines subsequent emotions and so on, and so forth.

[4]. As a matter of fact, not only early dialogues—a feeling of similar dizziness recurs in *Theaetetus*'s famous passage (155c: "sometimes when I regard them it really makes my head swim," transl. H. N. Fowler).

[5]. The fact that there is no clear solution reached (or even reachable) should not be considered as an argument against personal identity as such. One could easily appeal to a case of competing particle and wave theories of light. Nobody should infer from that duality in explanation),that there is no such thing as light.

Tragic Sense of Life: By Miguel de Unamuno, Multiple Editions

Marianna D. Falcón Cooper

It was back in 1999, my last year at University in Mexico City, when my philosophy teacher gave me a most valuable gift: Miguel de Unamuno's book, "*Tragic Sense of Life.*" He was convinced that I was a "natural existentialist," for our conversations outside the classroom often revolved around subjects such as anguish, mortality, the meaning of life, and the question about God. I was immediately drawn to it. The title alone made an impression on me, and gave me the intuitive feeling that its author and I would have a mutual understanding. I can honestly say that the reading of this book (years before I studied to become a logotherapist) was "auto-biblio-therapy."

From the first pages of this book, Unamuno presents his existential viewpoint. He is interested in the individual, concrete, substantive man: "The man of flesh and bone; the man who is born, suffers, and dies – above all, who dies; the man who eats and drinks and plays and thinks and wills; the man who is seen and heard; the brother, the real brother." (Unamuno 2006, 1)

He rejects reductionism and is not interested in the "abstract" man, that is, a "no-man," the man that is "merely an idea." He fights to reclaim the human heart and spirit, and does so by "operating upon himself," while he reflects upon the tragic sense of life. In other words, his "philosophy" expresses the integral spiritual yearning of its author, and he believes that this is how it should be, because "in a philosopher, what must needs most concern us is the man" (Unamuno 2006, 3).

Unamuno believes that the personal and affective starting point of all philosophy and religion is the tragic sense of life. "And the most tragic problem of philosophy is to reconcile intellectual necessities with the necessities of the heart and the will." (Unamuno 2006, 14).

M.D.F. Cooper (✉)
Centro Nous, Av. Insurgentes Sur 1971, local 383 nivel fuente. Col.
Guadalupe Inn. Del. Alvaro Obregón, Mexico City, Mexico
e-mail: marianna_f@yahoo.com

A. Batthyány (ed.), *Logotherapy and Existential Analysis*, Logotherapy and Existential Analysis: Proceedings of the Viktor Frankl Institute Vienna 1,
DOI 10.1007/978-3-319-29424-7_37

He wishes to shatter faith; faith in science, faith in reason, even "blind faith" in faith itself, and to shelter us from the "pedantry of specialists, against the philosophy of the professional philosophers" (Unamuno 2006, 267). He is an enemy of "philosophical systems" and asks that no theory or school be founded on him.

The Spanish novelist, essayist, poet, playwright, and philosopher, Miguel de Unamuno (1864–1936) is considered a precursor of existentialism, and, as Ortega y Gasset said of him: "all his life and all his philosophy have been a *meditatio mortis.*" In this particular book, considered his philosophical masterpiece (originally published in 1913), Unamuno insists "although this meditation upon mortality may soon induce in us a sense of anguish, it fortifies us in the end" (Unamuno 2006, 37).

From the "contradictions" that spring from what is deepest in him, and by uniquely blending intellect with sentiment, he reflects upon subjects such as "the hunger for immortality," "the essence of religion," "the rationalist dissolution," and, hand in hand, leads us "into the depths of the abyss of despair," into a battlefield where heart is at war with head, faith with reason, and he does not wish to make peace between them, for he is convinced that from these contradictions and conflicts can stem a basis for human action.

At his point, we find a practical purpose for all the theory that preceded it. And Unamuno dives into subjects such as: love, suffering, compassion, faith, hope, and charity.

By exposing his own suffering and despair, he dares to speak what others prefer to keep silent, because he knows he is expressing the suffering of humanity: "I have sought to strip naked, not only my soul, but the human soul" (Unamuno 2006, 110).

Unamuno considers the "attitude of despair" to be the most noble attitude of the spirit, the most profound, the most human, and the most fruitful. "I believe that many of the greatest heroes, perhaps the greatest of all, have been men of despair and that by despair they have accomplished their mighty works" (Unamuno 2006, 116).

And while reading Unamuno one cannot but think of the man Viktor Frankl, whose biography is inevitably intertwined with his philosophy. We cannot but assert that he, too, was a man who understood and possessed the tragic sense of life, as Unamuno said of his "brothers" Kierkegaard, St. Augustine, Marcus Aurelius, Pascal, among others. Frankl himself "confesses" that he had to "go through the hell of despair over the apparent meaninglessness of life, through total and ultimate nihilism" before he could develop logotherapy as an immunization against it (Frankl 1988, 166). Without a doubt, they would both agree that tragedy could be turned into triumph. And it is the astonishing similarities I found between Unamuno and Frankl's ideas, which bring me to share with you an interesting recent discovery:

A close friend and colleague, who is studying the works of Max Scheler, searching for clues that influenced Frankl's thought, came across the following paragraph in John Raphael Staude's book "*Max Scheler, An Intellectual Portrait*" (Staude 1967), and enthusiastically shared it with me:

"Inspired by his reading of Miguel de Unamuno's *Tragic Sense of Life*, a book that he felt he might have written himself, Scheler found that there was an amazing unity of style in the way things happened to him. Perhaps everything had been absolutely necessary after all." Could it be that Scheler, too, found solace and empathy in Unamuno's words? To what extent could his ideas have impacted Scheler, and these, in turn, had an influence on Frankl's thought, if we consider Frankl's admission that "logotherapy is the result of the application of Max Scheler's concepts to psychotherapy"? (Frankl 1988, 10). Of this we may never have certainty, but for me it is an idea, a possibility worth entertaining.

But even if there was no such thing, what is expressed in Unamuno's writings will not only echo our innermost concerns (where reasons do not avail), but will surely provide depth to our work as logotherapists and existential analysts. For there are many people out there who suffer from conflicts of conscience, crises of faith, from the struggle between mind and heart, from the hunger for God, and who search for finality, a personal one, to the Universe. And we must learn to consider and listen to the "values of the heart" of the "man of flesh and bone" that sits before us seeking spiritual first-aid, and I believe that there is no better way to do so, than in recognizing them, first, in ourselves, in order to truly offer empathy and compassion.

As Frankl noted, "one must go through his own existential despair if he is to learn how to immunize his patients against it" (Frankl 1988, 137), and we can rest assured that Unamuno will guide us through it.

References

Frankl, V. (1988). *The will to meaning. Foundations and applications of logotherapy*. New York: Penguin.

Staude, J. (1967). *Max Scheler, 1874–1928, An intellectual portrait*. New York: The Free Press.

Unamuno, M. (2006). *Tragic sense of life*. New York: Barnes and Noble.

Portrait of the Psychiatrist as a Young Man: The Early Writing and Work of R.D. Laing, 1927–1960: By Allan Beveridge, Oxford University Press, 2011

Sharon Packer

Even those who do not like Laing will love Beveridge's book about Laing. The reasons to relish this book? It does not convert non-believers into believers, but it contains a wealth of data, and contextualizes Laing's iconoclastic ideas about psychiatry into the currents of his times. Beveridge convinces us that Laingianism was a reaction to the excesses of 50s' era biologically based psychiatry, and that it was spiced up by a wide range of influences, from Buber's *I and Thou*, to Anton Chekhov's *Ward No. 6*, to his native Scotland, with its divided Highlands and Lowlands, plus his psychotic mother.

Beveridge's book is a very serious book, even though the very sound of the syllables, "R.D. Laing," conjures up images of the counterculture of the 1960s. We expect to hear electronic harpsichords chiming in the background, and the sweet smell of incense wafting through the air. For Laing became haute-counterculture, but not in the same way as one-time psych aid turned writer, Ken Kesey of *One Flew Over the Cuckoo's Nest* (1962), or Timothy Leary, the Harvard professor turned High Priest of LSD.

Laing was a practicing psychiatrist who wielded his greatest influence through writings such as *The Divided Self* (1960), and through his well-publicized but short-lived experiment at Kingsley Hall. There, doctors and patients bunked together as "equals," and patients were encouraged to experience unbridled psychosis, with the (naïve) hopes that this experiential approach would purge them of the psychic

Reprinted with kind permission from *Metapsychology* (metapsychology.mentalhelp.net). Acknowledgements go to Christian Perring for his kind support.

S. Packer (✉)
Private Practice, 270 Lafayette Street, New York, NY 10012, USA
e-mail: drpacker@hotmail.com

A. Batthyány (ed.), *Logotherapy and Existential Analysis*, Logotherapy and Existential Analysis: Proceedings of the Viktor Frankl Institute Vienna 1,
DOI 10.1007/978-3-319-29424-7_38

demons that possessed them. Laing claimed that psychosis was a sane reaction to an insane world. Unlike some other "anti-psychiatrists" of his day, Laing did not deny the reality of mental illness.

Unfortunately, Laing's theories did not work well in real life, and his approaches were abandoned by 1970, when Kingsley Hall was shuttered. Eventually, Laing himself abandoned himself to alcohol, but he lived on until 1989, long past the prime of the counter-culture, and long past the time when other youth cultures remembered his name. Laing is still taught in some psychiatry residency programs, mostly to provoke debate, but not to be taken literally. His writings are often assigned to philosophy students.

For better or for worse, this book does not delve into the outcomes of Laing's ideas and practices, although it does predict that Laing will become more relevant in our current day, as practitioners and patients alike bemoan the sterile approach of neuropsychiatry and psychopharmacology, and long for the days when more holistic approaches prevailed. This prediction is probably my only point of contention with Beveridge's assessment, although time will tell if he turns out to be right.

Beveridge's book covers a circumscribed time: 1927–1960. It ends when Kingsley Hall began, and when *The Divided Self* (1960)—Laing's most influential book—appeared. Like the title of *The Divided Self*, Laing's life and oeuvre are divided by the publication of *The Divided Self*. Because of this clearly defined endpoint, Beveridge does not trace the evolution of Laing's thought and treatments from start to finish.

There is a remarkable advantage to this circumscribed approach. By stopping before Laing's ideas became sensationalized, and just before they were co-opted by the fulminating counterculture of the mid-60s, Beveridge can trace Laing's thought back to other philosophical and cultural influences. In other words, this book looks backward, rather than forward. Unlike so many others, Beveridge does not address what Laing anticipated. Instead, he unearths elements from the past. It is hardly surprising that a psycho-dynamically inclined psychiatrist would valorize the past more than the future or the present.

Stripped of the "Sixties' stuff," Laing's intellectual approach is silhouetted against a backdrop that is far broader than lava lamps, love beads, and LSD-laced postage stamps. Beveridge does for Laing what Henri Ellenberger did for Freud, and for some of Freud's predecessors and some of his followers (and some of his detractors). Whether or not Laing deserves as much attention as the founding fathers of psychoanalysis deserve is another matter. What is important is that readers will benefit from the cram course on phenomenology and existentialism that is found in this volume.

The attention showered on existentialism and Existential Phenomenology is impressive. Nestled within this lengthy subsection of the book is an entire chapter on Laing and Individual Existential Thinkers. Beveridge explains that existentialism focuses on the individual, rather than on individual truths. Although existentialist philosophy existed earlier, its heyday peaked from the mid-1940s through 1960. The Second World War, and the horror of the holocaust, contributed to its popularity at that time.

Beveridge briefly addresses Frankl's contribution to this existential backdrop. He summarizes Frankl's thesis: that the most pressing question for humankind is to find a purpose to their individual existences. Unlike Laing, who denied the biological basis of behavior or perception, Frankl acknowledged the role played by biology. Yet he remained optimistic that existential psychology can override inherent obstacles. Mental health professionals who read these passages will wonder if Laing had greater reason to deny the significance of biology and genetics, given that his own mother suffered from psychosis.

Indeed, Frankl's own concentration camp experiences were formidable obstacles, as chronicled in his best seller, *Man's Search for Meaning* (1946). As horrific as they were, Frankl's experiences as an adult are qualitatively different from Laing's youthful experience of his mother. Frankl's poignant descriptions of camp inmates who withered and died, after they lost their sense of purpose, even before gas or gunshots or epidemic disease claimed their lives, remain etched in the memories of his readers. These details do not appear in Beveridge's book, but are easily retrievable through Frankl's writings.

When we realize how much existentialism and phenomenology molded Laing's ideas and how thoroughly he thought out the ideas that he articulated in his books, we realize that Laingian ideas were not based on negativism or nihilism. Nor were they the products of adolescent angst—even though his ideas were adopted by adolescents, who endured their own angst. That does not mean that we come to agree with Laingian thought. We simply come to understand its foundations better. (This is the same approach used when treating psychosis; we do not come to agree with delusions, but we are relieved to find the "kernel of truth" embedded within a delusion, before that full-blown delusion crystallized.)

The most valuable take-away lesson of Beveridge's book comes from his discussion of treatment trends from the 1950s, when Laing was a young psychiatrist. We are reminded that Thorazine (phenothiazine) had arrived in the early 1950s (earlier in Europe than in the U.S.). Lobotomies enjoyed their heyday in those years. With those facts in mind, we understand how Laing (and others) were pushed into the opposite camp, and why they were motivated to pursue alternative approaches. For, in the early days of CPZ (chlorpromazine), psychotic patients were over-sedated, until they walked like zombies, with the "Thorazine shuffle." It was not a pretty sight, even though it led to other advances.

We hear about Laing's personal friend, a neurosurgeon, who suffered from his own psychiatric ills, and who confided his antipathy toward psychosurgery to Laing. In this section, we are told that this neurosurgeon colleague also introduced Laing to Chasidic Jewish thinkers, such as Buber. The surgeon was a scion of a Chasidic clan, and was versed in both traditional and contemporary (Buber) thought. Beveridge emphasizes that other Jewish influences percolated through the Scottish medical system at that time, because Scotland had less stringent requirements for foreign-trained physicians than Britain, and so was more welcoming of the Jewish doctors who fled Nazi-controlled Europe in the 30s and 40s.

Beveridge reviews Laing's own Protestant religious upbringing, in search for influences on his ideas, just as Ellenberger and so many others probed Freud's formative influences, religious and otherwise. Most intriguingly, we learn that Laing's mother was frankly paranoid and that she spent time in and out of institutions. Fortunately, the text never becomes a "pathography" that attributes all professional, intellectual, and creative accomplishments to traumatic experiences or "bad childhoods."

There is no intimation that Laing had "bad genes," even though someone who is less of a Laing sympathizer might wonder about biological influences on Laing's belief that crazy societies drive people crazy. Was he speaking about the "society" created by his mother, in their own home, using "society" as metaphor for mother? Because this book stops before Laing's *Sanity, Madness and the Family* (1964), we are left wondering how much Laing's personal familial experiences color the ideas in that book.

Many, many intriguing factoids pepper this book and add depth and even drama. We read about comparisons between the Scottish divide (Highlands vs. Lowlands) and how that "divide" increased awareness of "the divided self." Again, we are reminded of theories about Austrian authoritarianism—a product of the Hapsburg monarchy—and its influence on Freud's autocratic approach to his psychoanalytic circle. At this point, those of us who delighted in Ellenberger's approach to *The Discovery of the History of the Unconscious: The History and Evolution of Dynamic Psychiatry* (New York: Basic Books, 1970), are enthralled, and cannot wait to see what is in store for Part II, which chronicles Laing's next 27 years, until his death at age 61. (Hopefully, there will be Part II.)

An especially gripping section revolves around literary influences on Laing. Parallels between a Chekhov story, *Ward No. 6* (A. Chekhov, *Ward No. 6 and Other Stories*, 1892–1895. New York: Penguin, 2002) and Laing's approach to patients, become obvious, after Beveridge explains them in plain prose. Chekhov, himself a physician who earned more from writing about his medical practice than from his actual practice, describes a staff psychiatrist who becomes engaged by a psychotic patient. He finds himself talking to this patient, day after day. Colleagues believe that the psychiatrist himself has gone mad, because they cannot understand how a sane person could find value in conversing with psychotics. Eventually, the doctor is committed to the asylum himself, and suffers the same mistreatment as all other patients.

Laing's life story proceeded in a very different direction than Chekhov's life story. Even though Beveridge bypasses Laing's later life in this book, most people who are inclined to read a book about Laing already know that Laing was eventually prohibited from practicing medicine. Chekhov, on the other hand, practiced almost continuously, treating the poor for free, and writing about abuses he witnesses at a Russian penal colony to the north of Japan.

For those who are accustomed to reading books about Laing's influence on culture, rather than the other way around, this book is a refreshing departure, because it takes the opposite approach. It also chronicles arguments against biological psychiatry that were made in the 1950s and 1960s. The reasoning behind those debates reminds me of arguments between Copernicus and his detractors, who refused to admit that the earth revolves around the sun. Even though most of those theories have no place in philosophical or scientific discourse today, that section is still worth reading, because it summarizes those outdated ideas eloquently, and makes us realize how far we have come since the mid-1950s.

In conclusion, I must confess that I am haunted by Beveridge's confidence that Laing will become more relevant to contemporary psychiatry as more and more practitioners, patients, and critics condemn the supposedly "soulless" neuropsychiatry of the early twenty-first century. For sure, the back-and-forth debates chronicled in *The New York Review of Books*, in the summer of 2011, confirm that questions about contemporary trends in psychiatry are mounting.

Yet I cannot imagine that anyone will find an antidote to these woes in Laing's theories. But one is sure to find intellectual stimulation in Beveridge's approach, and in the compendium of background information in this first installment. I look forward to reading the second half of his research, not so much because of his subject, but because he weaves such an interesting tapestry of the arts and the sciences, the theoretical and the practical, the past and the present.

Part VII
Institutional Section

The Viktor Frankl Institute Vienna

Internationale Vereinigung für Logotherapie und Existenzanalyse
International Association of Logotherapy and Existential Analysis
Asociación Internacional de Logoterapia y Análisis Existencial

Honorary President: DDr. h.c. Eleonore Frankl
Director: Prof. Dr. Alexander Batthyány
Vice-Director: Katharina Ratheiser, LLM, MAS
Secretary: Dr. Gabriele Vesely-Frankl

The Viktor Frankl Institute was founded in Vienna in 1992 by an international circle of colleagues and friends. It is a scientific society with the goal of maintaining and fostering the life work of Viktor Frankl and to provide access to authentic information about Logotherapy and Existential Analysis.

The institute offers the first state-accredited doctoral degree program for logotherapy, in the framework of the Viktor Frankl Chair of Philosophy and Psychology at the International Academy of Philosophy (University of the Principality of Liechtenstein). Also, a Master's program and psychotherapy training in logotherapy is offered in collaboration with the Department for Logotherapy, founded in 2012, at the Graduate Institute of Psychoanalysis in Moscow. The institute has exclusive access to Viktor Frankl's private archives and the world's largest collection of texts and research on Logotherapy and Existential Analysis. In collaboration with City of Vienna's "Viktor Frankl Fund," the institute grants scholarships and awards prizes for work in the field of meaning-oriented humanistic psychotherapy.

Key activities of the Viktor Frankl Institute include:

A. Batthyány (ed.), *Logotherapy and Existential Analysis*, Logotherapy and Existential Analysis: Proceedings of the Viktor Frankl Institute Vienna 1,
DOI 10.1007/978-3-319-29424-7_39

I. VIKTOR FRANKL´S PRIVATE ARCHIVES

- Member of the UNESCO Archives Portal (Paris)
- Cataloguing of Viktor Frankl´s private archives from 1925 to 1997
- Digitalization of historical audio and video recordings
- Bibliography (dissertations, theses, journal articles, media reports)
- Documentation of the international history of Logotherapy and Existential Analysis

II. ACADEMIC DEPARTMENT

- Supervision of theses, dissertations, and research projects
- Awarding of Research Fellowships (Viktor Frankl Fund of the City of Vienna for the Advancement of Meaning-Oriented Humanistic Psychotherapy)
- Comprehensive bibliography of research literature on logotherapy
- Research Group "Intellectual History of European Existential Psychology" at the International Academy of Philosophy in Bendern
- Research Group "Existential Cognition" at University of Vienna´s Cognitive Science Program
- Online Research Platform

III. UNIVERSITY TEACHING

- Accredited Doctoral Program in Logotherapy and Logotherapy-related Studies at the Viktor-Frankl-Chair, Bendern
- Viktor Frankl lecture and seminar at Vienna Medical School, Department of Psychiatry and Psychotherapy (continuation of the early Wednesday lectures on Logotherapy and Existential Analysis, which Viktor Frankl held between 1947 and 1996)
- Logotherapy Master Program, Department for Logotherapy and Existential Analysis at the Moscow University Institute for Psychoanalysis

IV. TEACHING AND TRAINING

- Biennial International Congress *Die Zukunft der Logotherapie/The Future of Logotherapy* in Vienna
- Viktor Frankl Award and Lectures (*Wiener Vorlesungen*), co-organized with the Cultural Department of the City of Vienna

- Seminars and lectures at conferences and congresses around the world
- Coordination of educational and training seminars in cooperation with universities and other academic and research institutions, e.g. the Danube University Krems, the Medical Society in Tokyo, the InfoSys Campus Bangalore, India, and others.

V. PUBLICATIONS OF THE VIKTOR FRANKL INSTITUTE

- *Logotherapy and Existential Analysis/Proceedings of the Viktor Frankl Institute Vienna*
- The Edition of the Collected Works of Viktor Frankl, 14 Volumes (annotated published and unpublished writings by Viktor Frankl)
- Publication of text collections about the theory and practice of Logotherapy and Existential Analysis
- Book series, published by the Viktor-Frankl-Chair in Bendern

VI. INTERNATIONAL ACCREDITATION AND MEMBERSHIP

- International Accreditation and Certification of Logotherapy Institutes and individuals (clinical psychologists and psychotherapists, coaches, counselors, etc.)
- International Association of Logotherapy and Existential Analysis (membership section of the Viktor Frankl Institute): cooperation with 110 logotherapy institutes and initiatives in 33 countries

If you are interested in joining our worldwide clinical and scientific community and would like to become a Professional or Associate Member of the Institute, please visit http://www.viktorfrankl.org/e/accreditation.html

- Seminars and lectures at conferences and congresses around the world
- Coordination of educational and training seminars in cooperation with universities and other academic and research institutions, e.g., the Danube University Krems, the Medical Society in Tokyo, the Inforum Campus in [illegible], and others

V. PUBLICATIONS OF THE VIKTOR FRANKL INSTITUTE

- *Logotherapy and Existential Analysis/Proceedings of the Viktor Frankl Institute Vienna*
- The Edition of the Collected Works of Viktor Frankl, including published and unpublished writings by Viktor Frankl
- Publication of text collections about the theory and practice of Logotherapy and Existential Analysis
- Book series published by the Viktor-Frankl-Chair in Brazil

VI. INTERNATIONAL ACCREDITATION AND MEMBERSHIP

- International Accreditation and Certification of Logotherapy institutes and individuals (clinical psychologists and psychotherapists, counselors, coaches, etc.)
- International Association of Logotherapy and Existential Analysis (membership section of the Viktor Frankl Institute): cooperation with 140 Logotherapy institutes and initiatives in 35 countries

If you are interested in joining our worldwide community of Logotherapists and would like to become a Professional or Associate Member or get further information, please visit http://www.viktorfrankl.org/accreditation.html

International Directory of Logotherapy Institutes and Initiatives

Institutes and initiatives on this list are affiliated with the Viktor Frankl Institute Vienna and/or are certified members of the International Association of Logotherapy and Existential Analysis (IALEA).

Inclusion in the Directory

Institutes and Initiatives on this list are affiliated with the Viktor Frankl Institute Vienna and/or are certified members of the International Association of Logotherapy and Existential Analysis (IALEA). Considering occasional questionable offers in the field, the International Association of Logotherapy and Existential Analysis at the Viktor Frankl Institute aims to safeguard the public and prospective clients and trainees in logotherapy and existential analysis; additionally, it tries to promote high excellence standards in the professional conduct of logotherapy training, practice, and research.

Ethical Principles and Professional Code of Conduct

Certified Member Institutes and Initiatives follow the Ethical Principles of Psychologists and Code of Conduct of the American Psychological Association (APA). This Ethics Code applies to all activities that are part of the logotherapists' scientific and therapeutic functions, such as the clinical or counseling practice of logotherapy, research, teaching, supervision of trainees, development of assessment instruments, conducting assessments, educational counseling, organizational consulting, social intervention, administration, and other activities as well.

A. Batthyány (ed.), *Logotherapy and Existential Analysis*, Logotherapy and Existential Analysis: Proceedings of the Viktor Frankl Institute Vienna 1,
DOI 10.1007/978-3-319-29424-7_40

International Certification of Trained Logotherapists

Many of the training and educational Institutes listed below offer accredited training programs and courses in Viktor Frankl's logotherapy and existential analysis. Successful completion of the full training entitles alumnis to apply for certified individual membership at the International Association. After approval of the application for individual membership and pledging to follow the Ethical Principles and Professional Code of Conduct mentioned above, accredited members will be listed in the International Directory of Logotherapists and will receive an accreditation certificate. Further benefits of individual membership include patient and client referrals and discount fees for the Biannual International Vienna "Future of Logotherapy" Congresses. For further information, please contact registration@viktorfrankl.info.

International

International Association of Logotherapy and Existential Analysis & International Curricular Advisory Panel at the Viktor Frankl Institute

Dir.: Prof. Dr. Elisabeth Lukas (Hon. Pres.)
Prof. Dr. Alexander Batthyány (Secr.)
Dipl. Psych. Michael Thir, MA
Post: Prinz Eugen Str. 18/12, A-1040 Vienna, Austria
T: +43 1 505 23 39
E: registration@viktorfrankl.info
W: www.viktorfrankl.org/e/accreditation.html
Focus: Curricular Accreditation/Accreditation of Institutes and Initiatives (International Certification)/Accreditation of Individual Logotherapists (International Certification)/Individual Membership Services/Institutional Membership Services/Patient and Client Referrals/Complaint Board and Conflict Resolution.

Europe

Europäische Akademie für Logotherapie und Psychologie (EALP)
[European Academy for Logotherapy and Psychology (EALP)]

Dir.: Dr. med. Klaus Gstirner
Post: Körblergasse 10, 8010 Graz, Austria
T: +43 650 3233050
E: office@ealp.at
W: www.ealp.at
Focus: Educational and Training:
Coordination of European University-Based M.A. Programs in Counselling; Logopedagocis; Psychology [with focus on Logotherapy and Franklian Psychology] at various European Universities

Iberoamerican

Asociacion Iberoamericana de Logoterapia
[Iberoamerican Association of Logotherapy]
Participating Institutions:
- Centro Viktor Frankl para la difusión de la Logoterapia (see Argentina)
- Asociacion Espanola de Logoterapia (AESLO) (see Spain)
- Sociedad Mexicana de Análisis Existencial y Logoterapia (see Mexico)

W: www.asil.com.ar

Red Internacional de Logoterapia Organizacional (RILO)
Red—International Organisational Logotherapy
Offices and representatives in:
Argentina, Columbia, Dominican Republic, Mexico, Guatemala, Uruguay
Dir.: Dr. Juan Carlos Carvajal Gómez
Post: Calle 98 A No 71 D 29, Ciudad: Bogotá, Colombia
T: +57 1 8101011
E: info@redinternacionaldelogoterapia.org
W: www.redinternacionaldelogoterapia.org
Focus: Educational/Therapy or Counselling Training Public information/dissemination of LT and EA Research.

Argentina

Centro Viktor Frankl para la difusión de la Logoterapia
[Centre Viktor Frankl for the Dissemination of Logotherapy]
Dir.: Prof. Dr. Gerónimo Acevedo
Post: Ciudad de la Paz 2139 Piso 9 F, 14 28 Ciudad de Buenos Aires CABA, Argentina
T: +54 1147828020
E: info@centroviktorfrankl.com.ar
W: www.centroviktorfrankl.com.ar
Focus: Educational/Therapy or Counselling Training Public information/dissemination of LT and EA Therapy and Counselling.

Fundación Argentina de Logoterapia "Viktor E. Frankl"
[Argentinian Foundation for Logotherapy "Viktor E. Frankl"]
Dir.: Dr. Oscar Ricardo Oro
Dr. Adriana Sosa Terradas
Post: Charcas 3151. Ciudad Autónoma de Buenos Aires, C.P. 1425, Argentina
T: +54 11 48229678
E: Info@logoterapia-arg.com.ar
W: www.logoterapia-arg.com.ar
Focus: Educational/Therapy or Counselling Training/Public information/dissemination of LT and EA/Therapy and Counselling/Research.

Cátedra Abierta Viktor Emil Frankl (CAVEF)
[Open Space Viktor Emil Frankl
Dir.: Prof. Dr. Claudio César Garcia Pintos
Post: Virrey del Pino 2878—1° "A", 1426—Ciudad Autónoma de Buenos Aires, Argentina
T: +54 11 47830416
E: cavef@yahoo.com
W: www.facebook.com/claudio.garciapintos.1
Focus: Educational and Training/Public information/dissemination of LT and EA.

Centro de Logoterapia y Análisis Existencial (CLAE) de la Universidad Católica Argentina
[Centre for Logotherapy and Existential Analysis at the Catholic University Argentina]
Dir.: Dr. Lucía Copello
Post: Av. Alicia Moreau de Justo 1500, C1107AAZ, Buenos Aires, Argentina
T: +54 11 43490200
E: clae.uca@gmail.com
W: www.uca.edu.ar/index.php/site/index/es/uca/facultad-de-psicologia-y-psicopedagogia/nuestra-facultad/centro-de-logoterapia-y-analisis-existencial/
Focus: Public information/dissemination of LT and EA/Research.

Centro de Análisis Existencial "Viktor Frankl"
[Center for Logotherapy and Existential Analysis "Viktor Frankl"
Dir.: Lic. Cecilia Saint Girons
Post: Santiago 1149 PB dto. 1, C.P. 2000 Rosario, Argentina
T: +54 341 4477091
E: logoterapiarosario@gmail.com
W: www.logoterapiarosario.com; www.logoterapiarosario.com.ar
Focus: Educational/Therapy or Counselling Training/Therapy and Counselling.

Metahumanitas. Centro de Formación en Logoterapia y Análisis Existencial
[Metahumanitas: Centre for Training in Logotherapy and Existential Analysis]
Dir.: Lic. Cecilia Barovero.
Post: Calle Obispo Trejo 459, 5000 Córdoba, Argentina
T: +54 3564-15580172
E: centrometahumanitas@gmail.com; lic.delossantoslima@gmail.com; cebarovero@gmail.com
W: metahumanitas.org/
Focus: Educational/Therapy or Counselling Training/Public information/dissemination of LT and EA.

Centro de Logoterapia de Tucuman
[Tucuman Center for Logotherapy]
Dir.: Lic. Maria Yolanda Veliz de Esper
Post: Marcos Paz 1594, San Miguel de Tucuman, C.P.4000, Argentina
T: +54 381 423 4284
E: centrologoterapiatuc@gmail.com
W: www.logoterapiatuc.com.ar
Focus: Educational/Therapy or Counselling Training/Public information/dissemination of LT and EA/Therapy and Counselling.

Centro Bonaerense de Logoterapia
[Buenos Aires Center for Logotherapy]
Dir.: Prof. Lic. Roberto Juan Mucci
Post: Perú N° 2995, San Justo, C.P.1754, Pcia.
T: +54 11 44822391
E: robertomucci@uolsinectis.com.ar
W: www.bsaslogoterapia.com.ar
Focus: Public information/dissemination of LT and EA.

Australia

Viktor Frankl Institute Australia
Dir.: Dr. Paul McQuillan
Post: PO Box 1126, Oxley, QLD, 4075, Australia
T: +61 408 740 749
E: paul@lifechange.net.au,
W: www.viktorfranklinstitute.net.au
Focus: Educational/Therapy or Counselling Training/Public information/dissemination of LT and EA.

Viktor Frankl Institute Sydney
Dir.: Dr. Reza Pishyar
Post: 12/2 O'Connell Street Parramatta NSW 2150, Australia
E: pishyarr@gmail.com
W: www.vfis.com.au
Focus: Educational/Therapy or Counselling Training/Therapy and Counselling.

Austria

Viktor Frankl Institute (VFI)

Dir.: Prof. Dr. Alexander Batthyány (Director)
Dr. h.c. Eleonore Frankl (Honorary President)
Post: Prinz Eugen Str. 18/12, A-1040 Wien, Österreich
T: +43 1 505 23 39
E: secretary@viktorfrankl.info; alexander.batthyany@univie.ac.at
W: www.viktorfrankl.org; www.viktorfrankl.info
Focus: Vienna HQ/Public information/dissemination of LT and EA/Coordination of University-based Programs in LT and EA/Coordination of International LT and EA/Publication/International Lecturing/Media Contacts.

International Association of Logotherapy and Existential Analysis & International Curricular Advisory Panel at the Viktor Frankl Institute

Dir.: Prof. Dr. Elisabeth Lukas (Honorary President)
Prof. Dr. Alexander Batthyány (Secretary)
Post: Prinz Eugen Str. 18/12, A-1040 Wien, Österreich
T: +43 1 505 23 39
E: registration@viktorfrankl.info
W: www.viktorfrankl.org/e/accreditation.html
Focus: Curricular Accreditation/International Accreditation of Institutes and Initiatives/International Accreditation of Individual Therapists, Clinicians and Counsellors/Membership Services.

Viktor Frankl Archives and History of Logotherapy Documentation Centre

Post: Mariannengasse 1, A-1090 Vienna, Austria
T: +43 676 9345 750
E: alexander.batthyany@gmail.com
Focus: Research Institution (by appointment only!)/Edition of the Collected Works of Viktor Frankl (14 Vols)

Ausbildungsinstitut für Logotherapie und Existenzanalyse (ABILE)

[Psychotherapy Training Institute for Logotherapy and Existential Analysis]

Dir.: Prof. Dr. Otmar Wiesmeyr
Post: Kaiser Franz-Josef Platz 52, A-4600 Wels, Österreich
T: +43 7242 207584
E: abileinstitut@aon.at
W: www.abile.org
Focus: Educational/Therapy Training/Supervision/University-Based M.A. Program in Logotherapy/Public information/dissemination of LT and EA/Research.

Ausbildungsinstitut für Logotherapie und Existenzanalyse West (ABILE WEST)
[Psychotherapy Training Institute for Logotherapy and Existential Analysis (ABILE WEST)]
Dir.: Dr. Heidi Vonwald
Post: Defreggerstraße 38, A-6020 Innsbruck, Österreich
T: +43 650 53 52 70 6
E: office@abile-west.at; heidi.vonwald@aon.at
W: www.abile-west.at
Focus: Educational/Therapy or Counselling Training/Public information/dissemination of LT and EA/Research.

Viktor Frankl Zentrum Wien: Museum & SeminarZentrum
[Viktor Frankl Centre Vienna: Museum & Seminar Centre]
Dir.: Elisabeth Gruber, M.A.
Johanna Schechner, MSc.
Post: Mariannengase 1/13 & 15, A-1090 Wien, Österreich
T: +43 699 1096 1068
E: office@franklzentrum.org
W: www.franklzentrum.org
Focus: Educational/Logopedagogics Training/Public information/dissemination of LT and EA/Museum/Public Lecture Program.

Europäische Akademie für Logotherapie und Psychologie (EALP)
European Academy for Logotherapy and Psychology (EALP)
Dir.: Dr. med. Klaus Gstirner
Post: Körblergasse 10, 8010 Graz, Österreich
T: +43 650 3233050
E: office@ealp.at
W: www.ealp.at
Focus: Educational and Training: Coordination of European University-Based M.A. Programs in Counselling; Logopedagocis; Psychology [with focus on Logotherapy and Franklian Psychology] at various European Universities.

Institut für Logotherapie und Existenzanalyse Europäische Akademie für Wertorientierte Persönlichkeitsbildung Salzburg
[Institute for Logotherapy and Existential Analysis/European Academy for Value Based Personality Development]
Dir.: Prof. Dr. Uwe Böschemeyer
Post: Getreidegasse 31/Universitätsplatz 3, A-5020 Salzburg, Österreich
T: +43 662 843154
E: office@boeschemeyer.at
W: www.boeschemeyer.at
Focus: Educational/Therapy or Counselling Training/Public information/dissemination of LT and EA/Research.

Institut für Logotherapie und Existenzanalyse Salzburg
[Institute for Logotherapy and Existential Analysis Salzburg]
Dir.: Mag. Christoph Schlick
Post: Berchtesgadner Strasse 11, A-5020 Salzburg-Gneis, Österreich
T: +43 662 828501-0; +43 662 890170 (F)
E: office@logotherapie-salzburg.at
W: www.logotherapie-salzburg.at
Focus: Educational/Therapy or Counselling Training/Public information/dissemination of LT and EA/Therapy and Counselling/Research.

Tiroler Institut für Logotherapie und Existenzanalyse nach Viktor E. Frankl
[Tyrolean Institute for Franklian Logotherapy and Existential Analysis]
Dir.: Inge Patsch
Post: Lizumstraße 34, A-6094 Axams/Tyrolia, Österreich
T: +43 699 1160 9455; +43 5234 68844
E: info@existenzanalyse.co.at; office@existenzanalyse.co.at
W: www.existenzanalyse.co.at
Focus: Educational/Therapy or Counselling Training/Public information/dissemination of LT and EA/.

Existential Cognition Research Group at the University of Vienna
Dir.: Prof. Dr. Alexander Batthyány
Cognitive Science Programm an der Universität Wien
Post: Universitätsstraße , A-1010 Wien, Österreich
E: alexander.batthyany@univie.ac.at
Focus: Research Initiative/Educational/University Courses in Logotherapy and Existential Analysis.

SinnAG
[Institute of Meaning-Centered and Systemic Work to Promote and Regain Mental Health]
Dir.: Mag. Dominik Hussak
Patrick Eder
Post: Straßerau 6, A-4020 Linz, Österreich
T: +43 664 26 87 700; +43 664 10 17 456
E: institut@sinnag.at
W: www.sinnag.at
Focus: Therapy and Counselling/Public Information/dissemination of LT and EA/Workshops and Groups.

Brazil

Centro Viktor Frankl de Logoterapia
[Viktor Frankl Centre for Logotherapy]
Dir.: Prof. Dr. Izar Aparecida de Moraes Xausa
Post: Rua 24 de Outubro, 1085, Apt. 1003—Moinho dos Ventos, 90510-003 Porto Alegre, Brasil
T: +55 51 3331 3328
E: izarxausa@terra.com.br
Focus: Educational/Therapy or Counselling Training.

Núcleo Viktor Frankl de Logoterapia da Universidade Estadual da Paraíba Centro de Ciências Biológicas e da Saúde, Departamento de Psicologia
[Viktor Frankl Working Group for Logotherapy at the University Estaual de Paraíba Centre for Biological Sciences and Health, Department of Psychology]
Dir.: Prof. Dr. Gilvan de Melo Santos
Post: University Estaual de Paraíba, Departamento de Psicologia, Rua Baraúnas, 351, Bairro Universitário, Campina Grande-PB, CEP 58429-500, Brasil
E: nucleovf@gmail.com
W: www.facebook.com/NucleoViktorFrankl, http://www.nvlogo.com.br/
Focus: Educational/Therapy or Counselling Training.

Associação Brasileira de Logoterapia e Análise Existencial (ABLAE)
[Brazilian Association for Logotherapy and Existential Analysis (ABLAE)]
Dir.: Dr. Guilherme Falcão
Lic. Sheila Maria Hesketh Rabuske.
Post: Rua Des. Ermelino de Leão no. 15, conj. 101, Curitiba, Paraná, Brasil
T: +55 41 3223-9101
E: logoterapia.brasil@yahoo.com.br
W: www.ablae.org.br/
Focus: Educational/Therapy or Counselling Training/Public information/dissemination of LT and EA.

Associação Brasileira de Logoterapia e Análise Existencial Frankliana (SOBRAL)
[Brazilian Association for Franklian Logotherapy and Existential Analysis (SOBRAL)]
Dir.: Lic. Diogo Arnaldo Corrêa
Post: Rua Luís Góis, 1238, Bairro: Mirandópolis, São Paulo – SP, CEP: 04.043-100, Brasil
T: +55 11 05581 6162
E: sobralog@terra.com.br
W: www.logoterapia.com.br
Focus: Educational/Therapy or Counselling Training.

Colégio Viktor Frankl
[Viktor Frankl College]
Dir.: Dr. Rita de Cássia Garnica Conterato
Prof. Dr. Marina Lemos Silveira Freitas
Post: Avenida do Café 1295—Vila Amélia, 14050-230, Ribeirão Preto, São Paulo, Brasil
T: +55 16 36335065
E: colegioviktorfrankl@colegioviktorfrankl.com.br
W: www.colegioviktorfrankl.com.br
Focus: Educational/Therapy or Counselling Training.

Instituto Geist
Dir.: Dr. Tatiana Oliveira De Carvalho
Av. Colares Moreira, Centro Empresarial Vinícius De Moraes, Loja 11, Calhau, Código Postal,
Post: 65.075-440, São Luís-Ma, Brasil
T: +55 98 32270006, +55 98 988216631
E: institutogeist@institutogeist.com.br
W: www.institutogeist.com.br
Focus: Educational/Therapy or Counselling Training/Public information/dissemination of LT and EA/Therapy and Counselling.

Instituto de Educação e Cultura Viktor Frankl
[Institute for Education and Culture Viktor Frankl]
Dir.: Prof. Dr. Marina Lemos Silveira Freitas
Post: Avenida do Café 1353, 14050-230, Ribeirão Preto, São Paulo, Brasil
T: +55 16 34464683
E: institutoviktorfranklrp@yahoo.com.br
W: www.iecvf.blogspot.com.br
Focus: Educational/Therapy or Counselling Training.

Instituto de Logoterapia Campinas
[Logotherapy Institute of Campinas]
Dir.: Dr. José Carlos Vitor Gomes
Post: Rua Irma serafina, 919 Ap. 801, CEP 13015-201 Campinas/SP, Brazil
Rua Ten Joaquim Nunes Cabral, 2673 Araraquara/SP, Brazil
T: +55 19 32337505
E: jcvitor@uol.com.br
W: www.sitedopsicologo.com.br
Focus: Educational/Therapy or Counselling Training/Public information/dissemination of LT and EA/Therapy and Counselling.

Agir3 – Núcleo de Logoterapia – Psicologia - Educação
[Agir 3: Logotherapy Working Group Psychology and Education]
Dir.: Dr. Simone Guedes
Post: Rua Joaquim Antunes, 490, cjto 31, CEP 05413-000, São Paulo,
T: +55 11 99299.0930
E: agir3@agir3.com.br; simoneguedesagir3@gmail.com
W: www.agir3.com.br; www.facebook.com/Agir3Logoterapia
Focus: Educational/Therapy or Counselling Training/Therapy and Counselling.

Nous: Espiritualidade e Sentido
[Nous: Spirituality and Health]
Dir.: Prof. Dr. Thiago A. Avellar de Aquino
Post: Centro de Educação, Universidade Federal da Paraíba, Programa de Pós-graduação em Ciências das Religiões,
Cidade Universitária, 58051-900, João Pessoa, Paraíba, Brazil
E: logosvitae@ig.com.br
W: www.espiritualidadesentido.yolasite.com/
Focus: Research Initiative/Postgraduate Study Program.

Bulgaria

Bulgarian Society for Logotherapy and Existential Analysis
Dir.: Dr. med. Klaus Gstirner
Post: Todor Kableshkov 8b , 4000 Plovdiv, Bulgaria
E: klaus@gstirner.com
W: www.logoterapiabg.com
Focus: Accredited University-Based M.A. Program in (1) Existential Counselling (2) Logopedagocis (3) Logotherapy (4) Psychology [with focus on Logotherapy and Franklian Psychology].

Canada

Canadian Institute of Logotherapy
Dir.: Dr. med. et phil. Dipl. Psych. Edward Marshall
Post: PO Box 45006, Ottawa, ON K2M 2G0, Canada
T: +1 613 599 3299
E: info@logotherapy.ca
W: www.logotherapy.ca; www.logotherapie.ca
Focus: Public information/dissemination of LT and EA.

Ottawa Institute of Logotherapy
Dir.: Dr. Maria Marshall
Post: 160—F1 Terence Matthews Crescent, Ottawa, ON K2M 0B2, Canada
T: +1 613 599 7027
E: info@ltea.ca
W: www.ltea.ca
Focus: Educational/Therapy or Counselling Training/Therapy and Counselling.

International Network on Personal Meaning (INPM)
Dir.: Prof. Dr. Paul T. P. Wong
Post: Pos13 Ballyconnor Court, Toronto, Ontario, M2M 4C5, Canada
T: +1 416 546-5588
E: drpaulwong@gmail.com
W: www.meaning.ca; www.existentialpsychology.org
Focus: Educational/Therapy or Counselling Training/Public information/dissemination of LT and EA/Research.

Chile

Instituto Chileno de Logoterapia Viktor Frankl
[Chilean Institute for Logotherapy Viktor Frankl]
Dir.: Ps. Carmen Gloria González Parra
Post: Gabriela Mistral 0850, Temuco 4780000, Chile
T: +45 2402612; +45 87575435
E: logoterapiachile@gmail.com
W: www.logoterapia.cl/; www.facebook.com/logoterapia.chile
Focus: Educational/Therapy or Counselling Training/Public information/dissemination of LT and EA/Therapy and Counselling.

China/Hong Kong

Logotherapy Group at the Chinese University of Hong Kong
Dir.: Assistenzprof. Dr. Wallace Chi Ho Chan
Post: Department of Social Work, 4/F, T.C. Cheng Building
United College, The Chinese University of Hong Kong, Shatin, Hong Kong
E: chchan@swk.cuhk.edu.hk
Focus: Research/Educational/Therapy or Counselling Training.

Colombia

Sociedad Para El Avance De La Psicoterapia Centrada En El Sentido (SAPS)
[Society for the Advancement of Meaning-Centered Psychotherapy]
Dir.: Prof. Dr. Efren Martinez Ortiz
Carrera 14a No 101–11 Oficina 403, Bogota, Colombia
E: info@saps-col.org
W: www.saps-col.org
Focus: Educational/Therapy or Counselling Training/Public information/dissemination of LT and EA/Therapy and Counselling/Research.

Corporación Instituto Colombiano de Análisis Existencial y Logoterapia Viktor Frankl
[Columbian Cooperate Viktor Frankl Institute for Existential Analysis and Logotherapy]
Dir.: Dr. José Arturo Luna Vargas
Post: Calle 152 A 18 A 28, Bogotá, Colombia
T: +57 1 3108707055; +57 1 3103294144; +57 1 2749908
E: institutodelogoterapia@gmail.com; info@iclogoterapia.com; lunalogo@gmail.com
W: www.iclogoterapia.com
Focus: Educational/Therapy or Counselling Training/Public information/dissemination of LT and EA/Therapy and Counselling/Research.

Instituto Logos
Dir.: Wilmer Palomares Potes, Mg.
Post: Calle 5D #38A-35 Edificio Vida Centro Profesional, Torre 2, oficina 714. Código, 760010, Cali, Colombia
T: +57 2 5185252 Ext. 714; +57 3006517270; +57 3002796626
E: director@institutologos.net; info@institutologos.net
W: www.institutologos.net
Focus: Educational/Therapy or Counselling Training/Public information/dissemination of LT and EA/Therapy and Counselling.

Red Internacional de Logoterapia Organizacional (RILO)
[Red—International Organisational Logotherapy]
Dir.: Dr. Juan Carlos Carvajal Gómez
Post: Calle 98 A No 71 D 29, Ciudad: Bogotá, Colombia
T: +57 1 8101011
E: info@redinternacionaldelogoterapia.org
W: www.redinternacionaldelogoterapia.org
Focus: Educational/Therapy or Counselling Training/Public information/dissemination of LT and EA/Research.

Croatia

LOGOS - Hrvatska udruga za logoterapiju
[LOGOS—Croatian Society for Logotherapy]
Dir.: Dr. med. Cvijeta Pahljina
Post: Ul.Vladimira Nazora 7, 10 408 Velika Mlaka, Croatia
T: +385 95 895 3283
E: cvijeta.pahljina@siol.com; cvijeta.pahljina@gmail.com
W: www.logoterapija.com
Focus: Educational/Therapy or Counselling Training/Public information/dissemination of LT and EA/Therapy and Counselling/Research.

Czech Republic

Ceskomoravska spolecnost pro logoterapii a existencialni analysu
[Czech and Moravian Society for Logotherapy and Existential Analysis]
Dir.: Prof. Dr. Vladimir Smekal, C.Sc.
Post: Faculty of Social Sciences, Masaryk University, Department of Psychology, Jostova 10, 602 00 Brno, Czechia
T: +420 5 49 49 6617
E: smekal@fss.muni.cz
Focus: Educational/Therapy or Counselling Training/Research.

Dominican Rep.

Instituto Dominicano de Logoterapia y Analisis Existencial
[Dominican Institute of Logotherapy and Existential Analysis]
Dir.: Dr. med. Miguel Angel Hernandez Latorre
Post: Ave Sarasota #79, Edificio Plaza Sarasota Apt 405-C, Bella Vista, Santo Domingo, Dominican Republic
T: +1809 998 5981
E: infologoterapia@gmail.com
W: www.logoterapiasentidodevida.blogspot.com/
Focus: Educational/Therapy or Counselling Training/Public information/dissemination of LT and EA/Therapy and Counselling/Research/Instagram: logoterapia/Twitter: @logoterapiaRD.

Ecuador

Centro Ecuatoriano de Analisis Existencial y Logoterapia CEAL
[Ecuadorian Centre for Existential Analysis and Logotherapy (CEAL)]
Dir.: Prof. Mgs. Eliana Cevallos
Post: Av. Gonzalo Díaz de Pineda 415 y Orellana, Casilla Postal 17171622, 170150 Distrito, Metropolitano de Quito, Ecuador
T: +59 3999231933
E: elianalogoterapia@gmail.com
W: www.logoterapiaecuador.com; www.wakeup.com.ec
Focus: Educational/Therapy or Counselling Training/Public information/dissemination of LT and EA/.

Finland

Suomen logoterapiayhdistys
[Finnish Logotherapy Association]
Dir.: Prof. Dr. Risto Nurmela
Post: Skogsgränd 10-12 D 19/FI-21600 Pargas,) Finland
T: +358 400 973534
E: president@logoterapiayhdistys.fi
W: www.logoterapiayhdistys.fi
Focus: Public information/dissemination of LT and EA/Research.

Logoterapiayhdistys
[Finland's Institute for the Theory of Viktor Frankl]
Dir.: Dr. Timo Purjo
Heinätie 8, 12700 Loppi, Finland
T: +358 400607792
E: timo.purjo@nfg.fi; timo.purjo@pp.inet.fi
W: www.logoteoria.net/
Focus: Educational/Therapy or Counselling Training/Public information/) dissemination of LT and EA/Research.

France

Ecole Française d'Analyse et de Thérapie Existentielles (Logothérapie) V. Frankl – EFRATE
[French School for Existential Analysis and Therapy (Logotherapy) V. Frankl—EFRATE]

Dir.:	Prof. Dr. Georges-Elia Sarfati
Post:	23, rue de Valmy, 94220 Charenton-le-Pont,)France
T:	+33 07 77 73 18 29
E:	exislog@gmail.com
W:	www.efrate.org
Focus:	Educational/Therapy or Counselling Training/Public information/dissemination of LT and EA/Therapy and Counselling/Research.

Association des Logothérapeutes Francophones
[French Association of Logotherapy – ALF]

Dir.:	Annick Boutin
Contact:	Nathalie Haberman
Post:	c/o Ms Salleron, 34 rue de Chartreux, F-69001 Lyon, France
E:	nathalie.haberman@gmail.com; annickboutin@hotmail.fr
W:	www.logotherapie-alf.org
Focus:	Public information / dissemination of LT & EA

Germany

AGIEL
Arbeitsgemeinschaft International für Existenzanalyse und Logotherapie in Deutschland
[Working Group and Association of Institutes for Logotherapy and Existential Analysis in Germany]

Dir.:	Institutsgremium; siehe Webseite Walter Cremer Waldweg 16, D-41352 Korschenbroich
T:	+49 2161 402 4684
E:	cremer@loginstitut.de; s.ruetter@leben-philosophie.de; u.tirier@cityweb.de
W:	www.agiel.de
Focus:	Viktor Frankl Institute-Affiliated Umbrella Organisation of German Logotherapy Institutes and Initiatives/Institution for Public Relations and Promotion of LT/Training and Educational Media Contacts.

Institut für Sinnorientierte Weiterbildung
Institute for Meaning-Oriented Continuing Education
Dir.: Dipl.Psych. Simone von Hoyningen
Dornfelder Str. 5, D-71384 Weinstadt, Germany
T: +49 177 3459318
E: info@sinn-wb.de
W: www.sinn-wb.de
Focus: Educational/Therapy or Counselling Training/Public information/dissemination of LT and EA/Therapy and Counselling/Research (in collaboration with the University of Heidelberg).

Akademie für Logotherapie im Elisabeth Lukas Archiv
[Academy for Logotherapy at the Elisabeth Lukas Archives]
Dir.: Dr. Heidi Schönfeld
Nürnberger Str. 103a, 96050 Bamberg, Germany
T: +49 951 222 00 399
E: dr.schoenfeld@arcor.de; elisabeth-lukas-archiv@online.de
W: www.elisabeth-lukas-archiv.de
Focus: Educational/Therapy or Counselling Training/Logotherapy Training Curriculum of Elisabeth Lukas

Akademie für Logotherapie und Existenzanalyse an der Volkshochschule Mainz
[Academy for Logotherapy and Existential Analysis at the Mainz Adult Education Centre]
Dir.: Prof. Dr. Randolph Ochsmann
Post: Karmeliterplatz 1, 55116 Mainz, Germany
T: +49 6131 2625 0
E: logotherapie@vhs-mainz.de
W: www.logotherapie-mainz.de
Focus: Educational/Therapy or Counselling Training/Public information/dissemination of LT and EA.

Viktor E. Frankl Häuser
[Viktor Frankl Halfway Houses]
Dir.: Wolfgang R. Hiller
Post: Grambeker Weg 37, 23879 Mölln, Germany
T: +49 4542/841607
E: info@vefh.de
W: www.vefh.de
Focus: Educational/Therapy or Counselling Training.

Akademie Leben und Philosophie
[Academy Life and Philosophy]
Dir.: Dr. Susanne Rütter
Post: Adlergasse 3, 78355 Hohenfels, Germany
T: +49 7775 938948
E: s.ruetter@leben-philosophie.de
W: www.leben-philosophie.de
Focus: Educational/Therapy or Counselling Training.

Institut für Logotherapie und Existenzanalyse Essen
[Institute for Logotherapy and Existential Analysis Essen]
Dir.: Dr. med. Ursula Tirier
Post: In der Borbeck 23, D-45239 Essen
T: +49 201 49 1381; +49 201 49 1381
E: u.tirier@cityweb.de
W: www.logotherapie-essen.de
Focus: Educational/Therapy or Counselling Training/Public information/dissemination of LT and EA/Therapy and Counselling.

logi Institut für Logotherapie und Existenzanalyse
[logi Institute for Logotherapy and Existential Analysis]
Dir.: Dipl. theol. Walter Cremer
Post: Waldweg 16, D-41352 Korschenbroich
T: +49 2161 402 4684
E: cremer@loginstitut.de
W: www.loginstitut.de
Focus: Educational/Therapy or Counselling Training/Public information/dissemination of LT and EA/Therapy and Counselling.

Institut für Logotherapie und Existenzanalyse Hamburg-Bergedorf
[Institute for Logotherapy and Existential Analysis Hamburg-Bergedorf]
Dir.: Dr. Stephan Peeck
Post: Am Baum 40, D-21029 Hamburg-Bergedorf, Germany
T: +49 40 72004952
E: speeck@imail.de
W: www.logotherapie-peeck.de/
Focus: Educational/Therapy or Counselling Training/Public information/dissemination of LT and EA/Therapy and Counselling.

Hamburger Akademie für Wertorientierte Persönlichkeitsbildung
[Hamburg Academy for Value Oriented Personality Development]
Dir.: Dipl. Sozpäd. Corinna Böschemeyer
Post: Friedrich-Legahn-Straße 2, 22587 Hamburg–Blankenese, Germany
T: +49 40 28668362
E: sekretariat@boeschemeyer.de
W: www.boeschemeyer.de
Focus: Educational/Therapy or Counselling Training.

Brühler Institut für Logotherapie
[Institute for Logotherapy Brühl]
Dir: Dipl theol. Sebastian J. Schmidt
Post: Friederikeweg 2, 50321 Brühl-Heide, Germany
T: +49 2232 578883
E: info@bilogo.de
W: www.bilogo.de
Focus: Educational/Therapy or Counselling Training (Supervision)/Therapy & Counselling.

Elisabeth Lukas Archiv
[Elisabeth Lukas Archives]
Dir.: Dr. Heidi Schönfeld
Univ.-Prof. Dr. Alexander Batthyany
Post: Nürnberger Str. 103a, 96050 Bamberg, Germany
T: +49 951 222 00 399
E: dr.schoenfeld@arcor.de
alexander.batthyany@univie.ac.at
W: www.elisabeth-lukas-archiv.de
Focus: Public information / dissemination of LT & EA
Archives, Library & Publications (Collected Works of Elisabeth Lukas)

Akademie LEA—Logotherapie und Existenzanalyse - Augsburg
[Academy LEA—Logotherapy and Existential Analysis in Augsburg]
Dir.: Lic. Maria de Lourdes Stiegeler
Post: Albert-Einstein-Strasse 17, 86179 Augsburg, Germany
T: +49 821 881835
E: akademie-lea@gmx.de
E: lourdes-stiegeler@gmx.de
W: www.logotherapie-in-augsburg.de
Focus: Educational/Therapy or Counselling Training/ Public information/ dissemination of LT & EA/Therapy & Counselling.

Institut für Logotherapie & Existenzanalyse & Seelsorge—ILES-Kiel
[Institute for Logotherapy and Existential Analysis and Pastoral Care]
Dir.: Dipl. Sozialarb./Sozpäd. Gerlinde Ghattas
Post: Am Wellsee 105, D-24146 Kiel, Germany
T: +49 17858938
E: iles-kiel@t-online.de
W: www.iles-kiel.de
Focus: Educational/Therapy or Counselling Training.

Akademie für Logotherapie nach Viktor E. Frankl
[Academy for Franklian Logotherapy]
Dir.: Petra Dau
Post: Borgfelder Str. 72, D-28215 Bremen, Germany
T: +49 421 355467
E: info@logotherapie-coach.com
W: www. logotherapie-coach.com
Focus: Coaching Training.

Logotherapeutischer Ansatz: Alter & Demenz (LAAD)
[Working Group: Logotherapy, Aging, and Dementia]
LAAD Herford
Dir.r: Dipl.Ing. LSB Heidrun Mildner
Post: Alter Markt 1, 32052 Herford, Germany
T: +49 5221 275 495
E: logotherapeutische-beratung@handelnde-herzen.de
W: www.herforderherzen.de/

LAAD Karlsruhe
Dir.: Elli Kobela
Akad. Rätin Sabine Rettinger
Post: Karlstrasse 119, 76137 Karlsruhe, Germany
T: +49 721 7540 6539
E: sabine.rettinger@logotherapeutische-beratung.de
E: elli.kobela@logotherapeutische-beratung.de
W: www.logotherapeutische-beratung.de/
Focus: Educational/Therapy or Counselling Training/Therapy & Counselling (focus on Aging and Dementia)/Research.

Europäische Gesellschaft für Krisenpädagogik
[European Society for Crisis Pedagogics]
Dir.: Prof. Dr. Bijan Amini
Post: Lindenstr. 7, 24118 Kiel, Germany
T: +49 431 81311/+43 1 8896184
F: +49 431 81490
E: prof.amini@t-online.de
W: www.krisenpaedagogik.de
Focus: Educational/Therapy or Counselling Training/Therapy & Counselling.

Süddeutsches Institut für Logotherapie und Existenzanalyse
[South German Institute for Logotherapy and Existential Analysis]
Dir.: Dr. Otto Zsok & Dipl.-Sozpäd. (FH) Nadja Palombo
Post: Hauptstraße 9, 82256 Fürstenfeldbruck, Germany
T: +49 8141 18041
E: si@logotherapie.de/zsok@logotherapie.de
W: www.logotherapie.de
Focus: Educational/Therapy or Counselling Training/Public information/dissemination of LT & EA/Therapy & Counselling.

Institut für Logotherapie und Existenzanalyse Tübingen
[Institute for Logotherapy and Existential Analysis Tübingen]
Dir.: Prof. Dr. theol. Wolfram Kurz
Dr. Boglarka Hadinger
Post: Haaggasse 37, 72070 Tübingen, Germany
T: +49 7071 51270
E: info@logotherapie.net
W: www.logotherapie.net
Focus: Educational/Therapy or Counselling Training/Therapy & Counselling.

Great Britain

UK Chapter of Logotherapy: Viktor Frankl's Psychology
Dir.: Dr. Doreen M. Francis
Post: 150 Bower Street, Carlisle, Cumbria, UK CA2 7DE, UK
E: dr.dm.francis@londonvfi.co.uk
W: www.londonvfi.co.uk
Focus: Educational/Therapy or Counselling Training/Public information/dissemination of LT and EA/Therapy and Counselling.

Guatemala

Instituto de Ciencias de la Familia
[Institute for Family Sciences]
Dir.: Maria de los Angeles de Mollinedo, MA
Post: 1a. avenida 10-20 zona 3 Mixco Colonia el Rosario, Guatemala C.A., C.P. 01057, Guatemala
T: +502 24313428; +502 24331631
E: nstitutocienciasfamilia.gt@gmail.com; icf.guate.edu@gmail.com; directoraicfguatemala@gmail.com
W: www.icfguate.org
Focus: Educational/Therapy or Counselling Training/Public information/dissemination of LT and EA/Therapy and Counselling.

Hungary

Hungarian Foundation for Logotherapy
Dir.: Assistant Prof. Dr. habil. Péter Sárkány
Post: Alkotás u. 49/c, H- 1125 Budapest, Hungary
E: logoterapiastudio@gmail.com
W: www.logoterapia.hu
Focus: Educational and Training Institution/Institution for Public Relations and Promotion of LT and EA.

Iran

Logotherapy Research Group at Allameh Tabataba'i University

Dir.: Dr. Somaye Robatmili
Dr. Hossein Eskandari
Post: Center for Behavioral Sciences, Allameh Tabataba'i University (ATU), Dehkadeh-ye-Olympic, Teheran, Iran
E: s.robatmeili@st.atu.ac.ir; somayemili@yahoo.com; sknd40@gmail.com
Focus: Therapy and Counselling/Research.

Ireland

Viktor Frankl Institute of Ireland

Dir.: Dr. Stephen J. Costello
Post: Dartmouth Terrace, Ranelagh, Dublin 6, Ireland.
T: +353 1 4971120
E: stephenjcostello@eircom.net
W: www.viktorfranklireland.com
Focus: Educational/Therapy or Counselling Training/Public information/dissemination of LT and EA/Therapy and Counselling/Research.

Israel

The Logotherapy Association in Israel

Dir.: Pninit Russo-Netzer, Ph.D.
Post: 8 Arbel st., Karkur P.O.B. 5247, Israel
T: +972 76 5408880; +972 524 215822
E: logotherapy@org.il
W: www.logotherapy.org.il
Focus: Educational/Therapy or Counselling Training/Public information/dissemination of LT and EA.

Israeli School of Existential Analysis and Logotherapy V. Frankl

Dir.: Prof. Dr. Georges-Elia Sarfati
Post: Avigaïl, 6 – Apt 18, 93 551 Abu Tor- Jerusalem, Israel
T: +972 058 644 65 76
E: exislog@gmail.com
Focus: Educational/Therapy or Counselling Training/Public information/dissemination of LT and EA/Therapy and Counselling.

The Viktor Frankl Center for Logotherapy in Israel

Dir.: Gideon Millul
Post: 4 Martin Buber st., Haifa 3486137, Israel
T: +972 4 8244059; +972 522 617853
E: otsmot@gmail.com
W: www.otsmot.com
Focus: Educational/Therapy or Counselling Training.

Italy

A.L.Æ.F. Associazione di Logoterapia e Analisi Esistenziale Frankliana
[A.L.Æ.F. Association for Franklian Logotherapy and Existential Analysis]
Dir.: Prof. Dr. Daniele Bruzzone
Post: Strada Marengo 3/C, 46044 Goito (Mantova), Italy
T: +39 3922184480
E: info@logoterapiaonline.it
W: www.logoterapiaonline.it
Focus: Educational/Therapy or Counselling Training/Public information/dissemination of LT and EA/Research.

Südtiroler Institut für Logotherapie & Existenzanalyse SILEA
[South Tyrolean Institute for Logotherapy and Existential Analysis SILEA]
Dir.: Hans Tscholl
Post: Lauben 9/2. Stock, 39100 Bozen, Italy
T: +39 0471 324409
E: silea@rolmail.net
W: www.silea.bz.it
Focus: Educational/Therapy or Counselling Training.

Japan

Japan Logotherapist Association
Dir.: Kayao Katsuta-Grandy, MA
Post: 15-10-102 Nishiyaizu, Yaizu-shi Shizuoka-ken 425-0075, Japan
E: klogotherapy@gmail.com; snb67003xyz@yahoo.co.jp
W: www.geocities.jp/japan_logo_semi/e_logo_html/index.html
Focus: Educational and Training Institution/Institution for Public Relations and Promotion of LT and EA.

Logotherapy Institute at the International Foundation of Comprehensive Medicine
Dir.: Prof. Dr. Katsutaro Nagata
Post: Kanda-Ogawamachi 1-7-901, Chiyoda-ku, Tokyo, 101-0052 Japan
T: +81 3 5577 6841
E: tklogos@nifty.com; vknagata@nifty.com
W: www.compmed.jp
Focus: Educational/Therapy or Counselling Training/Research.

Japan Society of Humanistic Anthropology Association
Dir.: Yoshimichi Katsumot
Post: Rm#308, 6-25-8 Nishi-shinjuku, Shinjuku-ku, 160-0023 Tokyo, Japan
T: +81 3 5909 7010
E: info@ningengakkai.or.jp
W: www.ningengakkai.or.jp/en/en_index.html
Focus: Public information/dissemination of LT and EA/Research.

Liechtenstein

Viktor Frankl Lehrstuhl für Philosophie und Psychologie im Fürstentum Liechtenstein
[The Viktor Frankl Chair for Philosophy and Psychology in the Principality of Liechtenstein]
Dir.: Prof. Dr. Alexander Batthyány
Post: Internationale Akademie für Philosophie im Fürstentum Liechtenstein, Im Schwibboga 7 Fl-9487 Bendern, Principality of Liechtenstein
T: +42 32654343
E: abatthyany@iap.li
W: www.abatthyany.li
Focus: Post-Graduate Studies in Logotherapy and Logotherapy-Related Studies/ Doctorate Studies in Logotherapy and Logotherapy-Related Studies/ Research/The Viktor Frankl Library on Existential Psychology, Psychotherapy, and Psychiatry/Lukas-Curriculum.

Mexico

Sociedad Mexicana de Análisis Existencial y Logoterapia
[Mexican Society for Existential Analysis and Logotherapy]
Dir.: Dr. Leticia Ascencio de García
Post: Narciso Mendoza #45, Lomas Ávila Camacho, 53900 Naucalpan, Edo. de México, México
T: +52 5589 1362
E: smael@logoterapia.com.mx; smaelsedelomas@prodigy.net.mx
W: www.logoterapia.com.mx
Focus: Educational/Therapy or Counselling Training/Public information/dissemination of LT and EA/Research.

Colegio De Posgrado En Desarrollo Humano Y Logoterapia, Universidad Lisieux
[Postgraduate College for Human Development and Logotherapy at the University Lisieux]
Dir.: Lic. Gilberto Hernandez Vázquez
Post: Calle Orizaba #29, Fracc. Pomona, C. P. 91040, Xalapa Veracruz, Mexico
T: +52 228 814 08 87
E: contacto@lisieux.edu.mx; sk_cpl@hotmail.com
W: www.lisieux.edu.mx/esplogoterapia.php
Focus: Educational/Therapy or Counselling Training/Postgraduate Studies in Logotherapy/Therapy and Counselling.

Instituto Especializado en Logoterapia
[Institute for Specialisation in Logotherapy]
Dir.: Lic. Jacqueline Marie Becker Duprat
Post: Fuente de las Platerías N°8, Tecamachalco, Naucalpan, México, 53950, México
T: +52 5294 0855
E: jacbecker20@gmail.com; jacbecker@prodigy.net.mx
W: www.ielogoterapia.com.mx
Focus: Educational/Therapy or Counselling Training/Public information/dissemination of LT and EA.

Colegio Viktor Frankl
[Viktor Frankl College]
Dir.: Prof. Dr. Constanza Basurto Soriano
Post: Fray Sebastián de Gallegos No. 300, Col Ejido El Retablo, C.P. 76900, Corregidora, Querétaro, México
T: +52 442 295 24 94 AL 97
E: contacto@colegioviktorfrankl.edu.mx
W: www.colegioviktorfrankl.edu.mx
Focus: Educational/Therapy or Counselling Training.

Logoforo Centro de Psicoterapia
[Logoforo Psychotherapy Centre]
Dir.: María Teresa Lemus de Vanek, MA
Post: Paraíso 3, Colonia Álamos, Querétaro C.P. 76150, México
T: +52 442 2186429
E: terevanek@logoforo.com
W: www.logoforo.com
Focus: Educational/Therapy or Counselling Training/Public information/dissemination of LT and EA/Therapy and Counselling/Research.

Instituto de Logoterapia y Tanatología
[Institute for Logotherapy and Thanatology]
Dir.: Blanca Isela Carrasco Loya, MA
Post: Av de la Raza 5385-73 Col Mascareñas, Ciudad Juárez, Chihuahua, C.P. 32340, México
T: +52 656 6290668; +52 656 6169988
E: info@institutodelogoterapia.org; institutodelogoterapiajuarez@gmail.com
W: www.institutodelogoterapia.org
Focus: Educational/Therapy or Counselling Training.

Instituto de Formación y Atención en Psicologia IFAPS
[Institute for Psychological Education and Care]
Dir.: Lic. Marta Concepción Mayela Azcué Carillo
Dr. Alberto Murguía Leines
Post: Aniceto Ortega 817 Colonia del Valle, Delegacioón Álvaro Obregón DF 01730, Mexico
E: administracion@ifaps.com.mx; academico@ifaps.com.mx
W: www.ifaps.com.mx
Focus: Educational/Therapy or Counselling Training/Therapy and Counselling/ Public information/dissemination of LT and EA.

Instituto de Logoterapia
[Institute for Logotherapy]
Dir.: Rocio Arocha Romero, MA
Post: Ahuehuetes 100-104, 05260, Mexico, D.F., Mexico
T: +55 50 68 59 70
E: rocioarocha@gmail.com
W: www.rocioarocha.com
Focus: Public information/dissemination of LT and EA.

Netherlands

Netherlands Logotherapy Information Center at the Department of Psychology, University Of Ibadan
Dir.: Mag. Jutta Jank Clarke, MA
Post: Statenlaan 130, 2582-GW Den Haag, Holland
T: 031 63 6489902
E: jutta.clarke@gmail.com
Focus: Public information/dissemination of LT and EA.

Nigeria

Nigerian Logotherapy Group at the Department of Psychology, University Of Ibadan

Dir.: Prof. Dr. Benjamin O Ehigie
Dr. Rachel B Asagba
Post: Department of Psychology, University Of Ibadan, Oyo Road, Ibadan, Nigeria
T: +234 809 2945144
E: nigerianlogotherapystudygroup@gmail.com
Focus: Public information/dissemination of LT and EA.

Peru

Instituto Peruano de Logoterapia - Dau Escuela de Vida

[Peruvian Institute for Logotherapy – Dau School of Life]
Dir.: Sandra Barbero, MA
Juan Davila, MA
Post: Jr. Medrano silva 260,Barranco/ Jr. Tacna 1250, Magdalena, Lima 04, Perú.
T: +51 1 2529639; +51 1 991212811
E: info@dauperu.com
W: www.dauperu.com
Focus: Educational/Therapy or Counselling Training/Public information/dissemination of LT and EA/Therapy and Counselling/Research.

Asociación Peruana de Análisis Existencial y Logoterapia (APAEL)

[Peruvian Association for Existential Analysis and Logotherapy (APAEL)]
Dir.: Dr. Edward Antonio Lozano Vargas
Psic. Dobereyner Hioel Jamanca Rojas
Post: Los Pinos 190 Oficina 1104 y 1107, Miraflores, CP 511 Lima, Perú
T: +51 1 942795190; +51 1 2475190; +51 1 2423591
E: info@logoterapia.pe
W: www.logoterapia.pe
Focus: Educational/Therapy or Counselling Training/Public information/dissemination of LT and EA/Therapy and Counselling/Research.

Centro de Estudios e Investigación de Logoterapia y Análisis Existencial—Humanitas
[Centre for Studies and Research in Logotherapy and Existential Analysis—Humanitas]
Dir.: Lic. Miguel Angel Molla Madueño
Post: Av. Caminos del Inca N° 1539,/1, Santiago de Surco, Lima 33, Perú
T: +51 1 986216531
E: migmolla@gmail.com; estudios.logoterapia@gmail.com
W: www.logotherapy-research.com
Focus: Research.

Centro Psicoterapéutico Logos
[Psychotherapy Centre Logos]
Dir.: Ps. Alejandro Khaled Salomón Paredes
Post: Av. Canadá 3264, San Borja, Lima 41, Perú
T: +51 1 727 1044; +51 1 3464197
E: informes@cpllogoterapia.com; asalomon@cpllogoterapia.com
W: www.cpllogoterapia.com
Focus: Educational/Therapy or Counselling Training/Public information/dissemination of LT and EA/Therapy and Counselling.

Poland

Institute of Biofeedback and Noo-Psychosomatic
Dir.: Prof. Dr. Kazimierz Popielski
Dr. Lilia Suchocka
Post: Ul. 3 Maja 18/4a,, 20-078 Lublin, Poland
E: info@ibnps.eu
W: www.ibnps.eu
Focus: Educational/Therapy or Counselling Training/Research.

Romania

Asociatia Stiintifica Internationala de Logoterapie si Analiza Existentiala
[Scientific Association for Logotherapy and Existential Analysis]
Dir.: Assistenzprof. Dr. János Vik
Assistenzprof. Dr. Péter Sárkány
Post: Str. Iuliu Maniu nr. 5/8, RO-400095 Cluj-Napoca, jud. Cluj, Romania
T: +40 757 048 568
E: logoterapia@logoterapia.ro
W: www.logoterapia.ro
Focus: Educational/Therapy or Counselling Training/Public information/dissemination of LT and EA.

RUSSIAN FEDERATION

Dept. of Logotherapy and Existential Analysis at the Moscow Univ. Institute of Psychoanalysis

Dir.: Dean Prof. Dr. Lev Surat.
Prof. Dr. Alexander Batthyány (Visiting Professor)
Post: Kutuzovsky prospect, 34 A, 121170, Moscow, Russian Federation
T: +7 495 225-5348
E: inpsycho@inpsycho.ru
W: www.inpsycho.ru
Focus: Educational/Therapy or Counselling Training/Therapy and Counselling/Clinical Dept./Research/Public information/dissemination of LT and EA.

Institut Smysl
[Meaning Institut]
Dir.: Prof. Dr. Dmitry Leontiev
Post: 103050 Moscow-50, a/ja 158, Russian Federation
E: institut@smysl.ru
W: www.smysl.ru
Focus: Public information/dissemination of LT and EA/Research.

Viktor Frankl Centre St. Petersburg
Dir.: Ekaterina Voulfson
Post: Public programs and exhibitions at varying locations in St. Petersburg, Russia
T: +7 963 303 02 12
E: info@viktorfranklcenter.ru; evoulfson@gmail.com
W: www.viktorfranklcenter.ru; www.viktorfrankl.ru
Focus: Public information/dissemination of LT and EA.

Slovakia

Slovak Institut of Logotherapy (SILOE)
Dir.: Assoc. Prof. Dr. Eva Naništová
Post: Čerešnová 5, 811 04 Bratislava, Slovakia
T: 42 1 949786700
E: institut.logoterapia@gmail.com; enanist@gmail.com
W: www.logoterapia.sk
Focus: Educational/Therapy or Counselling Training/Research.

Logotherapy Research Group at the Slovak Academy of Sciences
Dir.: Assoc. Prof. Dr. Peter Halama
Post: Institute of Experimental Psychology, Slovak Academy of Sciences, Dubravska cesta 9, Bratislava, Slovakia
E: peter.halama@savba.sk
Focus: Research.

Slovenia

Zavod Žički Tabor Za Duhovno Rast
[Institute for Spiritual and Existential Growth and Logotherapy]
Dir.: Dr.med Cvijeta Pahljina
Post: Šolska ul.3, 3215 Loče, Slovenia
T: +386 3 7523 103; +385 707 07 340
E: cvijeta.pahljina@siol.com; cvijeta.pahljina@gmail.com
Focus: Educational/Therapy or Counselling .Training/Public information/dissemination of LT and EA/Therapy and Counselling/Research.

Inštitut Antona Trstenjaka
[Anton Trstenjak Institute for Psychology, Logotherapy and Anthropohygiene]
Dir.: Prof. Dr. Joze Ramovs
Post: Resljeva 11, SI-1001 Ljubljana
T: +386 1 433 93 01
E: joze.ramovs@guest.arnes.si
W: www.inst-antonatrstenjaka.si
Focus: Educational/Therapy or Counselling Training/Research—Logotherapy and Aging/Intergenerational Relations/Public information/dissemination of LT and EA/Social Work.

South Africa

The Viktor Frankl Institute of Logotherapy, South Africa.
Dir.: Dr. Teria Shantall
Post: 20 Saddle Drive, Woodmead Office Park, Woodmead, 2128, Johannesburg, South Africa
E: teriashantall@gmail.com; klasie@streetschool.co.za; clubryall@iburtst.co.za
W: vfisa.co.za
Focus: Educational/Therapy or Counselling Training Public information/dissemination of LT and EA Research in collaboration with The Centre of Applied Psychology, University of South Africa, Pretoria.

Spain

Asociacion Espanola de Logoterapia (AESLO)
[Spanish Association for Logotherapy (AESLO)]
Dir.: Dr. Ana Maria Ozcariz
Dr. Maria Angeles Noblejas de la Flor
Post: C/ Chantada 2, 1/1, 28029 Madrid, Spain
T: +34 649 155 426
E: ma_aeslo@yahoo.es
W: www.logoterapia.net/
Focus: Educational/Therapy or Counselling Training/Publi.c information/dissemination of LT and EA/Research.

Asociación Viktor E. Frankl de Valencia
[Viktor Frankl Association of Valencia]
Dir.: Lic. Sebastián Tabernero Capella
Post: C/ Don Juan de Austria 34, Puerta 4,, 46002 Valencia, Spain
T: +34 96 351 0113
E: correo@asociacionviktorfrankl.org; sebastabernero@hotmail.com
W: www.asociacionviktorfrankl.org
Focus: Public information/dissemination of LT and EA.

Associació Catalana de Logoteràpia i Anàlisi Existencial
[Catalanian Association for Logotherapy and Existential Analysis]
Dir.: Lic. Cristina Visiers Würth
Post: Acadèmia de Ciències Mèdiques de Catalunya i Balears,
Carrer Major de Can Caralleu, 1-7, 08017 Barcelona, Spain
E: formacionlogoterapia@gmail.com
W: aclae.org
Focus: Educational and Training/Public information/dissemination of LT and EA.

Switzerland

Institut für Logotherapie und Existenzanalyse nach Viktor Frankl (ILE)
[Institute for Franklian Logotherapy and Existential Analysis (ILE)]
Dir.: Dr. Reto Parpan
Post: Freifeldstrasse 27, CH-7000 Chur., Switzerland
T: +41 81 250 50 83
E: info@logotherapie.ch; galbrecht@spin.ch
W: www.logotherapie.ch
Focus: Educational/Therapy or Counselling Training/Public information/dissemination of LT and EA/Research.

Schweizerische Gesellschaft für Logotherapie und Existenzanalyse (SGLE)
[Swiss Society for Logotherapy and Existential Analysis]
Dir.: Rosmarie Mühlbacher (interim)
Post: Espentobelstrasse 5, CH-9008 St. Gallen, Switzerland
T: +41 71 244 91 38
E: rmuehlbacher@bluewin.ch
W: www.sgle.ch
Focus: Public information/dissemination of LT and EA.

Schule für Logotherapie und Existenzanalyse
[School of Logotherapy and Existential Analysis]
Dir.: Dipl.Psych. Sven Reichmann
Post: Kientalerhof, Griesalpstrasse 44, CH-3723 Kiental
T: +41 33 676 2676
E: info@kientalerhof.ch; mail@svenreichmann.de
W: www.kientalerhof.ch
Focus: Educational/Therapy or Counselling Training/Public information/dissemination of LT & EA Therapy & Counselling.

Institut für Sinnzentrierte Führung, ISF
[Institute für Meaning-Centered Leadership]
Dir.: Stefan Schwarz, MSc
Post: Eulerstrasse 9, CH-4051 Basel, Switzerland
T: +41 061 271 11 28; +41 061 271 17 04 (F)
E: stefan.schwarz@i-s-f.ch
W: www.i-s-f.ch
Focus: Educational/Therapy or Counselling Training/Public information/dissemination of LT and EA/Therapy and Counselling.

Turkey

Society of Existential Psychotherapies of Turkey "EXISTanbul"/Logotherapy
Dir.: Ferhat Jak Icoz, MA, MSc, Clinical Psychologist
Post: Buyuk Hendek Cad. No:21/4 Galata Beyoglu, 34420, Istanbul, Turkey.
T: +90 212 2431543
E: varoluscupsikoterapilerdernegi@gmail.com; ferhatjakicoz@gmail.com; info@varoluscuakademi.com.
W: www.varoluscuakademi.com; www.existanbul.org
Focus: Educational/Therapy or Counselling Training/Public information/dissemination of LT and EA/Therapy and Counselling/Research.

Uruguay

Centro de Logoterapia y Análisis Existencial (CELAE)
[Centre for Logotherapy and Existential Analysis (CELAE)]
Dir.: Prof. Dr. Alejandro De Barbieri
Lic. Marcela Arocena
Post: Francisco Llambí 1410, C.P. 11600, Montevideo, Uruguay
T: +598 26281024; +598 94 303697
E: secretariacelae@gmail.com; celae@logoterapia.com.uy
W: www.logoterapia.com.uy
Focus: Educational/Therapy or Counselling Training/Public information/dissemination of LT and EA/Therapy and Counselling.

Sociedad de Logoterapia del Uruguay
[Uruguay Society for Logotherapy]
Dir.: Lic. María Soledad Olave
Post: José Enrique Rodó 1924, Código postal, ciudad 11200 Montevideo, Uruguay
T: +598 99194010
E: secretarialogo@gmail.com
W: www.facebook.com/logoterapiauruguaya
Focus: Educational/Therapy or Counselling Training/Public information/dissemination of LT and EA.

USA

Viktor Frankl Institute of Logotherapy
Dir.: Prof. Dr. Robert C. Barnes
Post: P.O. Box 15211, Abilene, TX 79605, USA
T: +1 325 692 9597; +1 325 692 9188 (F)
E: marshallhlewis@yahoo.com
W: www.logotherapyinstitute.org
Focus: Educational/Therapy or Counselling Training (Distance Learning Program in Logotherapy) Public information/dissemination of LT and EA/ (Bi-Annual World Congress every even year),

The Graduate Center for Pastoral Logotherapy at the Graduate Theological Foundation
Dir.: Prof. Dr. Ann V. Graber
Post: 415 Lincoln Way East, Mishawaka, Indiana 46544, USA
T: +1 800 423-5983
E: academicaffairs@gtfeducation.org
W: www.gtfeducation.org
Focus: Educational/Therapy or Counselling Training/Public information/dissemination of LT and EA/Research.

Arizona Institute of Logotherapy
Dir.: Rabbi Leo Michel Abrami
Post: 13315 W. Aleppo Drive, 85375 Sun City West Arizona, USA
T: +1 623 546 8639
E: azlogotherapy@gmail.com
Focus: Educational/Therapy or Counselling Training/Public information/dissemination of LT and EA/Research.

Viktor Frankl Collection and Memorabilia at GTU Library Archives
Dir.: Lucinda Glenn
Post: Graduate Theological Union, 2400 Ridge Road, Berkeley, CA 94709, USA
T: +1 510 649 2507; +1 510 649 2508 (F)
E: lglenn@gtu.edu
W: www.gtu.edu/library/special-collections/archives/frankl-logotherapy
Focus: American Collection of Viktor Frankl Memorabilia and Documents.

LogoTalk Radio
Dir.: Dr. Marshall H. Lewis
Post: P. O. Box 632, Ulysses, Kansas 67880, USA
T: +1 620 424 7480
E: logotalk@gmail.com
W: www.logotalkradio.com
Focus: Public information/dissemination of LT and EA/Logotherapy Radio Station/Interview and Lecture Repository.

Kansas Initiative for Meaningful Health
Dir.: Dr. Marshall H. Lewis
Post: P. O. Box 632, Ulysses, Kansas 67880, USA
T: +1 620 424 7480
E: marshallhlewis@yahoo.com
W: www.kansasinitiative.org
Focus: Research.

Southwest Guidance Center
Dir.: Dr. Leslie Bissell (Exec. Director)
Dr. Marshall H. Lewis (Clinical Director)
Post: 333 West 15th Street, Liberal, Kansas 67905, USA
T: +1 620 624 8171
E: mlewis@swguidance.org
W: www.southwestguidance.org
Focus: Educational/Therapy or Counselling Training/Therapy and Counselling.

Logotherapy Research Group at Yale University

Dir.: Prof. Dr. med. Steven M. Southwick,
Glenn H. Greenberg Professor of Psychiatry, PTSD and Resilience, Yale University School of Medicine
Post: Yale Child Study Center, National Center for PTSD, VA CT Healthcare System, 950 Campbell Ave./116A, West Haven, CT 06516, USA
T: +1 203 932 5711, x2464; +1 203 937 3481 (F)
Focus: Research.

Logotherapy Research Group at the Department of Psychology, University of Mississippi

Dir.: Assoc. Prof. Dr. Stefan E. Schulenberg
Post: Kinard Hall Suite 203, The University of Mississippi University, MS 38677-1848, USA
T: +1 662 915 3518
E: sschulen@olemiss.edu
W: psychology.olemiss.edu/stefan-e-schulenberg
Focus: Research/Clinical Application and Assessment Research.

Logotherapy Research Group at James Madison University

Dir.: Prof. Dr. William F. Evans
Post: MSC 7704 – 1173 Miller Hall, James Madison University,
Post: Harrisonburg, 22807 Virginia, USA
T: +1 540 568 6373; +1 540 568 3322 (F)
E: evanswf@jmu.edu
W: www.linkedin.com/in/wfevans/
Focus: Research.

Purpose Research, LLC

Dir.: Dr. Charles McLafferty, Jr.
Post: 803 Greensprings Hwy #19051, 35219, Birmingham, AL, USA
T: +01 205 223 2822
E: charles@purposeresearch.com
W: www.purposeresearch.com
Focus: Educational/Therapy or Counselling Training/Public information/dissemination of LT and EA/Research.

Venezuela

Instituto Venezolano de Logoterapia Viktor Frankl
[Venezuelan Institute for Logotherapy Viktor Frankl]

Dir.:	Colegio Universatario "Padre Isaias Ojeda" (CUPIO), Valencia-Edo Carabobo, Venezuela
T:	+58 414 595 49 42
E:	logoterapiavenezuela@gmail.com
W:	institutovenezolanodelogoterapiavf.blogspot.co.at/
Focus:	Educational/Therapy or Counselling Training/Public information/dissemination of LT and EA/Research.

Ph.D. Program in Logotherapy

Historical Background

In 1992, an Endowed University Chair for logotherapy and logotherapy-related interdisciplinary studies was established at the International Academy of Philosophy, University in the Principality of Liechtenstein. The main intention of establishing the Chair was to provide Ph.D. students with an excellent and supportive academic environment to pursue their studies and strive and flourish in their field. In 1994, Professor Dr. Giselher Guttmann (Dean of Psychology and Philosophy of the University of Vienna) was commissioned to teach and supervise Ph.D. students at the Chair. After the retirement of the Professor Guttmann in 2001, the University Chair, now called Viktor Frankl Chair of Philosophy and Psychology, became vacant. In 2012, Professor Alexander Batthyány was appointed Professor of the Chair and Professor Dr. Elisabeth Lukas was appointed as academic supervisor.

The Ph.D. Program in Logotherapy

The program in logotherapy and logotherapy-related studies is a Ph.D. program for philosophy and psychology. The doctoral degree is awarded for 30 ECTS points from tutorials, seminars, or lectures plus an excellent doctoral thesis, which is a work of rigorous and precise research.

A. Batthyány (ed.), *Logotherapy and Existential Analysis*, Logotherapy and Existential Analysis: Proceedings of the Viktor Frankl Institute Vienna 1,
DOI 10.1007/978-3-319-29424-7_41

Accreditation and University Ranking

The Ph.D. program in logotherapy and logotherapy-related interdisciplinary studies is a fully accredited Ph.D. program for philosophy and psychology. Mutual recognition agreements between the Principality Liechtenstein, Switzerland, the European Union, and the United States grant full accreditation to international Ph.D. students at the Viktor Frankl Chair.

On Campus and Distance Programs

Students can choose between living on campus and studying by distance with supervision by internet media. The normal length of a doctoral study is approximately 3 years, but exceptions are possible.

Academic Faculty

Univ.-Prof. Dr. phil. habil. Alexander Batthyány (Chair)
Univ.-Prof. Dr. phil. habil. Daniel von Wachter
Hon.-Prof. Dr. phil. habil. Elisabeth Lukas (Academic Supervisor)
Georg Kranz, Ph.D. (Research Assistant)
Michael Thir, MA (Assistant)

Contact

Admissions Office:

Mag.a Doris Hager-Hämmerle
Internationale Akademie für Philosophie
Universität im Fürstentum Liechtenstein
Im Schwibboga 7, FL-9487 Bendern, Fürstentum Liechtenstein
Email: admin@iap.li
Tel. +423 265 4343 or Fax +423 265 4341
www.iap.li

Index

A. Batthyány (ed.), *Logotherapy and Existential Analysis*, Logotherapy and Existential Analysis: Proceedings of the Viktor Frankl Institute Vienna 1,
DOI 10.1007/978-3-319-29424-7

MIX
Papier aus verantwortungsvollen Quellen
Paper from responsible sources
FSC® C105338

If you have any concerns about our products,
you can contact us on
ProductSafety@springernature.com

In case Publisher is established outside the EU,
the EU authorized representative is:
Springer Nature Customer Service Center GmbH
Europaplatz 3, 69115 Heidelberg, Germany

Printed by Libri Plureos GmbH
in Hamburg, Germany